The Best Books for Academic Libraries

The Best Books for Academic Libraries
10 Volumes (ISBN 0-7222-0014-5)

The Best Books for Academic Libraries

Music & Fine Arts

Volume 9

First Edition

The Best Books, Inc.
P. O. Box 893520
Temecula, CA. 92589-3520

ISBN 0-7222-0010-2 (10 Volume Set)
ISBN 0-7222-0019-6 (Volume 9)

Library of Congress Cataloging-in-Publication Data

The best books for academic libraries.-- 1st ed.
       v. cm.
Includes indexes.
Contents: v. 1. Science, technology, and agriculture -- v. 2. Medicine
-- v. 3. Language and literature -- v. 4. History of the Americas -- v.
5. World history -- v. 6. Social sciences -- v. 7. Political science,
law, education - v. 8. Religion and philosophy -- v. 9. Music & fine
arts -- v. 10. General works, military & naval, library science.
    ISBN 0-7222-0020-21-0.(set : alk. paper) -- ISBN 0-7222-0011-0 (v. 1 :
alk. paper. ISBN 0-7222-0012-9 (v. 2 : alk. paper) -- ISBN 0-7222-
0013-7 (v.3 : alk. paper) -- ISBN 0-7222-0014-5 (v. 4 : alk.
paper) -- ISBN 0-7222-0015-3 (v. 5 : alk. paper) ISBN 0-7222-0016-1
(v. 6 : alk. paper) -- ISBN 0-7222-0017-X (v. 7 : alk. paper) -- ISBN
0-7222-0018-8 (v. 8 : alk. paper) -- ISBN 0-7222-0019-6 (v. 9 : alk.
paper) -- ISBN 0-7222-0020-X (v. 10 : alk. paper).
    1.   Academic libraries--United States--Book lists.   I.   Best Books,
Inc.

Z1035 .B545 2002
011'.67—dc21   2002013790

For further information, contact:

The Best Books, Inc.
P.O. Box 893520
Temecula, CA 92589-3520
(Voice) 888-265-3531
(Fax) 888-265-3540

For product information/customer service, e-mail: customerservice@thebbooks.net

Visit our Web site: www.bestbooksfor.com

Table of Contents

Introduction

ABOUT THE PROJECT:

The Best Books for Academic Libraries was created to fill a need that has been growing in collection development for undergraduate and college libraries since the late 1980's. Our editorial department organized *The Best Books Database* (designed as a resource for university libraries) by consulting the leading book review journals, bibliographies, and reference books with subject bibliographies. It was compiled based upon the bibliographic standard from the Library of Congress (LC) MARC records. Each section was arranged by Library of Congress Classification Numbers.

PROCESSES FOR SUBJECT SELECTION AND COMPILATION:

To create *The Best Books for Academic Libraries,* the Editor conducted a comprehensive search of prominent Subject Librarians and Subject Specialists, experts in their area(s), to participate as Subject Advisors. The editorial processes utilized by The Best Books editorial staff are as follows:

1. Subject Advisors were asked to select the best books recommended for undergraduate and college libraries. Those who volunteered selected approximately one-third from over 170,000 books in *The Best Books Database* that they felt were essential to undergraduate work in their area(s) of expertise. Each Subject Advisor made their selections from subject surveys that were arranged by LC Classification Number. They added their choices of titles that were omitted from the surveys, and updated titles to the latest editions.

2. The Best Books editorial staff tabulated the returned surveys, and added the omissions into the database, following the LC MARC record standard, to arrive at a consensus of approximately the best 80,000 books.

3. Senior Subject Advisors were selected to conduct a final review of the surveys. They added any other titles they felt were essential to undergraduate work in their area(s) of expertise.

4. The final results were tabulated to create the First Edition of the 10 Volume set – *The Best Books for Academic Libraries.*

The actual title selection was left to the Subject Advisors. Each Advisor used the bibliographic resources available to them in their subject areas to make the best possible recommendations for undergraduate and college libraries. In order to achieve results that were well rounded, two to three Subject Advisors reviewed each section.

When there were discrepancies in the LC sorting and/or the description of any titles, The Best Books editorial staff defaulted to the information available on the LC MARC records.

The intention of this project, and The Best Books editorial staff, was to include only books in this listing. However, other titles may have been included, based upon recommendations by Subject Advisors and Senior Subject Advisors. In some cases, the Advisors did select annual reviews and multi-volume sets for inclusion in this work.

The editorial department has made every attempt to list the most recent publications for each title in this work. In the interest of maintaining a current core-collection bibliographic list, our Advisors were asked to note the most recent publications available, especially with regards to series and publishers that regularly produce new editions. Books were listed as the original edition (or latest reprint) when no information of a recent publication was available.

ARRANGEMENT BY LC CLASSIFICATION SCHEDULE:

Each section of this work was arranged by Library of Congress Classification Numbers (LCCN), using the Library of Congress Classification Schedule for ready reference. For the purposes of this project, we have organized a system of varying font sizes and the incorporation of Em-dashes (—) to identify whether the subject headings herein are **primary** (Main Class), **secondary** (Sub-Class), or **tertiary** (Sub-Sub-Class) in the LC Classification Schedule outline. The primary heading is presented in 14 point Times New Roman, the secondary in 12 point, and the tertiary in 10 point. This distinction can be viewed in the examples that follow:

Primary Classification:
(14 Point Times New Roman)

P49 Addresses, essays, lectures

P49.J35 1985
Jakobson, Roman,
Verbal art, verbal sign, verbal time / Roman Jakobson ; Krystyna Pomorska and Stephen Rudy, editors ; with the assistance of Brent Vine. Minneapolis : University of Minnesota Press, c1985. xiv, 208 p. :
84-007268   808/.00141   0816613583
Philology. Semiotics. Space and time in language.

Secondary Classification:
(12 Point Times New Roman)

P51 Study and teaching. Research — General

P51.L39 1998
Learning foreign and second languages : perspectives in research and scholarship / edited by Heidi Byrnes. New York : Modern Language Association of America, 1998. viii, 322 p.
98-039497   418/.007   087352800X
Language and languages — Study and teaching. Second language acquisition.

Tertiary Classification:
(10 Point Times New Roman)

P92 Communication. Mass media — By region or country — Individual regions or countries, A-Z

P92.C5.C52 2000
Chinese perspectives in rhetoric and communication / edited by D. Ray Heisey. Stamford, Conn. : Ablex Pub. Corp., 2000. xx, 297 p. ;
99-053426   302.2/0951   1567504949
Communication and culture — China. Rhetoric — Political aspects — China.

ERRORS, LACUNAE, AND OMISSIONS:

The Subject Advisors and Senior Subject Advisors were the sole source for recommending titles to include in the completed work, and no titles were intentionally added or omitted other than those that the Subject Advisors and Senior Subject Advisors recommended. There is no expressed or implied warranty or guarantee on this product.

The Best Books editorial department requests that any suggestions or errors be sent, via e-mail or regular mail, to be corrected in future editions of this project.

BEST BOOKS EDITORIAL STAFF:

This work is the ongoing product and group effort of a number of enthusiastic individuals: The Best Books editorial staff includes: Assistant Editor, Annette Wiles; Database Administrator, Richelle Tague; and Editor, Ashley Ludwig.

CONTRIBUTING ADVISORS:

This volume would not be possible without the dedicated work of our Subject Advisors and Senior Subject Advisors who donated their time, resources and knowledge towards creating this Best Books list. To them, we are truly grateful. *(Denotes Senior Subject Advisors for *Volume 9– Music & Fine Arts*.)

SUBJECT ADVISORS:

Donna Arnold, *Music Reference Librarian, Music Library – Willis Library, University of North Texas*
Subject Advisor for: ML, MT Music

Lisa Blankenship, *Head of Reference, James A. Michener Library, University of Northern Colorado – Greely, Colorado*
Subject Advisor for: N-NX - Fine Arts

Richard Griscom, *Music Librarian, University of Illinois Music Library, University of Illinois*
Subject Advisor for: ML, MT Music

Miguel Juarez, *Assistant Librarian, Center for Creative Photography Library, University of Arizona - Tucson, Arizona*
Subject Advisor for: N – NX – Fine Arts

Joon J. Mornes, *Architecture & Landscape Architecture Librarian, University of Minnesota – Minneapolis, Minnesota*
Subject Advisor for: NA - Architecture

Ericka Patillo, *Director, Music Library, Moores School of Music, University of Houston*
Subject Advisor for: ML, MT Music

Eunice Schroeder, *Music Librarian, Assistant Head, Arts Library, University of California – Santa Barbara*
Subject Advisor for: ML, MT Music

Deborah K. Ultan, *Art/Art History Librarian, University of Minnesota – Minneapolis, Minnesota*
Subject Advisor for: N-NX – 2003 Supplement

SENIOR SUBJECT ADVISORS:

Miguel Juarez,* *Assistant Librarian, Center for Creative Photography Library, University of Arizona - Tucson, Arizona.* Miguel Juarez earned his Master of Library Science at the University of Buffalo. He is working towards his Master of Arts degree, completing courses in Arts Management, Museum Studies and Chicano Research Studies. His Bachelor of Arts degree was earned from the University of Texas, El Paso. Miguel currently serves as Assistant Art and Photography Librarian at the University of Arizona, where he is a member of the Fine Arts/Humanities Team. Miguel is a member of the Ansel Adams Research Fellowship Committee for the Center for Creative Photography. He has served as a Project Consultant for Humanities Scholar for Americanos, and currently serves as Secretary for the Library Faculty Assembly. He is a member of many professional organizations, and has attended conferences for ARLIS/North America, the Society for Photographic Education (SPE), and the American Libraries Association (ALA). He has served as an External Reviewer for the National Endowment for the Humanities, a Moderator for the ARLIS/North America – VRA Joint Conference, as well as organizing and co-organizing meetings at various professional conferences for such discussions as the promotion of Visual Literacy, Librarians interested in Photography, and Multicultural Art Librarians seeking to increase the attendance of underrepresented librarians and library school students. Juarez has assisted in the organization of many professional exhibits and events as part of the University of Arizona Library Allies Group and the Center for Creative Photography. He has given several presentations for such conferences as ARLIS/North America, and the National Association of Chicana and Chicano Studies. He has recently has written an advanced book review for *The 21st Century Art Librarian*, as well as articles for *The Second REFORMA National Conference* and *Diversity in Libraries: Academic Library Residency Programs*. He remains actively involved in Web site development for art subjects.

Senior Subject Advisor for: N – NX – Fine Arts

Ericka Patillo,* *Director, Music Library, University of Houston.* Ericka Patillo earned her Masters of Library Science from the University of North Carolina at Chapel Hill. She graduated cum laude from Old Dominion University, in Norfolk, Virginia, with a Bachelors degree in Music History and a minor in journalism. Ericka has been a professional musician for twenty years, and studied harp at the Peabody Institute of the Johns Hopkins University in Baltimore, Maryland. Ericka is a member of the Music Library Association, and is a participant of multiple campus committees and task forces at the University of Houston. She performs as an alto in the University of Houston Women's Concert Choir. Ms. Patillo regularly works the reference desk at the main library, and serves on a variety of ad hoc and elected committees on the local and national level. Her current interests include library administration, the library as a learning organization, and electronic resources in musicological research, reference performance, and instruction in the music library.

Senior Subject Advisor for: ML, MT – Music

Eunice Schroeder,* *Music Librarian, Assistant Head, Arts Library, University of California, Santa Barbara.* Eunice Schroeder earned her Masters of Library Science from the University of Tennessee. She earned her Ph.D. in musicology from Stanford University, and her Bachelors in piano performance from Valparaiso University. Ms. Schroeder is currently serving as the Music Librarian and Assistant Head of the Arts Library at the University of California, Santa Barbara campus. Previously, she was employed at the Seeley G. Mudd Library at Lawrence University as Music Librarian, and at Oberlin College's Conservatory Library, as Summer Reference Intern. She has taught graduate and undergraduate courses in Music History and Literature. She has been a member of the Music Library Association since 1992 and has been active in the Midwest and Southern California chapters, as well as at the national level. Schroeder has also served as book review editor for *Notes: Quarterly Journal of the Music Library Association*. She has contributed to multiple publications, including *Encyclopedia of Library and Information Science, A Basic Music Library: Essential Scores and Sound Recordings, Lawrence Today, Journal of Musicology,* and *Musica Disciplina*. She has reviewed for *Notes: Quarterly Journal of the Music Library Association* and *Music Reference Services Quarterly,* and has given papers at regional and national meetings of the American Musicological Society. She has served on panel discussions for MLA/SCC, the MLA/Midwest Chapter, and the American Musicological Society. Ms. Schroeder is actively involved at UCSB, serving on multiple committees for the Library.

Senior Subject Advisor for: ML, MT – Music

ML Literature on music

ML1 Serials — United States

ML1.I83
International Repertory of Music Literature (Organization)
RILM abstracts of music literature. New York, RILM
70-200921   780/.5
Music -- Abstracts -- Periodicals.

ML12 Directories. Almanacs — International

ML12.M88
Musical America. Great Barrington, Mass.: ABC Leisure Magazines.
88-640608   780/.25 19
Music--United States--Directories. Performing arts--United States--Directories.

ML12.Z54 1999
Zietz, Karyl Lynn.
Opera companies and houses of western Europe, Canada, Australia, and New Zealand: a comprehensive illustrated reference/ by Karyl Lynn Zietz. Jefferson, N.C.: McFarland, c1999. xx, 480 p.
98-045854   792.5/025   0786406119
Opera companies -- Directories. Theaters -- Directories. Opera -- 20th century -- Directories.

ML13 Directories. Almanacs — United States — General works

ML13.D57
Directory of music faculties in colleges and universities, U. S. and Canada. [Binghamton, N.Y.] College Music Society.
75-644786   780/.92/2
Music teachers -- United States -- Directories. Music teachers -- Canada -- Directories.

ML13.Z54 1994
Zietz, Karyl Lynn.
Opera companies and houses of the United States: a comprehensive, illustrated reference/ by Karyl Lynn Zietz. Jefferson, N.C.: McFarland, c1995. xv, 335 p.
94-000943   782.1/06/073   089950955X
Opera companies -- United States -- Directories. Theaters -- United States -- Directories. Opera -- United States.

ML19 Directories. Almanacs — United States — Other (not A-Z)

ML19.L9 1994
Lynch, Richard Chigley, 1932-
Musicals!: a complete selection guide for local productions/ Richard Chigley Lynch. Chicago: American Library Association, 1994. vii, 404 p.
93-027387   782.1/4/02573   0838906273
Musicals -- Directories.

ML49-50 Librettos. Scenarios — Operas — Collections

ML49.M83 M42 1991
Mozart, Wolfgang Amadeus,
The Metropolitan Opera book of Mozart operas/ the Metropolitan Opera   Guild; translations by Judyth Schaubhut Smith, David Stivender, Susan Webb; executive editor Paul Gruber. New York, N.Y.: HarperCollins, c1991. x, 658 p.
91-055003   782.1/026/8 20   0062730517
Mozart, Wolfgang Amadeus, 1756-1791. Operas. Operas -- Librettos. Opera -- 18th century.

ML49.S9.A1 1996
Sullivan, Arthur, 1842-1900.
The complete annotated Gilbert and Sullivan/ introduced and edited by Ian Bradley. New York: Oxford University Press, 1996. xiii, 1197 p.
95-051813   782.1/2026/8   019816503X
Operas -- Librettos.

ML50.W14.R32 1993
Wagner, Richard, 1813-1883.
Wagner's Ring of the Nibelung: a companion: the full German text/ with a new translation by Stewart Spencer and commentaries by Barry Millington ... [et al.]. New York: Thames and Hudson, 1993. 383 p.
93-060196   782.1/0268   0500015678
Wagner, Richard, -- 1813-1883. -- Ring des Nibelungen. Operas -- Librettos.

ML53.8 Librettos. Scenarios — Cantatas, choruses, etc. — Collections

ML53.8.B3 C3613 2000
Bach, Johann Sebastian,
The complete church and secular cantatas/ Johann Sebastian Bach; translated by Richard Stokes; with an introduction by Martin Neary. Lanham, Md.: Scarecrow Press, [2000?] xviii, 378 p.
00-046361   782.2/40268 21   0810839334
Cantatas -- Texts.

ML54.6 Librettos. Scenarios —
Songs and cantatas for one voice, etc. — 1800-

ML54.6.B82.G52 1999
Brahms, Johannes, 1833-1897.
Brahms' complete song texts: in one volume containing solo songs, duets, Liebeslieder waltzes (both sets), the Alto rhapsody, folk song arrangements/ with International Phonetic Alphabet transcriptions, word for word translations, and commentary by Beaumont Glass. Geneseo, N.Y.: Leyerle, c1999. xiv, 329 p.
99-214695   782.42168/0268   1878617265
Songs -- Texts.

ML54.6.J76
Johnson, Graham, 1950-
A French song companion/ Graham Johnson; Richard Stokes. New York: Oxford University Press, 2000. xxxii, 530 p.
99-057524   782.42168/0268   0198164106
Songs, French -- Texts. Songs, French -- History and criticism.

ML54.6.M5 R5 1973
Miller, Philip Lieson,
The ring of words; an anthology of song texts. The original texts selected and translated, with an introd. by Philip L. Miller. New York, W. W. Norton [1973] xxviii, 518 p.
72-010270   781.9/6   0393006778
Songs--Texts.

ML54.6.R39 2000
Reading lyrics/ edited and with an introduction by Robert Gottlieb and Robert Kimball. New York: Pantheon Books, c2000. xxvi, 706 p.
99-088811   782.42164/0268   0375400818
Songs, English -- Texts. Popular music -- Texts. Musicals -- Excerpts -- Librettos.

ML54.6.S39.G515 1996
Schubert, Franz, 1797-1828.
Schubert's complete song texts/ with International Phonetic Alphabet transcriptions, word for word translations, and commentary by Beaumont Glass. Geneseo, N.Y.: Leyerle, c1996. 2 v.
99-217189   1878617192
Songs -- Texts.

ML55 Collected works (nonserial) —
Addresses. Essays. Lectures
— Several authors

ML55.B663 P5
Boretz, Benjamin,
Perspectives on Schoenberg and Stravinsky. Edited by Benjamin Boretz and Edward T. Cone. Princeton, N.J., Princeton University Press, 1968. x, 284 p.
68-028031   780/.922
Schoenberg, Arnold, -- 1874-1951. Stravinsky, Igor, -- 1882-1971. Music -- Addresses, essays, lectures.

ML55.E9 1998
The exotic in western music/ edited by Jonathan Bellman. Boston: Northeastern University Press, c1998. xiii, 370 p.
97-016407   780   1555533205
Music -- History and criticism. Exoticism in music.

ML55.M49
Mitchell, William J. 1906-
The Music forum. New York, Columbia University Press, [1967-] 4 v.
67-016204   780/.8
Musicology -- Periodicals. Musical analysis -- Periodicals. Music -- Theory -- Periodicals.

ML55.Q44 1993
Queering the pitch: the new gay and lesbian musicology/ edited by Philip Brett, Elizabeth Wood, Gary C. Thomas. New York: Routledge, 1994. ix, 357 p.
93-015025   780/.8/664   0415907527
Homosexuality and music. Sex in music. Gay musicians.

ML60 Collected works (nonserial) —
Addresses. Essays. Lectures
— Individual authors

ML60.A215.S6
Abraham, Gerald, 1904-
Slavonic and Romantic music; essays and studies, by Gerald Abraham. New York, St. Martin's Press [1968] 360 p.
68-013029   780
Music -- 19th century -- History and criticism.

ML60.A26513 1999
Adorno, Theodor W.,
Sound figures/ Theodor W. Adorno; translated by Rodney Livingstone. Stanford, Calif.: Stanford University Press, 1999. ix, 229 p.
98-033460   780 21   0804735581
Music -- 20th century -- History and criticism.

ML60.B47 1965
Bernstein, Leonard, 1918-
The joy of music. New York: Simon and Schuster, 1959. 303 p.
59-011162   780.15
Music -- Analysis, appreciation.

ML60.B688
Blume, Friedrich, 1893-
Classic and romantic music; a comprehensive survey. Translated by M. D. Herter Norton. New York, W. W. Norton [1970] viii, 213 p.
78-077390   780.9033   0393021378
Music -- Addresses, essays, lectures. Music -- 18th century -- History and criticism. Music -- 19th century -- History and criticism.

ML60.B71313 1991
Boulez, Pierre, 1925-
Stocktakings from an apprenticeship/ Pierre Boulez; collected and presented by Paule Thevenin; translated from the French by Stephen Walsh; with an introduction by Robert Piencikowski. Oxford: Clarendon Press; 1991. xxix, 316 p.
90-007655   780/.9   0193112108
Music -- History and criticism.

ML60.B796.R43
Boulez, Pierre, 1925-
Notes of an apprenticeship. Texts collected and presented by Paule Thevenin. Translated from the French by Herbert Weinstock. New York, A. A. Knopf, 1968. 398 p.
67-018625   780.15
Music -- History and criticism.

ML60.B84 1990
Brendel, Alfred.
Music sounded out: essays, lectures, interviews, afterthoughts/ Alfred Brendel. London: Robson Books, 1990. 258 p.
92-116914   780 20   0860516660
Music -- History and criticism.

ML60.C125 1993
Cage, John.
John Cage, writer: previously uncollected pieces/ selected and introduced by Richard Kostelanetz. New York: Limelight Editions, 1993. xviii, 281 p.
92-041359   780   0879101644
Music -- History and criticism.

ML60.C13.S5
Cage, John.
Silence; lectures and writings.   Middletown, Conn., Wesleyan University Press [1961] 276 p.
61-014238   780.8
Music -- History and criticism.

ML60.C22
Carter, Elliott, 1908-
The writings of Elliott Carter: an American composer looks at modern music/ compiled, edited, and annotated by Else Stone and Kurt Stone. Bloomington: Indiana University Press, c1977. xvii, 390 p.
76-048539   780/.904   0253367204
Music -- 20th century -- History and criticism -- Addresses, essays, lectures.

ML60.C85 2000
Cowell, Henry,
Essential Cowell: selected writings on music/ edited with an introduction by Dick Higgins; preface by Kyle Gann. Kingston, N.Y.: Documentext, 2000.
00-055904   780 21   0929701631
Music -- History and criticism.

ML60.D158 1987
Dahlhaus, Carl, 1928-
Schoenberg and the new music: essays/ by Carl Dahlhaus; translated by Derrick Puffett and Alfred Clayton. Cambridge [Cambridgeshire]; Cambridge University Press, 1987. viii, 305 p.
87-006360   780/.92/4   0521332516
Schoenberg, Arnold, -- 1874-1951 -- Criticism and interpretation.   Music -- 20th century -- History and criticism.

ML60.G68 1984
Gould, Glenn.
The Glenn Gould reader/ edited and with an introduction by Tim Page. New York: Knopf, 1984. xvi, 475 p.
84-047819   780   0394540670
Music -- History and criticism.

ML60.H2043
Hanslick, Eduard, 1825-1904.
Music criticisms, 1846-99. Translated and edited by Henry Pleasants. Baltimore, Penguin Books [1963, c1950] 312 p.
64-000143
Music -- 19th century -- History and criticism.

ML60.H33713 1989
Harnoncourt, Nikolaus.
The musical dialogue: thoughts on Monteverdi, Bach, and Mozart/ Nikolaus Harnoncourt; translated by Mary O'Neill; Reinhard G. Pauly, general editor. Portland, Or.: Amadeus Press, c1989. 220 p.
88-038033   780/.903/2   093134008X
Monteverdi, Claudio, -- 1567-1643. Bach, Johann Sebastian, -- 1685-1750. Mozart, Wolfgang Amadeus, -- 1756-1791. Music -- History and criticism. Music -- Interpretation (Phrasing, dynamics, etc.)

ML60.M499 1975
Mencken, H. L. 1880-1956.
H. L. Mencken on music; a selection of his writings on music together with an account of H. L. Mencken's musical life and a history of the Saturday Night Club/ by Louis Cheslock. New York: Schirmer Books, 1975, c1961. ix, 222 p.
61-013949   780.8
Mencken, H. L. -- (Henry Louis), -- 1880-1956. Music.

ML60.S374
Schoenberg, Arnold, 1874-1951.
Style and idea. New York, Philosophical Library [1950] vii, 224 p.
50-008187   780.4
Music.

ML60.S444.I5
Seeger, Pete, 1919-
The incompleat folksinger, by Pete Seeger. Edited by Jo Metcalf Schwartz. New York, Simon and Schuster [1972] viii, 596 p.
73-156161   784.4   067120954X
Folk music -- History and criticism. Folk songs -- History and criticism.

ML60.S513
Sessions, Roger, 1896-
Questions about music. Cambridge, Mass., Harvard University Press, 1970. 166 p.
72-102672   780   0674743504
Music -- Addresses, essays, lectures.

ML60.T515
Thomson, Virgil, 1896-
A Virgil Thomson reader/ by Virgil Thomson; with an introduction by John Rockwell. Boston: Houghton Mifflin, 1981. x, 582 p.
81-006375   780   0395313309
Music -- History and criticism.

ML60.T5533 1995
Tippett, Michael, 1905-
Tippett on music/ edited by Meirion Bowen. Oxford: Clarendon Press; 1995. xiv, 318 p.
94-034148   780   0198165412
Music -- History and criticism.

ML63 Special aspects of the subject as a whole — Topics not elsewhere provided for

ML63.C48
Copland, Aaron, 1900-
Copland on music. Garden City, N.Y., Doubleday, 1960. 280 p.
60-015171   780.8
Music.

ML65 Special aspects of the subject as a whole — Anecdotes, humor, etc.

ML65.S6
Slonimsky, Nicolas, 1894-
A thing or two about music, illus. by Maggi Fiedler. New York, Allen, Towne & Heath [1948] 304 p.
48-006965
Music -- Anecdotes, facetiae, satire, etc.

ML82 Special aspects of the subject as a whole — Women and music

ML82.A45
Ammer, Christine.
Unsung: a history of women in American music/ Christine Ammer. Westport, Conn.: Greenwood Press, c1980. x, 317 p.
79-052324   780/.92/2   0313220077
Women musicians. Women composers. Musicians -- United States.

ML82.H35 1997
Halstead, Jill.
The woman composer: creativity and the gendered politics of musical composition/ Jill Halstead. Aldershot [England]; Ashgate, c1997. xii, 286 p.
97-002419   780/.82/0941   1859281834
Women composers -- Great Britain -- Social conditions. Women composers -- Great Britain -- Psychology. Great Britain -- Social conditions -- 20th century.

ML82.M38 1990
McClary, Susan.
Feminine endings: music, gender, and sexuality/ Susan McClary. Minneapolis: University of Minnesota Press, c1991. viii, 220 p.
90-011169   780/.82   0816618992
Feminism and music. Sex in music.

ML82.M74 2000
Music and gender/ edited by Pirkko Moisala and Beverley Diamond; foreword by Ellen Koskoff. Urbana: University of Illinois Press, c2000. xiii, 376 p.
99-006791   780/.82   025202544X
Women musicians. Sex in music.

ML82.R43 1993
Rediscovering the muses: women's musical traditions/ edited by Kimberly Marshall. Boston: Northeastern University Press, c1993. xxvii, 304 p.
93-028495   780/.82   1555531733
Women musicians. Women composers. Music -- Social aspects.

ML82.R53 1995
Reynolds, Simon, 1963-
The sex revolts: gender, rebellion, and rock'n'roll/ Simon Reynolds and Joy Press. Cambridge, Mass.: Harvard University Press, 1995. xvii, 410 p.
94-030683   781.66/082   0674802721
Feminism and music. Rock music -- History and criticism. Women rock musicians.

ML82.W48 2000
Whiteley, Sheila, 1941-
Women and popular music: sexuality, identity, and subjectivity/ Shelia Whiteley. London; Routledge, 2000. x, 246 p.
99-058596   781.64/082   0415211891
Women musicians. Popular music -- Social aspects. Feminism and music.

ML82.W625 2002
Women and music in America since 1900: an encyclopedia/ edited by Kristine H. Burns. Westport, Conn.: Greenwood Press, 2002. 2 v.
2001-054570   780/.82/0973 21   1573563099
Women musicians -- United States -- History -- 20th century -- Encyclopedias. Music -- United States -- 20th century -- Encyclopedias.

ML82.W65 1996
Women in music: an anthology of source readings from the Middle Ages to the present/ edited by Carol Neuls-Bates. Boston: Northeastern University Press, 1996. xviii, 400 p.
95-017460   780/.82   155553239X
Women musicians. Women composers.

ML85 Special aspects of the subject as a whole — Music in art. Musical instruments in art

ML85.L4813
Lesure, Francois.
Music and art in society. Foreword by Denis Stevens. Preface by Pierre Francastel. [Translated by Denis and Sheila Stevens] University Park, Pennsylvania State University Press, 1968. xxvi, 59 p.
67-027113   780/.08
Music in art. Music -- Social aspects.

ML85.W58 1979
Winternitz, Emanuel.
Musical instruments and their symbolism in Western art: studies in musical iconology/ Emanuel Winternitz. New Haven: Yale University Press, 1979. 253 p.
78-065482   704.94/9/78191   0300023243
Musical instruments in art.

ML89 Special aspects of the subject as a whole — Pictorial works

ML89.K55
Kinsky, Georg, 1882-1951,
A history of music in pictures, edited by Georg Kinsky with the co-operation of Robert Haas, Hans Schnoor and other experts. With an introduction by Eric Blom. New York, Dover Publications [c1951] xiv, 363 p.
53-009805
Music in art Musicians -- Portraits Musical instruments

ML89.L15
Lang, Paul Henry, 1901-
A pictorial history of music [by] Paul Henry Lang and Otto Bettmann. New York, Norton [1960] vii, 242 p.
60-006822   780.9
Music -- History and criticism. Music in art. Musicians -- Portraits.

ML90 Special aspects of the subject as a whole — Writings of musicians (Collections)

ML90.C77 1997
Composers on music: eight centuries of writings. Boston: Northeastern University Press, c1997. xvi, 512 p.
96-027774   780   1555532780
Musicians as authors. Music -- History and criticism.

ML90.W44
Weiss, Piero,
Letters of composers through six centuries. Compiled and edited by Piero Weiss. Foreword by Richard Ellmann. Philadelphia, Chilton Book Co. [1967] xxix, 619 p.
67-028895   780/.922
Composers -- Correspondence.

ML96.4 Manuscripts, autographs, etc. Paleography — Compositions and musical sketches — Facsimiles

ML96.4.W5 1965
Winternitz, Emanuel.
Musical autographs from Monteverdi to Hindemith. New York, Dover Publications [1965] 2 v.
65-012261   781.969
Music -- Manuscripts -- Facsimiles. Composers -- Autographs. Musical notation.

ML100 Dictionaries. Encyclopedias — General works

ML100.G16 1998
The Garland encyclopedia of world music/ advisory editors, Bruno Nettl and Ruth M. Stone; founding editors, James Porter and Timothy Rice. New York: Garland Pub., 1998-2000. v. 1-2, 4-5
97-009671   780/.9   0824060350
Music -- Encyclopedias. Folk music -- Encyclopedias. Popular music -- Encyclopedias.

ML100.H36 1999
The Harvard concise dictionary of music and musicians/ edited by Don Michael Randel. Cambridge, Mass.: Belknap Press, 1999. viii, 757 p.
99-040644   780/.3   0674000846
Music -- Dictionaries. Music -- Bio-bibliography.

ML100.K35 1994
Kennedy, Michael, 1926-
The Oxford dictionary of music/ Michael Kennedy; associate editor, Joyce Bourne. Oxford; Oxford University Press, 1994. xv, 985 p.
94-004539   780/.3   0198691629
Music -- Dictionaries. Music -- Bio-bibliography.

ML100.N48 2001
The new Grove dictionary of music and musicians/ edited by Stanley Sadie; executive editor, John Tyrrell. New York: Grove, 2001. 29 v.
00-055156   780/.3   1561592390
Music -- Encyclopedias. Music -- Bio-bibliography.

ML100.N485 1986
The New Harvard dictionary of music/ edited by Don Michael Randel. Cambridge, Mass.: Belknap Press of Harvard University Press, 1986. xxi, 942 p.
86-004780   780/.3/21   0674615255
Music -- Dictionaries.

ML100.N5 1983
The New Oxford companion to music/ general editor, Denis Arnold. Oxford; Oxford University Press, 1983. 2 v.
83-233314   780/.3/21   0193113163
Music -- Dictionaries. Music -- Bio-bibliography.

ML100.S637 1989
Slonimsky, Nicolas,
Lectionary of music/ by Nicolas Slonimsky. New York: McGraw-Hill, c1989. 521 p.
89-002515   780/.3 19   007058222X
Music -- Encyclopedias.

ML101 Dictionaries. Encyclopedias — By region or country, A-Z

ML101.I73.V35 1999
The companion to Irish traditional music/ edited by Fintan Vallely. New York: New York University Press, c1999. xviii, 478 p.
99-010078   781.62/9162/003   0814788025
Folk music -- Ireland -- Encyclopedias.

ML101.U6.N48 1986
The New Grove dictionary of American music/ edited by H. Wiley Hitchcock and Stanley Sadie. New York, N.Y.: Grove's Dictionaries of Music, 1986. 4 v.
86-000404   781.773/03/21   0943818362
Music -- United States -- Encyclopedias. Music -- United States -- Bio-bibliography.

ML102 Dictionaries. Encyclopedias — By topic, A-Z

ML102.B35.R4 1991
Rehrig, William H., 1939-
The heritage encyclopedia of band music: composers and their music/ by William H. Rehrig; edited by Paul E. Bierley. Westerville, Ohio: Integrity Press, c1991-c1996. 3 v.
91-073637   016.784   0918048087
Band music -- Bio-bibliography.

ML102.B6.H3
Harris, Sheldon.
Blues who's who: a biographical dictionary of Blues singers/ Sheldon Harris. New Rochelle, N.Y.: Arlington House, c1979. 775 p.
78-027073   784/.092/2   0870004255
Blues (Music) -- Bio-bibliography. Blues musicians -- United States -- Biography -- Dictionaries.

ML102.F66.S7 1983
Stambler, Irwin.
Encyclopedia of folk, country & western music/ Irwin Stambler and Grelun Landon. New York, N.Y.: St. Martin's Press, c1983. 902 p.
82-005702   781.773/03/21   0312248180
Folk music -- United States -- Encyclopedias. Country music -- Encyclopedias. Folk singers -- United States -- Biography -- Encyclopedias.

ML102.I5.N48 1984
The New Grove dictionary of musical instruments/ edited by Stanley Sadie. London: Macmillan Press; c1984. 3 v.
84-009062   781.91/03/21   0943818052
Musical instruments -- Dictionaries.

ML102.I5 D5
Musical instruments of the world: an illustrated encyclopedia/ by the Diagram Group. New York: Paddington Press, c1976. 320 p.
76-021722   781.9/1/03   0846701340
Musical instruments -- Dictionaries.

ML102.J3.F39 1999
Feather, Leonard G.
The biographical encyclopedia of jazz/ Leonard Feather and Ira Gitler, with the assistance of Swing journal, Tokyo. New York: Oxford University Press, 1999. xx, 718 p.
98-015485   781.65/092/2   0195074181
Jazz -- Bio-bibliography. Jazz -- Discography.

ML102.J3.N48 2000
The New Grove dictionary of jazz/ edited by Barry Kernfeld. 2nd Edition London: Macmillan Press; 2002. 2 v.
87-025452   785.42/03   1561592846
Jazz -- Encyclopedias. Jazz -- Bio-bibliography.

ML102.M88.G3 2001
Ganzl, Kurt.
The encyclopedia of the musical theatre/ Kurt Ganzl. New York: Schirmer Books, 2001. 3 v.
2001-018361   782.1/4/03 21   0028649702
Musicals -- Encyclopedias.

ML102.M88.H59 1995
Hischak, Thomas S.
The American musical theatre song encyclopedia/ Thomas S. Hischak; foreword by Gerald Bordman. Westport, Conn.: Greenwood Press, 1995. xv, 543 p.
94-040853   782.1/4/0973   0313294070
Musicals -- Encyclopedias. Popular music -- Encyclopedias.

ML102.O6.L6 1978
Loewenberg, Alfred.
Annals of opera, 1597-1940/ compiled from the original sources by Alfred Loewenberg; with an introd. by Edward J. Dent. Totowa, N.J.: Rowman and Littlefield, 1978. xxv, 1756 p.
79-105243   782.1/09   0874718511
Opera -- Dictionaries. Operas -- Performances.

ML102.O6 N5 1992
The New Grove dictionary of opera/ edited by Stanley Sadie. New York: Grove's Dictionaries of Music , 1992. 4 v.
92-036276   782.1/03 20   0935859926
Opera--Dictionaries.

ML102.O6 V55 1993
The Viking opera guide/ edited by Amanda Holden with Nicholas Kenyon and Stephen Walsh; consultant editor, Rodney Milnes; recordings consultant, Alan Blyth; with a preface by Sir Colin Davis. 1st ed. London; Viking, 1993. xxii, 1305 p.
94-143500   782.1/0269/03 20   0670812927
Opera -- Dictionaries.

ML102.O6.W37 1992
Warrack, John Hamilton, 1928-
The Oxford dictionary of opera/ John Warrack and Ewan West. Oxford; Oxford University Press, 1992. xviii, 782 p.
92-006730   782.1/03   0198691645
Opera -- Dictionaries.

ML102.P66.F2 1993
Facts behind the songs: a handbook of American popular music from the nineties to the '90s/ Marvin E. Paymer, general editor. New York: Garland Pub., 1993. xxii, 564 p.
93-024342   781.64/0973   0824052404
Popular music -- United States -- Dictionaries.

ML102.P66 G84 1998
The encyclopedia of popular music/ compiled & edited by Colin Larkin. 3rd ed. London; Muze; 8 v.
98-037439   781.64/03 21   033374134X
Popular music--Encyclopedias.

ML102.P66 P5 1998
The Penguin encyclopedia of popular music/ edited by Donald Clarke; [contributors to the first edition, Alan Cackett ... et al.]. 2nd ed./ [contributors] to the second edition, Paul Balmer ... London, England; Penguin Books, 1998. xii, 1524 p.
99-213528   781.64/03 21   0140513701
Popular music -- Dictionaries. Popular music -- Bio-bibliography.

ML102.P66.R67 2000
Rosalsky, Mitch, 1943-
Encyclopedia of rhythm & blues and doo wop vocal groups/ Mitch Rosalsky. Lanham, MD: Scarecrow Press, 2000. xv, 703 p.
99-032194   781.643/03   0810836637
Popular music -- United States -- Dictionaries. Musical groups -- United States -- Dictionaries.

ML102.R6.H5 1996
Helander, Brock.
The rock who's who/ Brock Helander. New York: Schirmer Books; c1996. xii, 849 p.
96-028307   781.66/092/2   0028710312
Rock musicians -- Biography -- Dictionaries. Rock music -- Bio-bibliography. Rock music -- Discography.

ML102.S67.E5 1993
Encyclopedia of recorded sound in the United States/ Guy A. Marco, editor; Frank Andrews, contributing editor. New York: Garland Pub., 1993. xlix, 910 p.
93-018166   780.26/6/03   0824047826
Sound recordings -- United States -- Dictionaries. Sound recording industry -- United States -- Dictionaries.

ML102.W67 W67 1999
World music: the rough guide/ edited by Simon Broughton, Mark Ellingham and Richard Trillo, with Orla Duane and Vanessa Dowell. New ed. London: Rough Guides; v. <1 >
00-364709   780/.9 21   1858286352
World music--History and criticism. World music--Bio-bibliography. World music--Discography.

ML105 Dictionaries. Encyclopedias — Bio-bibliographical — International

ML105.B16 2001
Baker's biographical dictionary of musicians. Centennial ed./ Nicolas Slonimsky, editor emeritus; Laura Kuhn, New York: Schirmer Books, c2001. 6 v.
00-046375   780/.92/2 21   0028655710
Music--Bio-bibliography--Dictionaries.

ML105.F53 2002
Ficher, Miguel,
Latin American classical composers: a biographical dictionary/ compiled and edited by Miguel Ficher, Martha Furman Schleifer, John M. Furman. 2nd ed. Lanham, Md.: Scarecrow Press, 2002. xxi, 645 p.
2002-030430   780/.92/28 B 21   0810845172
Music -- Latin America -- Bio-bibliography -- Dictionaries. Composers -- Latin America -- Biography -- Dictionaries.

ML105.I5 1999
International dictionary of black composers/ editor Samuel A. Floyd Jr. Chicago; London: Fitzroy Dearborn, c1999. 2 v.
99-214303   780/.92/396   1884964273
Afro-American composers -- Bio-bibliography -- Dictionaries. Composers, Black -- Bio-bibliography -- Dictionaries.

ML105.I54
International who's who in classical music. London, England: Europa Publications Ltd., [c2002-   ]
2002-200068   780/.92/2 21
Music--Bio-bibliography--Periodicals. Music--Societies, etc.--Directories.

ML105.S67 1982
Southern, Eileen.
Biographical dictionary of Afro-American and African musicians/ Eileen Southern. Westport, Conn.: Greenwood Press, 1982. xviii, 478 p.
81-002586   780/.92/2   0313213399
Afro-American musicians -- Biography -- Encyclopedias. Musicians -- Africa -- Biography -- Encyclopedias.

**ML106 Dictionaries. Encyclopedias —
Bio-bibliographical — National. By country, A-Z**

ML106.C3 E5 1992
Encyclopedia of music in Canada/ edited by Helmut Kallmann, Gilles Potvin, Kenneth Winters. 2nd ed./ Helmut Kallmann and Gilles Potvin, editors; Robin Elliott Toronto; University of Toronto Press, c1992. 1524 p.
93-109483   780/.971 20   0802028810
Music -- Canada -- Encyclopedias. Music -- Canada -- Bio-bibliography -- Dictionaries.

ML106.S68 B56 1989
Biographical dictionary of Russian/Soviet composers/ editors-in-chief, Allan Ho and Dmitry Feofanov. New York: Greenwood Press, 1989. xxv, 739 p.
88-034810   780/.92/2 B 19   0313244855
Music -- Soviet Union -- Bio-bibliography -- Dictionaries. Music -- Soviet Union -- Discography.

ML106.U4 B66 2000
McGee, Marty,
Traditional musicians of the central Blue Ridge: old time, early country, folk and bluegrass label recording artists, with discographies/ by Marty McGee; with a foreword by Bobby Patterson. Jefferson, NC: McFarland & Co., c2000. ix, 235 p.
00-023671   781.642/09755 21   0786408766
Music -- Blue Ridge Mountains Region -- Bio-bibliography -- Dictionaries. Country musicians -- Blue Ridge Mountains Region -- Biography Folk musicians -- Blue Ridge Mountains Region -- Biography -- Dictionaries. Bluegrass musicians -- Blue Ridge Mountains Region -- Biography

**ML108 Dictionaries. Encyclopedias —
Terminological**

ML108.H64 1997
Hoffman, Miles.
The NPR classical music companion: terms and concepts from A to Z/ Miles Hoffman. Boston: Houghton Mifflin, 1997. x, 306 p.
97-010479   780/.3   0395707420
Music -- Dictionaries. Music -- Terminology

ML108.K37 1990
Kaufmann, Walter,
Selected musical terms of non-Western cultures: a notebook-glossary/ Walter Kaufmann. Warren, Mich.: Harmonie Park Press, 1990. x, 806 p.
90-040670   780/.89 20   0899900399
Ethnomusicology -- Terminology.

ML108.T4
Terminorum musicae index septem linguis redactus = Polyglottes Wörterbuch der musikalischen Terminologie: deutsch, englisch, französisch, italienisch, spanisch, ungarisch, russisch = Polyglot dictionary of musical terms: English, German, French, Ital [Commission internationale mixte; rédacteur en chef. Horst Leuchtmann]. Budapest: Akadémiai Kiadó, 1978. 798 p.
78-369482   780/.3   9630512769
Music -- Dictionaries -- Polyglot. Dictionaries, Polyglot.

ML108.T46 1989
Thomsett, Michael C.
Musical terms, symbols, and theory: an illustrated dictionary/ compiled by Michael C. Thomsett. Jefferson, N.C.: McFarland, c1989. ix, 277 p.
89-042758   780/.3 20   0899503926
Music -- Terminology.

**ML109 Dictionaries. Encyclopedias —
Pronouncing**

ML109.F73 1996
Fradkin, Robert A., 1951-
The well-tempered announcer: a pronunciation guide to classical music/ Robert A. Fradkin. Bloomington: Indiana University Press, c1996. xviii, 255 p.
95-000360   780/.14   025321064X
Music -- Terminology -- Pronunciation. Names, Personal -- Pronunciation.

**ML111 Music librarianship —
General works**

ML111.B77 1990
Bradley, Carol June.
American music librarianship: a biographical and historical survey/ Carol June Bradley. New York: Greenwood Press, 1990. xii, 237 p.
89-017103   026.78/0973 20   0313268207
Music librarianship -- United States. Music librarians -- United States -- Biography.

ML111.B83 1985
Bryant, E. T.
Music librarianship: a practical guide/ by E.T. Bryant with the assistance of Guy A. Marco. 2nd ed. Metuchen, N.J.: Scarecrow Press, 1985. xiv, 449 p.
84-027731   026/.78 19   0810817853
Music librarianship. Music--Bibliography. Cataloging of music.

ML111.M756 2000
Music librarianship at the turn of the century/ Richard Griscom, editor; Amanda Maple, assistant editor. Lanham, Md.: Scarecrow Press, 2000. 107 p.
00-032949   026/.78 21   0810838664
Music librarianship.

**ML112 Music printing and publishing —
General works**

ML112.D53 1977
Dichter, Harry, 1899-
Handbook of early American sheet music, 1768-1889/ by Harry Dichter and Elliott Shapiro. New York: Dover Publications, 1977. xxvii, 287 p.
77-070454   016.7817/73   0486233642
Music -- United States -- Bibliography. Publishers and publishing -- United States. Music printing -- United States.

ML112.K765 1992
Krummel, Donald William, 1929-
The literature of music bibliography: an account of the writings on the history of music printing & publishing/ D.W. Krummel. Berkeley, Calif.: Fallen Leaf Press, c1992. xix, 447 p.
92-010492   016.0705/794   0914913212
Music printing -- History -- Bibliography. Music -- Publishing -- History -- Bibliography.

ML113 Bibliography — International — General works

ML113.B3 1997
A basic music library: essential scores and sound recordings/ compiled by the Music Library Association; Elizabeth Davis, coordinating editor; Pamela Bristah and Jane Gottlieb, scores editors; Kent Underwood and William E. Anderson, sound recordings editors. Chicago: American Library Association, 1997. xvi, 665 p.
96-047351   016.78026   0838934617
Music -- Bibliography. Music libraries -- Collection development.

ML113.B39 1975
Berkowitz, Freda Pastor.
Popular titles and subtitles of musical compositions/ by Freda Pastor Berkowitz. 2d ed. Metuchen, N.J.: Scarecrow Press, 1975. viii, 209 p.
75-004751   016.78   0810808064
Titles of musical compositions -- Bibliography. Music -- Bibliography.

ML113.B85 1987
Brockman, William S.
Music: a guide to the reference literature/ William S. Brockman. Littleton, Colo.: Libraries Unlimited, 1987. xv, 254 p.
87-026462   016.78   0872875261
Music -- Bibliography. Music -- Reference books -- Bibliography.

ML113.C68 1993
Crabtree, Phillip.
Sourcebook for research in music/ Phillip D. Crabtree and Donald H. Foster. Bloomington: Indiana University Press, c1993. xiii, 236 p.
92-032038   016.7   0253314763
Music -- Bibliography. Music -- History and criticism -- Bibliography. Music -- Bibliography of bibliographies.

ML113.D83 1997
Duckles, Vincent H. 1913-
Music reference and research materials: an annotated bibliography. New York: Schirmer Books, c1997. xviii, 812 p.
97-011148   016.78   0028708210
Music -- Bibliography. Music -- History and criticism -- Bibliography. Music -- Bibliography -- Bibliography.

ML113.F8 2000
Fuld, James J.,
The book of world-famous music: classical, popular, and folk/ James J. Fuld. 5th ed., rev. and enl. New York: Dover Publications, 2000. xiii, 718 p.
00-702558   016.78 21   0486414752
Music -- Thematic catalogs. First editions.

ML113.H52 1980
Heyer, Anna Harriet, 1909-
Historical sets, collected editions, and monuments of music: a guide to their contents/ compiled by Anna Harriet Heyer. Chicago: American Library Association, 1980. 2 v.
80-022893   016.78   083890288X
Music -- Bibliography.

ML113.H55 1997
Hill, George Robert, 1943-
Collected editions, historical series & sets & monuments of music: a bibliography/ George R. Hill, Norris L. Stephens. Berkeley, Calif.: Fallen Leaf Press, c1997. xliv, 1349 p.
96-045419   016.78   0914913220
Music -- Bibliography.

ML113.M59 1996
Mixter, Keith E. 1922-
General bibliography for music research/ by Keith E. Mixter. [Warren,] Mich.: Harmonie Park Press, 1996. xxii, 200 p.
96-006364   016.78   0899901034
Music -- History and criticism -- Bibliography. Bibliography -- Bibliography -- Music.

ML113.R34 1999
Reader's guide to music: history, theory, criticism/ editor, Murray Steib. Chicago: Fitzroy Dearborn, 1999. xxxvi, 891 p.
2001-274620   780 21   1579581439
Music -- Bibliography.

ML118.M84
The Music index. Warren, Mich. Harmonie Park Press [etc.]
50-013627   016.78
Music--Periodicals--Indexes--Periodicals. Musicology--Periodicals--Indexes--Periodicals. Popular music--Periodicals--Indexes--Periodicals.

ML120 Bibliography — By region or country, A-Z

ML120.A35.G7 1991
Gray, John, 1962-
African music: a bibliographical guide to the traditional, popular, art, and liturgical musics of Sub-Saharan Africa/ John Gray. Westport, Conn.: Greenwood Press, 1991. xii, 499 p.
90-024517   016.78/0967   0313277699
Music -- Africa, Sub-Saharan -- History and criticism -- Bibliography.

ML120.C2.M67 1997
Morey, Carl.
Music in Canada: a research and information guide/ Carl Morey. New York: Garland Pub., 1997. xiii, 283 p.
96-029156   016.78/0971   0815316038
Music -- Canada -- History and criticism -- Bibliography.

ML120.D3.M35 1998
McLoskey, Lansing D., 1964-
Twentieth century Danish music: an annotated bibliography and research directory/ Lansing D. McLoskey. Westport, Conn.: Greenwood Press, 1998. xxi, 149 p.
97-042760   016.78/09489/0904   0313302936
Music -- Denmark -- 20th century -- Bibliography. Music -- Denmark -- 20th century -- Directories.

ML120.I5.H37 1991
Haroon, Mohammed, 1950-
Indian music literature/ Mohammed Haroon. Delhi: Indian Bibliographies Bureau, 1991. vi, 144 p.
91-901488   780/.954   8185004285
Music -- India -- Bibliography.

ML120.I75.T57 1988
Tischler, Alice.
A descriptive bibliography of art music by Israeli composers/ Alice Tischler. Warren, Mich.: Harmonie Park Press, 1988. xxiii, 424 p.
88-038301   016.78175694   0899900453
Composers -- Israel -- Bibliography.

ML120.P6.S6 1989
Smialek, William.
Polish music: a research and information guide/ William Smialek. New York: Garland Pub., 1989. xii, 260 p.
89-011965   016.78/09438   0824046145
Music -- Poland -- History and criticism -- Bibliography.

ML120.U5 C6 1988
Cohen-Stratyner, Barbara Naomi.
Popular music, 1900-1919: an annotated guide to American popular songs, including introductory essay, lyricists and composers index, important performances index, chronological index, and list of publishers/ Barbara Cohen-Stratyner, editor. Detroit, Mich.: Gale Research Inc., c1988. xxx, 656 p.
88-021191   784.5/00973 19   0810325950
Popular music -- United States -- Bibliography.

ML120.U5.H46 1990
Heintze, James R.
Early American music: a research and information guide/ James R. Heintze. New York: Garland Pub., c1990. xii, 511 p.
89-016904   016.78/0973/09033   0824041194
Music -- United States -- History and criticism -- Bibliography.

ML120.U5.H7 Suppl. 1
Horn, David, 1942-
The literature of American music in books and folk music collections. a fully annotated bibliography/ by David Horn with Richard Jackson. Metuchen, N.J.: Scarecrow Press, 1988. xvi, 570 p.
87-009630   016.781773   081081997X
Music -- United States -- History and criticism -- Bibliography.

ML120.U5.K78 1987
Krummel, Donald William, 1929-
Bibliographical handbook of American music/ D.W. Krummel. Urbana: University of Illinois Press, c1987. 269 p.
87-020597   780/.92/2   0252014502
Music -- United States -- Bibliography -- Catalogs.

ML120.U5.M133 1996
Marco, Guy A.
Checklist of writings on American music, 1640-1992/ Guy A. Marco. Lanham, Md.: Scarecrow Press, 1996. v, 237 p.
95-026773   016.78/0973   0810831333
Horn, David, -- 1942- -- Literature of American music in books and folk music collections -- Indexes. Marco, Guy A. -- Literature of American music III, 1983-1992 -- Indexes. Music -- United States -- History and criticism -- Indexes.

ML120.U5 M135 1996
Marco, Guy A.
Literature of American music III, 1983-1992/ Guy A. Marco. Lanham, Md.: Scarecrow Press, 1996. xviii, 451 p.
95-026774   016.78/0973 20   0810831325
Music -- United States -- History and criticism -- Bibliography.

ML120.U5.R47
Resources of American music history: a directory of source materials from Colonial times to World War II/ D. W. Krummel ... [et al.]. Urbana: University of Illinois Press, c1981. 463 p.
80-014873   016.78/0973   0252008286
Music -- United States -- Bibliography -- Union lists. Music -- United States -- Directories.

ML120.U5 H7
Horn, David,
The literature of American music in books and folk music collections: a fully annotated bibliography/ by David Horn. Metuchen, N.J.: Scarecrow Press, 1977. xiv, 556 p.
76-013160   016.7817/73   0810809966
Music -- United States -- History and criticism -- Bibliography.

ML125 Bibliography — Local, A-Z

ML125.P8 T55 1991
Thompson, Donald,
Music and dance in Puerto Rico from the age of
Columbus to modern times: an annotated bibliography/
by Donald Thompson and Annie F. Thompson.
Metuchen, N.J.: Scarecrow Press, 1991. xv, 339 p.
91-040519   016.78/097295 20   0810825155
Music -- Puerto Rico -- History and criticism -- Bibliography.
Dance -- Puerto Rico -- Bibliography.

ML128 Bibliography — By topic, A-Z

ML128.A7.D5 1991
Diamond, Harold J., 1934-
Music analyses: an annotated guide to the literature/
Harold J. Diamond. New York: Schirmer Books; c1991.
xi, 716 p.
90-013432   016.781   0028701100
Musical analysis -- Bibliography.

ML128.B45.F6 1983
Floyd, Samuel A.
Black music in the United States: an annotated
bibliography of selected reference and research materials/
Samuel A. Floyd, Marsha J. Reisser. Millwood, N.Y.:
Kraus International Publications, 1983. xv, 234 p.
82-049044   781.7/296073   0527301647
Afro-Americans -- Music -- History and criticism --
Bibliography. Music -- United States -- History and criticism --
Bibliography.

ML128.B45.G7 1988
Gray, John, 1962-
Blacks in classical music: a bibliographical guide to
composers, performers, and ensembles/ compiled by John
Gray. New York: Greenwood Press, c1988. x, 280 p.
87-037567   016.78/043/08996   0313260567
Musicians, Black -- Bibliography. Afro-American musicians --
Bibliography.

ML128.C4.H5
Hinson, Maurice.
The piano in chamber ensemble: an annotated guide/
Maurice Hinson. Bloomington: Indiana University Press,
c1978. xxxiii, 570 p.
77-009862   016.7857   025334493X
Piano with instrumental ensemble -- Bibliography. Chamber
music -- Bibliography.

ML128.C48.T5 1992
Tiemstra, Suzanne Spicer.
The choral music of Latin America: a guide to
compositions and research/ Suzanne Spicer Tiemstra.
New York: Greenwood Press, 1992. xx, 317 p.
91-046317   016.7825/098   0313282080
Choral music -- Latin America -- Bibliography.

ML128.C48.W5 1996
White, Evelyn Davidson.
Choral music by African American composers: a
selected, annotated bibliography/ compiled by Evelyn
Davidson White. Lanham, Md.: Scarecrow Press, c1996.
viii, 226 p.
95-031914   016.7825/089/96073   081083037X
Choral music -- Bibliography. Afro-Americans -- Music --
Bibliography.

ML128.C54.L4 1996
Laster, James, 1934-
Catalogue of choral music arranged in Biblical order/
James Laster. Lanham, Md.: Scarecrow Press, c1996. vi,
711 p.
95-033461   016.7834   081083071X
Church music -- Bibliography. Choral music -- Bibliography.

ML128.E8.S4 1992
Schuursma, Ann Briegleb, 1934-
Ethnomusicology research: a select annotated
bibliography/ Ann Briegleb Schuursma. New York:
Garland Pub., 1992. xxvii, 173 p.
90-003736   780/.89   082405735X
Ethnomusicology -- Bibliography.

ML128.F75.K44 1997
Keeling, Richard.
North American Indian music: a guide to published
sources and selected recordings/ Richard Keeling. New
York: Garland Pub., 1997. xlix, 420 p.
96-041847   016.78/089/97   0815302320
Indians of North America -- Music -- History and criticism --
Bibliography. Indians of North America -- Music --
Discography.

ML128.I64.K36 1997
Kantorski, Vincent.
A bibliography of source readings in music education/ by
Vincent J. Kantorski. Warren, Mich.: Harmonie Park
Press, 1997. xiv, 286 p.
97-033024   780/.71   0899900798
Music -- Instruction and study -- Bibliography.

ML128.I65 B3 1978
Barlow, Harold.
A dictionary of musical themes/ by Harold Barlow and
Sam Morgenstern; introd. by John Erskine. London: E.
Benn, 1978, c1975. xiii, 642 p.
78-317090   016.785/09/03   0510355013
Instrumental music -- Thematic catalogs.

ML128.J3.G7 1991
Gray, John, 1962-
Fire music: a bibliography of the new jazz, 1959-1990/
compiled by John Gray; foreword by Val Wilmer. New
York: Greenwood Press, 1991. xviii, 515 p.
91-020601   016.78165/5   031327892X
Jazz -- Bibliography.

ML128.J3.K45 1980
Kennington, Donald.
The literature of jazz: a critical guide/ by Donald Kennington and Danny L. Read. Chicago: American Library Association, 1980. xi, 236 p.
80-019837   016.781/57   0838903134
Jazz -- Bibliography.

ML128.M7.B6 1995
Bloom, Ken, 1949-
Hollywood song: the complete film & musical companion/ Ken Bloom. New York: Facts on File, c1995. 3 v.
90-022261   016.7821/4/0973   0816020027
Motion picture music -- Bibliography. Songs, English -- United States -- Indexes.

ML128.M7.M3 2000
McCarty, Clifford, 1929-
Film composers in America: a filmography, 1911-1970/ Clifford McCarty. New York: Oxford University Press, 2000. viii, 534 p.
98-042710   016.7815/42/09733   0195114736
Motion picture music -- United States -- Bibliography.

ML128.M78.B6 1996
Bloom, Ken, 1949-
American song: the complete musical theatre companion/ Ken Bloom. New York: Schirmer Books; c1996. 4 v.
95-049840   782.1/4/0973   0028704843
Musicals -- United States -- Bibliography. Songs, English -- United States -- Indexes.

ML128.M78.D48 1998
DeVenney, David P., 1958-
The Broadway song companion: an annotated guide to musical theatre literature by voice type and song style/ David P. DeVenney. Lanham, Md.: Scarecrow Press, 1998. xiii, 210 p.
97-042486   016.7821/4   0810833735
Musicals -- Bibliography. Popular music -- Bibliography. Voice types (Singing) -- Handbooks, manuals, etc.

ML128.M78.K7 1988
Krasker, Tommy.
Catalog of the American musical: musicals of Irving Berlin, George & Ira Gershwin, Cole Porter, Richard Rodgers & Lorenz Hart/ by Tommy Krasker and Robert Kimball. [Washington, D.C.]: National Institute for Opera and Musical Theater, c1988. xv, 442 p.
87-061421   016.7821/4/0973   0961857501
Musicals -- Bibliography.

ML128.O2.H55 1991
Haynes, Bruce, 1942-
Music for oboe, 1650-1800: a bibliography/ Bruce Haynes. Berkeley, Calif.: Fallen Leaf Press, c1992. xxv, 432 p.
91-034794   016.7885/2   0914913158
Oboe music -- 17th century -- Bibliography. Oboe music -- 18th century -- Bibliography. Music -- 17th century -- Bibliography.

ML128.O4 M28 2001
Marco, Guy A.
Opera: a research and information guide/ Guy A. Marco; foreword by Edward O.D. Downes. New York: Garland Pub., 2001. xx, 632 p.
00-050302   016.7821   0815335164
Opera -- Bibliography.

ML128.O4.S8 1989
Studwell, William E. 1936-
Opera plot index: a guide to locating plots and descriptions of operas, operettas, and other works of the musical theater, and associated material/ William E. Studwell, David A. Hamilton. New York: Garland Pub., 1990. xxi, 466 p.
89-037920   016.7821/026/9   0824046218
Operas -- Stories, plots, etc. -- Indexes. Musicals -- Stories, plots, etc. -- Indexes.

ML128.O5 D3 1996
Daniels, David,
Orchestral music: a handbook/ David Daniels. 3rd ed. Lanham, Md.: Scarecrow Press, 1996. xv, 611 p.
96-034819   016.7842 20   0810832283
Orchestral music--Bibliography.

ML128.P235.J3 1988
Jackson, Roland John, 1925-
Performance practice, medieval to contemporary: a bibliographic guide/ Roland Jackson. New York: Garland, 1988. xxix, 518 p.
87-025900   016.78/07/3   0824015126
Performance practice (Music) -- Bibliography.

ML128.P3 H5 2000
Hinson, Maurice.
Guide to the pianist's repertoire/ Maurice Hinson. 3rd ed. Bloomington: Indiana University Press, c2000. xli, 933 p.
99-058594   016.7862/0263 21   0253213487
Piano music--Bibliography. Piano music--Bibliography--Graded lists.

ML128.P3 H53 1993
Hinson, Maurice.
Music for piano and orchestra: an annotated guide/ Maurice Hinson. Enl. ed., 1st Midland ed. Bloomington: Indiana University Press, 1993. xxiv, 359 p.
93-020035   016.7842/62 20   0253208351
Piano with orchestra -- Bibliography. Concertos (Piano) -- Bibliography.

ML128.P3 H534 1998
Hinson, Maurice.
The pianist's bookshelf; a practical guide to books, videos, and other resources/ Maurice Hinson. Bloomington: Indiana University Press, c1998. xii, 323 p.
97-047307   016.7862 21   025321145X
Piano -- Bibliography. Piano music -- Bibliography.

ML128.P3.H536 1990
Hinson, Maurice.
The pianist's guide to transcriptions, arrangements, and paraphrases/ Maurice Hinson. Bloomington: Indiana University Press, 1990. xxi, 159 p.
89-045356   016.7862/138/026 20   0253327458
Piano music -- Bibliography. Piano music, Arranged -- Bibliography. Piano music -- Bibliography -- Graded lists.

ML128.P3.H54 1987
Hinson, Maurice.
The pianist's reference guide: a bibliographical survey/ Maurice Hinson. Los Angeles: Alfred Pub. Co., c1987. xi, 336 p.
87-001208   016.7861   0882843583
Piano -- Bibliography. Piano music -- History and criticism -- Bibliography.

ML128.P63.G65 1995
Goodfellow, William D., 1947-
SongCite: an index to popular songs/ William D. Goodfellow. New York: Garland, 1995. 433 p.
94-044768   016.78242164/0263   0815320590
Popular music -- Indexes.

ML128.P63 G65 1995 Suppl.
Goodfellow, William D.,
SongCite: an index to popular songs. William D. Goodfellow. New York: Garland Pub., 1999. 400 p.
98-039928   016.78242164/0263 21   081533298X
Popular music -- Indexes.

ML128.P63.H34 1995
Haggerty, Gary.
A guide to popular music reference books: an annotated bibliography/ Gary Haggerty. Westport, Conn.: Greenwood Press, 1995. xv, 210 p.
95-018177   016.78164   0313296618
Popular music -- Reference books -- Bibliography.

ML128.R28.M3 1992
McCoy, Judy, 1946-
Rap music in the 1980s: a reference guide/ by Judy McCoy. Metuchen, N.J.: Scarecrow Press, 1992. xiv, 261 p.
92-039684   782.42164   0810826496
Rap (Music) -- History and criticism -- Bibliography. Rap (Music) -- Discography.

ML128.R31 G75 2003
Griscom, Richard.
The recorder: a research and information guide/ Richard Griscom and David Lasocki. 2nd ed. New York: Routledge, 2003.
2003-001023   016.7883/6 21   0415937442
Recorder (Musical instrument) -- Bibliography.

ML128.R6.G37 1995
Gatten, Jeffrey N.
Rock music scholarship: an interdisciplinary bibliography/ Jeffrey N. Gatten. Westport, Conn.: Greenwood Press, 1995. xiv, 294 p.
95-036391   016.78166   0313294550
Rock music -- History and criticism -- Bibliography.

ML128.R6.H6
Hoffmann, Frank W., 1949-
The literature of rock/ by Frank Hoffmann. Metuchen, N.J.: Scarecrow Press, 1981-1995. 3 v. in 4.
80-023459   016.78166   0810813718
Rock music -- History and criticism -- Bibliography.

ML128.R6.P65 1997
Pollock, Bruce.
The rock song index: essential information on the 7,500 most important songs of rock and roll/ Bruce Pollock. New York: Schirmer Books; c1997. xviii, 524 p.
96-031950   016.78242166   0028720687
Rock music -- Bibliography.

ML128.S17.R87 1996
Rust, Ezra Gardner.
The music and dance of the world's religions: a comprehensive, annotated bibliography of materials in the English language/ E. Gardner Rust. Westport, Conn.: Greenwood Press, 1996. xx, 476 p.
96-018212   016.7817   0313295611
Sacred vocal music -- Bibliography. Music -- Bibliography. Dance -- Bibliography.

ML128.S3 C37 2001
Carman, Judith E.
Art song in the United States, 1759-1999: an annotated bibliography/ Judith E. Carman, William K. Gaeddert, Rita M. Resch; with Gordon Myers. 3rd ed./ edited by Judith E. Carman. Lanham, Md.: Scarecrow Press, 2001. xxiv, 475 p.
2001-042636   016.78242168/0973 21   0810841371
Songs -- United States -- Bibliography. Songs -- United States -- Indexes.

ML128.S3.D37
De Charms, Desiree.
Songs in collections; an index [by] Desiree de Charms & Paul F. Breed. [Detroit] Information Service [c1966] xxxix, 588 p.
65-027601   783.6016
Songs -- Indexes.

ML128.S3.E8
Espina, Noni.
Repertoire for the solo voice: a fully annotated guide to works for the solo voice published in modern editions and covering material from the 13th century to the present/ by Noni Espina; with a foreword by Berton Coffin. Metuchen, N.J.: Scarecrow Press, [1977-]
76-030441   016.784/3061   0810809435
Songs -- Bibliography.

ML128.S3 H4
Havlice, Patricia Pate.
Popular song index/ by Patricia Pate Havlice. Metuchen, N.J.: Scarecrow Press, 1975. 933 p.
75-009896   016.784   081080820X
Songs -- Indexes.

ML128.S3 H4 Suppl. 1
Havlice, Patricia Pate.
Popular song index: first supplement/ by Patricia Pate Havlice. Metuchen, N.J.: Scarecrow Press, 1978. 386 p.
77-025219   784   0810810999
Songs -- Indexes.

ML128.S3 H4 Suppl. 2
Havlice, Patricia Pate.
Popular song index. by Patricia Pate Havlice. Metuchen, N.J.: Scarecrow Press, 1984. iv, 530 p.
83-007692   016.784 19   0810816423
Songs -- Indexes.

ML128.S3 L4 1989
Lax, Roger.
The great song thesaurus/ Roger Lax, Frederick Smith. 2nd ed., updated and expanded. New York: Oxford University Press, 1989. 774 p.
88-031267   784.5/0016 19   0195054083
Popular music -- Indexes.

ML128.S3.S31 1966
Sears, Minnie Earl, 1873-1933.
Song index; an index to more than 12,000 songs in 177 song collections comprising 262 volumes and supplement, 1934. Assisted by Phyllis Crawford. [n.p.] Shoe String Press, 1966. 2 v. in 1.
66-025185   016.784
 Songs -- Indexes.

ML128.S3.S31 Suppl.
Sears, Minnie Earl, 1873-1933.
Song index. Supplement; an index to more than 7000 songs in 104 song collections, comprising 124 volumes, edited by Minnie Earl Sears, assisted by Phyliss Crawford. Preface by Isadore Gilbert Mudge. New York, The H. W. Wilson company, 1934.
27-026092
 Songs -- Dictionaries, indexes, etc.

ML128.S3 S66 1995
Snyder, Lawrence D.,
German poetry in song: an index of Lieder/ Lawrence D. Snyder. Berkeley, Calif.: Fallen Leaf Press, 1995. xviii, 730 p.
94-049170   016.78242168/0943 20   0914913328
Songs, German -- Indexes.

ML128.S4.A27 1999
Abromeit, Kathleen A., 1962-
An index to African-American spirituals for the solo voice/ compiled by Kathleen A. Abromeit; foreword by Francois Clemmons. Westport, Conn.: Greenwood Press, 1999. xiii, 199 p.
98-044409   016.78225/3   0313305773
 Spirituals (Songs) -- Indexes. Afro-Americans -- Music -- Bibliography.

ML128.V5.H66 1994
Homuth, Donald, 1920-
Cello music since 1960: a bibliography of solo, chamber & orchestral works for the solo cellist/ Donald Homuth. Berkeley, CA: Fallen Leaf Press, c1994. x, 451 p.
94-015453   016.7874/09/045   0914913271
 Violoncello music -- 20th century -- Bibliography. Chamber music -- 20th century -- Bibliography. Orchestral music -- 20th century -- Bibliography.

ML128.V5.M28 1989
Markevitch, Dimitry.
The solo cello: a bibliography of the unaccompanied violoncello literature/ Dimitry Markevitch. Berkeley, Calif.: Fallen Leaf Press, c1989. viii, 113 p.
89-023355   016.7874/026   0914913115
 Violoncello music -- Bibliography.

ML128.V7 B3 1976
Barlow, Harold.
A dictionary of opera and song themes: including cantatas, oratorios, lieder, and art songs = originally published as A dictionary of vocal themes / compiled by Harold Barlow and Sam Morgenstern. Rev. ed. New York: Crown Publishers, c1976. 547 p.
75-030751   016.784   0517525038
Vocal music -- Thematic catalogs.

ML128.V7.H67 1986
Hovland, Michael A.
Musical settings of American poetry: a bibliography/ compiled by Michael Hovland. Westport, Conn.: Greenwood Press, 1986. xli, 531 p.
86-000402   016.7843   0313229384
 Vocal music -- Bibliography. American poetry -- Musical settings -- Bibliography.

ML128.V7.K3 1968
Kagen, Sergius.
Music for the voice; a descriptive list of concert and teaching material. Bloomington, Indiana University Press [c1968] xx, 780 p.
68-027348   781/.97   0253339553
 Vocal music -- Bibliography.

ML128.V7 M4 1971
Mattfeld, Julius,
Variety music cavalcade, 1620-1969; a chronology of vocal and instrumental music popular in the United States. With an introd. by Abel Green. 3d ed. Englewood Cliffs, N.J., Prentice-Hall [1971] xx, 766 p.
70-129240   0139407189
Popular music -- United States -- Bibliography. Music -- United States -- Chronology.

ML128.V7.M45 1998
McTyre, Ruthann Boles, 1954-
Library resources for singers, coaches, and accompanists: an annotated bibliography, 1970-1997/ compiled by Ruthann Boles McTyre. Westport, Conn.: Greenwood Press, 1998. xxiv, 151 p.
98-023959   016.783   0313302669
 Singing -- Instruction and study -- Sources -- Bibliography.

ML128.W5.F3 1990
Fasman, Mark J.
Brass bibliography: sources on the history, literature, pedagogy, performance, and acoustics of brass instruments/ Mark J. Fasman. Bloomington: Indiana University Press, c1990. xii, 452 p.
89-045198   016.7889   0253321301
Brass instruments -- Bibliography.

ML128.W5.G52 1998
Gillaspie, Jon A.
The wind ensemble catalog/ Jon A. Gillaspie, Marshall Stoneham, and David Lindsey Clark. Westport, CT: Greenwood Press, 1998. xix, 444 p.
97-042759   016.7848/026   0313253943
Wind ensembles -- Bibliography.

ML128.W5.H62 1996
Horne, Aaron, 1940-
Brass music of black composers: a bibliography/ compiled by Aaron Horne; foreword by David N. Baker. Westport, Conn.: Greenwood Press, 1996. xxix, 521 p.
95-052946   016.7889/089/96   0313298262
Brass instruments -- Bibliography. Blacks -- Music -- Bibliography.

ML128.W5.H65 1990
Horne, Aaron, 1940-
Woodwind music of Black composers/ compiled by Aaron Horne. New York: Greenwood Press, 1990. xvii, 145 p.
89-025650   016.7882   0313272654
Woodwind instrument music -- Bibliography. Blacks -- Music -- Bio-bibliography.

ML128.W7.E75 1995
Ericson, Margaret D.
Women and music: a selective annotated bibliography on women and gender issues in music, 1987-1992/ Margaret D. Ericson. New York: G.K. Hall; c1995. xxii, 400 p.
94-045222   016.78/082   0816105804
Women musicians -- Bibliography. Feminism and music -- Bibliography.

ML134 Bibliography —
Individual composers, A-Z

ML134.A45 C53 1998
Clark, Walter Aaron.
Isaac Albéniz: a guide to research/ Walter A. Clark. New York: Garland Publishing, 1998. xii, 256 p.
98-023412   780/.92 21   0815320957
Albéniz, Isaac, 1860-1909 -- Bibliography.

ML134.B1.G74 2000
Green, Jonathan D., 1964-
A conductor's guide to the choral-orchestral works of J.S. Bach/ Jonathan D. Green. Lanham, Md.: Scarecrow Press, 2000. ix, 622 p.
99-048684   016.7825/092   0810837331
Bach, Johann Sebastian, -- 1685-1750. -- Choral music. Choruses with orchestra -- Bibliography. Choruses with orchestra -- Analysis, appreciation.

ML134.B1.M45 1998
Melamed, Daniel R.
An introduction to Bach studies/ Daniel R. Melamed, Michael Marissen. New York: Oxford University Press, 1998. xi, 189 p.
97-040406   016.780/92   0195122313
Bach, Johann Sebastian, -- 1685-1750 -- Bibliography.

ML134.B175 W46 2001
Wentzel, Wayne C.
Samuel Barber: a guide to research/ Wayne C. Wentzel. New York: Routledge, 2001.
00-066506   016.78/092 21   0815334966
Barber, Samuel, 1910- -- Bibliography.

ML134.B18.A7 1988
Antokoletz, Elliott.
Bela Bartok: a guide to research/ Elliott Antokoletz. New York: Garland Pub., 1988. xxxi, 356 p.
87-036053   016.78/092/4   0824077474
Bartok, Bela, -- 1881-1945 -- Bibliography.

ML134.B46.S56 1996
Simms, Bryan R.
Alban Berg: a guide to research/ Bryan R. Simms. New York: Garland Pub., 1996. xv, 293 p.
96-018210   016.78/092   0815320329
Berg, Alban, -- 1885-1935 -- Bibliography.

ML134.B5.L3 1989
Langford, Jeffrey Alan.
Hector Berlioz: a guide to research/ Jeffrey Langford, Jane Denker Graves. New York: Garland, 1989. xxi, 307 p.
89-001390   016.78/092   0824046358
Berlioz, Hector, -- 1803-1869 -- Bibliography.

ML134.B512 L35 2002
Laird, Paul R.
Leonard Bernstein: a guide to research/ Paul R. Laird. New York: Routledge, 2002. x, 306 p.
2001-019232   016.78/092 21   0815335172
Bernstein, Leonard, 1918- -- Bibliography.

ML134.B8.Q53 1998
Quigley, Thomas, 1954-
Johannes Brahms: an annotated bibliography of the literature from 1982 to 1996 with an appendix on Brahms and the Internet/ Thomas Quigley, in collaboration with Mary I. Ingraham. Lanham, MD: Scarecrow Press, 1998. xiii, 697 p.
97-041925   016.780/92   0810834391
Brahms, Johannes, -- 1833-1897 -- Bibliography.

ML134.B85.H63 1996
Hodgson, Peter John, 1929-
Benjamin Britten: a guide to research/ Peter J. Hodgson. New York: Garland Pub., 1996. 244 p.
96-019632   016.78/092   0815317956
Britten, Benjamin, -- 1913-1976 -- Bibliography.

ML134.C19 L56 2000
Link, John F.
Elliott Carter: a guide to research/ John F. Link. New York: Garland Pub., 2000. xiv, 331 p.
99-042718   016.780/92 21   0815324324
Carter, Elliott, 1908- -- Bibliography.

ML134.C42 P69 2002
Poznansky, Alexander.
The Tchaikovsky handbook: a guide to the man and his music/ compiled by Alexander Poznansky and Brett Langston. Bloomington: Indiana University Press, c2002. 2 v.
2001-039546   780/.92 B 21   0253339472
Tchaikovsky, Peter Ilich, 1840-1893 -- Bibliography. Tchaikovsky, Peter Ilich, 1840-1893 -- Thematic catalogs.

ML134.D26.B7 1990
Briscoe, James R., 1949-
Claude Debussy: a guide to research/ James R. Briscoe. New York: Garland, 1990. xxi, 504 p.
89-023691   016.78/092   0824057953
Debussy, Claude, -- 1862-1918 -- Bibliography.

ML134.D66.C37 2000
Cassaro, James P.
Gaetano Donizetti: a guide to research/ James P. Cassaro. New York: Garland Pub., 2000. xiii, 231 p.
00-029426   016.7821/092   0815323506
Donizetti, Gaetano, -- 1797-1848 -- Bibliography.

ML134.E613 K46 1993
Kent, Christopher,
Edward Elgar: a guide to research/ Christopher Kent. New York: Garland Pub., 1993. xvii, 523 p.
92-032217   016.78/092 20   0824084454
Elgar, Edward, 1857-1934 -- Bibliography.

ML134.F29.P55 2000
Phillips, Edward R.
Gabriel Faure: a guide to research/ Edward R. Phillips. New York: Garland Pub., 2000. xv, 429 p.
99-045622   016.780/92   0824070739
Faure, Gabriel, -- 1845-1924 -- Bibliography.

ML134.F6.E4 1988
Elliker, Calvin, 1949-
Stephen Collins Foster: a guide to research/ Calvin Elliker. New York: Garland Pub., 1988. xii, 197 p.
87-035853   016.784/092/4   0824066405
Foster, Stephen Collins, -- 1826-1864 -- Bibliography.

ML134.G29.C37 2000
Carnovale, Norbert, 1932-
George Gershwin: a bio-bibliography/ Norbert Carnovale. Westport, Conn.: Greenwood Press, 2000. xiv, 608 p.
99-046018   780/.92   0313260036
Gershwin, George, -- 1898-1937 -- Bibliography. Gershwin, George, -- 1898-1937 -- Discography.

ML134.G29.R5 1991
Rimler, Walter.
A Gershwin companion: a critical inventory & discography, 1916-1984/ Walter Rimler. Ann Arbor, MI: Popular Culture, 1991. xiv, 498 p.
91-061884   780/.92   1560750197
Gershwin, George, -- 1898-1937 -- Bibliography. Gershwin, George, -- 1898-1937 -- Discography.

ML134.G956.E3 1995
Earp, Lawrence Marshburn.
Guillaume de Machaut: a guide to research/ Lawrence Earp. New York: Garland Pub., 1995. xix, 669 p.
95-035044   016.841/1   0824023234
Guillaume, -- de Machaut, -- ca. 1300-1377 -- Bibliography. Music -- 500-1400 -- History and criticism -- Bibliography.

ML134.H16.P37 1988
Parker-Hale, Mary Ann, 1951-
G.F. Handel: a guide to research/ Mary Ann Parker-Hale. New York: Garland, 1988. xvii, 294 p.
88-027472   780/.92/4   0824084527
Handel, George Frideric, -- 1685-1759 -- Bibliography.

ML134.H272.G74 1990
Grave, Floyd K. 1945-
Franz Joseph Haydn: a guide to research/ Floyd K. Grave, Margaret G. Grave. New York: Garland Pub., 1990. xi, 451 p.
90-003533   016.78/092   082408487X
Haydn, Joseph, -- 1732-1809 -- Bibliography.

ML134.I9.B6 1988
Block, Geoffrey Holden.
Charles Ives: a bio-bibliography/ Geoffrey Block; foreword by J. Peter Burkholder. New York: Greenwood Press, 1988. xviii, 422 p.
88-021316   016.78/092/4   0313254044
Ives, Charles, -- 1874-1954 -- Bibliography. Ives, Charles, -- 1874-1954 -- Discography.

ML134.J75.P56 1998
Ping-Robbins, Nancy R., 1939-
Scott Joplin: a guide to research/ Nancy R. Ping-Robbins. New York: Garland Pub., 1998. vi, 419 p.
98-010988   016.78/092   0824083997
Joplin, Scott, -- 1868-1917 -- Bibliography.

ML134.J773 C5 1983
Charles, Sydney Robinson.
Josquin des Prez: a guide to research/ Sydney Robinson Charles. New York: Garland Pub., 1983. xi, 235 p.
81-048418   016.784/092/4 19   0824093879
Josquin, des Prez, d. 1521 -- Bibliography.

ML134.K64.H68 1998
Houlahan, Micheal.
Zoltan Kodaly: a guide to research/ Micheal Houlahan and Philip Tacka. New York: Garland Pub., 1998. xiv, 611 p.
97-049639   016.78/092   0815328532
Kodaly, Zoltan, -- 1882-1967 -- Bibliography.

ML134.L7.S2 1991
Saffle, Michael Benton, 1946-
Franz Liszt: a guide to research/ Michael Saffle; with discographical contributions by Ben Arnold, Keith Fagan, and Artis Wodehouse. New York: Garland Pub., 1991. xviii, 407 p.
91-011182   016.78/092   0824083822
Liszt, Franz, -- 1811-1886 -- Bibliography. Liszt, Franz, -- 1811-1886 -- Discography.

ML134.L86.H4 1991
Hartsock, Ralph.
Otto Luening: a bio-bibliography/ Ralph Hartsock. New York: Greenwood Press, 1991. xiii, 272 p.
90-022926   016.78/092   0313243204
Luening, Otto, -- 1900- -- Bibliography. Luening, Otto, -- 1900- -- Discography.

ML134.M34.F54 1989
Filler, Susan Melanie, 1947-
Gustav and Alma Mahler: a guide to research/ Susan M. Filler. New York: Garland Pub., 1989. li, 336 p.
89-023369   016.78/092   0824084837
Mahler, Gustav, -- 1860-1911 -- Bibliography. Mahler, Alma, -- 1879-1964 -- Bibliography.

ML134.M53 C6 2001
Cooper, John Michael.
Felix Mendelssohn Bartholdy: a guide to research: with an introduction to research concerning Fanny Hensel/ John Michael Cooper. New York: Routledge, 2001.
00-045737   016.78/092 21   0815315139
Mendelssohn-Bartholdy, Felix, 1809-1847 -- Bibliography. Hensel, Fanny Mendelssohn, 1805-1847 -- Bibliography.

ML134.M533 H59 2000
Hixon, Donald L.
Gian Carlo Menotti: a bio-bibliography/ Donald L. Hixon. Westport, CT: Greenwood Press, 2000. xii, 339 p.
99-054384   780/.92 B 21   0313261393
Menotti, Gian Carlo, 1911- -- Bibliography.

ML134.M66.A5 1989
Adams, K. Gary.
Claudio Monteverdi: a guide to research/ K. Gary Adams and Dyke Kiel. New York: Garland Pub., 1989. xviii, 273 p.
89-033040   016.782/0092   0824077431
Monteverdi, Claudio, -- 1567-1643 -- Bibliography.

ML134.P2 M37 2001
Marvin, Clara.
Giovanni Pierluigi da Palestrina: a guide to research/ Clara Marvin. New York: Routledge, 2001.
00-068435   016.7822/2/092 21   0815323514
Palestrina, Giovanni Pierluigi da, 1525?-1594 -- Bibliography.

ML134.P94.F35 1999
Fairtile, Linda Beard.
Giacomo Puccini: a guide to research/ Linda B. Fairtile. New York: Garland Pub., 1999. xvi, 381 p.
98-041182   782.1/092   0815320337
Puccini, Giacomo, 1858-1924 -- Bibliography.

ML134.R12.C86 2001
Cunningham, Robert, 1948-
Sergei Rachmaninoff: a bio-bibliography/ Robert E. Cunningham, Jr. Westport, CT: Greenwood Press, 2001. xi, 349 p.
00-042672   780/.92   0313309078
Rachmaninoff, Sergei, -- 1873-1943 -- Bibliography. Rachmaninoff, Sergei, -- 1873-1943 -- Discography.

ML134.R14.F7 1989
Foster, Donald H.
Jean-Philippe Rameau: a guide to research/ Donald H. Foster. New York: Garland Pub., 1989. xiii, 292 p.
88-037500   016.7821/092/4   0824056450
Rameau, Jean Philippe, -- 1683-1764 -- Bibliography.

ML134.S485 H8 2002
Hulme, Derek C.
Dmitri Shostakovich: a catalogue, bibliography, and discography/ Derek C. Hulme. 3rd ed. Lanham, Md.: Scarecrow Press, 2002. xiv, 701 p.
2002-011012   016.78/092 21   081084432X
Shostakovich, Dmitriæi Dmitrievich, 1906-1975 -- Bibliography. Shostakovich, Dmitriæi Dmitrievich, 1906-1975 -- Discography.

ML134.S49 G67 1998
Goss, Glenda Dawn.
Jean Sibelius: a guide to research/ Glenda D. Goss. New York: Garland Pub., 1998. xxi, 298 p.
97-033019   016.78/092 21   0815311710
Sibelius, Jean, 1865-1957 -- Bibliography.

ML134.S8.S75 1996
Still, Judith Anne.
William Grant Still: a bio-bibliography/ Judith Anne Still, Michael J. Dabrishus, and Carolyn L. Quin. Westport, Conn: Greenwood Press, 1996. xii, 331 p.
96-021946   016.78/092   0313252556
Still, William Grant, -- 1895- -- Bibliography.

ML134.V47.H37 1998
Harwood, Gregory W.
Giuseppe Verdi: a guide to research/ Gregory Harwood. New York: Garland Pub., 1998. xxx, 396 p.
98-012194   782.1/092   0824041178
Verdi, Giuseppe, -- 1813-1901 -- Bibliography.

ML134.V7.T34 1988
Talbot, Michael.
Antonio Vivaldi: a guide to research/ Michael Talbot. New York: Garland Pub., 1988. xlv, 197 p.
88-002521   016.78/092/4   0824083865
Vivaldi, Antonio, -- 1678-1741 -- Bibliography.

ML134.W1 S24 2002
Saffle, Michael,
Richard Wagner: a guide to research/ Michael Saffle. New York: Routledge, 2002.
2001-048162   016.7821/092 21   0824056957
Wagner, Richard, 1813-1883 -- Bibliography.

ML134.W75.O87 1988
Ossenkop, David, 1937-
Hugo Wolf: a guide to research/ David Ossenkop. New York: Garland, 1988. xxxii, 329 p.
88-016323   016.7843/0092/4   0824084748
Wolf, Hugo, -- 1860-1903 -- Bibliography.

ML134.5 Bibliography — Other individuals, A-Z

ML134.5.D5 L7 1992
Lowenberg, Carlton.
Musicians wrestle everywhere: Emily Dickinson & music/ Carlton Lowenberg. Berkeley, Calif.: Fallen Leaf Press, c1992. xxviii, 210 p.
92-009923   016.7824 20   0914913204
Dickinson, Emily, 1830-1886 -- Musical settings -- Bibliography. Dickinson, Emily, 1830-1886 -- Knowledge -- Music.

ML134.5.P73 H56 2001
Hinds, Mary Hancock.
Infinite Elvis: an annotated bibliography/ by Mary Hancock Hinds. Chicago: A Cappella, c2001. xvi, 512 p.
00-043063   016.78242166/092 21   1556524102
Presley, Elvis, 1935-1977 -- Bibliography.

ML134.5.S52.G6 1991
Gooch, Bryan N. S.
A Shakespeare music catalogue/ Bryan N.S. Gooch, David Thatcher; Odean Long, associate editor; incorporating material collected and contributed by Charles Haywood. Oxford: Clarendon Press, 1991. 5 v.
89-009270   016.78/00822   0198129416
Shakespeare, William, -- 1564-1616 -- Songs and music -- Bibliography. Shakespeare, William, -- 1564-1616 -- Musical settings -- Bibliography.

ML141 Bibliography — Catalogs — Exhibitions. By city, A-Z

ML141.N4.A76 1994
Louis Armstrong: a cultural legacy/ edited by Marc H. Miller; essays by Donald Bogle... [et al.]. Seattle: Queens Museum of Art, New York in association with University of Washington Press, c1994. 248 p.
94-021134   781.65/092   029597382X
Armstrong, Louis, -- 1901-1971 -- Exhibitions. Jazz -- Exhibitions.

ML156.4 Bibliography — Discography — By topic, A-Z

ML156.4.B6.A45 1996
All music guide to the blues: the experts' guide to the best blues recordings/ edited by Michael Erlewine ... [et al.]. San Francisco: Miller Freeman Books; 1996. xii, 424 p.
96-077864   016.781643/0266   0879304243
Blues (Music) -- Discography. Sound recordings -- Reviews.

ML156.4.B6.D59 1997
Dixon, Robert M. W.
Blues & gospel records, 1890-1943/ compiled by Robert M.W. Dixon, John Godrich, and Howard Rye. Oxford [England]: Clarendon Press; 1997. xlix, 1370 p.
96-006715   016.781643/0266   0198162391
Blues (Music) -- Discography. Gospel music -- Discography. Afro-Americans -- Music -- Discography.

ML156.4.C7.A45 1997
All music guide to country: the experts' guide to the best recordings in country music/ edited by Michael Erlewine ... [et al.]. San Francisco, CA: Miller Freeman; c1997. xxii, 611 p.
97-060980   781.642/0266   0879304758
Country music -- Discography. Sound recordings -- Reviews.

ML156.4.C7 M87 1997
MusicHound country: the essential album guide/ edited by Brian Mansfield and Gary Graff. Detroit: Visible Ink, c1997. xxiv, 642 p.
97-005277   016.781642/0266 21   157859006X
Country music--Discography. Sound recordings--Reviews. Country music--Bio-bibliography--Dictionaries.

ML156.4.F5 C64 1994
Cohen, Norm.
Traditional Anglo-American folk music: an annotated discography of published sound recordings/ Norm Cohen. New York: Garland Pub., 1994. xx, 517 p.
93-026934   016.78162/13/00266 20   0815303777
Folk music -- United States -- Discography. Folk songs, English -- United States -- Discography.

ML156.4.F5 S69 1990
Spottswood, Richard K.
Ethnic music on records: a discography of ethnic recordings produced in the United States, 1893 to 1942/ Richard K. Spottswood with a foreword by James H. Billington. Urbana: University of Illinois Press, c1990. 7 v.
89-020526   016.78162/0026/6 20   0252017188
Folk music -- Discography. Folk songs -- Discography. Popular music -- Discography. Sound recordings -- United States -- Catalogs.

ML156.4.J3 A45 1998
All music guide to jazz: the experts' guide to the best jazz recordings/ edited by Michael Erlewine ... [et al.]. 3rd ed. San Francisco: Miller Freeman Books; xvi, 1378 p.
00-268509   781.65/0266 21   0879305304
Jazz--Discography. Sound recordings--Reviews.

ML156.4.J3.B66 1995
The Blackwell guide to recorded jazz/ edited by Barry Kernfeld. Cambridge, Mass.: Blackwell, 1995. xx, 587 p.
95-000762   016.78165/026/6   0631195521
Jazz -- Discography. Jazz -- History and criticism.

ML156.4.J3 C67 2002
Cook, Richard,
The Penguin guide to jazz on CD/ Richard Cook and
Brian Morton. 6th ed. London; Penguin Books, c2002. x,
1730 p.
2003-269440   781.65/0266 22   0140515216
Jazz -- Discography. Compact discs -- Reviews.

ML156.4.J3.C87 2001
Cuscuna, Michael.
The Blue Note label: a discography/ compiled by Michael
Cuscuna and Michel Ruppli. Westport, Conn.:
Greenwood Press, 2001. xix, 913 p.
00-052112   016.78165/0266   0313318263
*Jazz -- Discography. Sound recordings -- United States --
Catalogs.*

ML156.4.J3 P53 1995
Piazza, Tom,
The guide to classic recorded jazz/ Tom Piazza. Iowa
City: University of Iowa Press, c1995. xviii, 391 p.
94-036373   016.78165/0266 20   0877454892
Jazz -- Discography. Sound recordings -- Reviews.

ML156.4.O46.M5 1993
The Metropolitan Opera guide to recorded opera/ edited
by Paul Gruber. New York: Metropolitan Opera Guild:
c1993. xv, 782 p.
92-032618   016.7821/026/6   0393034445
Operas -- Discography. Sound recordings -- Reviews.

ML156.4.P6.W497 1985
Whitburn, Joel.
Joel Whitburn's top pop albums, 1955-1985: compiled
from Billboard's pop album charts, 1955-1985.
Menomonee Falls, Wis.: Record Research Inc., c1985.
508 p.
85-216224   781.64/0973/09045   0898200547
*Popular music -- United States -- Discography. Popular music
-- United States -- Statistics.*

ML156.4.P6 W4977 1995
Whitburn, Joel.
Joel Whitburn's top pop singles CD guide, 1955-1979/
compiled by Jerry Reuss. Menomonee Falls, WI: Record
Research Inc., c1995. xi, 270 p.
95-195298   781.64/0973/09045 20   0898201071
Popular music -- United States -- Discography.

ML156.4.R6.K64 1988
Kocandrle, Mirek.
The history of rock and roll: a selective discography/
Mirek Kocandrle. Boston: G.K. Hall, c1988. xv, 297 p.
88-021200   789.9/12454   0816189560
Rock music -- Discography.

ML156.4.R6.M87 1999
MusicHound rock: the essential album guide/ edited by
Gary Graff and Daniel Durchholz. Detroit: Visible Ink
Press, c1999. xxv, 1497 p.
98-040006   781.66/0266   1578590612
Rock music -- Discography.

ML156.4.R6.S8 1998
Strong, M. C. 1960-
The great rock discography/ by Martin C. Strong. New
York: Times Books, 1998.
98-021875   016.78166/0266   0812931114
Rock music -- Discography.

ML156.4.W63.M87 2000
MusicHound world: the essential album guide/ edited by
Adam McGovern; photographs by Jack & Linda
Vartoogian; forewords by Angelique Kidjo & David
Byrne. Detroit, Mich.: Visible Ink, c2000. xxxi, 1096 p.
99-066755   1578590396
World music -- History and criticism.

ML156.5 Bibliography — Discography — Individual composers, A-Z

ML156.5.E45.T5 1988
Timner, W. E., 1930-
Ellingtonia: the recorded music of Duke Ellington and his
sidemen/ compiled by W.E. Timner. Metuchen, N.J.:
Institute of Jazz Studies: 1988. xiv, 534 p.
86-021967   016.7899/12542   0810819341
Ellington, Duke, -- 1899-1974 -- Discography.

ML156.7 Bibliography — Discography — Individual performers, A-Z

ML156.7.D97.K67 1991
Krogsgaard, Michael.
Positively Bob Dylan: a thirty-year discography, concert
& recording session guide, 1960-1991/ by Michael
Krogsgaard. Ann Arbor, MI: Popular Culture, 1991. xiv,
498 p.
89-092336   016.78242162/0092   1560750006
Dylan, Bob, -- 1941- -- Discography.

ML156.7.F594 J64 2001
Johnson, J. Wilfred, 1920-
Ella Fitzgerald: an annotated discography: including a
complete discography of Chick Webb/ J. Wilfred
Johnson. Jefferson, N.C.: McFarland, c2001. ix, 358 p.
00-053706   016.78242165/092   0786409061
Fitzgerald, Ella -- Discography. Sound recordings -- Catalogs.

ML156.9 Bibliography — Discography — Reviews, indexes, etc.

ML156.9.A38 2001
All music guide: the definitive guide to popular music/
edited by Vladimir Bogdanov, Chris Woodstra, Stephen
Thomas Erlewine. 4th ed. San Francisco: Backbeat
Books/All Media Guide, c2001. viii, 1491 p.
2001-052673   016.78026/6 21   0879306270
*Sound recordings--Reviews. Popular music--Discography.
Music--Discography.*

ML156.9.A39 1995
All music guide to rock: the best CDs, albums & tapes: rock, pop, soul, R&B and rap/ edited by Michael Erlewine, Vladimir Bogdanov, and Chris Woodstra. San Francisco, CA: Miller Freeman Books, c1995. x, 973 p.
95-040238   016.78164/0266   087930376X
Sound recordings -- Reviews. Rock music -- Discography. Popular music -- Discography.

ML156.9.G73 1999
March, Ivan.
The Penguin guide to compact discs/ Ivan March, Edward Greenfield and Robert Layton; edited by Ivan March. Completely rev. and updated. London, England: Penguin Books, 1999. xxiii, 1639 p.
2003-555559   780.26/6 21   0140513795
Music -- Discography. Compact discs -- Reviews.

ML158.4 Bibliography — Video recordings, films, etc. — General works

ML158.4.A46 1999
Almquist, Sharon G.
Opera singers in recital, concert, and feature film: a mediagraphy/ compiled by Sharon G. Almquist. Westport, Conn.: Greenwood Press, 1999. xiv, 376 p.
98-041642   016.7821/0267   0313295921
Concerts -- Video catalogs. Concerts -- Film catalogs. Motion pictures -- Catalogs.

ML159 History and criticism — General — Published through 1800

ML159.B96 1957
Burney, Charles, 1726-1814.
A general history of music, from the earliest ages to the present period (1789) With critical and historical notes by Frank Mercer. New York, Dover Publications [1957] 2 v.
58-000659   780.9
Music -- History and criticism.

ML159.H39 1963
Hawkins, John, 1719-1789.
A general history of the science and practice of music. With a new introd. by Charles Cudworth. New York, Dover Publications [1963] 2 v.
63-004484   780.9
Music -- History and criticism. Musicians -- Portraits.

ML160 History and criticism — General — Published 1801-

ML160.A27
Abraham, Gerald, 1904-
The concise Oxford history of music/ Gerald Abraham. London; Oxford University Press, 1979. 968 p.
79-040540   780/.9   0193113198
Music -- History and criticism.

ML160.B655.R5
Blume, Friedrich, 1893-
Renaissance and Baroque music; a comprehensive survey. Translated by M. D. Herter Norton. New York, W. W. Norton [1967] ix, 180 p.
65-013323   780.9031
Music -- 16th century -- History and criticism. Music -- 17th century -- History and criticism. Music -- 18th century -- History and criticism.

ML160.G872 2001
Grout, Donald Jay.
A history of western music/ Donald Jay Grout, Claude V. Palisca. 6th ed. New York: Norton, c2001. xvi, 843 p.
00-058411   780/.9 21   0393975274
Music--History and criticism.

ML160.H527 1989
Heritage of music/ edited by Michael Raeburn and Alan Kendall. Oxford; Oxford University Press, 1989. 4 v.
85-021429   780/.9   019520493X
Music -- History and criticism.

ML160.L25 1997
Lang, Paul Henry,
Music in Western civilization/ by Paul Henry Lang; with a new foreword by Leon Botstein. New York: W.W. Norton, c1997. xxii, 1107 p.
97-005883   780/.9 21   0393040747
Music -- History and criticism.

ML160.L83 1989
Lowinsky, Edward E. 1908-1985.
Music in the culture of the Renaissance and other essays/ Edward E. Lowinsky; edited and with an introduction by Bonnie J. Blackburn; with forewords by Howard Mayer Brown and Ellen T. Harris. Chicago: University of Chicago Press, 1989. 2 v.
88-004869   780/.903/1   0226494780
Music -- History and criticism. Music -- 15th century -- History and criticism. Music -- 16th century -- History and criticism.

ML160.N44 1990
New Oxford history of music. Oxford; Oxford University Press, <1990-2001 > v. <2, 3, pt. 1 >
88-022471   780/.9 19   0198162057
Music -- History and criticism.

ML160.S89 1998b
Source readings in music history/ Oliver Strunk, editor. Rev. ed./ Leo Treitler, general editor. New York: Norton, c1998. xv, 1552 p.
94-034569   780/.9 20   0393037525
Music -- History and criticism -- Sources.

ML162-169 History and criticism — By period — Ancient

ML162.S14
Sachs, Curt, 1881-1959.
The rise of music in the ancient world, East and West. New York, W. W. Norton & company, inc. [1943] 324 p.
43-016820   781.8
Music -- To 500 -- History and criticism. Music -- Asia -- History and criticism. Music, Greek and Roman -- History and criticism.

ML166.W43 1970
Werner, Eric, 1901-
The sacred bridge; liturgical parallels in synagogue and early church. New York, Schocken Books [1970] xviii, 364 p.
75-127818   783.2   0805202781
Judaism -- Liturgy -- History.

ML167.G73 1984
Greek musical writings/ edited by Andrew Barker. Cambridge; Cambridge University Press, 1984-1989. 2 v.
83-020924   781.738   0521235936
Music, Greek and Roman -- Sources. Music -- To 500 -- Sources.

ML169.A66 1994
Anderson, Warren D.
Music and musicians in Ancient Greece/ Warren D. Anderson. Ithaca [N.Y.]: Cornell University Press, 1994. 248 p.
94-028507   780/.9/01   0801430836
Music, Greek and Roman -- History and criticism. Musicians -- Greece.

ML169.C6513 1989
Comotti, Giovanni, 1931-
Music in Greek and Roman culture/ Giovanni Comotti; translated by Rosaria V. Munson. Baltimore: Johns Hopkins University Press, c1989. xii, 186 p.
88-045413   780/.938   0801833647
Music, Greek and Roman -- History and criticism.

ML169.L68
Lippman, Edward A.
Musical thought in ancient Greece/ Columbia Univ. Pr., 1964. 215 p.
64-022482   780.10938
Music, Greek and Roman. Music -- History and criticism.

ML169.W5 1992
West, M. L. 1937-
Ancient Greek music/ M.L. West. Oxford [England]: Clarendon Press; 1992. xiii, 409 p.
91-005170   780/.938   0198148976
Music, Greek and Roman -- History and criticism.

ML171-182 History and criticism — By period — Medieval. Renaissance

ML171.Y8 1989
Yudkin, Jeremy.
Music in medieval Europe/ Jeremy Yudkin. Englewood Cliffs, N.J.: Prentice Hall, c1989. xxi, 612 p.
88-032495   780/.902 19   0136081924
Music--500-1400--History and criticism.

ML172.A84 1998
Atlas, Allan W.
Renaissance music: music in Western Europe, 1400-1600/ Allan W. Atlas. 1st ed. New York: Norton, 1998. xxi, 729 p.
97-019816   780/.9/02 21   0393971694
Music--Europe, Western--15th century--History and criticism. Music--Europe, Western--16th century--History and criticism.

ML172.B86 1999
Brown, Howard Mayer.
Music in the Renaissance/ Howard Mayer Brown, Louise K. Stein. 2nd ed. Upper Saddle River, N.J.: Prentice Hall, c1999. xx, 396 p.
98-012248   780/.9/031 21   0134000455
Music--15th century--History and criticism. Music--16th century--History and criticism. Renaissance.

ML172.C28
Caldwell, John, 1938-
Medieval music/ John Caldwell. Bloomington: Indiana University Press, c1978. 304 p.
77-094060   780/.902   0253337313
Music -- 500-1400 -- History and criticism.

ML172.C65 1992
Companion to medieval and renaissance music/ edited by Tess Knighton and David Fallows. New York: Schirmer Books: 1992. xx, 428 p.
92-032213   780/.9/02   0028712218
Music -- 500-1400 -- History and criticism. Music -- 15th century -- History and criticism. Music -- 16th century -- History and criticism.

ML172.H8
Hoppin, Richard H.
Medieval music/ Richard H. Hoppin. New York: W. W. Norton, c1978. xxiii, 566 p.
78-007010   780/.902   0393090906
Music -- 500-1400 -- History and criticism.

ML172.P47 1999
Perkins, Leeman L.
Music in the age of the Renaissance/ Leeman L. Perkins. New York: W.W. Norton, c1999. 1147 p.
98-028961   780/.9/031 21   0393046087
Music -- 15th century -- History and criticism. Music -- 16th century -- History and criticism.

ML172.S4 1975
Seay, Albert.
Music in the medieval world/ Albert Seay. 2d ed. Englewood Cliffs, N.J.: Prentice-Hall, [1975] ix, 182 p.
74-023185   780/.902   0136081339
Music--500-1400--History and criticism.

ML172.W58 1995
Wilkins, Nigel E.
Music in the age of Chaucer/ Nigel Wilkins. 2nd ed., with Chaucer songs. Woodbridge, Suffolk: D.S. Brewer, 1995. xiv, 210 p.
95-002220   780/.9/02 20   0859914615
Chaucer, Geoffrey, d. 1400 -- Knowledge -- Music. Music -- 500-1400 -- History and criticism. Music and literature. Songs, Middle English. Part songs, English.

ML182.A78 1996
Aubrey, Elizabeth, 1951-
The music of the troubadours/ Elizabeth Aubrey. Bloomington: Indiana University Press, c1996. xxi, 326 p.
96-010358   782.4/3/0944809021   0253332079
Troubadours. Music -- 500-1400 -- History and criticism.

ML193-197 History and criticism — By period — 1601-

ML193.C56 1991
Companion to baroque music/ compiled and edited by Julie Anne Sadie; foreword by Christopher Hogwood. New York: Schirmer Books, 1991. xviii, 549 p.
91-027758   780/.9/032   0028722752
Music -- 17th century -- History and criticism. Music -- 18th century -- History and criticism.

ML193.P34 1991
Palisca, Claude V.
Baroque music/ Claude V. Palisca. 3rd ed. Englewood Cliffs, N.J.: Prentice Hall, [c1991] xi, 356 p.
90-046900   780/.9/032 20   0130584967
Music--17th century--History and criticism. Music--18th century--History and criticism.

ML193.S38 2001
Schulenberg, David.
Music of the Baroque/ David Schulenberg. New York: Oxford University Press, 2001. xiv, 349 p.
00-036679   780/.9/032 21   0195122321
Music -- 17th century -- History and criticism. Music -- 18th century -- History and criticism.

ML195.L13 1988
Larsen, Jens Peter, 1902-
Handel, Haydn, and the Viennese classical style/ by Jens Peter Larsen; translations by Ulrich Kramer. Ann Arbor, Mich.: UMI Research Press, c1988. xii, 332 p.
88-001206   781.7436/13   0835718514
Handel, George Frideric, -- 1685-1759 -- Criticism and interpretation. Haydn, Joseph, -- 1732-1809 -- Criticism and interpretation. Music -- 18th century -- History and criticism. Music -- Austria -- Vienna -- 18th century -- History and criticism. Classicism in music.

ML195.P38 2000
Pauly, Reinhard G.
Music in the classic period/ Reinhard G. Pauly. 4th ed. Upper Saddle River, N.J.: Prentice Hall, c2000. xvi, 272 p.
99-030849   780/.9/033 21   0130115029
Music -- 18th century -- History and criticism.

ML195.R38 1980
Ratner, Leonard G.
Classic music: expression, form, and style/ Leonard G. Ratner. New York: Schirmer Books; c1980. xvii, 475 p.
76-057808   780/.903/3   0028720202
Music -- 18th century -- History and criticism. Classicism in music.

ML195.R68 1997
Rosen, Charles,
The classical style: Haydn, Mozart, Beethoven/ Charles Rosen. Expanded ed. New York: W. W. Norton, c1997. xxx, 533 p.
96-027335   780/.9/033 20   0393040208
Haydn, Joseph, 1732-1809 -- Criticism and interpretation. Mozart, Wolfgang Amadeus, 1756-1791 -- Criticism and interpretation. Beethoven, Ludwig van, 1770-1827 -- Criticism and interpretation. Classicism in music. Music -- 18th century -- History and criticism.

ML196.C36 2001
The Cambridge history of nineteenth-century music/ edited by Jim Samson. Cambridge; Cambridge University Press, 2001. xv, 772 p.
00-067469   780/.9/034 21   0521590175
Music -- 19th century -- History and criticism.

ML196.D2513 1989
Dahlhaus, Carl, 1928-
Nineteenth-century music/ Carl Dahlhaus; English translation by J. Bradford Robinson. Berkeley: University of California Press, c1989. x, 417 p.
88-015472   780/.903/4   0520052919
Music -- 19th century -- History and criticism.

ML196.L65 1988
Longyear, Rey M.
Nineteenth-century romanticism in music/ Rey M. Longyear. 3rd ed. Englewood Cliffs, N.J.: Prentice Hall, c1988. xiv, 367 p.
87-018719   780/.903/4 19   0136226973
Music--19th century--History and criticism. Romanticism in music.

ML196.P6 1984
Plantinga, Leon.
Romantic music: a history of musical style in nineteenth-century Europe/ Leon Plantinga. New York: W.W. Norton, c1984. xiii, 523 p.
84-004012   780/.903/4   0393951960
Music -- 19th century -- History and criticism.

ML196.R27 1992
Ratner, Leonard G.
Romantic music: sound and syntax/ Leonard G. Ratner. New York: Schirmer Books; c1992. xix, 348 p.
92-010566   781/.09/034   0028720652
Music -- 19th century -- History and criticism. Romanticism in music. Musical analysis.

ML196.R67 1995
Rosen, Charles, 1927-
The romantic generation/ Charles Rosen. Cambridge, Mass.: Harvard University Press, 1995. xv, 723 p.
94-046239   780/.9/034   0674779339
Romanticism in music. Music -- 19th century -- History and criticism.

ML197.C748 1999
Composers on modern musical culture: an anthology of readings on twentieth-century music/ compiled and edited by Bryan R. Simms. New York: Schirmer Books, 1999.
98-014757   780/.9/04   0028647513
Music -- 20th century -- History and criticism.

ML197.C757 2001
Cope, David.
New directions in music/ David Cope. 7th ed. Prospect Heights, Ill.: Waveland Press, c2001. xiii, 259 p.
2001-266343   780/.9/04 21   1577661087
Music--20th century--History and criticism.

ML197.C76 1968
Copland, Aaron, 1900-
The new music, 1900-1960. New York, W. W. Norton [1968] 194 p.
68-010878   780/.904
Music -- 20th century -- History and criticism.

ML197.G76 1995
Griffiths, Paul, 1947 Nov. 24-
Modern music and after/ Paul Griffiths. Oxford; Oxford University Press, 1995. xv, 373 p.
95-013369   780/.9/04   0198165110
Music -- 20th century -- History and criticism.

ML197.M675 1990
Morgan, Robert P.
Twentieth-century music: a history of musical style in modern Europe and America/ Robert P. Morgan. 1st ed. New York: Norton, c1991. xvii, 554 p.
90-006986   780/.9/04 20   039395272X
Music--20th century--History and criticism. Style, Musical.

ML197.P76 2000
Prendergast, Mark J.
The ambient century: from Mahler to trance: the evolution of sound in the electronic age/ Mark Prendergast. 1st US ed. New York: Bloomsbury, c2000. xii, 498 p.
00-046800   780/.9/04 21   1582341346
Music -- 20th century -- History and criticism. Electronic music -- History and criticism. Composers -- Biography.

ML197.S17 2002
Salzman, Eric.
Twentieth-century music: an introduction/ Eric Salzman. 4th ed. Upper Saddle River, NJ: Prentice Hall, c2002. xiv, 337 p.
2001-021466   780/.9/04 21   0130959413
Music -- 20th century -- History and criticism.

ML197.S585 1996
Simms, Bryan R.
Music of the twentieth century: style and structure/ Bryan R. Simms. New York: Schirmer Books; c1996. xvii, 435 p.
96-002063   780/.9/04   0028723929
Music -- 20th century -- History and criticism. Musical analysis.

ML197.S634 1994
Slonimsky, Nicolas,
Music since 1900/ Nicolas Slonimsky. 5th ed. New York: Schirmer Books; xvi, 1260 p.
93-049052   780/.9/04 20   0028724186
Music -- 20th century -- History and criticism. Music -- 20th century -- Chronology.

ML197.S767 1990
Straus, Joseph Nathan.
Remaking the past: musical modernism and the influence of the tonal tradition/ Joseph N. Straus. Cambridge, Mass.: Harvard University Press, 1990. ix, 207 p.
89-024721   780/.9/04   0674759907
Music -- 20th century -- History and criticism. Sonata -- 20th century. Harmony.

ML197.W437 1994
Watkins, Glenn,
Pyramids at the Louvre: music, culture, and collage from Stravinsky to the postmodernists/ Glenn Watkins. Cambridge, Mass.: Belknap Press of Harvard University Press, 1994. ix, 571 p.
93-031703   780/.9/04 20   0674740831
Music -- 20th century -- History and criticism. Music -- Philosophy and aesthetics. Art and music.

ML198.5-200.5 History and criticism — By region or country — America

ML198.5.D75 1999
Driven into paradise: the musical migration from Nazi Germany to the United States/ edited by Reinhold Brinkmann and Christoph Wolff. Berkeley, Calif.: University of California Press, c1999. xiii, 373 p.
98-028956   780/.943/0973   0520214137
Music -- United States -- 20th century -- History and criticism. National socialism and music. Exiles -- Germany -- History -- 20th century.

ML200.C36 1998
The Cambridge history of American music/ edited by David Nicholls. Cambridge, UK; Cambridge University Press, 1998. xv, 637 p.
98-003814   780/.973   0521454298
Music -- United States -- History and criticism.

ML200.C5 1987
Chase, Gilbert, 1906-
America's music, from the pilgrims to the present/ Gilbert Chase; with a foreword by Richard Crawford and a discographical essay by William Brooks. Urbana: University of Illinois Press, c1987. xxiv, 712 p.
86-030795   781.773   025200454X
Music -- United States -- History and criticism.

ML200.C68 1993
Crawford, Richard, 1935-
The American musical landscape/ Richard Crawford.
Berkeley: University of California Press, c1993. xi,
381 p.
92-011237   780/.973   0520077644
Music -- United States -- History and criticism.

ML200.C69 2001
Crawford, Richard, 1935-
America's musical life: a history/ Richard Crawford. New
York: Norton, 2001. xv, 976 p.
99-047565   780/.973   0393048101
Music -- United States -- History and criticism.

ML200.H15 1996
Hall, Charles J.
A chronicle of American music, 1700-1995/ Charles J.
Hall. New York: Schirmer Books, c1996. xi, 825 p.
96-016458   780/.973 20   002860296X
Music -- United States -- Chronology.

ML200.H17 1983
Hamm, Charles.
Music in the New World/ Charles Hamm. 1st ed. New
York: Norton, c1983. xiv, 722 p.
82-006481   781.773 19   0393951936
Music--United States--History and criticism.

ML200.H58 2000
Hitchcock, H. Wiley
Music in the United States: a historical introduction/ H.
Wiley Hitchcock; with a final chapter by Kyle Gann. 4th
ed. Upper Saddle River, NJ: Prentice Hall, c2000. xviii,
413 p.
99-042121   780/.973 21   0139076433
Music -- United States -- History and criticism.

ML200.S263 1991
Sanjek, Russell.
American popular music business in the 20th century/
Russell Sanjek,   David Sanjek. New York: Oxford
University Press, 1991. xxii, 334 p.
90-047745   0195058283
*Popular music -- United States -- History and criticism. Music --
United States -- 20th century -- History and criticism. Music
trade -- United States.*

ML200.5.G36 1997
Gann, Kyle.
American music in the twentieth century/ Kyle Gann.
New York: Schirmer Books; c1997. xvi, 400 p.
97-019863   780/.973/0904   002864655X
Music -- United States -- 20th century -- History and criticism.

ML200.5.N55 1990
Nicholls, David,
American   experimental   music,   1890-1940/   David
Nicholls. Cambridge [England]; Cambridge University
Press, 1990. xiv, 239 p.
89-000563   781.773 19   0521345782
Music -- United States -- 20th century -- History and criticism.
Music -- United States -- 19th century -- History and criticism.
Composition (Music)

ML200.5.P48 1999
Perspectives on American music since 1950/ edited by
James R. Heintze. New York: Garland, 1999. xi, 482 p.
99-010967   780/.973/0904 21   0815321449
Music--United States--20th century--History and criticism.
Jazz--History and criticism.

ML240-315 History and criticism —
By region or country — Europe

ML240.B37 1993
Bellman, Jonathan,
The style hongrois in the music of Western Europe/
Jonathan Bellman. Boston: Northeastern University
Press, c1993. viii, 261 p.
93-010150   780/.9/033 20   1555531695
*Music -- Europe -- 18th century -- History and criticism. Music -
- Europe -- 19th century -- History and criticism. Music --
Europe -- Hungarian influences.*

ML240.2.S87 1993
Strohm, Reinhard.
The rise of European music, 1380-1500/ Reinhard
Strohm. Cambridge [England]; Cambridge University
Press, 1993. xv, 720 p.
92-002736   780/.9/02   0521417457
*Music -- Europe -- 500-1400 -- History and criticism. Music --
Europe -- 15th century -- History and criticism.*

ML240.5.R48 1996
Retuning culture: musical changes in Central and Eastern
Europe/ edited by Mark Slobin. Durham: Duke
University Press, 1996. vi, 310 p.
96-027983   780/.947/0904   0822318555
*Music -- Europe, Central -- 20th century -- History and
criticism. Music -- Europe, Eastern -- 20th century -- History
and criticism. Music -- Social aspects.*

ML270.J64 1995
Johnson, James H.,
Listening in Paris: a cultural history/ James H. Johnson.
Berkeley: University of California Press, c1995. xvi,
384 p.
94-006492   780/.944 20   0520085647
*Music -- France -- History and criticism. Music -- Social
aspects. Music appreciation.*

ML270.2.A6 1997
Anthony, James R.
French baroque music from Beaujoyeulx to Rameau/
James R. Anthony. Portland, Ore.: Amadeus Press,
c1997. 586 p.
96-038352   780/.944/09032   1574670212
Music -- France -- 16th century -- History and criticism.
*Music -- France -- 17th century -- History and criticism. Music -
- France -- 18th century -- History and criticism.*

ML270.2.P22 1993
Page, Christopher, 1952-
Discarding images: reflections on music and culture in medieval France/ Christopher Page. Oxford [England]: Clarendon Press; 1993. xxiv, 222 p.
93-008142   780/.9/02   0198163460
Music -- France -- 500-1400 -- History and criticism.   France -- Civilization -- 1000-1328. France -- Civilization -- 1328-1600.

ML270.3.M88 1992
Music and the French Revolution/ edited by Malcolm Boyd. Cambridge [England]; Cambridge University Press, 1992. x, 328 p.
91-010775   780/.944/09033   0521402875
Music -- France -- 18th century -- Congresses. Revolutionary music -- France -- Congresses. France -- History -- Revolution, 1789-1799 -- Songs and music -- Congresses.

ML270.3.V47 1993
Verba, Cynthia.
Music and the French enlightenment: reconstruction of a dialogue, 1750-1764/ Cynthia Verba. Oxford: Clarendon Press; 1993. vii, 163 p.
92-017495   780/.944/09033   0198162812
Music -- France -- 18th century -- History and criticism. Enlightenment. Music -- Philosophy and aesthetics.

ML270.4.C7
Cooper, Martin, 1910-
French music, from the death of Berlioz to the death of Faure.   London, New York, Oxford University Press 1951. viii, 239 p.
51-013449
Music, French -- History and criticism.

ML275.5.K38 1997
Kater, Michael H., 1937-
The twisted muse: musicians and their music in the Third Reich/ Michael H. Kater. New York: Oxford University Press, 1997. xv, 327 p.
96-006339   780/.943/09043   0195096207
Music -- Germany -- 20th century -- History and criticism. National socialism and music. Music and state -- Germany -- 20th century.

ML285.P18 1988
Palmer, Roy,
The sound of history: songs and social comment/ Roy Palmer. Oxford, [England]; Oxford University Press, 1988. xviii, 361 p.
87-030438   784.6/836123/0941 19   0192158902
Music -- Great Britain -- History and criticism. Music -- Social aspects. Protest songs -- Great Britain -- History and criticism.

ML285.5.B55 1997
Blake, Andrew, 1955-
The land without music: music, culture and society in twentieth-century Britain/ Andrew Blake. Manchester, UK; Manchester University Press; 1997. xiv, 256 p.
97-002600   780/.941/0904   0719042984
Music -- Great Britain -- 20th century -- History and criticism.

ML286.C28 1991
Caldwell, John, 1938-
The Oxford history of English music/ John Caldwell. Oxford [England]: Clarendon Press; 1991-c1999. 2 v.
90-014229   780/.942   0198161298
Music -- England -- History and criticism.

ML286.3.W4 1992
Weber, William, 1940-
The rise of musical classics in eighteenth-century England: a study in canon, ritual, and ideology/ William Weber. Oxford [England]: Clarendon Press; 1992. xiii, 274 p.
92-010567   780/.942/09033   0198162871
Concerts -- England -- London -- 18th century. Music -- England -- 18th century -- History and criticism.

ML286.4.S85 1993
Stradling, R. A.
The English musical Renaissance, 1860-1940: construction and deconstruction/ Robert Stradling and Meirion Hughes. London; Routledge, 1993. 270 p.
92-034087   780/.942/09034   0415034930
Music -- England -- 19th century -- History and criticism. Music -- England -- 20th century -- History and criticism.

ML286.8.L5.S44
Shaw, Bernard, 1856-1950.
Shaw on music; a selection from the music criticism of Bernard Shaw, made by Eric Bentley. Garden City, N.Y., Doubleday, 1955. 307 p.
55-005501   780.4
Music -- England -- London -- History and criticism.

ML290.2.B513 1987
Bianconi, Lorenzo.
Music in the seventeenth century/ Lorenzo Bianconi; translated   by   David   Bryant.   Cambridge [Cambridgeshire]; Cambridge University Press, c1987. xii, 346 p.
87-011685   780/.945   0521262909
Music -- Italy -- 17th century -- History and criticism.

ML290.2.C22 1992
Carter, Tim.
Music in late Renaissance & early baroque Italy/ Tim Carter. Portland, Or.: Amadeus Press, 1992. 288 p.
92-225174   780/.945/09031   0931340535
Music -- Italy -- 16th century -- History and criticism. Music -- Italy -- 17th century -- History and criticism.

ML290.2.G313 1995
Gallo, F. Alberto.
Music in the castle: troubadours, books, and orators in Italian courts of the thirteenth, fourteenth, and fifteenth centuries/ F. Alberto Gallo; translated from the Italian by Anna Herklotz; translations from Latin by Kathryn Krug. Chicago: University of Chicago Press, 1995. 147 p.
95-009257   780/.945/0902 20   0226279693
Music -- Italy -- 500-1400 -- History and criticism.

ML290.2.P34 1985
Palisca, Claude V.
Humanism in Italian Renaissance musical thought/ Claude V. Palisca. New Haven: Yale University Press, c1985. xiii, 471 p.
85-008190   781.745   0300033028
Music -- Italy -- 15th century -- History and criticism. Music -- Italy -- 16th century -- History and criticism. Renaissance -- Italy.

ML290.4.R65 1991
Rosselli, John.
Music & musicians in nineteenth-century Italy/ John Rosselli. London: B.T. Batsford, 1991. 160 p.
92-159960   780/.945/09034 20   0713461535
Music -- Italy -- 19th century -- History and criticism.

ML290.8.M4 K46 1996
Kendrick, Robert L.
Celestial sirens: nuns and their music in early modern Milan/ Robert L. Kendrick. Oxford [England]: Clarendon Press; xxi, 556 p.
95-044937   781.71/2/0082 20   0198164084
Music -- Italy -- Milan -- 16th century -- History and criticism.
Music -- Italy -- Milan -- 17th century -- History and criticism.
Nuns as musicians -- Italy -- Milan.

ML300.A16S8 1968
Abraham, Gerald, 1904-
Studies in Russian music; critical essays on the most important of Rimsky-Korsakov's operas, Borodin's Prince Igor, Dargomizhky's Stone guest, etc., with chapters on Glinka, Mussorgsky, Balakirev an by Gerald Abraham. Freeport, N.Y., Books for Libraries Press [1968] vi, 355 p.
68-020285   780/.9/47
Rimsky-Korsakov, Nikolay, -- 1844-1908.   Opera -- Russia -- 19th century. Music -- Russia -- 19th century -- History and criticism.

ML300.A16S82 1970
Abraham, Gerald, 1904-
On Russian music; critical and historical studies of Glinka's operas, Balakirev's works, etc., with chapters dealing with compositions by Borodin, Rimsky-Korsakov, Tchaikovsky, Mussorgsky, Glazunov, by Gerald E. H. Abraham. Freeport, N.Y., Books for Libraries Press [1970] 279 p.
73-134046   780/.947   0836919009
Music -- Soviet Union -- History and criticism. Opera -- Russia.

ML300.M1313 2002
Maes, Francis,
A history of Russian music: from Kamarinskaya to Babi Yar/ Francis Maes; translated by Arnold J. Pomerans and Erica Pomerans. Berkeley: University of California Press, c2002. xiv, 427 p.
2001-027617   780/.947 21   0520218159
Music -- Russia -- History and criticism. Music -- Soviet Union -- History and criticism.

ML300.T37 1997
Taruskin, Richard.
Defining Russia musically: historical and hermeneutical essays/ Richard Taruskin. Princeton, N.J.: Princeton University Press, c1997. xxxii, 561 p.
96-041182   780/.947   0691011567
Music -- Russia -- History and criticism.

ML300.4.R87 1994
Russians on Russian music, 1830-1880: an anthology/ edited and translated by Stuart Campbell. Cambridge; Cambridge University Press, 1994. xxi, 295 p.
93-017690   780/.947/09034   0521402670
Music -- Russia -- 19th century -- History and criticism. Opera -- Russia -- 19th century.

ML300.5.S37 1983
Schwarz, Boris, 1906-
Music and musical life in Soviet Russia/ Boris Schwarz. Bloomington: Indiana University Press, c1983. xiii, 722 p.
82-048267   780/.947   0253339561
Music -- Soviet Union -- 20th century -- History and criticism.

ML315.C4 1959
Chase, Gilbert, 1906-
The music of Spain.   New York, Dover Publications [1959] 383 p.
59-016808   780.946
Music -- Spain -- History and criticism. Music -- Latin America -- History and criticism. Music -- Portugal -- History and criticism.

ML330-345 History and criticism — By region or country — Asia

ML330.M3 1996
Malm, William P.
Music cultures of the Pacific, the Near East, and Asia/ William P. Malm. 3rd ed. Upper Saddle River, N.J.: Prentice Hall, c1996. xxiii, 278 p.
94-048578   780/.95 20   0131823876
Music--Asia--History and criticism. Music--Oceania--History and criticism.

ML338.C593 2000
Clayton, Martin.
Time in Indian music: rhythm, metre, and form in North Indian rag performance/ Martin Clayton. Oxford; Oxford University Press, 2000. xx, 230 p.
2001-267180   781.2/2/0954   0198166869
Music -- India -- History and criticism. Hindustani music -- History and criticism. Musical meter and rhythm.

ML338.F37 1997
Farrell, Gerry.
Indian music and the West/ Gerry Farrell.   Oxford: Clarendon Press; 1997. xi, 241 p.
96-034212   780/.954   0198163916
Music -- India -- History and criticism. Music -- Indic influences. Civilization, Western -- Indic influences.

ML338.P423 1999
Pesch, Ludwig.
The illustrated companion to South Indian classical music/ Ludwig Pesch. Delhi: Oxford University Press, 1999. xvii, 376 p.
99-932759   780/.954/8 21   0195643828
Carnatic music -- History and criticism. Music -- India -- History and criticism.

ML338.S475.M9
Shankar, Ravi, 1920-
My music, my life. With an introd. by Yehudi Menuhin. New York, Simon and Schuster [1968] 160 p.
68-028918   781.7/54
Music -- India -- History and criticism.

ML338.W318 1998
Wade, Bonnie C.
Imaging sound: an ethnomusicological study of music, art, and culture in Mughal India/ Bonnie C. Wade. Chicago: University of Chicago Press, c1998. lvi, 276 p.
97-014033   700/.954/0903   0226868400
Music -- India -- History and criticism. Music -- Mogul Empire -- History and criticism. Music in art.

ML338.W32
Wade, Bonnie C.
Music in India: the classical traditions/ Bonnie C. Wade. Englewood Cliffs, N.J.: Prentice-Hall, c1979. xix, 252 p.
77-028488   781.7/54   0136070361
Music -- India -- History and criticism.

ML338.2.W5 1995
Widdess, Richard.
The ragas of early Indian music: modes, melodies, and musical notations from the Gupta period to c. 1250/ Richard Widdess. Oxford: Clarendon Press; c1995. xvii, 429 p.
94-000074   781.2/64   0193154641
Raga. Music -- India -- Theory -- 500-1400 -- History.

ML340.M33
Malm, William P.
Nagauta: the heart of kabuki music. Rutland, Vt., C. E. Tuttle Co. [1963] xvi, 344 p.
62-009362   780.954   0837169003
Music -- History and criticism -- Japan -- History and criticism. Kabuki (Japanese drama and theater)

ML344.D86 1991
During, Jean, 1947-
The art of Persian music/ Jean During , Zia Mirabdolbaghi; lesson from Master Dariush Safvat; [translation from French and Persian by Manuchehr Anvar]. Washington, D.C.: Mage Publishers, 1991. 280 p.
90-043217   780/.955   0934211221
Music -- Iran -- History and criticism.

ML345.B3 M25 1976
McPhee, Colin,
Music in Bali: a study in form and instrumental organization in Balinese orchestral music/ by Colin McPhee, with photos. by the author. New York: Da Capo Press, 1976, c1966. xviii, 430 p.
76-004979   781.7/598/6   0306707780
Music -- Indonesia -- Bali Island. Gamelan. Musical instruments -- Indonesia -- Bali Island.

ML345.I5.B35 1999
Bakan, Michael B.
Music of death and new creation: experiences in the world of Balinese gamelan beleganjur/ Michael B. Bakan. Chicago: University of Chicago Press, 1999. xxii, 384 p.
98-042727   784.2/09598/6   0226034879
Music -- Indonesia -- Bali Island -- History and criticism. Gamelan. Gamelan music -- History and criticism.

ML345.I5.G73 1996
Gradenwitz, Peter, 1910-
The music of Israel: from the biblical era to modern times/ Peter Gradenwitz. Portland, Or.: Amadeus Press, c1996. 472 p.
95-047994   780/.89/924   1574670123
Music -- Israel -- History and criticism.

ML345.I5.S86 1995
Sumarsam.
Gamelan: cultural interaction and musical development in central Java/ Sumarsam. Chicago: University of Chicago Press, c1995. xviii, 350 p.
94-043013   780/.9598/2   0226780104
Music -- Indonesia -- Java -- History and criticism. Gamelan.

ML345.I8.B6 1989
Bohlman, Philip Vilas.
"The land where two streams flow": music in the German-Jewish community of Israel/ Philip V. Bohlman. Urbana: University of Illinois Press, c1989. xviii, 257 p.
88-025902   781.75694   0252015967
Jews, German -- Israel -- Music -- History and criticism. Music -- Israel -- History and criticism.

ML345.P3.H57 1995
Hirshberg, Jehoash.
Music in the Jewish community of Palestine, 1880-1948: a social history/ Jehoash Hirshberg. Oxford: Clarendon Press; 1995. xii, 297 p.
94-042448   780/.89/92405694
Jews -- Palestine -- Music -- History and criticism. Music -- Palestine -- 19th century -- History and criticism. Music -- Palestine -- 20th century -- History and criticism.

ML348 History and criticism — By region or country — Arab countries

ML348.T6913 1996
Touma, Habib, 1934-
The music of the Arabs/ Habib Hassan Touma; translated by Laurie Schwartz. Portland, Or.: Amadeus Press, c1996. xxi, 238 p.
94-043650   780/.89/927   0931340888
Music -- Arab countries -- History and criticism. Islamic music -- History and criticism.

ML350 History and criticism — By region or country — Africa

ML350.A7613 1991
Arom, Simha.
African polyphony and polyrhythm: musical structure and methodology/ Simha Arom; translated from French by Martin Thom, Barbara Tuckett, and Raymond Boyd. Cambridge; Cambridge University Press; 1991. xxviii, 668 p.
90-046665   781.2/84/0967   052124160X
Music -- Africa, Central -- History and criticism. Counterpoint. Musical meter and rhythm.

ML350.E77 1991
Erlmann, Veit.
African stars: studies in Black South African performance/ Veit Erlmann. Chicago: University of Chicago Press, 1991. xxi, 214 p.
91-013927   780/.89/968 20   0226217248
Blacks -- South Africa -- Music -- History and criticism. Music -- South Africa -- History and criticism.

ML360 History and criticism — By region or country — Australia, Oceania, etc.

ML360.M28 1999
McLean, Mervyn.
Weavers of song: Polynesian music and dance/ Mervyn McLean. Honolulu: University of Hawaii Press, c1999. x, 543 p.
99-034404   780/.996   0824822714
Music -- Polynesia -- History and criticism. Dance -- Polynesia.

ML385-406 History and criticism — Biography — Collective

ML385.D26
Dance, Stanley.
The world of Count Basie/ Stanley Dance. New York: C. Scribner's Sons, c1980. xxi, 399 p.
80-015641   785.42/092/4   0684166046
Basie, Count, -- 1904-   Jazz musicians -- United States -- Biography. Jazz -- History and criticism. Big bands.

ML385.D29 1990
Davis, Francis.
Outcats: jazz composers, instrumentalists, and singers/ Francis Davis. New York: Oxford University Press, 1990. x, 261 p.
89-023031   781.65/092/273   019505587X
Jazz musicians -- United States -- Biography.

ML385.G53 1998
Giddins, Gary.
Visions of jazz: the first century/ Gary Giddins. New York: Oxford University Press, 1998. xi, 690 p.
98-012199   781.65/092/2 B 21   0195076753
Jazz musicians -- Biography. Composers -- Biography. Jazz -- History and criticism.

ML385.G7 1995
Goss, Glenda Dawn.
Jean Sibelius and Olin Downes: music, friendship, criticism/ Glenda Dawn Goss. Boston: Northeastern University Press, c1995. xi, 274 p.
94-022367   780/.92/24897 B 20   1555532004
Sibelius, Jean, 1865-1957. Downes, Olin, 1886-1955. Composers -- Finland -- Biography. Music critics -- United States -- Biography.

ML390.A54 1982
Anderson, E. Ruth, 1928-
Contemporary American composers: a biographical dictionary/ compiled by E. Ruth Anderson. Boston, Mass.: G.K. Hall, 1982. 578 p.
81-007047   780/.92/2   081618223X
Composers -- United States -- Biography -- Dictionaries.

ML390.B64
The Black composer speaks/ edited by David N. Baker, Lida M. Belt, and Herman C. Hudson; a project of the Afro-American Arts Institute, Indiana University. Metuchen, N.J.: Scarecrow Press, 1978. v, 506 p.
77-024146   780/.92/2   081081045X
Composers -- United States -- Interviews. Afro-American composers -- Interviews.

ML390.F59 1997
Fleisher, Robert Jay, 1953-
Twenty Israeli composers: voices of a culture/ Robert Fleisher; foreword by Shulamit Ran. Detroit: Wayne State University Press, c1997. 380 p.
96-052284   780/.95694/09049   081432648X
Composers -- Israel -- Interviews. Music -- Israel -- 20th century -- History and criticism.

ML390.F69 1993
Ford, Andrew, 1957-
Composer to composer: conversations about contemporary music/ Andrew Ford; photographs by Malcolm Crowthers & Belinda Webster. St Leonards, NSW, Australia: Allen & Unwin, 1993. xi, 252 p.
94-107806   780/.92/2   1863734430
Composers -- Interviews. Music -- 20th century -- History and criticism.

ML390.J26 1998
Jasen, David A.
Spreadin' rhythm around: Black popular songwriters, 1880-1930/ David A. Jasen and Gene Jones. New York; Schirmer Books; c1998. xxvi, 435 p.
98-010639   781.64/092/396073   0028647424
Composers, Black -- Biography. Afro-Americans -- Music -- History and criticism.

ML390.K198 2000
Kater, Michael H., 1937-
Composers of the Nazi era: eight portraits/ Michael H. Kater. New York: Oxford University Press, 2000. xiii, 399 p.
99-013272   780/.92/243   0195099249
Composers -- Germany -- Biography. Music -- Germany -- 20th century -- History and criticism. National socialism.

ML390.K595 2001
Kivy, Peter.
The possessor and the possessed: Handel, Mozart, Beethoven, and the idea of musical genius/ Peter Kivy. New Haven: Yale University Press, c2001. xiv, 287 p.
2001-017785   781/.1 21   0300087586
Handel, George Frideric, 1685-1759. Mozart, Wolfgang Amadeus, 1756-1791. Beethoven, Ludwig van, 1770-1827. Genius -- History. Creation (Literary, artistic, etc.) -- History. Composers.

ML390.L79 1999
Lock, Graham,
Blutopia: visions of the future and revisions of the past in the work of Sun Ra, Duke Ellington, and Anthony Braxton/ Graham Lock. Durham: Duke University Press, 1999. xi, 314 p.
99-034402   781.65/092/2 21   0822324407
Sun Ra -- Criticism and interpretation. Ellington, Duke, 1899-1974 -- Criticism and interpretation. Braxton, Anthony -- Criticism and interpretation. Jazz -- History and criticism.

ML390.P745 1992
Pollack, Howard.
Harvard composers: Walter Piston and his students, from Elliott Carter to Frederic Rzewski/ by Howard Pollack. Metuchen, N.J.: Scarecrow Press, 1992. xviii, 490 p.
91-046438   780/.92/27444   0810824930
Piston, Walter, -- 1894-1976. Carter, Elliott, -- 1908- Rzewski, Frederic. Composers -- United States.

ML390.P759 1999
Potter, Keith.
Four musical minimalists: La Monte Young, Terry Riley, Steve Reich, Philip Glass/ Keith Potter. Cambridge, UK; Cambridge University Press, 2000. xv, 390 p.
99-011736   780/.92/273   052148250X
Young, La Monte. Riley, Terry, -- 1935- Reich, Steve, -- 1936- Composers -- United States -- Biography. Minimal music -- United States -- History and criticism.

ML390.S389 1999
Schoenberg, Berg, and Webern: a companion to the second Viennese school/ edited by Bryan R. Simms. Westport, Conn: Greenwood Press, 1999. xiv, 410 p.
98-028960   780/.9436/130904   0313296049
Schoenberg, Arnold, -- 1874-1951 -- Criticism and interpretation. Berg, Alban, -- 1885-1935 -- Criticism and interpretation. Webern, Anton, -- 1883-1945 -- Criticism and interpretation. Composers -- Austria -- Vienna. Music -- Austria -- Vienna -- 20th century -- History and criticism.

ML390.S393 1997
Schonberg, Harold C.
The lives of the great composers/ Harold C. Schonberg. 3rd ed. New York: W.W. Norton, c1997. 653 p.
96-013308   780/.92/2 B 20   0393038572
Composers -- Biography.

ML390.S6682 1993
Gagne, Cole, 1954-
Soundpieces 2: interviews with American composers/ by Cole Gagne; photographs by Gene Bagnato and Lona Foote. Metuchen, N.J.: Scarecrow Press, 1993. x, 557 p.
93-034663   780/.92/273   0810827107
Composers -- United States -- Interviews.

ML390.S942 1991
Strickland, Edward,
American composers: dialogues on contemporary music/ Edward Strickland. Bloomington: Indiana University Press, c1991. xi, 220 p.
90-046787   780/.92/273 20   025320643X
Composers -- United States -- Interviews. Music -- United States -- 20th century -- History and criticism.

ML390.W16 2002
Walker-Hill, Helen.
From spirituals to symphonies: African-American women composers and their music/ Helen Walker-Hill. Westport, Conn.: Greenwood Press, 2002. xvi, 401 p.
2001-040600   780/.89/96073 21   0313299471
African American women composers -- Biography. Composers -- United States -- Biography. Music by African American women composers -- History and criticism.

ML390.W274 1992
We'll understand it better by and by: pioneering African American gospel composers/ edited by Bernice Johnson Reagon. Washington: Smithsonian Institution Press, c1992. xii, 384 p.
91-037954   782.25   1560981660
Afro-American composers -- Biography. Gospel music -- History and criticism.

ML394.B66 1999
Blum, David,
Quintet: five journeys toward musical fulfillment/ David Blum; with a foreword by Arnold Steinhardt. Ithaca, NY: Cornell University Press, 1999. xiii, 185 p.
99-047562   780/.92/2 B 21   0801437318
Ma, Yo-Yo, 1955- Tate, Jeffrey. Gingold, Josef. Goode, Richard. Nilsson, Birgit. Musicians -- Biography.

ML394.D36 1996
Davis, Francis.
Bebop and nothingness: jazz and pop at the end of the century/ Francis Davis. New York: Schirmer Books, c1996. xix, 304 p.
95-024545   781.65/092/273   0028704711
Jazz musicians -- United States -- Biography. Jazz -- History and criticism. Singers -- United States -- Biography.

ML394.G84 1998
Griffiths, David, 1939-
Hot jazz: from Harlem to Storyville/ David Griffiths. Lanham, Md.: Scarecrow Press, 1998. xiii, 257 p.
98-028624   781.65/092/2   0810834154
Jazz musicians -- Interviews.

ML394.L39 1994
Lees, Gene.
Cats of any color: jazz black and white/ Gene Lees. New York: Oxford University Press, 1994. ix, 246 p.
94-008058   781.65/092/2   0195084489
Jazz musicians -- Biography. Jazz -- History and criticism. United States -- Race relations -- History.

ML394.L4 1988
Lees, Gene.
Meet me at Jim & Andy's: jazz musicians and their world/ Gene Lees. New York: Oxford University Press, 1988. xviii, 265 p.
88-004865   785.42/092/2   0195046110
Jazz musicians -- United States -- Biography. Jazz -- History and criticism.

ML394.L97 1989
Lyons, Leonard.
Jazz portraits: the lives and music of the jazz masters/ Len Lyons and Don Perlo. New York: Morrow, c1989. 610 p.
88-008929   785.42/092/2   068804946X
Jazz musicians -- Biography. Jazz -- History and criticism.

ML394.M5 2001
Metting, Fred,
The unbroken circle: tradition and innovation in the music of Ry Cooder and Taj Mahal/ Fred Metting. Lanham, Md.: Scarecrow Press, 2001. xviii, 293 p.
00-038760   781.64/092/273 21   0810838184
Cooder, Ry -- Criticism and interpretation. Taj Mahal (Musician) -- Criticism and interpretation. Folk music -- United States -- History and criticism.

ML394.M86 2001
Gerard, Charley.
Music from Cuba: Mongo Santamaria, Chocolate Armenteros, and Cuban musicians in the United States/ Charley Gerard. Westport, CT: Praeger, 2001. xi, 155 p.
00-045148   780/.89/687291   0275966828
Musicians -- Cuba. Musicians -- United States. Cuban Americans -- Music -- History and criticism.

ML394.T76 1997
Trouble girls: the Rolling Stone book of women in rock/ edited by Barbara O'Dair. New York: Random House, 1997. xxx, 575 p.
96-026673   781.66/082   0679768742
Women rock musicians -- Biography.

ML394.Y68 1997
Young, Alan.
Woke me up this morning: Black gospel singers and the gospel life/ Alan Young. Jackson, Miss.: University Press of Mississippi, c1997. xxxvi, 320 p.
96-028054   782.25/4/092276   0878059431
Gospel musicians -- United States -- Biography. Gospel music -- History and criticism.

ML395.B34 1986
Balliett, Whitney.
American musicians: fifty-six portraits in jazz/ Whitney Balliett. New York: Oxford University Press, 1986. x, 415 p.
86-012491   785.42/092/2 19   0195037588
Jazz musicians--United States--Biography.

ML395.B36 1996
Balliett, Whitney.
American musicians II: seventy-two portraits in jazz/ Whitney Balliett. New York: Oxford University Press, 1996. 520 p.
96-021232   785.65/092/273   0195095383
Jazz musicians -- United States -- Biography.

ML395.D44 1990
Deffaa, Chip, 1951-
Voices of the jazz age: profiles of eight vintage jazzmen/ Chip Deffaa. Urbana: University of Illinois Press, c1990. xix, 255 p.
89-005242   781.65/092/273   0252016815
Jazz musicians -- United States -- Biography.

ML395.P53 1998
Playin' around: the lives and careers of famous session musicians/ [compiled and edited by] Jennifer Ember Pierce. Lanham, MD: Scarecrow Press, 1998. xviii, 327 p.
97-045588   781.642/092/273 B 21   0810834340
Country musicians -- Biography.

ML395.S5 1975
Shapiro, Nat,
The jazz makers/ edited by Nat Shapiro and Nat Hentoff. Westport, Conn.: Greenwood Press, 1975. xiii, 368 p.
73-011864   780/.92/2   0837170982
Jazz musicians -- Biography. Jazz -- History and criticism.

ML396.M87 1998
Murray, Michael, 1943-
French masters of the organ: Saint-Saens, Franck, Widor, Vierne, Dupre, Langlais, Messiaen/ Michael Murray. New Haven: Yale University Press, c1998. 245 p.
97-041401   786.5/092/244   0300072910
Organists -- France -- Biography.

ML397.S3 1987
Schonberg, Harold C.
The great pianists/ Harold C. Schonberg. Rev. and updated. New York: Simon & Schuster, c1987. 525 p.
87-000341   786.1/092/2 B 19   0671638378
Pianists -- Biography.

ML398.G835 1998
Steinhardt, Arnold.
Indivisible by four: a string quartet in pursuit of harmony/ Arnold Steinhardt. 1st ed. New York: Farrar, Straus, Giroux, 1998. 308 p.
98-007978   785/.7194/0922 B 21   0374236704

ML398.R68 1986
Roth, Henry, 1916-
Great violinists in performance; critical evaluations of over 100 twentieth-century virtuosi/ by Henry Roth. Los Angeles: Panjandrum Books, c1987. xii, 266 p.
86-021248   787.1/092/2   0915572850
Violinists -- Biography.

ML399.B38 2000
Barnhart, Stephen L., 1950-
Percussionists: a biographical dictionary/ Stephen L. Barnhart; John Gillespie, advisory editor. Westport, Conn.: Greenwood Press, 2000. xvi, 429 p.
99-046021   786.8/092/2   0313296278
Percussionists -- Biography.

ML399.D54 1995
Dietrich, Kurt.
Duke's 'bones: Ellington's great trombonists/ Kurt Dietrich. Rottenburg am Neckar: Advance Music, c1995. 229 p.
97-176249   788.9/3165/092273
Jazz musicians -- United States -- Biography. Trombonists -- United States -- Biography.

ML399.K65 1998
Kononenko, Natalie O.
Ukrainian minstrels: and the blind shall sing/ by Natalie Kononenko. Armonk, N.Y.: M.E. Sharpe, c1998. xvi, 360 p.
97-028498   782.42162/91791 21   0765601443
Kobzari -- History. Minstrels -- Ukraine -- History. Blind musicians -- Ukraine -- Biography. Ukraine -- Social life and customs.

ML400.D4 1996
Deffaa, Chip, 1951-
Blue rhythms: six lives in rhythm and blues/ Chip Deffaa. Urbana: University of Illinois Press, c1996. xviii, 301 p.
95-004414   781.643/092/273   0252022033
Singers -- United States -- Biography. Rhythm and blues music -- History and criticism.

ML400.D53 1999
Dicaire, David, 1963-
Blues singers: biographies of 50 legendary artists of the early 20th century/ by David Dicaire. Jefferson, N.C.: McFarland, c1999. vii, 292 p.
99-016594   781.643/092/273   0786406062
Blues musicians -- United States -- Biography.

ML400.M34 1969
Marsh, J. B. T.
The story of the Jubilee Singers; with their songs, by J. B. T. Marsh. New York, Negro Universities Press [1969] viii, 243 p.
79-078583   783.8   0837114241
Afro-American musicians. Afro-Americans -- Music. Folk music -- United States.

ML400.S77 1996
Stancell, Steven.
Rap whoz who: the world of rap music/ Steven Stancell. New York: Schirmer Books, c1996. x, 339 p.
95-043926   782.42164   0028645200
Rap musicians -- United States -- Biography. Disc jockeys -- United States -- Biography. Rap (Music) -- Discography.

ML402.H36 1995
Handy, D. Antoinette, 1930-
Black conductors/ by D. Antoinette Handy. Metuchen, N.J.: Scarecrow Press, 1995. xii 557 p.
94-034560   781.45/092/273   0810829304
Afro-American conductors (Music) -- Biography.

ML402.S387.G7
Schonberg, Harold C.
The great conductors [by] Harold C. Schonberg. New York, Simon and Schuster [1967] 384 p.
67-019821   780.922
Conductors (Music) -- Biography.

ML405.C64 2000
Cohodas, Nadine.
Spinning blues into gold: the Chess brothers and the legendary Chess Records/ Nadine Cohodas. 1st ed. New York: St. Martin's Press, 2000. viii, 358 p.
00-025480   781.643/149 21   0312261330
Chess, Leonard, 1917- Chess, Phil, 1921- Sound recording executives and producers -- United States -- Biography.

ML406.W56 1998
Williams, Gilbert Anthony, 1951-
Legendary pioneers of Black radio/ Gilbert A. Williams. Westport, Conn.: Praeger, 1998. xi, 198 p.
97-038995   791.44/089/96073   0275958884
Disc jockeys -- United States -- Interviews. Afro-American disc jockeys -- United States -- Interviews. Afro-Americans in radio broadcasting.

ML410-429 History and criticism — Biography — Individual

ML410.A315.T37 1990
Talbot, Michael.
Tomaso Albinoni: the Venetian composer and his world/ Michael Talbot. Oxford [England]: Clarendon Press; 1990. vi, 308 p.
89-049221   780/.92   0193152452
Albinoni, Tomaso, -- 1671-1750. Composers -- Italy -- Biography.

ML410.A638 A3 1981
Antheil, George,
Bad boy of music/ by George Antheil; new introd. by Charles Amirkhanian. New York: Da Capo Press, 1981, c1945. vi, 378 p.
81-001169   780/.92/4 B 19   0306760843
Antheil, George, 1900-1959. Composers -- United States -- Biography.

ML410.B1.A96 1984
Arnold, Denis.
Bach/ Denis Arnold. Oxford; Oxford University Press, 1984. vii, 103 p.
83-015141　780/.92/4　019287554X
Bach, Johann Sebastian, -- 1685-1750.　Composers -- Germany -- Biography.

ML410.B1.B24513 1992
Badura-Skoda, Paul.
Interpreting Bach at the keyboard/ Paul Badura-Skoda; translated by Alfred Clayton. Oxford: Clarendon Press; 1993. xvi, 573 p.
92-012565　786/.146/092　0198161557
Bach, Johann Sebastian, -- 1685-1750. -- Harpsichord music. Harpsichord music -- Interpretation (Phrasing, dynamics, etc.) Performance practice (Music) -- 18th century.

ML410.B1 B73 2000
Boyd, Malcolm.
Bach/ Malcolm Boyd. 3rd ed. Oxford; Oxford University Press, 2000. xvi, 312 p.
00-033976　780/.92 21　0195142233
Bach, Johann Sebastian, 1685-1750.　Composers--Germany--Biography.

ML410.B1.B9 1990
Butt, John.
Bach interpretation: articulation marks in primary sources of J.S. Bach/ John Butt. Cambridge [England]; Cambridge University Press, 1990. xiii, 278 p.
89-007141　780/.92　0521372399
Bach, Johann Sebastian, -- 1685-1750 -- Criticism and interpretation.　Performance practice (Music) -- 18th century.

ML410.B1.B93 1991
Butt, John.
Bach, Mass in B minor/ John Butt. Cambridge; Cambridge University Press, 1991. x, 116 p.
90-002286　782.32/32　0521382807
Bach, Johann Sebastian, -- 1685-1750. -- Masses, -- BWV 232, -- B minor.

ML410.B1.D24 1998
The new Bach reader: a life of Johann Sebastian Bach in letters and documents/ edited by Hans T. David and Arthur Mendel; revised and enlarged by Christoph Wolff. New York: W.W. Norton, c1998. liv, 551 p.
97-041850　780/.92　0393045587
Bach, Johann Sebastian, -- 1685-1750.　Composers -- Germany -- Biography.

ML410.B1 D63 1996
Dreyfus, Laurence.
Bach and the patterns of invention/ Laurence Dreyfus. Cambridge, Mass.: Harvard University Press, 1996. 270 p.
96-032275　780/.92 B 20　0674060059
Bach, Johann Sebastian, 1685-1750 -- Criticism and interpretation. Composition (Music)

ML410.B1.J15 1999
J.S. Bach/ edited by Malcolm Boyd; consultant editor, John Butt. Oxford; Oxford University Press, 1999. xxv, 626 p.
98-019587　780/.92　0198662084
Bach, Johann Sebastian, -- 1685-1750 -- Dictionaries.

ML410.B1.W79 1991
Wolff, Christoph.
Bach: essays on his life and music/ Christoph Wolff. Cambridge, Mass.: Harvard University Press, 1991. xiv, 461 p.
90-005247　780/.92　0674059255
Bach, Johann Sebastian, -- 1685-1750. Bach, Johann Sebastian, -- 1685-1750 -- Criticism and interpretation.

ML410.B1.W793 2000
Wolff, Christoph.
Johann Sebastian Bach: the learned musician/ Christoph Wolff. New York: W.W. Norton, c2000. xvii, 599 p.
99-054364　780/.92　039304825X
Bach, Johann Sebastian, -- 1685-1750.　Composers -- Germany -- Biography.

ML410.B13 2000
Durr, Alfred, 1918-
Johann Sebastian Bach's St. John Passion: genesis, transmission, and meaning/ Alfred Durr; translated by Alfred Clayton.. Oxford; Oxford University Press, 1999. xiii, 182 p.
99-032937　782.23　0198162405
Bach, Johann Sebastian, -- 1685-1750. -- Johannespassion.

ML410.B13.B6 1993
Boyd, Malcolm.
Bach, the Brandenburg concertos/ Malcolm Boyd. New York, NY, USA: Cambridge University Press, 1993. x, 111 p.
92-039751　784.2/4/092　0521382769
Bach, Johann Sebastian, -- 1685-1750. -- Brandenburgische Konzerte.

ML410.B13.C36 1997
The Cambridge companion to Bach/ edited by John Butt. New York: Cambridge University Press, 1997. xv, 326 p.
96-022581　780/.92　052145350X
Bach, Johann Sebastian, -- 1685-1750.

ML410.B13 L52 2001
Little, Meredith,
Dance and the music of J.S. Bach/ Meredith Little and Natalie Jenne. Expanded ed. Bloomington: Indiana University Press, c2001. xii, 337 p.
2001-016944　784.18/82/092 21　0253214645
Bach, Johann Sebastian, 1685-1750 -- Criticism and interpretation. Dance music -- 18th century -- History and criticism.

ML410.B13.M28 1989
Marshall, Robert Lewis.
The music of Johann Sebastian Bach: the sources, the style, the significance/ Robert L. Marshall. New York: Schirmer Books, c1989. xxi, 375 p.
88-023921 780/.92/4 0028717813
Bach, Johann Sebastian, -- 1685-1750 -- Criticism and interpretation.

ML410.B13 S87 1996
Stinson, Russell.
Bach, the Orgelbüchlein/ Russell Stinson. New York: Schirmer Books; xv, 208 p.
96-024581 786.5/18992/092 20 0028725050
Bach, Johann Sebastian, 1685-1750. Orgelbüchlein. Chorale prelude.

ML410.B23.H5 1992
Heyman, Barbara B.
Samuel Barber: the composer and his music/ Barbara B. Heyman. New York: Oxford University Press, 1992. xviii, 586 p.
91-002454 780/.92 0195066502
Barber, Samuel, -- 1910- -- Criticism and interpretation.

ML410.B26.B272 1995
Bartok and his world/ edited by Peter Laki. Princeton, NJ: Princeton University Press, c1995. ix, 314 p.
95-013368 780/.92 0691006342
Bartok, Bela, -- 1881-1945.

ML410.B26.C35 2001
The Cambridge companion to Bartok/ edited by Amanda Bayley. Cambridge; Cambridge University Press, 2001. xv, 271 p.
00-036030 780/.92 0521660106
Bartok, Bela, -- 1881-1945 -- Criticism and interpretation.

ML410.B26 F75 1997
Frigyesi, Judit.
Béla Bartók and turn-of-the century Budapest/ Judit Frigyesi. Berkeley: University of California Press, c1998 x, 357 p.
97-019826 780/.92 21 0520207408
Bartók, Béla, 1881-1945 -- Aesthetics. Bartók, Béla, 1881-1945 -- Sources. Bartók, Béla, 1881-1945. Kékszakállú herceg vára. Ady, Endre, 1877-1919 -- Influence. Modernism (Aesthetics) -- Hungary -- Budapest. Budapest (Hungary) -- Intellectual life.

ML410.B26.G7 1984
Griffiths, Paul, 1947 Nov. 24-
Bartok/ Paul Griffiths. London: J.M. Dent, 1984. ix, 224 p.
84-141807 780/.92/4 0460031821
Bartok, Bela, -- 1881-1945. Composers -- Hungary -- Biography.

ML410.B26.H2
Haraszti, Emil, 1885-
Bela Bartok, his life and works, by Emil Haraszti. Paris, The Lyrebird press, Louise B. M. Dyer [c1938] 103 p.
39-014718 927.8
Bartok, Bela, -- 1881-1945.

ML410.B26.S83 1995
Suchoff, Benjamin.
Bartok, Concerto for orchestra: understanding Bartok's world/ Benjamin Suchoff. New York: Schirmer Books, c1995. xi, 266 p.
95-010440 784.2/186 002872495X
Bartok, Bela, -- 1881-1945 -- Criticism and interpretation. Bartok, Bela, -- 1881-1945. -- Concertos, -- orchestra. Bartok, Bela, -- 1881-1945 -- Influence.

ML410.B36.B56 1998
Block, Adrienne Fried.
Amy Beach, passionate Victorian: the life and work of an American composer, 1867-1944/ Adrienne Fried Block. New York: Oxford University Press, 1998. xiii, 409 p.
97-002710 780/.92 0195074084
Beach, H. H. A., -- Mrs., -- 1867-1944. Composers -- United States -- Biography. Women composers -- United States -- Biography.

ML410.B36 J46 1994
Jenkins, Walter S.,
The remarkable Mrs. Beach, American composer: a biographical account based on her diaries, letters, newspaper clippings, and personal reminiscences/ by Walter S. Jenkins; edited by John H. Baron. Warren, Mich.: Harmonie Park Press, 1994. xiv, 226 p.
94-021509 780/.92 B 20 0899900690
Beach, H. H. A., Mrs., 1867-1944. Composers -- United States -- Biography. Women composers -- United States -- Biography.

ML410.B4.A75 1971b
Arnold, Denis.
The Beethoven reader. Edited by Denis Arnold and Nigel Fortune. New York, W. W. Norton [1971] 542 p.
77-139374 780/.924 0303021491
Beethoven, Ludwig van, -- 1770-1827.

ML410.B4.B2813 1992
The Beethoven compendium: a guide to Beethoven's life and music/ Barry Cooper ... [et al.]; edited by Barry Cooper. New York: Thames and Hudson, 1992. 351 p.
91-065423 780/.92 0500015236
Beethoven, Ludwig van, -- 1770-1827. Composers -- Austria -- Biography.

ML410.B4.C24 2000
The Cambridge companion to Beethoven/ edited by Glenn Stanley. Cambridge, UK; Cambridge University Press, 2000. xiii, 373 p.
98-042732 780/.92 0521580749
Beethoven, Ludwig van, -- 1770-1827 -- Criticism and interpretation.

ML410.B4.D213 1991
Dahlhaus, Carl, 1928-
Ludwig van Beethoven: approaches to his music/ Carl Dahlhaus; translated by Mary Whittall. Oxford: Clarendon Press; 1991. xxviii, 254 p.
90-022249 780/.92 0198161484
Beethoven, Ludwig van, -- 1770-1827 -- Criticism and interpretation.

ML410.B4.K56 1995
Kinderman, William.
Beethoven/ William Kinderman. Berkeley: University of California Press, c1995. xvi, 374 p.
94-004813   780/.92   0520087968
Beethoven, Ludwig van, -- 1770-1827 -- Criticism and interpretation.

ML410.B4.L287
Landon, H. C. Robbins 1926-
Beethoven; a documentary study. Compiled and edited by H. C. Robbins Landon. New York] Macmillan [1970] 400 p.
77-101293   780/.924
Beethoven, Ludwig van, -- 1770-1827. Beethoven, Ludwig van, -- 1770-1827 -- Pictorial works.

ML410.B4.L595 1992
Lockwood, Lewis.
Beethoven: studies in the creative process/ Lewis Lockwood. Cambridge, Mass.: Harvard University Press, 1992. 283 p.
91-024796   780/.92   0674063627
Beethoven, Ludwig van, -- 1770-1827 -- Criticism and interpretation.

ML410.B4.N45 1988
Newman, William S.
Beethoven on Beethoven: playing his piano music his way/ William S. Newman. New York: Norton, c1988. 336 p.
87-018756   786.1/092/4   0393025381
Beethoven, Ludwig van, -- 1770-1827. -- Piano music. Piano music -- Interpretation (Phrasing, dynamics, etc.) Performance practice (Music) -- 18th century. Performance practice (Music) -- 19th century.

ML410.B4 S3333 1996
Schindler, Anton,
Beethoven as I knew him/ Anton Felix Schindler; edited by Donald W.　MacArdle; English translation by Constance S. Jolly. Mineola, N.Y.: Dover Publications, 1996. 547 p.
96-022901   780/.92 B 20   0486292320
Beethoven, Ludwig van, 1770-1827. Composers -- Austria -- Biography.

ML410.B4.S64 1998
Solomon, Maynard.
Beethoven/ Maynard Solomon. New York: Schirmer Books; c1998. xxii, 554 p.
97-051363   780/.92   0028647173
Beethoven, Ludwig van, -- 1770-1827.　Composers -- Austria -- Biography.

ML410.B4.W97 1998
Wyn Jones, David.
The life of Beethoven/ David Wyn Jones. Cambridge; Cambridge University Press, 1998. xii, 204 p.
98-003638   780/.92   0521560195
Beethoven, Ludwig van, -- 1770-1827.　Composers -- Austria -- Biography.

ML410.B42.B425 1991
Beethoven's compositional process/ edited by William Kinderman. Lincoln: University of Nebraska Press in association with the American Beethoven Society and the Ira F. Brilliant Center for Beethoven Studies, San Jose State University, c1991. xii, 195 p.
90-024227   780/.92   0803212224
Beethoven, Ludwig van, -- 1770-1827 -- Criticism and interpretation -- Congresses.

ML410.B42.D8 1991
Drabkin, William.
Beethoven, Missa solemnis/ William Drabkin. Cambridge, [England]; Cambridge University Press, 1991. xiii, 118 p.
91-011383   782.32/32   0521372291
Beethoven, Ludwig van, -- 1770-1827. -- Missa solemnis.

ML410.B42.L48 1995
Levy, David Benjamin.
Beethoven, the Ninth symphony/ David Benjamin Levy. New York: Schirmer Books; c1995. xi, 226 p.
94-029785   784.2/184   002871363X
Beethoven, Ludwig van, -- 1770-1827 -- Symphonies, -- no. 9, op. 125, -- D minor.

ML410.B42.M25 1995
Marston, Nicholas.
Beethoven's piano sonata in E, op. 109/ Nicholas Marston Oxford: Clarendon Press; 1995. xviii, 267 p.
94-010762   786.2/183   0193153327
Beethoven, Ludwig van, -- 1770-1827. -- Sonatas, -- piano, -- no. 30, op. 109, -- E major.

ML410.B42.P47 1994
Performing Beethoven/ edited by Robin Stowell. Cambridge; Cambridge University Press, 1994. xiv, 246 p.
93-031379   780/.92   0521416442
Beethoven, Ludwig van, -- 1770-1827 -- Criticism and interpretation.　Performance practice (Music) -- 18th century. Performance practice (Music) -- 19th century.

ML410.B42.P6 1999
Plantinga, Leon.
Beethoven's concertos: history, style, performance/ Leon Plantinga. New York: W.W. Norton, c1999. xi, 403 p.
98-022552   784.2/3/092   0393046915
Beethoven, Ludwig van, -- 1770-1827. -- Concertos. Concerto.

ML410.B42.S57 1998
Sipe, Thomas.
Beethoven, Eroica symphony/ Thomas Sipe. Cambridge; Cambridge University Press, 1998. xi, 146 p.
97-033020   784.2/184   0521475287
Beethoven, Ludwig van, -- 1770-1827. -- Symphonies, -- no. 3, op. 55, -- E major.

ML410.B44 K56 1998
Kimbell, David R. B.
Vincenzo Bellini, Norma/ David Kimbell. Cambridge; Cambridge University Press, 1998. xiii, 141 p.
97-032615   782.1 21   0521485142
Bellini, Vincenzo, 1801-1835. Norma.

ML410.B44 R77 1996
Rosselli, John.
The life of Bellini/ John Rosselli. Cambridge, [England]; Cambridge University Press, 1996.
95-039270   782.1/092 B 20   0521467810
Bellini, Vincenzo, 1801-1835. Composers -- Italy -- Biography.

ML410.B47.B53 1990
The Berg companion/ edited by Douglas Jarman. Boston: Northeastern University Press, 1990. xii, 301 p.
89-008581   780/.92   1555530680
Berg, Alban, -- 1885-1935 -- Criticism and interpretation.

ML410.B47.C38 1997
The Cambridge companion to Berg/ edited by Anthony Pople. Cambridge; Cambridge University Press, 1997. xv, 304 p.
96-039727   780/.92   0521563747
Berg, Alban, -- 1885-1935 -- Criticism and interpretation.

ML410.B47.H43 1996
Headlam, David John.
The music of Alban Berg/ Dave Headlam. New Haven [Conn.]: Yale University Press, c1996. xi, 460 p.
95-046936   780/.92   0300064004
Berg, Alban, -- 1885-1935 -- Criticism and interpretation.

ML410.B47.J28 1991
Jarman, Douglas.
Alban Berg, Lulu/ Douglas Jarman. Cambridge [England]; Cambridge University Press, 1991. xiii, 146 p.
90-001637   782.1   0521241502
Berg, Alban, -- 1885-1935. -- Lulu.

ML410.B47.J3 1989
Jarman, Douglas.
Alban Berg, Wozzeck/ Douglas Jarman. Cambridge [Cambridgeshire]; Cambridge University Press, 1989. ix, 181 p.
88-015965   782.1/092/4   0521241510
Berg, Alban, -- 1885-1935. -- Wozzeck.

ML410.B47.J33
Jarman, Douglas.
The Music of Alban Berg/ Douglas Jarman. Berkeley: University of California Press, c1979. xii, 266 p.
77-076687   780/.92/4   0520034856
Berg, Alban, -- 1885-1935 -- Criticism and interpretation.

ML410.B47.P48
Perle, George, 1915-
The operas of Alban Berg/ George Perle. Berkeley: University of California Press, c1980-c1985. 2 v.
76-052033   782.1/092/4   0520034406
Berg, Alban, -- 1885-1935. Berg, Alban, -- 1885-1935. -- Wozzeck. Berg, Alban, -- 1885-1935. -- Lulu.

ML410.B47.P6 1991
Pople, Anthony.
Berg, Violin concerto/ Anthony Pople. Cambridge; Cambridge University Press, 1991. ix, 121 p.
90-002542   784.2/72   0521390664
Berg, Alban -- 1885-1935. -- Concerto, -- violin, orchestra.

ML410.B4968.O55 1990
Osmond-Smith, David.
Berio/ David Osmond-Smith. Oxford; Oxford University Press, 1991. 158 p.
90-007368   780/.92   0193154781
Berio, Luciano, -- 1925- -- Criticism and interpretation.

ML410.B499.H36 1997
Hamm, Charles.
Irving Berlin: songs from the melting pot: the formative years, 1907-1914/ Charles Hamm. New York: Oxford University Press, 1997. xii, 292 p.
96-006335   782.42164/092   0195071883
Berlin, Irving, -- 1888- -- Criticism and interpretation. Popular music -- United States -- 1901-1910 -- History and criticism. Popular music -- United States -- 1911-1920 -- History and criticism.

ML410.B499 J33 1999
Jablonski, Edward.
Irving Berlin: American troubadour/ Edward Jablonski. 1st ed. New York: Henry Holt, 1999. viii, 406 p.
98-003058   782.42164/092 B 21   0805040773
Berlin, Irving, 1888- Composers -- United States -- Biography.

ML410.B5 A3 2002
Berlioz, Hector,
The memoirs of Hector Berlioz/ translated and edited by David Cairns. New York: A.A. Knopf, c2002. xxxv, 709 p.
2002-283060   780/.92 B 21   037541391X
Berlioz, Hector, 1803-1869. Composers -- France -- Biography.

ML410.B5.A33 1997
Berlioz, Hector, 1803-1869.
Selected letters of Berlioz/ edited by Hugh Macdonald; translated by Roger Nichols. New York: Norton, 1997. xiii, 479 p.
96-047015   780/.92   0393040623
Berlioz, Hector, -- 1803-1869. Composers -- France -- Correspondence.

ML410.B5 A533 1999
Berlioz, Hector,
Evenings with the orchestra/ Hector Berlioz; translated and edited with an introduction and notes by Jacques Barzun; with a new foreword by Peter Bloom. Chicago: University of Chicago Press, c1999. xxvi, 381 p.
98-054094   780/.944/36109034 21   0226043746
Music -- France -- Paris -- History and criticism. Music -- History and criticism.

ML410.B5.B2 1969
Barzun, Jacques, 1907-
Berlioz and the romantic century. New York, Columbia University Press, 1969. 2 v.
77-097504   780/.924   0231031351
Berlioz, Hector, -- 1803-1869.

ML410.B5 C25 1999
Cairns, David.
Berlioz/ David Cairns. Berkeley, Calif.: University of California Press, [1999-   ] v. <1 >
99-053825   780/.92 B 21   0520222008
Berlioz, Hector, 1803-1869. Composers -- France -- Biography.

ML410.B5.C27 2000
The Cambridge companion to Berlioz/ edited by Peter
Bloom. New York: Cambridge University Press, 2000.
xxiv, 301 p.
99-054359   780/.92   0521593883
Berlioz, Hector, -- 1803-1869 -- Criticism and interpretation.

ML410.B5.H58 1989
Holoman, D. Kern, 1947-
Berlioz/ D. Kern Holoman. Cambridge, Mass.: Harvard
University Press, 1989. 687 p.
88-035788   780/.92/4   0674067789
*Berlioz, Hector, -- 1803-1869.   Composers -- France --
Biography.*

ML410.B5 M13 2000
Macdonald, Hugh,
Berlioz/ Hugh Macdonald. Oxford; Oxford University
Press, 2000. 261 p.
00-040065   780/.92 B 21   0198164831
Berlioz, Hector, 1803-1869. Composers -- France -- Biography.

ML410.B566.G713 1987
Gradenwitz, Peter, 1910-
Leonard Bernstein: the infinite variety of a musician/
Peter Gradenwitz. Leamington Spa [Warwickshire];
Berg; 1987. 310 p.
86-026326   780/.92/4   0854965106
*Bernstein, Leonard, -- 1918-   Musicians -- United States --
Biography.*

ML410.B605.A35 2000
Adlington, Robert.
The music of Harrison Birtwistle/ Robert Adlington. New
York: Cambridge University Press, 2000. xiv, 242 p.
99-022678   780/.92   0521630827
Birtwistle, Harrison -- Criticism and interpretation.

ML410.B605.C76 2000
Cross, Jonathan, 1961-
Harrison Birtwistle: man, mind, music/ Jonathan Cross.
Ithaca, N.Y.: Cornell University Press, 2000. xiii, 295 p.
00-020553   780/.92   0801486726
Birtwistle, Harrison -- Criticism and interpretation.

ML410.B62 D35 1975
Dean, Winton.
Bizet/ by Winton Dean. [3rd ed.]. London: Dent, 1975. x,
306 p.
76-364220   780/.92/4   0460031635
Bizet, Georges, 1838-1875.

ML410.B62.M25 1992
McClary, Susan.
Georges Bizet, Carmen/ Susan McClary. Cambridge;
Cambridge University Press, 1992. xi, 163 p.
91-032840   782.1   0521393019
Bizet, Georges, -- 1838-1875. -- Carmen.

ML410.B773.J313 1990
Jameux, Dominique.
Pierre Boulez/ Dominique Jameux; translated by Susan
Bradshaw. Cambridge, Mass.: Harvard University Press,
1990. xiii, 422 p.
90-004715   780/.92   0674667409
Boulez, Pierre, -- 1925- Composers -- France -- Biography.

ML410.B773.S68 1987
Stacey, Peter F.
Boulez and the modern concept/ Peter F. Stacey. Lincoln:
University of Nebraska Press, c1987. x, 151 p.
86-030818   780/.92/4   0803241836
Boulez, Pierre, -- 1925- -- Criticism and interpretation.

ML410.B8.A4 1997
Brahms, Johannes, 1833-1897.
Johannes Brahms: life and letters/ selected and annotated
by Styra Avins; translations by Josef Eisinger and Styra
Avins. Oxford; Oxford University Press, 1997. xxviii,
858 p.
97-005417   780/.92   0198162340
*Brahms, Johannes, -- 1833-1897 -- Correspondence.
Composers -- Germany -- Correspondence.*

ML410.B8.B38 1995
Bell, A. Craig.
Brahms--the vocal music/ A. Craig Bell. Madison [N.J.]:
Fairleigh Dickinson University Press; c1995. 262 p.
94-043514   782.2/092   0838635970
*Brahms, Johannes, -- 1833-1897. -- Vocal music. Vocal music -
- 19th century -- History and criticism.*

ML410.B8.B65 1990
Brahms and his world/ edited by Walter Frisch.
Princeton, N.J.: Princeton University Press, c1990. viii,
223 p.
90-008623   780/.92   0691091390
Brahms, Johannes, -- 1833-1897.

ML410.B8 C36 1999
The Cambridge companion to Brahms/ edited by Michael
Musgrave. Cambridge, U.K.; Cambridge University
Press, 1999. xxii, 325 p.
98-003057   780/.92 21   0521485819
Brahms, Johannes, 1833-1897--Criticism and interpretation.

ML410.B8.F75 1996
Frisch, Walter, 1951-
Brahms, the four symphonies/ Walter Frisch. New York:
Schirmer Books; c1996. xiv, 226 p.
96-022951   784.2/184/092   0028707656
Brahms, Johannes, -- 1833-1897. -- Symphonies. Symphony.

ML410.B8 G42 1982
Geiringer, Karl,
Brahms, his life and work/ Karl Geiringer in
collaboration with Irene Geiringer. 3rd, enl. ed./ with a
new appendix ... New York: Da Capo Press, 1982. xv,
397 p.
81-012549   780/.92/4 B 19   0306760932
*Brahms, Johannes, 1833-1897. Composers -- Germany --
Biography.*

ML410.B8.M113 1990
MacDonald, Malcolm, 1948-
Brahms/ Malcolm MacDonald. New York: Schirmer Books, 1990. xiii, 490 p.
90-008545   780/.92   0028713931
Brahms, Johannes, -- 1833-1897.   Composers -- Germany -- Biography.

ML410.B8.M86 1996
Musgrave, Michael, 1942-
Brahms, A German requiem/ Michael Musgrave. Cambridge [England]; Cambridge University Press, 1996. xii, 97 p.
95-051987   782.2/9   052140200X
Brahms, Johannes, -- 1833-1897. -- Deutsches Requiem.

ML410.B8.M865 2000
Musgrave, Michael, 1942-
A Brahms reader/ Michael Musgrave. New Haven, CT: Yale University Press, c2000. xviii, 344 p.
99-011127   780/.92   0300068042
Brahms, Johannes, -- 1833-1897.   Composers -- Germany -- Biography.

ML410.B8 S93 1997
Swafford, Jan.
Johannes Brahms: a biography/ Jan Swafford. 1st ed. New York: Alfred A. Knopf: xxii, 699 p.
97-029308   780/.92 21   0679422617
Brahms, Johannes, 1833-1897.   Composers--Germany-- Biography.

ML410.B853.A4 1991
Britten, Benjamin, 1913-1976.
Letters from a life: the selected letters and diaries of Benjamin Britten, 1913-1976/ edited by Donald Mitchell and Philip Reed. Berkeley: University of California Press, [1991-] 2 v.
90-042998   780/.92   0520065204
Britten, Benjamin, -- 1913-1976 -- Correspondence. Britten, Benjamin, -- 1913-1976 -- Diaries.   Composers -- England -- Correspondence. Composers -- England -- Diaries.

ML410.B853.C37 1993
Carpenter, Humphrey.
Benjamin Britten: a biography/ Humphrey Carpenter. New York: C. Scribner's Sons, c1992. x, 677 p.
93-018146   780/.92   0684195690
Britten, Benjamin, -- 1913-1976.   Composers -- England -- Biography.

ML410.B853.E9 1979
Evans, Peter, 1929-
The music of Benjamin Britten/ Peter Evans; illustrated with over 300 music examples and diagrams. Minneapolis: University of Minnesota Press, 1979. vii, 564 p.
78-031606   780/.92/4   0816608369
Britten, Benjamin, -- 1913-1976 -- Criticism and interpretation.

ML410.B853 K45 2001
Kennedy, Michael,
Britten/ Michael Kennedy. [Rev. ed.] Oxford; Oxford University Press, 2001. xi, 359 p.
00-057119   780/.92 B 21   0198164793
Britten, Benjamin,   1913-1976. Composers -- England -- Biography.

ML410.B853.W4 1970
White, Eric Walter, 1905-
Benjamin Britten, his life and operas.   Berkeley, University of California Press, 1970. 256 p.
73-107655   782.1/0924   0520016793
Britten, Benjamin, -- 1913-1976.

ML410.B868.H35 1996
Hall, Fred, 1923-
It's about time: the Dave Brubeck story/ Fred M. Hall. Fayetteville: University of Arkansas Press, 1996. xiii, 182 p.
95-038531   781.65/092   1557284040
Brubeck, Dave.   Jazz musicians -- United States -- Biography.

ML410.B87.F53 1988
Fifield, Christopher.
Max Bruch: his life and works/ by Christopher Fifield. New York: G. Braziller, 1988. 351 p.
88-016689   780/.92/4   0807612049
Bruch, Max, -- 1838-1920.   Composers -- Germany -- Biography.

ML410.B88 H69 2002
Howie, Crawford,
Anton Bruckner: a documentary biography/ Crawford Howie. Lewiston, N.Y.: Edwin Mellen Press, c2002. 2 v.
2001-042755   780/.92 21   0773473009
Bruckner, Anton, 1824-1896.   Composers--Austria--Biography.

ML410.B88 W26 1996
Watson, Derek,
Bruckner/ Derek Watson. 2nd ed. Oxford; Oxford University Press, 1996. xiii, 158 p.
96-035599   780/.92 20   0198166176
Bruckner, Anton, 1824-1896.   Composers--Austria--Biography.

ML410.B98.A12 1965
Busoni, Ferruccio, 1866-1924.
The essence of music: and other papers/ Translated from the German by Rosamond Ley. New York: Dover Publications, [1965, c1957] 204 p.
65-026072   780.8
Music

ML410.B99.S6 1987
Snyder, Kerala J.
Dieterich Buxtehude, organist in Lubeck/ Kerala J. Snyder. New York: Schirmer Books; c1987. xxiii, 551 p.
87-018505   780/.92/4   0028730801
Buxtehude, Dietrich, -- 1637-1707.   Composers -- Germany -- Biography.

ML410.B996.H37 1997
Harley, John, 1928-
William Byrd: gentleman of the Chapel Royal/ John Harley. Aldershot, Hants, England: Scolar Press; c1997. xvi, 480 p.
96-037221   780/.92   1859281656
Byrd, William, -- 1542 or 3-1623.   Composers -- England -- Biography.

ML410.C24.A5 1995
Cage, John.
Musicage: Cage muses on words, art, music/ Joan Retallack, editor. Hanover, NH: Wesleyan University Press: c1996. xlvii, 360 p.
95-009497   780/.92   0819552852
Cage, John -- Interviews.   Composers -- United States -- Interviews.

ML410.C24 J54 1991
John Cage: an anthology/ edited by Richard Kostelanetz. New York, N.Y.: Da Capo Press, c1991. xvi, 239 p.
90-027392   780/.92 20   0306804352
Cage, John -- Criticism and interpretation. Cage, John -- Chronology. Cage, John -- Bibliography. Cage, John -- Discography. Music -- Philosophy and aesthetics.

ML410.C24.K68 1988
Kostelanetz, Richard.
Conversing with Cage/ Richard Kostelanetz. New York: Limelight Editions, 1988, c1987. xi, 299 p.
87-022853   780/.92/4   0879101008
Cage, John -- Interviews.   Composers -- United States -- Interviews.

ML410.C24.R5 1992
Revill, David, 1965-
The roaring silence: John Cage, a life/ David Revill. New York: Arcade Pub., c1992. 375 p.
92-005917   780/.92   1559701668
Cage, John.   Composers -- United States -- Biography.

ML410.C327 S83 2002
Sudhalter, Richard M.
Stardust melody: the life and music of Hoagy Carmichael/ Richard M. Sudhalter. Oxford; Oxford University Press, 2002. xiii, 432 p.
2001-034612   782.42164/092 B 21   0195131207
Carmichael, Hoagy, 1899- Composers -- United States -- Biography.

ML410.C3293.E3
Edwards, Allen, 1944-
Flawed words and stubborn sounds; a conversation with Elliott Carter. New York, W. W. Norton [1972, c1971] 128 p.
77-152660   780/.924   0393021599
Carter, Elliott, -- 1908- Music -- 20th century -- History and criticism.

ML410.C395.Y4 1990
Yellin, Victor Fell.
Chadwick, Yankee composer/ by Victor Fell Yellin. Washington: Smithsonian Institution Press, c1990. xvi, 238 p.
89-039869   780/.92   0874749883
Chadwick, G. W. -- (George Whitefield), -- 1854-1931. Chadwick, G. W. -- (George Whitefield), -- 1854-1931 -- Criticism and interpretation. Composers -- United States -- Biography.

ML410.C4.A4 1993
Tchaikovsky, Peter Ilich, 1840-1893.
To my best friend: correspondence between Tchaikovsky and Nadezhda von Meck, 1876-1878/ translated by Galina von Meck; edited by Edward Garden and Nigel Gotteri; with an introduction by Edward Garden. Oxford: Clarendon Press, 1993. lxxi, 439 p.
92-000422   780/.92   0198161581
Tchaikovsky, Peter Ilich, -- 1840-1893 -- Correspondence. Meck, Nadezhda Filaretovna von, -- 1831-1894 -- Correspondence.   Composers -- Russia -- Correspondence. Benefactors -- Russia -- Correspondence.

ML410.C4 B74
Brown, David,
Tchaikovsky: a biographical and critical study/ by David Brown. London: Gollancz, 1978-<1991 > v. <1-2, 4 >
79-309079   780/.92/4   0575050942
Tchaikovsky, Peter Ilich, 1840-1893.   Composers--Russia--Biography.

ML410.C4 P85 1991
Poznansky, Alexander.
Tchaikovsky: the quest for the inner man/ Alexander Poznansky. New York: Schirmer Books; xix, 679 p.
91-010095   780/.92 B 20   0028718852
Tchaikovsky, Peter Ilich, 1840-1893. Composers -- Russia -- Biography.

ML410.C4.P856 1996
Poznansky, Alexander.
Tchaikovsky's last days: a documentary study/ Alexander Poznansky. Oxford: Clarendon Press; 1996. xvii, 236 p.
96-013332   780/.92   019816596X
Tchaikovsky, Peter Ilich, -- 1840-1893 -- Death and burial. Composers -- Russia -- Biography.

ML410.C4.T36 1998
Tchaikovsky and his world/ edited by Leslie Kearney. Princeton, N.J.: Princeton University Press, c1998. xiii, 369 p.
98-025777   780/.92   0691004293
Tchaikovsky, Peter Ilich, -- 1840-1893 -- Criticism and interpretation.

ML410.C433.C4713 1995
Cessac, Catherine, 1952-
Marc-Antoine Charpentier/ Catherine Cessac; translated from the French by E. Thomas Glasow; Reinhard G. Pauly, general editor. Portland, Or.: Amadeus Press, c1995. 558 p.
94-029786   782.1/092   0931340802
Charpentier, Marc Antoine, -- 1634-1704.   Composers -- France -- Biography.

ML410.C54.C2 1992
The Cambridge companion to Chopin/ edited by Jim Samson. Cambridge [England]; Cambridge University Press, 1992. xi, 341 p.
91-024533   786.2/092   0521404908
Chopin, Frederic, -- 1810-1849 -- Criticism and interpretation.
Chopin, Frederic, -- 1810-1849. -- Piano music.

ML410.C54.K16 1996
Kallberg, Jeffrey, 1954-
Chopin at the boundaries: sex, history, and musical genre/ Jeffrey Kallberg. Cambridge, Mass.: Harvard University Press, 1996. xiii, 301 p.
95-042776   786.2/092
Chopin, Frederic, -- 1810-1849 -- Criticism and interpretation.
Music -- 19th century -- History and criticism. Music -- Social aspects.

ML410.C54.L738
Liszt, Franz, 1811-1886.
Frederic Chopin. Translated with an introd. by Edward N. Waters. London [New York] Free Press of Glencoe, Collier-Macmillan [1963] vii, 184 p.
63-010651   927.8
Chopin, Frederic, -- 1810-1849.

ML410.C57.R67 1999
Rossi, Nick, 1924-
Domenico Cimarosa: his life and his operas/ Nick Rossi and Talmage Fauntleroy. Westport, Conn.: Greenwood Press, 1999. x, 225 p.
98-023934   782.1/092   0313301123
Cimarosa, Domenico, -- 1749-1801. Cimarosa, Domenico, -- 1749-1801. -- Operas. Composers -- Italy -- Biography. Opera -- 18th century.

ML410.C64.P5
Plantinga, Leon.
Clementi: his life and music/ Leon Plantinga. London; Oxford University Press, 1977. xiii, 346 p.
77-359247   786.1/092/4   0193152274
Clementi, Muzio, -- 1752-1832.

ML410.C756 A3 1989
Copland, Aaron,
Copland. by Aaron Copland and Vivian Perlis. 1st ed. New York: St. Martin's Press, 1989. xii, 463 p.
89-034847   780/.92 B 20   0312033133
Copland, Aaron, 1900- Composers -- United States -- Biography.

ML410.C756.P6 1999
Pollack, Howard.
Aaron Copland: the life and work of an uncommon man/ Howard Pollack. New York: Henry Holt, 1999. xi, 690 p.
98-029179   780/.92   0805049096
Copland, Aaron, -- 1900- Composers -- United States -- Biography.

ML410.C78.A8 1999
Allsop, Peter,
Arcangelo Corelli: new Orpheus of our times/ Peter Allsop. Oxford [England]; Oxford University Press, c1999. viii, 260 p.
98-007973   787.2/092   0198165625
Corelli, Arcangelo, -- 1653-1713.   Composers -- Italy -- Biography.

ML410.C78.P52 1979
Pincherle, Marc, 1888-1974.
Corelli: his life, his work/ Marc Pincherle; translated from the French by Hubert E. M. Russell. New York: Da Capo Press, 1979, c1956. 236 p.
79-009155   787/.1/0924   0306795760
Corelli, Arcangelo, -- 1653-1713.   Composers -- Italy -- Biography.

ML410.C855.B413 1990
Beaussant, Philippe.
Francois Couperin/ Philippe Beaussant; translated from the French by Alexandra Land; musical examples transcribed by Dominique Visse; Reinhard G. Pauly, general editor. Portland, Or.: Amadeus Press, c1990. 422 p.
89-028729   780/.92   0931340276
Couperin, Francois, -- 1668-1733.   Composers -- France -- Biography.

ML410.D138.V6 1977
Vlad, Roman, 1919-
Luigi Dallapiccola/ Roman Vlad; [English translation by Cynthia Jolly]. St. Clair Shores, Mich.: Scholarly Press, 1977. 62 p.
76-051492   780/.92/4   0403072158
Dallapiccola, Luigi, -- 1904-1975 -- Criticism and interpretation.

ML410.D28.A333
Debussy, Claude, 1862-1918.
Debussy on music: the critical writings of the great French composer Claude Debussy/ collected and introduced by Francois Lesure; translated and edited by Richard Langham Smith. New York: A. A. Knopf, 1977. xxv, 353 p.
76-013717   780/.8   0394481208
Music -- 19th century -- History and criticism.

ML410.D28.A42 1987
Debussy, Claude, 1862-1918.
Debussy letters/ selected and edited by Francois Lesure and Roger Nichols; translated by Roger Nichols. Cambridge, Mass.: Harvard University Press, 1987. xxvi, 355 p.
87-000385   780/.92/4   0674194292
Debussy, Claude, -- 1862-1918 -- Correspondence. Composers -- France -- Correspondence.

ML410.D28.D385 1999
Debussy in performance/ edited by James R. Briscoe.
New Haven [Conn.]: Yale University Press, c1999. xi,
301 p.
99-038223   780/.92   0300076266
Debussy, Claude, -- 1862-1918 -- Criticism and interpretation.
Performance practice (Music) -- 19th century. Performance
practice (Music) -- 20th century.

ML410.D28.D5513 1990
Dietschy, Marcel.
A portrait of Claude Debussy/ Marcel Dietschy; edited
and translated from the French by William Ashbrook and
Margaret G. Cobb. Oxford [England]: Clarendon Press;
1990. xvi, 254 p.
89-023215   780/.92   0193154692
Debussy, Claude, -- 1862-1918.   Composers -- France --
Biography.

ML410.D28.L8 1980
Lockspeiser, Edward, 1905-1973.
Debussy/ by Edward Lockspeiser. London: Dent, 1980.
xvi, 301 p.
80-491637   780/.92/4   0460031732
Debussy, Claude, -- 1862-1918.   Composers -- France --
Biography.

ML410.D28.P24 1989
Parks, Richard S., 1942-
The music of Claude Debussy/ Richard S. Parks. New
Haven: Yale University Press, c1989. xiv, 366 p.
89-031406   780/.92/4   0300044399
Debussy, Claude, -- 1862-1918 -- Criticism and interpretation.

ML410.D28.R56 1996
Roberts, Paul, 1949-
Images: the piano music of Claude Debussy/ Paul
Roberts. Portland, Or.: Amadeus Press, c1996. xxi, 372 p.
95-011283   786.2/092   0931340977
Debussy, Claude, -- 1862-1918. -- Piano music.   Piano music --
History and criticism. Art and music.

ML410.D28.T7 1994
Trezise, Simon.
Debussy, La mer/ Simon Trezise. Cambridge; Cambridge
University Press, 1994. xii, 109 p.
93-042789   784.2/1896   0521441005
Debussy, Claude, -- 1862-1918. -- Mer.

ML410.D35 A4 1983
Delius, Frederick,
Delius, a life in letters/ [compiled and edited by] Lionel
Carley. Cambridge, Mass.: Harvard University Press,
1983-1988. 2 v.
83-016626   780/.92/4 B 19   0859677176
Delius, Frederick,   1862-1934. Composers -- England --
Correspondence.

ML410.D35 D44 1980
A Delius companion/ edited, with a preface by
Christopher Redwood. Rev. ed. London: J. Calder; 1980.
270 p.
81-102245   780/.92/4 19   0714535265
Delius, Frederick, 1862-1934.

ML410.D367.I6 1971
Josquin des Prez: proceedings of the International
Josquin Festival-Conference held at the Julliard School at
Lincoln Center in New York City, 21-25 June 1971/
sponsored by the American Musicological Society, in
cooperation with the International Musicological Society,
and the Renaissance Society of America; edited by
Edward E. Lowinsky, in collaboration with Bonnie J.
Blackburn. London; Oxford University Press, 1976. xviii,
787 p.
77-361746   780/.92/4   0193152290
Josquin, -- des Prez, -- d. 1521 -- Congresses.   Music --
Congresses. Renaissance -- Congresses.

ML410.D7.A83 1982
Ashbrook, William, 1922-
Donizetti and his operas/ William Ashbrook. Cambridge,
[Eng.]: Cambridge University Press, 1982. viii, 744 p.
81-012235   782.1/092/4   052123526X
Donizetti, Gaetano, -- 1797-1848. -- Operas.

ML410.D808 P7 1982
Poulton, Diana.
John Dowland/ Diana Poulton. New and rev. ed.
Berkeley, Calif.: University of California Press, 1982.
528 p.
81-043686   780/.92/4 B 19   0520046498
Dowland, John,   1563?-1626. Composers -- England --
Biography.

ML410.D99 B42 2003
Beckerman, Michael Brim,
New worlds of Dvořák: searching in America for the
composer's inner   life/ Michael B. Beckerman. New
York: Norton, 2003.
2002-026590   780/.92 B 21   0393047067
Dvořák, Antonín,   1841-1904 -- Travel -- United States.
Composers -- Czech Republic -- Biography. United States --
Description and travel.

ML410.D99.D88 1993
Dvorak and his world/ edited by Michael Beckerman.
Princeton, N.J.: Princeton University Press, c1993. x,
284 p.
93-004037   780/.92   0691033862
Dvorak, Antonin, -- 1841-1904.

ML410.D99.D9 1993
Dvorak in America, 1892-1895/ edited by John C.
Tibbetts. Portland, Or.: Amadeus Press, c1993. x, 447 p.
92-019768   780/.92   093134056X
Dvorak, Antonin, -- 1841-1904 -- Journeys -- United States.
Composers -- Czech Republic -- Biography.   United States --
Description and travel.

ML410.D99.R6 1974
Robertson, Alec.
Dvorak/ by Alec Robertson. London: Dent, 1974. ix,
234 p.
75-314527   780/.92/4   0460031163
Dvorak, Antonin, -- 1841-1904.

ML410.E41.A4 1990
Elgar, Edward, 1857-1934.
Edward Elgar: letters of a lifetime/ [selected] by Jerrold Northrop Moore. Oxford: Clarendon Press; 1990. xviii, 524 p.
90-007473   780/.92   0193154722
Elgar, Edward, -- 1857-1934 -- Correspondence. Composers -- England -- Correspondence.

ML410.E41.A65 1993
Anderson, Robert, 1927-
Elgar/ Robert Anderson. New York: Schirmer Books: 1993. xv, 493 p.
93-015280   780/.92   0028701852
Elgar, Edward, -- 1857-1934. Composers -- England -- Biography.

ML410.E41 M65 1984
Moore, Jerrold Northrop.
Edward Elgar: a creative life/ Jerrold Northrop Moore. Oxford; Oxford University Press, 1984. xiv, 841 p.
83-023616   780/.92/4 B 19   0193154471
Elgar, Edward, 1857-1934. Composers -- England -- Biography.

ML410.E41.R87 1998
Rushton, Julian.
Elgar, Enigma variations/ Julian Rushton. New York: Cambridge University Press, 1998. ix, 114 p.
98-022042   784.2/1825   0521631750
Elgar, Edward, -- 1857-1934. -- Variations on an original theme.

ML410.E44.D84 1993
The Duke Ellington reader/ edited by Mark Tucker. New York: Oxford University Press, 1993. xxi, 536 p.
92-037233   781.65/092   0195054105
Ellington, Duke, -- 1899-1974 -- Criticism and interpretation. Jazz -- History and criticism.

ML410.E44.H37 1993
Hasse, John Edward, 1948-
Beyond category: the life and genius of Duke Ellington/ John Edward Hasse. New York: Simon & Schuster, c1993. 479 p.
93-004285   781.65/092   0671703870
Ellington, Duke, -- 1899-1974. Jazz musicians -- United States -- Biography.

ML410.E44.L33 1999
Lambert, Eddie.
Duke Ellington: a listener's guide/ Eddie Lambert. Lanham, Md.: Scarecrow Press, 1999. xiii, 374 p.
98-036431   781.65/092   0810831619
Ellington, Duke, -- 1899-1974 -- Criticism and interpretation.

ML410.E44.N53 1999
Nicholson, Stuart.
Reminiscing in tempo: a portrait of Duke Ellington/ Stuart Nicholson. Boston: Northeastern University Press, c1999. xix, 538 p.
99-010873   781.65/092   1555533809
Ellington, Duke, -- 1899-1974. Jazz musicians -- United States -- Biography.

ML410.E44 T8 1990
Tucker, Mark,
Ellington: the early years/ Mark Tucker. Urbana: University of Illinois Press, c1991. xvii, 343 p.
90-036360   781.65/092 B 20   0252014251
Ellington, Duke, 1899-1974. Jazz musicians -- United States -- Biography.

ML410.E55.M27 1990
Malcolm, Noel.
George Enescu: his life and music/ Noel Malcolm; with a preface by Sir Yehudi Menuhin. [London]: Toccata Press, 1990. 320 p.
91-194575   780/.92   0907689329
Enesco, Georges, -- 1881-1955. Composers -- Romania -- Biography.

ML410.F215 D43 1983
Demarquez, Suzanne.
Manuel de Falla/ by Suzanne Demarquez; translated from the French by Salvator Attanasio. New York: Da Capo Press, 1983, c1968. viii, 253 p.
82-023640   780/.92/4 B 19   0306762048
Falla, Manuel de, 1876-1946. Composers -- Spain -- Biography.

ML410.F215 H47 2001
Hess, Carol A.
Manuel de Falla and modernism in Spain, 1898-1936/ Carol A. Hess. Chicago: University of Chicago Press, 2001. xiii, 347 p.
2001-001222   780/.92 21   0226330389
Falla, Manuel de, 1876-1946 -- Criticism and interpretation. Music -- Spain -- 20th century -- History and criticism. Modernism (Aesthetics) -- Spain.

ML410.F228.C8 1992
Culbertson, Evelyn Davis.
He heard America singing: Arthur Farwell, composer and crusading music educator/ by Evelyn Davis Culbertson. Metuchen, N.J.: Scarecrow Press, 1992. xxix, 852 p.
92-011172   780/.92   0810825805
Farwell, Arthur, -- 1872-1952. Farwell, Arthur, -- 1872-1952 -- Criticism and interpretation. Music teachers -- United States -- Biography. Composers -- United States -- Biography.

ML410.F27.N413 1991
Nectoux, Jean Michel.
Gabriel Faure: a musical life/ Jean-Michel Nectoux; translated by Roger Nichols. Cambridge [England]; Cambridge University Press, 1991. xxv, 646 p.
90-001530   780/.92   0521235243
Faure, Gabriel, -- 1845-1924 -- Criticism and interpretation.

ML410.F2957.M87 1996
The music of Morton Feldman/ Thomas DeLio, [editor]. Westport, Conn.: Greenwood Press, 1996. xvi, 242 p.
95-024022   780/.92   0313298033
Feldman, Morton, -- 1926- -- Criticism and interpretation. Musical analysis.

ML410.F75.T38 1997
Tawa, Nicholas E.
Arthur Foote: a musician in the frame of time and place/ Nicholas E. Tawa. Lanham, Md: Scarecrow Press, 1997. xvi, 489 p.
97-010070   780/.92   081083295X
Foote, Arthur, -- 1853-1937.   Composers -- United States -- Biography.

ML410.F78.E46 1997
Emerson, Ken.
Doo-dah!: Stephen Foster and the rise of American popular culture/ Ken Emerson. New York: Simon & Schuster, c1997. 400 p.
96-029816   782.42164/092   0684810107
Foster, Stephen Collins, -- 1826-1864.   Composers -- United States -- Biography. Music -- Social aspects -- United States. Popular culture -- United States -- History -- 19th century.

ML410.F78 H6 1962
Howard, John Tasker,
Stephen Foster, America's troubadour/ by John Tasker Howard. New York: T. Y. Crowell Co., 1962, c1953. x, 433 p.
77-379301   784/.092/4 B   0815200323
Foster, Stephen Collins, 1826-1864. Composers -- United States -- Biography.

ML410.F82 D29 1977
Davies, Laurence.
César Franck and his circle/ Laurence Davies. New York: Da Capo Press, 1977, c1970. 380 p.
77-004231   780/.92 B   0306774100
Franck, César, 1822-1890 -- Friends and associates. Composers -- France -- Biography.

ML410.F82.I63 1965
Indy, Vincent d', 1851-1931.
Cesar Franck; a translation from the French. With an introd. by Rosa Newmarch. New York, Dover Publications [1965] 286 p.
65-014031   780.92
Franck, Cesar, -- 1822-1890.

ML410.F99.J6 1992
Johann Joseph Fux and the music of the Austro-Italian Baroque/ edited by Harry White. Aldershot, Hants, England: Scolar Press; c1992. xiv, 330 p.
92-106568   780/.92   0859678326
Fux, Johann Joseph, -- 1660-1741 -- Criticism and interpretation.

ML410.G26.C3 1993
Careri, Enrico.
Francesco Geminiani, 1687-1762/ Enrico Careri. Oxford [England]: Clarendon Press; 1993. 300 p.
92-041355   787.2/092   0198163002
Geminiani, Francesco, -- 1687-1762. Geminiani, Francesco, -- 1687-1762. -- Thematic catalogs. Composers -- Biography.

ML410.G288.G49 1999
The Gershwin style: new looks at the music of George Gershwin/ edited by Wayne Schneider. New York: Oxford University Press, 1999. xiv, 290 p.
97-050590   780/.92   0195090209
Gershwin, George, -- 1898-1937 -- Criticism and interpretation.

ML410.G288.J3 1996
Jablonski, Edward.
The Gershwin years: George and Ira/ by Edward Jablonski and Lawrence D. Stewart; with an introduction by Carl van Vechten. New York: Da Capo Press, 1996. 402 p.
96-022950   780/.92/2   0306807394
Gershwin, George, -- 1898-1937. Gershwin, Ira, -- 1896- Composers -- United States -- Biography. Lyricists -- United States -- Biography.

ML410.G288.R67 1991
Rosenberg, Deena, 1951-
Fascinating rhythm: the collaboration of George and Ira Gershwin/ Deena Rosenberg. New York: Dutton, c1991. xxv, 516 p.
91-017717   780/.92/2   0525933565
Gershwin, George, -- 1898-1937. Gershwin, Ira, -- 1896- Composers -- United States -- Biography. Lyricists -- United States -- Biography.

ML410.G29 W4 1991
Watkins, Glenn,
Gesualdo: the man and his music/ Glenn Watkins; preface by Igor Stravinsky. 2nd ed. Oxford [England]: Clarendon Press; xxiv, 414 p.
92-212547   782.4/3/092 20   0198161972
Gesualdo, Carlo, principe di Venosa, 1560 (ca.)-1613-- Criticism and

ML410.G398.A3 1987
Glass, Philip.
Music by Philip Glass/ by Philip Glass; edited and with supplementary material by Robert T. Jones. New York: Harper & Row, c1987. xvii, 222 p.
87-045051   780/.92/4   0060158239
Glass, Philip.   Composers -- United States -- Biography. Operas -- Librettos.

ML410.G46.O813 1988
Orlova, Aleksandra Anatolevna, 1911-
Glinka's life in music: a chronicle/ by Alexandra Orlova; translated by Richard Hoops. Ann Arbor: UMI Research Press, c1988. xxiv, 823 p.
88-004870   780/.92/4   0835718646
Glinka, Mikhail Ivanovich, -- 1804-1857 -- Chronology. Composers -- Soviet Union -- Biography.

ML410.G5.N3 1967
Newman, Ernest, 1868-1959.
Gluck and the opera; a study in musical history. London, Gollancz, 1967. ix, 300 p.
74-355466   782/.0924
Gluck, Christoph Willibald, -- Ritter Von, -- 1714-1787.   Opera.

ML410.G6448.T5 1997
Thomas, Adrian, 1947-
Gorecki/ Adrian Thomas. Oxford: Clarendon Press; 1997.
xviii, 187 p.
96-026034　780/.92　0198163932
Gorecki, Henryk Mikolaj, -- 1933- -- Criticism and interpretation.

ML410.G68.A3 1979
Gottschalk, Louis Moreau, 1829-1869.
Notes of a pianist/ Louis Moreau Gottschalk; edited, with a prelude, a postlude, and explanatory notes, by Jeanne Behrend. New York: Da Capo Press, 1979, c1964.
xxxviii, 420 p.
79-001260　786.1/092/4　0306795086
Gottschalk, Louis Moreau, -- 1829-1869.　Pianists -- United States -- Biography.

ML410.G68.S7 1995
Starr, S. Frederick.
Bamboula!: the life and times of Louis Moreau Gottschalk/ S. Frederick Starr. New York: Oxford University Press, 1995. xii, 564 p.
93-011539　780/.92　0195072375
Gottschalk, Louis Moreau, -- 1829-1869.　Composers -- United States -- Biography. Pianists -- United States -- Biography.

ML410.G695 G66 2000
Goodman, Peter W.
Morton Gould: American salute/ by Peter W. Goodman.
Portland, Or.: Amadeus Press, c2000. 382 p.
99-059948　780/.92 B 21　1574670557
Gould, Morton, 1913- Composers -- United States -- Biography.

ML410.G7.H8 1990
Huebner, Steven.
The operas of Charles Gounod/ Steven Huebner. Oxford [England]: Clarendon Press; 1990. viii, 314 p.
89-035988　782.1/092　0193153297
Gounod, Charles, -- 1818-1893. -- Operas.　Opera -- France -- 19th century.

ML410.G75.B64 1987
Blacking, John.
"A commonsense view of all music": reflections on Percy Grainger's contribution to ethnomusicology and music education/ John Blacking. Cambridge [Cambridgeshire]; Cambridge University Press, 1987. xiii, 201 p.
87-006628　781.7　0521265002
Grainger, Percy, -- 1882-1961 -- Contributions in ethnomusicology.

ML410.G75.M4 1992
Mellers, Wilfrid Howard, 1914-
Percy Grainger/ Wilfrid Mellers. Oxford; Oxford University Press, 1992. ix, 166 p.
92-000152　786.2/092　0198162693
Grainger, Percy, -- 1882-1961.　Composers -- Biography.

ML410.G9.A25 2001
Grieg, Edvard, 1843-1907.
Edvard Grieg: diaries, articles, speeches/ edited and translated by Finn Benestad & William H. Halverson. Columbus, Ohio: Peer Gynt Press, c2001. xiii, 455 p.
00-135386　0964523833
Grieg, Edvard, -- 1843-1907 -- Diaries.　Composers -- Norway -- Diaries. Music -- History and criticism.

ML410.G9.B413 1988
Benestad, Finn.
Edvard Grieg: the man and the artist/ by Finn Benestad and Dag Schjelderup-Ebbe; translated by William H. Halverson and Leland B. Sateren. Lincoln: University of Nebraska Press, c1988. xiii, 441 p.
87-020608　780/.92/4　080321202X
Grieg, Edvard, -- 1843-1907.　Composers -- Norway -- Biography.

ML410.G9134.A8 1993
Anderson, Donna K.
Charles T. Griffes: a life in music/ Donna K. Anderson. Washington: Smithsonian Institution Press, c1993. xvii, 313 p.
92-021844　780/.92　1560981911
Griffes, Charles Tomlinson, -- 1884-1920.　Composers -- United States -- Biography.

ML410.G966.L3 1990
Leech-Wilkinson, Daniel.
Machaut's Mass: an introduction/ Daniel Leech-Wilkinson. Oxford: Clarendon Press; 1990. xi, 212 p.
89-023005　782.32/32　0193163330
Guillaume, -- de Machaut, -- ca. 1300-1377. -- Messe de Nostre Dame.

ML410.G978.H37 1999
Hard travelin': the life and legacy of Woody Guthrie/ edited by Robert Santelli and Emily Davidson. [S.l.]: Wesleyan University Press; c1999. xxii, 256 p.
99-021098　782.42162/13/0092　0819563668
Guthrie, Woody, -- 1912-1967.

ML410.G978.Y9
Yurchenco, Henrietta.
A mighty hard road; the Woody Guthrie story, by Henrietta Yurchenco, assisted by Marjorie Guthrie. Introd. by Arlo Guthrie. New York, McGraw-Hill [1970] 159 p.
73-110963　784.4/9/24
Guthrie, Woody, -- 1912-1967.

ML410.H13.B94 1994b
Burrows, Donald.
Handel/ Donald Burrows. New York: Schirmer Books: c1994. xii, 491 p.
93-015279　780/.92　0028703278
Handel, George Frideric, -- 1685-1759.　Composers -- Biography.

ML410.H13 B95 1991
Burrows, Donald,
Handel, Messiah/ Donald Burrows. Cambridge; Cambridge University Press, 1991. x, 127 p.
90-002566   782.23 20   0521376203
Handel, George Frideric, 1685-1759. Messiah.

ML410.H13.D37 1987
Dean, Winton.
Handel's operas, 1704-1726/ Winton Dean and John Merrill Knapp. Oxford [Oxfordshire]: Clarendon Press; 1987. xx, 751 p.
85-011580   782.1/092/4   0193152193
Handel, George Frideric, -- 1685-1759. -- Operas. Opera.

ML410.H13.H57 1985
Hogwood, Christopher.
Handel/ Christopher Hogwood; chronological table by Anthony Hicks. New York: Thames and Hudson, 1985, c1984. 312 p.
85-203040   780/.92/4
Handel, George Frideric, -- 1685-1759. Composers -- Biography.

ML410.H13.K33 1985
Keates, Jonathan, 1946-
Handel, the man and his music/ by Jonathan Keates. New York: St. Martin's Press, c1985. 346 p.
85-040017   780/.92/4   0312358466
Handel, George Frideric, -- 1685-1759. Composers -- Biography.

ML410.H13.L23 1995
LaRue, C. Steven.
Handel and his singers: the creation of the Royal Academy operas, 1720-1728/ C. Steven LaRue. Oxford: Clarendon Press; 1995. xiii, 213 p.
94-031871   782.1/092   0198163150
Handel, George Frideric, -- 1685-1759. -- Operas. Singers -- England -- London. Opera.

ML410.H13.M36 1996
Mann, Alfred, 1917-
Handel, the orchestral music: orchestral concertos, organ concertos, Water music, Music for the royal fireworks/ Alfred Mann. New York: Schirmer Books; c1996. xii, 182 p.
95-010441   784.2/092   0028713826
Handel, George Frideric, -- 1685-1759. -- Instrumental music. Instrumental music -- History and criticism.

ML410.H13.S58 1995
Smith, Ruth, 1947-
Handel's oratorios and eighteenth-century thought/ Ruth Smith. Cambridge; Cambridge University Press, 1995. xiii, 484 p.
94-020603   782.23/0268   0521402654
Handel, George Frideric, -- 1685-1759. -- Oratorios. Librettos. Libretto -- 18th century. Great Britain -- History -- 18th century.

ML410.H18.A3 1985
Handy, W. C. 1873-1958.
Father of the blues: an autobiography/ by W.C. Handy; edited by Arna Bontemps; with a foreword by Abbe Niles. New York: Da Capo Press, 1985, c1941. xiv, 317 p.
84-017663   784.5/3/00924   0306762412
Handy, W. C. -- (William Christopher), -- 1873-1958. Composers -- United States -- Biography.

ML410.H2066.M55 1998
Miller, Leta E.
Lou Harrison: composing a world/ Leta E. Miller, Fredric Lieberman. New York: Oxford University Press, 1998. xiv, 385 p.
97-009712   780/.92   0195110226
Harrison, Lou, -- 1917- -- Criticism and interpretation.

ML410.H4 G4 1982
Geiringer, Karl,
Haydn: a creative life in music/ by Karl Geiringer in collaboration with Irene Geiringer. 3rd rev. and enl. ed. Berkeley: University of California Press, c1982. xii, 403 p.
82-002821   780/.92/4 B 19   0520043170
Haydn, Joseph, 1732-1809. Composers -- Austria -- Biography.

ML410.H4.H314 1998
Harrison, Bernard, 1958-
Haydn, the "Paris" symphonies/ Bernard Harrison. Cambridge; Cambridge University Press, 1998. ix, 124 p.
97-042606   784.2/184/092   0521471648
Haydn, Joseph, -- 1732-1809. -- Symphonies, -- H. I, 82-87. Symphony -- 18th century.

ML410.H4.H315 1997
Harrison, Bernard, 1958-
Haydn's keyboard music: studies in performance practice/ Bernard Harrison. Oxford: Clarendon Press; 1997. xxxv, 418 p.
95-049505   786/.143   0198163258
Haydn, Joseph, -- 1732-1809. -- Piano music. Performance practice (Music) -- 18th century.

ML410.H4 H3177 2002
Haydn/ edited by David Wyn Jones; consultant editor Otto Biba. Oxford; Oxford University Press, 2002. xxi, 515 p.
2002-510033   780/.92 B 21
Haydn, Joseph, 1732-1809 -- Dictionaries.

ML410.H4.H318 1997
Haydn and his world/ edited by Elaine R. Sisman. Princeton, N.J.: Princeton University Press, c1997. xiii, 474 p.
97-019850   780/.92   0691057982
Haydn, Joseph, -- 1732-1809 -- Criticism and interpretation. Music -- 18th century -- History and criticism.

ML410.H4.L257
Landon, H. C. Robbins 1926-
Haydn, a documentary study/ H.C. Robbins Landon. New York: Rizzoli, c1981. 224 p.
81-050279   780/.92/4   0847803880
Haydn, Joseph, -- 1732-1809.   Composers -- Austria -- Biography.

ML410.H4.L265 1988
Landon, H. C. Robbins 1926-
Haydn: his life and music/ H.C. Robbins Landon and David Wyn Jones. Bloomington: Indiana University Press, c1988. 383 p.
88-002685   780/.92/4   0253372658
Haydn, Joseph, -- 1732-1809.   Composers -- Austria -- Biography.

ML410.H4 S83 1992
Sutcliffe, W. Dean.
Haydn, string quartets, op. 50/ W. Dean Sutcliffe. Cambridge [England]; Cambridge University Press, 1992. ix, 114 p.
91-014804   785/.7194 20   0521399955
Haydn, Joseph, 1732-1809. Quartets, strings, H. III, 44-49.

ML410.H4.T36 1991
Temperley, Nicholas.
Haydn, The Creation/ Nicholas Temperley. Cambridge; Cambridge University Press, 1991. vii, 135 p.
90-001859   782.23   0521372550
Haydn, Joseph, -- 1732-1809. -- Schopfung.

ML410.H482.T513 1996
Tillard, Francoise.
Fanny Mendelssohn/ by Francoise Tillard; translated by Camille Naish. Portland, Or.: Amadeus Press, c1996. 399 p.
95-017336   786.2/092   0931340969
Hensel, Fanny Mendelssohn, -- 1805-1847.   Women composers -- Germany -- Biography.

ML410.H685.A4 1995
Hindemith, Paul, 1895-1963.
Selected letters of Paul Hindemith/ edited and translated from the German by Geoffrey Skelton. New Haven: Yale University Press, c1995. xiii, 255 p.
95-017335   780/.92   0300064519
Hindemith, Paul, -- 1895-1963 -- Correspondence.   Composers -- Correspondence.

ML410.H685 N5 1986
Neumeyer, David.
The music of Paul Hindemith/ David Neumeyer. New Haven: Yale University Press, c1986. viii, 294 p.
85-014495   780/.92/4 19   0300032870
Hindemith, Paul, 1895-1963 -- Criticism and interpretation.

ML410.H685 N7 1989
Noss, Luther.
Paul Hindemith in the United States/ Luther Noss. Urbana: University of Illinois Press, c1989. xii, 219 p.
88-010694   780/.92/4 B 19   0252015630
Hindemith, Paul, 1895-1963. Composers -- Biography.

ML410.H748 G74 1995
Greene, Richard.
Holst, The planets/ Richard Greene. Cambridge [England]; Cambridge University Press, 1995. ix, 99 p.
94-017175   784.2/1858 20   0521456339
Holst, Gustav, 1874-1934. Planets.

ML410.H748.S5 1990
Short, Michael, 1937-
Gustav Holst: the man and his music/ Michael Short. Oxford; Oxford University Press, 1990. xiv, 530 p.
89-022260   780/.92   019314154X
Holst, Gustav, -- 1874-1934.   Composers -- England -- Biography.

ML410.H79.H313 1999
Halbreich, Harry.
Arthur Honegger/ by Harry Halbreich; translated by Roger Nichols; Reinhard G. Pauly, general editor. Portland, Or.: Amadeus Press, 1999. 677 p.
98-014759   780/.92   1574670417
Honegger, Arthur, -- 1892-1955. Honegger, Arthur, -- 1892-1955 -- Bibliography. Composers -- Biography.

ML410.H886.S73 1998
Spicer, Paul.
Herbert Howells/ Paul Spicer. Bridgend, Wales: Seren, c1998. 205 p.
99-206418   780/.92   1854112325
Howells, Herbert, -- 1892- Musicians -- England -- Biography.

ML410.I94.B87 1995
Burkholder, J. Peter
All made of tunes: Charles Ives and the uses of musical borrowing/ J. Peter Burkholder. New Haven: Yale University Press, c1995. xii, 554 p.
95-013537   780/.92   0300056427
Ives, Charles, -- 1874-1954 -- Criticism and interpretation. Ives, Charles, -- 1874-1954 -- Sources.

ML410.I94.C33 1996
Charles Ives and his world/ edited by J. Peter Burkholder. Princeton, N.J.: Princeton University Press, c1996. xiv, 452 p.
96-021393   780.92   0691011648
Ives, Charles, -- 1874-1954 -- Criticism and interpretation. Ives, Charles, -- 1874-1954 -- Correspondence.

ML410.I94.C35 1996
Charles Ives and the classical tradition/ edited by Geoffrey Block and J. Peter Burkholder. New Haven: Yale University Press, c1996. viii, 192 p.
95-031915   780/.92   0300061773
Ives, Charles, -- 1874-1954 -- Criticism and interpretation.

ML410.I94.L36 1997
Lambert, Philip, 1958-
The music of Charles Ives/ Philip Lambert. New Haven: Yale University Press, c1997. xii, 244 p.
96-038979   780/.92   0300065221
Ives, Charles, -- 1874-1954 -- Criticism and interpretation.

ML410.I94 S7 1992
Starr, Larry.
A union of diversities: style in the music of Charles Ives/
by Larry Starr. New York: Schirmer Books; xii, 170 p.
91-022486   780/.92 20   0028724658
Ives, Charles, 1874-1954 -- Criticism and interpretation. Style,
Musical.

ML410.J18.L49 1982
Leos Janacek, Kata Kabanova/ compiled by John Tyrrell.
Cambridge [Cambridgeshire]; Cambridge University
Press, 1982. xv, 234 p.
81-038505   782.1/092/4   0521231809
Janacek, Leos, -- 1854-1928. -- Kata Kabanova.

ML410.J18.V712 1981
Vogel, Jaroslav.
Leos Janacek, a biography/ by Jaroslav Vogel; with a
foreword by Sir Charles Mackerras. London: Orbis Pub.,
c1981. 439 p.
82-107499   780/.92/4   0856130451
Janacek, Leos, -- 1854-1928.   Composers -- Czechoslovakia --
Biography.

ML410.J18.W56 1992
Wingfield, Paul.
Janacek, Glagolitic mass/ Paul Wingfield. Cambridge;
Cambridge University Press, 1992. x, 135 p.
91-016986   782.32/3   0521380138
Janacek, Leos, -- 1854-1928. -- Msa glagolskaja.

ML410.J445.J6 1996
John Jenkins and his time: studies in English consort
music/ edited by Andrew Ashbee and Peter Holman.
Oxford: Clarendon Press; c1996. xxiii, 421 p.
95-051814   780/.92   0198164610
Jenkins, John, -- 1592-1678.   Chamber music -- England -- 17th
century -- History and criticism.

ML410.J75.C87 1994
Curtis, Susan, 1956-
Dancing to a black man's tune: a life of Scott Joplin/
Susan Curtis. Columbia: University of Missouri Press,
c1994. xx, 265 p.
93-046116   780/.92   0826209491
Joplin, Scott, -- 1868-1917.   Composers -- United States --
Biography.

ML410.J815.J68 2000
The Josquin companion/ edited by Richard Sherr. Oxford;
Oxford University Press, c2000. xxix, 691 p.
00-056654   782.2/2/092   0198163355
Josquin, des Prez, -- d. 1521 -- Criticism and interpretation.

ML410.K385.B7
Bordman, Gerald Martin.
Jerome Kern: his life and music/ Gerald Bordman. New
York: Oxford University Press, 1980. viii, 438 p.
79-013826   782.8/1/0924   0195026497
Kern, Jerome, -- 1885-1945.   Composers -- United States --
Biography.

ML410.K732.E582
Eosze, Laszlo.
Zoltan Kodaly: his life and work. [Translated by Istvan
Farkas and Gyula Gulyas] London, Collet's [1962] 183 p.
67-059649
Kodaly, Zoltan, -- 1882-1967.

ML410.K732 Y7 1976
Young, Percy M.
Zoltán Kodály: a Hungarian musician/ Percy M. Young.
Westport, Conn.: Greenwood Press, 1976, c1964. xvi,
231 p.
75-045268   780/.92/4   0837186501
Kodály, Zoltán, 1882-1967.

ML410.K7356 C37 1997
Carroll, Brendan G.
The last prodigy: a biography of Erich Wolfgang
Korngold/ Brendan G. Carroll. Portland, Or.: Amadeus
Press, c1997. 464 p.
97-004963   780/.92 B 21   1574670298
Korngold, Erich Wolfgang, 1897-1957. Composers -- Austria --
Biography.

ML410.K7365.S7 1991
Stewart, John L.
Ernst Krenek: the man and his music/ John L. Stewart.
Berkeley: University of California Press, c1991. xi,
445 p.
90-003900   780/.92   0520070143
Krenek, Ernst, -- 1900- Composers -- Biography.

ML410.L2487 L33 2000
Labounsky, Ann.
Jean Langlais: the man and his music/ Ann Labounsky.
Portland, Or.: Amadeus Press, 2000. 392 p.
99-042129   780/.92   1574670549
Langlais, Jean, -- 1907- Composers -- France -- Biography.

ML410.L3 F74 2000
Freedman, Richard.
The chansons of Orlando di Lasso and their Protestant
listeners: music, piety, and print in sixteenth-century
France/ Richard Freedman. Rochester, NY: University of
Rochester Press, 2001. xxiv, 259 p.
00-059945   782.4/3/092   1580460755
Lasso, Orlando di, -- 1532-1594. -- Chansons.   Polyphonic
chansons -- 16th century -- History and criticism. Music --
Religious aspects -- Protestantism. Protestantism -- France --
History -- 16th century.

ML410.L7.A4 1998
Liszt, Franz, 1811-1886.
Selected letters/ Franz Liszt; translated and edited by
Adrian Williams. Oxford: Clarendon Press; 1998. xxxix,
1063 p.
97-050595   780/.92   0198166885
Liszt, Franz, -- 1811-1886 -- Correspondence.   Composers --
Correspondence.

ML410.L7.B913 1989
Burger, Ernst, 1937-
Franz Liszt: a chronicle of his life in pictures and documents/ Ernst Burger; translated by Stewart Spencer; foreword by Alfred Brendel. Princeton, N.J.: Princeton University Press, c1989. 358 p.
88-039348   780/.92/4   0691091331
Liszt, Franz, -- 1811-1886 -- Chronology. Liszt, Franz, -- 1811-1886 -- Pictorial works. Composers -- Pictorial works.

ML410.L7 W27 1983
Walker, Alan,
Franz Liszt/ by Alan Walker. 1st American ed. New York: Knopf: 1983-1996. 3 v.
82-047821   780/.92/4 B 19   0394525426
Liszt, Franz, 1811-1886. Composers -- Biography.

ML410.L7 W35 2000
Watson, Derek,
Liszt/ Derek Watson. Oxford; Oxford University Press, 2000.
00-057105   780/.92 B 21   0198164998
Liszt, Franz, 1811-1886. Composers -- Biography.

ML410.L78.M3 1984
McKnight, Gerald.
Andrew Lloyd Webber/ Gerald McKnight. New York: St. Martin's Press, c1984. 278 p.
84-052069   782.81/092/4   0312036477
Lloyd Webber, Andrew, -- 1948- Composers -- England -- Biography.

ML410.L798 K6 1992
Knight, Ellen E.
Charles Martin Loeffler: a life apart in American music/ Ellen Knight. Urbana: University of Illinois Press, c1993. xv, 345 p.
91-039540   780/.92 B 20   0252019083
Loeffler, Charles Martin, 1861-1935. Composers -- United States -- Biography.

ML410.L947.A3
Luening, Otto, 1900-
The Odyssey of an American composer: the autobiography of Otto Luening. New York: Scribner, c1980. x, 605 p.
80-011624   780/.92/4   0684164965
Luening, Otto, -- 1900- Composers -- United States -- Biography.

ML410.L965.S8
Stucky, Steven.
Lutoslawski and his music/ Steven Stucky. Cambridge [Eng.]; Cambridge University Press, 1981. ix, 252 p.
80-040982   780/.92/4   0521227992
Lutoslawski, Witold, -- 1913- Composers -- Poland -- Biography.

ML410.M23.F5513 1993
Floros, Constantin.
Gustav Mahler: the symphonies/ Constantin Floros; translated from the German by Vernon Wicker; Reinhard G. Pauly, general editor. Portland, Or.: Amadeus Press, c1993. 363 p.
92-021193   784.2/184/092   0931340624
Mahler, Gustav, -- 1860-1911. -- Symphonies.

ML410.M23 F69 1997
Franklin, Peter.
The life of Mahler/ Peter Franklin. Cambridge; Cambridge University Press, 1997. ix, 228 p.
96-025105   780/.92 B 20   0521467616
Mahler, Gustav, 1860-1911. Composers -- Austria -- Biography.

ML410.M23 F7 1991
Franklin, Peter.
Mahler, Symphony no. 3/ Peter Franklin. Cambridge; Cambridge University Press, 1991. xiii, 127 p.
90-025620   784.2/184 20   0521379474
Mahler, Gustav, 1860-1911. Symphonies, no. 3, -- D minor.

ML410.M23.L3413 1995
La Grange, Henry-Louis de, 1924-
Gustav Mahler/ Henry-Louis de La Grange. Oxford; Oxford University Press, 1995. v. 2
94-018322   780/.92   0193151596
Mahler, Gustav, -- 1860-1911. Composers -- Austria -- Biography.

ML410.M23 M1963 2002
Mahler and his world/ edited by Karen Painter. Princeton, N.J.: Princeton University Press, c2002. xiii, 393 p.
2002-104405   780/.92 21   0691092435
Mahler, Gustav, 1860-1911 -- Criticism and interpretation.

ML410.M23.M232 1999
The Mahler companion/ edited by Donald Mitchell & Andrew Nicholson. Oxford; Oxford University Press, 1999. xviii, 633 p.
98-045827   780/.92   0198163762
Mahler, Gustav, -- 1860-1911.

ML410.M23.M48 1986
Mitchell, Donald, 1925-
Gustav Mahler: songs and symphonies of life and death: Donald Mitchell. Berkeley: University of California Press, [1986], c1985 659 p.
85-040494   780/.92/4   0520055780
Mahler, Gustav, -- 1860-1911. Mahler, Gustav, -- 1860-1911. -- Songs. Mahler, Gustav, -- 1860-1911. -- Symphonies. Composers -- Austria -- Biography.

ML410.M23.W532 1969
Werfel, Alma (Schindler) Mahler.
Gustav Mahler; memories and letters, by Alma Mahler. New York, Viking Press [1969] xl, 369 p.
69-018800   780/.924   0670358096
Mahler, Gustav, -- 1860-1911.

ML410.M41.H4 1971
Harding, James.
Massenet. New York, St. Martin's Press [1971, c1970]
229 p.
70-132189   782.1/0924
Massenet, Jules, -- 1842-1912.

ML410.M41.I8 1994
Irvine, Demar.
Massenet: a chronicle of his life and times/ Demar Irvine.
Portland, Or.: Amadeus Press, c1994. xix, 398 p.
93-024443   782.1/092   0931340632
Massenet, Jules, -- 1842-1912.   Composers -- France --
Biography.

ML410.M5.M47 1991
Mendelssohn and his world/ edited by R. Larry Todd.
Princeton, N.J.: Princeton University Press, c1991. xiii,
401 p.
91-016124   780/.92   0691091439
Mendelssohn-Bartholdy, Felix, -- 1809-1847.

ML410.M5.M55 2001
The Mendelssohn companion/ edited by Douglass Seaton.
Westport, CT: Greenwood Press, 2001. xii, 799 p.
00-033129   780/.92   0313284458
Mendelssohn-Bartholdy, Felix, -- 1809-1847.

ML410.M5.M66 2000
Mercer-Taylor, Peter Jameson.
The life of Mendelssohn/ Peter Mercer-Taylor. New
York: Cambridge University Press, 2000. viii, 238 p.
99-058441   780/.92   0521630258
Mendelssohn-Bartholdy, Felix, -- 1809-1847.   Composers --
Germany -- Biography.

ML410.M5.T64 1993
Todd, R. Larry.
Mendelssohn, the Hebrides and other overtures: A
midsummer night's dream, Calm sea and prosperous
voyage, The Hebrides (Fingal's cave)/ R. Larry Todd.
New York, NY, USA: Cambridge University Press, 1993.
vii, 121 p.
92-036005   784.2/18926/092   0521404193
Mendelssohn-Bartholdy, Felix, -- 1809-1847. -- Overtures.
Overture.

ML410.M595.A3 1994
Messiaen, Olivier, 1908-
Music and color: conversations with Claude Samuel/
Olivier Messiaen; translated by E. Thomas Glasow.
Portland, Or.: Amadeus Press, c1994. 296 p.
93-028281   780/.92   0931340675
Messiaen, Olivier, -- 1908- -- Interviews. Composers -- France
-- Interviews.

ML410.M595.G7 1985
Griffiths, Paul, 1947 Nov. 24-
Olivier Messiaen and the music of time/ Paul Griffiths.
Ithaca, N.Y.: Cornell University Press, 1985. 274 p.
84-045797   780/.92/4   0801418135
Messiaen, Olivier, -- 1908- -- Criticism and interpretation.

ML410.M595.P58 1998
Pople, Anthony.
Messiaen, Quatuor pour la fin du temps/ Anthony Pople.
Cambridge, U.K.; Cambridge University Press, 1998. x,
115 p.
98-023937   785/.24194   0521584973
Messiaen, Olivier, -- 1908- -- Quatuor pour la fin du temps.

ML410.M61.A3 1999
Meyerbeer, Giacomo, 1791-1864.
The diaries of Giacomo Meyerbeer/ translated, edited,
and annotated by Robert Ignatius Letellier. Madison,
[NJ]: Fairleigh Dickinson University Press, [1999-   ]
v. 1
98-052129   782.1/092   0838637892
Meyerbeer, Giacomo, -- 1791-1864 -- Diaries.   Composers --
France -- Diaries.

ML410.M61.A4 1989
Meyerbeer, Giacomo, 1791-1864.
Giacomo Meyerbeer, a life in letters/ [edited by] Heinz
and Gudrun Becker; translated by Mark Violette.
Portland, Or.: Amadeus Press, c1989. 215 p.
89-000045   782.1/092/4   0931340195
Meyerbeer, Giacomo, -- 1791-1864 -- Correspondence.
Composers -- Correspondence.

ML410.M674.A32 1970
Milhaud, Darius, 1892-1974.
Notes without music; an autobiography. [Translated from
the French by Donald Evans] New York, Da Capo Press,
1970 [c1953] x, 355 p.
72-087419   780/.924   0306715651
Milhaud, Darius, -- 1892-1974.   Musicians -- France --
Biography.

ML410.M77.A4 1995
Monteverdi, Claudio, 1567-1643.
The letters of Claudio Monteverdi/ translated and
introduced by Denis Stevens. Oxford: Clarendon Press;
1995. xviii, 458 p.
94-040349   782/.0092   0198164149
Monteverdi, Claudio, -- 1567-1643 -- Correspondence.
Composers -- Italy -- Correspondence.

ML410.M77 A8 1990
Arnold, Denis.
Monteverdi/ Denis Arnold. 3rd ed./ rev. by Tim Carter.
London: J.M. Dent, 1990. x, 245 p.
90-229780   782/.0092 20   0460860267
Monteverdi, Claudio, 1567-1643 -- Criticism and
interpretation.

ML410.M77.L513 1990
Leopold, Silke.
Monteverdi: music in transition/ Silke Leopold; translated
from the German by Anne Smith. Oxford: Clarendon
Press; 1991. xii, 262 p.
90-007074   780/.92   0193152487
Monteverdi, Claudio, -- 1567-1643 -- Criticism and
interpretation.

ML410.M77 N5 1985
The New Monteverdi companion/ edited by Denis Arnold and Nigel Fortune. London; Faber and Faber, 1985. 361 p.
85-006845   784/.092/4 19   0571133576
Monteverdi, Claudio, 1567-1643.

ML410.M82 L6 2001
Lomax, Alan,
Mister Jelly Roll: the fortunes of Jelly Roll Morton, New Orleans Creole and "inventor of jazz"/ Alan Lomax; drawings by David Stone Martin. Berkeley: University of California Press, 2001.
00-064430   781.65/092 B 21   0520225309
Morton, Jelly Roll, d. 1941. Jazz musicians -- United States -- Biography.

ML410.M9 A187 1990
Mozart, Wolfgang Amadeus,
Mozart's letters: an illustrated selection/ translated by Emily Anderson. 1st U.S. ed. Boston: Little, Brown, c1990. 254 p.
90-055577   780/.92 B 20   0821218050
Mozart, Wolfgang Amadeus, 1756-1791 -- Correspondence. Composers -- Austria -- Correspondence.

ML410.M9 A4 2000
Mozart, Wolfgang Amadeus, 1756-1791.
Mozart's letters, Mozart's life: selected letters/ edited and newly translated by Robert Spaethling. New York: Norton, c2000. xiii, 479 p.
00-025530   780/.92   0393047199
Mozart, Wolfgang Amadeus, -- 1756-1791 -- Correspondence. Composers -- Austria -- Correspondence.

ML410.M9.A813 1988
Angermuller, Rudolph.
Mozart's operas/ Rudolph Angermuller; preface and translation by Stewart Spencer. New York: Rizzoli, 1988. 295 p.
88-042743   782.1/092/4   0847809935
Mozart, Wolfgang Amadeus, -- 1756-1791. -- Operas. Opera.

ML410.M9.B1413 1986
Badura-Skoda, Eva.
Interpreting Mozart on the keyboard/ Eva and Paul Badura-Skoda; translated by Leo Black; new preface by Eva Badura-Skoda. New York: Da Capo Press, 1986. ix, 319 p.
85-024566   786.1/092/4   030676265X
Mozart, Wolfgang Amadeus, -- 1756-1791. -- Instrumental music. Piano music -- Interpretation (Phrasing, dynamics, etc.) Performance practice (Music) -- 18th century.

ML410.M9 B185 1987
Bauman, Thomas,
W.A. Mozart, Die Entführung aus dem Serail/ Thomas Bauman. Cambridge [Cambridgeshire]; Cambridge University Press, xiii, 141 p.
87-010326   782.1/092/4 19   0521310601
Mozart, Wolfgang Amadeus, 1756-1791. Entführung aus dem Serail.

ML410.M9.B76 1991
Branscombe, Peter.
W.A. Mozart, die Zauberflote/ Peter Branscombe. Cambridge; Cambridge University Press, 1991. xv, 247 p.
90-040403   782.1   052126491X
Mozart, Wolfgang Amadeus, -- 1756-1791. -- Zauberflote.

ML410.M9.B7813 1990
Braunbehrens, Volkmar.
Mozart in Vienna, 1781-1791/ Volkmar Braunbehrens; translated from the German by Timothy Bell. New York: Grove Weidenfeld, 1990. ix, 481 p.
88-013940   780/.92/4   0802110096
Mozart, Wolfgang Amadeus, -- 1756-1791. Composers -- Austria -- Biography. Music -- Austria -- Vienna -- 18th century -- History and criticism.

ML410.M9.B819 1995
Brown, Bruce Alan.
W.A. Mozart, Cosi fan tutte/ Bruce Alan Brown. Cambridge; Cambridge University Press, 1995. viii, 208 p.
95-009885   782.1   0521431344
Mozart, Wolfgang Amadeus, -- 1756-1791. -- Cosi fan tutte.

ML410.M9.C33 1987
Carter, Tim.
W.A. Mozart, Le nozze di Figaro/ Tim Carter. Cambridge [Cambridgeshire]; Cambridge University Press, c1987. xii, 180 p.
87-011597   782.1/092/4   0521302676
Mozart, Wolfgang Amadeus, -- 1756-1791. -- Nozze di Figaro.

ML410.M9.D4782 Suppl.
New Mozart documents: a supplement to O.E. Deutsch's documentary biography/ [compiled by] Cliff Eisen. Stanford, Calif.: Stanford University Press, 1991. xvii, 192 p.
91-065554   016.78/092   0804719551
Mozart, Wolfgang Amadeus, -- 1756-1791. Composers -- Austria -- Biography.

ML410.M9 G96 1999
Gutman, Robert W.
Mozart: a cultural biography/ Robert W. Gutman. New York: Harcourt Brace, c1999. xxii, 839 p.
99-031953   780/.92 B 21   015100482X
Mozart, Wolfgang Amadeus, 1756-1791. Composers -- Austria -- Biography.

ML410.M9.H2 1990
Heartz, Daniel.
Mozart's operas/ Daniel Heartz; edited, with contributing essays, by Thomas Bauman. Berkeley: University of California Press, c1990. xvi, 363 p.
89-020435   782.1/092   0520068629
Mozart, Wolfgang Amadeus, -- 1756-1791. -- Operas. Opera.

ML410.M9 K25 2001
Keefe, Simon P.,
Mozart's piano concertos: dramatic dialogue in the Age of Enlightenment/ Simon P. Keefe. Rochester, NY: Boydell Press, 2001. x, 205 p.
2001-025775   784.2/62/092 21   085115834X
Mozart, Wolfgang Amadeus, 1756-1791. Concertos, piano, orchestra.

ML410.M9.L236 1988
Landon, H. C. Robbins 1926-
1791, Mozart's last year/ H.C. Robbins Landon. New York: Schirmer Books, 1988. 240 p.
88-003169   780/.92/4   0028725921
Mozart, Wolfgang Amadeus, -- 1756-1791 -- Last years. Composers -- Austria -- Biography.

ML410.M9.L239 1991
Landon, H. C. Robbins 1926-
Mozart and Vienna/ H.C. Robbins Landon. New York: Schirmer Books: 1991. 208 p.
91-007648   780/.92   0028713176
Mozart, Wolfgang Amadeus, -- 1756-1791. Composers -- Austria -- Vienna -- Biography. Music -- Austria -- Vienna -- 18th century -- History and criticism. Vienna (Austria) -- Social life and customs.

ML410.M9.L245 1989
Landon, H. C. Robbins 1926-
Mozart, the golden years, 1781-1791/ by H.C. Robbins Landon. New York: Schirmer Books, 1989. 271 p.
89-005848   780/.92/4   0028720253
Mozart, Wolfgang Amadeus, -- 1756-1791. Composers -- Austria -- Biography.

ML410.M9.M6995 1990
The Mozart compendium: a guide to Mozart's life and music/ edited by H.C. Robbins Landon. New York: Schirmer Books, 1990. 452 p.
90-009071   780/.92   0028713214
Mozart, Wolfgang Amadeus, -- 1756-1791.

ML410.M9.R54 1991
Rice, John A.
W.A. Mozart, La clemenza di Tito/ John A. Rice. Cambridge [England]; Cambridge University Press, 1991. xii, 181 p.
90-002068   782.1   0521361427
Mozart, Wolfgang Amadeus, -- 1756-1791. -- Clemenza di Tito.

ML410.M9 R847 1998
Rosselli, John.
The life of Mozart/ John Rosselli. Cambridge, U.K.; Cambridge University Press, 1998. xii, 171 p.
97-033013   780/.92 B 21   0521587441
Mozart, Wolfgang Amadeus, 1756-1791. Composers -- Austria -- Biography.

ML410.M9.R89 1993
Rushton, Julian.
W.A. Mozart, Idomeneo/ Julian Rushton. Cambridge [England]; Cambridge University Press, 1993. x, 187 p.
92-025833   782.1   0521431441
Mozart, Wolfgang Amadeus, -- 1756-1791. -- Idomeneo.

ML410.M9 S56 1993
Sisman, Elaine Rochelle.
Mozart, the "Jupiter" symphony, no. 41 in C major, K. 551/ Elaine Sisman. Cambridge [England]: Cambridge University Press, 1993. xii, 110 p.
92-039074   784.2/184 20   0521409241
Mozart, Wolfgang Amadeus, 1756-1791. Symphonies, K. 551, C major.

ML410.M9 S65 1995
Solomon, Maynard.
Mozart: a life/ Maynard Solomon. 1st ed. New York, NY: HarperCollinsPublishers, c1995. xvi, 640 p.
94-042277   780/.92 B 20   0060190469
Mozart, Wolfgang Amadeus, 1756-1791. Composers -- Austria -- Biography.

ML410.M9 S815 1991
Stafford, William.
The Mozart myths: a critical reassessment/ William Stafford. Stanford, Calif.: Stanford University Press, 1991. viii, 285 p.
91-065301   780/.92 20   0804719373
Mozart, Wolfgang Amadeus, 1756-1791 -- Criticism and interpretation.

ML410.M9.S86 1988
Steptoe, Andrew.
The Mozart-Da Ponte operas: the cultural and musical background to Le nozze di Figaro, Don Giovanni, and Cosi fan tutte/ Andrew Steptoe. Oxford: Clarendon Press, 1988. 273 p.
87-034873   782.1/092/4   019313215X
Mozart, Wolfgang Amadeus, -- 1756-1791. -- Operas. Mozart, Wolfgang Amadeus, -- 1756-1791. -- Nozze di Figaro. Mozart, Wolfgang Amadeus, -- 1756-1791. -- Don Giovanni. Opera -- 18th century.

ML410.M9.Z28 1989
Zaslaw, Neal, 1939-
Mozart's symphonies: context, performance practice, reception/ Neal Zaslaw. Oxford [Oxfordshire]: Clarendon Press; 1989. xxv, 617 p.
88-019009   785.1/1/0924   0193152401
Mozart, Wolfgang Amadeus, -- 1756-1791. -- Symphonies. Performance practice (Music) -- 18th century. Symphony. Performance practice (Music) -- 18th century.

ML410.M97 B75 2002
Brown, David,
Musorgsky: his life and works/ David Brown. Oxford; Oxford University Press, 2002. xvii, 391 p.
2002-020154   780/.92 B 21   0198165870
Mussorgsky, Modest Petrovich, 1839-1881. Composers -- Russia -- Biography.

ML410.M97 E42 1999
Emerson, Caryl.
The life of Musorgsky/ Caryl Emerson. New York: Cambridge University Press, 1999. 194 p.
98-047948   780/.92 B 21   052148507X
Mussorgsky, Modest Petrovich, 1839-1881. Composers -- Russia -- Biography.

ML410.M97.L5 1970
Leyda, Jay, 1910-
The Musorgsky reader; a life of Modeste Petrovich Musorgsky in letters and documents. Edited and translated by Jay Leyda and Sergei Bertensson. New York, Da Capo Press, 1970 [c1947] xxiii, 474 p.
70-087393   780/.924   0306715341
Mussorgsky, Modest Petrovich, -- 1839-1881.

ML410.M97.M2213 1991
Musorgsky remembered/ compiled and edited by Alexandra Orlova; translated by Veronique Zaytzeff and Frederick Morrison. Bloomington: Indiana University Press, c1991. xiii, 186 p.
90-025310   780/.92   0253342643
Mussorgsky, Modest Petrovich, -- 1839-1881. Composers -- Russia.

ML410.M97.R9 1992
Russ, Michael.
Musorgsky, Pictures at an exhibition/ Michael Russ. Cambridge [England]; Cambridge University Press, 1992. xi, 99 p.
91-032687   786.2/1896   0521384427
Mussorgsky, Modest Petrovich, -- 1839-1881. -- Kartinki s vystavki.

ML410.M97.T37 1992
Taruskin, Richard.
Musorgsky: eight essays and an epilogue/ Richard Taruskin. Princeton, N.J.: Princeton University Press, c1993. xxxiv, 415 p.
92-012124   780/.92   0691091471
Mussorgsky, Modest Petrovich, -- 1839-1881 -- Criticism and interpretation.

ML410.O5834.V6 1983
Von Gunden, Heidi, 1940-
The music of Pauline Oliveros/ by Heidi Von Gunden. Metuchen, N.J.: Scarecrow Press, 1983. ix, 195 p.
82-021443   780/.92/4   0810816008
Oliveros, Pauline, -- 1932- -- Criticism and interpretation. Oliveros, Pauline, -- 1932- -- Bibliography.

ML410.O65.L57 1966a
Liess, Andreas, 1903-
Carl Orff: his life and his music; Translated by Adelheid and Herbert Parkin. New York, St. Martin's Press [1966] 184 p.
64-016423   782.0924
Orff, Carl, -- 1895-

ML410.P163 K4 1990
Kearns, William,
Horatio Parker, 1863-1919: his life, music, and ideas/ by William K. Kearns. Metuchen, N.J.: Scarecrow Press, 1990. xvii, 356 p.
89-070355   780/.92 B 20   081082292X
Parker, Horatio W. (Horatio William), 1863-1919. Composers -- United States -- Biography.

ML410.P173.D5 1992
Dibble, Jeremy.
C. Hubert H. Parry: his life and music/ Jeremy Dibble. Oxford [England]: Clarendon Press; 1992. xvi, 554 p.
92-006634   780/.92   0193153300
Parry, C. Hubert H. -- (Charles Hubert Hastings), -- 1848-1918. Composers -- England -- Biography.

ML410.P176.A3 1991
Partch, Harry, 1901-1974.
Bitter music: collected journals, essays, introductions, and librettos/ Harry Partch; edited with an introduction by Thomas McGeary. Urbana: University of Illinois Press, c1991. xxx, 487 p.
89-020344   780/.92   0252016602
Partch, Harry, -- 1901-1974. Composers -- United States -- Biography. Music -- United States -- 20th century -- History and criticism.

ML410.P176 G55 1998
Gilmore, Bob,
Harry Partch: a biography/ Bob Gilmore. New Haven, [Conn.]: Yale University Press, c1998. xii, 468 p.
97-039140   780/.92 B 21   0300065213
Partch, Harry, 1901-1974. Composers -- United States -- Biography.

ML410.P176.H37 1997
Harry Partch/ [produced by] Philip Blackburn. Saint Paul, MN: American Composers Forum, c1997. 523 p.
97-014032   780/.92   096565690X
Partch, Harry, -- 1901-1974 -- Archives. Composers -- United States -- Biography.

ML410.P2925.A3 1990
Perle, George, 1915-
The listening composer/ George Perle. Berkeley: University of California Press, c1990. 202 p.
89-020436   780/.92   0520069919
Perle, George, -- 1915- -- Criticism and interpretation. Music -- 20th century -- History and criticism.

ML410.P32.M47 1998
Mercier, Richard, 1949-
The songs of Hans Pfitzner: a guide and study/ Richard Mercier. Westport, Conn.: Greenwood Press, 1998. xiii, 207 p.
97-041922   782.42168/092   0313305331
Pfitzner, Hans Erich, -- 1869-1949. -- Songs. Songs -- Analysis, appreciation.

ML410.P7844.M33 1998
McBrien, William.
Cole Porter: a biography/ by William McBrien. New York: Alfred A. Knopf, 1998. xiii, 459 p.
97-046116   782.1/4/092   0394582357
Porter, Cole, -- 1891-1964. Composers -- United States -- Biography.

ML410.P787.M44 1993
Mellers, Wilfrid Howard, 1914-
Francis Poulenc/ Wilfrid Mellers. Oxford; Oxford University Press, 1993. xvii, 186 p.
93-004412   780/.92   0198163371
Poulenc, Francis, -- 1899-1963 -- Criticism and interpretation.

ML410.P865 R55 2002
Robinson, Harlow.
Sergei Prokofiev: a biography/ by Harlow Robinson [with a new foreword and afterword by the author]. Boston: Northeastern University Press, 2002. xxiv, 584 p.
2002-070919   780/.92 B 21   1555535178
Prokofiev, Sergey, 1891-1953. Composers -- Soviet Union -- Biography.

ML410.P89 B83 2002
Budden, Julian.
Puccini: his life and works/ Julian Budden. Oxford; Oxford University Press, 2002. ix, 527 p.
2002-020155   782.1/092 B 21   0198164688
Puccini, Giacomo, 1858-1924. Composers -- Italy -- Biography.

ML410.P89.G5713 2000
Girardi, Michele.
Puccini: his international art/ Michele Girardi; translated by Laura Basini. Chicago: University of Chicago Press, 2000. xvi, 530 p.
99-045342   782.1/092   0226297578
Puccini, Giacomo, -- 1858-1924 -- Criticism and interpretation.

ML410.P93.H3 1987
Harris, Ellen T.
Henry Purcell's Dido and Aeneas/ by Ellen T. Harris. Oxford: Clarendon Press; 1987. xii, 184 p.
87-005621   782.1/092/4   0193152533
Purcell, Henry, -- 1659-1695. -- Dido and Aeneas.

ML410.P93.H63 1994
Holman, Peter, 1946-
Henry Purcell/ Peter Holman. Oxford; Oxford University Press, 1994. xvii, 250 p.
94-031870   780/.92   0198163401
Purcell, Henry, -- 1659-1695 -- Criticism and interpretation.

ML410.P93.K4 1996
Keates, Jonathan, 1946-
Purcell: a biography/ Jonathan Keates. Boston: Northeastern University Press, 1996. xi, 304 p.
96-026031   780/.92   155553287X
Purcell, Henry, -- 1659-1695. Composers -- England -- Biography.

ML410.P93 P868 1995
Purcell remembered/ [compiled by] Michael Burden. Portland, Or.: Amadeus, 1995. xxv, 188 p.
96-101747   780/.92 B 20   1574670034
Purcell, Henry, 1659-1695 -- Archives. Composers -- England -- Biography.

ML410.R12.M17 1990
Martyn, Barrie.
Rachmaninoff: composer, pianist, conductor/ Barrie Martyn. Aldershot, Hants, England: Scolar Press; c1990. xvi, 584 p.
89-024085   780/.92   0859678091
Rachmaninoff, Sergei, -- 1873-1943. Composers -- Biography. Pianists -- Biography.

ML410.R12.N67 1994
Norris, Geoffrey.
Rachmaninoff/ Geoffrey Norris. New York: Schirmer Books: 1994. xi, 194 p.
93-013932   780/.92   0028706854
Rachmaninoff, Sergei, -- 1873-1943. Composers -- Biography. Pianists -- Biography.

ML410.R23.A4 1990
Ravel, Maurice, 1875-1937.
A Ravel reader: correspondence, articles, interviews/ compiled and edited by Arbie Orenstein. New York: Columbia University Press, 1990. xvi, 653 p.
89-025228   780/.92   0231049625
Ravel, Maurice, -- 1875-1937 -- Correspondence. Ravel, Maurice, -- 1875-1937 -- Interviews.

ML410.R23.C36 2000
The Cambridge companion to Ravel/ edited by Deborah Mawer. New York: Cambridge University Press, 2000. xv, 294 p.
99-047568   780/.92   0521640261
Ravel, Maurice, -- 1875-1937 -- Criticism and interpretation.

ML410.R23.I97 2000
Ivry, Benjamin.
Maurice Ravel: a life/ Benjamin Ivry. New York: Welcome Rain Publishers, 2000.
00-040899   780/.92   1566491525
Ravel, Maurice, -- 1875-1937. Composers -- France -- Biography.

ML410.R23 N53 1988
Nichols, Roger.
Ravel remembered/ Roger Nichols. 1st American ed. New York: Norton, 1988, c1987. xxviii, 203 p.
87-034867   780/.92/4 B 19   039302573X
Ravel, Maurice, 1875-1937. Composers -- France -- Biography.

ML410.R233 M33 1998
McCabe, John,
Alan Rawsthorne: portrait of a composer/ John McCabe. Oxford: Oxford University Press, 1999. xvii, 311 p.
98-024508   780/.92 21   0198166931
Rawsthorne, Alan, 1905-1971. Composers -- England -- Biography.

ML410.R6315.M7 1992
Mordden, Ethan, 1947-
Rodgers & Hammerstein/ Ethan Mordden. New York: H.N. Abrams, 1992. 224 p.
91-046586   782.1/4/0922   0810915677
Rodgers, Richard, -- 1902- -- Musicals. Hammerstein, Oscar, -- 1895-1960. Musicals -- History and criticism.

ML410.R6315 R53 2002
The Richard Rodgers reader/ edited by Geoffrey Block. Oxford; Oxford University Press, 2002. xii, 356 p.
2001-037505   782.1/4/092 21   0195139542
Rodgers, Richard, 1902- -- Criticism and interpretation.

ML410.R693 A27 2000
Rorem, Ned,
The later diaries of Ned Rorem, 1961-1972/ Ned Rorem.
1st Da Capo Press ed. Cambridge, MA: Da Capo Press,
2000.
00-060223   780/.92 21   0306809648
Rorem, Ned, 1923---Diaries.   Composers--United States--
Diaries.

ML410.R8.K43 1992
Kendall, Alan, 1939-
Gioacchino Rossini, the reluctant hero/ Alan Kendall.
London: V. Gollancz, 1992. 276 p.
94-167553   782.1/092   0575051787
Rossini, Gioacchino, -- 1792-1868.   Composers -- Biography.

ML410.R8 O9 2001
Osborne, Richard,
Rossini/ Richard Osborne. Oxford; Oxford University
Press, 2001. xiv, 332 p.
00-057106   782.1/092 B 21   0198164904
Rossini, Gioacchino, 1792-1868. Composers -- Biography.

ML410.S15.S78 1999
Studd, Stephen.
Saint-Saens: a critical biography/ Stephen Studd.
London: Cygnus Arts; 1999. x, 356 p.
99-025256   780/.92   0838638422
Saint-Saens, Camille, -- 1835-1921.   Composers -- France --
Biography.

ML410.S16.B713 1992
Braunbehrens, Volkmar.
Maligned master: the real story of Antonio Salieri/ by
Volkmar Braunbehrens; translated from the German by
Eveline L. Kanes. New York: Fromm International Pub.
Corp., c1992. x, 276 p.
92-028067   780/.92   0880641401
Salieri, Antonio, -- 1750-1825.   Composers -- Biography.

ML410.S16.R53 1998
Rice, John A.
Antonio Salieri and Viennese Opera/ John A. Rice.
Chicago, Ill.: University of Chicago Press, c1998. xx,
648 p.
97-032585   782.1/092   0226711250
Salieri, Antonio, -- 1750-1825 -- Criticism and interpretation.
Opera -- Austria -- Vienna -- 18th century.

ML410.S196.A4 1988
Satie, Erik, 1866-1925.
Satie seen through his letters/ [edited by] Ornella Volta;
translated by Michael Bullock; introduced by John Cage.
London; M. Boyars, 1989. 239 p.
87-026872   780/.92/4   0714528110
Satie, Erik, -- 1866-1925 -- Correspondence.   Composers --
France -- Correspondence.

ML410.S196.G54 1988
Gillmor, Alan M.
Erik Satie/ Alan M. Gillmor. Boston: Twayne Publishers,
c1988. xxvi, 387 p.
87-037381   780/.92/4   0805794727
Satie, Erik, -- 1866-1925.   Composers -- France -- Biography.

ML410.S196.O74 1990
Orledge, Robert.
Satie the composer/ Robert Orledge. Cambridge;
Cambridge University Press, 1990. xliii, 394 p.
89-022309   780/.92   0521350379
Satie, Erik, -- 1866-1925 -- Criticism and interpretation.

ML410.S196.P47 1991
Perloff, Nancy Lynn.
Art and the everyday: popular entertainment and the
circle of Erik Satie/ Nancy Perloff. Oxford [England]:
Clarendon Press; 1991. x, 227 p.
90-041301   780/.92   0198161948
Satie, Erik, -- 1866-1925 -- Criticism and interpretation. Satie,
Erik, -- 1866-1925 -- Friends and associates. Popular culture --
France -- Paris. Popular music -- France -- Paris -- History and
criticism.

ML410.S196.W55 1999
Whiting, Steven Moore, 1953-
Satie the bohemian: from cabaret to concert hall/ Steven
Moore Whiting. Oxford; Oxford University Press, 1999.
596 p.
97-032611   780/.92   0198164580
Satie, Erik, -- 1866-1925.   Popular music -- France -- Paris --
To 1901 -- History and criticism. Music-halls (Variety-theaters,
cabarets, etc.) -- France -- Paris -- History -- 19th century.
Montmartre (Paris, France)

ML410.S22.D2 1960
Dent, Edward Joseph, 1876-1957.
Alessandro Scarlatti: his life and works. London, E.
Arnold [1960] xii, 252 p.
60-004215   927.8
Scarlatti, Alessandro, -- 1660-1725.

ML410.S221 B7 1987
Boyd, Malcolm.
Domenico Scarlatti--master of music/ Malcolm Boyd. 1st
American ed. New York: Schirmer Books, 1987, c1986.
xi, 302 p.
86-021743   780/.92/4 19   0028702913
Scarlatti, Domenico, 1685-1757 -- Criticism and interpretation.

ML410.S221 K5 1983
Kirkpatrick, Ralph.
Domenico Scarlatti/ by Ralph Kirkpatrick. Princeton,
N.J.: Princeton University Press, 1983, c1953. xviii,
491 p.
83-011007   780/.92/4 19   0691027080
Scarlatti, Domenico, 1685-1757.   Composers--Biography.

ML410.S283.A745 1998
The Arnold Schoenberg companion/ edited by Walter B.
Bailey. Westport, Conn.: Greenwood Press, 1998. xiv,
335 p.
97-041923   780/.92   0313287791
Schoenberg, Arnold, -- 1874-1951.

ML410.S283.D83 1992
Dunsby, Jonathan.
Schoenberg, Pierrot lunaire/ Jonathan Dunsby. Cambridge [England]; Cambridge University Press, 1992. x, 84 p.
91-036068   782.4/7   0521382793
Schoenberg, Arnold, -- 1874-1951. -- Pierrot Lunaire.

ML410.S283 M15
MacDonald, Malcolm,
Schoenberg/ [by] Malcolm MacDonald. London: Dent, 1976. xiv, 289 p.
77-359244   780/.92/4 B   0460031430
Schoenberg, Arnold, 1874-1951. Composers -- Biography.

ML410.S283.R43 1971b
Reich, Willi, 1898-
Schoenberg: a critical biography. Translated by Leo Black. New York, Praeger [1971] xi, 268 p.
73-134527   780/.924
Schoenberg, Arnold, -- 1874-1951.

ML410.S283.R55 1990
Ringer, Alexander L.
Arnold Schoenberg-- the composer as Jew/ Alexander L. Ringer. Oxford [England]: Clarendon Press; 1990. xii, 260 p.
89-023030   780/.92   0193154668
Schoenberg, Arnold, -- 1874-1951. Judaism -- Influence.

ML410.S283.S36 1999
Schoenberg and his world/ edited by Walter Frisch. Princeton, N.J.: Princeton University Press, c1999. xi, 352 p.
99-031792   780/.92   0691048606
Schoenberg, Arnold, -- 1874-1951.

ML410.S283.S45 2000
Simms, Bryan R.
The atonal music of Arnold Schoenberg, 1908-1923/ Bryan R. Simms. New York: Oxford University Press, 2000. ix, 265 p.
99-035938   780/.92   0195128265
Schoenberg, Arnold, -- 1874-1951 -- Criticism and interpretation. Atonality.

ML410.S283.S93 1977
Stuckenschmidt, Hans Heinz, 1901-
Schoenberg: his life, world, and work/ H. H. Stuckenschmidt; translated from the German by Humphrey Searle. London: Calder, 1977. 581 p.
77-376619   780/.92/4   071453532X
Schoenberg, Arnold, -- 1874-1951.   Composers -- Austria -- Biography.

ML410.S3.A413 1970b
Schubert, Franz, 1797-1828.
Franz Schubert's letters and other writings. Edited by Otto Erich Deutsch and translated by Venetia Savile. With a foreword by Ernest Newman. Westport, Conn., Greenwood Press, [1970] xx, 143 p.
76-109840   780/.924   0837143319
Schubert, Franz, -- 1797-1828.

ML410.S3.A56 1969
Abraham, Gerald, 1904-
The music of Schubert, edited by Gerald Abraham. Port Washington, N.Y., Kennikat Press [1969] 342 p.
68-008226   780/.924
Schubert, Franz, -- 1797-1828.

ML410.S3.C18 1997
The Cambridge companion to Schubert/ edited by Christopher H. Gibbs. Cambridge [England]; Cambridge University Press, 1997. xiii, 340 p.
96-014260   780/.92   0521482291
Schubert, Franz, -- 1797-1828.

ML410.S3.D52
Deutsch, Otto Erich, 1883-1967.
The Schubert reader, a life of Franz Schubert in letters and documents; translated by Eric Blom; being an English version of Franz Schubert: die Dokumente seines Lebens. Rev. and augm., with a commentary by the author. New York, W. W. Norton [1947] xxxii, 1039 p.
47-012315   927.8
Schubert, Franz, -- 1797-1828.

ML410.S3.F3313 1988
Feil, Arnold.
Franz Schubert, Die schone Mullerin, Winterreise (The lovely miller maiden, Winter journey)/ Arnold Feil; with an essay Wilhelm Muller and romanticism by Rolf Vollmann; translated by Ann C. Sherwin; Reinhard G. Pauly, general editor. Portland, Or.: Amadeus Press, c1988. 179 p.
88-008111   784.3/0092/4   0931340098
Schubert, Franz, -- 1797-1828. -- Schone Mullerin. Schubert, Franz, -- 1797-1828. -- Winterreise. Muller, Wilhelm, -- 1794-1827.

ML410.S3 G53 2000
Gibbs, Christopher Howard.
The life of Schubert/ Christopher H. Gibbs. Cambridge; Cambridge University Press, 2000. xiii, 211 p.
99-032936   780/.92 B 21   052159426X
Schubert, Franz, 1797-1828. Composers -- Austria -- Biography.

ML410.S3.H5613 1988
Hilmar, Ernst.
Franz Schubert in his time/ Ernst Hilmar; translated by Reinhard G. Pauly. Portland, Or.: Amadeus Press, c1988. 157 p.
88-010408   780/.92/4   0931340071
Schubert, Franz, -- 1797-1828.   Composers -- Austria -- Biography.

ML410.S3.M34 1996
McKay, Elizabeth Norman.
Franz Schubert: a biography/ Elizabeth Norman McKay. New York: Oxford University Press, 1996.
95-051812   780/.92   0198165234
Schubert, Franz, -- 1797-1828.   Composers -- Austria -- Biography.

ML410.S3.N48 1997
Newbould, Brian, 1936-
Schubert, the music and the man/ Brian Newbould.
Berkeley: University of California Press, c1997. 465 p.
96-049876   780/.92   0520210654
Schubert, Franz, -- 1797-1828 -- Criticism and interpretation.

ML410.S3 R265 1997
Reed, John,
The Schubert song companion/ John Reed; with prose
translations by Norma Deane and Celia Larner; and a
foreword by Dame Janet Baker. Manchester, UK;
Mandolin: xii, 510 p.
98-179605   782.42168/092 21   1901341003
Schubert, Franz, 1797-1828. Songs.

ML410.S3.S29975 1997
Schubert's Vienna/ edited by Raymond Erickson. New
Haven: Yale University Press, c1997. xvi, 283 p.
97-010707   780/.92   0300070802
Schubert, Franz, -- 1797-1828.   Music -- Austria -- Vienna --
19th century -- History and criticism. Arts, Austrian -- Austria --
Vienna.   Vienna (Austria) -- Social life and customs. Vienna
(Austria) -- Politics and government.

ML410.S3.Y7 1992
Youens, Susan.
Schubert, Die schone Mullerin/ Susan Youens.
Cambridge [England]; Cambridge University Press, 1992.
vi, 123 p.
91-028960   782.42168   0521410916
Schubert, Franz, -- 1797-1828. -- Schone Mullerin.

ML410.S3.Y72 1997
Youens, Susan.
Schubert, Muller, and Die schone Mullerin/ Susan
Youens. Cambridge; Cambridge University Press, 1997.
xviii, 245 p.
96-014037   782.4/7   052156364X
Schubert, Franz, -- 1797-1828. -- Schone Mullerin. Muller,
Wilhelm, -- 1794-1827. -- Schone Mullerin.

ML410.S3.Y73 1996
Youens, Susan.
Schubert's poets and the making of lieder/ Susan Youens.
Cambridge; Cambridge University Press, c1996. xv,
384 p.
95-019069   782.42168/092   0521552575
Schubert, Franz, -- 1797-1828. -- Songs.   Songs, German --
19th century -- History and criticism. Poets, German -- 18th
century. Poets, German -- 19th century.

ML410.S35.A4 1990
Schutz, Heinrich, 1585-1672.
Letters and documents of Heinrich Schutz, 1656-1672: an
annotated translation/ by Gina Spagnoli; with a foreword
by Werner Breig. Ann Arbor, Mich.: UMI Research
Press, c1990. xx, 395 p.
89-005204   782.2/2/092   0835719022
Schutz, Heinrich, -- 1585-1672 -- Correspondence. Schutz,
Heinrich, -- 1585-1672 -- Archives.   Music -- Germany -- 17th
century -- History and criticism.

ML410.S35.S6 2000
Smallman, Basil.
Schutz/ Basil Smallman. Oxford; Oxford University
Press, 2000. xvii, 218 p.
99-042131   782.2/2/092   0198166745
Schutz, Heinrich, -- 1585-1672 -- Criticism and interpretation.

ML410.S4 A124 1983
Schumann, Robert,
On music and musicians/ Robert Schumann; [edited by
Konrad Wolff;   translated by Paul Rosenfeld]. 1st
California pbk. ed. Berkeley: University of California
Press, 1983, c1946. 274 p.
82-070650   780 19   0520046854
Music -- 19th century -- History and criticism. Musicians.

ML410.S4.D38 1997
Daverio, John.
Robert Schumann: herald of a "new poetic age"/ John
Daverio. New York: Oxford University Press, 1997. xi,
607 p.
96-023177   780/.92   0195091809
Schumann, Robert, -- 1810-1856.   Composers -- Germany --
Biography.

ML410.S4.F47 2000
Ferris, David, 1960-
Schumann's Eichendorff Liederkreis and the genre of the
romantic cycle/ David Ferris. New York: Oxford
University Press, 2000. viii, 270 p.
00-036740   782.4/7/092   0195124472
Schumann, Robert, -- 1810-1856. -- Liederkreis, -- op. 39.
Eichendorff, Joseph, -- Freiherr von, -- 1788-1857 -- Musical
settings -- History and criticism.   Song cycles -- History and
criticism.

ML410.S4 J45 2001
Jensen, Eric Frederick,
Schumann/ Eric Frederick Jensen. New York: Oxford
University Press, 2001. xv, 380 p.
00-027866   780/.92 B 21   0195135660
Schumann, Robert,   1810-1856. Composers -- Germany --
Biography.

ML410.S4.M65
Moore, Gerald.
Poet's love: the songs and cycles of Schumann/ Gerald
Moore. New York: Taplinger Pub. Co., 1981. xii, 247 p.
81-050607   784.3/007   0800863909
Schumann, Robert, -- 1810-1856. -- Songs.

ML410.S4.P6
Plantinga, Leon.
Schumann as critic, by Leon B. Plantinga. New Haven,
Yale University Press, 1967. xiii, 354 p.
67-013446
Schumann, Robert, -- 1810-1856.   Musical criticism.

ML410.S4.S323 1994
Schumann and his world/ edited by R. Larry Todd.
Princeton, N.J.: Princeton University Press, c1994. x,
393 p.
94-009686   780/.92   0691036977
Schumann, Robert, -- 1810-1856.

ML410.S4446.S77 1995
Straus, Joseph Nathan.
The music of Ruth Crawford Seeger/ Joesph N. Straus.
Cambridge [England]; Cambridge University Press, 1995.
xii, 260 p.
94-021135   780/.92   0521416469
Seeger, Ruth Crawford, -- 1901-1953 -- Criticism and interpretation.

ML410.S4446 T5 1997
Tick, Judith.
Ruth Crawford Seeger: a composer's search for American music/ Judith Tick. New York: Oxford University Press, 1997. xiv, 457 p.
95-030085   780/.92 B 20   0195065093
Seeger, Ruth Crawford, 1901-1953. Composers -- United States -- Biography.

ML410.S473.A4 1992
Sessions, Roger, 1896-
The correspondence of Roger Sessions/ edited by Andrea Olmstead. Boston: Northeastern University Press, c1992. xxviii, 539 p.
91-039197   780.92   1555531229
Sessions, Roger, -- 1896- -- Correspondence. Composers -- United States -- Correspondence.

ML410.S473 O4 1985
Olmstead, Andrea.
Roger Sessions and his music/ by Andrea Olmstead. Ann Arbor, Mich.: UMI Research Press, c1985. xvii, 218 p.
84-028110   780/.92/4 B 19   0835716333
Sessions, Roger, 1896- Sessions, Roger, 1896- -- Criticism and interpretation. Composers -- United States -- Biography.

ML410.S53.F39 2000
Fay, Laurel E.
Shostakovich: a life/ Laurel E. Fay. New York: Oxford University Press, 2000. 458 p.
99-025255   780/.92   0195134389
Shostakovich, Dmitrii Dmitrievich, -- 1906-1975. Composers -- Soviet Union -- Biography.

ML410.S53.W55 1994
Wilson, Elizabeth.
Shostakovich: a life remembered/ Elizabeth Wilson. Princeton, N.J.: Princeton University Press, c1994. xxiv, 550 p.
94-021130   780/.92   0691029717
Shostakovich, Dmitrii Dmitrievich, -- 1906-1975. Composers -- Soviet Union -- Biography.

ML410.S54.A5
Abraham, Gerald, 1904-
The music of Sibelius. New York, W. W. Norton [1947] 218 p.
47-011886   780.81
Sibelius, Jean, -- 1865-1957.

ML410.S54 H4 1993
Hepokoski, James A.
Sibelius, Symphony no. 5/ James Hepokoski. Cambridge [England]; Cambridge University Press, 1993. xi, 107 p.
92-021614   784.2/184 20   0521409586
Sibelius, Jean, 1865-1957. Symphonies, no. 5, op. 82, E major.

ML410.S54 S53 1996
The Sibelius companion/ edited by Glenda Dawn Goss. Westport, Conn: Greenwood Press, 1996. xvi, 449 p.
96-005833   780/.92 20   0313283931
Sibelius, Jean, 1865-1957 -- Criticism and interpretation.

ML410.S5988.S313 1987
Schloezer, Boris de, 1881-1969.
Scriabin: artist and mystic/ by Boris de Schloezer; translated from the Russian by Nicolas Slonimsky; with introductory essays by Marina Scriabine. Berkeley: University of California Press, c1987. xii, 334 p.
86-040109   780/.92/4   0520043847
Scriabin, Aleksandr Nikolayevich, -- 1872-1915. Composers -- Soviet Union -- Biography.

ML410.S5988 M2
Macdonald, Hugh,
Skryabin/ Hugh Macdonald. London; Oxford University Press, c1978. 71 p.
78-322912   786.1/092/4 B   0193154382
Scriabin, Aleksandr Nikolayevich, 1872-1915 -- Criticism and

ML410.S6872.B3 1993
Banfield, Stephen, 1951-
Sondheim's Broadway musicals/ Stephen Banfield. Ann Arbor: University of Michigan Press, c1993. xvi, 453 p.
93-012818   782.1/4/092   0472102230
Sondheim, Stephen. -- Musicals. Musicals -- New York (State) -- New York -- History and criticism.

ML410.S6872.S43 1998
Secrest, Meryle.
Stephen Sondheim: a life/ Meryle Secrest. New York: Knopf, 1998. ix, 461 p.
98-014258   782.1/4/092   0679448179
Sondheim, Stephen. Composers -- United States -- Biography.

ML410.S688.M3
Sousa, John Philip, 1854-1932.
Marching along: recollections of men, women and music/ by John Philip Sousa. Boston: Hale, Cushman & Flint, 1928. 384 p.
28-012968
   Musicians -- Correspondence, reminiscences, etc.

ML410.S688 P47 1983
Perspectives on John Philip Sousa/ edited and with an introduction by Jon Newsom (Music Division, Research Services). Washington: Library of Congress: viii, 144 p.
83-600076   785/.092/4 19   084440425X
Sousa, John Philip, 1854-1932.

ML410.S855 S65 2000
Smith, Catherine Parsons,
William Grant Still: a study in contradictions/ Catherine Parsons Smith; with contributed essays by Gayle Murchison and Willard B. Gatewood, chronology by Carolyn L. Quin, and contemporary sources from the 1930s, Verna Arvey ... [et al.]. Berkeley, Calif.: University of California Press, c2000. xvi, 368 p.
99-043232   780/.92 21   0520215435
Still, William Grant, 1895- -- Criticism and interpretation.

ML410.S858.A5 1989
Stockhausen, Karlheinz, 1928-
Stockhausen on music: lectures and interviews/ Karlheinz Stockhausen; compiled by Robin Maconie. London; M. Boyars; 1989. 220 p.
88-022242 780 0714528870
Stockhausen, Karlheinz, -- 1928- Music -- History and criticism.

ML410.S858.M3 1990
Maconie, Robin.
The works of Karlheinz Stockhausen/ Robin Maconie; with a foreword by Karlheinz Stockhausen. Oxford [England]: Clarendon Press; 1990. xiii, 318 p.
89-020989 780/.92 0193154773
Stockhausen, Karlheinz, -- 1928- -- Criticism and interpretation.

ML410.S93 A372 1974
Strauss, Richard,
Recollections and reflections. Edited by Willi Schuh. English translation by L. J. Lawrence. Westport, Conn., Greenwood Press [1974, c1953] 173 p.
74-000072 780/.8 0837173663
Strauss, Richard, 1864-1949. Composers -- Biography.

ML410.S93.A453
Strauss, Richard, 1864-1949.
A working friendship/ the correspondence between Richard Strauss and Hugo von Hofmannsthal; translated by Hanns Hammelmann and Ewald Osers; introd. by Edward Sackville-West. New York, Vienna House, 1974, c1961. xx, 558 p.
61-013839 927.8
Strauss, Richard, -- 1864-1949.

ML410.S93.B5 1989
Birkin, Kenneth.
Richard Strauss, Arabella/ Kenneth Birkin. Cambridge; Cambridge University Press, 1989. xiii, 162 p.
88-029953 782.1/092/4 0521340314
Strauss, Richard, -- 1864-1949. -- Arabella.

ML410.S93 D4 1986
Del Mar, Norman,
Richard Strauss: a critical commentary on his life and works/ by Norman Del Mar. Ithaca, N.Y.: Cornell University Press, 1986. 3 v.
85-019033 780/.92/4 B 19 080141783X
Strauss, Richard, 1864-1949. Composers -- Germany -- Biography.

ML410.S93.G53 1999
Gilliam, Bryan Randolph.
The life of Richard Strauss/ Bryan Gilliam. Cambridge, UK; Cambridge University Press, 1999. viii, 201 p.
98-047947 780/.92 0521570190
Strauss, Richard, -- 1864-1949. Composers -- Germany -- Biography.

ML410.S93.K46 1999
Kennedy, Michael, 1926-
Richard Strauss: man, musician, enigma/ Michael Kennedy. New York: Cambridge University Press, 1999. xvi, 451 p.
98-035860 780/.92 0521581737
Strauss, Richard, -- 1864-1949. Composers -- Germany -- Biography.

ML410.S93 R44 1992
Richard Strauss and his world/ edited by Bryan Gilliam. Princeton, N.J.: Princeton University Press, c1992. xi, 425 p.
92-015748 780/.92 B 20 0691027625
Strauss, Richard, 1864-1949. Strauss, Richard, 1864-1949 -- Criticism and interpretation.

ML410.S93.R485 1989
Richard Strauss, Elektra/ edited by Derrick Puffett. Cambridge [Cambridgeshire]; Cambridge University Press, 1989. vii, 179 p.
89-000499 782.1/092/4 0521351731
Strauss, Richard, -- 1864-1949. -- Elektra.

ML410.S93.R52 1989
Richard Strauss, Salome/ edited by Derrick Puffett. Cambridge [England]; Cambridge University Press, 1989. ix, 211 p.
89-000500 782.1/092/4 0521351723
Strauss, Richard, -- 1864-1949. -- Salome.

ML410.S932.A13 1970
Stravinsky, Igor Fedorovich, 1882-1971.
Poetics of music in the form of six lessons [by] Igor Stravinsky. English translation by Arthur Knodell and Ingolf Dahl. Pref. by George Seferis. Cambridge, Mass., Harvard University Press, 1970. ix, 187 p.
79-099520 780 0674678559
Music -- Addresses, essays, lectures.

ML410.S932 A22 1962
Stravinsky, Igor Fedorovich, 1882-1971.
Igor Stravinsky: an autobiography. New York, Norton [1962, c1936] 176 p.
63-000197
Stravinsky, Igor, -- 1882-1971. Composers -- Biography.

ML410.S932.A33 1980
Stravinsky, Igor Fedorovich, 1882-1971.
Conversations with Igor Stravinsky/ Igor Stravinsky and Robert Craft. Berkeley: University of California Press, 1980, c1959. 140 p.
79-019367 780 0520040406
Stravinsky, Igor, -- 1882-1971. Composers -- Interviews.

ML410.S932 A335 1982
Stravinsky, Igor,
Dialogues/ Igor Stravinsky and Robert Craft. Berkeley: University of California Press, 1982. 152 p.
82-050247 780/.92/4 B 19 0520046501
Stravinsky, Igor, 1882-1971. Composers -- Interviews.

ML410.S932.A38
Stravinsky, Igor Fedorovich, 1882-1971.
Themes and episodes New York, A. A. Knopf, 1966. x, 352 p.
66-019373
Music.

ML410.S932.C8 1994
Craft, Robert.
Stravinsky: chronicle of a friendship/ Robert Craft. Nashville: Vanderbilt University Press, 1994. xv, 588 p.
94-012666   780/.92   0826512585
Stravinsky, Igor, -- 1882-1971 -- Friends and associates. Craft, Robert -- Diaries. Composers -- Biography.

ML410.S932.C87 1998
Cross, Jonathan, 1961-
The Stravinsky legacy/ Jonathan Cross. Cambridge; Cambridge University Press, 1998. xii, 282 p.
98-017405   780/.92   0521563658
Stravinsky, Igor, -- 1882-1971 -- Criticism and interpretation.
Stravinsky, Igor, -- 1882-1971 -- Influence.

ML410.S932.G76 1993
Griffiths, Paul, 1947 Nov. 24-
Stravinsky/ Paul Griffiths. New York: Schirmer Books: 1993, c1992. xiii, 253 p.
92-046649   780/.92   0028714830
Stravinsky, Igor, -- 1882-1971. Composers -- Biography.

ML410.S932 H55 2000
Hill, Peter,
Stravinsky, The rite of spring/ Peter Hill. Cambridge; Cambridge University Press, 2000. x, 170 p.
00-023703   784.2/1556 21   0521627141
Stravinsky, Igor, 1882-1971. Vesna svëïïashchennaëïïa.

ML410.S932.L44
Libman, Lillian.
And music at the close: Stravinsky's last years, a personal memoir. New York, W. W. Norton [1972] 400 p.
72-004499   780/.92/4   0393021130
Stravinsky, Igor, -- 1882-1971.

ML410.S932.S787
Stravinsky, Vera.
Stravinsky in pictures and documents/ by Vera Stravinsky and Robert Craft. New York: Simon and Schuster, c1978. 688 p.
78-015375   780/.92/4   0671243829
Stravinsky, Igor, -- 1882-1971. Composers -- Biography.

ML410.S932.T38 1996
Taruskin, Richard.
Stravinsky and the Russian traditions: a biography of the works through Mavra/ Richard Taruskin. Berkeley: University of California Press, c1996. 2 v.
93-028500   780/.92   0520070992
Stravinsky, Igor, -- 1882-1971 -- Criticism and interpretation.
Stravinsky, Igor, -- 1882-1971 -- Sources. Music -- Russia -- History and criticism.

ML410.S932 W34 1988
Walsh, Stephen,
The music of Stravinsky/ Stephen Walsh. London; Routledge, 1988. 317 p.
87-012896   780/.92/4 19   0415001986
Stravinsky, Igor, 1882-1971 -- Criticism and interpretation.

ML410.S932 W345 1999
Walsh, Stephen,
Stravinsky: a creative spring: Russia and France, 1882-1934/ Stephen Walsh. 1st ed. New York: Alfred A. Knopf, 1999. xvii, 698 p.
99-462433   780/.92 B 21   0679414843
Stravinsky, Igor, 1882-1971. Composers -- Biography.

ML410.S9325.H35 1996
Hajdu, David.
Lush life/ a biography of Billy Strayhorn/ David Hajdu. New York: Farrar, Straus, Giroux, 1996. xii, 305 p.
95-044707   781.65/092   0374194386
Strayhorn, Billy. Composers -- United States -- Biography.
Jazz musicians -- United States -- Biography.

ML410.S95.J28 1984
Jacobs, Arthur, 1922-
Arthur Sullivan, a Victorian musician/ Arthur Jacobs. Oxford; Oxford University Press, 1984. xvi, 470 p.
83-008207   782.81/092/4   0193154439
Sullivan, Arthur, -- Sir, -- 1842-1900. Composers -- England -- Biography.

ML410.T452.A4 1988
Thomson, Virgil, 1896-
Selected letters of Virgil Thomson/ edited by Tim Page and Vanessa Weeks Page. New York: Summit Books, c1988. 413 p.
88-002220   780/.92/4   0671621173
Thomson, Virgil, -- 1896- -- Correspondence. Composers -- United States -- Correspondence.

ML410.T452.T58 1997
Tommasini, Anthony, 1948-
Virgil Thomson: composer on the aisle/ Anthony Tommasini. New York: W.W. Norton, c1997. xiii, 605 p.
96-031695   780/.92   0393040062
Thomson, Virgil, -- 1896- Composers -- United States -- Biography.

ML410.V27.O83
Ouellette, Fernand.
Edgard Varese. Translated from the French by Derek Coltman. New York, Orion Press [1968] ix, 270 p.
68-015461   780/.924
Varese, Edgard, -- 1883-1965.

ML410.V3.D4.H37 2001
Heffer, Simon.
Vaughan Williams/ Simon Heffer. Boston, Mass.: Northeastern University Press, 2001. 167 p.
00-052725   780/.92   1555534724
Vaughan Williams, Ralph, -- 1872-1958. Composers -- England -- Biography.

ML410.V3 K4 1980
Kennedy, Michael,
The works of Ralph Vaughan Williams/ Michael Kennedy. New ed. London; Oxford University Press, 1980. 454 p.
80-508763   780/.92/4 19   0193154544
Vaughan Williams, Ralph,   1872-1958 -- Criticism and interpretation.

ML410.V3.V46 1996
Vaughan Williams studies/ edited by Alain Frogley. Cambridge; Cambridge University Press, 1996. xvii, 241 p.
95-050620   780/.92   0521480310
Vaughan Williams, Ralph, -- 1872-1958 -- Criticism and interpretation.

ML410.V4.A4 1994
Verdi, Giuseppe, 1813-1901.
The Verdi-Boito correspondence/ edited by Marcello Conati & Mario Medici; with a new introduction by Marcello Conati; English-language edition prepared by William Weaver. Chicago: University of Chicago Press, 1994. lxiv, 321 p.
93-022598   782.1/092/2   0226853047
Verdi, Giuseppe, -- 1813-1901 -- Correspondence. Boito, Arrigo, -- 1842-1918 -- Correspondence. Composers -- Italy -- Correspondence. Librettists -- Italy -- Correspondence. Opera -- Italy -- 19th century.

ML410.V4 B88 1991
Budden, Julian.
The operas of Verdi/ Julian Budden. Rev. ed. Oxford; Clarendon Press, 1992. 3 v.
91-036272   782.1/092 20   0198162634
Verdi, Giuseppe, 1813-1901. Operas. Opera.

ML410.V4 H46 1983
Hepokoski, James A.
Giuseppe Verdi, Falstaff/ James A. Hepokoski. Cambridge; Cambridge University Press, 1983. x, 181 p.
82-023493   782.1/092/4 19   0521280168
Verdi, Giuseppe, 1813-1901. Falstaff. Falstaff, John, Sir (Fictitious character)

ML410.V4 H48 1987
Hepokoski, James A.
Giuseppe Verdi, Otello/ James A. Hepokoski. Cambridge [Cambridgeshire]; Cambridge University Press,   xi, 209 p.
86-017189   782.1/092/4 19   0521277493
Verdi, Giuseppe, 1813-1901. Otello.

ML410.V4.P43 1993
Phillips-Matz, Mary Jane.
Verdi: a biography/ Mary Jane Phillips-Matz; with a foreword by Andrew Porter. Oxford [England]; Oxford University Press, 1993. xxx, 941 p.
92-037841   782.1/092   0193132044
Verdi, Giuseppe, -- 1813-1901.   Composers -- Italy -- Biography.

ML410.V4.R73 1995
Rosen, David, 1938-
Verdi, Requiem/ David Rosen. Cambridge, [England]; Cambridge University Press, 1995. ix, 115 p.
94-033380   782.32/38   0521394481
Verdi, Giuseppe, -- 1813-1901. -- Messa da Requiem.

ML410.V4.R74 2000
Rosselli, John.
The life of Verdi/ John Rosselli. New York: Cambridge University Press, 2000. x, 204 p.
99-059952   782.1/092   0521660114
Verdi, Giuseppe, -- 1813-1901.   Composers -- Italy -- Biography.

ML410.V4.V29
Verdi: a documentary study/ compiled, edited, and translated by William Weaver. [London]: Thames & Hudson, [1977?] 256 p.
77-376231   782.1/092/4   0500011842
Verdi, Giuseppe, -- 1813-1901.   Composers -- Italy -- Biography.

ML410.V4.V295
The Verdi companion/ edited by William Weaver and Martin Chusid. New York: W. W. Norton, c1979. xvi, 366 p.
79-014793   782.1/092/4   0393012158
Verdi, Giuseppe, -- 1813-1901.

ML410.V76.B44 1994
Behague, Gerard.
Heitor Villa-Lobos: the search for Brazil's musical soul/ by Gerard Behague. Austin: Institute of Latin American Studies, University of Texas at Austin, c1994. xvii, 202 p.
94-021638   780/.92   0292708238
Villa-Lobos, Heitor.   Composers -- Brazil -- Biography.

ML410.V76.W7 1992
Wright, Simon.
Villa-Lobos/ Simon Wright. Oxford; Oxford University Press, 1992. xii, 146 p.
91-034731   780/.92   0193154765
Villa-Lobos, Heitor -- Criticism and interpretation.

ML410.V82 E84 1996
Everett, Paul.
Vivaldi, The four seasons and other concertos, op. 8/ Paul Everett. Cambridge, [England]; Cambridge University Press, 1996. xiv, 104 p.
95-018173   784.2/72 20   0521406927
Vivaldi, Antonio,   1678-1741.   Cimento dell'armonia e dell'inventione.

ML410.V82 H4413 1997
Heller, Karl,
Antonio Vivaldi: the red priest of Venice/ by Karl Heller; translated from the German by David Marinelli. Portland, Ore.: Amadeus Press, c1997. 360 p.
96-006730   780/.92 B 20   1574670158
Vivaldi, Antonio, 1678-1741. Composers -- Italy -- Biography.

ML410.V82.T34 1993
Talbot, Michael.
Vivaldi/ Michael Talbot. New York: Schirmer Books:
1993. xi, 237 p.
93-015281   780/.92   0028726650
*Vivaldi, Antonio, -- 1678-1741. Vivaldi, Antonio, -- 1678-1741 -
- Criticism and interpretation. Composers -- Italy -- Biography.*

ML410.W1.A317 1988
Wagner, Richard, 1813-1883.
Selected letters of Richard Wagner/ translated and edited
by Stewart Spencer and Barry Millington; with original
texts of passages omitted from existing printed editions.
New York: W.W. Norton, 1988, c1987. ix, 1030 p.
87-032470   782.1/092/4   0393025004
*Wagner, Richard, -- 1813-1883 -- Correspondence. Composers
-- Germany -- Correspondence.*

ML410.W1 M58 1999
Millington, Barry.
Wagner/ Barry Millington. Oxford [England]; Oxford
University Press, 1999.
99-046523   782.1/092 B 21   0198164874
*Wagner, Richard, 1813-1883. Composers -- Germany --
Biography.*

ML410.W1.W146 1983
Wagner, Richard, 1813-1883.
My life/ Richard Wagner; translated by Andrew Gray;
edited by Mary Whittall. Cambridge [Cambridgeshire];
Cambridge University Press, 1983. ix, 786 p.
82-023568   782.1/092/4   0521229294
*Wagner, Richard, -- 1813-1883. Composers -- Germany --
Biography.*

ML410.W1.W38 1981
Watson, Derek, 1948-
Richard Wagner: a biography/ Derek Watson. New York:
Schirmer Books, 1981, c1979. 352 p.
81-001161   780/.92/4   0028727002
*Wagner, Richard, -- 1813-1883. Composers -- Germany --
Biography.*

ML410.W11.W122
Wagner, Richard, 1813-1883.
The diary of Richard Wagner 1865-1882: the brown
book/ presented and annotated by Joachim Bergfeld;
translated by George Bird. London; Cambridge
University Press, 1980. 218 p.
79-056128   782.1/092/4   0521233119
*Wagner, Richard, -- 1813-1883 -- Diaries. Composers --
Germany -- Diaries.*

ML410.W13.D153
Dahlhaus, Carl, 1928-
Richard Wagner's music dramas/ Carl Dahlhaus;
translated by Mary Whittall. Cambridge; Cambridge
University Press, 1979. 161 p.
78-068359   782.1/092/4   0521223970
Wagner, Richard, -- 1813-1883. -- Operas.

ML410.W13.W122 1992
The Wagner compendium: a guide to Wagner's life and
music/ edited by Barry Millington. New York: Schirmer
Books, 1992. 431 p.
92-032214   782.1/092   0028713591
Wagner, Richard, -- 1813-1883.

ML410.W131.R41613 1992
Wagner handbook/ edited by Ulrich Muller, Peter
Wapnewski; translation edited by John Deathridge.
Cambridge, Mass.: Harvard University Press, 1992. vii,
711 p.
91-042202   782.1/092   0674945301
Wagner, Richard, -- 1813-1883.

ML410.W15.E9 1983
Ewans, Michael, 1946-
Wagner and Aeschylus: the Ring and the Oresteia/
Michael Ewans. Cambridge [Cambridgeshire];
Cambridge University Press, 1983, c1982. 271 p.
82-012762   782.1/092/4   0521250730
*Wagner, Richard, -- 1813-1883. -- Ring des Nibelungen.
Aeschylus. -- Oresteia.*

ML410.W19.W12 1992
Wagner in performance/ edited by Barry Millington and
Stewart Spencer. New Haven: Yale University Press,
1992. x, 214 p.
92-004964   782.1/092   0300057180
*Wagner, Richard, -- 1813-1883 -- Performances. Opera --
Production and direction. Performance practice (Music) -- 19th
century. Performance practice (Music) -- 20th century.*

ML410.W19.W23 1995
Weiner, Marc A.
Richard Wagner and the anti-Semitic imagination/ Marc
A. Weiner. Lincoln: University of Nebraska Press, c1995.
xii, 439 p.
94-012187   782.1/092   0803247753
*Wagner, Richard, -- 1813-1883 -- Symbolism. Antisemitism.
Body, Human, in literature.*

ML410.W2.B265 1980
Bayreuth, the early years: an account of the early decades
of the Wagner festival as seen by the celebrated visitors
& participants/ compiled, edited, and introduced by
Robert Hartford. London; Cambridge University Press,
1980. 284 p.
80-067459   782.1/07/94331   0521238226
Wagner, Richard, -- 1813-1883.

ML410.W22.H65 1996
Holman, J. K.
Wagner's Ring: a listener's companion & concordance/
J.K. Holman. Portland, Or.: Amadeus Press, c1996.
440 p.
96-001829   782.1   157467014X
*Wagner, Richard, -- 1813-1883. -- Ring des Nibelungen.
Wagner, Richard, -- 1813-1883. -- Ring des Nibelungen --
Concordances.*

ML410.W292.K4 1989
Kennedy, Michael, 1926-
Portrait of Walton/ Michael Kennedy. Oxford; Oxford
University Press, 1989. x, 348 p.
88-038917   780/.92/4   0193154188
Walton, William, -- 1902- Composers -- England -- Biography.

ML410.W292.W3 1988
Walton, Susana.
William Walton: behind the facade/ Susana Walton.
Oxford [Oxfordshire]; Oxford University Press, 1988. xi,
255 p.
87-024054   780/.92/4   0193151561
Walton, William, -- 1902- Composers -- England -- Biography.

ML410.W2953.S6 1994
Smith, Barry, 1939-
Peter Warlock: the life of Philip Heseltine/ Barry Smith.
Oxford; Oxford University Press, 1994. xviii, 347 p.
93-044931   782.2/092   019816310X
*Warlock, Peter, -- 1894-1930.   Composers -- England --
Biography.*

ML410.W3.T9 1991
Tusa, Michael Charles.
Euryanthe and Carl Maria von Weber's dramaturgy of
German opera/ Michael C. Tusa. Oxford: Clarendon
Press; 1991. xvi, 293 p.
90-043678   782.1   0193153254
Weber, Carl Maria von, -- 1786-1826. -- Euryanthe.

ML410.W3.W26 1976
Warrack, John Hamilton, 1928-
Carl Maria von Weber/ John Warrack. Cambridge, Eng.:
Cambridge University Press, c1976. 411 p.
76-026655   780/.92/4   0521213541
*Weber, Carl Maria von, -- 1786-1826. Composers -- Germany
-- Biography.*

ML410.W33.B32 1998
Bailey, Kathryn.
The life of Webern/ Kathryn Bailey. Cambridge,
[England]; Cambridge University Press, 1998. xix, 217 p.
97-025751   780/.92   052157336X
*Webern, Anton, -- 1883-1945.   Composers -- Austria --
Biography.*

ML410.W33.K63
Kolneder, Walter.
Anton Webern; an introduction to his works. Translated
by Humphrey Searle. Berkeley, University of California
Press, 1968. 232 p.
68-010663   780/.924
Webern, Anton, -- 1883-1945.

ML410.W33.M55 1979
Moldenhauer, Hans.
Anton von Webern, a chronicle of his life and work/ Hans
Moldenhauer and Rosaleen Moldenhauer. New York:
Knopf: distributed by Random House, 1979, c1978.
803 p.
77-020370   780/.92/4   0394472373
*Webern, Anton, -- 1883-1945.   Composers -- Austria --
Biography.*

ML410.W395.F37 1999
Farneth, David.
Kurt Weill: a life in pictures and documents/ David
Farneth. Woodstock: Overlook Press, 1999. xv, 312 p.
99-033577   782.1/092   0879517212
*Weill, Kurt, -- 1900-1950 -- Chronology. Weill, Kurt, -- 1900-
1950 -- Pictorial works.*

ML410.W395.J37 1982
Jarman, Douglas.
Kurt Weill, an illustrated biography/ Douglas Jarman.
Bloomington: Indiana University Press, c1982. 160 p.
82-047949   782.81/092/4   025314650X
Weill, Kurt, -- 1900-1950. Composers -- Biography.

ML410.W395 K87 1990
Kurt Weill, The threepenny opera/ edited by Stephen
Hinton. Cambridge; Cambridge University Press, 1990.
xv, 229 p.
91-109557   782.1/4 20   0521338883
Weill, Kurt, 1900-1950. Dreigroschenoper.

ML410.W648.T5 1987
Thomson, Andrew, 1944-
Widor: the life and times of Charles-Marie Widor, 1844-
1937/ Andrew Thomson. Oxford [Oxfordshire]; Oxford
University Press, 1987. ix, 116 p.
87-015176   780/.92/4   0193164175
*Widor, Charles Marie, -- 1844-1937.   Composers -- France --
Biography.*

ML410.W6975.S76 1996
Stone, Desmond.
Alec Wilder in spite of himself: a life of the composer/
Desmond Stone. New York: Oxford University Press,
1996. x, 244 p.
95-008968   780/.92   0195096002
Wilder, Alec. Composers -- United States -- Biography.

ML410.W8.N5 1966
Newman, Ernest, 1868-1959.
Hugo Wolf. With a new introd. by Walter Legge. New
York, Dover Publications [1966] xxv, 279 p.
66-023973   784/.0924
Wolf, Hugo, -- 1860-1903.

ML410.W8.Y68 2000
Youens, Susan.
Hugo Wolf and his Morike songs/ Susan Youens.
Cambridge; Cambridge University Press, 2000. xii,
203 p.
99-054035   782.42168/092   052165159X
*Wolf, Hugo, -- 1860-1903. -- Morike-Lieder Morike, Eduard
Friedrich, -- 1804-1875 -- Musical settings -- History and
criticism.*

ML410.W8.Y7 1992
Youens, Susan.
Hugo Wolf: the vocal music/ Susan Youens. Princeton,
N.J.: Princeton University Press, c1992. xix, 384 p.
91-045446   782.42168/092   0691091455
*Wolf, Hugo, -- 1860-1903. -- Vocal music. Vocal music -- 19th
century -- History and criticism.*

ML410.X45.B6
Bois, Mario.
Iannis Xenakis, the man and his music; a conversation with the composer and a description of his works [by Mario Bois] London, Boosey & Hawkes Music Publishers, 1967. 40 p.
68-005108   780/.924
Xenakis, Iannis, -- 1922-

ML416.S33.M9 1994
Murray, Michael, 1943-
Albert Schweitzer, musician/ Michael Murray. Aldershot, Hants, England: Scolar Press; c1994. xiv, 161 p.
93-037090   786.5/092   1859280315
Schweitzer, Albert, -- 1875-1965. Organists -- Biography.

ML417.B2.A3 1992
Barenboim, Daniel, 1942-
Daniel Barenboim: a life in music/ Daniel Barenboim; edited by Michael Lewin. New York: C. Scribner's Sons: 1992. x, 198 p.
92-007459   780/.92   0684193264
Barenboim, Daniel, -- 1942- Pianists -- Biography. Conductors (Music) -- Biography.

ML417.C67.R44 1993
Reich, Howard.
Van Cliburn/ Howard Reich. Nashville: T. Nelson Publishers, c1993. 428 p.
92-041082   786.2/092   0840776810
Cliburn, Van, -- 1934- Pianists -- United States -- Biography.

ML417.E9.P53 1998
Pettinger, Peter, 1945-
Bill Evans: how my heart sings/ Peter Pettinger. New Haven: Yale Univeristy Press, c1998. xiii, 346 p.
97-049991   781.65/092   0300071930
Evans, Bill, -- 1929- Pianists -- United States -- Biography. Jazz musicians -- United States -- Biography.

ML417.F286.M43 1995
McCarthy, Margaret William, 1931-
Amy Fay: America's notable woman of music/ by Margaret William McCarthy. Warren, Mich.: Harmonie Park Press, 1995. xviii, 196 p.
95-010196   786.2/092   0899900747
Fay, Amy, -- 1844-1928. Pianists -- United States -- Biography.

ML417.G68.F7 1989
Friedrich, Otto, 1929-
Glenn Gould: a life and variations/ Otto Friedrich. New York: Random House, c1989. xviii, 441 p.
88-029676   786.1/092/4   0394562992
Gould, Glenn. Pianists -- Canada -- Biography.

ML417.L26.A33
Landowska, Wanda.
Landowska on music. Stein, [1964-] 434 p.
64-022698   780.8
   Music -- Instruction and study. Music -- History and criticism. Music appreciation.

ML417.L64.A35
Levant, Oscar, 1906-1972.
The unimportance of being Oscar. New York, Putnam [1968] 255 p.
68-020949   786.1/0924
Levant, Oscar, -- 1906-1972. Levant, Oscar, -- 1906-1972. Musicians -- Biography.

ML417.L64.K37 1994
Kashner, Sam.
A talent for genius: the life and times of Oscar Levant/ Sam Kashner and Nancy Schoenberger. New York: Villard Books, 1994. xii, 512 p.
93-040647   780/.92   0679404899
Levant, Oscar, -- 1906-1972. Musicians -- United States -- Biography.

ML417.M85.A3 1979
Moore, Gerald.
Am I too loud?: memoirs of an accompanist/ by Gerald Moore. London: Hamish Hamilton, 1979, c1962. 304 p.
82-108251   786.1/092/4   0241900190
Moore, Gerald. Pianists -- England -- Biography.

ML417.R79.A28
Rubinstein, Artur, 1887-
My many years/ Arthur Rubinstein. New York: Knopf: distributed by Random House, 1980. 626 p.
79-002231   786.1/092/4   0394422538
Rubinstein, Artur, -- 1887- Pianists -- Biography.

ML417.R79.A3
Rubinstein, Artur, 1887-
My young years [by] Arthur Rubinstein. New York, Knopf; [distributed by Random House] 1973. xi, 478 p.
70-171147   786.1/092/4   0394468902
Rubinstein, Artur, -- 1887- Rubinstein, Artur, -- 1887- Pianists -- Biography.

ML417.R79.S23 1995
Sachs, Harvey, 1946-
Rubinstein: a life/ Harvey Sachs; with a discography compiled and edited by Donald Manildi. New York: Grove Press, c1995. xviii, 525 p.
95-013539   786.2/092   0802115799
Rubinstein, Artur, -- 1887- Rubinstein, Artur, -- 1887- -- Discography. Pianists -- Biography.

ML417.S36.A3 1972
Schnabel, Artur, 1882-1951.
My life and music; &, Reflections on music. With a foreword by Sir Robert Mayer and an introd. by Edward Crankshaw. New York, St. Martin's Press [1972, c1961] xv, 248 p.
70-166527   786.1/092/4
Schnabel, Artur, -- 1882-1951. Schnabel, Artur, -- 1882-1951. Pianists -- Biography. Music -- Philosophy and aesthetics.

ML417.S4.R4 1985
Reich, Nancy B.
Clara Schumann, the artist and the woman/ Nancy B.
Reich. Ithaca, N.Y.: Cornell University Press, 1985.
346 p.
84-045798   786.1/042/4   0801417481
Schumann, Clara, -- 1819-1896.   Pianists -- Germany --
Biography.

ML417.T2.L47 1994
Lester, James.
Too marvelous for words: the life and genius of Art
Tatum/ James Lester. New York: Oxford University
Press, 1994. ix, 240 p.
93-004284   786.2/165/092   0195083652
Tatum, Art, -- 1910-1956.   Jazz musicians -- United States --
Biography.

ML417.W15 S5 2002
Shipton, Alyn.
Fats Waller: the cheerful little earful/ Alyn Shipton. Rev.
ed. London; Continuum, 2002. xi, 180 p.
2001-047404   786.2/165/092 21   0826457967
Waller, Fats, 1904-1943.   Jazz musicians--United States--
Biography.

ML417.W515.D34 1999
Dahl, Linda, 1949-
Morning glory: a biography of Mary Lou Williams/ Linda
Dahl. New York: Pantheon Books, c1999. viii, 463 p.
99-034970   786.2/165/092   0375408991
Williams, Mary Lou, -- 1910-   Pianists -- United States --
Biography.

ML418.B9 H38 1992
Haugen, Einar Ingvald,
Ole Bull: Norway's romantic musician and cosmopolitan
patriot/ Einar Haugen and Camilla Cai. Madison:
University of Wisconsin Press, c1993. xxx, 354 p.
91-050989   787.2/092 B 20   0299132501
Bull, Ole, 1810-1880. Violinists -- Norway -- Biography.

ML418.C4.A35
Casals, Pablo, 1876-1973.
Joys and sorrows; reflections, by Pablo Casals as told to
Albert E. Kahn. New York, Simon and Schuster [1970]
314 p.
73-101879   787/.3/0924   0671204858
Casals, Pablo, -- 1876-1973. Casals, Pablo, -- 1876-1973.
Violoncellists -- Biography.

ML418.C4.B28 1993
Baldock, Robert, 1950-
Pablo Casals/ Robert Baldock. Boston: Northeastern
University Press, 1993. 334 p.
93-010115   787.4/092   1555531768
Casals, Pablo, -- 1876-1973. Violoncellists -- Biography.

ML418.D85.W55 1999
Wilson, Elizabeth.
Jacqueline du Pre: her life, her music, her legend/
Elizabeth Wilson. New York: Arcade, 1999. xiii, 466 p.
98-049664   787.4/092   155970490X
Du Pre, Jacqueline, -- 1945-   Violoncellists -- England --
Biography.

ML418.E48.K7 1990
Kozinn, Allan.
Mischa Elman and the romantic style/ Allan Kozinn.
Chur Switzerland; Harwood Academic Publishers, c1990.
xiv, 405 p.
89-030876   787.1/092/4   3718604973
Elman, Mischa, -- 1891-1967.   Violinists -- Biography.

ML418.F81.F6 1990
Flesch, Carl F., 1910-
And do you also play the violin?/ Carl F. Flesch; with a
foreword by Sir Yehudi Menuhin. [London]: Toccata
Press, 1990. 382 p.
91-142564   787.2/092   0907689361
Flesch, Carl, -- 1873-1944.   Violinists -- Biography.

ML418.F814.H84 1998
Hughes, Angela, 1926-
Pierre Fournier: cellist in a landscape with figures/
Angela Hughes. Aldershot, Hants, England; Ashgate,
c1998. xvi, 227 p.
97-033080   787.4/092   1859284221
Fournier, Pierre, -- 1906- Violoncellists -- Biography.

ML418.K9.B53 1998
Biancolli, Amy.
Fritz Kreisler: love's sorrow, love's joy/ by Amy
Biancolli. Portland, Or.: Amadeus Press, c1998. 453 p.
98-012200   787.2/092   1574670379
Kreisler, Fritz, -- 1875-1962.   Violinists -- Biography.

ML418.M27.A3 1997
Menuhin, Yehudi, 1916-
Unfinished journey: twenty years later/ Yehudi Menuhin.
New York: Fromm International, 1997. xiv, 490 p.
97-009122   787.2/092   0880641797
Menuhin, Yehudi, -- 1916- Violinists -- Biography.

ML418.M27.B87 2001
Burton, Humphrey, 1931-
Yehudi Menuhin: a life/ Humphrey Burton. Boston,
Mass.: Northeastern University Press, 2001. xiii, 561 p.
00-056607   787.2/092   1555534651
Menuhin, Yehudi, -- 1916- Violinists -- Biography.

ML418.M27.D8 1992
Menuhin, Yehudi, 1916-
Conversations with Menuhin/ David Dubal. New York:
Harcourt Brace Jovanovich, c1992. xv, 256 p.
91-029829   787.2/0992   0151225869
Menuhin, Yehudi, -- 1916- -- Interviews.   Violinists --
Interviews.

ML418.M45.S26 2000
Santoro, Gene.
Myself when I am real: the life and music of Charles
Mingus/ Gene Santoro. New York: Oxford University
Press, 2000. x, 452 p.
99-046734   781.65/092   0195097335
Mingus, Charles, -- 1922- Jazz musicians -- United States --
Biography.

ML419.A32 S76 1996
Stock, Jonathan P. J.,
Musical creativity in twentieth-century China: Abing, his music, and its changing meanings/ by Jonathan P.J. Stock. Rochester, N.Y.: University of Rochester Press, 1996. xii, 209 p.
96-028056   781.62/951/0092 20   1878822764
A-ping, 1893-1950. Folk musicians -- China -- Biography. Folk music -- China -- History and criticism. Wuxi (Jiangsu Sheng, China) -- History.

ML419.A75.A3 1999
Armstrong, Louis, 1901-1971.
Louis Armstrong, in his own words: selected writings/ Louis Armstrong; edited and with an introduction by Thomas Brothers; annotated index by Charles Kinzer. Oxford; Oxford University Press, 1999. xxvii, 255 p.
99-017040   781.65/092   0195119584
Armstrong, Louis, -- 1901-1971.   Jazz musicians -- United States -- Biography. Jazz -- History and criticism.

ML419.A75.A7
Armstrong, Louis, 1901-1971.
Louis Armstrong--a self-portrait. The interview by Richard Meryman. New York, Eakins Press [1971] 59 p.
70-152507   788/.1/0924

ML419.A75.L68 1999
The Louis Armstrong companion: eight decades of commentary/ edited by Joshua Berrett. New York: Schirmer Books, c1999. xvi, 299 p.
98-029206   781.65/092   002864669X
Armstrong, Louis, -- 1901-1971.   Jazz musicians -- United States -- Biography. Jazz -- History and criticism.

ML419.B23.C5 1987
Chilton, John, 1932-
Sidney Bechet: the wizard of jazz/ by John Chilton. New York: Oxford University Press, 1987. 331 p.
88-117773   788/.66/0924   0195206231
Bechet, Sidney, -- 1897-1959.   Jazz musicians -- Biography.

ML419.B735.R3 1993
Radano, Ronald Michael.
New musical figurations: Anthony Braxton's cultural critique/ Ronald M. Radano. Chicago: University of Chicago Press, c1993. xv, 315 p.
93-001878   788.7/165/092   0226701956
Braxton, Anthony. Jazz -- History and criticism. Jazz musicians -- United States -- Biography.

ML419.B75.C37 2000
Catalano, Nick.
Clifford Brown: the life and art of the legendary jazz trumpeter/ Nick Catalano. Oxford; Oxford University Press, 2000. xv, 208 p.
99-027887   788.9/2165/092   0195100832
Brown, Clifford.   Jazz musicians -- United States -- Biography.

ML419.B89 A3 1998
Bushell, Garvin,
Jazz from the beginning/ by Garvin Bushell as told to Mark Tucker; introduction by Lawrence Gushee; new preface by Stanley Crouch. New York: Da Capo Press, 1998. xviii, 196 p.
98-007966   781.65/092 21   030680848X
Bushell, Garvin, 1902-   Jazz musicians--United States--Biography.

ML419.C645.C6
Cole, Bill, 1937-
John Coltrane/ by Bill Cole. New York: Schirmer Books, c1976. vi, 264 p.
76-014289   788/.66/0924   0028706609
Coltrane, John, -- 1926-1967.   Jazz musicians -- United States -- Biography.

ML419.C645 P65 1998
Porter, Lewis.
John Coltrane: his life and music/ Lewis Porter. Ann Arbor: University of Michigan Press, c1998. xvii, 409 p.
97-041995   788.7/165/092 B 21   0472101617
Coltrane, John, 1926-1967. Jazz musicians -- United States -- Biography.

ML419.D39.A3 1990
Davis, Miles.
Miles, the autobiography/ Miles Davis with Quincy Troupe. New York: Simon and Schuster, 1990. 441 p.
90-037501   788.9/2165/092   0671635042
Davis, Miles. Jazz musicians -- United States -- Biography.

ML419.D39 C35 1998
Carr, Ian.
Miles Davis: the definitive biography/ by Ian Carr. New York: Thunder's Mouth Press, c1998. xii, 658 p.
99-029423   788.9/2165/092 B 21   1560252413
Davis, Miles. Jazz musicians -- United States -- Biography.

ML419.D39.T56 2001
Tingen, Paul.
Miles beyond: the electric explorations of Miles Davis, 1967-1991/ by Paul Tingen. New York: Billboard Books, 2001. 352 p.
2001-016194   788.9/2165/092   0823083462
Davis, Miles.   Jazz musicians -- United States -- Biography.

ML419.F74.A3 1989
Freeman, Bud, 1906-
Crazeology: the autobiography of a Chicago jazzman/ Bud Freeman, as told to Robert Wolf; with a foreword by Studs Terkel. Urbana: University of Illinois Press, c1989. xii, 103 p.
89-004704   788/.42/0924   0252016343
Freeman, Bud, -- 1906-   Jazz musicians -- United States -- Biography.

ML419.G48.M34 1996
Maggin, Donald L.
Stan Getz: a life in jazz/ by Donald L. Maggin. New York: W. Morrow & Co., c1996. viii, 417 p.
95-047748   788.7/165/092   0688123155
Getz, Stan, -- 1927-   Jazz musicians -- United States -- Biography.

ML419.G54.A3
Gillespie, Dizzy, 1917-
To be, or not ... to BOP: memoirs/ Dizzy Gillespie, with Al Fraser. Garden City, N.Y.: Doubleday, 1979. xix, 552 p.
77-076237   785.420924   0385120524
Gillespie, Dizzy, -- 1917-   Jazz musicians -- United States -- Biography.

ML419.G54.M4 1988
McRae, Barry.
Dizzy Gillespie: his life & times/ Barry McRae. New York: Universe Books, 1988. 136 p.
87-035752   785.42/092/4   0876636865
Gillespie, Dizzy, -- 1917-   Jazz musicians -- United States -- Biography.

ML419.G54.S55 1999
Shipton, Alyn.
Groovin' high: the life of Dizzy Gillespie/ Alyn Shipton. New York: Oxford University Press, 1999. x, 422 p.
98-027684   788.9/2165/092   0195091329
Gillespie, Dizzy, -- 1917-   Jazz musicians -- United States -- Biography.

ML419.H26.A3 1989
Hampton, Lionel.
Hamp: an autobiography/ by Lionel Hampton with James Haskins. New York, NY: Warner Books, c1989. ix, 286 p.
89-080365   786.8/43/092   0446710059
Hampton, Lionel. Jazz musicians -- United States -- Biography.

ML419.H35.C5 1990
Chilton, John, 1932-
The song of the Hawk: the life and recordings of Coleman Hawkins/ John Chilton. Ann Arbor: University of Michigan Press, c1990. viii, 429 p.
90-047644   788.7/165/092   0472102125
Hawkins, Coleman.   Jazz musicians -- United States -- Biography.

ML419.H45 C53 1995
Clancy, William D.
Woody Herman: chronicles of the Herds/ William D. Clancy with Audree Coke Kenton; foreword by Steve Allen. New York: Schirmer Books; xiii, 430 p.
94-042276   781.65/092 B 20   0028704967
Herman, Woody, 1913-1987. Jazz musicians -- United States -- Biography.

ML419.J36.L48 1999
Levinson, Peter J.
Trumpet blues: the life of Harry James/ Peter Levinson. New York: Oxford University Press, 1999. xvii, 334 p.
99-011507   781.64/092   0195110307
James, Harry, -- 1916-   Trumpet players -- United States -- Biography. Jazz musicians -- United States -- Biography.

ML419.J62.B47 1999
Berrett, Joshua.
The musical world of J.J. Johnson/ Joshua Berrett & Louis G. Bourgois, III. Lanham, Md.: Scarecrow Press; 1999. xxiv, 440 p.
99-010077   788.9/3165/092   0810836483
Johnson, J. J., -- 1924-   Jazz musicians -- United States -- Biography.

ML419.M69.M3 1994
McCutchan, Ann.
Marcel Moyse: voice of the flute/ by Ann McCutchan; discography by Susan Nelson and William Shaman. Portland, Or.: Amadeus Press, c1994. 326 p.
93-033357   788.3/2/092   0931340683
Moyse, Marcel, -- 1889-   Flute players -- France -- Biography.

ML419.P48 A3 2000
Pepper, Art,
Straight life: the story of Art Pepper/ by Art & Laurie Pepper;   introduction by Gary Giddins; discography by Todd Selbert. Edinburgh: Mojo Books, 2000. 558 p.
2001-339011   788.7/3165/092 VB 21   1841950645
Pepper, Art,   1925- Jazz musicians -- United States -- Biography. Saxophonists -- United States -- Biography.

ML419.P82.L6 1999
Loza, Steven Joseph.
Tito Puente and the making of Latin music/ Steven Loza. Urbana: University of Illinois Press, c1999. xvi, 260 p.
98-025507   784.4/81888/092   0252023323
Puente, Tito, -- 1923-   Musicians -- Latin America -- Biography.

ML419.R52.T7 1991
Torme, Mel, 1925-
Traps, the drum wonder: the life of Buddy Rich/ Mel Torme. New York: Oxford University Press, 1991. xiii, 233 p.
90-022594   786.9/165/092   0195070380
Rich, Buddy, -- 1917- Drummers (Musicians) -- United States -- Biography.

ML419.R84 A3 1991
Ruff, Willie.
A call to assembly: the autobiography of a musical storyteller/ Willie Ruff. New York, NY: Viking, 1991. xvi, 432 p.
90-050514   788.9/4165/092 B 20   0670838004
Ruff, Willie. Jazz musicians -- United States -- Biography.

ML419.S52.S56 2000
Simosko, Vladimir.
Artie Shaw: a musical biography and discography/ Vladimir Simosko. Lanham, Md.: Scarecrow Press, 2000. xiii, 279 p.
99-024345   788.6/2165/092   0810833972
Shaw, Artie, -- 1910- Shaw, Artie, -- 1910- -- Discography. Jazz musicians -- United States -- Biography.

ML419.T68.A3 1999
Townsend, Henry.
A blues life/ Henry Townsend as told to Bill Greensmith. Urbana: University of Illinois Press, c1999.
99-006216   781.643/092   0252025261
Townsend, Henry.   Guitarists -- Missouri -- Saint Louis -- Biography. Blues musicians -- Missouri -- Saint Louis -- Biography.

ML419.Y7.B75 1990
Buchmann-Moller, Frank.
You just fight for your life: the story of Lester Young/ Frank Buchmann-Moller; foreword by Lewis Porter. New York: Praeger, 1990. xvi, 282 p.
89-003786   788/.66/0924   0275932656
Young, Lester, -- 1909-1959.   Jazz musicians -- United States -- Biography.

ML419.Y7 D36 2002
Daniels, Douglas Henry.
Lester leaps in: the life and times of Lester "Pres" Young/ Douglas Henry Daniels. Boston: Beacon Press, c2002. 524 p.
2001-037387   788.7/165/092 B 21   0807071021
Young, Lester, 1909-1959. Jazz musicians -- United States -- Biography.

ML419.Y7.L47 1991
A Lester Young reader/ edited by Lewis Porter. Washington: Smithsonian Institution Press, c1991. xiii, 323 p.
90-024922   788.7/165/092   1560980648
Young, Lester, -- 1909-1959.

ML420.A6 A3 2002
Anderson, Marian,
My Lord, what a morning: an autobiography/ Marian Anderson;   foreword by James Anderson DePreist. Urbana: University of Illinois Press, c2002. xv, 319 p.
2001-040980   782.1/092 B 21   0252070534
Anderson, Marian,   1897-1993. Contraltos -- United States -- Biography.

ML420.A77.S77 1997
Streissguth, Michael.
Eddy Arnold, pioneer of the Nashville sound/ Michael Streissguth. New York: Schirmer Books; c1997. xi, 290 p.
97-003009   002864719X
Arnold, Eddy.   Country musicians -- United States -- Biography.

ML420.B365.A3 1987
Berry, Chuck.
Chuck Berry: the autobiography. New York: Harmony Books, 1987. xxii, 346 p.
87-011825   784.5/4/00924   0517566664
Berry, Chuck. Rock musicians -- United States -- Biography.

ML420.B365.D5 1985
DeWitt, Howard A.
Chuck Berry, rock 'n' roll music/ by Howard A. DeWitt; with research assistance and a discography by Morten Reff. Ann Arbor, MI: Pierian Press, 1985. xvi, 291 p.
84-061230   784.5/4/00924   0876501714
Berry, Chuck. Rock musicians -- United States -- Biography.

ML420.B6 B48 1996
Björling, Anna-Lisa.
Jussi/ by Anna-Lisa Björling and Andrew Farkas; chronology by   Harald Henrysson. Portland, Or.: Amadeus Press, c1996. 456 p.
95-050104   782.1/092 B 20   1574670107
Björling, Jussi, 1911-1960. Tenors (Singers) -- Biography.

ML420.B78.A3 1964
Broonzy, Big Bill, 1893-1958.
Big Bill blues, William Broonzy's story as told to Yannick Bruynoghe. With 9 pages of half-tone illus. and 4 drawings by Paul Oliver. Foreword by Charles Edward Smith. New York, Oak Publications [1964, c1955] 176 p.
64-008787   927.8
Musicians -- Correspondence.

ML420.B899.A3 2000
Butler, Jerry.
Only the strong survive: memoirs of a soul survivor/ Jerry Butler, with Earl Smith. Bloomington: Indiana University Press, c2000. xvii, 266 p.
00-032002   782.421643//092   0253337968
Butler, Jerry. Soul musicians -- United States -- Biography.

ML420.C18.K513 1993
Kesting, Jurgen.
Maria Callas/ Jurgen Kesting; translated by John Hunt. Boston: Northeastern University Press, 1993. xvi, 416 p.
93-001757   782.1/092   1555531792
Callas, Maria, -- 1923-1977. Sopranos (Singers) -- Biography.

ML420.C18.S35 1992
Scott, Michael.
Maria Meneghini Callas/ Michael Scott. Boston: Northeastern University Press, 1992. 312 p.
92-017103   782.1/092   1555531466
Callas, Maria, -- 1923-1977. Sopranos (Singers) -- Biography.

ML420.C259.C3 1990
Caruso, Enrico, 1904-1987.
Enrico Caruso: my father and my family/ by Enrico Caruso, Jr. & Andrew Farkas; chronologies by Thomas G. Kaufman; discographies by William R. Moran and Richard Koprowski; bibliography by Opritsa Popa. Portland, Or.: Amadeus Press, c1990. 724 p.
89-017917   782.1/092   0931340241
Caruso, Enrico, -- 1873-1921. Tenors (Singers) -- Biography.

ML420.C259.S3 1988
Scott, Michael.
The great Caruso/ by Michael Scott. New York: Knopf: 1988. xix, 322 p.
87-046107   782.1/092/4   0394536819
Caruso, Enrico, -- 1873-1921. Tenors (Singers) -- Biography.

ML420.C46 A3 1992
Charles, Ray,
Brother Ray: Ray Charles' own story/ Ray Charles and David Ritz. 1st Da Capo Press ed. New York: Da Capo Press, 1992. xii, 348 p.
92-017010   782.42164/092 B 20   0306804824
Charles, Ray, 1930- Singers -- United States -- Biography.

ML420.C63.E67 1999
Epstein, Daniel Mark.
Nat King Cole/ Daniel Mark Epstein. New York: Farrar, Straus & Giroux, 1999. viii, 437 p.
99-032940   782.42164/092   0374219125
Cole, Nat King, -- 1917-1965. Singers -- United States -- Biography.

ML420.C63 G7 1991
Gourse, Leslie.
Unforgettable: the life and mystique of Nat King Cole/ Leslie Gourse. 1st ed. New York: St. Martin's Press, 1991. xxi, 309 p.
90-027409   782.42164/092 B 20   0312059825
Cole, Nat King, 1917-1965. Singers -- United States -- Biography.

ML420.C93.G53 2001
Giddins, Gary.
Bing Crosby: a pocketful of dreams/ Gary Giddins. Boston, Mass.: Little, Brown, [c2001-] v. 1
00-044403   782.42164/092   0316881880
Crosby, Bing, -- 1904-1977. Singers -- United States -- Biography.

ML420.D98.M16 1997
Marcus, Greil.
Invisible republic: Bob Dylan's Basement tapes/ Greil Marcus. New York: H. Holt & Co., c1997. xvi, 286 p.
96-050893   782.42164/092   0805033939
Dylan, Bob, -- 1941- -- Basement tapes. Popular music -- United States -- 1961-1970.

ML420.D98.M25 1993
McKeen, William, 1954-
Bob Dylan: a bio-bibliography/ William McKeen. Westport, Conn.: Greenwood Press, 1993. xii, 307 p.
92-032212   782.42162/0092   0313279985
Dylan, Bob, -- 1941- Dylan, Bob, -- 1941- -- Bibliography. Rock musicians -- United States -- Biography.

ML420.D98.S6 1989
Spitz, Bob.
Dylan: a biography/ Bob Spitz. New York: McGraw-Hill, c1989. xv, 639 p.
88-012912   784/.092/4   0070603308
Dylan, Bob, -- 1941- Singers -- United States -- Biography.

ML420.E28.A3 1997
Edwards, Honeyboy.
The world don't owe me nothing: the life and times of Delta bluesman Honeyboy Edwards/ David Honeyboy Edwards; as told to Janis Martinson and Michael Robert Frank. Chicago: Chicago Review Press, c1997. xv, 287 p.
97-002599   781.643/092   1556522754
Edwards, Honeyboy. Blues musicians -- United States -- Biography.

ML420.F27 A2 1970b
Farrar, Geraldine,
The autobiography of Geraldine Farrar: Such sweet compulsion. New York, Da Capo Press, 1970 [c1938] xii, 303 p.
70-100656   782.1/0924 B   0306718634
Farrar, Geraldine, 1882-1967. Sopranos (Singers) -- United States -- Biography.

ML420.F275.A3 1999
Farrell, Eileen.
Can't help singing: the life of Eileen Farrell/ Eileen Farrell and Brian Kellow. Boston: Northeastern University Press, c1999. xii, 255 p.
99-034401   782/.0092   1555534066
Farrell, Eileen. Sopranos (Singers) -- United States -- Biography.

ML420.F51.A3 1989
Fischer-Dieskau, Dietrich, 1925-
Reverberations: the memoirs of Dietrich Fischer-Dieskau/ translated by Ruth Hein. New York: Fromm International Pub. Corp., c1989. 376 p.
89-030749   782.1/092/4   0880641371
Fischer-Dieskau, Dietrich, -- 1925- Singers -- Germany (West) -- Biography.

ML420.G23.R33 2000
Radomski, James.
Manuel Garcia: 1775-1832: chronicle of the life of a bel canto tenor at the dawn of romanticism/ James Radomski. Oxford; Oxford University Press, 2000. xiv, 367 p.
99-048687   782.1/092   0198163738
Garcia, Manuel, -- 1775-1832. Tenors (Singers) -- Biography. Composers -- Biography.

ML420.G25.T87 1997
Turnbull, Michael, 1941-
Mary Garden/ Michael T.R.B. Turnbull. Portland, Ore.: Amadeus Press, 1997. xii, 234 p.
96-021686   782.1/092   1574670174
Garden, Mary, -- 1874-1967. Singers -- Biography.

ML420.G253.C58 2000
Clarke, Gerald, 1937-
Get happy: the life of Judy Garland/ Gerald Clarke. New York: Random House, 2000. 510 p.
99-036285   782.42164/092   0375503781
Garland, Judy. Singers -- United States -- Biography.

ML420.H452.A3
Hines, Jerome, 1921-
This is my story, this is my song. Westwood, N.J., F. H. Revell Co. [1968] 160 p.
68-019054   782.1/0924
Hines, Jerome, -- 1921- Basses (Singers) -- United States -- Biography.

ML420.H58.A3 1984
Holiday, Billie, 1915-1959.
Lady sings the blues/ Billie Holiday with William Dufty; with a new discography by Vincent Pelote. Harmondsworth, Middlesex, England; Penguin Books, 1984. 199 p.
83-022014   784.5/3/00924   0140067620
Holiday, Billie, -- 1915-1959 Holiday, Billie, -- 1915-1959 -- Discography. Singers -- United States -- Biography.

ML420.H58.N53 1995
Nicholson, Stuart.
Billie Holiday/ Stuart Nicholson. Boston: Northeastern University Press, 1995. 311 p.
95-016155   782.42165/092   1555532489
Holiday, Billie, -- 1915-1959.   Singers -- United States -- Biography.

ML420.H65 A3 1986
Horne, Lena.
Lena/ by Lena Horne and Richard Schickel. 1st Limelight ed. New York: Limelight Editions: 1986, 300 p.
86-005035   784.5/0092/4 B 19   0879100664
Horne, Lena. Singers -- United States -- Biography.

ML420.J17.S4 1992
Schwerin, Jules Victor.
Got to tell it: Mahalia Jackson, Queen of Gospel/ Jules Schwerin. New York: Oxford University Press, 1992. 204 p.
91-043947   782.25   0195071441
Jackson, Mahalia, -- 1911-1972.   Gospel musicians -- United States -- Biography.

ML420.J74.G6 1988
Goldman, Herbert G.
Jolson: the legend comes to life/ Herbert G. Goldman. New York: Oxford University Press, 1988. xii, 411 p.
88-004222   782.81/092/4   0195055055
Jolson, Al, -- d. 1950. Singers -- United States -- Biography.

ML420.J75.A3 1983
Jones, Bessie, 1902-
For the ancestors: autobiographical memories/ Bessie Jones; collected and edited by John Stewart. Urbana: University of Illinois Press, c1983. xxv, 203 p.
82-008593   783.6/7/0924   0252009592
Jones, Bessie, -- 1902- Singers -- United States -- Biography.

ML420.J77.E25 1999
Echols, Alice.
Scars of sweet paradise: the life and times of Janis Joplin/ Alice Echols. New York: Metropolitan Books, 1999. xxii, 408 p.
98-042562   782.42166/092   0805053875
Joplin, Janis.   Singers -- United States -- Biography. Rock musicians -- United States -- Biography.

ML420.J777.C55 1994
Chilton, John, 1932-
Let the good times roll: the story of Louis Jordan and his music/ John Chilton. Ann Arbor: University of Michigan Press, 1994, c1992. 286 p.
94-197772   781.643/092   0472105299
Jordan, Louis, -- 1908-1975.   Jazz musicians -- United States -- Biography. Afro-American musicians -- Biography.

ML420.K473.D36 1998
Danchin, Sebastian.
Blues Boy: the life and music of B.B. King/ Sebastian Danchin. Jackson: University Press of Mississippi, c1998. xii, 156 p.
97-009716   781.643/092   1578060176
King, B. B. Blues musicians -- United States -- Biography.

ML420.K5.A32
Kitt, Eartha.
Alone with me: a new autobiography/ by Eartha Kitt. Chicago: H. Regnery Co., c1976. xii, 276 p.
75-013229   784/.092/4   0809283514
Kitt, Eartha.   Musicians -- Illinois -- Biography.

ML420.L277.W6 1992
Wolfe, Charles K.
The life and legend of Leadbelly/ Charles Wolfe and Kip Lornell. New York, NY: HarperCollins Publishers, c1992. xv, 333 p.
92-052606   782.42162/0092   0060168625
Leadbelly, -- 1885-1949.   Blues musicians -- United States -- Biography.

ML420.L33.G6 1988
Glass, Beaumont, 1925-
Lotte Lehmann, a life in opera & song/ Beaumont Glass. Santa Barbara: Capra Press, 1988. xviii, 330 p.
87-032574   782.1/092/4   0884962776
Lehmann, Lotte. Singers -- Biography.

ML420.L38.E45 1999
Elliott, Anthony.
The mourning of John Lennon/ Anthony Elliott. Berkeley: University of California Press, c1999. xi, 219 p.
98-003637   782.42166/092   0520215486
Lennon, John, -- 1940-1980. Popular culture. Fame.

ML420.L38.R6 1991
Robertson, John.
The art & music of John Lennon/ by John Robertson. New York: Carol Pub. Group, 1991. xiv, 218 p.
90-028953   782.42166/092   155972076X
Lennon, John, -- 1940-1980. Rock musicians -- Biography. Artists -- Biography.

ML420.L38.W52 1999
Wiener, Jon.
Gimme some truth: the John Lennon FBI files/ Jon Wiener. Berkeley [Calif.]: University of California Press, c1999. 344 p.
99-015216   782.42166/092   0520216466
Lennon, John, -- 1940-1980 -- Archives.   Singers -- United States -- Archives.

ML420.L67.A3 1993
Lipscomb, Mance, 1895-1976.
I say me for a parable: the oral autobiography of Mance Lipscomb, Texas songster/ compiled and edited by Glen Alyn. New York: W.W. Norton, c1993. 508 p.
92-046560   782.42/1643/092   039303500X
Lipscomb, Mance, -- 1895-1976.   Blues musicians -- Texas -- Biography.

ML420.L7.S5
Shultz, Gladys Denny.
Jenny Lind: the Swedish nightingale.   Philadelphia, Lippincott [1962] 345 p.
62-010537   927.8
Lind, Jenny, -- 1820-1887.   Musicians.

ML420.L947.A3
Lynn, Loretta.
Loretta Lynn: Coal miner's daughter/ Loretta Lynn, with George Vecsey. Chicago: Regnery, c1976. xiv, 204 p.
75-032976   784/.092/4   0809281228
Lynn, Loretta.   Country musicians -- Biography.

ML420.M13863.R36 1997
Whiteside, Jonny.
Ramblin' Rose: the life and career of Rose Maddox/ Jonny Whiteside; with a previously unpublished foreword by Woody Guthrie. Nashville, TN: Country Music Foundation Press: c1997. xxi, 229 p.
96-034377   782.42/1642/092   0826512690
Maddox, Rose.   Country musicians -- Biography.

ML420.M2 F6 1987
Fitzlyon, April.
Maria Malibran: diva of the romantic age/ by April Fitzlyon. London: Souvenir Press, 1987. 330 p.
88-215834   782.1/092 B 20   0285650300
Malibran, Maria, 1808-1836. Mezzo-sopranos -- Biography.

ML420.M332.A3
Martin, Mary, 1913-
My heart belongs/ by Mary Martin. New York: Morrow, 1976. 320 p.
75-031857   782.81/092/4   0688030092
Martin, Mary, -- 1913- Singers -- United States -- Biography.

ML420.M35.M41
Melba, Nellie, 1861-1931
Melodies and memories, by Nellie Melba ... New York, George H. Doran company [c1926] 339 p.
26-008666
  Musicians -- Correspondence, reminiscences, etc.

ML420.M352.E4 1990
Emmons, Shirlee.
Tristanissimo: the authorized biography of heroic tenor Lauritz Melchior/ Shirlee Emmons; foreword by Birgit Nilsson. New York: Schirmer Books; c1990. xvi, 462 p.
89-010938   782.1/092   0028730607
Melchior, Lauritz.   Tenors (Singers) -- Biography.

ML420.M388.H4 1987
Haskins, James, 1941-
Mabel Mercer: a life/ by James Haskins. New York: Atheneum, 1987. xvii, 217 p.
87-027027   784.5   0689115954
Mercer, Mabel, -- 1900-1984.   Singers -- United States -- Biography.

ML420.M39.A32
Merman, Ethel.
Merman/ by Ethel Merman with George Eells. New York: Simon and Schuster, c1978. 320 p.
78-000092   782.8/1/0924   0671227122
Merman, Ethel.   Singers -- United States -- Biography.

ML420.M42.A3
Merrill, Robert, 1917-
Between acts, an irreverent look at opera and other madness/ by Robert Merrill, with Robert Saffron. New York: McGraw-Hill, c1976. 240 p.
76-020467   784/.092/4   0070415013
Merrill, Robert, -- 1919-   Musicians -- Correspondence, reminiscences, etc.

ML420.M5595.B55 2000
The Bill Monroe reader/ edited by Tom Ewing. Urbana: University of Illinois Press, c2000. 301 p.
00-008015   781.642/092   0252025008
Monroe, Bill, -- 1911- -- Criticism and interpretation. Bluegrass music -- History and criticism.

ML420.M5595.S65 2000
Smith, Richard D., 1949-
Can't you hear me callin': the life of Bill Monroe, father of bluegrass/ Richard D. Smith. Boston: Little, Brown and Co., c2000. xviii, 365 p.
99-054372   781.642/092   0316803812
Monroe, Bill, -- 1911- Bluegrass musicians -- United States -- Biography.

ML420.O29.S43 1996
Schumacher, Michael.
There but for fortune: the life of Phil Ochs/ Michael Schumacher. New York: Hyperion, 1996. xii, 386 p.
96-006340   782.42162/13/0092   0786860847
Ochs, Phil.   Singers -- United States -- Biography.

ML420.P32.C66 1993
Cone, John Frederick.
Adelina Patti: queen of hearts/ by John Frederick Cone; chronology by Thomas G. Kaufman; discography by William R. Moran. Portland, Or.: Amadeus Press, c1993. xxi, 400 p.
92-039331   782.1/092   0931340608
Patti, Adelina, -- 1843-1919.   Singers -- Biography.

ML420.P52.A3 1990
Piaf, Edith, 1915-1963.
My life/ Edith Piaf with Jean Noli; translated from the French and edited by Margaret Crosland. London; Peter Owen, 1990. 120 p.
90-229787   782.42164/092   0720607973
Piaf, Edith, -- 1915-1963.   Singers -- France -- Biography.

ML420.P96.D49 1993
DeWitt, Howard A.
Elvis, the Sun years: the story of Elvis Presley in the
fifties/ by Howard A. Dewitt. Ann Arbor, MI: Popular
Culture, Ink, 1993. xi, 362 p.
91-061883   782.42164/092   1560750200
*Presley, Elvis, -- 1935-1977.   Rock music -- To 1961 -- History
and criticism. Rock musicians -- United States -- Biography.*

ML420.P96.G66
Goldman, Albert Harry, 1927-
Elvis/ by Albert Goldman. New York: McGraw-Hill,
c1981. x, 598 p.
81-008130   784.5/4/00924   0070236577
*Presley, Elvis, -- 1935-1977.   Rock musicians -- United States --
Biography.*

ML420.P96.G87 1994
Guralnick, Peter.
Last train to Memphis: the rise of Elvis Presley/ Peter
Guralnick. Boston: Little, Brown, and Co., c1994. xiv,
560 p.
94-010763   782.42166/092   0316332208
*Presley, Elvis, -- 1935-1977 -- Childhood and youth.   Rock
musicians -- United States -- Biography.*

ML420.R274.L5
Lieb, Sandra R.
Mother of the blues: a study of Ma Rainey/ Sandra R.
Lieb. [Amherst]: University of Massachusetts Press,
1981. xvii, 226 p.
81-001168   784.5/3/00924   0870233343
*Rainey, Ma, -- 1886-1939.   Afro-American singers --
Biography.*

ML420.S388.P8 1993
Puritz, Gerd.
Elisabeth Schumann: a biography/ by Gerd Puritz; edited
and translated by Joy Puritz. London: A. Deutsch, 1993.
375 p.
93-190299   782.1/092   0233987940
Schumann, Elisabeth.   Sopranos (Singers) -- Biography.

ML420.S445.D8
Dunaway, David King.
How can I keep from singing: Pete Seeger/ David King
Dunaway. New York: McGraw-Hill Book Co., c1981.
386 p.
80-029374   784.7/92/4   0070181500
*Seeger, Pete, -- 1919-   Folk singers -- United States --
Biography.*

ML420.S565.F73 1998
Frank Sinatra and popular culture: essays on an American
icon/ edited by Leonard Mustazza. Westport, Conn.:
Praeger, 1998. xv, 311 p.
98-023933   782.42164/092   0275964957
*Sinatra, Frank, -- 1915- -- Criticism and interpretation.
Popular music -- United States -- History and criticism. Popular
culture.*

ML420.S565 F78 1995
Friedwald, Will,
Sinatra! the song is you: a singer's art/ Will Friedwald.
New York: Scribner, c1995. 557 p.
95-011317   782.42164/092 20   068419368X
Sinatra, Frank, 1915- Singers--United States--Biography.

ML420.S565.M9 1998
Mustazza, Leonard, 1952-
Ol' Blue Eyes: a Frank Sinatra encyclopedia/ Leonard
Mustazza. Westport, Conn.: Greenwood Press, 1998. xii,
436 p.
97-033017   782.42164/092   0313304866
Sinatra, Frank, -- 1915- -- Encyclopedias.

ML420.S565 R6 1984
Rockwell, John,
Sinatra: an American classic/ John Rockwell. 1st ed. New
York: Random House, c1984. 251 p.
84-042738   784.5/0092/4 B 19   039453977X
Sinatra, Frank, 1915- Singers -- United States -- Biography.

ML420.S8115.W74 1993
Wright, John, 1941-
Traveling the high way home: Ralph Stanley and the
world of traditional bluegrass music/ John Wright.
Urbana: University of Illinois Press, c1993. xiv, 273 p.
92-043830   781.642/092   0252020243
*Stanley, Ralph.   Bluegrass musicians -- United States.
Bluegrass music -- History and criticism.*

ML420.S96.A3 1997
Sutherland, Joan, 1926-
A prima donna's progress: the autobiography of Joan
Sutherland. Washington, D.C.: Regnery Pub., 1997. x,
486 p.
97-041866   782.1/092   0895263742
Sutherland, Joan, -- 1926- Sopranos (Singers) -- Biography.

ML420.T52.L4 1989
Lawrence Tibbett, singing actor/ edited by Andrew
Farkas; with an introduction and discography by William
R. Moran. Portland, Or.: Amadeus Press, c1989. 160 p.
88-026272   782.1/092/4   0931340179
*Tibbett, Lawrence, -- 1896-1960.   Singers -- United States --
Biography.*

ML420.T87.P84 1996
Pugh, Ronnie.
Ernest Tubb: the Texas troubadour/ Ronnie Pugh.
Durham: Duke University Press, 1996. xii, 456 p.
96-007918   782.42/1642/092   0822318598
*Tubb, Ernest, -- 1914-   Country musicians -- United States --
Biography.*

ML420.V367.W55 1999
Williams, Jeannie, 1942-
Jon Vickers: a hero's life/ Jeannie Williams; foreword by
Birgit Nilsson. Boston: Northeastern University Press,
c1999. xvi, 391 p.
99-036261   782.1/092   1555534082
Vickers, Jon.   Tenors (Singers) -- Canada -- Biography.

ML420.W24 A3 1992
Waters, Ethel,
His eye is on the sparrow: an autobiography/ by Ethel Waters with Charles Samuels; new preface by Donald Bogle. 1st Da Capo Press ed. New York: Da Capo Press, 1992. xv, 278 p.
91-045598   782.42164/092 B 20   0306804778
Waters, Ethel, 1896-1977. Singers -- United States -- Biography.

ML420.W55 W5 1981
Williams, Roger M.,
Sing a sad song: the life of Hank Williams/ Roger M. Williams. 2d ed./ with a discography by Bob Pinson. Urbana: University of Illinois Press, c1981. ix, 318 p.
80-015520   784.5/2/00924 B   0252008618
Williams, Hank, 1923-1953. Country musicians -- United States -- Biography.

ML421.B4.B436 2000
The Beatles, popular music, and society: a thousand voices/ edited by Ian Inglis. New York: St. Martin's Press, 1999. xxii, 211 p.
98-053894   782.42166/092/2   0312222351
Rock musicians -- England -- Biography. Rock music -- 1961-1970 -- Analysis, appreciation. Music -- Social aspects.

ML421.B4.M66 1997
Moore, Allan F.
The Beatles, Sgt. Pepper's Lonely Hearts Club Band/ Allan F. Moore. Cambridge; Cambridge University Press, 1997. xi, 98 p.
96-006714   782.42166/092/2   0521573815
Rock music -- England -- History and criticism.

ML421.C28.C6 1994
Coleman, Ray.
The Carpenters: the untold story: an authorized biography/ Ray Coleman. New York: HarperCollins, c1994. xiii, 359 p.
93-041139   782.42164/092/2   0060183454
Singers -- United States -- Biography.

ML421.J77.W37 2000
Ward, Andrew, 1946-
Dark midnight when I rise: the story of the Jubilee Singers, who introduced the world to the music of Black America/ Andrew Ward. New York: Farrar, Straus, and Giroux, 2000. xv, 493 p.
99-086036   782.42162/96073/00922   0374187711
Afro-American musicians -- Biography.

ML421.S8 T7 1993
Tribe, Ivan M.
The Stonemans: an Appalachian family and the music that shaped their lives/ Ivan M. Tribe. Urbana: University of Illinois Press, c1993. xxi, 361 p.
92-022232   781.642/092/2 B 20   0252019784
Stoneman, Ernest V. Country musicians -- United States -- Biography.

ML422.B33 A2 1976
Beecham, Thomas,
A mingled chime: an autobiography/ by Sir Thomas Beecham, bart. Westport, Conn.: Greenwood Press, 1976, c1943. viii, 330 p.
76-040238   785/.092/4 B   0837192749
Beecham, Thomas, Sir, 1879-1961. Conductors (Music) -- England -- Biography.

ML422.B79.K4 1987
Kennedy, Michael, 1926-
Adrian Boult/ by Michael Kennedy. London: H. Hamilton, 1987. x, 342 p.
87-175183   785/.092/4   0241120713
Boult, Adrian, -- Sir, -- 1889- Conductors (Music) -- England -- Biography.

ML422.E87.B2 1995
Badger, Reid.
A life in ragtime: a biography of James Reese Europe/ Reid Badger. New York: Oxford University Press, 1995. x, 328 p.
93-042407   781.65/092   019506044X
Europe, James Reese, -- 1881-1919. Jazz musicians -- United States -- Biography. Bandmasters -- United States -- Biography. Ragtime music -- History and criticism.

ML422.F92.A85 1994
Ardoin, John.
The Furtwangler record/ by John Ardoin; discography by John Hunt. Portland, Or.: Amadeus Press, c1994. 376 p.
93-032503   784.2/092   0931340691
Furtwangler, Wilhelm, -- 1886-1954. Furtwangler, Wilhelm, -- 1886-1954 -- Discography. Conductors (Music) -- Germany -- Biography.

ML422.F92.P7513 1994
Prieberg, Fred K.
Trial of strength: Wilhelm Furtwangler in the Third Reich/ Fred K. Prieberg; translated by Christopher Dolan. Boston: Northeastern University Press, 1994. ix, 394 p.
94-006520   784.2/092   1555531962
Furtwangler, Wilhelm, -- 1886-1954. Conductors (Music) -- Germany -- Biography. National socialism and music.

ML422.G65.C6 1989
Collier, James Lincoln, 1928-
Benny Goodman and the Swing Era/ James Lincoln Collier. New York: Oxford University Press, 1989. xii, 404 p.
89-016030   781.65/092   0195052781
Goodman, Benny, -- 1909- Jazz musicians -- United States -- Biography. Jazz -- History and criticism.

ML422.G65.F6 1992
Firestone, Ross.
Swing, swing, swing: the life & times of Benny Goodman/ Ross Firestone. New York: Norton, c1993. 522 p.
92-009485   781.65/092   0393033716
Goodman, Benny, -- 1909- Clarinetists -- United States -- Biography. Jazz musicians -- United States -- Biography.

ML422.K22.O83 2000
Osborne, Richard, 1943-
Herbert von Karajan: a life in music/ Richard Osborne.
Boston: Northeastern University Press, 2000. x, 851 p.
99-059108   784.2/092   1555534252
Karajan, Herbert von.   Conductors (Music) -- Biography.

ML422.K67 H53 1996
Heyworth, Peter,
Otto Klemperer, his life and times/ Peter Heyworth.
Cambridge [England]; Cambridge University Press, 1996.
2 v.
97-111686   784.2/092 B 21   0521244889
Klemperer, Otto, 1885-1973. Conductors (Music) -- Germany --
Biography.

ML422.L38.A3
Leinsdorf, Erich, 1912-
Cadenza: a musical career/ Erich Leinsdorf. Boston:
Houghton Mifflin, 1976. x, 321 p.
76-003553   785/.092/4   0395244013
Leinsdorf, Erich, -- 1912- Conductors (Music) -- Biography.

ML422.M125 S3 1994
Schabas, Ezra,
Sir Ernest MacMillan: the importance of being Canadian/
Ezra Schabas. Toronto; University of Toronto Press,
c1994. xv, 374 p.
95-103515   780/.92 B 20   0802028497
MacMillan, Ernest, Sir, 1893-1973. MacMillan, Ernest, Sir,
1893-1973. Music -- Canada -- 20th century -- History and
criticism. Conductors (Music) -- Canada -- Biography.
Musicians -- Canada -- Biography. Composers -- Canada --
Biography. Musique -- Canada -- 20e siècle -- Histoire et
critique. Chefs d'orchestre -- Canada -- Biographies. Musiciens
-- Canada -- Biographies.

ML422.M59.T76 1995
Trotter, William R., 1943-
Priest of music: the life of Dimitri Mitropoulos/ by
William R. Trotter. Portland, Or.: Amadeus Press, 1995.
495 p.
94-023928   780/.92   0931340810
Mitropoulos, Dimitri, -- 1896-1960.   Conductors (Music) --
Biography.

ML422.M9 A32 1978
Munch, Charles,
I am a conductor/ Charles Munch; translated by Leonard
Burkat. Westport, Conn.: Greenwood Press, 1978, c1955.
xxxiii, 104 p.
78-003638   785/.092/4 B   0313203725
Munch, Charles, 1891-1968. Conducting.

ML422.R38 H37 1994
Hart, Philip,
Fritz Reiner: a biography/ Philip Hart. Evanston, Ill.:
Northwestern University Press, c1994. xii, 330 p.
94-017316   784.2/092 B 20   081011125X
Reiner, Fritz, 1888-1963. Conductors (Music) -- United States -
- Biography.

ML422.S76 D3 1982
Daniel, Oliver.
Stokowski: a counterpoint of view/ by Oliver Daniel.
New York: Dodd, Mead & Co., c1982. xxviii, 1090 p.
82-002443   785/.092/4 B 19   0396079369
Stokowski, Leopold, 1882-1977. Conductors (Music) -- United
States -- Biography.

ML422.T46.S3 1989
Schabas, Ezra, 1924-
Theodore Thomas: America's conductor and builder of
orchestras, 1835-1905/ Ezra Schabas; with a foreword by
Valerie Solti. Urbana: University of Illinois Press, c1989.
xvi, 308 p.
88-038072   785/.092/4   0252016106
Thomas, Theodore, -- 1835-1905.   Conductors (Music) --
United States.

ML422.T67.S338 1991
Sachs, Harvey, 1946-
Reflections on Toscanini/ Harvey Sachs. New York:
Grove Weidenfeld, 1991. xiii, 191 p.
91-013121   784.2/092   0802114253
Toscanini, Arturo, -- 1867-1957.   Conductors (Music) --
Biography.

ML422.T67 S34 1981
Sachs, Harvey,
Toscanini/ Harvey Sachs. New York: Da Capo Press,
[1981] c1978. 380 p.
80-029199   785/.092/4 B 19   030680137X
Toscanini, Arturo, 1867-1957. Conductors (Music) --
Biography.

ML422.W27.A312
Walter, Bruno, 1876-1962.
Of music and music-making. Translated by Paul
Hamburger. New York, W. W. Norton [1961] 222 p.
61-005616   927.8
Walter, Bruno, -- 1876-1962.   Conductors (Music) --
Biography. Music.

ML422.W27.A32
Walter, Bruno, 1876-1962.
Theme and variations: an autobiography/ by Bruno
Walter; translated from the German by James A. Galston.
New York: A.A. Knopf, 1946. xi, 344 p.
46-005672   927.8
Walter, Bruno, -- 1876-1962.   Conductors (Music) --
Biography. Musicians -- Correspondence, reminiscences, etc.

ML422.W27 R93 2001
Ryding, Erik S.,
Bruno Walter: a world elsewhere/ Erik Ryding and
Rebecca Pechefsky. New Haven [CT]: Yale University
Press, c2001. xvii, 487 p.
00-043842   784.2/092 B 21   0300087136
Walter, Bruno, 1876-1962. Conductors (Music) -- Biography.

ML422.W63.A3 1975
Willson, Meredith, 1902-
And there I stood with my piccolo/ Meredith Willson. Westport, Conn.: Greenwood Press, 1975, c1948. 255 p.
75-026870   780/.92/4   083718486X
Willson, Meredith, -- 1902- Musicians -- Correspondence, reminiscences, etc.

ML423.B52.K4
Kendall, Alan, 1939-
The tender tyrant, Nadia Boulanger: a life devoted to music: a biography/ by Alan Kendall; introduction by Yehudi Menuhin. London: Macdonald and Jane's, 1976. xvi, 144 p.
76-382568   780/.92/4   0356084035
Boulanger, Nadia. Music teachers -- Biography.

ML423.B9.A3 1988
Burney, Charles, 1726-1814.
Memoirs of Dr. Charles Burney, 1726-1769/ edited from autograph fragments by Slava Klima, Garry Bowers, and Kerry S. Grant. Lincoln: University of Nebraska Press, c1988. xxxix, 233 p.
87-006060   780/.92/4   080321197X
Burney, Charles, -- 1726-1814. Musicologists -- England -- Biography.

ML423.D15 A3 2000
Da Ponte, Lorenzo,
Memoirs/ Lorenzo Da Ponte; translated by Elisabeth Abbott; edited, annotated, and with an introduction by Arthur Livingston; preface by Charles Rosen. New York: New York Review Books, 2000. xxxii, 472 p.
99-046014   782.1/092 B 21   0940322358
Da Ponte, Lorenzo, 1749-1838. Librettists -- Biography.

ML423.G334.F87 1996
Furia, Philip, 1943-
Ira Gershwin: the art of the lyricist/ Philip Furia. New York: Oxford University Press, 1996. vii, 278 p.
94-045715   782.1/4/092   0195082990
Gershwin, Ira, -- 1896- Lyricists -- United States -- Biography.

ML423.H24.F7
Fordin, Hugh, 1935-
Getting to know him: a biography of Oscar Hammerstein II/ Hugh Fordin. New York: Random House, c1977. xiv, 383 p.
77-006021   782.8/1/0924   0394494415
Hammerstein, Oscar, -- 1895-1960. Librettists -- United States -- Biography.

ML423.H32.N6 1994
Nolan, Frederick W., 1931-
Lorenz Hart: a poet on Broadway/ Frederick Nolan. New York: Oxford University Press, 1994. x, 390 p.
92-041968   782.1/4/092   0195068378
Hart, Lorenz, -- 1895-1943. Lyricists -- United States -- Biography.

ML423.L3.A3 1978b
Lerner, Alan Jay, 1918-
The street where I live/ Alan Jay Lerner. New York: W. W. Norton, c1978. 333 p.
78-018381   782.8/1/0924   039307532X
Lerner, Alan Jay, -- 1918- Musicals -- Anecdotes.

ML423.L3 J3 1996
Jablonski, Edward.
Alan Jay Lerner: a biography/ Edward Jablonski. 1st ed. New York: H. Holt and Co., 1996. xvii, 345 p.
95-037656   782.1/4/092 B 20   0805040765
Lerner, Alan Jay, 1918- Librettists -- United States -- Biography. Lyricists -- United States -- Biography.

ML423.L635.P67 1996
Porterfield, Nolan.
Last cavalier: the life and times of John A. Lomax, 1867-1948/ Nolan Porterfield. Urbana: University of Illinois Press, c1996. 580 p.
95-050212   781.62/13/0092   0252022165
Lomax, John Avery, -- 1867-1948. Ethnomusicologists -- United States -- Biography.

ML423.S346.H613 1990
Honolka, Kurt, 1913-
Papageno: Emanuel Schikaneder, man of the theater in Mozart's time/ Kurt Honolka; translated by Jane Mary Wilde; Reinhard G. Pauly, general editor. Portland, Or.: Amadeus Press, c1990. 236 p.
89-017574   782.1/092   0931340217
Schikaneder, Emanuel, -- 1751-1812. Librettists -- Austria -- Biography. Dramatists, Austrian -- Biography.

ML423.S498.P5 1992
Pescatello, Ann M.
Charles Seeger: a life in American music/ Ann M. Pescatello. Pittsburgh: University of Pittsburgh Press, c1992. xii, 346 p.
92-004679   780/.92   0822937131
Seeger, Charles, -- 1886-1979. Musicians -- United States -- Biography.

ML423.S74 A3 1977
Spaeth, Sigmund Gottfried,
Fifty years with music/ Sigmund Spaeth. Westport, Conn.: Greenwood Press Publishers, 1977, c1959. 288 p.
77-013488   780/.8   0837198623
Spaeth, Sigmund Gottfried, 1885-1965. Music -- Addresses, essays, lectures.

ML424.D65.D57 1980
Dolmetsch, Mabel.
Personal recollections of Arnold Dolmetsch/ Mabel Dolmetsch. New York: Da Capo Press, 1980, c1957. viii, 198 p.
79-024413   781.9/1/0924   0306760223
Dolmetsch, Arnold, -- 1858-1940. Musicians -- England -- Biography. Musical instruments.

ML424.S76.L54 1995
Lieberman, Richard K.
Steinway & Sons/ Richard K. Lieberman. New Haven:
Yale University Press, c1995. ix, 374 p.
95-017330   786.2/197471   0300063644
   *Steinway piano. Piano makers -- New York (State) -- New York
-- History.*

ML424.S8.H62 1963
Hill, William Henry, 1857-1927.
Antonio Stradivari, his life and work, 1644-1737, by W.
Henry Hill, Arthur F. Hill, and Alfred E. Hill. With a new
introd. by Sydney Beck and new supplementary indexes
by Rembert Wurlitzer. New York, Dover Publications
[1963] xxiv, 314 p.
63-017904   787.12
Stradivari, Antonio, -- d. 1737.

ML429.A83.G65 1998
Goldsmith, Peter David, 1952-
Making people's music: Moe Asch and Folkways records/
Peter D. Goldsmith. Washington, D.C.: Smithsonian
Institution Press, c1998. xi, 468 p.
97-033293   781.62/13/0092   1560988126
*Asch, Moses.   Sound recording executives and producers --
United States -- Biography. Folk music -- United States --
History and criticism.   United States -- Civilization -- 1918-
1945. United States -- Civilization -- 1945-*

ML429.B52.A3
Bing, Rudolf, 1902-
5000 nights at the opera. Garden City, N.Y. Doubleday,
1972. 360 p.
72-076124   782.1/092/4   0385092598
*Bing, Rudolf, -- Sir, -- 1902- Bing, Rudolf, -- Sir, -- 1902-
Impresarios -- Biography.*

ML429.C64.B37 1998
Barr, Cyrilla.
Elizabeth Sprague Coolidge: American patron of music/
Cyrilla Barr; foreword by Gunther Schuller. New York:
Schirmer Books; c1998. xxiv, 436 p.
97-031635   780/.92   0028648889
*Coolidge, Elizabeth Sprague, -- 1864-1953.   Music patrons --
United States -- Biography.*

ML429.F75.J3 1991
Jackson, John A., 1943-
Big beat heat: Alan Freed and the early years of rock &
roll/ John A. Jackson. New York: Schirmer Books;
c1991. xiv, 400 p.
90-020437   781.66/092   0028711556
*Freed, Alan. Disc jockeys -- United States -- Biography. Rock
music -- United States -- History and criticism.*

ML429.G95.A3 1976
Guthrie, Woody, 1912-1967.
Bound for glory/ Woody Guthrie; illustrated with
sketches by the author; with an introd. by Studs Terkel.
New York: E. P. Dutton, 1976, c1943.
76-364186   784.4/92/4   0525070257
*Guthrie, Woody, -- 1912-1967.   Folk singers -- United States --
Biography.*

ML429.G95.K6
Klein, Joe, 1946-
Woody Guthrie: a life/ Joe Klein. New York: A.A.
Knopf: Distributed by Random House, 1980. xv, 475 p.
80-007634   784.4/924   0394501527
*Guthrie, Woody, -- 1912-1967.   Folk singers -- United States --
Biography.*

ML429.H87.R6 1994
Robinson, Harlow.
The last impresario: the life, times, and legacy of Sol
Hurok/ Harlow Robinson. New York: Viking, 1994. xxii,
521 p.
93-022138   780/.92   0670825298
Hurok, Sol, -- 1888-1974.   Impresarios -- Biography.

ML429.J2.S6 1990
Spector, Irwin.
Rhythm and life: the work of Emile Jaques-Dalcroze/ by
Irwin Spector. Stuyvesant, NY: Pendragon Press, [1990]
xvii, 411 p.
89-028139   780/.92   0945193009
*Jaques-Dalcroze, Emile, -- 1865-1950.   Music teachers --
Switzerland -- Biography.*

ML429.K74.A3 1993
Koestenbaum, Wayne.
The queen's throat: opera, homosexuality, and the
mystery of desire/ Wayne Koestenbaum. New York:
Poseidon Press, c1993. 271 p.
92-034911   782.1/092   0671754572
*Koestenbaum, Wayne.   Opera -- Biography. Gay men --
Biography. Sex in music.*

ML429.L68.A3 1947
Lomax, John Avery, 1867-1948,
Adventures of a ballad hunter, by John A. Lomax;
sketches by Ken Chamberlain. New York, Macmillan,
1947.
47-030155   927.8
   Ballads, English -- United States -- History and criticism.

ML429.P78.H6 1989
Hirsch, Foster.
Harold Prince and the American musical theatre/ Foster
Hirsch. Cambridge; Cambridge University Press, 1989.
xvii, 187 p.
88-029941   792/.023/0924   0521333148
Prince, Harold, -- 1928- -- Criticism and interpretation.

ML429.T43
Glinsky, Albert.
Theremin: ether music and espionage/ Albert Glinsky;
foreword by Robert Moog. Urbana: University of Illinois
Press, c2000. xvi, 403 p.
00-008024   786.7/3   0252025822
*Theremin, Leon, -- 1896-1993. Musicians -- Biography. Spies -
- Biography. Theremin. United States -- Foreign relations --
Soviet Union. Soviet Union -- Foreign relations -- United States.*

ML430 History and criticism — Composition — General works

ML430.L46 1992
Lester, Joel.
Compositional theory in the eighteenth century/ Joel Lester. Cambridge, Mass.: Harvard University Press, 1992. 355 p.
92-005083   781.3/09/033   067415522X
Music -- Theory -- 18th century -- History. Composition (Music) -- History -- 18th century.

ML430.M28 1987
Mann, Alfred, 1917-
Theory and practice: the great composer as student and teacher/ Alfred Mann. New York: Norton, c1987. viii, 167 p.
86-012584   781   0393023524
Music -- Theory -- 18th century -- History. Music -- Theory -- 19th century -- History. Composition (Music)

ML430.M5
Mickelsen, William C.
Hugo Riemann's Theory of harmony: a study/ by William C. Mickelsen and History of music theory, book III/ by Hugo Riemann; translated and edited by William C. Mickelsen. Lincoln: University of Nebraska Press, c1977. xv, 263 p.
76-015366   781.3   080320891X
Riemann, Hugo, -- 1849-1919. -- Geschichte der Musiktheorie im IX.-XIX. Jahrhundert.   Composition (Music) -- History. Harmony.

ML430.O94 1997
Owens, Jessie Ann.
Composers at work: the craft of musical composition 1450-1600/ Jessie Ann Owens. New York: Oxford University Press, 1997. xxi, 345 p.
95-038533   781/.3/09031   0195095774
Composition (Music) -- History. Music -- 15th century -- History and criticism. Music -- 16th century -- History and criticism.

ML430.R563
Riemann, Hugo, 1849-1919.
History of music theory, books I and II: polyphonic theory to the sixteenth century. Translated, with a preface, commentary, and notes by Raymond H. Haggh. Lincoln, University of Nebraska Press, 1962. xx, 431 p.
62-008280
Composition (Music) -- History.

ML430.5 History and criticism — Composition — Style

ML430.5.C76
Crocker, Richard L.
A history of musical style [by] Richard L. Crocker. New York, McGraw-Hill [1966] vii, 573 p.
65-028233   781.63
Style, Musical. Music -- Performance -- History.

ML430.5.D3 1967
Dart, Thurston, 1921-1971.
The interpretation of music. London, Hutchinson, 1967. 190 p.
67-101007   781.6/3
Music -- Interpretation (Phrasing, dynamics, etc.) Music -- Performance.

ML430.5.D66.H5
Dorian, Frederick, 1902-
The history of music in performance; the art of musical interpretation from the renaissance to our day. By Frederick Dorian. New York, N.Y., W.W. Norton & Company, Inc. [c1942] 387 p.
43-002216   781.63
Music -- Performance -- History. Music appreciation. Musical analysis.

ML430.5.M5 1989
Meyer, Leonard B.
Style and music: theory, history, and ideology/ Leonard B. Meyer. Philadelphia: University of Pennsylvania Press, c1989. xi, 376 p.
89-031354   781   0812281780
Style, Musical. Music -- 19th century -- Philosophy and aesthetics. Romanticism in music.

ML437 History and criticism — Composition — Rhythm

ML437.H43 1993
Hefling, Stephen E.
Rhythmic alteration in seventeenth- and eighteenth-century music: notes inegales and overdotting/ Stephen E. Hefling. New York: Schirmer Books; c1993. xvi, 232 p.
92-011958   781.2/2/09032   0028710355
Notes inegales. Musical meter and rhythm. Performance practice (Music) -- 17th century.

ML437.S3
Sachs, Curt, 1881-1959.
Rhythm and tempo: a study in music history/ by Curt Sachs. New York: c1953. 391 p.
52-004911   781.62
Musical meter and rhythm. Musical meter and rhythm. Music -- History and criticism.

ML442 History and criticism — Composition — Continuo

ML442.A7 1965
Arnold, F. T. 1861-1940.
The art of accompaniment from a thorough-bass, as practised in the XVIIth & XVIIIth centuries, by F. T. Arnold. With a new introd. by Denis Stevens. New York, Dover Publications [1965] 2 v.
65-024022   781.660903
Thorough bass. Musical accompaniment.

ML444 History and criticism — Composition — Harmony

ML444.R92 1979
Rufer, Josef, 1893-
Composition with twelve notes related only to one another/ Josef Rufer; translated by Humphrey Searle. Westport, Conn.: Greenwood Press, 1979, c1954. xiv, 186 p.
78-009838   781.6/1   0313212368
Schoenberg, Arnold, -- 1874-1951.   Composition (Music) Twelve-tone system.

ML444.S55.T3 1955
Shirlaw, Matthew, 1873-
The theory of harmony; an inquiry into the natural principles of harmony, with an examination of the chief systems of harmony from Rameau to the present day. DeKalb, Ill., B. Coar, 1955. xvi, 484 p.
56-000398   781.3
Harmony.

ML448 History and criticism — Composition — Musical form

ML448.M25 1987
Mann, Alfred,
The study of fugue/ Alfred Mann. New York: Dover Publications, 1987, c1965. xii, 339 p.
87-006663   781.4/2 19   0486254399
Fugue.

ML448.O4 1986
Oldroyd, George.
The technique and spirit of fugue: an historical study/ George Oldroyd; with a foreword by Sir Stanley Marchant. Westport, Conn.: Greenwood Press, 1986, c1948. viii, 220 p.
85-027089   781.4/2   0313250529
Fugue.

ML448.W25 2000
Walker, Paul, 1953-
Theories of fugue from the age of Josquin to the age of Bach/ Paul Mark Walker. Rochester, NY; University of Rochester Press, 2000. 485 p.
2001-316929   784.18/72   1580460291
Fugue.

ML455 History and criticism — Composition — Instrumentation

ML455.C32 1964
Carse, Adam von Ahn, 1878-1958.
The history of orchestration.   New York, Dover Publications [1964] xiii, 348 p.
64-017314
Instrumentation and orchestration -- History.

ML455.R4
Read, Gardner,
Style and orchestration/ Gardner Read; foreword by Nicolas Slonimsky. New York: Schirmer Books, c1979 xvi, 304 p.
77-015884   781.6/4   0028721101
Instrumentation and orchestration -- History. Style, Musical.

ML457 History and criticism — Interpretation. Performance practice

ML457.A98 1988
Authenticity and early music: a symposium/ edited by Nicholas Kenyon. Oxford; Oxford University Press, 1988. xv, 219 p.
88-015464   781.6/3   0198161522
Performance practice (Music) -- Congresses. Style, Musical -- Congresses. Music -- History and criticism -- Congresses.

ML457.B76 1999
Brown, Clive, 1947-
Classical and Romantic performing practice 1750-1900/ Clive Brown. Oxford; Oxford University Press, 1999. xiii, 662 p.
97-050572   781.4/3/09033   0198161654
Performance practice (Music) -- 18th century. Performance practice (Music) -- 19th century.

ML457.B9 1994
Butt, John.
Music education and the art of performance in the German baroque/ John Butt. Cambridge; Cambridge University Press, 1994. xviii, 237 p.
93-017691   781.4/3/0943   0521433274
Performance practice (Music) -- Germany -- 17th century. Performance practice (Music) -- Germany -- 18th century. Music -- Instruction and study -- Germany -- History -- 17th century.

ML457.C9 1992
Cyr, Mary.
Performing baroque music/ Mary Cyr; Reinhard G. Pauly, general editor. Portland, Or.: Amadeus Press, c1992. 254 p.
92-000097   781.4/3/09032   0931340497
Performance practice (Music) -- 17th century. Performance practice (Music) -- 18th century.

ML457.G3 1988
Galkin, Elliott W.
A history of orchestral conducting: in theory and practice/ Elliott W. Galkin. New York, NY: Pendragon Press, c1988. xlii, 893 p.
85-028433   781.6/35   0918728444
Conducting.

ML457.H313 1988
Harnoncourt, Nikolaus.
Baroque music today: music as speech: ways to a new understanding of music/ Nikolaus Harnoncourt; translated by Mary O'Neill; Reinhard G. Pauly, general editor. Portland, Or.: Amadeus Press, c1988. 205 p.
88-006207   780/.903/2   0931340055
Performance practice (Music) -- 17th century. Performance practice (Music) -- 18th century.

ML457.H83 1994
Hudson, Richard, 1924-
Stolen time: the history of tempo rubato/ Richard Hudson. Oxford: Clarendon Press, 1994. xiv, 473 p.
94-036464   781.46   0198161697
Rubato.

ML457.K58 1995
Kivy, Peter.
Authenticities: philosophical reflections on musical performance/ Peter Kivy. Ithaca: Cornell University Press, 1995. xiv, 299 p.
94-036842   781.4/3/01   0801430461
Performance practice (Music) Music -- Philosophy and aesthetics.

ML457.L39 1999
Lawson, Colin
The historical performance of music: an introduction/ Colin Lawson and Robin Stowell. Cambridge, UK; Cambridge University Press, 1999. xiii, 219 p.
98-042731   781.4/3/09 21   0521627389
Performance practice (Music) -- 18th century. Performance practice (Music) -- 19th century.

ML457.N46 1993
Neumann, Frederick.
Performance practices of the seventeenth and eighteenth centuries/ Frederick Neumann; prepared with the assistance of Jane Stevens. New York: Schirmer Books, c1993. xiii, 605 p.
92-033205   781.4/3/09032   0028733002
Performance practice (Music) -- 17th century. Performance practice (Music) -- 18th century.

ML457.R4
Readings in the history of music in performance/ selected, translated, and edited by Carol MacClintock. Bloomington: Indiana University Press, c1979. xii, 432 p.
78-009511   780/.9   0253144957
Performance practice (Music) Music -- History and criticism -- Sources.

ML457.S52 1997
Sherman, Bernard D.
Inside early music: conversations with performers/ Bernard D. Sherman. New York: Oxford University Press, 1997. xi, 414 p.
96-006341   781.4/3   0195097084
Performance practice (Music) Style, Musical. Musicians -- Interviews.

ML457.T37 1995
Taruskin, Richard.
Text and act: essays on music and performance/ Richard Taruskin. New York: Oxford University Press, 1995. vi, 382 p.
94-024903   781.4/3   0195094379
Performance practice (Music) Style, Musical.

ML460 History and criticism —
Instruments and instrumental music —
General works

ML460.B14 1966a
Baines, Anthony.
Musical instruments through the ages; edited by Anthony Baines for the Galpin Society. New York, Walker [1966, c1961] 344 p.
66-022505   785.09
Musical instruments -- History.

ML460.D63 1982
Donington, Robert.
Music and its instruments/ Robert Donington. London; Methuen, 1982. xii, 232 p.
82-008012   781.91   0416722709
Musical instruments.

ML460.G14.T35 1976
Galpin, Francis W. 1858-1945.
A textbook of European musical instruments, their origin, history, and character. New York, J. De Graff [1956, c1937] 256 p.
56-058142   781.9109
Musical instruments -- History.

ML460.P34 1992
Parakilas, James.
Ballads without words: Chopin and the tradition of the instrumental ballade/ James Parakilas. Portland, Or.: Amadeus Press, c1992. 358 p.
91-030216   784.18/96 20   0931340470
Chopin, Frédéric, 1810-1849. Ballades, piano. Ballades (Instrumental music) -- History and criticism. Instrumental music -- History and criticism.

ML460.S24.H5
Sachs, Curt, 1881-1959.
The history of musical instruments [by] Curt Sachs. New York, W. W. Norton & company, inc. [c1940] 505 p.
41-000559   781.9109
Musical instruments -- History.

ML465 History and criticism —
Instruments and instrumental music —
By period

ML465.M65
Montagu, Jeremy.
The world of baroque and classical musical instruments/ Jeremy Montagu. Woodstock, N.Y.: Overlook Press, 1979. 136 p.
78-025814   781.9/1/0903
Musical instruments.

ML480-499.2 History and criticism — Instruments and instrumental music — By region or country

ML480.E88 1991
Essays on Cuban music: North American and Cuban perspectives/ edited by Peter Manuel. Lanham, Md.: University Press of America, c1991. xvi, 327 p.
91-027250   780/.97291   0819184306
Music -- Cuba -- History and criticism. Cuban Americans -- New York (State) -- New York -- Music -- History and criticism.

ML497.2.L4 1987
Ledbetter, David.
Harpsichord and lute music in 17th-century France/ by David Ledbetter. Bloomington: Indiana University Press, c1987. xvi, 194 p.
87-017041   786.2/21/0944   0253327075
Instrumental music -- France -- 17th century -- History and criticism. Keyboard instrument music -- 17th century -- History and criticism. Lute music -- 17th century -- History and criticism.

ML497.2.P33 1990
Page, Christopher, 1952-
The owl and the nightingale: musical life and ideas in France, 1100-1300/ Christopher Page. Berkeley: University of California Press, 1990. xi, 279 p.
89-040538   780/.944/0902   0520069447
Music -- France -- 500 to 1400 -- History and criticism.

ML499.2.P64 1992
Polk, Keith.
German instrumental music of the late Middle Ages: players, patrons, and performance practice/ Keith Polk. Cambridge [England]; Cambridge University Press, 1992. xvi, 272 p.
91-033751   784/.0943/0902   0521385210
Instrumental music -- Germany -- 500-1400 -- History and criticism. Instrumental music -- Germany -- 15th century -- History and criticism. Performance practice (Music) -- Germany -- 500-1400.

ML549-734 History and criticism — Instruments and instrumental music — Instruments — Keyboard instruments

ML549.K49 1995
Keyboard music before 1700/ edited by Alexander Silbiger. New York: Schirmer Books; c1995. xiii, 373 p.
95-010439   786/.09   0028723910
Keyboard instrument music -- History and criticism.

ML549.M38 1998
Maunder, C. R. F.
Keyboard instruments in eighteenth-century Vienna/ Richard Maunder. Oxford: Clarendon Press; 1998. xi, 266 p.
97-032613   786/.1943613/09033   0198166370
Keyboard instruments -- Austria -- Vienna -- History -- 18th century.

ML550.C35 1998
The Cambridge companion to the organ/ edited by Nicholas Thistlethwaite and Geoffrey Webber. Cambridge; Cambridge University Press, 1998. xiv, 340 p.
97-041723   786.5   0521573092
Organ (Musical instrument) Organ music -- History and criticism.

ML550.W38
Williams, Peter F.
A new history of the organ from the Greeks to the present day/ Peter Williams. Bloomington: Indiana University Press, c1980. 233 p.
79-002176   786.6/2   0253157048
Organ -- History.

ML574.D69 1995
Douglass, Fenner.
The language of the classical French organ: a musical tradition before 1800/ Fenner Douglass. New Haven: Yale University Press, [1995] xiii, 251 p.
94-045846   786.5/0946   0300064268
Organs -- France. Organ -- History.

ML578.B53 1996
Bicknell, Stephen.
The history of the English organ/ Stephen Bicknell. Cambridge; Cambridge University Press, c1996. xxii, 407 p.
95-042779   786.5/1942   0521550262
Organ (Musical instrument) -- Great Britain -- History.

ML600.A76 1995
Arnold, Corliss Richard.
Organ literature: a comprehensive survey/ by Corliss Richard Arnold. Metuchen, N.J.: Scarecrow Press, 1995. 2 v.
94-040388   786.5/09   0810829649
Organ music -- History and criticism. Organ music -- Bibliography.

ML624.F74 1995
French organ music: from the revolution to Franck and Widor/ edited by Lawrence Archbold and William J. Peterson. Rochester, N.Y.: University of Rochester Press, 1995. xiii, 323 p.
95-021601   786.5/0944   1878822551
Organ music -- France -- History and criticism.

ML624.O25 1994
Ochse, Orpha Caroline, 1925-
Organists and organ playing in nineteenth-century France and Belgium/ by Orpha Ochse. Bloomington: Indiana University Press, c1994. xii, 270 p.
94-002589   786.5/0944/09034   0253341612
Organists -- France. Organists -- Belgium. Organ -- France -- Performance -- History -- 19th century.

ML650.C3 1998
The Cambridge companion to the piano/ edited by David Rowland. Cambridge; Cambridge University Press, c1999. xiv, 244 p.
97-041860   786.2   0521474701
Piano.

ML650.L64 1990
Loesser, Arthur,
Men, women, and pianos: a social history/ Arthur Loesser; with a new foreword by Edward Rothstein and a preface by Jacques Barzun. New York: Dover Publications, 1990. xviii, 654 p.
90-044829   786.2/09 20   0486265439
Piano -- History.

ML650.P37 1999
Parakilas, James.
Piano roles: three hundred years of life with the piano/ James Parakilas with E. Douglas Bomberger ... [et al.]; foreword by Noah Adams. New Haven, [Conn.]: Yale University Press, c1999. x, 461 p.
99-029430   786.2/09   0300080557
Piano -- History. Music -- Social aspects.

ML651.B66 1997
Bond, Ann.
A guide to the harpsichord/ Ann Bond. Portland, Or.: Amadeus Press, c1997. 267 p.
96-041086   786.4/19   1574670271
Harpsichord.

ML651.H83
Hubbard, Frank.
Three centuries of harpsichord making/ by Frank Hubbard. Cambridge, Mass.: Harvard University Press, c1967. xvi, 373 p.
65-012784   681.816221   0674888456
Harpsichord -- Construction.

ML651.P3 1989
Palmer, Larry.
Harpsichord in America: a twentieth-century revival/ Larry Palmer. Bloomington: Indiana University Press, c1989. xiv, 202 p.
88-045446   786.2/21/0973   0253327105
Harpsichord. Harpsichordists -- United States. Harpsichord makers -- United States.

ML652.B666 1995
Boalch, Donald H.
Makers of the harpsichord and clavichord 1440-1840/ Donald H. Boalch. Oxford: Clarendon Press, 1995. xxxii, 788 p.
95-022105   786.4/19/0922   019318429X
Harpsichord makers. Clavichord makers. Harpsichord.

ML652.E4 1990
Ehrlich, Cyril.
The piano: a history/ Cyril Ehrlich. Oxford: Clarendon Press; 1990. 254 p.
89-023161   786.2/19/09   0198161816
Piano -- History.

ML652.G6 2001
Good, Edwin M. 1928-
Giraffes, black dragons, and other pianos: a technological history from Cristofori to the modern concert grand/ Edwin M. Good. Stanford, Calif.: Stanford University Press, c2001. xxv, 369 p.
00-061241   786.2/19/09   0804733163
Piano -- History. Piano -- Construction.

ML655.C63 1998
Cole, Michael.
The pianoforte in the classical era/ Michael Cole. Oxford [England]: Clarendon Press, 1998. xiv, 398 p.
97-015105   786.2/09/033   0198166346
Piano -- History -- 18th century.

ML655.P64 1995
Pollens, Stewart.
The early pianoforte/ Stewart Pollens. Cambridge; Cambridge University Press, 1995. xx, 297 p.
93-041231   786.2/19/09 20   0521417295
Piano -- History. Piano -- Construction.

ML661.R64 1989
Roell, Craig H.
The piano in America, 1890-1940/ Craig H. Roell. Chapel Hill: University of North Carolina Press, c1989. xix, 396 p.
88-014326   381/.4568181621/0973   080781802X
Piano -- History. Music trade -- United States. Music -- United States -- 19th century -- History and criticism.

ML700.A6
Apel, Willi, 1893-
Masters of the keyboard; a brief survey of pianoforte music. Cambridge, Harvard Univ. Press, 1947. 323 p.
47-012245   786.409   0674553004
Piano music -- History and criticism. Organ music -- History and criticism.

ML700.G65 1996
Gordon, Stewart, 1930-
A history of keyboard literature: music for the piano and its forerunners/ Stewart Gordon. New York: Schirmer Books; c1996. viii, 566 p.
95-031762   786   0028709659
Keyboard instrument music -- History and criticism. Piano music -- History and criticism.

ML700.K45 1995
Kirby, F. E.
Music for piano: a short history/ F.E. Kirby; foreword by Maurice Hinson. Portland, Or.: Amadeus Press, c1995. 466 p.
94-042642   786.2/09   0931340861
Piano music -- History and criticism.

ML700.K56 1996
Kopelson, Kevin, 1960-
Beethoven's kiss: pianism, perversion, and the mastery of desire/ Kevin Kopelson. Stanford, Calif.: Stanford University Press, c1996. 198 p.
95-023459   786.2/08/664   0804725977
Piano music -- 19th century -- History and criticism. Piano music -- 20th century -- History and criticism. Pianists -- Sexual behavior.

ML700.M39 1993
Maxwell, Grant L. 1960-
Music for three or more pianists: a historical survey and catalogue/ by Grant L. Maxwell. Metuchen, N.J.: Scarecrow Press, 1993. ix, 467 p.
92-037842   785.62   0810826313
Piano ensembles -- History and criticism. Piano ensembles -- Bibliography.

ML700.T4 1982
Taylor, Billy, 1921-
Jazz piano: history and development/ Billy Taylor. Dubuque, Iowa: W.C. Brown, c1982. viii, 264 p.
82-070521   786.4/041   0697034941
Piano music (Jazz) -- History and criticism. Jazz -- History and criticism.

ML705.E37 1994
Eighteenth-century keyboard music/ edited by Robert L. Marshall. New York: Schirmer Books, c1994. xvi, 443 p.
93-045594   786/.09/033   0028713559
Keyboard instrument music -- 18th century -- History and criticism. Performance practice (Music) -- 18th century. Keyboard instruments.

ML705.R67 1988
Rosenblum, Sandra P., 1928-
Performance practices in classic piano music: their principles and applications/ Sandra P. Rosenblum. Bloomington: Indiana University Press, c1988. xxviii, 516 p.
87-045437   786.3/041   0253343143
Piano -- Performance. Performance practice (Music) -- 18th century. Performance practice (Music) -- 19th century.

ML705.W64 1990
Wolff, Konrad, 1907-
Masters of the keyboard: individual style elements in the piano music of Bach, Haydn, Mozart, Beethoven, Schubert, Chopin, and Brahms/ Konrad Wolff. Bloomington: Indiana University Press, 1990. xii, 314 p.
89-045570   786.2/09/033   0253364582
Piano music -- 18th century -- History and criticism. Piano music -- 19th century -- History and criticism.

ML706.N56 1990
Nineteenth-century piano music/ edited by R. Larry Todd. New York: Schirmer Books; c1990. xvi, 426 p.
90-008681   786.2/09/034   0028725514
Piano music -- 19th century -- History and criticism.

ML707.B87 1990
Burge, David, 1930-
Twentieth-century piano music/ David Burge. New York: Schirmer Books; c1990. x, 284 p.
90-008663   786.2/09/04   0028703219
Piano music -- 20th century -- History and criticism.

ML724.T54 1999
Timbrell, Charles, 1942-
French pianism: a historical perspective/ by Charles Timbrell; foreword by Gaby Casadesus. Portland, Or.: Amadeus Press, 1999. 370 p.
98-028634   786.2/0944/0904   157467045X
Piano music -- Interpretation (Phrasing, dynamics, etc.) Pianists -- France -- Interviews. Performance practice (Music) -- France -- 19th century.

ML734.R6 1993
Roberts, Peter Deane.
Modernism in Russian piano music: Skriabin, Prokofiev, and their Russian contemporaries/ Peter Deane Roberts. Bloomington, Ind.: Indiana University Press, c1993. 2 v.
91-032124   786.2/0947   0253349923
Scriabin, Aleksandr Nikolayevich, -- 1872-1915. Prokofiev, Sergey, -- 1891-1953. Music -- Soviet Union -- 20th century -- History and criticism. Piano music -- 20th century -- History and criticism. Music -- Russia -- 20th century -- History and criticism.

ML756-880.2 History and criticism — Instruments and instrumental music — Instruments — Stringed instruments. Bowed stringed instruments

ML756.H64 1993
Holman, Peter, 1946-
Four and twenty fiddlers: the violin at the English court, 1540-1690/ Peter Holman. Oxford: Clarendon Press; 1993. xxvii, 491 p.
92-047231   787.2/0942/09031   019816145X
String ensembles -- 16th century -- History and criticism. String ensembles -- 17th century -- History and criticism. Music -- England -- 16th century -- History and criticism. Great Britain -- Court and courtiers -- History -- 16th century. Great Britain -- Court and courtiers -- History -- 17th century.

ML760.V55.W66 1984
Woodfield, Ian.
The early history of the viol/ Ian Woodfield. Cambridge [Cambridgeshire]; Cambridge University Press, 1984. xiii, 266 p.
83-018876   787/.42/09031   0521242924
Viol -- History.

ML800.B13 1966
Bachmann, Alberto, 1875-1963.
An encyclopedia of the violin [by] Alberto Bachmann. Original introd. by Eugene Ysaye. Preface to the Da Capo ed. by Stuart Canin. [Translated by Frederick H. Martens] New York, Da Capo Press, 1966. vi, 470 p.
65-023406   787.1
Violin. Violinists, violoncellists, etc. Violin makers.

ML800.B6 1984
The Book of the violin/ edited by Dominic Gill. New York: Rizzoli, [1984] 256 p.
84-042683   787.1 19   0847805484
Violin.

ML800.K6413 1998
Kolneder, Walter.
The Amadeus book of the violin: construction, history, and music/ Walter Kolneder; translated and edited by Reinhard G. Pauly. Portland, Or.: Amadeus Press, c1998. 597 p.
97-046198   787.2 21   1574670387
Violin. Violin music -- History and criticism.

ML880.2.A6313 1990
Apel, Willi, 1893-
Italian violin music of the seventeenth century/ Willi Apel; edited by Thomas Binkley. Bloomington: Indiana University Press, c1990. ix, 306 p.
88-045503   787.2/0945/09032   0253306833
Violin music -- 17th century -- History and criticism. Instrumental music -- Italy -- 17th century -- History and criticism. Composers -- Italy.

ML930-990 History and criticism — Instruments and instrumental music — Instruments — Wind instruments

ML930.B3 1963
Baines, Anthony.
Woodwind instruments and their history. With a forward by Sir Adrian Boult. New York, W.W. Norton [1963] 384 p.
63-001528   788.5
Wind instruments.

ML930.C38.M9 1965
Carse, Adam von Ahn, 1878-1958.
Musical wind instruments, by Adam Carse. With an introd. to the Da Capo ed. by Himie Voxman. New York, Da Capo Press, 1965. xi, 381 p.
65-018502   788
Wind instruments.

ML933.B33 1978
Baines, Anthony.
Brass instruments: their history and development/ Anthony Baines. New York: Scribner, [1978] c1976. 298 p.
77-074716   788/.01   0684152290
Brass instruments.

ML933.W52 1989
Whitener, Scott.
A complete guide to brass: instruments and pedagogy/ Scott Whitener; foreword by Charles Schlueter; illustrations by Cathy L. Whitener. New York: Schirmer Books; c1990. xvi, 336 p.
89-004132   788/.01   0028728610
Brass instruments. Brass instruments -- Instruction and study.

ML935.B25
Bate, Philip.
The flute: a study of its history, development and construction. London, Benn; 1969. xvi, 268 p.
74-382066   788/.51   0510363512
Flute -- History. Flute -- Construction.

ML935.H85
Hunt, Edgar, 1909-
The recorder and its music. London, H. Jenkins [1962] 176 p.
62-006190   788.53
Recorder (Musical instrument) -- History. Recorder (Musical instrument) -- Instruction and study.

ML935.T65 1996
Toff, Nancy.
The flute book: a complete guide for students and performers/ Nancy Toff. New York: Oxford University Press, 1996. xviii, 495 p.
96-023178   788.3   0195105028
Flute. Flute music -- History and criticism. Flute music -- Bibliography.

ML940.B37 1975
Bate, Philip.
The oboe: an outline of its history, development, and construction/ Philip Bate. 3d ed. London: E. Benn; 1975. xv, 236 p.
75-317958   788/.7   0393021161
Oboe -- History.

ML945.B8 1977
Brymer, Jack.
Clarinet/ Jack Brymer. New York: Schirmer Books, 1977, c1976. xii, 267 p.
77-000275   788/.62   002871430X
Clarinet.

ML945.C36 1995
The Cambridge companion to the clarinet/ edited by Colin Lawson. Cambridge [England]; Cambridge University Press, xiv, 240 p.
94-047624   788.6/2 20   0521476682
Clarinet.

ML945.L39 2000
Lawson, Colin
The early clarinet: a practical guide/ Colin Lawson. Cambridge, UK; Cambridge University Press, 2000. xiii, 128 p.
99-032934   788.6/2/09033   0521624592
Clarinet. Clarinet music -- 18th century -- History and criticism. Clarinet music -- 19th century -- History and criticism.

ML950.L29
Langwill, Lyndesay Graham, 1897-
The bassoon and contrabassoon [by] Lyndesay G. Langwill. London, E. Benn; [1965] xiv, 269 p.
65-029708   788.8
Bassoon -- History. Bassoonists. Bassoon music -- Bibliography.

ML955.G7 1969b
Gregory, Robin.
The horn; a comprehensive guide to the modern instrument & its music. New York, F. A. Praeger [1969] 410 p.
69-020022   781/.97
Horn (Musical instrument) Horn music -- Bibliography.

ML955.H86 2000
Humphries, John, 1956-
The early horn: a practical guide/ John Humphries. Cambridge; Cambridge University Press, 2000. ix, 138 p.
99-054036   788.9/4/09   0521632102
Horn (Musical instrument) Horn music -- 18th century -- History and criticism. Horn music -- 19th century -- History and criticism.

ML955.J313 1988
Janetzky, Kurt.
The horn/ Kurt Janetzky and Bernhard Bruchle; translated by James Chater. Portland, Or.: Amadeus Press, 1988. 127 p.
88-019282   788/.4   0931340144
Horn (Musical instrument)

ML960.B38 1978
Bate, Philip.
The trumpet and trombone: an outline of their history, development, and construction/ [by] Philip Bate. London: E. Benn; 1978. xix, 300 p.
78-313868   788/.1   0393021297
Trumpet -- History. Trumpet -- Construction. Trombone -- History.

ML960.T3713 1988
Tarr, Edward H.
The trumpet/ Edward Tarr; translated from the German by S.E. Plank and Edward Tarr. Portland, Or.: Amadeus Press, 1988. 221 p.
88-019280   788/.12/09   0931340136
Trumpet -- History.

ML970.B48 1978
Bevan, Clifford.
The tuba family/ by Clifford Bevan. New York: Scribner, c1978. 303 p.
77-082241   788/.48   0684154773
Tuba -- History.

ML975.C36 1998
The Cambridge companion to the saxophone/ edited by Richard Ingham. New York: Cambridge University Press, 1998. xvi, 226 p.
98-017404   788.7   0521593484
Saxophone.

ML980.G53 1998
Gibson, John G. 1941-
Traditional Gaelic bagpiping, 1745-1945/ John G. Gibson. Montreal: McGill-Queen's University Press, c1998.
99-488654   788.4/9/089916   0773515410
Bagpipe -- Scotland -- Highlands -- History. Bagpipe -- Nova Scotia -- History. Bagpipe music -- History and criticism.

ML990.R4 C35 1995
The Cambridge companion to the recorder/ edited by John Mansfield Thomson; assistant editor, Anthony Rowland-Jones. Cambridge; Cambridge University Press, 1995. xxiii, 238 p.
94-031992   788.3/6 20   0521358167
Recorder (Musical instrument)

ML990.R4.O5 1990
O'Kelly, Eve.
The recorder today/ Eve O'Kelly. Cambridge [England]; Cambridge University Press, 1990. xiv, 179 p.
89-035680   788.3/6   0521366607
Recorder (Musical instrument) Recorder music -- Interpretation (Phrasing, dynamics, etc.)

ML1005-1015 History and criticism — Instruments and instrumental music — Instruments — Plucked instruments

ML1005.R43 1989
Rensch, Roslyn.
Harps and harpists/ Roslyn Rensch. Bloomington: Indiana University Press, c1989. xiv, 329 p.
88-037609   787/.5/09   0253349036
Harp -- History. Harpists.

ML1015.A6 S63 1997
Smith, Ralph Lee,
Appalachian dulcimer traditions/ Ralph Lee Smith. Lanham, Md.: Scarecrow Press, 1997. ix, 167 p.
97-020990   787.7/4 21   0810833786
Appalachian dulcimer -- History.

ML1015.B3.G87 1999
Gura, Philip F., 1950-
America's instrument: the banjo in the nineteenth-century/ Philip F. Gura & James F. Bollman. Chapel Hill: The University of North Carolina Press, 1999. xvi, 303 p.
98-046164   787.8/81973/09034   0807824844
Banjo -- United States -- History -- 19th century.

ML1015.B3.L5 1991
Linn, Karen, 1957-
That half-barbaric twang: the banjo in American popular culture/ Karen Linn. Urbana: University of Illinois Press, c1991. xiii, 185 p.
90-044638   787.8/80973   0252017803
Banjo. Musical instruments -- United States. Popular music -- United States -- History and criticism.

ML1015.G9.C85 1987
Cumpiano, William R.
Guitarmaking, tradition and technology: a complete reference for the design and construction of the steel-string folk guitar and the classical guitar/ William R. Cumpiano, Jonathan D. Natelson; photographs by Clyde Herlitz; line drawings by William R. Cumpiano. Amherst, Mass.: Rosewood Press, c1987. 387 p.
84-005809   787.6/12   0442268459
Guitar -- Construction.

ML1015.G9.G76 1993
Gruhn, George.
Acoustic guitars and other fretted instruments: a photographic history/ [text by] George Gruhn & Walter Carter. San Francisco: GPI Books, c1993. 313 p.
92-044435   787.87/1973   0879302402
Guitar -- United States -- Pictorial works. Banjo -- Pictorial works. Mandolin -- Pictorial works.

ML1015.G9.G763 1994
Gruhn, George.
Electric guitars and basses: a photographic history/ George Gruhn & Walter Carter. San Francisco: GPI Books, c1994. 249 p.
94-010418   787.87/1973   087930328X
Guitar -- United States -- Pictorial works.

ML1015.G9.G825 1988
The Guitar: a guide for students and teachers/ compiled and edited by Michael Stimpson. Oxford; Oxford University Press, 1988. xviii, 284 p.
87-005622   787.6/1   0193174197
Guitar. Guitar -- Instruction and study.

ML1015.G9.T95
Tyler, James.
The early guitar: a history and handbook/ by James Tyler. London: Music Dept., Oxford University Press, 1980. xiii, 176 p.
80-504118   787.6/1   0193231824
Guitar.

ML1015.G9.W24 1999
Waksman, Steve.
Instruments of desire: the electric guitar and the shaping of musical experience/ Steve Waksman. Cambridge, Mass.: Havard University Press, 1999. x, 373 p.
99-039764   787.87/19   067400065X
Electric guitar -- History. Popular music -- Social aspects. Gender identity in music.

ML1015.M2 S63 1995
Sparks, Paul.
The classical mandolin/ Paul Sparks. Oxford: Clarendon Press; xiv, 225 p.
94-030665   787.8/4 20   0198162952
Mandolin.

ML1015.M2.T9 1989
Tyler, James.
The early mandolin/ by James Tyler and Paul Sparks. Oxford [Oxfordshire]: Clarendon Press; 1989. x, 186 p.
88-018103   787/.65/09   0193185164
Mandolin.

**ML1030-1041 History and criticism —
Instruments and instrumental music —
Instruments — Percussion instruments**

ML1030.B6 1992
Blades, James.
Percussion instruments and their history/ James Blades. Rev. ed. Westport, Conn.: Bold Strummer; 513 p.
93-162831   786.8/19/09 20   0933224613
Percussion instruments.

ML1030.H64 1981
Holland, James, 1933-
Percussion/ James Holland; foreword by Pierre Boulez. New York: Schirmer Books, 1981, c1978. xii, 283 p.
81-001171   789/.01   0028716000
Percussion instruments.

ML1038.T3 K36 1988
Kippen, James.
The tabla of Lucknow: a cultural analysis of a musical tradition/ James Kippen. Cambridge; Cambridge University Press, 1988. xxv, 222 p.
87-030943   789/.1 19   0521335299
Tabla. Music -- India -- Lucknow -- History and criticism. Lucknow (India) -- Social life and customs.

ML1041.G54 2001
Gifford, Paul M.
The hammered dulcimer: a history/ Paul M. Gifford. Lanham, Md.: Scarecrow Press, 2001. xxiv, 439 p.
00-061946   787.7/4 21   0810839431
Dulcimer.

**ML1055 History and criticism —
Instruments and instrumental music —
Instruments —
Mechanical instruments, devices, etc.**

ML1055.D37 2000
Day, Timothy.
A century of recorded music: listening to musical history/ Timothy Day. New Haven: Yale University Press, c2000. x, 306 p.
00-043490   780/.26/6   0300084420
Sound recordings -- History. Sound -- Recording and reproducing -- History. Sound recording industry -- History.

**ML1092 History and criticism —
Instruments and instrumental music —
Instruments — Electronic instruments**

ML1092.D54 1997
Dodge, Charles,
Computer music: synthesis, composition, and performance/ Charles Dodge, Thomas A. Jerse. [2nd ed.]. New York: Schirmer Books, 1997.
96-053478   786.7/13 21   0028646827
Computer music -- Instruction and study. Computer composition.

ML1092.P68 1992
Pressing, Jeff.
Synthesizer performance and real-time techniques/ Jeff Pressing. Madison, Wis.: A-R Editions, c1992. xiii, 462 p.
91-039700   786.7/4   0895792575
Synthesizer (Musical instrument)

ML1092.V25 1993
Vail, Mark.
Keyboard presents Vintage synthesizers: groundbreaking instruments and pioneering designers of electronic music synthesizers/ by Mark Vail. San Francisco: GPI Books; c1993. x, 300 p.
93-024714   786.7/419   0879302755
Synthesizer (Musical instrument) -- History.

ML1100-1331.1 History and criticism — Instruments and instrumental music — Ensembles

ML1100.C7 1963
Cobbett, Walter Willson, 1847-1937,
Cyclopedic survey of chamber music. Compiled and edited by Walter Willson Cobbett. With supplementary material edited by Colin Mason. London, Oxford University Press, 1963. 3 v.
64-001302   785.7003
Chamber music -- Dictionaries. Music -- Bio-bibliography.

ML1100.U4 1966
Ulrich, Homer, 1906-
Chamber music. New York, Columbia University Press, 1966. xvi, 401 p.
66-017909   785.7009
Chamber music -- History and criticism.

ML1104.N56 1998
Nineteenth-century chamber music/ edited by Stephen E. Hefling. New York: Schirmer Books; c1998. xv, 389 p.
97-021884   785/.009/034   0028710347
Chamber music -- 19th century -- History and criticism.

ML1156.A44.I8 1992
Allsop, Peter,
The Italian 'trio' sonata: from its origins until Corelli/ Peter Allsop. Oxford: Clarendon Press; 1992. ix, 334 p.
92-001001   785/.13183/0945   0198162294
Trio sonata. Chamber music -- Italy -- 17th century -- History and criticism.

ML1156.N42 1983
Newman, William S.
The sonata in the baroque era/ by William S. Newman. 4th ed. New York: W.W. Norton, 1983. xiv, 476 p.
82-024574   781/.52/09032 19   0393952754
Sonata -- 17th century. Sonata -- 18th century.

ML1156.N43 1983
Newman, William S.
The sonata in the classic era/ by William S. Newman. 3rd ed. New York: W.W. Norton, 1983. xxii, 933 p.
82-024575   781/.52/09033 19   039395286X
Sonata -- 18th century. Classicism in music.

ML1156.N44 1983
Newman, William S.
The sonata since Beethoven/ by William S. Newman. 3rd ed. New York: W.W. Norton, c1983. xxvi, 870 p.
82-024573   781/.52/09034 19   0393952908
Sonata -- 19th century. Sonata -- 20th century.

ML1156.N4S63
Newman, William S.
The sonata since Beethoven; the third and final volume of a history of the sonata idea, by William S. Newman. Chapel Hill, University of North Carolina Press [1969] xxvi, 854 p.
76-080924   785.3/1
Sonata.

ML1156.R67 1988
Rosen, Charles,
Sonata forms/ by Charles Rosen. Rev. ed. New York: Norton, c1988. 415 p.
88-167680   781/.52 19   0393026582
Sonata form.

ML1160.G74 1983
Griffiths, Paul, 1947 Nov. 24-
The string quartet/ Paul Griffiths. New York, N.Y.: Thames and Hudson, 1983. 240 p.
83-070402   785.7/0471   050001311X
String quartet.

ML1165.S59 1994
Smallman, Basil.
The piano quartet and quintet: style, structure, and scoring/ Basil Smallman. Oxford: Clarendon Press; 1994. ix, 196 p.
94-009685   785/.2194   0198163746
Piano quartets -- History and criticism. Piano quintets -- History and criticism.

ML1165.S6 1989
Smallman, Basil.
The piano trio: its history, technique, and repertoire/ Basil Smallman. Oxford [England]: Clarendon Press; 1990. viii, 230 p.
89-009412   785/.28193   0193183072
Piano trios -- History and criticism.

ML1200.D45
Del Mar, Norman, 1919-
Anatomy of the orchestra/ Norman Del Mar. Berkeley: University of California Press, c1981. 528 p.
81-011559   785/.06/61   0520045009
Orchestra. Music -- Performance.

ML1200.U4
Ulrich, Homer, 1906-
Symphonic music, its evolution since the Renaissance. New York, Columbia University Press, 1952. 352 p.
52-012033   785.11
Orchestral music -- History and criticism.

ML1251.I53 L56 1992
Lindsay, Jennifer.
Javanese gamelan: traditional orchestra of Indonesia/
Jennifer Lindsay. 2nd ed. Singapore; Oxford University
Press, 1992. vii, 76 p.
92-000163   784.2/09598/2 20   0195885821
Gamelan. Music -- Indonesia -- Java -- History and criticism.

ML1255.B67 1996
Bonds, Mark Evan.
After Beethoven: imperatives of originality in the
symphony/ Mark Evan Bonds. Cambridge, Mass.:
Harvard University Press, 1996. 212 p.
96-028053   784.2/184/09034   0674008553
Symphony -- 19th century. Originality.

ML1255.C9 1995
Cuyler, Louise Elvira, 1908-
The symphony/ Louise Cuyler. Warren, Mich.: Harmonie
Park Press, 1995. x, 248 p.
95-013538   784.2/184   0899900720
Symphony.

ML1255.N5 1996
The nineteenth-century symphony/ edited by D. Kern
Holoman. New York: Schirmer Books; c1997. xvii,
468 p.
96-024580   784.2/184/09034   002871105X
Symphony -- 19th century.

ML1263.C64 1989
A Companion to the concerto/ edited by Robert Layton.
New York: Schirmer Books, 1989, c1988. xiv, 369 p.
88-026417   785.6   0028719611
Concerto.

ML1263.K47 1999
Kerman, Joseph, 1924-
Concerto conversations/ Joseph Kerman. Cambridge,
Mass.: Harvard University Press, 1999. 175 p.
99-030919   784.2/3   0674158911
Concerto.

ML1263.R64 1994
Roeder, Michael Thomas.
A history of the concerto/ Michael Thomas Roeder.
Portland, Or.: Amadeus Press, c1994. 480 p.
92-041967   784.2/3/09   0931340616
Concerto.

ML1263.S74 1998
Steinberg, Michael,
The concerto: a listener's guide/ Michael Steinberg. New
York: Oxford University Press, 1998. xv, 506 p.
97-042678   784.2/3/015 21   0195103300
Concerto.

ML1263.W53 1992
White, Chappell.
From Vivaldi to Viotti: a history of the early classical
violin concerto/ Chappell White. Philadelphia: Gordon
and Breach, c1992. xxviii, 375 p.
91-008775   784.2/72/09033 20   2881244955
*Vivaldi, Antonio, 1678-1741. Viotti, Giovanni Battista, 1755-
1824. Concertos (Violin with string orchestra) -- 18th century --
History and Concertos (Violin) -- 18th century -- History and
criticism.*

ML1263.W55 1991
Whitmore, Philip.
Unpremeditated art: the cadenza in the classical keyboard
concerto/ Philip Whitmore. Oxford [England]: Clarendon
Press; 1991. xviii, 227 p.
90-007831   784.2/62/09033   0193152630
*Concertos (Piano) -- 18th century -- Cadenzas -- History and
criticism. Improvisation (Music)*

ML1300.F33 1970
Farmer, Henry George, 1882-
The rise & development of military music. With an
introd. by Albert Williams. Freeport, N.Y., Books for
Libraries Press [1970] xxi, 156 p.
79-107801   785.06/71   0836952049
Military music -- History and criticism.

ML1300.G65
Goldman, Richard Franko, 1910-
The wind band, its literature and technique. Boston,
Allyn and Bacon, 1961 [c1962] xvi, 286 p.
62-008835   785.12
Bands (Music)

ML1311.7.P4 K73 1990
Kreitner, Kenneth.
Discoursing sweet music: town bands and community life
in turn-of-the-century Pennsylvania/ Kenneth Kreitner.
Urbana: University of Illinois Press, c1990. xvi, 205 p.
89-004766   785/.06/70974823 19   0252016610
*Bands (Music) -- Pennsylvania -- Wayne County -- History --
19th century. Bands (Music) -- Pennsylvania -- Wayne County --
History -- 20th century.*

ML1331.1.B75 2000
The British brass band: a musical and social history/
edited by Trevor Herbert. Oxford: Clarendon Press; xii,
381 p.
99-057637   784.9/0941 21   0198166982
Brass bands -- Great Britain.

ML1400 History and criticism —
Vocal music — General works

ML1400.P3 1974
Partch, Harry, 1901-1974.
Genesis of a music; an account of a creative work, its
roots and its fulfillments. New York, Da Capo Press,
1974. xxv, 517 p.
76-087373   780/.92/4   030671597X
*Vocal music -- History and criticism. Musical intervals and
scales. Musical instruments.*

ML1406 History and criticism — Vocal music — By period

ML1406.T5 1989
Thomson, Virgil, 1896-
Music with words: a composer's view/ Virgil Thomson.
New Haven: Yale University Press, c1989. x, 178 p.
89-030709   784/.028   0300045050
Vocal music -- 20th century -- History and criticism.
Composition (Music) Libretto.

ML1460 History and criticism — Vocal music — Vocal technique

ML1460.C28 2000
The Cambridge companion to singing/ edited by John
Potter. Cambridge, UK; Cambridge University Press,
2000. x, 286 p.
99-032948   782/.009   0521622255
Singing -- History. Choral singing -- History. Vocal music --
History and criticism.

ML1460.H46 1982
Hines, Jerome, 1921-
Great singers on great singing/ Jerome Hines. Garden
City, N.Y.: Doubleday, 1982. 356 p.
81-043280   784.9/3   0385146388
Singing. Singers -- Interviews.

ML1460.R68 1992
Rosselli, John.
Singers of Italian opera: the history of a profession/ John
Rosselli. Cambridge; Cambridge University Press, 1992.
xvi, 272 p.
91-040160   782.1/023/45   0521416833
Singers. Opera -- Italy. Singing -- History.

ML1460.S73 1992
Steane, J. B.
Voices, singers & critics/ J.B. Steane. Portland, Or.:
Amadeus Press, c1992. x, 294 p.
93-123440   783/.009 20   0931340543
Singing -- History. Singers. Musical criticism.

ML1500 History and criticism — Vocal music — Choral music

ML1506.S76 2002
Strimple, Nick.
Choral music in the twentieth century/ Nick Strimple.
Portland, Or.: Amadeus Press, c2002. 389 p.
2002-066536   782.5/09/04 21   1574670743
Choral music -- 20th century.

ML1700-2831 History and criticism — Vocal music — Secular vocal music

ML1700.A7 1992
Arblaster, Anthony.
Viva la liberta!: politics in opera/ Anthony Arblaster.
London; Verso, 1992. vii, 340 p.
92-027541   782.1/1599   0860913910
Opera -- Political aspects.

ML1700.B79 1996
Brener, Milton E., 1930-
Opera offstage: passion and politics behind the great
operas/ Milton Brener. New York: Walker and Co., 1996.
xv, 240 p.
95-030180   782.1/09   0802713130
Opera -- Social aspects. Opera -- Political aspects.

ML1700.C58 1999
Clum, John M.
Something for the boys: musical theater and gay culture/
John M. Clum. New York: St. Martin's Press, c1999. vii,
317 p.
99-025435   782.1/4/086642   0312210582
Gay men and musicals.

ML1700.D4 1990
Dean, Winton.
Essays on opera/ Winton Dean. Oxford [England]:
Clarendon Press; 1990. x, 323 p.
89-048621   782.1   0193152657
Opera.

ML1700.D66
Donington, Robert.
The opera/ Robert Donington. New York: Harcourt Brace
Jovanovich, 1978. x, 238 p.
77-093589   782.1   0155675362
Opera.

ML1700.D665 1990
Donington, Robert.
Opera and its symbols: the unity of words, music, and
staging/ Robert Donington. New Haven: Yale University
Press, c1990. viii, 248 p.
89-039530   782.1   0300047134
Opera. Symbolism in music.

ML1700.D67
Donington, Robert.
The rise of opera/ Robert Donington. New York: C.
Scribner's Sons, c1981. 399 p.
81-050730   782.1/09/032   0684171651
Opera.

ML1700.G322 1997
Ganzl, Kurt.
The musical: a concise history/ Kurt Ganzl. Boston:
Northeastern University Press, c1997. xv, 432 p.
97-003008   782.1/4/09   1555533116
Musicals -- History and criticism.

ML1700.G738 B7
Goldovsky, Boris.
Bringing opera to life; operatic acting and stage direction.
New York, Appleton-Century-Crofts [1968] x, 424 p.
68-015228   782.1/07
Opera. Opera -- Production and direction.

ML1700.G83 2003
Grout, Donald Jay.
A short history of opera/ Donald Jay Grout and Hermine Weigel Williams. 4th ed. New York: Columbia University Press, 2003.
2002-041470   782.1/09 21   0231119585
Opera.

ML1700.H42 1987
Headington, Christopher.
Opera: a history/ Christopher Headington, Roy Westbrook, Terry Barfoot. London: Bodley Head, 1987. 399 p.
87-166487   782.1/09 19   0370308891
Opera.

ML1700.H57 1990
History of opera/ edited by Stanley Sadie. 1st American ed. New York: W.W. Norton, 1990. xiii, 485 p.
90-197183   782.1/09 20   0393028100
Opera.

ML1700.H87 1996
Hutcheon, Linda, 1947-
Opera: desire, disease, death/ Linda Hutcheon & Michael Hutcheon. Lincoln: University of Nebraska Press, c1996. xvi, 294 p.
95-018825   782.1   0803223676
Sex in opera. Diseases in opera. Death in opera.

ML1700.O644 2002
Opera: a history in documents/ [compiled by] Piero Weiss. New York; Oxford University Press, 2002. xii, 338 p.
2001-032179   782.1/09 21   0195116380
Opera -- Sources.

ML1700.O95 1994
The Oxford illustrated history of opera/ edited by Roger Parker. Oxford [England]; Oxford University Press, 1994. xv, 541 p.
93-024898   782.1/03   0198162820
Opera. Opera -- Pictorial works.

ML1700.S13 1997
Sacher, Jack.
Opera: a listener's guide/ Jack Sacher. New York: Schirmer Books, c1997. xv, 511 p.
97-011271   782.1 21   0028722728
Opera.

ML1700.S9485 1996
Sutcliffe, Tom.
Believing in opera/ by Tom Sutcliffe. Princeton, NJ: Princeton University Press, c1996. xv, 464 p.
96-034342   782.1   0691015635
Opera. Musical theater.

ML1704.D46
Dent, Edward Joseph, 1876-1957.
The rise of romantic opera/ Edward J. Dent; edited by Winton Dean. Cambridge; Cambridge University Press, 1976. x, 198 p.
76-014029   782.1/094   0521213371
Opera.

ML1705.M67
Mordden, Ethan, 1947-
Opera in the twentieth century: sacred, profane, Godot/ Ethan Mordden. New York: Oxford University Press, 1978. ix, 357 p.
77-023745   782.1/09   0195022882
Opera -- 20th century.

ML1711.B66 1982
Bordman, Gerald Martin.
American musical comedy: from Adonis to Dreamgirls/ Gerald Bordman. New York: Oxford University Press, 1982. vi, 244 p.
81-022444   782.81/0973 19   0195031040
Musicals -- United States -- History and criticism.

ML1711.B665 1985
Bordman, Gerald Martin.
American musical revue: from The passing show to Sugar babies/ Gerald Bordman. New York: Oxford University Press, 1985. vi, 184 p.
85-004816   782.81/0973   0195036301
Musicals -- United States -- History and criticism.

ML1711.B67 2001
Bordman, Gerald Martin.
American musical theatre: a chronicle/ Gerald Bordman. 3rd ed. Oxford; Oxford University Press, 2001. xvi, 917 p.
00-059812   782.1/4/0973 21   019513074X
Musicals--United States--History and criticism.

ML1711.C63 1997
Cockrell, Dale.
Demons of disorder: early blackface minstrels and their world/ Dale Cockrell. Cambridge; Cambridge University Press, 1997. xx, 236 p.
96-045566   791/.12/0973   0521560748
Dixon, George Washington, -- 1808-1861. Minstrel music -- United States -- History and criticism. Blackface entertainers -- United States. Minstrel shows -- History. United States -- Social conditions -- 19th century. United States -- Race relations.

ML1711.F57 1997
Flinn, Denny Martin.
Musical!: a grand tour: the rise, glory, and fall of an American institution/ Denny Martin Flinn. New York: Schirmer Books; c1997. xv, 556 p.
96-046030   782.1/4/0973   002864610X
Musicals -- United States -- History and criticism.

ML1711.G74 1980
Green, Stanley.
The world of musical comedy: the story of the American musical stage as told through the careers of its foremost composers and lyricists/ Stanley Green; photo. by Martha Swope. 4th ed., rev. and enl. San Diego, CA: A.S. Barnes; c1980. xiv, 480 p.
80-016915   782.81/0973   0498023443
Musicals--United States--History and criticism. Composers--United States. Librettists--United States.

ML1711.K56 2001
Kirk, Elise K. 1932-
American opera/ Elise K. Kirk. Urbana: University of Illinois Press, c2001. xii, 459 p.
00-009959   782.1/0973   0252026233
Opera -- United States.

ML1711.L67 1993
Lott, Eric.
Love and theft: blackface minstrelsy and the American working class/ Eric Lott. New York: Oxford University Press, 1993. 314 p.
92-041071   791/.12/097309034   0195078322
Minstrel shows -- United States -- History and criticism. Working class -- United States. United States -- Race relations. United States -- History -- Civil War, 1861-1865.

ML1711.M39 1987
Mast, Gerald, 1940-
Can't help singin': the American musical on stage and screen/ Gerald Mast. Woodstock, N.Y.: Overlook Press, 1987. x, 389 p.
87-007986   782.81/0973   0879512830
Musicals -- United States -- History and criticism. Musical films -- United States -- History and criticism.

ML1711.W64 1989
Woll, Allen L.
Black musical theatre: from Coontown to Dreamgirls/ Allen Woll. Baton Rouge: Louisiana State University Press, c1989. xiv, 301 p.
88-008904   782.81/08996073   0807114693
Musicals -- United States -- History and criticism. Revues -- United States -- History and criticism. Afro-Americans -- Music -- History and criticism.

ML1711.8.N3.B56 1997
Block, Geoffrey Holden.
Enchanted evenings: the Broadway musical from Show boat to Sondheim/ Geoffrey Block. New York: Oxford University Press, 1997. xx, 410 p.
96-053477   782.1/4/097471   0195107918
Musicals -- New York (State) -- New York -- History and criticism.

ML1711.8.N3 M434 1992
Jackson, Paul,
Saturday afternoons at the old Met: the Metropolitan Opera broadcasts, 1931-1950/ by Paul Jackson. Portland, Or.: Amadeus Press, c1992. xvi, 569 p.
91-033533   782.1/09747/1 20   0931340489
Opera -- New York (State) -- New York -- 20th century. Radio and music -- United States.

ML1711.8.N3 M4343 1997
Jackson, Paul,
Sign-off for the old Met: the Metropolitan Opera broadcasts, 1950-1966/ by Paul Jackson. Portland, Or.: Amadeus Press, c1997. xv, 644 p.
97-019864   782.1/09747/1 21   1574670301
Opera -- New York (State) -- New York -- 20th century. Radio and music -- United States.

ML1711.8.N3.R5 1989
Riis, Thomas Laurence.
Just before jazz: Black musical theater in New York, 1890-1915/ Thomas L. Riis. Washington: Smithsonian Institution Press, c1989. xxiv, 309 p.
88-600332   782.81/0899607307471   0874747880
Musical theater -- New York (State) -- New York -- History. Afro-Americans -- New York (State) -- New York -- Music -- History and criticism. Afro-American musicians -- New York (State) -- New York.

ML1711.8.N3.R67 1993
Rosenberg, Bernard, 1923-
The Broadway musical: collaboration in commerce and art/ Bernard Rosenberg and Ernest Harburg. New York: New York University Press, c1993. xxii, 356 p.
93-022380   792.6/09747/1   0814774334
Musicals -- New York (State) -- New York -- History and criticism.

ML1720.R6 1985
Robinson, Paul A., 1940-
Opera & ideas: from Mozart to Strauss/ by Paul A. Robinson. New York: Harper & Row, c1985. 279 p.
84-048822   782.1/09   0060154500
Opera. Song cycles -- History and criticism. Europe -- Intellectual life.

ML1723.8.V6.H86 1999
Hunter, Mary Kathleen, 1951-
The culture of opera buffa in Mozart's Vienna: a poetics of entertainment/ Mary Hunter. Princeton, N.J.: Princeton University Press, c1999. xiii, 329 p.
98-012583   782.1/09436/1309033   0691058121
Mozart, Wolfgang Amadeus, -- 1756-1791. -- Operas. Opera -- Austria -- Vienna -- 18th century.

ML1723.8.V6.O64 1997
Opera buffa in Mozart's Vienna/ edited by Mary Hunter and James Webster. New York: Cambridge University Press, 1997. xii, 459 p.
96-050282   782.1/09436/1309033   0521572398
Mozart, Wolfgang Amadeus, -- 1756-1791. Opera -- Austria -- Vienna -- 18th century.

ML1727.8.P2.B313 1995
Barbier, Patrick.
Opera in Paris, 1800-1850: a lively history/ by Patrick Barbier; translated by Robert Luoma. Portland, Or.: Amadeus Press, c1995. vii, 243 p.
94-026952   782.1/0944/36109034   0931340837
Opera -- France -- Paris -- 19th century.

ML1727.8.P2.G3813 1998
Gerhard, Anselm, 1958-
The urbanization of opera: music theater in Paris in the nineteenth century/ by Anselm Gerhard; translated by Mary Whittall. Chicago: University of Chicago Press, c1998. xxi, 503 p.
97-046199   782.1/0944/36109034   0226288579
Opera -- France -- Paris -- 19th century. Opera -- Social aspects.

ML1731.W58 1983
White, Eric Walter, 1905-
A history of English opera/ Eric Walter White. London: Faber and Faber, 1983. 472 p.
83-001599   782.1/0942   0571107885
Opera -- England.

ML1733.K55 1990
Kimbell, David R. B.
Italian opera/ David Kimbell. Cambridge [England]; Cambridge University Press, 1991. xvii, 684 p.
89-017414   782.1/0945   0521235332
Opera -- Italy.

ML1733.R78 1984
Rosselli, John.
The opera industry in Italy from Cimarosa to Verdi: the role of the impresario/ John Rosselli. Cambridge [Cambridgeshire]; Cambridge University Press, 1984. viii, 214 p.
83-007688   782.1/0945   0521257328
Opera -- Italy -- 18th century. Opera -- Italy -- 19th century. Impresarios -- Italy.

ML1733.8.V4.R67 1991
Rosand, Ellen.
Opera in seventeenth-century Venice: the creation of a genre/ Ellen Rosand. Berkeley: University of California Press, c1991. xxii, 684 p.
90-040399   782.1/0945/3109032   0520068084
Opera -- Italy -- Venice -- 17th century.

ML1737.B83 2000
Buckler, Julie A.
The literary lorgnette: attending opera in imperial Russia/ Julie A. Buckler. Stanford, Calif.: Stanford University Press, c2000. xii, 294 p.
99-086375   782.1/0947 21   0804732477
Opera -- Russia.

ML1751.C4.M32 1997
Mackerras, Colin.
Peking opera/ Colin Mackerras. Hong Kong; Oxford University Press, 1997. viii, 72 p.
97-006887   782.1/0951   0195877292
Operas, Chinese -- History and criticism.

ML1751.C4.Y9 1989
Yung, Bell.
Cantonese opera: performance as creative process/ Bell Yung. Cambridge [Cambridgeshire]; Cambridge University Press, 1989. xiv, 205 p.
88-020297   782.1/0951/27   0521305063
Operas, Chinese -- China -- Guangdong Sheng -- History and criticism.

ML1751.M4.M35 1993
Matusky, Patricia Ann.
Malaysian shadow play and music: continuity of an oral tradition/ Patricia Matusky. Kuala Lumpur; Oxford University Press, 1993. xii, 149 p.
93-001647   782.1/09595   9676530484
Dramatic music -- Malaysia -- History and criticism. Wayang. Music -- Malaysia -- History and criticism.

ML1751.M4.T34 1993
Tan, Sooi Beng.
Bangsawan: a social and stylistic history of popular Malay opera/ Tan Sooi Beng. Singapore; Oxford University Press, 1993. xxiii, 261 p.
92-025275   782.1/09595/1   0195885996
Bangsawan -- Malaysia -- Malaya -- History and criticism. Malaysia -- Social life and customs. Malaya -- Social life and customs.

ML1900.T7 1983
Traubner, Richard.
Operetta: a theatrical history/ Richard Traubner. Garden City, N.Y.: Doubleday, 1983. xvii, 461 p.
77-027684   782.81/09   0385132328
Operetta.

ML2075.B76 1994
Brown, Royal S.
Overtones and undertones: reading film music/ Royal S. Brown. Berkeley: University of California Press, c1994. x, 396 p.
93-046924   781.5/42/09 20   0520085442
Motion picture music -- History and criticism.

ML2075.D33 1990
Darby, William, 1942-
American film music: major composers, techniques, trends, 1915-1990/ William Darby and Jack Du Bois. Jefferson, N.C.: McFarland, c1990. xvii, 605 p.
90-005973   781.5/42/0973   089950468X
Motion picture music -- United States -- History and criticism. Motion picture music -- United States -- Analysis, appreciation.

ML2075.G33 1996
Gabbard, Krin.
Jammin' at the margins: jazz and the American cinema/ Krin Gabbard. Chicago: University of Chicago Press, 1996. xi, 350 p.
95-025337   791.43/657   0226277887
Motion pictures and music. Jazz -- History and criticism. Musical films -- History.

ML2075.K37 1994
Karlin, Fred.
Listening to movies: the film lover's guide to film music/ Fred Karlin; foreword by Leonard Maltin. New York: Schirmer Books; xv, 429 p.
93-014304   781.5/42 20   0028733150
Motion picture music -- History and criticism.

ML2075.K58 2000
Knowing the score: film composers talk about the art, craft, blood, sweat, and tears of writing music for cinema/ by David Morgan [interviewer]. New York: HarperEntertainment, c2000. xix, 313 p.
00-038285   781.5/42/0922 21   0380804824
Motion picture music--History and criticism. Composers--Interviews.

ML2075.M242 1997
Marks, Martin Miller.
Music and the silent film: contexts and case studies, 1895-1924/ Martin Miller Marks. New York: Oxford University Press, 1997. xvi, 303 p.
93-025082   781.5/42   0195068912
Silent film music -- History and criticism.

ML2075.M875 2000
Music and cinema/ edited by James Buhler, Caryl Flinn, and David Neumeyer. Hanover, NH: University Press of New England, c2000. vi, 397 p.
00-023696   781.5/42   0819564109
Motion picture music -- History and criticism. Musical films -- History and criticism.

ML2075.P28 1990
Palmer, Christopher.
The composer in Hollywood/ Christopher Palmer. London; Marion Boyars; 1990. 346 p.
89-022401   781.5/42/0979493   0714528854
Motion picture music -- History and criticism. Music -- California -- Los Angeles -- 20th century -- History and criticism. Hollywood (Los Angeles, Calif.) -- History.

ML2075.P73 1991
Prendergast, Roy M.,
Film music: a neglected art: a critical study of music in films/ Roy M. Prendergast. 2nd ed. New York: W.W. Norton, c1992. xxii, 329 p.
90-021393   781.5/42/09 20   039330874X
Motion picture music--History and criticism.

ML2075.S65 1998
Smith, Jeff
The sounds of commerce: marketing popular film music/ Jeff Smith. New York: Columbia University Press, c1998. x, 288 p.
98-017923   781.5/42/0688   0231108621
Motion picture music -- Economic aspects. Music trade -- United States. Motion picture music -- History and criticism.

ML2080.B39 1997
Baxter, Joan, 1927-
Television musicals: plots, critiques, casts, and credits for 222 shows written for and presented on television, 1944-1996/ by Joan Baxter. Jefferson, N.C.: McFarland, c1997. xi, 204 p.
97-013655   016.79145/6   0786402865
Television musicals -- United States -- Stories, plots, etc.

ML2100.C613 1988
Clement, Catherine, 1939-
Opera, or, The undoing of women/ Catherine Clement; translated by Betsy Wing; foreword by Susan McClary. Minneapolis: University of Minnesota Press, c1988. xviii, 201 p.
87-034322   782.1/09   0816616531
Women in opera.

ML2533.L25 1989
Lakeway, Ruth C.
Italian art song/ Ruth C. Lakeway and Robert C. White, Jr. Bloomington: Indiana University Press, c1989. ix, 399 p.
87-046370   784.3/00945 19   0253331544
Songs with piano -- 20th century -- History and criticism. Music -- Italy -- History and criticism.

ML2631.F45 1972
Fellowes, Edmund Horace, 1870-1951.
The English madrigal. Freeport, N.Y., Books for Libraries Press [1972] 111 p.
72-006997   784/.1   0836969294
Madrigals, English -- History and criticism. Composers, English. Music -- 16th century -- History and criticism.

ML2631.F46 1948
Fellowes, Edmund Horace, 1870-1951.
The English madrigal composers. London, Oxford University Press, 1948. 364 p.
49-009603
Composers -- England. Madrigals -- History and criticism.

ML2631.K47
Kerman, Joseph, 1924-
The Elizabethan madrigal; a comparative study. [New York?] American Musicological Society; distributor: Galaxy Music Corp., New York [1962] xxii, 318 p.
62-052131   784.1
Music -- History and criticism. Music -- England -- History and criticism. Madrigals -- History and criticism.

ML2633.F46 1988
Fenlon, Iain.
The Italian madrigal in the early sixteenth century: sources and interpretation/ Iain Fenlon & James Haar. Cambridge; Cambridge University Press, 1988. x, 369 p.
88-011119   784.1/2/00945   0521252288
Madrigals, Italian -- 16th century -- History and criticism. Madrigals, Italian -- 16th century -- Bibliography.

ML2800.S8 1961
Stevens, Denis, 1922-
A history of song. New York, W. W. Norton [1961, c1960] 491 p.
61-005622   784.09
Songs -- History and criticism.

ML2829.B76
Brody, Elaine.
The German lied and its poetry [by] Elaine Brody and Robert A. Fowkes. New York, New York University Press, 1971. viii, 316 p.
76-124520   784/.3/00943   0814709583
Songs, German -- History and criticism. German poetry -- 19th century -- History and criticism.

ML2829.K7 1996
Kravitt, Edward F.
The lied: mirror of late romanticism/ Edward F. Kravitt. New Haven: Yale University Press, c1996. xii, 323 p.
95-042761   782.42168/0943   0300063652
Songs, German -- 19th century -- History and criticism. Songs, German -- 20th century -- History and criticism.

ML2829.S55 1987
Smeed, J. W.
German song and its poetry, 1740-1900/ J.W. Smeed. London; Croom Helm, c1987. xiv, 246 p.
87-006786   784.3/00943 19   0709944071
Songs, German -- 18th century -- History and criticism. Songs, German -- 19th century -- History and criticism. German poetry -- 18th century -- History and criticism. German poetry -- 19th century -- History and criticism. Music and literature.

ML2829.W5 1984
Whitton, Kenneth S.
Lieder: an introduction to German song/ Kenneth Whitton; foreword by Dietrich Fischer-Dieskau. London: J. MacRae; 1984. xii, 203 p.
84-050908   784.3/00943 19   0531097595
Songs -- Germany -- History and criticism. Songs -- Austria -- History and criticism.

ML2831.B35 1985
Banfield, Stephen,
Sensibility and English song: critical studies of the early 20th century/ Stephen Banfield. Cambridge [Cambridgeshire]; Cambridge University Press, 2 v.
83-007801   784.3/00942 19   0521303605
Songs -- England -- 20th century -- History and criticism. Music and literature.

ML2900-3195 History and criticism —
Vocal music — Sacred vocal music

ML2900.S2 1992
Sacred sound and social change: liturgical music in Jewish and Christian experience/ edited by Lawrence A. Hoffman and Janet R. Walton. Notre Dame: University of Notre Dame Press, 1992. vi, 352 p.
91-051120   782.3   026801745X
Church music. Music -- Religious aspects -- Christianity. Synagogue music -- History and criticism.

ML2929.W43 1996
Webber, Geoffrey.
North German church music in the age of Buxtehude/ Geoffrey Webber. Oxford: Clarendon Press; 1996. viii, 236 p.
95-035104   782.2/2/094309032   019816212X
Buxtehude, Dietrich, -- 1637-1707. Church music -- Germany, Northern -- 18th century. Music -- Social aspects. Church music -- Germany, Northern -- 17th century.

ML2931.S8 1966a
Stevens, Denis, 1922-
Tudor church music, by Denis Stevens. New York, W. W. Norton [1966] 97 p.
65-013528   783.0942
Church music -- England -- 16th century. Great Britain -- History -- Tudors, 1485-1603.

ML3000.P53 1994
Plank, Steven Eric.
"The way to heavens doore": an introduction to liturgical process and musical style/ by Steven Plank. Metuchen, N.J.: Scarecrow Press, 1994. xiv, 183 p.
94-034082   781.71 20   0810829533
Church music. Liturgics.

ML3003.J362 1970
Jeppesen, Knud, 1892-
The style of Palestrina and the dissonance. With an introd. by Edward J. Dent. New York, Dover Publications [1970] 306 p.
69-018888   781.3   0486223868
Palestrina, Giovanni Pierluigi da, -- 1525?-1594 -- Harmony. Dissonance (Music) Music -- 16th century -- History and criticism.

ML3027.8.P2.W7 1989
Wright, Craig M.
Music and ceremony at Notre Dame of Paris, 500-1550/ Craig Wright. Cambridge [England]; Cambridge University Press, 1989. xvii, 400 p.
88-029924   783.2/00944/361   0521244927
Church music -- France -- Paris -- 500-1400. Church music -- France -- Paris -- 15th century. Church music -- France -- Paris -- 16th century.

ML3082.A64
Apel, Willi, 1893-
Gregorian chant. Bloomington, Indiana University Press [1958] xiv, 529 p.
57-010729   783.5
Chants (Plain, Gregorian, etc.) -- History and criticism.

ML3082.C73 2000
Crocker, Richard L.
An introduction to Gregorian chant/ Richard L. Crocker. New Haven, CT: Yale University Press, c2000. 248 p.
99-088603   782.32/22   0300083106
Chants (Plain, Gregorian, etc.) -- History and criticism.

ML3082.H54 1993
Hiley, David.
Western plainchant: a handbook/ David Hiley. Oxford [England]: Clarendon Press; 1993. xcvii, 661 p.
92-013020   782.32/22   0198162898
  Chants (Plain, Gregorian, etc.) -- History and criticism.

ML3082.L44 1998
Levy, Kenneth, 1927-
Gregorian chant and the Carolingians/ Kenneth Levy. Princeton, N.J.: Princeton University Press, c1998. x, 271 p.
97-021957   782.32/22/009021   0691017336
  Chants (Plain, Gregorian, etc.) -- History and criticism.

ML3088.R62 1968
Robertson, Alec.
Requiem: music of mourning and consolation.   New York, F. A. Praeger [1968, c1967] xii, 300 p.
68-019860   783.2/9
  Requiems -- History and criticism. Holy Week music -- History and criticism. Funeral music -- History and criticism.

ML3100.B5913
Blume, Friedrich,
Protestant church music; a history. By Friedrich Blume, in collaboration with Ludwig Finscher [and others] Foreword by Paul Henry Lang. [1st ed.] New York, W. W. Norton [1974] xv, 831 p.
74-008392   783/.026   0393021769
  Church music--Protestant churches.

ML3111.C6
Cobb, Buell E.
The sacred harp: a tradition and its music/ Buell E. Cobb, Jr. Athens: University of Georgia Press, c1978. ix, 245 p.
77-006323   783.6/7   0820304263
  White, Benjamin Franklin, -- comp. -- Sacred harp.   Hymns, English -- Southern States -- History and criticism. Church music -- Southern States.

ML3111.F6.T4 1961
Foote, Henry Wilder, 1875-1964.
Three centuries of American hymnody. Hamden, Conn.: Shoe String Press, 1961 [c1940] x, 418 p.
61-004914   245.2
  Hymns, English -- History and criticism. Church music -- United States -- History and criticism. Psalmody.

ML3131.F3 1969
Fellowes, Edmund Horace, 1870-1951.
English cathedral music [by] Edmund H. Fellowes. London, Methuen, 1969. xi, 283 p.
70-456990   783/.0942   0416148506
  Church music -- Church of England. Church music -- England.

ML3131.H88
Hutchings, Arthur, 1906-
Church music in the nineteenth century.   New York, Oxford University Press, 1967. 166 p.
67-016679   783/.0942
  Church music -- Protestant churches. Music -- 19th century -- History and criticism. Church music -- England -- History and criticism.

ML3131.L6
Long, Kenneth R.
The music of the English church, by Kenneth R. Long. London, Hodder and Stoughton, 1972. 480 p.
72-181799   783/.026/342   0340149620
  Church music -- England. Church music -- Church of England.

ML3131.R68
Routley, Erik.
Twentieth century church music.   New York, Oxford University Press, 1964. 244 p.
64-005901
  Church music -- England -- History and criticism. Church music -- Protestant churches. Music -- History and criticism -- 20th cent.

ML3131.T44
Temperley, Nicholas.
The music of the English parish church/ Nicholas Temperley. Cambridge; Cambridge University Press, 1979. 2 v.
77-084811   783/.026/342   0521220459
  Church music -- England. Church music -- Church of England. Sacred vocal music -- England.

ML3160.P28 1995
Patterson, Beverly Bush, 1939-
The sound of the dove: singing in Appalachian Primitive Baptist churches/ Beverly Bush Patterson. Urbana: University of Illinois Press, c1995. x, 238 p.
94-001697   782.32/261/00974   0252021231
  Church music -- Primitive Baptists. Church music -- Appalachian Region. Choral singing.

ML3178.S5.P4
Patterson, Daniel W.
The Shaker spiritual/ by Daniel W. Patterson. Princeton, N.J.: Princeton University Press, c1979. xix, 562 p.
77-085557   783/.026/98   0691091242
  Folk songs, English -- United States -- History and criticism. Folk dancing -- United States. Folk music -- United States -- History and criticism.

ML3186.W2 1998
Wasson, D. DeWitt.
Hymntune index and related hymn materials/ compiled by D. DeWitt Wasson. Lanham, MD: Scarecrow Press, 1998. 3 v.
97-034320   016.78225/026/3   0810834367
  Hymn tunes -- Indexes. Hymns -- Indexes.

ML3187.B7 1995
Boyer, Horace Clarence, 1935-
How sweet the sound: the golden age of gospel/ text by Horace Clarence Boyer, photography by Lloyd Yearwood. Washington, D.C.: Elliott & Clark, c1995. 272 p.
95-234266   782.25/4/09   1880216191
  Gospel music -- History and criticism.

ML3187.G64 2002
Goff, James R.,
Close harmony: a history of southern gospel/ James R. Goff Jr. Chapel Hill: University of North Carolina Press, c2002. xiv, 394 p.
2001-043372   782.25/4/0975 21   0807853461
Gospel music -- History and criticism. Contemporary Christian music -- History and criticism.

ML3187.H37 1992
Harris, Michael W.
The rise of gospel blues: the music of Thomas Andrew Dorsey in the urban church/ Michael W. Harris. New York: Oxford University Press, 1992. xxiii, 324 p.
91-008987   782.25   0195063767
Dorsey, Thomas Andrew.   Gospel music -- History and criticism.

ML3187.H44 1985
Heilbut, Anthony.
The gospel sound: good news and bad times/ Anthony Heilbut. Updated and rev., 1st Limelight ed. New York: Limelight Editions; 1985. xxxv, 370 p.
84-026122   783.7 19
Gospel music--History and criticism. Afro-American musicians.

ML3195.S4 1992
Shiloah, Amnon.
Jewish musical traditions/ Amnon Shiloah. Detroit: Wayne State University Press, 1992. 274 p.
91-039456   781.62/924   0814322344
Jews -- Music -- History and criticism.

ML3195.S55 1989
Slobin, Mark.
Chosen voices: the story of the American cantorate/ Mark Slobin. Urbana: University of Illinois Press, c1989. xxv, 318 p.
88-017310   783.2/096/0973   0252015657
Cantors (Judaism) -- United States.

ML3406 History and criticism — Dance music — By period

ML3406.G55 1999
Gilbert, Jeremy, 1971-
Discographies: dance music, culture, and the politics of sound/ Jeremy Gilbert and Ewan Pearson. London; Routledge, 1999. xii, 195 p.
99-010971   784.18/8   041517032X
Dance music -- 20th century -- History and criticism. Dance music -- Social aspects.

ML3460-3465 History and criticism — Dance music — Forms and types

ML3460.T4 1989
Teck, Katherine.
Music for the dance: reflections on a collaborative art/ Katherine Teck. New York: Greenwood Press, 1989. viii, 230 p.
88-038551   782.9/5   0313263760
Ballet. Modern dance. Music and dance.

ML3465.A95 1997
Austerlitz, Paul,
Merengue: Dominican music and Dominican identity/ Paul Austerlitz; foreword by Robert Farris Thompson. Philadelphia, Pa.: Temple University Press, 1997. xvii, 195 p.
96-024778   784.18/88 20   1566394848
Merengue (Dance) Dance music -- Dominican Republic -- History and criticism.

ML3465.V5313 1999
Vianna, Hermano,
The mystery of samba: popular music & national identity in Brazil/ Hermano Vianna; edited and translated by John Charles Chasteen. Chapel Hill: University of North Carolina Press, c1999. xx, 147 p.
98-022170   784.18/88 21   0807847666
Sambas -- History and criticism. Popular music -- Brazil -- History and criticism. Music -- Social aspects -- Brazil.

ML3470 History and criticism — Popular music — General works

ML3470.B45 1999
Bennett, Andy, 1963-
Popular music and youth culture: music, identity, and place/ Andy Bennett. New York: St. Martin's Press, 1999. viii, 223 p.
99-016789   306.4/84   0312227531
Popular music -- Social aspects. Music and youth. Popular culture.

ML3470.B73 1995
Brackett, David.
Interpreting popular music/ David Brackett. Cambridge [England]; Cambridge University Press, 1995. xiv, 260 p.
94-043515   781.64 21   0521473373
Popular music -- History and criticism. Popular music -- Analysis, appreciation.

ML3470.M33 1988
Manuel, Peter Lamarche.
Popular musics of the non-Western world: an introductory survey/ Peter Manuel. New York: Oxford University Press, 1988. x, 287 p.
87-034861   780/.42   0195053427
Popular music -- History and criticism.

ML3470.N44 1997
Negus, Keith.
Popular music in theory: an introduction/ Keith Negus. Hanover, NH: University Press of New England, 1997. 243 p.
96-061301   781.64/01   0819563102
Popular music -- Social aspects. Popular culture -- History -- 20th century.

ML3470.P7 1990
Pratt, Ray.
Rhythm and resistance: explorations in the political uses of popular music/ Ray Pratt. New York: Praeger, 1990. xii, 241 p.
89-016197   306.4/84   0275926249
Popular music -- Political aspects. Music -- Social aspects.

ML3470.S48 1988b
Shapiro, Harry.
Waiting for the man: the story of drugs and popular music/ Harry Shapiro. New York: Morrow, c1988. x, 276 p.
89-003028   362.2/9   0688089615
Drugs and popular music. Musicians -- Drug use. Rock musicians -- Drug use.

ML3470.S54 2001
Shuker, Roy.
Understanding popular music/ Roy Shuker. London; Routledge, 2001.
00-053356   781.64/0973 21   0415235103
Popular music -- History and criticism. Popular culture -- History -- 20th century.

ML3470.V36 1989
Van der Merwe, Peter.
Origins of the popular style: the antecedents of twentieth-century popular music/ Peter van der Merwe. Oxford [Oxfordshire]: Clarendon Press; 1989. xiii, 352 p.
87-028794   780/.42/09   0193161214
Popular music -- History and criticism.

ML3475-3503 History and criticism — Popular music — By region or country

ML3475.B63 1992
Boggs, Vernon.
Salsiology: Afro-Cuban music and the evolution of salsa in New York City/ Vernon W. Boggs. New York: Greenwood Press, 1992. xvii, 386 p.
91-043983   781.62/969729107471   0313284687
Salsa (Music) -- History and criticism. Popular music -- Caribbean Area -- History and criticism. Popular music -- New York (State) -- New York -- History and criticism.

ML3477.A42 2001
American popular music: new approaches to the twentieth century/ edited by Rachel Rubin and Jeffrey Melnick. Amherst [MA]: University of Massachusetts Press, 2001. viii, 280 p.
00-048881   781.64/0973   1558492674
Popular music -- United States -- History and criticism.

ML3477.F55 1994
Finson, Jon W.
The voices that are gone: themes in nineteenth-century American popular song/ Jon W. Finson. New York: Oxford University Press, 1994. xiii, 336 p.
93-028889   782.42164/0973/09034   0195057503
Popular music -- United States -- To 1901 -- History and criticism.

ML3477.F67 1995
Forte, Allen.
The American popular ballad of the golden era, 1924-1950/ Allen Forte. Princeton, N.J.: Princeton University Press, c1995. 366 p.
94-047249   782.42164/0973/09041   069104399X
Popular music -- United States -- History and criticism.

ML3477.G36 2000
Garman, Bryan K.
A race of singers: Whitman's working-class hero from Guthrie to Springsteen/ Bryan K. Garman. Chapel Hill: University of North Carolina Press, c2000. ix, 338 p.
99-058448   781.5/9   0807825581
Whitman, Walt, -- 1819-1892 -- Influence. Guthrie, Woody, -- 1912-1967 -- Influence. Springsteen, Bruce -- Influence. Working class -- United States -- Songs and music -- History and criticism. Popular music -- Social aspects -- United States.

ML3477.H35
Hamm, Charles.
Yesterdays: popular song in America/ Charles Hamm. New York: Norton, c1979. xxii, 533 p.
79-012953   784   0393012573
Popular music -- United States -- History and criticism.

ML3477.H95 1995
Hyland, William, 1929-
The song is ended: songwriters and American music, 1900-1950/ William G. Hyland. New York: Oxford University Press, 1995. xiv, 336 p.
94-016949   782.42164/0973/09041   0195086112
Popular music -- United States -- History and criticism.

ML3477.I44 1998
Iger, Arthur L., 1926-
Music of the golden age, 1900-1950 and beyond: a guide to popular composers and lyricists/ Arthur L. Iger. Westport, Conn.: Greenwood Press, 1998. xiii, 269 p.
98-012203   781.64/0973/0904   0313306915
Popular music -- United States -- History and criticism. Composers -- United States. Lyricists -- United States.

ML3477.K46 1999
Kenney, William Howland.
Recorded music in American life: the phonograph and popular memory, 1890-1945/ William Howland Kenney. New York: Oxford University Press, 1999. xix, 258 p.
98-008611   306.4/84   0195100468
Popular music -- Social aspects -- United States. Phonograph -- Social aspects -- United States. Sound recording industry -- United States -- History.

ML3477.L43 1987
Lees, Gene.
Singers and the song/ Gene Lees. New York: Oxford University Press, 1987. xii, 257 p.
86-033233   784.5/00973   019504293X
Popular music -- United States -- History and criticism. Singers -- United States.

ML3477.M45 1999
Melnick, Jeffrey Paul.
A right to sing the blues: African Americans, Jews, and American popular song/ Jeffrey Melnick. Cambridge, Mass.: Harvard University Press, 1999. ix, 277 p.
98-033877   781.64/089/924073   0674769767
Popular music -- United States -- History and criticism. Afro-Americans -- Music -- History and criticism. Jews -- United States -- Music -- History and criticism.

ML3477.R63 1999
Roberts, John Storm.
The Latin tinge: the impact of Latin American music on the United States/ John Storm Roberts. 2nd ed. New York: Oxford University Press, 1999. xi, 294 p.
98-019580   780/.89/68073 21   0195121015
Popular music -- United States -- Latin American influences.

ML3477.S2 1996
Sanjek, Russell.
Pennies from heaven: the American popular music business in the twentieth century/ Russell Sanjek; updated by David Sanjek. New York: Da Capo Press, 1996. xx, 769 p.
96-023223   338.4/778164/09730904   0306807068
Popular music -- United States -- History and criticism. Music trade -- United States.

ML3477.S475 1987
Shaw, Arnold.
The jazz age: popular music in the 1920's/ Arnold Shaw. New York: Oxford University Press, 1987. x, 350 p.
86-033234   780/.42/0973   0195038916
Popular music -- United States -- 1921-1930 -- History and criticism. Jazz -- 1921-1930 -- History and criticism. Musicals -- United States -- History and criticism. United States -- History -- 1919-1933.

ML3477.T42 1990
Tawa, Nicholas E.
The way to Tin Pan Alley: American popular song, 1866-1910/ Nicholas E. Tawa. New York: Schirmer Books; c1990. xii, 296 p.
89-038174   782.42164/0973/09034   0028725417
Popular music -- United States -- To 1901 -- History and criticism. Popular music -- United States -- 1901-1910 -- History and criticism.

ML3479.C37 1998
California soul: music of African Americans in the West/ edited by Jacqueline Cogdell DjeDje and Eddie S. Meadows. Berkeley: University of California Press, c1998. x, 507 p.
96-049288   780/.89/960730794   0520206274
Afro-Americans -- California -- Music -- History and criticism. Popular music -- California -- History and criticism.

ML3479.W37 1998
Ward, Brian, 1961-
Just my soul responding: rhythm and blues, Black consciousness, and race relations/ Brian Ward. Berkeley [Calif.]: University of California Press, c1998. xi, 600 p.
97-039138   781.643/0973   0520212975
Rhythm and blues music -- History and criticism. Afro-Americans -- Music -- History and criticism. Popular music -- United States -- History and criticism.

ML3481.G53 1995
Glasser, Ruth.
My music is my flag: Puerto Rican musicians and their New York communities, 1917-1940/ Ruth Glasser. Berkeley: University of California Press, c1995. xxiv, 253 p.
94-009015   780/.8968729507471   0520081226
Puerto Ricans -- New York (State) -- New York -- Music -- History and criticism. Popular music -- New York (State) -- New York -- History and criticism. Popular music -- Puerto Rico -- History and criticism.

ML3481.P44 1999
Pena, Manuel H., 1942-
The Mexican American orquesta: music, culture, and the dialectic of conflict/ Manuel Pena. Austin: University of Texas Press, 1999. xii, 350 p.
99-006098   781.64/089/6872079   029276586X
Mexican Americans -- Southwestern States -- Music -- History and criticism. Mexican Americans -- Southwestern States -- Social life and customs. Popular music -- Political aspects -- Southwestern States.

ML3486.C8.M66 1997
Moore, Robin, 1964-
Nationalizing blackness: afrocubanismo and artistic revolution in Havana, 1920-1940/ Robin Moore. Pittsburgh, Pa.: University of Pittsburgh Press, c1997. xii, 320 p.
97-021045   781.63/089/9607291   082294040X
Popular music -- Cuba -- African influences. Blacks -- Cuba -- Music. Popular culture -- Cuba -- African influences.

ML3486.H3.A94 1997
Averill, Gage.
A day for the hunter, a day for the prey: popular music and power in Haiti/ Gage Averill. Chicago: University of Chicago Press, 1997. xxix, 276 p.
96-034209   781.63/097294   0226032914
Popular music -- Haiti -- History and criticism. Power (Social sciences) -- Haiti -- History -- 20th century.

ML3486.T7.S78 1995
Stuempfle, Stephen.
The steelband movement/ the forging of a national art in Trinidad and Tobago/ Stephen Stuempfle. Philadelphia: University of Pennsylvania Press, c1995. xx, 287 p.
95-038564   784.6/8   0812233298
Steel bands (Music) -- Trinidad and Tobago -- History. Popular music -- Trinidad and Tobago -- History and criticism.

ML3487.B7.B76 2001
Brazilian popular music & globalization/ edited by Charles A. Perrone & Christopher Dunn. Gainesville: University Press of Florida, c2001. xii, 288 p.
00-069055   781.64/0981   0813018218
Popular music -- Brazil -- History and criticism. Globalization.

ML3502.A785.L6 1998
Lockard, Craig A.
Dance of life: popular music and politics in Southeast Asia/ Craig A. Lockard. Honolulu, HI: University of Hawaii Press, c1998. xix, 390 p.
96-039802   306.4/84   0824818482
Popular music -- Asia, Southeastern -- History and criticism. Music and state -- Asia, Southeastern.

ML3502.5.B4613 1991
Bender, Wolfgang, 1946-
Sweet mother: modern African music/ Wolfgang Bender; with a foreword by John M. Chernoff; translated by Wolfgang Freis. Chicago: University of Chicago Press, c1991. xx, 235 p.
90-020316   780/.96   0226042537
Popular music -- Africa -- History and criticism.

ML3502.5.G7 1988
Graham, Ronnie.
The Da Capo guide to contemporary African music/ by Ronnie Graham. New York: Da Capo Press, 1988. xii, 315 p.
87-031073   780/.42/096   0306803259
Popular music -- Africa -- History and criticism. Folk music -- Africa -- History and criticism. Popular music -- Africa -- Discography.

ML3502.5.S73 1992
Stewart, Gary, 1944-
Breakout: profiles in African rhythm/ Gary Stewart. Chicago: University of Chicago Press, 1992. x, 157 p.
91-030279   781.63/096   0226774058
Popular music -- Africa -- History and criticism. Musicians -- Africa -- Biography.

ML3503.S6.H35 1988
Hamm, Charles.
Afro-American music, South Africa, and apartheid/ Charles Hamm. Brooklyn, N.Y.: Institute for Studies in American Music, Conservatory of Music, Brooklyn College of the City University of New York, c1988. 42 p.
88-080431   781.64/0968   0914678310
Blacks -- South Africa -- Music -- History and criticism. Popular music -- South Africa -- History and criticism. Afro-Americans -- Music -- History and criticism.

ML3503.Z55
Turino, Thomas.
Nationalists, cosmopolitans, and popular music in Zimbabwe/ Thomas Turino. Chicago: University of Chicago Press, c2000. x, 401 p.
00-008067   781.63/096891   0226817016
Popular music -- Zimbabwe -- History and criticism. Music -- Social aspects -- Zimbabwe.

ML3506-3541 History and criticism — Popular music — Types and styles

ML3506.B475 1994
Berliner, Paul.
Thinking in jazz: the infinite art of improvisation/ Paul F. Berliner. Chicago: University of Chicago Press, 1994. xix, 883 p.
93-034660   781.65/136   0226043800
Jazz -- History and criticism. Improvisation (Music) Jazz musicians -- Interviews.

ML3506.D43 1989
Deffaa, Chip, 1951-
Swing legacy/ by Chip Deffaa; foreword by George T. Simon. Metuchen, N.J.: Scarecrow Press; 1989. xi, 379 p.
89-070029   781.65/4   0810822822
Jazz -- History and criticism.

ML3506.D433 1993
Deffaa, Chip, 1951-
Traditionalists and revivalists in jazz/ Chip Deffaa. Metuchen, N.J.: Scarecrow Press; c1993. x, 391 p.
93-001875   781.65/3   0810827042
Jazz -- History and criticism. Jazz musicians.

ML3506.D48 1997
DeVeaux, Scott Knowles.
The birth of bebop: a social and musical history/ Scott DeVeaux. Berkeley: University of California Press, c1997. xv, 572 p.
96-046887   781.65/5 21   0520205790
Bop (Music) -- History and criticism. Jazz -- 1931-1940 -- History and criticism. Jazz -- 1941-1950 -- History and criticism. Music -- Social aspects.

ML3506.G54 1997
Gioia, Ted.
The history of jazz/ Ted Gioia. New York: Oxford University Press, 1997. 471 p.
97-000102   781.65/09   0195090810
Jazz -- History and criticism.

ML3506.G74 2003
Gridley, Mark C.,
Jazz styles: history & analysis/ Mark C. Gridley; with contributions by David Cutler. 8th ed. Upper Saddle River, N.J.: Prentice Hall, c2003. xx, 442 p.
2001-058796   781.65 21   0130992828
Jazz -- Analysis, appreciation. Style, Musical. Jazz musicians.

ML3506.J47 2000
Jazz: the first century/ edited by John Edward Hasse. New York: William Morrow, 2000.
99-046071   781.65/09 21   0688170749
Jazz -- History and criticism.

ML3506.K47 1995
Kernfeld, Barry Dean, 1950-
What to listen for in jazz/ Barry Kernfeld. New Haven: Yale University Press, c1995. xvii, 247 p.
94-018324   781.65/17   0300059027
Jazz -- Analysis, appreciation.

ML3506.M64 1996
Monson, Ingrid T.
Saying something: jazz improvisation and interaction/ Ingrid Monson. Chicago: University of Chicago Press, c1996. xii, 253 p.
96-023224　781.65/136　0226534774
Jazz -- History and criticism. Improvisation (Music)

ML3506.M66 1993
Moody, Bill, 1941-
The jazz exiles: American musicians abroad/ Bill Moody; foreword by Stanley Dance. Reno: University of Nevada Press, c1993. xix, 193 p.
92-026936　781.65/089/13　0874172144
Jazz -- History and criticism. Jazz musicians -- United States. Expatriate musicians -- Europe.

ML3506.S35 1986
Schuller, Gunther.
Early jazz: its roots and musical development/ Gunther Schuller. New York: Oxford University Press, 1986, c1968. xxi, 401 p.
86-002403　781/.57 19　0195040430
Jazz--History and criticism.

ML3506.S36 1968 vol. 2
Schuller, Gunther.
The swing era: the development of jazz, 1930-1945/ Gunther Schuller. New York: Oxford University Press, 1989. xviii, 919 p.
87-001664　781/.57　019504312X
Jazz -- 1931-1940 -- History and criticism. Jazz -- 1941-1950 -- History and criticism. Swing (Music) -- History and criticism.

ML3506.S47 2001
Shipton, Alyn.
A new history of jazz/ Alyn Shipton. London; Continuum, 2001 x, 965 p.
2001-017177　781.65/09 21　0826447546
Jazz--History and criticism.

ML3506.S87 1991
Stokes, W. Royal.
The jazz scene: an informal history from New Orleans to 1990/ W. Royal Stokes. New York: Oxford University Press, 1991. viii, 261 p.
90-014208　781.65/09　0195054091
Jazz -- History and criticism. Jazz musicians -- Interviews.

ML3506.T57 1993
Tirro, Frank.
Jazz: a history/ Frank Tirro. 2nd ed. New York: Norton, c1993. xxi, 210 p.
92-032682　781.65/09 20　0393963683
Jazz--History and criticism.

ML3506.W54 1980
Williams, Martin T.
Jazz masters in transition, 1957-69/ by Martin Williams. New York: Da Capo Press, 1980, c1970. 288 p.
79-027874　785.42/092/2　0306796120
Jazz -- History and criticism. Jazz musicians -- Biography.

ML3507.B35 1983
Balliett, Whitney.
Jelly Roll, Jabbo, and Fats: 19 portraits in jazz/ Whitney Balliett. New York: Oxford University Press, 1983. x, 197 p.
82-022557　785.42/092/2　0195032756
Jazz musicians. Jazz -- History and criticism.

ML3507.G5 1985
Giddins, Gary.
Rhythm-a-ning: jazz tradition and innovation in the '80s/ Gary Giddins. New York: Oxford University Press, 1985. xviii, 291 p.
84-020658　785.42　0195035585
Jazz -- History and criticism.

ML3507.G52
Giddins, Gary.
Riding on a blue note: jazz and American pop/ Gary Giddins. New York: Oxford University, 1981. xv, 313 p.
80-021238　785.42　019502835X
Jazz -- History and criticism. Popular music -- United States -- History and criticism.

ML3507.J42 1997
Jazz: a century of change/ readings and new essays, Lewis Porter. New York: Schirmer Books; xi, 298 p.
97-025600　781.65 21　0028647130
Jazz -- History and criticism.

ML3507.L47 1991
Lees, Gene.
Waiting for Dizzy/ Gene Lees. New York: Oxford University Press, 1991. vii, 251 p.
90-047883　781.65　0195056701
Jazz -- History and criticism.

ML3507.M38 2003
McPartland, Marian.
Marian McPartland's jazz world: All in good time/ Marian McPartland; foreword by James T. Maher. Urbana: University of Illinois Press, 2003. xxviii, 165 p.
2002-007126　781.65 21　0252028015
Jazz--History and criticism. Jazz musicians.

ML3507.O94 2000
The Oxford companion to jazz/ edited by Bill Kirchner. Oxford; Oxford University Press, 2000. xi, 852 p.
99-088598　781.65/09　019512510X
Jazz -- History and criticism.

ML3507.R54 2001
Riffs & choruses: a new jazz anthology/ edited by Andrew Clark. London; Continuum by arrangement with Bayou Press, xvi, 486 p.
00-043025　781.65 21　0826447562
Jazz -- History and criticism.

ML3507.W53 1985
Williams, Martin T.
Jazz heritage/ Martin Williams. New York: Oxford University Press, 1985. xiv, 253 p.
85-004815　785.42　0195036115
Jazz -- History and criticism. Jazz musicians.

ML3507.W535 1989
Williams, Martin T.
Jazz in its time/ Martin Williams. New York: Oxford University Press, 1989. xii, 272 p.
88-031954   785.42   0195054598
Jazz -- History and criticism.

ML3508.B34
Balliett, Whitney.
Night creature: a journal of jazz, 1975-1980/ Whitney Balliett. New York: Oxford University Press, 1981. 285 p.
80-024678   785.42/09747/1   0195029089
Jazz -- New York (State) -- New York -- 1971-1980 -- History and criticism.

ML3508.C5 1981
Charters, Samuel Barclay.
Jazz: a history of the New York scene/ Samuel B. Charters and Leonard Kunstadt; new foreword by Samuel B. Charters. New York: Da Capo Press, 1981, c1962. viii, 382 p.
81-001173   785.42/09747/1 19   030676055X
Jazz--New York (State)--New York--History and criticism. Jazz musicians.

ML3508.C62 1993
Collier, James Lincoln, 1928-
Jazz: the American theme song/ James Lincoln Collier. New York: Oxford University Press, 1993. 326 p.
92-043644   781.65   0195079434
Jazz -- History and criticism. Music -- Social aspects.

ML3508.F74 1990
Friedwald, Will, 1961-
Jazz singing: America's great voices from Bessie Smith to Bebop and beyond/ Will Friedwald. New York: C. Scribner's Sons, c1990. xvi, 477 p.
89-028172   782.4165/092/273   0684185229
Jazz vocals -- History and criticism. Singers -- United States.

ML3508.G47 1998
Gerard, Charley.
Jazz in Black and White: race, culture, and identity in the jazz community/ Charley Gerard. Westport, Conn.: Greenwood Press, 1998. xx, 202 p.
97-033018   781.65/0973   0313305811
Jazz -- History and criticism. Music and race. Afro-Americans -- Race identity. United States -- Race relations.

ML3508.H46 1994
Hennessey, Thomas J.,
From jazz to swing: African-American jazz musicians and their music, 1890-1935/ Thomas J. Hennessey. Detroit: Wayne State University Press, c1994. 217 p.
93-033865   781.65/0973 20   0814321798
Jazz -- History and criticism. African American musicians. African American jazz musicians.

ML3508.J38 1998
The jazz cadence of American culture/ edited by Robert G. O'Meally. New York: Columbia University Press, c1998. xvi, 665 p.
98-014768   781.65 21   0231104499
Jazz -- History and criticism. Blues (Music) -- History and criticism. Afro-Americans -- Music -- History and criticism.

ML3508.O37 1989
Ogren, Kathy J.
The jazz revolution: twenties America & the meaning of jazz/ Kathy J. Ogren. New York: Oxford University Press, 1989. vii, 221 p.
88-022596   781/.57/0973   019505153X
Jazz -- 1921-1930 -- History and criticism. Music -- Social aspects. Popular culture -- United States -- History -- 20th century.

ML3508.P45 1992
Peretti, Burton W. 1961-
The creation of jazz: music, race, and culture in urban America/ Burton W. Peretti. Urbana: University of Illinois Press, c1992. xii, 277 p.
91-034772   306.4/84   0252017080
Jazz -- History and criticism. Afro-Americans -- Music -- History and criticism.

ML3508.P58 1982
Placksin, Sally.
American women in jazz: 1900 to the present: their words, lives, and music/ Sally Placksin. New York: Seaview Books, c1982. xvii, 332 p.
81-050324   785.42/092/2   0872237567
Women jazz musicians -- United States. Jazz -- History and criticism.

ML3508.S85 1999
Sudhalter, Richard M.
Lost chords: white musicians and their contribution to jazz, 1915-1945/ Richard M. Sudhalter. New York: Oxford University Press, 1999. xxii, 890 p.
97-042470   781.65/089/13   0195055853
White jazz musicians -- United States -- History. Jazz -- History and criticism.

ML3508.7.C28.G5 1992
Gioia, Ted.
West Coast jazz: modern jazz in California, 1945-1960/ Ted Gioia. New York: Oxford University Press, 1992. xii, 404 p.
91-023902   781.65/5/09794   0195063104
Jazz -- California -- 1941-1950 -- History and criticism. Jazz -- California -- 1951-1960 -- History and criticism.

ML3508.7.T4.O45 1996
Oliphant, Dave.
Texan jazz/ by Dave Oliphant. Austin: University of Texas Press, c1996. ix, 481 p.
95-004416   781.65/09764   0292760442
Jazz -- Texas -- History and criticism.

ML3508.8.C5.K46 1993
Kenney, William Howland.
Chicago jazz: a cultural history, 1904-1930/ William Howland Kenney. New York: Oxford University Press, 1993. xv, 233 p.
92-027397   781.65/0973/1109042   0195064534
Jazz -- Illinois -- Chicago -- History and criticism. Popular culture -- Illinois -- Chicago. Chicago (Ill.) -- Race relations. Chicago (Ill.) -- Social conditions.

ML3508.8.L7.C46 1998
Central Avenue sounds: jazz in Los Angeles/ edited by Clora Bryant ... [et al.]. Berkeley: University of California Press, c1998. xxiii, 442 p.
97-002560   781.65/09794/94   0520211898
Jazz -- California -- Los Angeles -- History and criticism. Jazz musicians -- California -- Los Angeles -- Interviews. Central Avenue (Los Angeles, Calif.)

ML3508.8.N48.C3 1991
Carter, William, 1934-
Preservation Hall: music from the heart/ by William Carter. New York: W.W. Norton, c1991. vii, 315 p.
91-205263   781.65/3   0393029158
Jazz musicians -- Louisiana -- New Orleans -- Biography. Jazz -- Louisiana -- New Orleans -- History and criticism. New Orleans (La.) -- History.

ML3509.G3.K37 1992
Kater, Michael H., 1937-
Different drummers: jazz in the culture of Nazi Germany/ Michael H. Kater. New York: Oxford University Press, 1992. xiv, 291 p.
91-017866   781.65/0943/09043   0195050096
Jazz -- Germany -- 1931-1940 -- History and criticism. Jazz -- Germany -- 1941-1950 -- History and criticism. National socialism.

ML3518.E74 1998
Erenberg, Lewis A., 1944-
Swingin' the dream: big band jazz and the rebirth of American culture/ Lewis A. Erenberg. Chicago: The University of Chicago Press, c1998. xxi, 320 p.
97-039135   781.65/4/0973   0226215164
Big band music -- History and criticism. Jazz -- History and criticism. Popular culture -- United States.

ML3518.S55 1981
Simon, George Thomas.
The big bands/ George T. Simon; with a foreword by Frank Sinatra. New York: Schirmer Books; c1981. xvii, 614 p.
81-051633   785/.06/66   0028724208
Big bands -- United States. Jazz musicians -- United States -- Biography.

ML3520.F6 2001
Fleischhauer, Carl.
Bluegrass odyssey: a documentary in pictures and words, 1966-86/ Carl Fleischhauer and Neil V. Rosenberg. Urbana: University of Illinois Press, c2001. xii, 189 p.
00-008713   781.642/09   0252026152
Bluegrass music -- History and criticism. Bluegrass musicians -- Portraits.

ML3520.R67 1985
Rosenberg, Neil V.
Bluegrass: a history/ Neil V. Rosenberg. Urbana: University of Illinois Press, c1985. xii, 447 p.
84-015747   784.5/2/00973 19   0252002652
Bluegrass music -- History and criticism.

ML3521.B36 1989
Barlow, William,
"Looking up at down": the emergence of blues culture/ William Barlow. Philadelphia: Temple University Press, 1989. xii, 404 p.
88-015921   784.5/3/00973 19   0877225834
Blues (Music) -- History and criticism.

ML3521.B39 1986
Bastin, Bruce, 1938-
Red River blues: the blues tradition in the Southeast/ Bruce Bastin. Urbana: University of Illinois Press, c1986. xiii, 379 p.
85-008571   784.5/3/00975   0252012135
Blues (Music) -- Southern States -- History and criticism. Afro-Americans -- Southern States -- Music -- History and criticism. Folk songs, English -- Southern States -- History and criticism.

ML3521.C55 1997
Conversation with the blues/ [compiled by] Paul Oliver; illustrated with photographs by the author. Cambridge; Cambridge University Press, c1997. xvi, 208 p.
96-047887   781.643/0973   0521591813
Blues (Music) -- History and criticism. Blues musicians -- Interviews.

ML3521.D355 1998
Davis, Angela Yvonne, 1944-
Blues legacies and Black feminism: Gertrude "Ma" Rainey, Bessie Smith, and Billie Holiday/ Angela Y. Davis. New York: Pantheon Books, c1998. xx, 427 p.
97-033021   782.421643/082   067945005X
Rainey, Ma, -- 1886-1939. Smith, Bessie, -- 1898?-1937. Holiday, Billie, -- 1915-1959. Women blues musicians -- United States. Afro-American women. Blues (Music) -- History and criticism.

ML3521.D36 1995
Davis, Francis.
The history of the blues: the roots, the music, the people: from Charley Patton to Robert Clay/ Francis Davis. New York: Hyperion, c1995. viii, 309 p.
94-023370   781.643/09   0786860529
Blues (Music) -- History and criticism.

ML3521.E9 1982
Evans, David, 1944-
Big road blues: tradition and creativity in the folk blues/ David Evans. Berkeley: University of California Press, c1982. xi, 379 p.
77-076177   784.5/3   0520034848
Blues (Music) -- History and criticism.

ML3521.G9 1986
Guralnick, Peter.
Sweet soul music: rhythm and blues and the southern dream of freedom / Peter Guralnick. 1st ed. New York: Harper & Row, c1986. ix, 438 p.
85-045202   784.5/3/0975 19   0060960493
Soul music -- History and criticism.

ML3521.H38 1988
Harrison, Daphne Duval, 1932-
Black pearls: blues queens of the 1920s/ Daphne Duval Harrison. New Brunswick, [N.J.]: Rutgers University Press, c1988. xv, 295 p.
87-014084   784.5/3/00922   0813512794
  Blues (Music) -- United States -- History and criticism. Blues musicians -- United States -- Biography. Afro-American women musicians -- Biography.

ML3521.K83 1999
Kubik, Gerhard, 1933-
Africa and the blues/ Gerhard Kubik. Jackson [Miss.]: University Press of Mississippi, 1999. xviii, 240 p.
99-024343   781.643/096   1578061458
  Blues (Music) -- African influences. Blacks -- Africa -- Music -- History and criticism. Music -- Africa -- History and criticism.

ML3521.L64 1993
Lomax, Alan, 1915-
The land where the blues began/ Alan Lomax. New York: Pantheon Books, c1993. xv, 539 p.
91-052627   781.643/09762/4   0679404244
  Blues (Music) -- Mississippi -- Delta (Region) -- History and criticism. Afro-Americans -- Mississippi -- Delta (Region) -- Music -- History and criticism. Afro-Americans -- Mississippi -- Delta (Region) -- Social life and customs.

ML3521.N68 1993
Nothing but the blues: the music and the musicians/ Lawrence Cohn... [et. al.]. New York: Abbeville Press, c1993. 432 p.
93-002791   781.643/09 20   1558592717
Blues (Music) -- History and criticism.

ML3521.O42 1990
Oliver, Paul, 1927-
Blues fell this morning: meaning in the blues/ Paul Oliver; with a foreword by Richard Wright. Cambridge [England]; Cambridge University Press, 1990. xxiv, 348 p.
89-025402   781.643/09   0521374375
  Blues (Music) -- History and criticism.

ML3521.S63 1993
Spencer, Jon Michael.
Blues and evil/ Jon Michael Spencer. Knoxville: University of Tennessee Press, c1993. xxx, 177 p.
92-033008   781.643 20   0870497839
Blues (Music) -- History and criticism. Blues (Music) -- Religious aspects.

ML3521.T58 1994
Titon, Jeff Todd,
Early downhome blues: a musical and cultural analysis/ Jeff Todd Titon; with a new foreword by Alan Trachtenberg and a new afterword by the author. 2nd ed. Chapel Hill: University of North Carolina Press, c1994. xxii, 318 p.
94-006953   781.643/09 20   0807844829
Blues (Music) -- History and criticism.

ML3521.Y66 2001
Yonder come the blues: the evolution of a genre/ Paul Oliver ... [et al.]. Cambridge; Cambridge University Press, c2001. xiii, 358 p.
00-028917   781.643   0521782597
  Blues (Music) -- History and criticism. African Americans -- Music -- History and criticism.

ML3524.A45 1993
All that glitters: country music in America/ edited by George H. Lewis. Bowling Green, Ohio: Bowling Green State University Popular Press, 340 p.
92-074544   781.642/09 20   0879725745
Country music -- History and criticism.

ML3524.E4 1995
Ellison, Curtis W.
Country music culture: from hard times to Heaven/ Curtis W. Ellison. Jackson [Miss.]: University Press of Mississippi, c1995. xxiii, 314 p.
94-036518   781.642/09   0878057218
  Country music -- History and criticism.

ML3524.J46 1998
Jensen, Joli.
The Nashville sound: authenticity, commercialization, and country music/ Joli Jensen. Nashville: Vanderbilt University Press, 1998. x, 218 p.
97-045428   781.642   082651314X
  Country music -- History and criticism.

ML3524.M34 2002
Malone, Bill C.
Country music, U.S.A./ by Bill C. Malone. 2nd rev. ed. Austin: University of Texas Press, 2002. xv, 628 p.
2002-004792   781.642/0973 21   0292752628
  Country music--History and criticism.

ML3524.M344 2002
Malone, Bill C.
Don't get above your raisin': country music and the southern working   class/ Bill C. Malone. Urbana: University of Illinois Press, c2002. xvi, 392 p.
2001-001219   781.642/0975 21   0252026780
  Country music--Social aspects. Working class--Southern States--Songs and music--History and

ML3524.R43 1998
Reading country music: steel guitars, opry stars, and honky tonk bars/ Cecelia Tichi, editor. Durham: Duke University Press, 1998. 408 p.
97-049637   781.642   0822321564
  Country music -- History and criticism. Country musicians.

ML3524.T5 1994
Tichi, Cecelia, 1942-
High lonesome: the American culture of country music/ Cecelia Tichi. Chapel Hill: University of North Carolina Press, c1994. xiii, 318 p.
93-036130   781.642/0973   0807821349
Country music -- History and criticism.

ML3524.W64 1999
Wolfe, Charles K.
A good-natured riot: the birth of the Grand Ole Opry/ Charles K. Wolfe. Nashville: Country Music Foundation Press and Vanderbilt University Press, c1999. xv, 312 p.
98-040104   791.44/72   082651331X
Country music -- History and criticism.

ML3527.G75 1992
Gribin, Anthony J.
Doo-wop: the forgotten third of rock 'n' roll/ by Anthony J. Gribin & Matthew M. Schiff. Iola, WI: Krause Publications, c1992. 616 p.
92-219147   782.42166   0873411978
Doo-wop (Music) -- History and criticism. Doo-wop (Music) -- Discography.

ML3527.P78 1996
Pruter, Robert, 1944-
Doowop: the Chicago scene/ Robert Pruter. Urbana, Ill.: University of Illinois Press, c1996. xiv, 304 p.
95-019593   782.42164   0252022084
Doo-wop (Music) -- Illinois -- Chicago -- History and criticism.

ML3528.8.S26 1999
Sapoznik, Henry.
Klezmer!: from old world to our world/ Henry Sapoznik. New York: Schirmer Books, 1999. xviii, 340 p.
99-031627   781.62/924   002864574X
Klezmer music -- History and criticism. Jews -- Music -- History and criticism.

ML3528.8.S58 2000
Slobin, Mark.
Fiddler on the move: exploring the klezmer world/ Mark Slobin. Oxford; Oxford University Press, 2000. 154 p.
99-048683   781.62/924   019513124X
Klezmer music -- History and criticism. Jews -- Music -- History and criticism.

ML3530.B47
Berlin, Edward A.
Ragtime: a musical and cultural history/ Edward A. Berlin. Berkeley: University of California Press, c1980. xix, 248 p.
78-051759   781/.572/09   0520036719
Ragtime music -- History and criticism.

ML3530.R33 1985
Ragtime: its history, composers, and music/ edited by John Edward Hasse. New York: Schirmer Books, 1985. x, 400 p.
84-013952   781/.572   0028716507
Ragtime music -- History and criticism.

ML3531.P68 1995
Potter, Russell A., 1960-
Spectacular vernaculars: hip-hop and the politics of postmodernism/ Russell A. Potter. Albany: State University of New York Press, c1995. x, 197 p.
94-024990   782.42164   0791426254
Rap (Music) -- Political aspects. Postmodernism.

ML3531.R67 1994
Rose, Tricia.
Black noise: rap music and black culture in contemporary America/ Tricia Rose. Hanover, NH: University Press of New England, c1994. xvi, 237 p.
93-041386   782.42164   0819552712
Rap (Music) -- History and criticism. Afro-Americans -- Music -- History and criticism. Popular culture -- United States.

ML3534.E55 1992
Ennis, Philip H.
The seventh stream: the emergence of rocknroll in American popular music/ Philip H. Ennis. [Middletown, Conn.]: Wesleyan University Press; c1992. xii, 445 p.
92-053859   781.66/0973   0819552380
Rock music -- United States -- History and criticism. Popular music -- United States -- History and criticism.

ML3534.F75 1988
Frith, Simon.
Music for pleasure: essays in the sociology of pop/ Simon Frith. New York: Routledge, c1988. viii, 232 p.
88-006678   784.5/4/009   0415900514
Rock music -- History and criticism. Music trade.

ML3534.H53 1999
Hicks, Michael, 1956-
Sixties rock: garage, psychedelic, and other satisfactions/ Michael Hicks. Urbana: University of Illinois Press, c1999. x, 162 p.
98-008992   781.66   0252024273
Rock music -- United States -- 1961-1970 -- History and criticism.

ML3534.N44 1997
Nehring, Neil, 1957-
Popular music, gender, and postmodernism: anger is an energy/ Neil Nehring. Thousand Oaks, Calif.: Sage Publications, c1997. xxxi, 203 p.
97-004590   781.66   0761908358
Punk rock music -- History and criticism. Feminism and music. Anger in music.

ML3534.R3844 1999
Reading rock and roll: authenticity, appropriation, aesthetics/ edited by Kevin J.H. Dettmar and William Richey; with a foreword by Anthony DeCurtis. New York: Columbia University Press, c1999. x, 347 p.
99-011659   781.66   0231113986
Rock music -- History and criticism. Music -- Philosophy and aesthetics.

ML3534.R613 2000
Rock and roll is here to stay: an anthology/ edited by
William McKeen; introduction by Peter Guralnick. New
York: W.W. Norton, c2000. 672 p.
99-031759   781.66   0393047008
Rock music -- History and criticism.

ML3534.R64 1992
The Rolling stone illustrated history of rock & roll: the
definitive history of the most important artists and their
music/ edited by Anthony DeCurtis and James Henke
with Holly George-Warren; original editor, Jim Miller.
3rd ed. New York: Random House, c1992. viii, 710 p.
92-006339   781.66/09 20   0679737286
Rock music--History and criticism. Rock musicians--
Biography.

ML3534.W29 1993
Walser, Robert.
Running with the Devil: power, gender, and madness in
heavy metal music/ Robert Walser. Hanover, NH:
University Press of New England, c1993. xviii, 222 p.
92-056911   781.66   0819552526
Heavy metal (Music) -- History and criticism.

ML3534.W33 1986
Ward, Ed,
Rock of ages: the Rolling stone history of rock & roll/ by
Ed Ward, Geoffrey Stokes, Ken Tucker; with an
introduction by Jann S. Wenner. New York: Rolling
Stone Press: 649 p.
86-014553   784.5/4/009 19   0671544381
Rock music--History and criticism.

ML3534.W5713 1990
Wicke, Peter.
Rock music: culture, aesthetics, and sociology/ Peter
Wicke; translated by Rachel Fogg. Cambridge;
Cambridge University Press, 1990. xii, 228 p.
91-132534   306.4/84   0521365554
Rock music -- History and criticism. Music -- Philosophy and
aesthetics. Music -- Social aspects.

ML3535.M67 1996
Morrison, Craig, 1952-
Go cat go!: rockabilly music and its makers/ Craig
Morrison. Urbana: University of Illinois Press, c1996. xii,
326 p.
95-041807   781.66   0252022076
Rockabilly music -- History and criticism.

ML3535.5.A63 1998
Aparicio, Frances R.
Listening to salsa: gender, Latin popular music, and
Puerto Rican cultures/ Frances R. Aparicio. Hanover,
NH: University Press of New England, c1998. xxi, 290 p.
97-009121   781.64   0819553069
Salsa (Music) -- Puerto Rico -- History and criticism.
Feminism and music.

ML3537.P78 1991
Pruter, Robert, 1944-
Chicago soul/ Robert Pruter. Urbana: University of
Illinois Press, c1991. xx, 408 p.
89-078326   781.644/09773/11   0252016769
Soul music -- Illinois -- Chicago -- History and criticism.

ML3541.B69 1998
Boyd, Jean Ann.
The jazz of the Southwest: an oral history of western
swing/ by Jean A. Boyd. Austin: University of Texas
Press, 1998. x, 269 p.
97-033740   781.65/3   0292708599
Western swing (Music) -- History and criticism.

ML3541.G56 1994
Ginell, Cary.
Milton Brown and the founding of western swing/ Cary
Ginell; with special assistance from Roy Lee Brown.
Urbana: University of Illinois Press, c1994. xxxii, 330 p.
93-029364   781.642   0252020413
Brown, Milton. Western swing (Music) -- History and criticism.

ML3545 History and criticism —
National music — General works

ML3545.B64 1988
Bohlman, Philip Vilas.
The study of folk music in the modern world/ Philip V.
Bohlman. Bloomington: Indiana University Press, c1988.
xx, 159 p.
87-045401   781.7/09   0253355559
Folk music -- History and criticism.

ML3545.C54 1994
Cleveland, Les.
Dark laughter: war in song and popular culture/ Les
Cleveland. Westport, Conn.: Praeger, 1994. xiv, 178 p.
93-026432   782.42/1599   0275947645
War songs -- History and criticism. Folk songs, English --
History and criticism. Folk music -- History and criticism.

ML3545.L63
Lomax, Alan, 1915-
Folk song style and culture. With contributions by the
cantometrics staff and with the editorial assistance of
Edwin E. Erickson. Washington, American Association
for the Advancement of Science, [1968] xix, 363 p.
68-021545   784.4/9
Folk songs -- History and criticism.

ML3545.N285 1990
Nettl, Bruno,
Folk and traditional music of the Western continents/
Bruno Nettl; with chapters on Latin America by Gerard
Béhague. 3rd ed./ revised and edited by Valerie
Woodring Goertzen. Englewood Cliffs, N.J.: Prentice-
Hall, c1990. xv, 286 p.
89-034653   781.62/009182/1 20   0133232476
Folk music--History and criticism.

ML3545.S486 1995
Shiloah, Amnon.
Music in the world of Islam: a socio-cultural study/ Amnon Shiloah. Detroit: Wayne State University Press, c1995. xviii, 243 p.
94-047620   780/.917/671   0814325890
Music -- Islamic Countries -- History and criticism. Music, Islamic -- History and criticism.

ML3545.W67 2002
Worlds of music: an introduction to the music of the world's peoples / Jeff Todd Titon, general editor. 4th ed. Belmont, Calif.: Schirmer/Thomson Learning, 2001, c2002. xix, 484 p.
2001-044676   780/.9 21   0534591035
World music--History and criticism. Ethnomusicology.

ML3551-3770 History and criticism — National music — By region or country

ML3551.C36 1996
Cantwell, Robert, 1945-
When we were good: the folk revival/ Robert Cantwell. Cambridge, Mass.: Harvard University Press, 1996. viii, 412 p.
95-020951   781.62/13/00904   0674951328
Folk music -- United States -- History and criticism. Folk songs, English -- United States -- History and criticism.

ML3551.C57
Cohen, Norm.
Long steel rail: the railroad in American folksong/ Norm Cohen; music edited by David Cohen. Urbana: University of Illinois Press, c1981. xx, 710 p.
80-014874   784.6/8385/0973   0252003438
Folk songs, English -- United States -- History and criticism. Railroads -- Songs and music -- History and criticism. Railroads -- Songs and music.

ML3551.F55 2000
Filene, Benjamin.
Romancing the folk: public memory & American roots music/ Benjamin Filene. Chapel Hill: University of North Carolina Press, c2000. xi, 325 p.
99-054367   781.62/13/00904   0807825506
Folk music -- United States -- History and criticism. Popular music -- United States -- History and criticism.

ML3551.J2 1965
Jackson, George Pullen, 1874-1953.
White spirituals in the southern uplands; the story of the fasola folk, their songs, singings, and "buckwheat notes." New York, Dover Publications [1965] xvi, 444 p.
65-024348   784.4
Solmization. Folk songs, English -- Appalachian Region, Southern -- History and criticism. Folk music -- Appalachian Region, Southern -- History and criticism.

ML3551.M26 1993
Malone, Bill C.
Singing cowboys and musical mountaineers: southern culture and the roots of country music/ Bill C. Malone. Athens: University of Georgia Press, c1993. viii, 155 p.
92-012430   781.62/13075   0820314838
Folk music -- Southern States -- History and criticism. Country music -- Southern States -- History and criticism.

ML3551.N47 1976
Nettl, Bruno, 1930-
Folk music in the United States: an introduction/ by Bruno Nettl. Detroit: Wayne State University Press, 1976. 187 p.
76-000084   781.7/73   0814315569
Folk music -- United States.

ML3551.T72 1993
Transforming tradition: folk music revivals examined/ edited by Neil V. Rosenberg; foreword by Alan Jabbour. Urbana: University of Illinois Press, c1993. xiii, 340 p.
92-026727   781.62/13   0252019822
Folk music -- United States -- History and criticism.

ML3551.W38 1995
"Wasn't that a time!": firsthand accounts of the folk music revival/ edited by Ronald D. Cohen. Metuchen, N.J.: Scarecrow Press, 1995. 232 p.
94-024902   781.62/13   081082955X
Folk music -- United States -- Congresses.

ML3551.7.S68.W65 1997
Wolfe, Charles K.
The devil's box: masters of southern fiddling/ Charles Wolfe; foreword by Mark O'Connor. Nashville: Country Music Foundation Press: 1997. xxiv, 232 p.
96-051254   787.2/1642/09   0826512836
Fiddling -- History and criticism. Fiddlers -- Southern States -- Biography. Fiddle tunes -- History and criticism.

ML3551.7.W4.M55 1999
Milnes, Gerald.
Play of a fiddle: traditional music, dance, and folklore in West Virginia/ Gerald Milnes. Lexington, Ky.: University Press of Kentucky, c1999. 211 p.
98-040733   781.62/1307546   0813120802
Folk music -- West Virginia -- History and criticism.

ML3554.G75 1996
Grimes, Robert R.
How shall we sing in a foreign land?: music of Irish-Catholic immigrants in the antebellum United States/ Robert R. Grimes. Notre Dame: University of Notre Dame Press, c1996. xi, 237 p.
95-018803   780/.89/9162073   0268011109
Irish Americans -- Music -- History and criticism. Music -- United States -- 19th century -- History and criticism. Music -- Ireland -- 19th century -- History and criticism.

ML3554.W77 1996
Williams, W. H. A.
'Twas only an Irishman's dream: the image of Ireland and the Irish in American popular song lyrics, 1800-1920/ William H.A. Williams. Urbana: University of Illinois Press, c1996. xii, 311 p.
96-004491   782.42/089/9162073 20   0252065514
Irish Americans -- Songs and music -- Texts -- History and criticism. Irish -- Songs and music -- Texts -- History and criticism. Popular music -- United States -- Texts -- History and criticism.

ML3556.C667 1995
Conway, Cecelia.
African banjo echoes in Appalachia: a study of folk traditions/ Cecelia Conway. Knoxville: University of Tennessee Press, c1995. xxviii, 394 p.
94-018762   787.8/8/08996073075   0870498932
Afro-Americans -- Appalachian Region -- Music -- History and criticism. Folk music -- Appalachian Region -- History and criticism. Folk songs, English -- Appalachian Region -- History and criticism.

ML3556.E8
Epstein, Dena J. Polacheck, 1916-
Sinful tunes and spirituals: Black folk music to the Civil War/ Dena J. Epstein. Urbana: University of Illinois Press, c1977. xix, 433 p.
77-006315   784.7/56/009   0252005201
Afro-Americans -- Music -- History and criticism. Spirituals (Songs) -- History and criticism.

ML3556.F65 1995
Floyd, Samuel A.
The power of Black music: interpreting its history from Africa to the United States/ Samuel A. Floyd, Jr. New York: Oxford University Press, c1995. 316 p.
94-000021   780/.89/96073   0195082354
Afro-Americans -- Music -- History and criticism. Music -- United States -- History and criticism.

ML3556.K43
Keil, Charles.
Urban blues. Chicago, University of Chicago Press [1966] ix, 231 p.
66-013876   781.57
Blues (Music) -- History and criticism. Blues musicians -- United States. Afro-American musicians.

ML3556.R34 1983
Readings in Black American music/ compiled and edited by Eileen Southern. 2nd ed. New York: W.W. Norton, c1983. xii, 338 p.
83-004192   781.7/296073 19   0393952800
Afro-Americans -- Music. Music -- United States.

ML3556.S65 1987
Small, Christopher, 1927-
Music of the common tongue: survival and celebration in Afro-American music/ Christopher Small. London: J. Calder; 1987. 495 p.
86-031381   781.7/296073   0714540951
Afro-Americans -- Music -- History and criticism. Music -- United States -- History and criticism. Music -- Social aspects.

ML3556.S738 2000
Southern, Eileen.
Images: iconography of music in African-American culture (1770s-1920s)/ by Eileen Southern and Josephine Wright. New York: Garland Pub., c2000. xxiii, 299 p.
00-029362   780/.89/96073   0815328753
African Americans -- Music -- History and criticism. African Americans -- Music -- History and criticism -- Pictorial works. Music in art.

ML3556.S74 1997
Southern, Eileen.
The music of black Americans: a history/ Eileen Southern. 3rd ed. New York: Norton, c1997. xxii, 678 p.
96-028811   780/.89/96073 20   0393971414
Afro-Americans--Music--History and criticism.

ML3556.S8 1990
Spencer, Jon Michael.
Protest & praise: sacred music of Black religion/ Jon Michael Spencer. Minneapolis: Fortress Press, c1990. x, 262 p.
89-023573   781.71/0089/96073   0800624041
Afro-Americans -- Music -- History and criticism. Afro-Americans -- Religion.

ML3556.S83 1996
Spencer, Jon Michael.
Re-searching Black music/ Jon Michael Spencer. Knoxville: University of Tennessee Press, c1996. xi, 154 p.
95-041760   780/.89/96073   0870499297
Afro-Americans -- Music -- History and criticism. Music -- United States -- History and criticism.

ML3556.S87 1998
Stewart, Earl L.
African American music: an introduction/ Earl L. Stewart. New York: Schirmer Books: c1998. xiii, 380 p.
97-042487   780/.89/96073   0028602943
Afro-Americans -- Music -- History and criticism. Music -- United States -- History and criticism.

ML3556.T75 2001
The triumph of the soul: cultural and psychological aspects of African American music/ edited by Ferdinand Jones and Arthur C. Jones. Westport, Conn.: Praeger, 2001. xviii, 228 p.
00-039200   780/.89/96073   0275953653
African Americans -- Music -- History and criticism. Music -- United States -- Psychological aspects. Popular culture -- United States.

ML3556.8.N5.B6 1990
Black music in the Harlem Renaissance: a collection of essays/ edited by Samuel A. Floyd, Jr. New York: Greenwood Press, 1990. x, 228 p.
89-011985   780/.89/9607307471   0313265461
Afro-Americans -- New York (State) -- New York -- Music -- History and criticism. Music -- New York (State) -- New York -- 20th century -- History and criticism. Harlem Renaissance. Harlem (New York, N.Y.) -- Intellectual life -- 20th century.

ML3557.G53 1994
Giglio, Virginia, 1953-
Southern Cheyenne women's songs/ by Virginia Giglio; with a foreword by David P. McAllester. Norman: University of Oklahoma Press, c1994. xxi, 243 p.
93-023221   782.42162/973   0806126051
Cheyenne Indians -- Music -- History and criticism. Cheyenne women -- Songs and music -- History and criticism. Folk music -- Oklahoma -- History and criticism.

ML3557.K43 1992
Keeling, Richard.
Cry for luck: sacred song and speech among the Yurok, Hupa, and Karok Indians of northwestern California/ Richard Keeling. Berkeley: Unversity of California Press, c1992. xii, 325 p.
91-039128   782.25/089/970794   0520075609
Yurok Indians -- Music -- History and criticism. Hupa Indians -- Music -- History and criticism. Karok Indians -- Music -- History and criticism.

ML3557.N38 1989
Nettl, Bruno, 1930-
Blackfoot musical thought: comparative perspectives/ Bruno Nettl. Kent, Ohio: Kent State University Press, c1989. xii, 198 p.
88-028450   781.7/297   0873383702
Siksika Indians -- Music -- History and criticism. Indians of North America -- Great Plains -- Music -- History and criticism.

ML3557.U53 1976
Underhill, Ruth Murray, 1884-1984.
Singing for power: the song magic of the Papago Indians of southern Arizona/ Ruth Murray Underhill. Berkeley: University of California Press, 1976, c1938. vii, 158 p.
77-354970   299/.7   0520033108
Tohono O'Odham Indians -- Music -- History and criticism. Folk music -- Arizona -- History and criticism. Tohono O'Odham Indians -- Arizona -- Rites and ceremonies.

ML3557.V36 1988
Vander, Judith.
Songprints: the musical experience of five Shoshone women/ Judith Vander. Urbana: University of Illinois Press, c1988. xxvi, 317 p.
87-024488   784.7/51   0252014928
Shoshoni Indians -- Music -- History and criticism. Indians of North America -- Wyoming -- Music -- History and criticism. Shoshoni women. Wind River Indian Reservation (Wyo.)

ML3558.H47 1993
Herrera-Sobek, Maria.
Northward bound: the Mexican immigrant experience in ballad and song/ Maria Herrera-Sobek. Bloomington: Indiana University Press, c1993. xxv, 340 p.
92-022209   782.42162/6872073   0253327377
Mexican Americans -- Music -- History and criticism. Folk songs, Spanish -- United States -- History and criticism. Folk music -- United States -- History and criticism.

ML3558.L69 1992
Loza, Steven Joseph.
Barrio rhythm: Mexican American music in Los Angeles/ Steven Loza. Urbana: University of Illinois Press, c1993. xx, 320 p.
91-035181   781.62/6872079494   0252062884
Mexican Americans -- California -- Los Angeles -- Music -- History and criticism. Popular music -- Mexico -- History and criticism. Popular music -- California -- Los Angeles -- History and criticism.

ML3561.A74.S8
Armstrong, Louis, 1900-1971.
Swing that music, by Louis Armstrong, with an introduction by Rudy Vallee. Music section edited by Horace Gerlach, with special examples of swing music contributed by Benny Goodman, Tommy Dorsey, Joe Venuti [and others]. London, New York [etc.] Longmans, Green and co., 1936.
36-036408   780.973
Jazz.

ML3561.B63 S53
Shaw, Arnold.
Honkers and shouters: the golden years of rhythm and blues/ Arnold Shaw. New York: Macmillan, c1978. xxvii, 555 p.
77-018511   784   0026100002
Blues (Music) -- History and criticism.

ML3561.J3.B24
Balliett, Whitney.
Dinosaurs in the morning; 41 pieces on jazz. Philadelphia, Lippincott [1962] 224 p.
62-015202
Jazz.

ML3561.J3.B244
Balliett, Whitney.
Ecstasy at the Onion; thirty-one pieces on jazz. Indianapolis, Bobbs-Merrill [1971] 284 p.
76-161239   785.4/2/08
Jazz -- History and criticism.

ML3561.J3.B25
Balliett, Whitney.
The sound of surprise; 46 pieces on jazz. New York, Dutton, 1959. 237 p.
59-005832   781.57
Jazz.

ML3561.J3.B255
Balliett, Whitney.
Such sweet thunder; forty-nine pieces on jazz. Indianapolis, Bobbs-Merrill Co. [1966] 366 p.
66-028030   780.973
Jazz.

ML3561.J3.S46 1966
Shapiro, Nat,
Hear me talkin' to ya; the story of jazz as told by the men who made it. Edited by Nat Shapiro [and] Nat Hentoff. New York, Dover Publications [1966, c1955] xvi, 429 p.
66-028271   785.4/2
Jazz -- History and criticism.

ML3561.J3.W53 1979
Williams, Martin T.,
The art of jazz: essays on the nature and development of jazz/ edited by Martin T. Williams. New York: Da Capo Press, 1979, c1959. 248 p.
79-010083   785.4/2   0306795566
Jazz -- History and criticism. Jazz musicians.

ML3561.J3.W5317
Williams, Martin T.
The jazz tradition [by] Martin Williams. New York, Oxford University Press, 1970. viii, 232 p.
71-083058   785.4/2
Jazz -- History and criticism. Jazz musicians.

ML3565.M36 1995
Manuel, Peter Lamarche.
Caribbean currents: Caribbean music from rumba to reggae/ Peter Manuel with Kenneth Bilby and Michael Largey. Philadelphia: Temple University Press, 1995. xvi, 272 p.
95-003152   780/.9729   1566393388
Music -- West Indies -- History and criticism. Music -- Caribbean Area -- History and criticism.

ML3575.B7.S313 1993
Schreiner, Claus, 1943-
Musica brasileira: a history of popular music and the people of Brazil/ Claus Schreiner; translated from the German by Mark Weinstein. New York: Marion Boyars, 1993. viii, 306 p.
92-019894   781.64/0981   071452946X
Folk music -- Brazil -- History and criticism. Popular music -- Brazil -- History and criticism. Jazz -- Brazil -- History and criticism.

ML3575.B7.S36 1987
Seeger, Anthony.
Why Suya sing: a musical anthropology of an Amazonian people/ Anthony Seeger. Cambridge [Cambridgeshire]; Cambridge University Press, 1987. xxi, 147 p.
87-006352   781.7/298   0521341736
Suya Indians -- Music -- History and criticism.

ML3575.P4.T87 1993
Turino, Thomas.
Moving away from silence: music of the Peruvian Altiplano and the experience of urban migration/ Thomas Turino. Chicago: University of Chicago Press, 1993. xii, 324 p.
92-026935   781.62/688508536   0226816990
Folk music -- Peru -- Conima (District) -- History and criticism. Folk music -- Peru -- Lima -- History and criticism. Rural-urban migration -- Peru.

ML3575.V3 O47 1996
Olsen, Dale A.
Music of the Warao of Venezuela: song people of the rain forest/ Dale A. Olsen. Gainesville: University Press of Florida, c1996. xxxiv, 444 p.
95-046549   781.62/98 20   0813013909
Warao Indians -- Music -- History and criticism. Folk music -- Venezuela -- History and criticism. Folk songs, Warao -- Venezuela -- History and criticism.

ML3602.R5 1994
Rice, Timothy, 1945-
May it fill your soul: experiencing Bulgarian music/ Timothy Rice. Chicago: University of Chicago Press, c1994. xxv, 370 p.
93-034083   781.62/91811   0226711218
Folk music -- Bulgaria -- History and criticism. Folk songs, Bulgarian -- Bulgaria -- History and criticism. Folk dancing, Bulgarian.

ML3621.R48.M37 1996
Mason, Laura.
Singing the French Revolution: popular culture and politics, 1787-1799/ Laura Mason. Ithaca: Cornell University Press, 1996. xi, 268 p.
96-017694   781.5/99/094409033   0801432332
Revolutionary ballads and songs -- France -- History and criticism. Popular culture -- France -- History -- 18th century. France -- History -- Revolution, 1789-1799.

ML3650.B82
Bronson, Bertrand Harris, 1902-
The traditional tunes of the Child ballads; with their texts, according to the extant records of Great Britain and America. Princeton, N.J., Princeton University Press, 1959-72. 4 v.
57-005468   784.3
English ballads and songs. Ballads, English -- England. Ballads, Scots -- Scotland.

ML3654.S54 1993
Shields, Hugh.
Narrative singing in Ireland: lays, ballads, come-all-yes, and other songs/ Hugh Shields. Blackrock, Co. Dublin: Irish Academic Press, c1993. ix, 283 p.
93-141147   0716524627
Ballads -- Ireland -- History and criticism. Lays (Music) -- History and criticism. Folk songs -- Ireland -- History and criticism.

ML3680.W33 1990
Warner, Elizabeth.
Russian traditional folk song/ Elizabeth A. Warner and Evgenii S. Kustovskii. [Hull]: Hull University Press, 1990. x, 120 p.
89-145876   781.62/9717/009   0859584739
Folk music -- Soviet Union -- History and criticism. Folk songs, Russian -- Soviet Union -- History and criticism. Folk songs, Russian -- Texts.

ML3740.B7
Brandel, Rose.
The music of Central Africa; an ethnomusicological study: former French Equatorial Africa, the former Belgian Congo, Ruanda-Urundi, Uganda, Tanganyika. The Hague, M. Nijhoff, 1961. xii, 272 p.
62-006547
Ethnomusicology. Music, African. Music -- Africa, Central -- History and criticism.

ML3746.J66 1995
Jones, Stephen.
Folk music of China: living instrumental traditions/ Stephen Jones. Oxford: Clarendon Press; c1995. xxvii, 422 p.
94-003457   781.62/0951   0198162006
Folk music -- China -- History and criticism. Instrumental music -- China -- History and criticism.

ML3758.A3.B3 1988
Baily, John, 1943-
Music of Afghanistan: professional musicians in the city of Herat/ John Baily. Cambridgeshire [England]; Cambridge University Press, 1988. xiv, 183 p.
87-035525   780/.958/1   0521250005
Music -- Afghanistan -- Herat -- History and criticism. Musicians -- Afghanistan -- Herat -- Social life and customs. Herat (Afghanistan) -- Social life and customs.

ML3758.A783.L48 1996
Levin, Theodore Craig.
The hundred thousand fools of God: musical travels in Central Asia (and Queens, New York)/ Theodore Levin. Bloomington: Indiana University Press, c1996. xvi, 318 p.
96-007607   780/.958   0253332060
Music -- Asia, Central -- History and criticism. Jews, Bukharan -- New York (State) -- New York -- Music -- History and criticism. Ethnomusicology. Queens (New York, N.Y.)

ML3758.I53.H47 1997
Herbst, Edward.
Voices in Bali: energies and perceptions in vocal music and dance theater/ Edward Herbst; foreword by Judith Becker; afterword by Rene T.A. Lysloff. Hanover, NH: University Press of New England, c1997. xxvii, 198 p.
97-019855   781.62/9922   0819563161
Folk music -- Indonesia -- Bali Island -- History and criticism. Dance -- Indonesia -- Bali Island. Theater -- Indonesia -- Bali Island.

ML3760.C38 2000
Charry, Eric S.
Mande music: traditional and modern music of the Maninka and Mandinka of Western Africa/ Eric Charry. Chicago: University of Chicago Press, 2000. xxxi, 500 p.
99-046011   781.62/9634   0226101614
Mandingo (African people) -- Music -- History and criticism. Music -- Africa, West -- History and criticism.

ML3760.C48
Chernoff, John Miller.
African rhythm and African sensibility: aesthetics and social action in African musical idioms/ John Miller Chernoff. Chicago: University of Chicago Press, 1979. xv, 261 p.
79-000189   780/.96   0226103447
Music -- Africa -- History and criticism. Aesthetics, African.

ML3760.E76 1995
Erlmann, Veit.
Nightsong: performance, power, and practice in South Africa/ Veit Erlmann; with an introduction by Joseph Shabalala. Chicago: University of Chicago, 1995. xxv, 446 p.
94-024977   782.42162/963986068   0226217205
Isicathamiya -- History and criticism. Zulu (African people) -- South Africa -- Music -- History and criticism. Folk music -- South Africa -- History and criticism.

ML3760.1.A37 2000
The African diaspora: a musical perspective/ edited by Ingrid Monson. New York: Garland Pub., 2000. viii, 366 p.
99-045341   780/.89/96   0815323824
Blacks -- Music -- History and criticism. Music -- Africa -- History and criticism.

ML3770.M35 1996
McLean, Mervyn.
Maori music/ Mervyn McLean. Auckland: Auckland University Press, 1996. xii, 418 p.
96-232016   781.62/99442 21   1869401441
Maori (New Zealand people) -- Music -- History and criticism. Folk music -- New Zealand -- History and criticism.

ML3776 History and criticism — Music of the Jews

ML3776.F62 1992
Flam, Gila, 1956-
Singing for survival: songs of the Lodz ghetto, 1940-45/ Gila Flam. Urbana: University of Illinois Press, c1992. xv, 207 p.
90-027846   782.42162/92404384   0252018176
Jews -- Poland -- Lodz -- Music -- History and criticism. Jews -- Persecutions -- Poland -- Lodz. Holocaust, Jewish (1939-1945) -- Poland -- Lodz.

ML3776.I3 1967
Idelsohn, A. Z. 1882-1938.
Jewish music in its historical development, by A. Z. Idelsohn. New York, Schocken Books [1967, c1956] xi, 535 p.
67-025236   781.7/2924
Jews -- Music -- History and criticism. Synagogue music -- History and criticism. Folk music -- History and criticism.

ML3785 History and criticism — Musical criticism

ML3785.S5 1965
Slonimsky, Nicolas, 1894-
Lexicon of musical invective; critical assaults on composers since Beethoven's time. New York, Coleman-Ross Co., 1965. 325 p.
65-026270   780.922
Musical criticism. Composers.

ML3790 Music trade — General works

ML3790.D32 1990
Dannen, Fredric.
Hit men: power brokers and fast money inside the music business/ Fredric Dannen. New York: Times Books, c1990. 387 p.
89-040187   338.4/778166/0266   0812916581
Sound recording industry -- United States. Rock music -- United States -- History and criticism.

ML3790.F74
Frith, Simon.
Sound effects: youth, leisure, and the politics of rock'n'roll/ Simon Frith. 1st American ed. New York: Pantheon Books, c1981. vii, 294 p.
81-047195   784.5/4 19   0394748115
Sound recording industry -- United States. Rock music -- History and criticism.

ML3790.N4 1999
Negus, Keith.
Music genres and corporate cultures/ Keith Negus. London; Routledge, 1999. ix, 209 p.
98-051909   781.64   041517399X
Sound recording industry. Popular music -- History and criticism.

ML3790.S385 1994
Segrave, Kerry, 1944-
Payola in the music industry: a history, 1880-1991/ by Kerry Segrave. Jefferson, N.C.: McFarland, c1994. x, 278 p.
92-056691   364.1/68   0899508820
Music trade -- Corrupt practices -- United States.

ML3790.S5 2003
Krasilovsky, M. William.
This business of music: the difinitive guide to the music industry/ M. William Krasilovsky and Sidney Schemel; contributions by John M. Gross. 9th ed. New York: Billboard Books, 2003. xviii, 526 p.
2003-103779   0823077284

ML3792 Music trade — Individual record companies and labels, A-Z

ML3792.S65 1999
Smith, Suzanne E.,
Dancing in the street: Motown and the cultural politics of Detroit/ Suzanne E. Smith. Cambridge, Mass.: Harvard University Press, 1999. 319 p.
99-034399   781.644/09774/34 21   0674000633
Afro-Americans -- Michigan -- Detroit -- Music. Music -- Social aspects -- Michigan -- Detroit. Civil rights movements -- Michigan -- Detroit.

ML3795 Music as a profession. Vocational guidance

ML3795.B33 2001
Baskerville, David.
Music business handbook and career guide/ David Baskerville. 7th ed. Thousand Oaks, Calif.: Sage Publications, c2001. xxviii, 676 p.
00-008014   780/.23/73 21   0761916679
Music -- Vocational guidance -- United States -- Handbooks, manuals, etc. Music trade -- Vocational guidance -- United States -- Handbooks, manuals,

ML3795.B6313 1992
Blaukopf, Kurt.
Musical life in a changing society: aspects of music sociology/ by Kurt Blaukopf; translated by David Marinelli. Portland, Or.: Amadeus Press, c1992. 308 p.
92-017805   306.4/84   0931340527
Music -- Social aspects. Music -- History and criticism.

ML3795.D34
Denisoff, R. Serge.
Great day coming; folk music and the American left [by] R. Serge Denisoff. Urbana, University of Illinois Press [1971] 219 p.
74-155498   784.6   0252001796
Music -- Social aspects. Radicalism -- Songs and music -- History and criticism. Right and left (Political science)

ML3795.L44 1989
Lieberman, Robbie, 1954-
My song is my weapon: People's Songs, American communism, and the politics of culture, 1930-1950/ Robbie Lieberman. Urbana: University of Illinois Press, c1989. xxiii, 201 p.
88-012226   324.273/75   0252015592
Communism and music. Music -- Political aspects -- United States. Communism -- United States.

ML3795.M14 1993
MacLeod, Bruce A., 1950-
Club date musicians: playing the New York party circuit/ Bruce A. MacLeod. Urbana: University of Illinois Press, c1993. x, 213 p.
92-010010   780/.23/7471   0252019547
Musicians -- Employment -- New York Metropolitan Area. Music trade -- New York Metropolitan Area. New York Metropolitan Area -- Social life and customs.

ML3795.M188 1995
Martin, Peter J., 1947-
Sounds and society: themes in the sociology of music/ Peter J. Martin. Manchester; Manchester University Press; c1995. xiii, 298 p.
94-037797   306.4/84   0719032237
Music -- Social aspects.

ML3795.M78 1987
Music and society: the politics of composition, performance, and reception/ edited by Richard Leppert and Susan McClary. Cambridge [Cambridgeshire]; Cambridge University Press, 1987. xx, 202 p.
86-031672   780/.07   0521327806
Music -- Social aspects.

ML3795.S36 1989
Seltzer, George,
Music matters: the performer and the American Federation of Musicians / by George Seltzer. Metuchen, N.J.: Scarecrow Press, 1989. ix, 343 p.
88-033671   331.88/1178 19
Musicians -- Labor unions -- United States. Music -- Economic aspects -- United States.

ML3795.T66 1993
Towse, Ruth, 1943-
Singers in the marketplace: the economics of the singing profession/ Ruth Towse. Oxford [England]: Clarendon Press; 1993. ix, 252 p.
93-018832   338.4/7782/00941   0198163479
Singers -- Great Britain -- Economic conditions. Singing teachers -- Great Britain -- Economic conditions.

ML3797 Musical research — Musicology — General works

ML3797.D2313 1983
Dahlhaus, Carl, 1928-
Foundations of music history/ Carl Dahlhaus; translated by J.B. Robinson. Cambridge, [Cambridgeshire]; Cambridge University Press, 1983. x, 177 p.
82-009591   780/.01   0521232813
Music -- Historiography.

ML3797.K47 1985
Kerman, Joseph, 1924-
Contemplating music: challenges to musicology/ Joseph Kerman. Cambridge, Mass.: Harvard University Press, 1985. 255 p.
84-025217   780/.01   0674166779
Musicology.

ML3797.P67 1998
Potter, Pamela Maxine.
Most German of the arts: musicology and society from the Weimar Republic to the end of Hitler's Reich/ Pamela M. Potter. New Haven: Yale University Press, c1998. xx, 364 p.
97-050585   780/.7/2043   0300072287
Musicology -- Germany -- History -- 20th century. Music -- Social aspects -- Germany. Nationalism in music.

ML3797.S3
Sachs, Curt, 1881-1959.
The wellsprings of music. Edited by Jaap Kunst. The Hague, M. Nijhoff, 1962. 228 p.
63-004764   781.71
Ethnomusicology.

ML3797.W54 2002
Wingell, Richard,
Writing about music: an introductory guide/ Richard J. Wingell. 3rd ed. Upper Saddle River, N.J.: Prentice Hall, c2002. xvi, 171 p.
2001-045945   808/.06678 21   0130406031
Music -- Historiography -- Handbooks, manuals, etc. Musical criticism -- Authorship -- Handbooks, manuals, etc. Academic writing -- Handbooks, manuals, etc.

ML3797.1 Musical research — Musicology — Addresses, essays, lectures

ML3797.1.D5 1992
Disciplining music: musicology and its canons/ edited by Katherine Bergeron and Philip V. Bohlman. Chicago: University of Chicago Press, 1992. xi, 220 p.
91-037836   780/.7   0226043681
Musicology. Ethnomusicology. Music -- Theory.

ML3798 Musical research — Ethnomusicology — General works

ML3798.E84 1992
Ethnomusicology/ edited by Helen Myers. 1st American ed. New York: W.W. Norton, 1992-1993. 2 v.
94-103100   780/.89 20   0393033783
Ethnomusicology.

ML3798.M87
Musics of many cultures: an introduction/ Elizabeth May, editor; foreword by Mantle Hood. Berkeley: University of California Press, c1980. xix, 431 p.
76-050251   781.7   0520033930
Ethnomusicology. Music -- History and criticism. Music -- Social aspects.

ML3798.N47 1983
Nettl, Bruno, 1930-
The study of ethnomusicology: twenty-nine issues and concepts/ Bruno Nettl. Urbana: University of Illinois Press, c1983. xii, 410 p.
82-007065   781.7   025200986X
Ethnomusicology.

ML3799 Musical research — Ethnomusicology — Addresses, essays, lectures

ML3799.C69 1990
Comparative musicology and anthropology of music: essays on the history of ethnomusicology/ edited by Bruno Nettl and Philip V. Bohlman. Chicago: University of Chicago Press, c1991. xvii, 378 p.
90-038366   780/.89   0226574083
Ethnomusicology. Music and anthropology.

ML3800 Philosophy and physics of music — General works

ML3800.B79 1998
Bowman, Wayne D., 1947-
Philosophical perspectives on music/ Wayne D. Bowman.
New York: Oxford University Press, 1998. viii, 488 p.
97-025601   781/.1   0195112962
Music -- Philosophy and aesthetics.

ML3800.C165 2002
The Cambridge history of Western music theory/ edited by Thomas Christensen. Cambridge; Cambridge University Press, 2002. xxiii, 998 p.
00-050366   781/.09 21   0521623715
Music theory -- History.

ML3800.G576 1992
Goehr, Lydia.
The imaginary museum of musical works: an essay in the philosophy of music/ Lydia Goehr. Oxford [England]: Clarendon Press; 1992. vii, 314 p.
91-028284   780/.1   0198248180
Music -- Philosophy and aesthetics.

ML3800.H43 2000
Herissone, Rebecca.
Music theory in seventeenth-century England/ Rebecca Herissone. New York: Oxford University Press, 2000. xv, 316 p.
00-040066   781/.0942/09032   0198167008
Music theory -- History. Music -- England -- 17th century -- History and criticism.

ML3800.H55
Hindemith, Paul, 1895-1963.
A composer's world, horizons and limitations. Cambridge, Harvard University Press, 1952. 221 p.
52-005033   780.1
Music -- Philosophy and aesthetics.

ML3800.M63
Meyer, Leonard B.
Emotion and meaning in music. [Chicago] University of Chicago Press [1956] 307 p.
56-009130   780.1
Music -- Philosophy and aesthetics. Music -- Psychological aspects.

ML3800.M633
Meyer, Leonard B.
Music, the arts, and ideas; patterns and predictions in twentieth-century culture, by Leonard B. Meyer. Chicago, University of Chicago Press [1967] xi, 342 p.
67-025515   780.15
Music -- Philosophy and aesthetics. Music -- 20th century -- History and criticism.

ML3805 Philosophy and physics of music — Acoustics and physics — General works

ML3805.B245 A3 1977
Backus, John.
The acoustical foundations of music/ John Backus. 2d ed.
New York: Norton, c1977. xiv, 368 p.
77-010334   781/.1   0393090965
Music -- Acoustics and physics.

ML3805.B328 1990
Benade, Arthur H.
Fundamentals of musical acoustics/ Arthur H. Benade.
New York: Dover Publications, 1990. xii, 596 p.
90-040159   781.2 20   048626484X
Music -- Acoustics and physics.

ML3805.H153 2002
Hall, Donald E.
Musical acoustics/ Donald E. Hall. 3rd ed. Pacific Grove, Calif.: Brooks/Cole Pub. Co., c2002. xiv, 480 p.
2001-037422   781.2 21   0534377289
Music -- Acoustics and physics.

ML3805.R74 1995
Roederer, Juan G., 1929-
The physics and psychophysics of music: an introduction/ Juan G. Roederer. New York: Springer-Verlag, c1995. x, 219 p.
94-016447   781.2   038794298X
Music -- Acoustics and physics.

ML3805.S3
Schafer, R. Murray.
The tuning of the world/ R. Murray Schafer. New York: Knopf, 1977. xii, 301 p.
76-049508   781/.1   0394409663
Music -- Acoustics and physics. Sound. Music -- Philosophy and aesthetics.

ML3807 Philosophy and physics of music — Acoustics and physics — Musical sounds

ML3807.H39 2002
Haynes, Bruce,
A history of performing pitch: the story of "A"/ Bruce Haynes. Lanham, Md.: Scarecrow Press, 2002. xii, 568 p.
2002-075248   781.2/32 21   0810841851
Musical pitch. Musical temperament.

ML3809 Philosophy and physics of music — Acoustics and physics — Intervals, temperament, etc.

ML3809.B234 1953
Barbour, J. Murray 1897-
Tuning and temperament, a historical survey. East Lansing, Michigan State College Press, 1953 [c1951] 228 p.
53-003973   781.22
Tuning. Musical temperament.

ML3809.L55 1979
Lloyd, Llewelyn S.
Intervals, scales, and temperaments/ Ll. S. Lloyd and Hugh Boyle. [Rev. and expanded ed.]. New York: St. Martin's Press, 1979, c1978. xix, 322 p.
78-007124   781/.22   0312425333
Musical intervals and scales. Musical temperament.

ML3811 Philosophy and physics of music — Acoustics and physics — Tonality, atonality, polytonality, etc.

ML3811.D3913 1990
Dahlhaus, Carl, 1928-
Studies on the origin of harmonic tonality/ Carl Dahlhaus; translated by Robert O. Gjerdingen. Princeton, NJ: Princeton University Press, c1990. xv, 389 p.
90-008696   781.2/6   0691091358
Tonality.

ML3820 Philosophy and physics of music — Physiology — General works

ML3820.H42 1954
Helmholtz, Hermann von, 1821-1894.
On the sensations of tone as a physiological basis for the theory of music. New York, Dover Publications [1954] xix, 576 p.
54-003730   781.1
Sound -- Physiological effect. Music -- Physiological aspects. Music -- Acoustics and physics.

ML3830 Philosophy and physics of music — Psychology — General works

ML3830.D28 1978b
Davies, John Booth.
The psychology of music/ John Booth Davies. Stanford, Calif.: Stanford University Press, 1978. 240 p.
77-092339   781/.15   0804709807
Music -- Psychological aspects.

ML3830.H23 1986
Hargreaves, David J. 1948-
The developmental psychology of music/ David J. Hargreaves. Cambridge [Cambridgeshire]; Cambridge University Press, 1986. x, 260 p.
86-013660   781/.15   0521306655
Music -- Psychological aspects. Developmental psychology. Child psychology.

ML3830.M983 1994
Musical perceptions/ edited by Rita Aiello with John A. Sloboda. New York: Oxford University Press, 1994. xiii, 290 p.
93-028888   781/.11   0195064755
Musical perception. Music -- Philosophy and aesthetics.

ML3830.P9 1999
The psychology of music/ edited by Diana Deutsch. 2nd ed. San Diego: Academic Press, c1999. xvi, 807 p.
98-085210   781/.11 21   0122135652
Music -- Psychological aspects.

ML3830.S56 2000
Snyder, Bob,
Music and memory: an introduction/ Bob Snyder. Cambridge, Mass.: MIT Press, c2000. xxii, 291 p.
99-086731   781/.11 21   0262692376
Music -- Psychological aspects. Memory. Music theory -- Elementary works.

ML3830.S57 1997
The social psychology of music/ edited by David J. Hargreaves and Adrian C. North. Oxford; 1997. xv, 319 p.
96-045586   781/.11   019852384X
Music -- Psychological aspects. Music -- Social aspects.

ML3830.S87 1992
Storr, Anthony.
Music and the mind/ Anthony Storr. New York: Free Press; c1992. xii, 212 p.
92-021743   781/.11   0029316219
Music -- Psychological aspects. Music -- Physiological aspects. Music -- Philosophy and aesthetics.

ML3838 Philosophy and physics of music — Psychology — Other (not A-Z)

ML3838.B76 1995
Brinner, Benjamin Elon.
Knowing music, making music: Javanese gamelan and the theory of musical competence and interaction/ Benjamin Brinner. Chicago: University of Chicago Press, 1995. xxiv, 363 p.
95-030177   780/.9598/2   0226075095
Musical ability. Gamelan.

ML3838.G38
Generative processes in music: the psychology of performance, improvisation, and composition/ edited by John A. Sloboda. Oxford [England]: Clarendon Press; 2000. xiii, 298 p.
2001-271717   781.4/3111   0198508468
Music -- Performance -- Psychological aspects. Improvisation (Music) -- Psychological aspects. Composition (Music) -- Psychological aspects.

ML3838.M96 1993
Musicology and difference: gender and sexuality in music scholarship/ edited by Ruth A. Solie. Berkeley: University of California Press, c1993. xi, 355 p.
92-016317   780/.82   0520079272
Sex in music. Music -- Psychological aspects. Musicology.

ML3838.S48 1988
Serafine, Mary Louise.
Music as cognition: the development of thought in sound/
Mary Louise Serafine. New York: Columbia University
Press, 1988. x, 247 p.
87-005122   781/.15   0231057423
Music -- Psychological aspects. Cognition.

ML3845 Philosophy and physics of music —
Aesthetics —
General works

ML3845.B837 1990
Burrows, David L.
Sound, speech, and music/ David Burrows. Amherst:
University of Massachusetts Press, c1990. viii, 138 p.
89-004947   780/.1   0870236857
Music -- Philosophy and aesthetics. Sound. Speech.

ML3845.C36 1996
Cameron, Catherine M.
Dialectics in the arts: the rise of experimentalism in
American music/ Catherine M. Cameron. Westport,
Conn.: Praeger, 1996. xiv, 163 p.
96-014784   780/.973   0275956105
*Music -- United States -- 20th century -- Philosophy and
aesthetics. Music and anthropology. Music -- Social aspects.*

ML3845.C67 1990
Cook, Nicholas, 1950-
Music, imagination, and culture/ Nicholas Cook. Oxford;
Oxford University Press, 1990. 265 p.
89-003352   781/.11
*Music -- Philosophy and aesthetics. Music -- Psychological
aspects.*

ML3845.D2913 1982
Dahlhaus, Carl, 1928-
Esthetics of music/ Carl Dahlhaus; translated by William
W. Austin. Cambridge; Cambridge University Press,
1982. xii, 115 p.
81-010080   780/.1   0521235081
Music -- Philosophy and aesthetics.

ML3845.I62 1993
The Interpretation of music: philosophical essays/ edited
with an introduction by Michael Krausz. Oxford:
Clarendon Press; 1993. ix, 288 p.
92-016508   781/.1   0198239580
Music -- Philosophy and aesthetics.

ML3845.K58
Kivy, Peter.
The corded shell: reflections on musical expression/ by
Peter Kivy. Princeton: Princeton University Press,
c1980. xiv, 167 p.
80-007539   780/.1 19   0691020140
*Music -- Philosophy and aesthetics. Music -- 17th century --
History and criticism. Music -- 18th century -- History and
criticism.*

ML3845.K583 1993
Kivy, Peter.
The fine art of repetition: essays in the philosophy of
music/ Peter Kivy. Cambridge [England]; Cambridge
University Press, 1993. x, 373 p.
92-025274   781/.1   0521434629
Music -- Philosophy and aesthetics.

ML3845.K585 1990
Kivy, Peter.
Music alone: philosophical reflections on the purely
musical experience/ Peter Kivy. Ithaca: Cornell
University Press, 1990. xii, 226 p.
89-035570   780/.1   0801423317
Music -- Philosophy and aesthetics.

ML3845.K59 1984
Kivy, Peter.
Sound   and   semblance: reflections   on   musical
representation/ by Peter Kivy. Princeton, N.J.: Princeton
University Press, c1984. 235 p.
83-043081   780/.1   0691072825
Music -- Philosophy and aesthetics. Music -- Theory.

ML3845.L47 1997
Levinson, Jerrold.
Music in the moment/ Jerrold Levinson. Ithaca, N.Y.:
Cornell University Press, 1997. xii, 184 p.
97-019847   781.1/7   0801431298
*Music -- Philosophy and aesthetics. Musical perception. Music
-- Psychological aspects.*

ML3845.S13 1991
Said, Edward W.
Musical elaborations/ Edward W. Said. New York:
Columbia University Press, c1991. xxi, 109 p.
90-026685   781   0231073186
*Music -- Philosophy and aesthetics. Music -- Social aspects.
Music -- Performance.*

ML3845.S628 1998
Small, Christopher, 1927-
Musicking: the meanings of performing and listening/
Christopher Small. Hanover: University Press of New
England, c1998. 230 p.
97-049996   781/.1   0819522562
*Music -- Philosophy and aesthetics. Music -- Performance --
Psychological aspects.*

ML3845.T77 1989
Treitler, Leo, 1931-
Music and the historical imagination/ Leo Treitler.
Cambridge, Mass.: Harvard University Press, 1989.
336 p.
88-018066   780/.1   0674591283
*Music -- Philosophy and aesthetics. Music -- History and
criticism.*

ML3845.W59 1997
Williams, Alastair.
New music and the claims of modernity/ Alastair
Williams. Aldershot, England; Ashgate, c1997. xi, 163 p.
96-045418   780/.9/04   1859283683
*Adorno, Theodor W., -- 1903-1969 -- Aesthetics. Music -- 20th
century -- Philosophy and aesthetics.*

ML3847 Philosophy and physics of music — Aesthetics — The beautiful in music

ML3847.H3 1957
Hanslick, Eduard, 1825-1904.
The beautiful in music. Translated by Gustav Cohen. Edited, with an introd., by Morris Weitz. New York, Liberal Arts Press [1957] 127 p.
57-014627   780.1
Music -- Philosophy and aesthetics.

ML3847.R53 1995
Ridley, Aaron.
Music, value, and the passions/ Aaron Ridley. Ithaca: Cornell University Press, 1995. xi, 199 p.
94-042018   781/.1   0801430356
Music -- Philosophy and aesthetics. Emotions (Philosophy)

ML3849 Philosophy and physics of music — Aesthetics — Relations between music and other arts

ML3849.K7 1984
Kramer, Lawrence, 1946-
Music and poetry, the nineteenth century and after/ Lawrence Kramer. Berkeley: University of California Press, c1984. xiii, 251 p.
83-001173   780/.08   0520048733
Music and literature. Music -- 19th century -- Philosophy and aesthetics. Music -- 20th century -- Philosophy and aesthetics.

ML3849.M935 1991
Music and text: critical inquiries/ edited by Steven Paul Sher. Cambridge; Cambridge University Press, 1992. xvii, 327 p.
90-023762   780/.08   0521401585
Music and language. Music and literature. Music -- Philosophy and aesthetics.

ML3849.P27 1997
Panish, Jon.
The color of jazz: race and representation in postwar American culture/ Jon Panish. Jackson: University Press of Mississippi, c1997. xxiii, 166 p.
97-011364   306.4/84   1578060354
Jazz in literature. Jazz -- Social aspects -- United States. Race in literature. United States -- Race relations.

ML3849.W58
Winn, James Anderson, 1947-
Unsuspected eloquence: a history of the relations between poetry and music/ James Anderson Winn. New Haven, CT: Yale University Press, c1981. xiv, 381 p.
80-027055   780/.08   0300026153
Music and literature.

ML3850 Philosophy and physics of music — Aesthetics — Rhythm

ML3850.K72 1988
Kramer, Jonathan D., 1942-
The time of music: new meanings, new temporalities, new listening strategies/ Jonathan D. Kramer. New York: Schirmer Books; c1988. xviii, 493 p.
88-004505   781.2/2   0028725905
Time in music. Time perception. Music -- Philosophy and aesthetics.

ML3853 Philosophy and physics of music — Aesthetics — Interpretation

ML3853.C7
Copland, Aaron, 1900-
Music and imagination.   Cambridge, Harvard University Press, 1952. 116 p.
52-009385   780.1
Creation (Literary, artistic, etc.). Music -- 20th century -- History and criticism. Imagination.

ML3854 Philosophy and physics of music — Aesthetics — Absolute music

ML3854.D3413 1989
Dahlhaus, Carl, 1928-
The idea of absolute music/ Carl Dahlhaus; translated by Roger Lustig. Chicago: University of Chicago Press, 1989. x, 176 p.
89-004829   781.1/7   0226134865
Absolute music. Music -- Philosophy and aesthetics. Music -- 19th century -- History and criticism.

ML3858 Philosophy and physics of music — Aesthetics — Dramatic music

ML3858.A2 1991
Abbate, Carolyn.
Unsung voices: opera and musical narrative in the nineteenth century/ Carolyn Abbate. Princeton, N.J.: Princeton University Press, c1991. xvi, 288 p.
90-008972   782.1/09/034   0691091404
Opera -- 19th century. Music -- 19th century -- Philosophy and aesthetics.

ML3858.K4 1988
Kerman, Joseph, 1924-
Opera as drama/ Joseph Kerman. Berkeley: University of California Press, c1988. xvii, 232 p.
88-004829   782.1   0520062736
Opera -- Dramaturgy.

ML3858.K53 1988
Kivy, Peter.
Osmin's rage: philosophical reflections on opera, drama, and text/ by Peter Kivy. Princeton, N.J.: Princeton University Press, c1988. xiii, 303 p.
87-026339   782.1/01   0691073244
Opera. Music -- Philosophy and aesthetics.

ML3858.S373 1990
Schmidgall, Gary, 1945-
Shakespeare & opera/ Gary Schmidgall. New York: Oxford University Press, 1990. xxii, 394 p.
90-006861   782.1   019506450X
Shakespeare, William, -- 1564-1616.   Opera. Music in literature. Music -- Philosophy and aesthetics.

ML3858.T66 1999
Tomlinson, Gary.
Metaphysical song: an essay on opera/ Gary Tomlinson. Princeton, N.J.: Princeton University Press, c1999. x, 192 p.
98-025780   782.1   0691004099
Opera. Music -- Philosophy and aesthetics.

ML3877 Philosophy and physics of music — Aesthetics — Other (not A-Z)

ML3877.C6 1983
Clifton, Thomas, 1935-1978.
Music as heard: a study in applied phenomenology/ Thomas Clifton. New Haven: Yale University Press, c1983. xi, 316 p.
82-010944   780/.1   0300020910
Music -- Philosophy and aesthetics. Phenomenology.

ML3880 Philosophy and physics of music — Criticism — General works

ML3880.K7 1990
Kramer, Lawrence, 1946-
Music as cultural practice, 1800-1900/ Lawrence Kramer. Berkeley: University of California Press, c1990. xv, 226 p.
89-020445   780/.9/034   0520068572
Music -- 19th century -- Philosophy and aesthetics.

ML3890 Philosophy and physics of music — Criticism — The musical canon

ML3890.C58 1993
Citron, Marcia J.
Gender and the musical canon/ Marcia J. Citron. Cambridge [England]; Cambridge University Press, 1993. xii, 307 p.
92-002468   780/.82   0521392926
Musical canon. Music by women composers -- History and criticism.

ML3918 Philosophy and physics of music — Social aspects of music — Forms and types, A-Z

ML3918.F65
Reuss, Richard A.
American folk music and left-wing politics, 1927-1957/ Richard A. Reuss; with JoAnne C. Reuss. Lanham, Md.: Scarecrow Press, c2000. xviii, 297 p.
00-023240   781.62/1301599   081083684X
Folk music -- Political aspects -- United States.

ML3918.R63
Bertrand, Michael T., 1961-
Race, rock, and Elvis/ Michael T. Bertrand. Urbana: University of Illinois Press, c2000. xii, 327 p.
99-050895   781.66/0975   0252025865
Presley, Elvis, -- 1935-1977 -- Criticism and interpretation. Music and race. Rock music -- Social aspects -- Southern States. Rock music -- United States -- To 1961 -- History and criticism.

ML3920 Philosophy and physics of music — Moral influence and therapeutic use of music — General works

ML3920.M89795 1998
Music therapy in palliative care: new voices/ edited by David Aldridge London; Jessica Kingsley Publishers, 1998. 175 p.
98-045893   615.8/5154   1853027391
Music therapy. Palliative treatment.

MT Musical instruction and study

MT1 Theory and history of music education — General works

MT1.C22 1991
Campbell, Patricia Shehan.
Lessons from the world: a cross-cultural guide to music teaching and learning/ Patricia Shehan Campbell. New York: Schirmer Books; c1991. xv, 331 p.
90-042513   780/.7   0028723619
Music -- Instruction and study.

MT1.C226 1995
Campbell, Patricia Shehan.
Music in childhood: from preschool through the elementary grades/ Patricia Shehan Campbell, Carol Scott-Kassner; technology for music instruction (chapter 12) by Kirk Kassner; photographs by Jerry Gay. New York: Schirmer Books; c1995. xvii, 398 p.
94-030663   372.87/044   0028705521
Music -- Instruction and study -- Juvenile. School music -- Instruction and study.

MT1.C536
Choksy, Lois.
The Kodaly context: creating an environment for musical learning/ Lois Choksy. Englewood Cliffs, N.J.: Prentice-Hall, c1981. xxi, 281 p.
80-022149   780/.7   0135166748
Kodaly, Zoltan, -- 1882-1967.   School music -- Instruction and study.

MT1.F53 1987
Fletcher, Peter, 1936-
Education and music/ Peter Fletcher. Oxford
[Oxfordshire]; Oxford University Press, 1987. xvi, 208 p.
86-016358   780/.7   0193174200
Music in education.

MT1.H138 1992
Handbook of research on music teaching and learning: a
project of the Music Educators National Conference/
editor, Richard Colwell. New York: Schirmer Books;
c1992. xvi, 832 p.
91-029363   780/.7   0028705017
Music -- Instruction and study.

MT1.J676 1997
Jorgensen, Estelle Ruth.
In search of music education/ Estelle R. Jorgensen.
Urbana: University of Illinois Press, c1997. xv, 126 p.
96-025326   780/.7   025206609X
Music -- Instruction and study.

MT1.R435 1989
Reimer, Bennett.
A philosophy of music education/ Bennett Reimer.
Englewood Cliffs, N.J.: Prentice Hall, c1989. xiv, 252 p.
88-021654   780/.7   0136638813
*Music -- Instruction and study. Music -- Philosophy and
aesthetics.*

MT1.T38 2001
Teaching music in the twenty-first century/ Lois Choksy
... [et al.]. 2nd ed. Upper Saddle River, N.J.: Prentice
Hall, c2001. x, 342 p.
00-031368   780/.71 21   0130280275
School music--Instruction and study.

MT1.W33 1991
Warner, Brigitte, 1928-
Orff-Schulwerk: applications for the classroom/ Brigitte
Warner. Englewood Cliffs, N.J.: Prentice Hall, c1991. xi,
305 p.
90-040203   780/.7   0136398243
*Orff, Carl, -- 1895- -- Orff-Schulwerk.   School music --
Instruction and study.*

MT3 History and criticism —
By region or country, A-Z

MT3.U5.M32 1996
Mark, Michael L.
Contemporary music education/ Michael L. Mark. New
York: Schirmer Books; c1996. xv, 350 p.
96-000270   780/.7/073   0028719158
School music -- Instruction and study -- United States.

MT3.U5.M76 1988
Music education in the United States: contemporary
issues/ edited by J. Terry Gates. Tuscaloosa: University
of Alabama Press, c1988. xi, 328 p.
87-005836   780/.7/2973   0817303693
Music -- Instruction and study -- United States -- Congresses.

MT3.U5.R43
Regelski, Thomas A., 1941-
Teaching general music: action learning for middle and
secondary schools/ Thomas A. Regelski. New York:
Schirmer Books; c1981. 421 p.
80-005561   780/.7/2973   0028720709
School music -- Instruction and study -- United States.

MT4 History and criticism —
Individual institutions.
By city and institution, A-Z —
United States

MT4.N5.J846 1999
Olmstead, Andrea.
Juilliard: a history/ Andrea Olmstead. Urbana: University
of Illinois Press, c1999. 368 p.
98-058043   780/.71/17471   0252024877
Conservatories of music -- New York (State) -- New York.

MT5.5 Music theory —
Early works to 1600

MT5.5.B613 1989
Boethius, Anicius Manlius Severinus, d. 524.
Fundamentals of music/ Anicius Manlius Severinus
Boethius; translated, with introduction and notes by
Calvin M. Bower; edited by Claude V. Palisca. New
Haven: Yale University Press, c1989. xliv, 205 p.
88-019939   781   0300039433
Music -- Theory -- 500-1400 -- Early works to 1800.

MT5.5.F63 1989
The Florentine Camerata: documentary studies and
translations/ Claude V. Palisca. New Haven: Yale
University Press, c1989. vi, 234 p.
88-001711   781   0300039166
*Music -- Theory -- 16th century -- Early works to 1800. Music,
Greek and Roman -- Instruction and study -- Early works to
1800. Camerata (Group of music theorists)*

MT5.5.G2613 1993
Gaffurius, Franchinus, 1451-1522.
The theory of music/ Franchino Gaffurio; translated, with
introduction and notes, by Walter Kurt Kreyszig; edited
by Claude V. Palisca. New Haven: Yale University Press,
c1993. xxxix, 236 p.
92-033709   781   0300054971
*Music -- Theory -- To 500 -- Early works to 1800. Music,
Greek and Roman -- Early works to 1800. Music -- Acoustics
and physics -- Early works to 1800.*

MT5.5.M8713 1995
Musica enchiriadis; and, Scolica enchiriadis/ translated,
with introduction and notes, by Raymond Erickson;
edited by Claude V. Palisca. New Haven: Yale University
Press, c1995. liv, 106 p.
94-034601   781/.09/02 20   0300058187
Music theory -- Early works to 1800.

MT5.5.V5313 1996
Vicentino, Nicola, 1511-ca. 1576
Ancient music adapted to modern practice/ Nicola Vicentino; translated with introduction and notes by Maria Rika Maniates; edited by Claude V. Palisca. New Haven: Yale University Press, c1996. lxix, 487 p.
95-049843   780.1   0300066015
Music -- Theory -- 16th century. Musical intervals and scales -- Early works to 1800. Archicembalo.

MT5.5.V573.B8 1993
Virdung, Sebastian, b. 1465?
Musica getutscht: a treatise on musical instruments (1511)/ by Sebastian Virdung; translated and edited by Beth Bullard. Cambridge; Cambridge University Press, 1993. xii, 275 p.
92-019194   784.19   0521308305
Virdung, Sebastian, -- b. 1465? -- Musica getutscht. Musical instruments -- Europe -- Early works to 1800. Tablature (Musical notation) -- Early works to 1800.

MT5.5.Z3813 1983
Zarlino, Gioseffo, 1517-1590.
On the modes: part four of Le istitutioni harmoniche, 1558/ Gioseffo Zarlino; translated by Vered Cohen; edited with an introduction by Claude V. Palisca. New Haven: Yale University Press, c1983. xxiii, 120 p.
83-002477   781/.22   0300029373
Music -- Theory -- 16th century -- Early works to 1800. Musical intervals and scales -- Early works to 1800.

MT6 Music theory —
1601-
—General works

MT6.A766 1983
Aspects of Schenkerian theory/ edited by David Beach. New Haven: Yale University Press, c1983. xi, 222 p.
82-013498   781   0300028008
Schenkerian analysis.

MT6.B465.M9 1989
Berry, Wallace.
Musical structure and performance/ Wallace Berry. New Haven: Yale University Press, c1989. xvi, 240 p.
88-027958   781   0300043279
Brahms, Johannes, -- 1833-1897. -- Stucke, -- piano, -- op. 76. -- Intermezzo, -- B major. Berg, Alban, -- 1885-1935. -- Stucke, -- clarinet, piano, -- op. 5. -- Nr. 3. Debussy, Claude, -- 1862-1918. -- Ariettes oubliees. -- C'est l'extase. Music -- Performance. Musical analysis.

MT6.C775 M88 1998
Cook, Nicholas,
Music/ Nicholas Cook. Oxford; Oxford University Press, 1998.
98-012197   780 21   0192853406
Music appreciation.

MT6.D92.M9 1988
Dunsby, Jonathan.
Music analysis in theory and practice/ Jonathan Dunsby and Arnold Whittall. New Haven: Yale University Press, 1988. 250 p.
86-051282   781   0300037139
Musical analysis. Atonality.

MT6.F642.I6 1982
Forte, Allen.
Introduction to Schenkerian analysis/ Allen Forte, Steven E. Gilbert. New York: Norton, c1982. vii, 397 p.
81-022502   781   0393951928
Schenkerian analysis.

MT6.K365 2000
Kerman, Joseph,
Listen/ Joseph Kerman, Gary Tomlinson; with Vivian Kerman. 4th brief ed. Boston: Bedford/St. Martin's, c2000. xxv, 445 p.
99-065254   781.1/7 21   157259795X
Music appreciation.

MT6.L146 G8 1992
LaRue, Jan,
Guidelines for style analysis/ Jan LaRue. 2nd ed. Warren, Mich.: Harmonie Park Press, c1992. xviii, 286 p.
92-025439   781 20   0899900623
Musical analysis. Style, Musical.

MT6.L36.G4 1983
Lerdahl, Fred, 1943-
A generative theory of tonal music/ Fred Lerdahl, Ray Jackendoff. Cambridge, Mass.: MIT Press, c1983. xiv, 368 p.
82-017104   781   0262120941
Music -- Theory. Music -- Psychological aspects. Music and language.

MT6.M313 1997
Marx, Adolf Bernhard, 1795-1866.
Musical form in the age of Beethoven: selected writings on theory and method/ A.B. Marx; edited and translated by Scott Burnham. Cambridge, U.K.; Cambridge University Press, 1997. xvi, 197 p.
96-049875   781/.09/034   0521452740
Music -- Theory -- 19th century. Musical analysis.

MT6.M86 1953
Morley, Thomas, 1557-1603?.
A plain and easy introduction to practical music. Edited by R. Alec Harman; with a foreword by Thurston Dart. New York, Norton [1953] xxix, 326 p.
52-012671   781
Music -- Theory -- 16th-17th century.

MT6.M96205 1993
Music theory and the exploration of the past/ edited by Christopher Hatch and David W. Bernstein. Chicago: University of Chicago Press, 1993. xii, 561 p.
91-046985   781   0226319016
Music -- Theory. Musical analysis.

MT6.R24 1977
Ratner, Leonard G.
Music, the listener's art/ Leonard G. Ratner. 3d ed. New York: McGraw-Hill, c1977. xii, 306 p.
76-023395   780/.15   0070512213
Music appreciation.

MT6.R87.M9 1992
Rowell, Lewis Eugene, 1933-
Music and musical thought in early India/ Lewis Rowell. Chicago: University of Chicago Press, 1992. xvii, 409 p.
91-038791   781/.0954/0902   0226730328
Music -- India -- Theory.

MT6.S354.M9
Schwartz, Elliott, 1936-
Music, ways of listening/ Elliott Schwartz. New York: Holt, Rinehart, and Winston, c1982. xvi, 534 p.
81-020327   780/.1/5   0030446767
Music -- Analysis, appreciation.

MT6.S457 1990
Schenker studies/ edited by Hedi Siegel. Cambridge; Cambridge University Press, 1990-1999. v. 1-2
89-000467   780   0521360382
Schenker, Heinrich, -- 1868-1935 -- Congresses.   Music -- Theory -- Congresses.

MT6.Y86 U53 1999
Yudkin, Jeremy.
Understanding music/ Jeremy Yudkin. 2nd ed. Upper Saddle River, NJ: Prentice Hall, c1999. xxvii, 494 p.
98-036428   780 21   0130811254
Music appreciation. Music--History and criticism.

MT6.5 Music theory — 1601- — Collections of music for analysis and appreciation

MT6.5.A55 1994
Anthology for musical analysis/ Charles Burkhart. 5th ed. Fort Worth, TX: Harcourt Brace College Publishers, c1994. xiv, 593 p.
93-077044   0030553180
Musical analysis -- Music collections. Music appreciation -- Music collections.

MT6.5.B87 1986
Burkhart, Charles
Anthology for musical analysis/ Charles Burkhart. New York: Holt, Rinehart and Winston, c1986. xv, 602 p.
85-008513   781   0030012899
Musical analysis -- Music collections.

MT22 Specific systems and methods — Jaques-Dalcroze

MT22.A74 1972
Jaques-Dalcroze, Emile, 1865-1950.
Eurhythmics, art, and education. Translated from the French by Frederick Rothwell. Edited and prepared for the press by Cynthia Cox. New York, B. Blom, 1972. ix, 265 p.
78-180027   780/.77
Jaques-Dalcroze, Emile, -- 1865-1950.   Musical meter and rhythm. Musico-callisthenics. Music -- Instruction and study.

MT22.B313 1991
Bachmann, Marie-Laure.
Dalcroze today: an education through and into music/ Marie-Laure Bachmann; translated by David Parlett; translation edited by Ruth Stewart; preface by Jack P.B. Dobbs. Oxford: Clarendon Press; 1991. x, 377 p.
91-008214   781.2/2   0193174243
Jaques-Dalcroze, Emile, -- 1865-1950.   Musical meter and rhythm. Musico-callisthenics. Music -- Instruction and study.

MT35 Notation — General works

MT35.H55 1987
Heussenstamm, George.
The Norton manual of music notation/ by George Heussenstamm. 1st ed. New York: W.W. Norton, c1987. viii, 168 p.
86-016449   781/.24 19   0393955265
Musical notation.

MT35.H6
Hindemith, Paul, 1895-1963.
Elementary training for musicians, by Paul Hindemith. New York, Associated music publishers, inc. [1946] xiii, 237 p.
47-000003   780.77
Sight-reading (Music) Music -- Instruction and study. Ear training.

MT35.M56 1991
Mender, Mona, 1926-
Music manuscript preparation: a concise guide/ by Mona Mender. Metuchen, N.J.: Scarecrow Press, 1991. ix, 212 p.
90-008373   780.26/2   0810822946
Musical notation.

MT35.R252 1990
Read, Gardner, 1913-
20th-century microtonal notation/ Gardner Read. New York: Greenwood Press, 1990. viii, 198 p.
90-002782   780/.148   0313273987
Musical notation. Microtonal music.

MT35.R253.M6
Read, Gardner, 1913-
Modern rhythmic notation/ Gardner Read. Bloomington: Indiana University Press, c1978. ix, 202 p.
77-009860   781.6/2   0253338670
Musical notation. Musical meter and rhythm.

MT35.R253.M9 1969
Read, Gardner, 1913-
Music notation; a manual of modern practice. Boston,
Allyn and Bacon [1969] x, 482 p.
68-054213   781.2/4
Musical notation.

MT35.S87
Stone, Kurt.
Music notation in the twentieth century: a practical
guidebook/ by Kurt Stone. New York: W. W. Norton,
c1980. xxii, 357 p.
79-023093   781/.24/0904   0393950530
Musical notation.

MT40 Composition.
Elements and techniques of music —
Composition

MT40.F83 1965
Fux, Johann Joseph, 1660-1741.
The study of counterpoint from Johann Joseph Fux's
Gradus ad parnassum. Translated and edited by Alfred
Mann, with the collaboration of John Edmunds. New
York, W. W. Norton [1965] xvi, 156 p.
65-004836   781.42
Counterpoint. Composition (Music)

MT40.H523
Hindemith, Paul, 1895-1963.
The craft of musical composition, by Paul Hindemith ...
New York, Associated music publishers, inc.; [1945-]
45-018358   781.61
Composition (Music) Harmony.

MT40.P45 1991
Perle, George,
Serial composition and atonality: an introduction to the
music of Schoenberg, Berg, and Webern/ by George
Perle. 6th ed., rev. Berkeley, Calif.: University of
California Press, 1991. xv, 164 p.
90-050902   781.2/67 20   0520074300
Twelve-tone system. Composition (Music) Atonality.

MT40.R394.T6
Reti, Rudolph, 1885-1957.
Tonality, atonality, pantonality; a study of some trends in
twentieth century music. New York, Macmillan, 1958.
166 p.
58-002758   781.22
Composition (Music) Music -- Theory.

MT40.R46
Reti, Rudolph, 1885-1957.
The thematic process in music/ Rudolph Reti. New York:
Macmillan, 1951. x, 362 p.
51-010953   781.61
*Music -- Theory. Music -- Analysis, appreciation. Composition
(Music)*

MT40.S2 1962
Salzer, Felix.
Structural hearing; tonal coherence in music. With a
foreword by Leopold Mannes. New York, Dover
Publications [1962] 2 v.
63-005537   781.22
Schenker, Heinrich, -- 1868-1935. Music -- Theory. Harmony.

MT40.S2912
Schenker, Heinrich, 1868-1935.
Harmony. Edited and annotated by Oswald Jonas.
Translated by Elisabeth Mann Borgese. [Chicago]
University of Chicago Press [1954] xxxii, 359 p.
54-011213   781
Schenkerian analysis.

MT40.S29213
Schenker, Heinrich,
Free composition = (Der freie Satz): volume III of New
musical theories and fantasies/ Heinrich Schenker;
translated and edited by Ernst Oster. New York:
Longman, c1979. xiv, 166 p.
79-014797   781   0582280737
Schenkerian analysis. Musical form.

MT40.S33.F8 1967b
Schoenberg, Arnold, 1874-1951.
Fundamentals of musical composition. Edited by Gerald
Strang. With an introd. by Leonard Stein. New York, St.
Martin's Press [1967] xiv, 224 p.
67-010150   781.6/1
Composition (Music)

MT40.S96 2000
Straus, Joseph Nathan.
Introduction to post-tonal theory/ Joseph N. Straus. 2nd
ed. Upper Saddle River, N.J.: Prentice Hall, c2000. x,
260 p.
99-016851   781.2/67 21   0130143316
Music theory. Atonality. Twelve-tone system. Musical analysis.

MT40.S98 1988
Swados, Elizabeth.
Listening out loud: becoming a composer/ by Elizabeth
Swados. New York: Harper & Row, c1988. 208 p.
88-045064   781.6/1   0060159928
Composition (Music)

MT41 Composition.
Elements and techniques of music —
Composition using mechanical devices
or prescribed formulas

MT41.M38
Mathews, Max V.
The technology of computer music [by] Max V.
Mathews. With the collaboration of Joan E. Miller [and
others] Cambridge, Mass., M.I.T. Press [1969] 188 p.
69-012754   789.7
Computer composition. Computer sound processing.

MT42 Composition.
Elements and techniques of music — Rhythm

MT42.C642
Cooper, Grosvenor.
The rhythmic structure of music [by] Grosvenor W. Cooper and Leonard B. Meyer. [Chicago] University of Chicago [1960] ix, 212 p.
60-014068   781.62
Musical meter and rhythm.

MT42.L48 1986
Lester, Joel.
The rhythms of tonal music/ Joel Lester. Carbondale: Southern Illinois University Press, c1986. viii, 284 p.
85-022293   781.6/2 19   0809312824
Musical meter and rhythm. Musical analysis.

MT42.R84 1989
Rothstein, William Nathan.
Phrase rhythm in tonal music/ William Rothstein. New York: Schirmer Books; xi, 349 p.
88-039325   781.6/2 19   0028721918
Musical meter and rhythm. Musical analysis. Music -- 18th century -- History and criticism. Music -- 19th century -- History and criticism.

MT45 Composition.
Elements and techniques of music — Scales

MT45.S55
Slonimsky, Nicolas, 1894-
Thesaurus of scales and melodic patterns/ Nicolas Slonimsky. New York: Scribner, 1947. 243 p.
47-003541   781.22
Musical intervals and scales.

MT49 Composition.
Elements and techniques of music — Continuo

MT49.B84 1986
Buelow, George J.
Thorough-bass accompaniment according to Johann David Heinichen/ George J. Buelow. Rev. ed. Ann Arbor, Mich.: UMI Research Press, c1986. xvi, 462 p.
85-021005   781.3/2 19   0835716481
Continuo.

MT50 Composition.
Elements and techniques of music — Harmony

MT50.A444 2003
Aldwell, Edward.
Harmony & voice leading/ Edward Aldwell, Carl Schachter. 3rd ed. Australia; Thomson/Schirmer, c2003. xiv, 656 p.
2002-537209   781.2/5 21   0155062425
Harmony.

MT50.F713.T7 1979
Forte, Allen.
Tonal harmony in concept and practice/ Allen Forte. New York: Holt, Rinehart and Winston, c1979. 564 p.
78-012229   781.3   0030207568
Harmony.

MT50.K85 2000
Kostka, Stefan M.
Tonal harmony, with an introduction to twentieth-century music/ Stefan Kostka, Dorothy Payne. 4th ed. Boston: McGraw-Hill, c2000. xix, 680 p.
99-017042   781.2/5 21   0072897821
Harmony.

MT50.M153
McHose, Allen Irvine, 1902-1986.
The contrapuntal harmonic technique of the 18th century, by Allen Irvine McHose. New York, F. S. Crofts & company, 1947. xvi, 333 p.
47-002163   781.3
Chorales -- Analysis, appreciation. Harmony. Music -- Theory.

MT50.O923 2000
Ottman, Robert W.
Advanced harmony: theory and practice/ Robert W. Ottman. 5th ed. Upper Saddle River, NJ: Prentice Hall, c2000. viii, 488 p.
99-042122   781.2/5 21   0130833398
Harmony.

MT50.O924 1998
Ottman, Robert W.
Elementary harmony: theory and practice/ Robert W. Ottman. 5th ed. Upper Saddle River, N.J.: Prentice Hall, c1998. x, 468 p.
97-025707   781.2/5 21   0132816105
Harmony.

MT50.P665 1987
Piston, Walter, 1894-1976.
Harmony/ Walter Piston. New York: Norton, c1987. xvi, 575 p.
86-023901   781.3   0393954803
Harmony.

MT50.R2
Ratner, Leonard G.
Harmony: structure and style. New York: McGraw-Hill, [1962] ix, 336 p.
62-010851   781.3
Harmony.

MT50.S37413 1978b
Schoenberg, Arnold, 1874-1951.
Theory of harmony/ Arnold Schoenberg; translated by Roy E. Carter. Berkeley: University of California Press, 1978. xxi, 440 p.
77-073502   781.3   0520034643
Harmony.

MT50.S37417 1969
Schoenberg, Arnold, 1874-1951.
Structural functions of harmony. New York, W. W. Norton [1969] xvi, 203 p.
74-081181   781.3
Harmony.

MT55 Composition.
Elements and techniques of music —
Counterpoint. Polyphony

MT55.B446 1986
Benjamin, Thomas.
Counterpoint in the style of J.S. Bach/ Thomas Benjamin. New York: Schirmer Books; c1986. xvi, 448 p.
85-018444   781.4/2/09033 19   0028702808
Bach, Johann Sebastian, 1685-1750 -- Criticism and interpretation. Counterpoint -- Textbooks. Musical analysis -- Music collections.

MT55.B447
Benjamin, Thomas.
The craft of modal counterpoint: a practical approach/ Thomas Benjamin. New York: Schirmer Books, c1979. ix, 230 p.
77-090012   781.4/2   0028704800
Counterpoint.

MT55.J45.K63
Jeppesen, Knud, 1892-
Counterpoint, the polyphonic vocal style of the sixteenth century, by Knud Jeppesen. Translated, with an introduction, by Glen Haydon. New York, Prentice-Hall, inc., 1939. xviii, 302 p.
39-015933   781.4
Counterpoint. Performance practice (Music) -- 16th century.

MT55.K53 1999
Kennan, Kent Wheeler,
Counterpoint: based on eighteenth-century practice/ Kent Kennan. 4th ed. Upper Saddle River, NJ: Prentice Hall, c1999. 292 p.
98-022174   781.2/86 21   013080746X
Counterpoint--18th century.

MT55.O97 1992
Owen, Harold,
Modal and tonal counterpoint: from Josquin to Stravinsky/ Harold Owen. New York: Schirmer Books; x, 389 p.
91-004775   781.2/86/09 20   0028721454
Counterpoint. Counterpoint--History.

MT55.P67
Piston, Walter, 1894-1976.
Counterpoint, by Walter Piston. New York, W. W. Norton & company, inc. [1947] 235 p.
47-001928   781.4
Counterpoint.

MT55.S2413 1987
Schenker, Heinrich, 1868-1935.
Counterpoint: a translation of Kontrapunkt/ by Heinrich Schenker; translated by John Rothgeb and Jurgen Thym; edited by John Rothgeb. New York: Schirmer Books; c1987. 2 v.
86-018645   781.4/2   0028732219
Counterpoint.

MT56 Composition.
Elements and techniques of music —
Electronic music. Computer music

MT56.C69 2001
Cope, David.
Virtual music: computer synthesis of musical style/ David Cope; with commentary by Douglas Hofstadter; and with perspectives and analysis by Eleanor Selfridge-Field ... [et al.]. Cambridge, Mass.: MIT Press, c2001. xiii, 565 p.
00-035506   781.3/4   026203283X
Cope, David. -- EMI. Composition (Music) -- Computer programs.

MT58 Composition.
Elements and techniques of music —
Forms and genres —
General works

MT58.B34 1986
Berry, Wallace.
Form in music: an examination of traditional techniques of musical form and their applications in historical and contemporary styles/ Wallace Berry. Englewood Cliffs, N.J.: Prentice-Hall, c1986. xx, 439 p.
85-003374   781/.5   0133292851
Musical form.

MT58.C37 1998
Caplin, William Earl,
Classical form: a theory of formal functions for the instrumental music of Haydn, Mozart, and Beethoven/ William E. Caplin. New York: Oxford University Press, 1998. xii, 307 p.
97-025561　　0195104803
Haydn, Joseph, 1732-1809 -- Criticism and interpretation. Mozart, Wolfgang Amadeus, 1756-1791 -- Criticism and interpretation. Beethoven, Ludwig van, 1770-1827 -- Criticism and interpretation. Musical form. Instrumental music -- 18th century -- Analysis, appreciation. Instrumental music -- 19th century -- Analysis, appreciation. Musical analysis. Classicism in music. Music theory -- History -- 18th century.

MT58.E67
Epstein, David, 1930-
Beyond Orpheus: studies in musical structure/ David Epstein. Cambridge, Mass.: MIT Press, c1979. xiv, 244 p.
78-000232　781.3　0262050161
Music -- Theory. Musical form. Music -- Philosophy and aesthetics.

MT59 Composition.
Elements and techniques of music —
Forms and genres —
Canon and fugue

MT59.G4.T75
Gedalge, Andre, 1856-1926.
Treatise on the fugue. Translated and edited by Ferdinand Davis, with a foreword by Darius Milhaud. Norman, University of Oklahoma Press [c1965] xi, 435 p.
65-011241　781.42
Fugue

MT59.R27 1995
Renwick, William,
Analyzing fugue: a Schenkerian approach/ by William Renwick. Stuyvesant, NY: Pendragon Press, c1995. viii, 229 p.
94-047622　784.18/72 20　0945193521
Fugue. Schenkerian analysis.

MT64 Composition.
Elements and techniques of music —
Forms and genres —
Other, A-Z

MT64.M65 B87 1994
Burt, George,
The art of film music: special emphasis on Hugo Friedhofer, Alex North, David Raksin, Leonard Rosenman/ George Burt. Boston: Northeastern University Press, c1994. xi, 266 p.
94-006521　781.5/42 20　1555531938
Motion picture music--Instruction and study. Motion picture music--Analysis, appreciation.

MT67 Composition.
Elements and techniques of music —
Forms and genres —
Popular music

MT67.C54 1991
Citron, Stephen.
The musical from the inside out/ Stephen Citron. Chicago: I.R. Dee, c1992. 336 p.
91-027825　782.1/4　0929587790
Musicals -- Writing and publishing. Musicals -- Production and direction.

MT68 Improvisation.
Accompaniment. Transposition

MT68.M6 1984
Moore, Gerald.
The unashamed accompanist/ Gerald Moore; with a foreword by Geoffrey Parsons and an afterword by Graham Johnson. Rev. ed. London; J. MacRae Books, 1984. 125 p.
84-050909　781.47 20　0531097714
Musical accompaniment.

MT70 Instrumentation and orchestration —
Orchestra —
General works

MT70.A3 2002
Adler, Samuel,
The study of orchestration/ Samuel Adler. 3rd ed. New York: W.W. Norton, c2002. xii, 839 p.
99-055023　781.3/74 21　039397572X
Instrumentation and orchestration.

MT70.B4813 1991
Berlioz, Hector,
Treatise on instrumentation/ Hector Berlioz & Richard Strauss; translated by Theodore Front. New York: Dover, 1991. iii, 424 p.
91-024083　781.3/74 20　0486269035
Instrumentation and orchestration.

MT70.B56 1997
Blatter, Alfred, 1937-
Instrumentation and orchestration/ Alfred Blatter. New York: Schirmer Books, c1997. xix, 508 p.
96-033608　781.3/7　0028645707
Instrumentation and orchestration.

MT70.K37 2002
Kennan, Kent Wheeler,
The technique of orchestration/ Kent Kennan, Donald Grantham. 6th ed. Upper Saddle River, N.J.: Prentice Hall, c2002. xiv, 414 p.
2001-026709　781.3/74 21　0130407712
Instrumentation and orchestration.

MT70.P56
Piston, Walter, 1894-1976.
Orchestration. New York, Norton [1955] 477 p.
55-014230 781.632
Instrumentation and orchestration.

MT70.R37 1969
Read, Gardner, 1913-
Thesaurus of orchestral devices. New York, Greenwood Press, [1969] xxi, 631 p.
69-014045 785/.0284 0837118840
Instrumentation and orchestration. Musical instruments.

MT70.R62 1964
Rimsky-Korsakov, Nikolay, 1844-1908.
Principles of orchestration, with musical examples drawn from his own works [by] Nikolay Rimsky-Korsakov. Edited by Maximilian Steinberg. English translation by Edward Agate. New York, Dover Publications [1964] 2 v. in 1.
64-024418 781.632
Instrumentation and orchestration.

MT75 Interpretation

MT75.L44
Leinsdorf, Erich, 1912-
The composer's advocate: a radical orthodoxy for musicians/ Erich Leinsdorf. New Haven: Yale University Press, c1981. viii, 216 p.
80-017614 781.6/3 0300024274
Music -- Interpretation (Phrasing, dynamics, etc.) Conducting. Music -- Performance.

MT75.W38 1993
Weisberg, Arthur.
Performing twentieth-century music: a handbook for conductors and instrumentalists/ Arthur Weisberg. New Haven: Yale University Press, c1993. 142 p.
93-004003 781.4/3 20 0300050100
Music -- Interpretation (Phrasing, dynamics, etc.) Music -- 20th century -- Performance. Conducting. Musical meter and rhythm.

MT85 Conducting. Score reading and playing

MT85.C444 1988
Choral conducting symposium/ edited by Harold A. Decker, Julius Herford. Englewood Cliffs, N.J.: Prentice Hall, c1988. xii, 290 p.
87-022744 784.9/63 0131333720
Choral conducting -- Congresses.

MT85.D36 1995
Demaree, Robert W.
The complete conductor: a comprehensive resource for the professional conductor of the twenty-first century/ Robert W. Demaree, Jr., Don V Moses. Englewood Cliffs, N.J.: Prentice-Hall, c1995. xvi, 491 p.
93-048392 781.45 20 0131730142
Conducting.

MT85.G785 1997
Green, Elizabeth A. H.
The modern conductor: a college text on conducting based on the technical principles of Nicolai Malko as set forth in his The conductor and his baton/ Elizabeth A.H. Green. 6th ed. Upper Saddle River, N.J.: Prentice Hall, c1997. xvii, 286 p.
96-028810 781.45 20 0132514818
Conducting.

MT85.M125 1989
McElheran, Brock.
Conducting technique: for beginners and professionals/ Brock McElheran; [foreword by Lukas Foss]. Rev. ed. New York: Oxford University Press, 1989. xiv, 134 p.
88-039211 781.6/35 19 0193858304
Conducting.

MT85.R8 1993
Rudolf, Max,
The grammar of conducting: a comprehensive guide to baton technique and interpretation/ Max Rudolf. 3rd ed./ prepared with the assistance of Michael Stern. New York: Schirmer Books; xvii, 481 p.
93-012310 781.45 20 0028722213
Conducting.

MT85.S46 1997
Schuller, Gunther.
The compleat conductor/ Gunther Schuller. New York: Oxford University Pres, 1997. xii, 571 p.
96-048362 784.2/145 21 0195063775
Conducting. Orchestral music--Interpretation (Phrasing, dynamics, etc.)

MT90 Analysis and appreciation of musical works — General works

MT90.M23 2003b
Machlis, Joseph,
The enjoyment of music: an introduction to perceptive listening/ Joseph Machlis, Kristine Forney. 9th ed., standard. New York: Norton, 2003.
2002-044892 780 21 039397877X
Music appreciation.

MT90.S58 1993
Sisman, Elaine Rochelle.
Haydn and the classical variation/ Elaine R. Sisman. Cambridge, Mass.: Harvard University Press, 1993. xii, 311 p.
92-028292 781.8/25/09033 067438315X
Haydn, Joseph, -- 1732-1809 -- Variations. Mozart, Wolfgang Amadeus, -- 1756-1791. -- Variations. Beethoven, Ludwig van, -- 1770-1827. -- Variations. Variation (Music) -- Analysis, appreciation.

MT91 Analysis and appreciation of musical works — Collections of music for analysis and appreciation

MT91.N67 2001
Norton anthology of western music/ edited by Claude V. Palisca. 4th ed. New York: W.W. Norton, c2001. 2 v.
2001-545308   0393976912
Musical analysis--Music collections. Music appreciation--Music collections.

MT91.T74 2000
A treasury of early music: masterworks of the Middle Ages, the Renaissance, and the Baroque Era/ complied and edited, with notes, by Carl Parrish. Mineola, New York: Dover Publications, 2000. x, 331 p.
00-727311   0486410889
Music appreciation--Music collections.

MT92 Analysis and appreciation of musical works — Individual composers

MT92.M14.C66
Cooke, Deryck.
Gustav Mahler: an introduction to his music/ Deryck Cooke. Cambridge [Eng.]; Cambridge University Press, 1980. 127 p.
79-008588   780/.92/4   0521231752
Mahler, Gustav, -- 1860-1911 -- Criticism and interpretation.

MT92.S24.K7 1999
Krebs, Harald, 1955-
Fantasy pieces: metrical dissonance in the music of Robert Schumann/ Harald Krebs. New York: Oxford University Press, 1999. xiv, 290 p.
98-012647   781.2/26/092   0195116232
Schumann, Robert, -- 1810-1856 -- Criticism and interpretation. Musical meter and rhythm.

MT95 Analysis and appreciation of musical works — Dramatic music — Two or more composers

MT95.A59 1989
Analyzing opera: Verdi and Wagner/ edited by Carolyn Abbate and Roger Parker. Berkeley: University of California Press, c1989. ix, 304 p.
88-021072   782.1/092/2   0520061578
Verdi, Giuseppe, -- 1813-1901. -- Operas -- Congresses. Wagner, Richard, -- 1813-1883. -- Operas -- Congresses. Operas -- Analysis, appreciation -- Congresses.

MT95.B3 1977
Balanchine, George.
Balanchine's Complete stories of the great ballets/ by George Balanchine; and Francis Mason. Garden City, N.Y.: Doubleday, 1977. xxvi, 838 p.
76-055684   792.8/4   0385113811
Ballets -- Stories, plots, etc.

MT95.K52 1997
The new Kobbé's opera book/ Anthony Peattie, general editor; the Earl of Harewood, consultant editor. New York: Putnam, 1997.
97-010981   782.1/0269 21   0399143327
Operas--Stories, plots, etc.

MT95.L5 1990
Lazarus, John.
The opera handbook/ John Lazarus. Boston, Mass.: G.K. Hall, [1990], c1987 242 p.
89-077758   782.1   0816190941
Operas -- Stories, plots, etc.

MT95.M49 1984
The Metropolitan Opera stories of the great operas/ by John W. Freeman. New York: Metropolitan Opera Guild: c1984-c1997. 2 v.
84-008030   782.1/3   0393018881
Operas -- Stories, plots, etc.

MT100 Analysis and appreciation of musical works — Dramatic music — One composer. By composer, A-Z

MT100.M76.M3
Mann, William, 1924-
The operas of Mozart/ William Mann. New York: Oxford University Press, 1977. 656 p.
76-009279   782.1/092/4   0195198913
Mozart, Wolfgang Amadeus, -- 1756-1791. -- Operas.

MT100.S84 M3 1966
Mann, William,
Richard Strauss; a critical study of the operas, by William Mann. New York, Oxford University Press, 1966 [c1964] xiv, 402 p.
66-002148   782.10924
Strauss, Richard, 1864-1949. Operas.

MT100.W2 N53 1991
Newman, Ernest,
The Wagner operas/ by Ernest Newman. Princeton, N.J.: Princeton University Press, [1991], c1949. xii, 729 p.
91-019248   782.1/092 20   0691027161
Wagner, Richard, 1813-1883. Operas. Wagner, Richard, 1813-1883 -- Stories, plots, etc. Operas -- Analysis, appreciation.

MT100.W25.S5 1967
Shaw, Bernard, 1856-1950.
The perfect Wagnerite; a commentary on the Niblung's ring. New York, Dover Publications [1967] xx, 136 p.
66-029055   782.1/0924
Wagner, Richard, -- 1813-1883. -- Ring des Nibelungen.

MT110 Analysis and appreciation of musical works — Oratorios, cantatas, etc. — Two or more composers

MT110.P3313 1990
Pahlen, Kurt, 1907-
The world of the oratorio: oratorio, Mass, Requiem, Te Deum, Stabat Mater, and large cantatas/ Kurt Pahlen, with the collaboration of Werner Pfister, Rosemarie Konig; additional material for the English language edition by Thurston Dox; translated by Judith Schaeffer; Reinhard G. Pauly, general editor. Portland, Ore.: Amadeus Press, c1990. 357 p.
89-017757   782.23
Oratorios -- Analysis, appreciation. Masses -- Analysis, appreciation. Requiems -- Analysis, appreciation.

MT115 Analysis and appreciation of musical works — Oratorios, cantatas, etc. — One composer. By composer, A-Z

MT115.B17.T4
Terry, Charles Sanford, 1864-1936.
Bach: the cantatas and oratorios, by Charles Sanford Terry. London, Oxford University Press, H. Milford, 1925. 2 v.
26-009480   780.9
Bach, Johann Sebastian, -- 1685-1750.

MT115.B2 T38 1970
Terry, Charles Sanford,
Bach: The passions. Westport, Conn., Greenwood Press [1970] 2 v. in 1.
75-109864   783.3/0924
Bach, Johann Sebastian, 1685-1750. Passions. Passion music -- Analysis, appreciation.

MT115.B2.Y7 1989
Young, W. Murray, 1920-
The cantatas of J.S. Bach: an analytical guide/ W. Murray Young. Jefferson, N.C.: MacFarland, c1989. xvi, 307 p.
89-042762   782.2/4   0899503942
Bach, Johann Sebastian, -- 1685-1750. -- Cantatas. Cantatas -- 18th century -- Analysis, appreciation.

MT115.B73 S7 1998
Stark, Lucien,
Brahms's vocal duets and quartets with piano: a guide with full texts and translations/ Lucien Stark. Bloomington: Indiana University Press, c1998. x, 160 p.
97-045142   782.42168/092 21   0253334020
Brahms, Johannes, 1833-1897. Vocal music. Vocal ensembles with piano -- Analysis, appreciation.

MT115.B73.S73 1995
Stark, Lucien, 1929-
A guide to the solo songs of Johannes Brahms/ Lucien Stark. Bloomington: Indiana University Press, c1995. x, 374 p.
94-045737   782.42168/092   0253328918
Brahms, Johannes, -- 1833-1897. -- Songs. Songs -- 19th century -- Analysis, appreciation.

MT115.S37.Y7 1991
Youens, Susan.
Retracing a winter's journey: Schubert's Winterreise/ Susan Youens. Ithaca: Cornell University Press, 1991. xvi, 330 p.
91-055234   782.4/7   0801425999
Schubert, Franz, -- 1797-1828. -- Winterreise.

MT115.W6 S3 1992
Sams, Eric.
The songs of Hugo Wolf/ Eric Sams. 1st Midland ed. Bloomington: Indiana University Press, 1992. xii, 401 p.
92-028981   782.42168/092 20   0253207908
Wolf, Hugo, 1860-1903. Songs. Songs -- Analysis, appreciation.

MT120 Analysis and appreciation of musical works — Songs, song cycles, etc. — Two or more composers

MT120.S74 1996
Stein, Deborah J.
Poetry into song: performance and analysis of lieder/ Deborah Stein, Robert Spillman; foreword by Elly Ameling with Max Deen Larsen. New York: Oxford University Press, 1996. xvii, 413 p.
95-005398   782.42168/0943   0195093283
Songs -- Analysis, appreciation. Songs -- Interpretation (Phrasing, dynamics, etc.) Songs -- 19th century -- History and criticism.

MT121 Analysis and appreciation of musical works — Songs, song cycles, etc. — One composer. By composer, A-Z

MT121.B73 S36 2000
Sams, Eric.
The songs of Johannes Brahms/ Eric Sams. New Haven, Conn.: Yale University Press, c2000. xii, 370 p.
99-088597   782.42168/092 21   0300079621
Brahms, Johannes, 1833-1897. Songs. Songs -- Analysis, appreciation.

MT121.S38.M55 1999
Miller, Richard, 1926-
Singing Schumann: an interpretive guide for performers/ Richard Miller. Cambridge; Oxford University Press, c1999. xiv, 245 p.
98-031645   782.42168/092   0195119045
Schumann, Robert, -- 1810-1856 -- Songs. Schumann, Robert, -- 1810-1856 -- Criticism and interpretation. Songs, German -- History and criticism. Songs, German -- Analysis, appreciation.

MT125 Analysis and appreciation of musical works — Orchestral music — Two or more composers

MT125.D68 1981
Downes, Edward, 1911-
Guide to symphonic music/ by Edward Downes. New York: Walker, c1981. xxix, 1058 p.
81-007442   785/.01/5   0802771777
Orchestral music -- Analysis, appreciation.

MT125.H62 1992
Holoman, D. Kern,
Evenings with the orchestra: a Norton companion for concertgoers/ D. Kern Holoman. First ed. New York, N.Y.: W.W. Norton, c1992. xviii, 734 p.
91-003441   784.2 20   0393029360
Orchestral music -- Analysis, appreciation.

MT125.K72 1988
Kramer, Jonathan D.,
Listen to the music: a self-guided tour through the orchestral repertoire/ Jonathan D. Kramer. New York: Schirmer Books; c1988. xxv, 816 p.
88-009248   785/.01/5 19   0028718429
Orchestral music -- Analysis, appreciation.

MT125.S79 1995
Steinberg, Michael,
The symphony: a listener's guide/ Michael Steinberg. New York: Oxford University Press, 1995. xvii, 678 p.
95-005568   784.2/184/015 20   0195061772
Symphonies -- Analysis, appreciation.

MT130 Analysis and appreciation of musical works — Orchestral music — One composer. By composer, A-Z

MT130.B43.S313 1992
Schenker, Heinrich, 1868-1935.
Beethoven's ninth symphony: a portrayal of its musical content, with running commentary on performance and literature as well/ Heinrich Schenker; translated and edited by John Rothgeb. New Haven: Yale University Press, c1992. xvii, 332 p.
91-036684   784.2/184
Beethoven, Ludwig van, -- 1770-1827. -- Symphonies, -- no. 9, op. 125, -- D minor.

MT130.M8.G62 1964
Girdlestone, Cuthbert Morton, 1895-1975.
Mozart and his piano concertos/ Cuthbert Girdlestone. New York: Dover Publications, 1964. 509 p.
64-008198   785.6   0486212718
Mozart, Wolfgang Amadeus, -- 1756-1791. Mozart, Wolfgang Amadeus, -- 1756-1791 -- Concertos -- Piano. Composers -- Austria -- Biography.

MT130.M8.H8 1950
Hutchings, Arthur, 1906-
A companion to Mozart's piano concertos. London, Oxford University Press, 1950. 211 p.
50-014482
Mozart, Johann Chrysostom Wolfgang Amadeus. -- Concertos piano. Mozart, Johann Chrysostom Wolfgang Amadeus -- Thematic catalogs.

MT140 Analysis and appreciation of musical works — Chamber and solo instrumental music — Two or more composers

MT140.R6 1968
Chamber music/ edited by Alec Robertson. [Harmondsworth, Middlesex]: Penguin Books, 1967 427 p.
68-093208   785.709
Chamber music -- Analysis, appreciation

MT140.T69
Tovey, Donald Francis, 1875-1940.
Essays in musical analysis; chamber music, by Donald Francis Tovey ... With an editor's note by Hubert J. Foss. London, Oxford University Press, 1944. viii, 217 p.
44-005779
Chamber music -- Analysis, appreciation.

MT145 Analysis and appreciation of musical works — Chamber and solo instrumental music — One composer. By composer, A-Z

MT145.B14.S415 1992
Schulenberg, David.
The keyboard music of J.S. Bach/ David Schulenberg. New York: Schirmer Books; c1992. xv, 475 p.
91-039348   786/.092   0028732758
Bach, Johann Sebastian, -- 1685-1750. -- Keyboard music. Keyboard instrument music -- Analysis, appreciation.

MT145.B14.W53 1980
Williams, Peter F.
The organ music of J.S. Bach/ by Peter Williams. Cambridge [Eng.]; Cambridge University Press, 1980-1984. 3 v.
77-071431   786.6/22/4   0521217237
Bach, Johann Sebastian, -- 1685-1750. -- Organ music. Organ music -- Analysis, appreciation.

MT145.B42 R67 2002
Rosen, Charles,
Beethoven's piano sonatas: a short companion/ Charles Rosen. New Haven: Yale University Press, c2002. xii, 256 p.
2001-093745   786.2/183/092 21   0300090706
Beethoven, Ludwig van, 1770-1827. Sonatas, -- piano. Sonatas (Piano) -- Analysis, appreciation.

MT145.B42.T6 1976
Tovey, Donald Francis, 1875-1940.
A companion to Beethoven's pianoforte sonatas: complete analyses/ by Donald Francis Tovey. New York: AMS Press, 1976. xiv, 301 p.
74-024243   786.4/1/0924   0404131174
Beethoven, Ludwig van, -- 1770-1827. -- Sonatas, -- piano. Sonatas (Piano) -- Analysis, appreciation.

MT145.B425.B4 1994
The Beethoven quartet companion/ edited by Robert Winter and Robert Martin. Berkeley: University of California Press, c1994. xi, 300 p.
92-040668   785/.7194/092   0520082117
Beethoven, Ludwig van, -- 1770-1827. -- Quartets, -- strings. String quartets -- Analysis, appreciation.

MT145.B425.K47 1982
Kerman, Joseph, 1924-
The Beethoven quartets/ Joseph Kerman. Westport, Conn.: Greenwood Press, 1982, c1966. 386 p.
81-020275   785.7/0092/4   0313233721
Beethoven, Ludwig van, -- 1770-1827. -- Quartets, -- strings. String quartets -- Analysis, appreciation.

MT145.M7.Z4 1990
Zaslaw, Neal Alexander, 1939-
Compleat Mozart: a guide to the musical works of Wolfgang Amadeus Mozart. edited by Neal Zaslaw with William Cowdery. Mozart Bicentennial at Lincoln Center: Norton, 1990. 352 p.
90-030833   780/.92   0393028860
Mozart, Wolfgang Amadeus, -- 1756-1791 -- Criticism and interpretation.

MT165 Tuning

MT165.J667 1991
Jorgensen, Owen.
Tuning: containing the perfection of eighteenth-century temperament, the lost art of nineteenth-century temperament, and the science of equal temperament, complete with instructions for aural and e Owen H. Jorgensen. East Lansing, Mich.: Michigan State University Press, 1991. xxiii, 798 p.
90-050887   784.192/8   0870132903
Tuning. Musical temperament. Musical intervals and scales.

MT170 Instrumental techniques — General works

MT170.R38 1993
Read, Gardner, 1913-
Compendium of modern instrumental techniques/ Gardner Read; foreword by Gunther Schuller. Westport, Conn.: Greenwood Press, 1993. xiv, 276 p.
92-017854   784.193   0313285128
Musical instruments -- Instruction and study. Music -- 20th century -- History and criticism. Instrumentation and orchestration.

MT180-189 Instrumental techniques — Keyboard instruments — Organ

MT180.H94 1988
Hurford, Peter.
Making music on the organ/ Peter Hurford. Oxford [Oxfordshire]; Oxford University Press, 1988. viii, 157 p.
88-005139   786.7   0193222647
Organ -- Instruction and study. Organ -- Performance. Organ music -- Interpretation (Phrasing, dynamics, etc.)

MT182.G55 1988
Gleason, Harold,
Method of organ playing/ Harold Gleason; edited by Catharine Crozier Gleason. 7th ed. Englewood Cliffs, N.J.: Prentice Hall, c1988. x, 337 p.
87-015626   0135794595
Organ (Musical instrument) -- Methods.

MT189.O94 1997
Owen, Barbara.
The registration of baroque organ music/ Barbara Owen. Bloomington, Ind.: Indiana University Press, c1997. ix, 284 p.
96-033081   786.5/09/032   0253332400
Organ -- Registration. Organ music -- 17th century -- History and criticism. Organ music -- 18th century -- History and criticism.

MT220-239 Instrumental techniques — Keyboard instruments — Piano

MT220.B515 2000
Berman, Boris.
Notes from the pianist's bench/ Boris Berman. New Haven: Yale University Press, c2000. xi, 223 p.
00-036514   786.2/193 21   0300083750
Piano -- Instruction and study. Piano -- Performance.

MT220.F83 1993
Friedberg, Ruth C.,
The complete pianist: body, mind, synthesis/ by Ruth C. Friedberg. Metuchen, N.J.: Scarecrow Press, 1993. xx, 132 p.
92-039275   786.2/19 20   0810826305
Piano -- Instruction and study. Piano -- Instruction and study -- Physiological aspects. Piano -- Performance. Practicing (Music)

MT220.N5 1984
Newman, William S.
The pianist's problems: a modern approach to efficient practice and musicianly performance/ William S. Newman; with a foreword by Arthur Loesser; illustrated by John V. Allcott. 4th ed./ new preface by the author. New York: Da Capo Press, 1984. xiii, 210 p.
83-019020   786.3/041 19   0306762137
Piano -- Instruction and study. Practicing (Music)

MT224.B132
Bach, Carl Philipp Emanuel, 1714-1788.
Essay on the true art of playing keyboard instruments, translated and edited by William J. Mitchell. New York, W. W. Norton [1949] xiii, 449 p.
48-009749   786.3
Piano -- Instruction and study -- Early works to 1800. Musical accompaniment -- Early works to 1800. Harpsichord -- Instruction and study -- Early works to 1800.

MT227.B2 1985
Banowetz, Joseph.
The pianist's guide to pedaling/ Joseph Banowetz; contributors, Dean Elder ... [et al.]. Bloomington: Indiana University Press, c1985. x, 309 p.
84-047534   786.3/5   0253344948
Piano -- Pedaling.

MT227.R72 1993
Rowland, David,
A history of pianoforte pedalling/ David Rowland. Cambridge [England]; Cambridge University Press, 1993. viii, 194 p.
92-037065   786.2/1938/09   0521402662
Piano -- Pedaling -- History. Piano -- Performance -- History.

MT239.L46 1989
Levine, Mark,
The jazz piano book/ by Mark Levine. Petaluma, CA: Sher Music Co., c1989. viii 306 p.
93-704247   0961470151
Piano -- Methods (Jazz) Jazz -- Instruction and study.

MT260-262 Instrumental techniques — Stringed instruments — Violin

MT260.G34 1985
Galamian, Ivan.
Principles of violin playing & teaching/ Ivan Galamian. 2nd ed./ with a postscript by Elizabeth A.H. Green. Englewood Cliffs, N.J.: Prentice-Hall, c1985. xii, 144 p.
84-011597   787.1/07/12 19   0137107730
Violin -- Instruction and study.

MT260.S99 1970
Szigeti, Joseph, 1892-1973.
Szigeti on the violin. New York, F. A. Praeger [1970, c1969] x, 234 p.
71-095361   787.1/07/12
Violin -- Instruction and study.

MT262.M93 1951
Mozart, Leopold, 1719-1787.
A treatise on the fundamental principles of violin playing. Translated by Editha Knocker. With a pref. by Alfred Einstein. London, Oxford University Press, [1951, 1963] xxxv, 234 p.
51-007192   787.1
Violin -- Instruction and study.

MT280 Instrumental techniques — Stringed instruments — Viola

MT280.D34 1988
Dalton, David
Playing the viola: conversations with William Primrose/ David Dalton. Oxford [England]; Oxford University Press, 1988. xii, 244 p.
87-025087   787/.2/071   0193185148
Viola -- Instruction and study.

MT338 Instrumental techniques — Stringed instruments — Early stringed instruments

MT338.C93 1989
Crum, Alison.
Play the viol: the complete guide to playing the treble, tenor, and bass viol/ Alison Crum with Sonia Jackson. Oxford; Oxford University Press, 1989. xii, 185 p.
88-019508   787/.42/0712 19   0193174227
Viol -- Instruction and study.

MT339.5 Instrumental techniques — Wind instruments — Woodwind instruments (General)

MT339.5.B37 1982
Bartolozzi, Bruno.
New sounds for woodwind/ Bruno Bartolozzi; translated and edited by Reginald Smith Brindle. London; Oxford University Press, 1982. 113 p.
80-040519   788/.05/0712   0193186071
Woodwind instruments -- Instruction and study.

MT340-342 Instrumental techniques — Wind instruments — Flute

MT340.M73 1991
Morris, Gareth.
Flute technique/ Gareth Morris. Oxford; Oxford University Press, 1991. vi, 68 p.
91-006597   788.3/2193   019318432X
Flute -- Instruction and study.

MT342.Q313 1985
Quantz, Johann Joachim,
On playing the flute/ Johann Joachim Quantz; translated with notes and an introduction by Edward R. Reilly. 2nd ed. New York: Schirmer Books, 1985. xliii, 412 p.
85-008840   788/.51/071 19   0028701607
Flute--Methods--Early works to 1800. Flute music-- Interpretation (Phrasing, dynamics, etc.)--Early works to Musical accompaniment--Early works to 1800.

MT360 Instrumental techniques — Wind instruments — Oboe

MT360.G66
Goossens, Leon, 1897-
Oboe/ Leon Goossens and Edwin Roxburgh. New York: Schirmer Books, 1977. xv, 238 p.
77-015886   788/.7/07   0028714504
Oboe -- Instruction and study.

MT380 Instrumental techniques — Wind instruments — Clarinet

MT380.T5 1977
Thurston, Frederick.
Clarinet technique/ by Frederick Thurston. London; Oxford University Press, 1977. viii, 94 p.
78-309842   788/.62/0712   0193186101
Clarinet -- Instruction and study. Clarinet music -- Bibliography.

MT418 Instrumental techniques — Wind instruments — Brass instruments (General)

MT418.J64 2002
Johnson, Keith,
Brass performance and pedagogy/ Keith Johnson. Upper Saddle River, NJ: Prentice Hall, c2002. xiv, 97 p.
2001-021981   788.9/193/071 21   0130914835
Brass instruments--Instruction and study. Brass instruments--Performance.

MT420 Instrumental techniques — Wind instruments — Horn

MT420.R49 1996
Reynolds, Verne.
The horn handbook/ Verne Reynolds. Portland, Or.: Amadeus Press, 1996. 253 p.
96-013672   788.9/4193   1574670166
Horn (Musical instrument) -- Instruction and study -- Handbooks, manuals, etc.

MT420.S35 1991
Schuller, Gunther.
Horn technique/ Gunther Schuller. 2nd ed. Oxford; Oxford University Press, 1992. xi, 137 p.
91-004338   788.9/4193 20   0198162774
Horn (Musical instrument) -- Instruction and study. Horn music -- Bibliography.

MT440 Instrumental techniques — Wind instruments — Trumpet. Cornet

MT440.D34 1985
Dale, Delbert A.
Trumpet technique/ Delbert A. Dale. 2nd ed. Oxford [Oxfordshire]; Music Dept., Oxford University xi, 102 p.
86-162172   788/.1/0714 19   0193221284
Trumpet -- Instruction and study.

MT580 Instrumental techniques — Plucked instruments — Guitar

MT580.Q56 1990
Quine, Hector.
Guitar technique: intermediate to advanced/ Hector Quine. Oxford; Oxford University Press, 1990. vi, 105 p.
89-023232   787.87/193   0193223236
Guitar -- Instruction and study.

MT723 Instrumental techniques — Percussion and other instruments — Computer sound processing

MT723.C77 2000
The Csound book: perspectives in software synthesis, sound design, signal processing, and programming/ edited by Richard Boulanger. Cambridge, Mass.: MIT Press, c2000. xli, 740 p.
99-014922   786.7/413453042 21   0262522616
Computer music -- Instruction and study. Computer composition. CSound (Computer program language)

MT723.M6 1990
Moore, F. Richard.
Elements of computer music/ F. Richard Moore. Englewood Cliffs, N.J.: Prentice Hall, c1990. xiv, 560 p.
89-008679   786.7/6 20   0132525526
Computer sound processing. Computer music -- Instruction and study.

MT820 Singing and vocal technique — General works

MT820.C17 1987
Callas, Maria, 1923-1977.
Callas at Juilliard: the master classes/ [edited] by John Ardoin. New York: Knopf, 1987. xvii, 300 p.
87-045375   784.9/32   0394563670
Singing -- Instruction and study.

MT820.D27 1998
Davis, Richard,
A beginning singer's guide/ Richard Davis. Lanham, Md.: Scarecrow Press, 1998. xi, 215 p.
98-008656   783/.014 21   0810835568
Singing -- Instruction and study.

MT820.H1413 1990
Hahn, Reynaldo,
On singers and singing: lectures and an essay/ Reynaldo Hahn; translated by Leopold Simoneau; introduction by Lorraine Gorrell; discography by William R. Moran; Reinhard G. Pauly, general editor. Portland, Or.: Amadeus Press, c1990. 244 p.
89-014987   783/.007 20   0931340225
Singing -- Instruction and study. Music -- Performance.

MT820.M599 1996
Miller, Richard,
On the art of singing/ Richard Miller. New York: Oxford University Press, 1996. xii, 318 p.
95-030176   783 20   0195098250
Singing--Instruction and study. Singing--Interpretation (Phrasing, dynamics, etc.) Singing--Vocational guidance.

MT820.M5995 2000
Miller, Richard, 1926-
Training soprano voices/ Richard Miller. New York: Oxford University Press, 2000. 177 p.
99-027828   783.6/6143   0195130189
Singing -- Instruction and study. Sopranos (Singers) -- Training of.

MT820.M6 1993
Miller, Richard, 1926-
Training tenor voices/ Richard Miller. New York:
Schirmer Books; c1993. xi, 173 p.
91-025936   782.8/7143   0028713974
Singing -- Instruction and study. Tenors (Singers) -- Training of.

MT820.R365
Reid, Cornelius L.
The free voice, a guide to natural singing [by] Cornelius
L. Reid. New York, Coleman-Ross Co., 1965. ix, 225 p.
65-018533   784.93
Singing -- Instruction and study.

MT821 Singing and vocal technique — Physiology and care of the voice

MT821.C65 1987
Coffin, Berton.
Coffin's sounds of singing: principles and applications of
vocal techniques with chromatic vowel chart/ by Berton
Coffin; foreword by Nicolai Gedda. Metuchen, N.J.:
Scarecrow Press, 1987. 308 p.
86-015491   784.9/32   0810819333
Singing -- Instruction and study.

MT821.S913 1987
Sundberg, Johan, 1936-
The science of the singing voice/ Johan Sundberg.
DeKalb, Ill.: Northern Illinois University Press, 1987. x,
216 p.
87-005499   784.9   087580120X
Singing. Voice.

MT823 Singing and vocal technique — History of vocal instruction and study

MT823.M55
Miller, Richard, 1926-
English, French, German, and Italian techniques of
singing: a study in national tonal preferences and how
they relate to functional efficiency/ by Richard Miller.
Metuchen, N.J.: Scarecrow Press, 1977. xviii, 257 p.
76-058554   784.9/32   0810810204
Singing -- Instruction and study -- History.

MT823.M55 1997
Miller, Richard, 1926-
National schools of singing: English, French, German,
and Italian techniques of singing revisited/ Richard
Miller. Lanham, Md.: Scarecrow Press, 1997. xl, 237 p.
96-035557   783/.0094   0810832372
Singing -- Instruction and study -- History.

MT825 Singing and vocal technique — Systems and methods — American

MT825.M646 1986
Miller, Richard,
The structure of singing: system and art in vocal
technique/ Richard Miller. New York: Schirmer Books;
c1986. xxii, 372 p.
85-011492   784.9/3 19   002872660X
Singing--Methods.

MT870 Singing and vocal technique — Special techniques — Sight-singing

MT870.O86 2001
Ottman, Robert W.
Music for sight singing/ Robert W. Ottman. 5th ed. Upper
Saddle River, N.J.: Prentice-Hall, c2001. xvi, 378 p.
2002-536900   0130262633
Sight-singing.

MT875 Singing and vocal technique — Special techniques — Chorus and part-singing

MT875.C68 1987
Corp, Ronald.
The choral singer's companion/ Ronald Corp. New York,
N.Y.: Facts on File Publications, 1987. 192 p.
86-031913   784.9/6 19   081601776X
Choral singing -- Instruction and study. Choirs (Music) Choral music -- Dictionaries.

MT875.S63 1999
Smith, Brenda
Choral pedagogy/ Brenda Smith, Robert Thayer Sataloff.
San Diego: Singular, [1999], c2000. xv, 200 p.
99-022677   782.5/071 21   0769300510
*Choral singing -- Instruction and study. Choral conducting.
Voice -- Care and hygiene.*

MT883 Singing and vocal technique — Special techniques — Pronunciation. Diction

MT883.A23 1999
Adams, David, 1950-
A handbook of diction for singers: Italian, German,
French/ David Adams. New York: Oxford University
Press, 1999. xii, 180 p.
98-012204   783/.043   0195125673
*Singing -- Diction. Italian language -- Pronunciation. French
language -- Pronunciation.*

MT883.D53 1990
Diction for singers: a concise reference for English,
Italian, Latin, German, French, and Spanish
pronunciation/ Joan Wall... [et al.]. Dallas: Pst, c1990.
279 p.
90-061008   783/.043 21   1877761516
Singing -- Diction.

MT883.S56 1996
Singing early music: the pronunciation of European languages in the Late Middle Ages and Renaissance/ edited by Timothy J. McGee with A.G. Rigg and David N. Klausner. Bloomington: Indiana University Press, c1996. xiii, 299 p.
95-022575   783/.043   0253329612
Singing -- Diction. Romance languages -- Pronunciation. Germanic languages -- Pronunciation.

MT892 Singing and vocal technique — Interpretation, phrasing, expression, etc.

MT892.B4
Bernac, Pierre.
The interpretation of French song. Translations of song texts, by Winifred Radford. New York, Praeger [1970] xiv, 326 p.
76-079069   784.9/34
Songs -- France -- Interpretation (Phrasing, dynamics, etc.)

MT892.E54
Emmons, Shirlee.
The art of the song recital/ Shirlee Emmons, Stanley Sonntag. New York: Schirmer Books, c1979. xx, 571 p.
78-066978   784.9/34 19   0028705300
Singing -- Instruction and study. Songs -- Interpretation (Phrasing, dynamics, etc.) Musical accompaniment.

MT892.E55 1998
Emmons, Shirlee.
Power performance for singers: transcending the barriers/ Shirlee Emmons, Alma Thomas. New York: Oxford University Press, 1998. xvi, 320 p.
97-031732   783/.043   0195112245
Singing -- Psychological aspects.

MT892.H44 1993
Helfgot, Daniel.
The third line: the opera performer as interpreter/ Daniel Helfgot with William O. Beeman. New York: Schirmer Books; c1993. xi, 242 p.
93-012311   782.1/146   0028710363
Singing -- Interpretation (Phrasing, dynamics, etc.) Acting in opera.

MT955 Musical theater — Production

MT955.K82 1990
Kornick, Rebecca Hodell.
Recent American opera: a production guide/ Rebecca Hodell Kornick. New York: Columbia University Press, c1991. xvii, 352 p.
90-002576   792.5/0232/0973   0231069200
Opera -- United States -- 20th century -- Production and direction.

MT955.O54 1998
Opera in context: essays on historical staging from the late Renaissance to the time of Puccini/ edited by Mark A. Radice. Portland, Or.: Amadeus Press, c1998. 410 p.
97-002712   792.5/023   1574670328
Opera -- Production and direction.

MT955.V36
Van Witsen, Leo, 1912-
Costuming for opera: who wears what and why/ Leo Van Witsen. Bloomington: Indiana University Press, c1981. xxiii, 232 p.
79-003250   782.1/07/3   0253132258
Operas -- Stage guides. Costume. Opera -- Production and direction.

MT955.W35 1999
White, Matthew, 1963-
Staging a musical/ Matthew White. New York: Routledge/Theatre Arts Books, c1999. v, 137 p.
99-031790   792.6/4   0878301089
Musicals -- Production and direction.

MT956 Musical theater — Performing

MT956.C7 1987
Craig, David,
On performing: a handbook for actors, dancers, singers on the musical stage/ David Craig; foreword by Robert Lewis. New York: McGraw-Hill, c1987. xv, 298 p.
86-021010   782.81/07/1 19   0070133417
Musicals -- Instruction and study. Singing -- Vocational guidance. Acting -- Vocational guidance. Dance -- Vocational guidance. Entertainers -- United States -- Interviews.

MT956.D4 2000
De Mallet Burgess, Thomas, 1964-
The singing and acting handbook: games and exercises for the performer/ Thomas De Mallet Burgess and Nicholas Skilbeck. London; Routledge, 2000. xv, 204 p.
99-029440   792.6/028   0415166578
Acting in musical theater.

MT956.R63 2000
Robison, Kevin.
The actor sings: discovering a musical voice for the stage/ Kevin Robison. Portsmouth, NH: Heinemann, c2000. xvi, 107 p.
99-086171   792.6/028   0325001774
Musical theater -- Instruction and study. Singing -- Instruction and study.

N Visual art

N31 Encyclopedias

N31.D5 1996
The dictionary of art/ editor, Jane Turner. New York: Grove, 1996. 34 v.
96-013628   703   1884446000
Art -- Encyclopedias.

N31.E4833
Encyclopedia of world art.   New York, McGraw-Hill [1959-c1987] 17 v.
59-013433   703
Art -- Encyclopedias.

N33 Dictionaries

N33.L353 2000
Langmuir, Erika.
The Yale dictionary of art and artists/ Erika Langmuir and Norbert Lynton. New Haven, CT: Yale University Press, c2000. viii, 753 p.
00-025800   703   0300064586
Art -- Dictionaries. Artists -- Dictionaries.

N33.M23
McGraw-Hill dictionary of art. Edited by Bernard S. Myers. Assistant editor: Shirley D. Myers. New York, McGraw-Hill [1969] 5 v.
68-026314   703
Art -- Dictionaries.

N33.M37 1992
Mayer, Ralph, 1895-
The HarperCollins dictionary of art terms and techniques/ Ralph Mayer; revised and edited by Steven Sheehan. New York, N.Y.: HarperPerennial, c1991. v, 474 p.
91-055395   703   0062715186
Art -- Dictionaries. Art -- Technique.

N33.O93 1988
The Oxford dictionary of art/ edited by Ian Chilvers and Harold Osborne; consultant editor, Dennis Farr. Oxford [Oxfordshire]; Oxford University Press, 1988. x, 548 p.
88-005138   703/.21   0198661339
Art -- Dictionaries.

N33.P74 2000
The Prestel dictionary of art and artists of the 20th century. Munich; Prestel, c2000. 383 p.
99-069078   709/.04/003   3791323253
Art, Modern -- 20th century -- Dictionaries. Artists -- Biography -- Dictionaries.

N34 Terminology

N34.C75 1996
Critical terms for art history/ edited by Robert S. Nelson and Richard Shiff. Chicago: University of Chicago Press, 1996. xvi, 364 p.
95-049975   701/.4   0226571645
Art -- Historiography -- Terminology. English language -- Terms and phrases.

N34.W34 1977
Walker, John Albert, 1938-
Glossary of art, architecture, and design since 1945: terms and labels describing movements styles and groups derived from the vocabulary of artists and critics/ John A Walker. London: Bingley; 1977. 352 p.
77-003201   709/.04   0208015434
Art -- Terminology.

N40 Biography — Collective — General

N40.B53 1995
A Biographical dictionary of artists/ general editor, Sir Lawrence Gowing. New York, NY: Facts on File, c1995. xiii, 784 p.
94-038801   709/.2/2   0816032521
Artists -- Biography -- Dictionaries.

N40.I55 1990
International dictionary of art and artists/ with a foreword by Cecil Gould; editor, James Vinson. Chicago: St. James Press, c1990. 2 v.
91-186208   709/.2/2   1558620001
Artists -- Biography -- Dictionaries. Art -- Dictionaries.

N40.J33 1999
Jackson, Christine E. 1936-
Dictionary of bird artists of the world/ Christine E. Jackson. Woodbridge, Suffolk: Antique Collectors' Club, 1999. 550 p.
00-300585   1851492038
Artists -- Biography -- Dictionaries. Ornithological illustration -- History. Birds in art.

N40.M63
Modern arts criticism.   Detroit: Gale Research, [c1991-] 4 v.
91-649722   709/.2/2
Artists -- Biography -- History and criticism -- Periodicals. Art criticism -- History -- 20th century -- Periodicals.

N40.P45 1976
Petersen, Karen,
Women artists: recognition and reappraisal from the early Middle Ages to the twentieth century/ Karen Petersen & J. J. Wilson. 1st ed. New York: Harper & Row, 1976. 212 p.
75-039543   709/.2/2 B   0060903872
Women artists -- Biography.

N40.S78 1997
St. James guide to Black artists/ with a preface by
Howard Dodson; editor, Thomas Riggs. Detroit: St.
James Press, c1997. xxiv, 625 p.
97-003068   709/.2/396   1558622209
Artists, Black -- Biography.

N43 Biography — Collective —
Women artists (Collective)

N43.F56 1978
Fine, Elsa Honig.
Women & art: a history of women painters and sculptors
from the renaissance to the 20th century. Montclair, N.J.:
Allanheld & Schram/Prior, c1978. xiii, 240 p.
77-015897   709/.2/2   0839001878
Women artists -- Biography. Art, Renaissance. Art, Modern.

N43.P47 1985
Petteys, Chris.
Dictionary of women artists: an international dictionary
of women artists born before 1900/ Chris Petteys, with
the assistance of Hazel Gustow, Ferris Olin, Verna
Ritchie. Boston, Mass.: G.K. Hall, c1985. xviii, 851 p.
84-022511   709/.2/2   0816184569
Women artists -- Biography -- Dictionaries.

N43.S57 1985
Slatkin, Wendy.
Women artists in history: from antiquity to the 20th
century/ Wendy Slatkin. Englewood Cliffs, N.J.:
Prentice-Hall, c1985. xv, 191 p.
84-011481   709/.2/2   013961821X
Women artists -- Biography.

N43.W26 1991
Waller, Susan, 1948-
Women artists in the modern era: a documentary history/
by Susan Waller. Metuchen, N.J.: Scarecrow Press, 1991.
xii, 392 p.
91-017047   709/.2/2   0810824051
*Women artists -- Biography -- History and criticism. Art,
Modern -- History.*

N45 Artists' marks and monograms

N45.C374 1991
Castagno, John, 1930-
Artists' monograms and indiscernible signatures: an
international directory, 1800-1991/ by John Castagno.
Metuchen, N.J.: Scarecrow Press, 1991. xviii, 538 p.
91-023003   702/.78   0810824159
*Artists' marks -- Directories. Monograms -- Directories.
Autographs -- Directories.*

N58 Communication of information —
Information services

N58.A78 1995
Art marketing sourcebook for the fine artist/ [editor,
Constance Smith]. Penn Valley, CA: ArtNetwork, c1995.
216 p.
96-113481   702/.5/73   0940899264
*Art -- United States -- Information services -- Directories. Art
-- Information services -- Directories. Art -- United States --
Marketing.*

N59 Communication of information —
Computer network resources

N59.J66 1999
Jones, Lois Swan.
Art information and the internet: how to find it, how to
use it/ by Lois Swan Jones. Phoenix, Ariz.: Oryx Press,
c1999. xv, 279 p.
98-034061   025.067   1573561622
Art -- Computer network resources.

N66-69 Theory. Philosophy.
Aesthetics of the visual arts —
Theories of the visual arts.
By language — Recent writings, 1870-

N66.R4 1965
Read, Herbert Edward, 1893-1968.
Icon and idea: the function of art in the development of
human consciousness/ Herbert Read. New York:
Schocken Books, c1965. 161 p.
65-025410   701
Art -- Philosophy. Aesthetics.

N67.S243
Sartre, Jean Paul, 1905-
Essays in aesthetics. Selected and translated by Wade
Baskin. New York, Citadel Press, [1963] 94 p.
63-011486   701.17
Art -- Philosophy. Artists.

N68.W613
Worringer, Wilhelm, 1881-1965.
Abstraction and empathy; a contribution to the
psychology of style. Translated by Michael Bullock. New
York, International Universities Press, 1953. 144 p.
53-012034   701.16
Aesthetics Art -- Philosophy.

N69.C813
Croce, Benedetto, 1866-1952.
Guide to aesthetics (Breviario di estetica) Translated,
with an introd., by Patrick Romanell. Indianapolis,
Bobbs-Merrill [1965] xxxii, 88 p.
65-026527   111.85
Aesthetics

N70 Theory. Philosophy. Aesthetics of the visual arts — Theories of the visual arts. By language — General special

N70.A69
Arnheim, Rudolf.
Toward a psychology of art; collected essays. Berkeley, University of California Press, 1966. viii, 369 p.
66-010692   701.15
Art -- Psychology. Perception.

N70.A693
Arnheim, Rudolf.
Visual thinking. Berkeley, University of California Press [1969] xi, 345 p.
71-076335   701
Visual perception. Art -- Philosophy.

N70.B2 1990
Barasch, Moshe.
Modern theories of art/ Moshe Barasch. New York: New York University Press, 1990-c1998. 2 v.
89-034682   701   0814711332
Art -- Philosophy. Aesthetics, Modern -- 18th century. Aesthetics, Modern -- 19th century.

N70.B55 1949
Blanshard, Frances Margaret Bradshaw, 1895-1966.
Retreat from likeness in the theory of painting. New York, Columbia Univ. Press, 1949. x, 178 p.
49-010859   701.16
Painting. Aesthetics.

N70.J67
Aesthetic inquiry; essays on art criticism and the philosophy of art. Edited by Monroe C. Beardsley [and] Herbert M. Schueller. Belmont, Calif., Dickenson Pub. Co. [1967] viii, 305 p.
66-028324   701.17
Aesthetics.

N70.L28
Langer, Susanne Katherina (Knauth) 1895-
Problems of art; ten philosophical lectures. New York, Scribner [1957] 184 p.
57-006068   701
Art -- Philosophy. Aesthetics -- Addresses, essays, lectures.

N70.S48 1991
Shlain, Leonard.
Art & physics: parallel visions in space, time, and light/ Leonard Shlain. New York: Morrow, c1991. 480 p.
91-014655   701   0688097529
Art -- Philosophy. Physics -- Influence.

N71 Theory. Philosophy. Aesthetics of the visual arts — Special topics — Psychology of art and the artist

N71.B398 1980
Berger, John.
About looking/ John Berger. New York: Pantheon Books, c1980. 198 p.
79-003615   701/.1/5   0394511247
Art -- Psychology. Visual perception. Meaning (Psychology)

N71.B673 1998
Borzello, Frances.
Seeing ourselves: women's self-portraits/ Frances Borzello. New York: Harry N. Abrams, Inc., 1998. 224 p.
97-041441   704/.042   0810941880
Women artists -- Psychology. Self-perception in women. Women artists -- Portraits.

N71.D57 1988
Dissanayake, Ellen.
What is art for?/ Ellen Dissanayake. Seattle: University of Washington Press, c1988. xv, 249 p.
87-031648   701/.1/5   0295966122
Art -- Psychology. Art appreciation. Behavior evolution.

N71.E5 1967
Ehrenzweig, Anton, 1908-1966.
The hidden order of art; a study in the psychology of artistic imagination. Berkeley, University of California Press, 1967. xiv, 306 p.
67-020443   701.15
Art -- Psychology. Imagination.

N71.F65 1989
Freedberg, David.
The power of images: studies in the history and theory of response/ David Freedberg. Chicago: University of Chicago Press, 1989. xxv, 534 p.
88-027638   701/.1/5   0226261441
Art -- Psychology. Symbolism in art.

N71.F655 1993
Freeman, Mark Philip, 1955-
Finding the muse: a sociopsychological inquiry into the conditions of artistic creativity/ Mark Freeman. Cambridge [England]; Cambridge University Press, 1993. viii, 330 p.
93-003468   709/.73/09046   0521392187
Artists -- United States -- Psychology. Creation (Literary, artistic, etc.) Art and society -- United States.

N71.H45 1993
Herwitz, Daniel Alan, 1955-
Making theory/constructing art: on the authority of the avant-garde/ Daniel Herwitz. Chicago: University of Chicago Press, 1993. xv, 353 p.
92-043483   701   0226328910
Art -- Philosophy. Constructivism (Philosophy) Avant-garde (Aesthetics) -- History -- 20th century.

N71.K56 1998
Kimmelman, Michael.
Portraits: talking with artists at the Met, the Modern, the Louvre, and elsewhere/ Michael Kimmelman. New York: Random House, c1998. xviii, 265 p.
98-009589   701/.15   0679452192
Artists -- Interviews. Artists -- Psychology. Artists and museums.

N71.M35 1998
McNiff, Shaun.
Trust the process: an artist's guide to letting go/ Shaun McNiff. Boston: Shambhala; 1998. ix, 210 p.
97-040182   701/.15   1570623570
Creative ability -- Psychological aspects. Self-actualization (Psychology) Artists -- Psychology.

N71.P32 1997
Patin, Thomas, 1958-
Artwords: a glossary of contemporary art theory/ Thomas Patin and Jennifer McLerran. Westport, Conn.: Greenwood Press, 1997. xiii, 153 p.
96-029274   701/.09045   0313292728
Art -- Philosophy -- History -- 20th century -- Terminology.

N71.P64 1998
Podro, Michael.
Depiction/ Michael Podro. New Haven, CT: Yale University Press, c1998. viii, 193 p.
98-015247   701/.15   0300069146
Artists -- Psychology. Visual perception. Imagery (Psychology) in art.

N71.R33
Rank, Otto, 1884-1939.
Art and artist; creative urge and personality development, by Otto Rank, with a preface by Ludwig Lewisohn; translated from the German by Charles Francis Atkinson. New York, A.A. Knopf, 1932. xlix, 431 p.
32-025675
Art -- Psychology. Artists.

N71.S18 1990
Sarason, Seymour Bernard, 1919-
The challenge of art to psychology/ Seymour B. Sarason. New Haven: Yale University Press, c1990. xi, 188 p.
89-021479   701/.15   0300047541
Art -- Psychology. Creation (Literary, artistic, etc.) Art and society.

N71.S35
Schaefer-Simmern, Henry, 1896-
The unfolding of artistic activity, its basis, processes, and implications. With a foreword by John Dewey. Berkeley, Univ. of California Press, 1948. xiii, 201 p.
48-002132   701.15
Art -- Psychology. Creation (Literary, artistic, etc.)

N71.S7 1997
Soussloff, Catherine M.
The absolute artist: the historiography of a concept/ Catherine M. Soussloff. Minneapolis, Minn.: University of Minnesota Press, c1997. xi, 204 p.
96-036005   701/.18   0816628963
Artists -- Psychology. Art -- Historiography.

N71.W54
Wittkower, Rudolf.
Born under Saturn; the character and conduct of artists: a documented history from antiquity to the French Revolution [by] Rudolf and Margot Wittkower. New York, Random House [1963] 344 p.
63-007128   706.972
Artists. Artists -- Psychology.

N72 Theory. Philosophy.
Aesthetics of the visual arts — Special topics —
Art in relation to other subjects, A-Z

N72.E53.P66 1993
Popper, Frank, 1918-
Art of the electronic age/ Frank Popper. New York: Harry N. Abrams, 1993. 192 p.
92-037367   700/.9/048   0810919281
Art and electronics. Art, Modern -- 20th century -- Themes, motives.

N72.F45.B43 1988
Beckett, Wendy.
Contemporary women artists/ Wendy Beckett. New York: Universe Books, 1988. 127 p.
88-004413   704/.042/0904   0876636911
Feminism and art. Women artists -- Biography -- History and criticism. Art, Modern -- 20th century.

N72.F45.F44 1982
Feminism and art history: questioning the litany/ edited by Norma Broude and Mary D. Garrard. New York: Harper & Row, c1982. ix, 358 p.
81-048062   701/.03   0064305252
Feminism and art. Feminism in art.

N72.F45.G37 1994
Garb, Tamar.
Sisters of the brush: women's artistic culture in late nineteenth-century Paris/ Tamar Garb. New Haven: Yale University Press, 1994. viii, 207 p.
93-043147   701/.03   0300059035
Feminism and art -- France -- History -- 19th century.

N72.F45.J33 1997
Jacobs, Fredrika Herman.
Defining the Renaissance virtuosa: women artists and the language of art history and criticism/ Fredrika H. Jacobs. Cambridge; Cambridge University Press, 1997. xii, 229 p.
96-037798   704/.042/094509031   0521572703
Feminism and art -- Italy. Women artists -- Italy -- Biography -- History and criticism. Art, Italian.

N72.F45.M34 1991
McCarthy, Kathleen D.
Women's culture: American philanthropy and art, 1830-1930/ Kathleen D. McCarthy. Chicago: University of Chicago Press, 1991. xvii, 324 p.
91-016632   701/.03   0226555836
Feminism and art -- East (U.S.) -- History. Feminism and art -- Middle West -- History.

N72.F45.N45 1995
New feminist art criticism: critical strategies/ edited by Katy Deepwell. Manchester; Manchester University Press; c1995. xv, 201 p.
94-005414   701/.03   0719042577
Feminism and art. Feminist art criticism.

N72.F45.N64 1988
Nochlin, Linda.
Women, art, and power: and other essays/ Linda Nochlin. New York: Harper & Row, c1988. xvi, 181 p.
88-045118   701/.03   0064358526
Feminism and art. Women artists -- Biography -- History and criticism.

N72.F45.P64 1988
Pollock, Griselda.
Vision and difference: femininity, feminism, and histories of art/ Griselda Pollock. London; Routledge, 1988. 239 p.
87-030783   704/.042   0415007224
Feminism and art.

N72.F45.P68 1994
The power of feminist art: the American movement of the 1970s, history and impact/ edited by Norma Broude and Mary D. Garrard; contributors, Judith K. Brodsky ... [et al.]. New York: H.N. Abrams, 1994. 318 p.
94-001543   701/.03   0810937328
Feminism and art -- United States. Art, American. Art, Modern -- 20th century -- United States.

N72.G68
Greenberg, Clement, 1909-
Art and culture; critical essays.   Boston: Beacon Press, [1961] 278 p.
61-007248   704.91
Art and society. Art. Artists.

N72.H58.L38 1993
Lavin, Irving, 1927-
Past-present: essays on historicism in art from Donatello to Picasso/ Irving Lavin. Berkeley: University of California Press, c1993. xx, 374 p.
91-028489   709   0520068165
Art and history. Historicism.

N72.L413
Leeuw, G. van der 1890-1950.
Sacred and profane beauty; the holy in art. Pref. by Mircea Eliade. Translated by David E. Green. New York, Holt, Rinehart and Winston [1963] 357 p.
63-011867   701
Art and religion. Religion and literature.

N72.M28.W34 1994
Walker, John Albert, 1938-
Art in the age of mass media/ John A. Walker. Boulder: Westview Press, 1994. vi, 200 p.
94-000254   700/.1/05
Mass media and art. Popular culture.

N72.P5.C6 1972
Coke, Van Deren, 1921-
The painter and the photograph; from Delacroix to Warhol. Albuquerque, University of New Mexico Press [1972] 324 p.
75-129804   759/.06
Painting from photographs. Painting -- Exhibitions. Photography -- Exhibitions.

N72.P5.K67 1999
Kosinski, Dorothy M.
The artist and the camera: Degas to Picasso/ Dorothy Kosinski. Dallas, TX: Dallas Museum of Art; c1999. 335 p.
99-038276   701/.05   0300081685
Art and photography -- Europe -- History -- 19th century -- Exhibitions. Art and photography -- Europe -- History -- 20th century -- Exhibitions.

N72.P74.K8 1983
Kuhns, Richard Francis, 1924-
Psychoanalytic theory of art: a philosophy of art on developmental principles/ Richard Kuhns. New York: Columbia University Press, 1983. xi, 169 p.
82-023499   701   0231056206
Psychoanalysis and art. Art -- Philosophy.

N72.S3.K5
Kepes, Gyorgy
The new landscape in art and science.   Paul Theobald & Co., [c1956] 383 p.
57-000576   701.1
Art and science. Art -- Essays. Nature (Aesthetics)

N72.S3.P53 1998
Picturing science, producing art/ Caroline A. Jones, Peter Galison, editors; with Amy Slaton. New York: Routledge, 1998. x, 518 p.
97-040521   701/.1/05   0415919118
Art and science.

N72.S3.S77 1999
Strosberg, Eliane.
Art and science/ Eliane Strosberg. New York: Abbeville Press, 2001. 245 p.
00-052571   700/.1/05   0789207133
Art and science.

N72.S6.C73 1987
Crane, Diana, 1933-
The transformation of the avant-garde: the New York art world, 1940-1985/ Diana Crane. Chicago: University of Chicago Press, 1987. ix, 194 p.
87-005013   701/.03/097471   0226117898
Art and society -- New York (State) -- New York -- History -- 20th century. Avant-garde (Aesthetics) -- New York (State) -- New York -- History -- 20th century. Art, American -- New York (State) -- New York. New York (N.Y.) -- Intellectual life.

N72.S6.D34 1999
Dakers, Caroline.
The Holland Park circle: artists and Victorian society/ Caroline Dakers. New Haven, Conn.: Yale University Press, 1999. vii, 303 p.
99-016247   709/.421/34   0300081642
Art and society -- England -- London -- History -- 19th century. Artists -- Homes and haunts -- England -- London -- History -- 19th century. Artists' studios -- England -- London -- History -- 19th century. Holland Park (London, England) London (England) -- Buildings, structures, etc.

N72.S6.D775 1993
Duncan, Carol.
The aesthetics of power: essays in critical art history/ Carol Duncan. Cambridge; Cambridge University Press, 1993. xvii, 230 p.
92-020448   701/.03   052142044X
Art and society. Feminism and art. Art -- Political aspects.

N72.S6.H32 1993
Halle, David.
Inside culture: art and class in the American home/ David Halle. Chicago: University of Chicago Press, 1993. xvi, 261 p.
93-007335   306.4/7   0226313670
Art and society -- United States. Art -- Psychology.

N72.S6.L39 1981
Layton, Robert, 1944-
The anthropology of art/ Robert Layton. New York: Columbia University Press, 1981. x, 227 p.
80-039919   709/.01/1   0231052820
Art and anthropology. Art and society.

N72.S6.L46 1996
Leppert, Richard D.
Art and the committed eye: the cultural functions of imagery/ Richard Leppert. Boulder, CO: Westview Press, 1996. xvii, 348 p.
95-019092   701/.03   0813315395
Art and society -- Europe. Artists -- Europe -- Psychology. Art and society -- United States.

N72.S6.M23 1996
Macleod, Dianne Sachko.
Art and the Victorian middle class: money and the making of cultural identity/ Dianne Sachko Macleod. New York: Cambridge University Press, 1996. xx, 530 p.
95-024299   701/.03   0521550904
Art and society -- England -- History -- 19th century. Art patronage -- England -- History -- 19th century. Middle class -- England -- Identification.

N72.S6.N63 1989
Nochlin, Linda.
The politics of vision: essays on nineteenth-century art and society/ Linda Nochlin. New York: Harper & Row, c1989. xxiv, 200 p.
89-045055   701/.03/094409034   0064358542
Art and society -- France -- History -- 19th century. Art, Modern -- 19th century -- France.

N72.S6.S29 2000
Sassower, Raphael.
The golden avant-garde: idolatry, commercialism, and art/ Raphael Sassower and Louis Cicotello. Charlottesville; University Press of Virginia, 2000. 147 p.
99-055194   701.03   0813919347
Art and society -- History -- 20th century. Avant-garde (Aesthetics) -- History -- 20th century.

N72.S6.V59 1994
Visual culture: images and interpretations/ edited by Norman Bryson, Michael Ann Holly, and Keith Moxey. Hanover: University Press of New England [for] Wesleyan University Press, c1994. xxix, 429 p.
93-013614   701/.03   0819552607
Art and society -- Congresses. Masculinity in art -- Congresses. Art -- Historiography -- Congresses.

N72.S6.Z65 1990
Zolberg, Vera L.
Constructing a sociology of the arts/ Vera L. Zolberg. Cambridge; Cambridge University Press, 1990. xii, 252 p.
89-038446   701/.03   0521351464
Art and society.

N76 Theory. Philosophy.
Aesthetics of the visual arts — Special topics — Symmetry. Proportion. Rhythm

N76.K4
Kepes, Gyorgy, 1906-
Module, proportion, symmetry, rhythm. New York, G. Braziller [1966] 233 p.
66-013044   701.17
Bartok, Bela, -- 1881-1945. Symmetry (Art)

N79 Theory. Philosophy.
Aesthetics of the visual arts — Special topics — Miscellaneous. Essays, etc.

N79.L2
Langer, Susanne Katherina Knauth, 1895-
Reflections on art; a source book of writings by artists, critics, and philosophers. Baltimore, Johns Hopkins Press [1959, c1958] 364 p.
58-059767   701.17
Music -- Philosophy and aesthetics. Art -- Philosophy. Aesthetics.

N85 Study and teaching.
Research — General works

N85.C6
Conant, Howard.
Art in education [by] Howard Conant and Arne Randall. Peoria, Ill., C.A. Bennett [1959] 345 p.
58-005510   707
Art -- Study and teaching.

N85.J64
Jones, Lois Swan.
Art research methods and resources: a guide to finding art information/ Lois Swan Jones. Dubuque, Iowa: Kendall/Hunt Pub. Co., c1978. xii, 243 p.
77-093281   707/.2   0840318464
Art -- Research.

N105-108 Study and teaching. Research — History — Special regions or countries

N105.E35 1990
Efland, Arthur, 1929-
A history of art education: intellectual and social currents in teaching the visual arts/ Arthur D. Efland. New York: Teachers College Press, c1990. xi, 305 p.
89-035255   707/.073   0807729779
Art -- Study and teaching -- United States -- History. Art -- Study and teaching -- History.

N105.L48 1991
Levi, Albert William, 1911-
Art education: a critical necessity/ Albert William Levi and Ralph A. Smith. Urbana: University of Illinois Press, c1991. xxi, 254 p.
90-026637   707/.073   0252018133
Art -- Study and teaching -- United States.

N108.W55 1997
Wilson, Brent.
The quiet evolution: changing the face of arts education/ Brent Wilson. Los Angeles: Getty Education Institute for the Arts, 1997. 255 p.
97-008882   707/.073   0892364092
Art -- Study and teaching -- United States.

N330-332 Study and teaching. Research — Art schools — Special countries

N330.B55.C74 1983
Design in America: the Cranbrook vision, 1925-1950/ text by Robert Judson Clark ... [et al.]; [catalog coordinator, Andrea P.A. Belloli]. New York: Abrams, in association with the Detroit Institute of Arts and the Metropolitan Museum of Art, c1983. 352 p.
83-006343   709/.774/38   0810908018
Art, Modern -- 20th century -- Michigan -- Bloomfield -- Exhibitions. Design -- Michigan -- Bloomfield -- History -- 20th century -- Exhibitions.

N332.B38.W513
Wingler, Hans Maria.
The Bauhaus: Weimar, Dessau, Berlin, Chicago [by] Hans M. Wingler. [Translated by Wolfgang Jabs and Basil Gilbert. Edited by Joseph Stein. Cambridge, Mass., MIT Press, [1969] xv, 653 p.
68-020052   707/.1/5   026223033X
Bauhaus.

N332.F83.P33
Boime, Albert.
The Academy and French painting in the Nineteenth century. London, Phaidon, 1971. xi, 330 p.
78-112622   759.4   0714814016
Academic art -- France. Painting, French -- History. Painting, Modern -- 19th century -- France.

N332.G33.B4455 1997
Hochman, Elaine S.
Bauhaus: crucible of modernism/ Elaine S. Hochman; foreword by Dore Ashton. New York: Fromm International, 1997. xii, 371 p.
96-037073   707/.1/143155   0880641754
Bauhaus -- History.

N332.G33.B447513 1999
Kentgens-Craig, Margret, 1948-
The Bauhaus and America: first contacts, 1919-1936/ Margret Kentgens-Craig. Cambridge, Mass.: MIT Press, c1999. xx, 283 p.
99-018804   724/.6   026211237X
Architecture, German -- United States. Architecture, Modern -- 20th century -- United States.

N332.G33.B487 1984
Whitford, Frank.
Bauhaus/ Frank Whitford. London: Thames and Hudson, c1984. 216 p.
83-050527   707/.114322   0500201935
Bauhaus.

N332.G33.B487 1993
The Bauhaus: masters & students by themselves/ edited by Frank Whitford; with additional research by Julia Englehardt. Woodstock, N.Y.: Overlook Press, 1993. 328 p.
93-001954   707/.1/143184   0879515074
Bauhaus.

N346 Study and teaching. Research — Art study in universities and colleges — By region or country

N346.A1
Elkins, James, 1955-
Why art cannot be taught: a handbook for art students/ James Elkins. Urbana: University of Illinois Press, c2001. 213 p.
00-011150   707/.1/173   0252026381
Art -- Study and teaching (Higher) -- United States.

N350 Study and teaching. Research — Art study in elementary and secondary schools — General works

N350.S67 1983
Smith, Nancy R.
Experience and art: teaching children to paint/ Nancy R. Smith. New York: Teachers College, Columbia University, 1983. xv, 120 p.
82-010287   372.5/2   0807727008
Painting -- Study and teaching (Elementary) Child artists. Children's art.

N351 Study and teaching. Research —
Art study in elementary and secondary schools —
Children as artists

N351.M54 1998
Milbrath, Constance, 1943-
Patterns of artistic development in children: comparative studies of talent/ Constance Milbrath. Cambridge; Cambridge University Press, 1998. xvi, 422 p.
97-032148   704/.054   052144313X
Child artists -- Psychology. Creative ability in children.

N366 Study and teaching. Research —
Picture study in the school and the home —
General works

N366.A78 1992
Art on screen: a directory of films and videos about the visual arts/ compiled and edited by the Program for Art on Film; Nadine Covert, editor; Elizabeth Scheines ... [et al.]. Boston, Mass.: G.K. Hall, c1991. xiv, 283 p.
91-034548   016.7   0816172943
Art -- Film catalogs. Art -- Video tape catalogs. Motion picture producers and directors -- Directories.

N380 Study and teaching. Research —
Study of the history of art — General works

N380.M556 1994
Minor, Vernon Hyde.
Art history's history/ Vernon Hyde Minor. Englewood Cliffs, N.J.: Prentice Hall, c1994. xii, 211 p.
93-028088   707/.2   0131946064
Art -- Historiography.

N380.P53 1982
Podro, Michael.
The critical historians of art/ Michael Podro. New Haven: Yale University Press, 1982. xxvi, 257 p.
82-004934   701/.1/80943   0300028628
Art -- Historiography. Art criticism.

N380.P68 1989
Preziosi, Donald, 1941-
Rethinking art history: meditations on a coy science/ Donald Preziosi. New Haven: Yale University Press, c1989. xvi, 269 p.
89-030733   707/.2   0300044623
Art -- Historiography.

N380.R66 1989
Roskill, Mark W., 1933-
The interpretation of pictures/ Mark Roskill. Amherst: University of Massachusetts Press, 1989. xvi, 124 p.
88-022112   701/.1/8   0870236601
Art -- Historiography.

N385 Study and teaching. Research —
Study of the history of art — Special countries

N385.E27 1993
The Early years of art history in the United States: notes and essays on departments, teaching, and scholars/ edited by Craig Hugh Smyth and Peter M. Lukehart. Princeton, N.J.: Dept. of Art and Archaeology, Princeton University, c1993. xxiii, 205 p.
93-023894   707/.2   0691036454
Art -- Historiography. Art -- Study and teaching (Higher) -- United States. Art schools -- United States -- History.

N510-858 Art museums, galleries, etc. —
Special countries and special museums —
United States

N510.A43 1996
Alexander, Victoria D.
Museums and money: the impact of funding on exhibitions, scholarship, and management/ Victoria D. Alexander. Bloomington: Indiana University Press, c1996. xiii, 167 p.
95-049863   708.13/068/1   0253332052
Art museums -- United States -- Management. Art museums -- United States -- Finance. Art patronage -- United States.

N510.A777 2000
Art across America: a comprehensive guide to American art museums and exhibition galleries/ edited by John J. Russell and Thomas S. Spencer. Monkton, Md.: Friar's Lantern, 2000. 898 p.
00-106757   708.13   0966714415
Art museums -- United States -- Directories.

N510.C3
Cartwright, W. Aubrey.
Guide to art museums in the United States. New York, Duell, Sloan and Pearce [1958-   ]
58-006767   708.1
Art museums -- United States.

N510.E27 1991
The Economics of art museums/ edited and with an introduction by Martin Feldstein. Chicago: University of Chicago Press, c1991. x, 363 p.
91-027088   338.4/770813   0226240738
Art museums -- Economic aspects -- United States.

N526.A84 1996
Harvard University.
Harvard's art museums: 100 years of collecting/ James Cuno ... [et al.]. Cambridge, Mass.: Harvard University Museums; 1996. 364 p.
95-052347   708.144/4   0810934272
Art -- Massachusetts -- Cambridge.

N530.A74 2000
Art Institute of Chicago.
Treasures from the Art Institute of Chicago/ selected by James N. Wood, with commentaries by Debra N. Mancoff; [edited by Laura J. Kozitka and Catherine A. Steinmann]. Chicago: Art Institute of Chicago; c2000. 344 p.
99-069501 708.173/11 0865591822
Art -- Illinois -- Chicago -- Catalogs.

N611.L43.M46 1987
Metropolitan Museum of Art (New York, N.Y.)
The Robert Lehman Collection. New York: The Museum; c1987-c1999.
86-012519 708.147/1 0870994794
Lehman, Robert, -- 1892-1969 -- Art collections -- Catalogs. Art -- Private collections -- New York (State) -- New York -- Catalogs.

N618.B47 1990
Berman, Avis.
Rebels on Eighth Street: Juliana Force and the Whitney Museum of American Art/ Avis Berman. New York: Atheneum, 1990. xvi, 572 p.
89-014968 709/.2 0689120869
Force, Juliana, -- 1876-1948.   Art patrons -- United States -- Biography. Art museum directors -- United States -- Biography.

N620.M9.A57 1999
Museum of Modern Art (New York, N.Y.)
ModernStarts: people, places, things/ edited by John Elderfield ... [et al.]. New York: Museum of Modern Art: 1999. 360 p.
99-074802 709/.4/00747471 0870700251
Art, Modern -- 20th century -- Exhibitions. Art, Modern -- 19th century -- Exhibitions.

N620.M9.A72 2000
Museum of Modern Art (New York, N.Y.)
Modern contemporary: art at MoMA since 1980/ edited by Kirk Varnedoe, Paola Antonelli, Joshua Siegel. New York, NY: Museum of Modern Art: c2000. 560 p.
00-108144 709/.04/00747471 0870700219
Arts, Modern -- 20th century -- Catalogs. Arts -- New York (State) -- New York -- Catalogs.

N856.W33 1984
Walker, John, 1906 Dec. 24-
National Gallery of Art, Washington/ by John Walker; foreword by J. Carter Brown. New York: H.N. Abrams, [1984]
83-027545 708.153 0810913704
National Gallery of Art (U.S.)

N857.A617 1995
National Museum of American Art (U.S.)
National Museum of American Art/ [foreword by Elizabeth Broun; introduction by William Kloss]. [Washington, D.C.]: The Museum, c1995. 279 p.
94-037723 709/.73/074753 0821222163
Art -- Washington (D.C.) -- Catalogs. Art, American -- Catalogs.

N858.P4.A87 1999
Phillips, Duncan, 1886-1966.
The eye of Duncan Phillips: a collection in the making/ editor, Erika D. Passantino; consulting editor, David W. Scott; researchers, Virginia Speer Burden ... [et al.]. Washington, DC: Phillips Collection in association with Yale University New Haven, c1999. xix, 820 p.
99-015182 750/.74/753 0300080905
Phillips, Duncan, -- 1886-1966. -- Art patronage.   Art, American -- Catalogs. Art -- Washington (D.C.) -- Catalogs. Art, European -- Catalogs.

N2030-3350 Art museums, galleries, etc. — Special countries and special museums — Europe

N2030.H8 1960
Huyghe, Rene.
Art treasures of the Louvre. Text adapted from the French of Rene Huyghe. Commentary by Mme. Rene Huyghe. With a brief history of the Louvre by Milton S. Fox. New York, H. N. Abrams [1960] 211 p.
60-008496 708.4
Art -- France -- Paris.

N2280.M413
Menz, Henner.
The Dresden Gallery. [Translated from the German by Daphne Woodward] New York, Abrams [1962] 320 p.
62-018732 708.3
Painting -- Dresden.

N3350.D4
Descargues, Pierre.
The Hermitage Museum, Leningrad. New York: H.N. Abrams, [1961] 320 p.
61-014628 759.074
Painting -- Leningrad (R.S.F.S.R.) Art museums -- Soviet Union.

N3350.N67 1998
Norman, Geraldine.
The Hermitage: the biography of a great museum/ Geraldine Norman. New York: Fromm International, 1998. xiv, 386 p.
97-039655 708.7/453 0880641908
Gosudarstvennyœi çErmitazh (Russia) -- History.

N3750 Art museums, galleries, etc. — Special countries and special museums — Asia

N3750.T32.A66 1996
Kuo li ku kung po wu yuan.
Splendors of Imperial China: treasures from the National Palace Museum, Taipei/ Maxwell K. Hearn. New York: Metropolitan Museum of Art; c1996. 144 p.
95-046590 709/.51/0747471 0870997661
Art -- Taiwan -- Taipei -- Exhibitions. Art, Chinese -- Exhibitions.

N3750.T32.A87 1996
Kuo li ku kung po wu yuan.
Possessing the past: treasures from the National Palace
Museum, Taipei/ Wen C. Fong, James C.Y. Watt; with
contributions by Richard M. Barnhart ... [et al.]. New
York: Metropolitan Museum of Art: 1996. xv, 648 p.
95-049102   709/.51/0747471   0870997653
Art -- Taiwan -- Taipei -- Catalogs. Art, Chinese -- Catalogs.

N4039 Catalogs of photographs and picture collections in art museums, libraries, etc. — Catalogs of slides of works of art — General

N4039.V58 1995
The visual resources directory: art slide and photograph
collections in the United States and Canada/ editor, Carla
Conrad Freeman; Canadian editor, Barbara Stevenson.
Englewood, Colo.: Libraries Unlimited, 1995. xvii,
174 p.
95-036610   026/.7797/02573   1563081962
*Art -- Slides -- Directories. Slides (Photography) -- United
States -- Directories. Photograph collections -- United States --
Directories.*

N4395 Exhibitions — General works. History. Organization, etc.

N4395.H37 2000
Haskell, Francis, 1928-
The ephemeral museum: old master paintings and the rise
of the art exhibition/ Francis Haskell. New Haven
[Conn.]: Yale University Press, c2000. xiv, 200 p.
00-040836   750/.74   0300085346
Art -- Exhibitions -- History.

N5015 Exhibitions — Other general exhibitions. By place held — America

N5015.A8.B7
Brown, Milton Wolf, 1911-
The story of the Armory show. New York: Joseph H.
Hirshhorn Foundation; [1963] 320 p.
63-013496   707.4
Art -- Exhibitions.

N5220 Private collections and collectors — Private patronage and collections — American

N5220.G26.S48 1997
Shand-Tucci, Douglass, 1941-
The art of scandal: the life and times of Isabella Stewart
Gardner/ Douglass   Shand-Tucci.   New   York:
HarperCollins, c1997. xvi, 351 p.
97-010676   709/.2   0060186437
*Gardner, Isabella Stewart, -- 1840-1924. Art -- Collectors and
collecting -- United States -- Biography. Women art collectors --
United States -- Biography.*

N5220.G886.A36 1979
Guggenheim, Marguerite, 1898-1979.
Out of this century: confessions of an art addict/ Peggy
Guggenheim; foreword by Gore Vidal; introd. by Alfred
H. Barr. New York: Universe Books, c1979. xviii, 396 p.
78-068475   704/.7   0876633378
*Guggenheim, Peggy, -- 1898-   Art patrons -- United States --
Biography.*

N5220.G886 G55 2002
Gill, Anton.
Art lover: a biography of Peggy Guggenheim/ Anton Gill.
1st ed. New York: HarperCollins, 2002.
2001-051731   709/.2.B 21   0060196971
*Guggenheim, Peggy, 1898- Art -- Collectors and collecting --
United States -- Biography. Art -- Collectors and collecting --
Europe -- Biography.*

N5276.2 Private collections and collectors — Private patronage and collections — European

N5276.2.S5.K4 1983
Kean, Beverly Whitney.
All the empty palaces: the merchant patrons of modern
art in pre-Revolutionary Russia/ Beverly Whitney Kean.
New York: Universe Books, 1983. xviii, 342 p.
82-008536   759.4/074/07   0876634129
*Shchukin, Sergei Ivanovich, -- 1854-1936 -- Art collections.
Morozov, Ivan Abramovich -- Art collections. Art patronage --
Soviet Union -- History -- 20th century. Impressionism (Art) --
France. Post-impressionism -- France.*

N5300 History — General works

N5300.A33 1994
Adams, Laurie.
A history of Western art/ Laurie Schneider Adams. New
York: H.N. Abrams, 1994. 512 p.
93-070606   709   0810934256
Art -- History.

N5300.G25 1980
Gardner, Helen, d. 1946.
Gardner's Art through the ages/ revised by Horst de la
Croix and Richard G. Tansey. New York: Harcourt Brace
Jovanovich, c1980. xiii, 922 p.
79-065963   709   0155037587
Art -- History.

N5300.G643 1984
Gombrich, Ernst Hans Josef, 1909-
The story of art. New York, Phaidon Publishers;
distributed by Oxford University Press [1964, 1963] vi,
462 p.
64-009844   709
Art -- History.

N5300.H68 1999
Honour, Hugh.
The visual arts: a history/ Hugh Honour, John Fleming.
New York: Henry N. Abrams, 1999. 928 p.
99-072250   709   0810939355
Art -- History.

N5300.J3 1986b
Janson, H. W. 1913-
History of art/ by H.W. Janson. New York: H.N. Abrams;
1986. 824 p.
85-012406   709   013389388X
Art -- History.

N5300.W82
Wolfflin, Heinrich, 1864-1945.
Principles of art history; the problem of the development
of style in later art. Translated by M. D. Hottinger. [New
York] Dover Publications [194-?] xvi, 237 p.
50-004154   709
Art -- History.

N5301 History —
General works — Illustrations

N5301.J3
Janson, H. W. 1913-
Key monuments of the history of art; a visual survey,
edited by H. W. Janson, with Dora Jane Janson.
Englewood Cliffs, N.J., Prentice-Hall [1959] 1068 p.
59-006934   709
Art -- History.

N5303 History — General special

N5303.E45 1981
Elsen, Albert Edward, 1927-
Purposes of art: an introduction to the history and
appreciation of art/ Albert E. Elsen. New York: Holt,
Rinehart, and Winston, c1981. x, 452 p.
80-026290   709   0030497663
Art -- History. Art -- Themes, motives. Art appreciation.

N5303.H762
Holt, Elizabeth Basye (Gilmore)
A documentary history of art.   Garden City, N.Y.,
Doubleday, [1957-   ]
57-010457   709
Art -- History -- Sources.

N5303.L35 1991
The Language of art history/ edited by Salim Kemal and
Ivan Gaskell. Cambridge [England]; Cambridge
University Press, 1991. x, 245 p.
90-028256   709   052135384X
Art -- History. Object (Aesthetics) Communication in art.

N5303.R68
Rowland, Benjamin, 1904-1972.
The classical tradition in Western art.   Cambridge,
Harvard University Press, 1963. xx, 379 p.
63-017211
Art -- History. Classicism in art.

N5303.S2
Sachs, Curt, 1881-1959.
The commonwealth of art; style in the fine arts, music
and the dance. New York, W. W. Norton & company,
inc. [1946]
46-008437   709
*Art -- History. Music -- History and criticism. Dance --
History.*

N5310 History — Prehistoric art.
Origins of art — General works

N5310.B34 1998
Bahn, Paul G.
The Cambridge illustrated history of prehistoric art/ by
Paul G. Bahn. Cambridge, U.K.; New York: 1998. xxxii,
302 p.
96-051099   709/.01/1   0521454735
Art, Prehistoric.

N5310.C54
Christensen, Erwin Ottomar, 1890-
Primitive art. New York, Crowell [1955] 384 p.
55-011109   709.01
Art, Primitive.

N5310.S32
Sandars, N. K.
Prehistoric art in Europe [by] N. K. Sandars.
Harmondsworth, Penguin, 1968. xlix, 350 p.
79-352957   709/.01/10936
Art, Prehistoric -- Europe. Europe -- Antiquities.

N5310.W764 1949
Windels, Fernand.
The Lascaux Cave paintings/ Fernand Windels; personal
note by Henry Breuil; preface by C.F.C. Hawkes;
introduction by A. Leroi-Gourhan; text prepared in
collaboration with Annette Laming. New York: Viking
Press, c1949. 139 p.
50-009739   571.72
*Cave paintings -- France. Painting, Prehistoric -- France.
Lascaux Cave (France)*

N5310.W766
Wingert, Paul S. 1900-1974.
Primitive art: its traditions and styles/ Paul S. Wingert.
New York: New American Library, 1962. 421 p.
62-020161   709.011   0529019469
Art, Primitive.

N5310.5 History — Prehistoric art. Origins of art — Special continents, regions, countries, etc., A-Z

N5310.5.F7.C4713 1996
Chauvet, Jean-Marie.
Dawn of art: the Chauvet Cave: the oldest known paintings in the world/ Jean-Marie Chauvet, Eliette Brunel Deschamps, and Christian Hillaire; epilogue by Jean Clottes; foreword by Paul G. Bahn; [translated from the French by Paul G. Bahn]. New York: H.N. Abrams, 1996. 135 p.
95-047571 759.01/12/094482 0810932326
Cave paintings -- France -- Vallon-Pont-d'Arc. Art, Prehistoric -- France -- Vallon-Pont-d'Arc. Chauvet Cave (France)

N5335 History — Ancient art. Artistic archaeology — Museums. Collections. Exhibitions

N5335.C56.C566 1996
Mistress of the House, Mistress of Heaven: women in ancient Egypt/ Anne K. Capel and Glenn E. Markoe, editors; essays by Catharine H. Roehrig, Betsy M. Bryan, and Janet H. Johnson; catalogue by Anne K. Capel and Glenn E. Markoe with contributions by Richard A. Fazzini ... [et al.]. New York: Hudson Hills Press in association with Cincinnati Art Museum; [Lanham, MD]: c1996. 235 p.
96-009376 704.9/424/093207477178 1555951295
Women in art -- Exhibitions. Art, Egyptian -- Exhibitions. Art, Ancient -- Egypt -- Exhibitions.

N5345 History — Ancient art. Artistic archaeology — Classic Orient (Egypt and southwestern Asia)

N5345.A7413 1980
Amiet, Pierre.
Art of the ancient Near East/ Pierre Amiet; translated from the French by John Shepley and Claude Choquet; [editor, Naomi Noble Richard]. New York: H. N. Abrams, 1980, c1977. 618 p.
79-004411 709/.39 0810906384
Art, Ancient -- Middle East. Art -- Middle East. Middle East -- Antiquities.

N5345.L55 1961a
Lloyd, Seton.
The art of the ancient Near East. New York, Praeger [1961] 303 p.
61-015605 709.56
Art -- Middle East -- History. Art, Ancient. Art, Asian.

N5350-5390 History — Ancient art. Artistic archaeology — pecial countries and groups of countries

N5350.A586 1961
Aldred, Cyril.
New kingdom art in ancient Egypt: during the eighteenth dynasty; 1570 to 1320 B. C./ by Cyril Aldred. London: A. Tiranti, 1961. v, 93 p.
62-051980 0854588396
Art, Egyptian -- History.

N5350.E37 1999
Egyptian art in the age of the pyramids. New York: Metropolitan Museum of Art: c1999. xxiii, 536 p.
99-022246 709/.32/0747471 0870999060
Art, Egyptian -- Exhibitions. Art, Ancient -- Egypt -- Exhibitions. Egypt -- Antiquities -- Exhibitions.

N5350.E87 2001
Eternal Egypt: masterworks of ancient art from the British Museum/ Edna R. Russmann; preface by W.V. Davies; essays by T.G.H. James and Edna R. Russmann; entries by Carol Andrews ... [et al.]. Berkeley, Calif.: University of California Press; 2001. 288 p.
00-067590 709/.32/07442142 1885444192
Art, Ancient -- Egypt -- Exhibitions. Art -- England -- London -- Exhibitions. Art, Egyptian -- Exhibitions. Egypt -- Antiquities -- Exhibitions.

N5350.R65 1994
Robins, Gay.
Proportion and style in ancient Egyptian art/ by Gay Robins; drawings by Ann S. Fowler. Austin: University of Texas Press, 1994. x, 283 p.
93-000065 709/.32 029277060X
Art, Egyptian. Art, Ancient -- Egypt. Proportion (Art)

N5350.S5
Smith, William Stevenson.
The art and architecture of ancient Egypt. [Harmondsworth, Middlesex] Penguin Books [1958] xxvii, 301 p.
58-003043 709.32
Art, Egyptian. Architecture -- Egypt. Egypt -- Antiquities.

N5350.W49 1992
Wilkinson, Richard H.
Reading Egyptian art: a hieroglyphic guide to ancient Egyptian painting and sculpture/ Richard H. Wilkinson. London: Thames and Hudson, c1992. 224 p.
91-067312 709/.32
Art, Egyptian -- Themes, motives. Art, Ancient -- Egypt -- Themes, motives. Symbolism in art -- Egypt.

N5350.W492 1994
Wilkinson, Richard H.
Symbol & magic in Egyptian art/ Richard H. Wilkinson. New York, N.Y.: Thames and Hudson, 1994. 224 p.
93-060424 704.9/46/0932 0500236631
Art, Egyptian. Symbolism in art.

N5370.M6613
Moortgat, Anton, 1897-
The art of ancient Mesopotamia; the classical art of the Near East. [Translated by Judith Filson] London, Phaidon [1969] x, 356 p.
69-012789   709/.35   0714813710
Art, Assyro-Babylonian. Art, Ancient -- Iraq.   Iraq -- Antiquities.

N5370.P333
Parrot, Andre, 1901-
The arts of Assyria. Translated by Stuart Gilbert and James Emmons. New York, Golden Press [1961] xviii, 383 p.
61-011170   709.35
Art, Assyro-Babylonian. Art -- Iraq.

N5370.P343
Parrot, Andre, 1901-
Sumer: the dawn of art. Translated by Stuart Gilbert and James Emmons. New York: Golden Press, 1961. l, 397 p.
61-006746   709.35
Art, Sumerian -- History.

N5370.S713
Strommenger, Eva.
5000 years of the art of Mesopotamia. Photos. by Max Hirmer. [Translated by Christina Haglund] New York, H. N. Abrams [1964] 480 p.
64-015231   709.35
Art -- Iraq -- History.

N5390.P613
Porada, Edith, 1912-
The art of ancient Iran; pre-Islamic cultures [by] Edith Porada with the collaboration of R. H. Dyson and contributions by C. K. Wilkinson. New York Crown Publishers [1965] 279 p.
65-015839
Art, Iranian -- History.

N5610-5865 History
Ancient art. Artistic archaeology — Classical art

N5610.O5 1999
Onians, John, 1942-
Classical art and the cultures of Greece and Rome/ John Onians. New Haven: Yale University Press, c1999. xiii, 306 p.
98-043738   709/.38   0300075332
Art, Classical. Art and society -- Greece. Art and society -- Rome.

N5630.C45713
Charbonneaux, Jean, 1895-1969.
Archaic Greek art (620-480 B.C.) [by] Jean Charbonneaux, Roland Martin [and] Francois Villard. [Translated from the French by James Emmons [and] Robert Allen. New York, G. Braziller [1971] xi, 437 p.
78-136166   709/.38   0807605875
Art, Greek -- History.

N5630.F85 2000
Fullerton, Mark D.
Greek art/ Mark D. Fullerton. Cambridge; Cambridge University Press, 2000. 176 p.
00-500521   709/.38   0521779731
Art, Greek.

N5630.S65 1997
Spivey, Nigel Jonathan.
Greek art/ Nigel Spivey. London: Phaidon Press, 1997. 447 p.
0714833681
Art, Greek.   Greece -- Antiquities.

N5740.H3
Hanfmann, George Maxim Anossov, 1911-
Roman art; a modern survey of the art of imperial Rome, by George M. A. Hanfmann. Greenwich, Conn., New York Graphic Society [1964] 224 p.
64-021814   709.37
Art, Roman.

N5760.B513
Bianchi Bandinelli, Ranuccio, 1900-1975.
Rome, the center of power, 500 B.C. to A.D. 200. Translated by Peter Green. New York, G. Braziller [1970] xii, 437 p.
70-116985   709/.37   080760559X
Art, Roman.   Rome -- Antiquities.

N5760.K313
Kahler, Heinz.
The art of Rome and her empire. [Translated by J. R. Foster] New York, Crown Publishers [1963, c1962] 262 p.
63-014558   709.37
Art, Roman -- History.

N5760.R45
Richter, Gisela Marie Augusta, 1882-1972.
Ancient Italy; a study of the interrelations of its peoples as shown in their arts.   Ann Arbor, University of Michigan Press, 1955. xxiv, 137 p.
55-010726
Art, Greco-Roman. Art, Greek. Art, Roman.

N5760.W5
Wheeler, Robert Eric Mortimer, 1890-
Roman art and architecture [by] Sir Mortimer Wheeler. New York, F. A. Praeger [1964] 250 p.
64-022933   709.37
Art, Roman.

N5843.T6 1962
Toynbee, J. M. C. d. 1985.
Art in Roman Britain. With 230 illus. from original photos. by Otto Fein. [London] Published by Phaidon Press for the Society for the Promotion of Roman Studies [1962] 219 p.
62-003788   913.42
Art -- Great Britain. Art, Roman.

N5865.A75
Kondoleon, Christine.
Antioch: the lost ancient city/ edited by Christine Kondoleon. Princeton, N.J.: Princeton University Press; c2000. xiii, 253 p.
00-032637   709/.39/43   0691049327
Art, Classical -- Turkey -- Antioch -- Exhibitions. Antioch (Turkey) -- Antiquities -- Exhibitions. Antioch (Turkey) -- Civilization -- Exhibitions.

N5963-5970 History — Medieval art — General works

N5963.K5 1969
Kitzinger, Ernst, 1912-
Early medieval art in the British Museum. London, British Museum, 1969. x, 115 p.
76-391330   709.021   0714113271
Art, Medieval.

N5970.B4
Beckwith, John, 1918-
Early medieval art. New York, Praeger [1964] 270 p.
64-019953   709/.02/1
Art, Medieval -- History.

N5970.C34 1979
Calkins, Robert G.
Monuments of medieval art/ Robert G. Calkins. New York: Dutton, c1979. xx, 299 p.
78-075288   709/.02   0525159320
Art, Medieval.

N5970.D64 1993
Dodwell, C. R.
The pictorial arts of the West, 800-1200/ C.R. Dodwell. New Haven: Yale University Press, 1993. 461 p.
92-032502   709/.02/1   0300053487
Art, Medieval.

N5970.D8313
Duby, Georges.
The age of the cathedrals: art and society, 980-1420/ Georges Duby; translated by Eleanor Levieux and Barbara Thompson. Chicago: University of Chicago Press, c1981. v, 312 p.
80-022769   701/.03   0226167690
Art, Medieval. Art and society. Civilization, Medieval.

N5970.H813
Huyghe, Rene,
Larousse encyclopedia of Byzantine and medieval art. New York, Prometheus Press [1963] 416 p.
63-012755   709.02
Art, Medieval -- History. Art, Byzantine -- History. Art -- History.

N5970.M6
Morey, Charles Rufus, 1877-1955.
Mediaeval art [by] Charles Rufus Morey. New York, W. W. Norton & company, inc. [1942] xv, 412 p.
42-051542   709.02
Art, Medieval.

N5975 History — Medieval art — General special

N5975.S58 1989
Snyder, James.
Medieval art: painting-sculpture-architecture, 4th-14th century/ James Snyder. New York: H.N. Abrams, 1989. 511 p.
88-010394   709/.02   0810915324
Art, Medieval. Christian art and symbolism -- Medieval, 500-1500.

N6245-6320 History — Medieval art — Special types

N6245.H813
Hubert, Jean, 1902-
The Carolingian renaissance [by] J. Hubert, J. Porcher [and] W. F. Volbach. New York, G. Braziller [1970] xi, 380 p.
72-099513   709/.4
Art, Carolingian. Art, Medieval -- France. Architecture, Carolingian.

N6250.A613 1961
Ainalov, D. V. 1862-1939
The Hellenistic origins of Byzantine art. Translated from the Russian by Elizabeth Sobolevitch and Serge Sobolevitch. Edited by Cyril Mango New Brunswick, N.J., Rutgers University Press [1961] xv, 322 p.
61-010252
Hellenism Art, Byzantine

N6250.B76 1991
Brend, Barbara, 1940-
Islamic art/ Barbara Brend. Cambridge, Mass.: Harvard University Press, 1991. 240 p.
90-025589   709/.17/671   0674468651
Art, Islamic -- History.

N6250.G6713
Grabar, Andre, 1896-
The golden age of Justinian, from the death of Theodosius to the rise of Islam. Translated by Stuart Gilbert and James Emmons. New York, Odyssey Press [1967] 408 p.
66-029363   709.02/1
Art, Byzantine -- History.

N6250.M33 1998
Mathews, Thomas F.
Byzantium: from antiquity to the Renaissance/ Thomas Mathews. New York: Abrams, 1998.
97-042413   709/.02/14   0810927004
Art, Byzantine.

N6250.R46 1959a
Rice, David Talbot, 1903-1972.
The art of Byzantium/ text and notes by David Talbot Rice, photographs by Max Hirmer. London: Thames and Hudson, c1959. 348 p.
60-001215   709.02
Art, Byzantine. Art -- Turkey -- Istanbul.

N6260.B57 1997
Bloom, Jonathan
Islamic arts/ Jonathan Bloom and Sheila Blair. London:
Phaidon Press, 1997. 447 p.
97-202635   071483176X
Art, Islamic. Architecture, Islamic.

N6260.K7783 1966
Kuhnel, Ernst, 1882-1964,
Islamic art & architecture. Translated by Katherine
Watson. Ithaca, N.Y., Cornell University Press [1966]
200 p.
66-019223   704.94897
Art, Islamic -- History. Architecture, Islamic -- History.

N6263.W3.A785 1991
Islamic art & patronage: treasures from Kuwait/ edited by
Esin Atil. New York: Rizzoli, c1990. 313 p.
90-028571   709/.17/67107473   0847813665
Sabah, Nasser Sabah al-Ahmad -- Art collections -- Exhibitions.
Sabah, Hussah -- Art collections -- Exhibitions. Art, Islamic --
Exhibitions. Art -- Private collections -- Kuwait -- Exhibitions.

N6280.F613 1969
Focillon, Henri, 1881-1943.
The art of the West in the Middle Ages; edited and
introduced by Jean Bony; [translated from the French by
Donald King]. London, Phaidon, 1969. 2 v.
71-444367   709/.4   0714813524
Art, Romanesque. Art, Medieval. Art, Gothic.

N6310.C36 1996
Camille, Michael.
Gothic art: glorious visions/ Michael Camille. New York:
Harry N. Abrams, 1996. 192 p.
96-003899   709.02/2   0810927012
Art, Gothic. Gothic revival (Art)

N6310.D813
Dvorak, Max, 1874-1921.
Idealism and naturalism in Gothic art. Translated with
notes and bibliography by Randolph J. Klawiter. Pref. by
Karl Maria Swoboda. [Notre Dame, Ind.] University of
Notre Dame Press, 1967. xxx, 252 p.
67-022143   709.02
Idealism in art. Naturalism in art. Art, Gothic.

N6310.F7
Frisch, Teresa Grace.
Gothic art 1140-c. 1450; sources and documents [by]
Teresa G. Frisch. Englewood Cliffs, N.J., Prentice-Hall
[1971] x, 181 p.
77-135403   709.02/2   0133605450
Art, Gothic -- History -- Sources. Art, Medieval -- Sources.

N6310.W6 1964a
Worringer, Wilhelm, 1881-1965.
Form in Gothic. Authorized translation edited with an
introd. by Sir Herbert Read. Containing the original illus.
New York, Schocken [1964, c1957] xv, 181 p.
64-004440
Architecture, Gothic. Aesthetics. Art, Gothic.

N6320.S92 1977b
Swaan, Wim.
The late Middle Ages: art and architecture from 1350 to
the advent of the Renaissance/ Wim Swaan; with photos.
by the author. Ithaca, N.Y.: Cornell University Press,
1977. 232 p.
77-077552   709/.02/3   0801411416
Art, Late Gothic. Architecture, Medieval. Architecture, Gothic.

N6350 History — Modern art — General works

N6350.A7
Artz, Frederick Binkerd, 1894-
From the Renaissance to romanticism; trends in style in
art, literature, and music, 1300-1830.   [Chicago]
University of Chicago Press [1962] 311 p.
62-020021   901.93
Arts -- History. Renaissance. Romanticism.

N6350.G76 2000
The Grove dictionary of art.   styles and movements in
western art, 1400-1900/ edited by Jane Turner. New
York, NY: St. Martin's Press, 2000. xii, 377 p.
99-089533   709 21   0312229755
Art, Modern -- Encyclopedias.

N6350.H35 1976
Harris, Ann Sutherland.
Women artists, 1550-1950/ Ann Sutherland Harris, Linda
Nochlin. Los Angeles: Los Angeles County Museum of
Art; 1976. 368 p.
76-039955   709/.03/074019494   0875870732
Art, Modern -- Exhibitions. Women artists.

N6350.H813
Huyghe, Rene.
Larousse encyclopedia of Renaissance and Baroque art.
New York, Prometheus Press [1964] 444 p.
64-013787   709.03
Art, Renaissance -- History Art, Baroque -- History.

N6350.P4 1968b
Pevsner, Nikolaus, 1902-
Studies in art, architecture, and design.   New York,
Walker [1968] 2 v.
68-027371   709.03
Art, Modern.

N6350.S9
Sypher, Wylie.
Rococo to Cubism in art and literature.   New York,
Random House [1960] 353 p.
60-008373   709
Arts -- History. Rococo literature.

N6370-6494 History — Modern art — By century

N6370.A58 2000
Ames-Lewis, Francis, 1943-
The intellectual life of the early Renaissance artist/ Francis Ames-Lewis. New Haven: Yale University Press, c2000. x, 322 p.
99-086289   709/.02/4   0300083041
Artists -- Europe -- Intellectual life -- 15th century. Artists -- Europe -- Intellectual life -- 16th century. Art, Renaissance.

N6370.E27 1987
Earls, Irene.
Renaissance art: a topical dictionary/ Irene Earls. New York: Greenwood Press, 1987. xv, 345 p.
87-000250   709/.02/4   0313246580
Art, Renaissance -- Italy -- Dictionaries. Art, Renaissance -- Europe, Northern -- Dictionaries. Artists -- Biography -- Dictionaries.

N6370.H25 1990
Hale, J. R. 1923-
Artists and warfare in the Renaissance/ J.R. Hale. New Haven: Yale University Press, 1990. ix, 278 p.
90-012295   760/.09/024   0300048408
Art, Renaissance. Art and war.

N6370.P3 1962
Panofsky, Erwin, 1892-1968.
Studies in iconology; humanistic themes in the art of the Renaissance. New York, Harper & Row [1962] xliii, 262 p.
62-006203   709.03
Art, Renaissance. Humanism.

N6370.R36 1995
Reframing the Renaissance: visual culture in Europe and Latin America, 1450-1650/ edited with an introduction by Claire Farago. New Haven: Yale University Press, c1995. x, 394 p.
95-012148   709/.02/4   0300062958
Art, Renaissance. Art, Colonial -- Latin America -- Foreign influences. Art, Latin American -- Foreign influences.

N6370.S48 1967
Shearman, John K. G.
Mannerism [by] John Shearman. Harmondsworth, Penguin, 1967. 216 p.
67-098470   709.03/1
Mannerism (Art)

N6370.S6 1985
Snyder, James.
Northern Renaissance art: painting, sculpture, the graphic arts from 1350 to 1575/ James Snyder. New York: Abrams, 1985. 559 p.
84-011435   709/.02/4   0136235964
Art, Renaissance -- Europe, Northern. Art -- Europe, Northern.

N6370.S95
Sypher, Wylie.
Four stages of Renaissance style; transformations in art and literature, 1400-1700. Garden City, N.Y., Doubleday, 1955. 312 p.
55-006749   709.03
Arts, Renaissance.

N6410.A713
Argan, Giulio Carlo.
The Europe of the capitals, 1600-1700. Translated from the Italian by Anthony Rhodes. Geneva Skira; [distributed in the U.S. by World Pub. Co., Cleveland, [1965, c1964] 222 p.
64-023257   709.033
Art, Baroque. Art and society. Art, Modern -- 17th-18th centuries -- History.

N6415.B3.B313 1968b
Bazin, Germain.
The baroque: principles, styles, modes, themes. [Translation by Pat Wardroper] Greenwich, Conn., New York Graphic Society [c1968] 368 p.
68-025737   709/.03/2
Art, Baroque.

N6415.B3.H4
Held, Julius Samuel, 1905-
17th and 18th century art; baroque painting, sculpture, architecture [by] Julius S. Held [and] Donald Posner. New York, H. N. Abrams [1971] 439 p.
79-127417   709/.03/2   0810900327
Art, Baroque. Art, Modern -- 17th-18th centuries.

N6415.B3.M37 1977b
Martin, John Rupert.
Baroque/ John Rupert Martin. New York: Harper & Row, c1977. 367 p.
77-156098   709/.03/2   006435332X
Art, Baroque -- History.

N6415.B3.S4
Sewter, A. C.
Baroque and rococo [by] A. C. Sewter. [New York] Harcourt Brace Jovanovich [1972] 224 p.
73-152765   709/.03/2   0155048902
Art, Baroque. Art, Rococo.

N6425.N4.B6 1987
Boime, Albert.
Art in an age of revolution, 1750-1800/ Albert Boime. Chicago: University of Chicago Press, 1987. xxvii, 521 p.
87-005944   709/.03/3   0226063321
Art and revolutions. Neoclassicism (Art) Art, Modern -- 17th-18th centuries.

N6425.N4.E35
Eitner, Lorenz,
Neoclassicism and romanticism, 1750-1850; sources and documents [compiled by] Lorenz Eitner. Englewood Cliffs, N.J., Prentice-Hall [1970] 2 v.
74-094425   709/.03/41   0136109071
Neoclassicism (Art) Romanticism in art.

N6425.N4.R65 1984
Rosenblum, Robert.
19th century art/ painting by Robert Rosenblum, sculpture by H.W. Janson. New York: Abrams, 1984. 527 p.
83-003882   709/.03/4   0810913623
Neoclassicism (Art) Art, Modern -- 19th century.

N6447.C36 1981
Canaday, John, 1907-
Mainstreams of modern art/ John Canaday. New York: Holt, Rinehart and Winston, c1981. xii, 484 p.
80-025696   709/.03/4   0030576385
Art, Modern -- 19th century. Art, Modern -- 20th century.

N6447.D86
Dunlop, Ian, 1940-
The shock of the new; seven historic exhibitions of modern art. New York, American Heritage Press [1972] 272 p.
77-039481   709/.04/074   0070182671
Art, Modern -- 19th century -- Exhibitions -- History. Art, Modern -- 20th century -- Exhibitions -- History. Art and society.

N6447.H83 1981
Hughes, Robert, 1938-
The Shock of the new/ Robert Hughes. New York: Knopf: 1981, c1980. 423 p.
80-007631   709/.04   0394513789
Art, Modern -- 19th century. Art, Modern -- 20th century.

N6447.M88 1992
Museum of Modern Art (New York, N.Y.)
The William S. Paley collection/ William Rubin, Matthew Armstrong. New York: Museum of Modern Art: c1992. xi, 180 p.
91-061563   709/.04/00747471
Paley, William S. -- (William Samuel), -- 1901- -- Art collections -- Exhibitions. Art, Modern -- 19th century -- Exhibitions. Art -- Private collections -- New York (State) -- New York -- Exhibitions. Art, Modern -- 20th century -- Exhibitions.

N6447.R87 1981
Russell, John, 1919-
The meanings of modern art/ John Russell. New York: Museum of Modern Art: c1981. 429 p.
80-008217   709/.04   0060137010
Art, Modern -- 19th century. Art, Modern -- 20th century.

N6447.S33
Schapiro, Meyer, 1904-
Modern art, 19th & 20th centuries/ Meyer Schapiro. New York: G. Braziller, 1978, 1979. xi, 277 p.
78-006831   709/.04   0807608998
Art, Modern -- 19th century. Art, Modern -- 20th century.

N6447.V37 1990
Varnedoe, Kirk, 1946-
A fine disregard: what makes modern art modern/ Kirk Varnedoe. New York: H.N. Abrams, c1990. 319 p.
89-018074   709/.04   0810931060
Art, Modern -- 19th century. Art, Modern -- 20th century.

N6447.W3 1992
Watson, Peter.
From Manet to Manhattan: the rise of the modern art market/ Peter Watson. New York: Random House, c1992. xxviii, 558 p.
92-005138   709/.04   0679404724
Art, Modern -- 19th century -- Marketing. Art, Modern -- 20th century -- Marketing. Art auctions.

N6450.B52
Brion, Marcel, 1895-
Romantic art. New York: McGraw-Hill, [1960] 240 p.
60-012761   709.035
Romanticism in art. Art -- History. Painting.

N6450.C7 1940
Craven, Thomas, 1889-
Modern art: the men, the movements, the meaning. New York: Simon and Schuster, 1940. xxii, 387 p.
40-007043   709.03
Art, Modern -- 19th century -- History. Art, Modern -- 20th century -- History. Artists.

N6450.E39 1994
Eisenman, Stephen.
Nineteenth century art: a critical history/ Stephen F. Eisenman; Thomas Crow ... [et al.]. New York: Thames and Hudson, 1994. 376 p.
93-061271   709/.03/4   0500236755
Art, Modern -- History -- 19th century. Art, Modern -- 19th century.

N6450.G23
Galassi, Peter.
Before photography: painting and the invention of photography/ Peter Galassi. New York: Museum of Modern Art; c1981. 151 p.
81-080568   760/.09/034074013   0870702548
Art, Modern -- 19th century -- Exhibitions. Art and photography -- Exhibitions. Photography, Artistic -- Exhibitions.

N6450.H29
Hamilton, George Heard.
19th and 20th century art: painting, sculpture, architecture. New York, H. N. Abrams [1970] 483 p.
70-100401   709.04   0810903466
Art, Modern -- 19th century. Art, Modern -- 20th century.

N6450.H62 1980
Holt, Elizabeth Basye Gilmore.
The triumph of art for the public: the emerging role of exhibitions and critics/ selected and edited by Elizabeth Gilmore Holt. Washington, D.C.: Decatur House Press, c1980. xxviii, 530 p.
80-013208   709/.03/4   0916276082
Art, Modern -- 19th century. Art -- Exhibitions. Art exhibition audiences.

N6450.R46
Reynolds, Donald M.
The nineteenth century/ Donald Martin Reynolds. Cambridge [Cambrideshire]; Cambridge University Press, 1985. vi, 138 p.
82-004381   709/.03/4   0521298695
Art, Modern -- 19th century.

N6460 1900.R68 2000
Rosenblum, Robert.
1900: art at the crossroads/ Robert Rosenblum, MaryAnne Stevens, Ann Dumas. New York: Harry N. Abrams, 2000. 445 p.
99-069361   0810943034
Art, Modern -- 19th century -- Themes, motives -- Exhibitions.

N6465.P74.R48 1994
Rhodes, Colin.
Primitivism and modern art/ Colin Rhodes. New York: Thames and Hudson, 1994. 216 p.
94-060286   709/.04   0500202761
Primitivism in art. Art, Modern -- 19th century. Art, Modern -- 20th century.

N6465.S9.D4413
Delevoy, Robert L.
Symbolists and symbolism/ by Robert L. Delevoy; [translated from the French by Barbara Bray, Elizabeth Wrightson, and Bernard C. Swift]. New York: Skira, 1978. 247 p.
77-079717   700/.94   0847801411
Symbolism (Art movement) Art, Modern -- 19th century.

N6487.N4.M85 1984
McShine, Kynaston.
An international survey of recent painting and sculpture/ Kynaston McShine; [edited by Harriet Schoenholz Bee and Jane Fluegel]. New York: Museum of Modern Art, 1984. 364 p.
84-192888   709/.04/807401471   0870703919
Art, Modern -- 20th century -- Exhibitions.

N6489.L83 1999
Lucie-Smith, Edward.
Lives of the great 20th-century artists/ Edward Lucie-Smith. New York: Thames and Hudson, 1999. 352 p.
98-075076   709/.2/2   0500237395
Artists -- Biography. Art, Modern -- 20th century.

N6490.A612 1994
Altshuler, Bruce.
The avant-garde in exhibition: new art in the 20th century/ Bruce Altshuler. New York: Abrams, 1994. 288 p.
93-034281   709/.04   0810936372
Avant-garde (Aesthetics) -- History -- 20th century -- Exhibitions -- History. Art, Modern -- 20th century -- Exhibitions -- History.

N6490.A669 1997
Archer, Michael.
Art since 1960/ Michael Archer. London; Thames and Hudson, 1997. 224 p.
96-061018   0500202982
Art, Modern -- 20th century -- History.

N6490.A713 1986b
Arnason, H. Harvard.
History of modern art: painting, sculpture, architecture/ H.H. Arnason. Englewood Cliffs, N.J.: Prentice-Hall; 1986. 744 p.
86-003411   709/.04   0133903605
Art, Modern -- 20th century.

N6490.C584 1999
Clark, T. J.
Farewell to an idea: episodes from a history of modernism/ T.J. Clark. New Haven: Yale University Press, c1999. vii, 451 p.
98-049433   709/.04   0300075324
Modernism (Art)

N6490.C6567 1983
Contemporary artists/ Muriel Emanuel ... [et al.], editors. New York: St. Martin's Press, 1983. vii, 1041 p.
82-025048   709/.2/2   0312166435
Art, Modern -- 20th century. Artists -- Biography.

N6490.D377 1989
Deconstruction: omnibus volume/ edited by Andreas Papadakis, Catherine Cooke, & Andrew Benjamin. New York: Rizzoli, 1989. 264 p.
89-003611   709/.04   0847810631
Art, Modern -- 20th century -- Themes, motives. Art -- Philosophy. Deconstruction.

N6490.F727 1998
Fried, Michael.
Art and objecthood: essays and reviews/ Michael Fried. Chicago: University of Chicago Press, 1998. xviii, 333 p.
97-014836   709/.04   0226263185
Art, Modern -- 20th century. Art.

N6490.H45
Herbert, Robert L., 1929-
Modern artists on art; ten unabridged essays, edited by Robert L. Herbert. Englewood Cliffs, N.J., Prentice-Hall [1965, c1964] ix, 149 p.
64-007568   709.04
Art, Modern -- 20th century -- Addresses, essays, lectures.

N6490.J3 1967
Janis, Harriet (Grossman)
Collage: personalities, concepts [and] techniques [by] Harriet Janis and Rudi Blesh. Philadelphia, Chilton Book Co. [1967] 342 p.
67-005494   751.4/9
Collage.

N6490.K4
Kepes, Gyorgy, 1906-
The visual arts today.   Middletown, Conn., Wesleyan University Press [1960] 272 p.
60-013159   709.04
Art, Modern -- 20th century -- Addresses, essays, lectures. Art -- Philosophy.

N6490.K553 1966
Klee, Paul, 1879-1940.
On modern art; translated [from the German] by Paul Findlay with an introd. by Herbert Read. London, Faber, 1966. 55 p.
71-356501   709.04   0571066828
Modernism (Art)

N6490.K727 1985
Krauss, Rosalind E.
The originality of the avant-garde and other modernist myths/ Rosalind E. Krauss. Cambridge, Mass.: MIT Press, c1985. 307 p.
84-011315   709/.04   0262110938
Avant-garde (Aesthetics) -- History -- 20th century. Modernism (Art) -- Themes, motives. Creation (Literary, artistic, etc.) -- Psychological aspects.

N6490.K86 1993
Kuspit, Donald B. 1935-
The cult of the avant-garde artist/ Donald Kuspit. Cambridge; Cambridge University Press, 1993. 175 p.
92-001733   701   0521413451
Avant-garde (Aesthetics) -- History -- 20th century. Art, Modern -- 20th century.

N6490.K87 1988
Kuspit, Donald B. 1935-
The new subjectivism: art in the 1980s/ by Donald Kuspit; with a foreword by Diane Waldman. Ann Arbor: UMI Research Press, c1988. xxiv, 578 p.
88-012224   709/.04/8   0835718883
Art, Modern -- 20th century -- Themes, motives. Art, Modern -- 20th century -- Psychological aspects.

N6490.L792 1997
Lucie-Smith, Edward.
Visual arts in the twentieth century/ Edward Lucie-Smith. New York: Harry N. Abrams, 1997. 400 p.
96-018460   709/.04   0810939347
Art, Modern -- 20th century.

N6490.L93 1980b
Lynton, Norbert.
The story of modern art/ Norbert Lynton. Ithaca, N.Y.: Cornell University Press, 1980. 382 p.
80-067606   709/.04   0801413516
Art, Modern -- 20th century -- History.

N6490.N374 1968
Museum of Modern Art (New York, N.Y.)
Fantastic art, dada, surrealism. Edited by Alfred H. Barr, Jr. Essays by Georges Hugnet. New York, Museum of Modern Art. [New York] Published for the Museum of Modern Art by Arno Press, 1968 [c1947] 271 p.
68-008367   709.04
Dadaism. Surrealism. Fantasy in art.

N6490.N38
Museum of Modern Art (New York, N.Y.)
Masters of modern art; edited by Alfred H. Barr, Jr. New York, Distributed by Simon and Schuster [1954] 239 p.
54-013277   709.04
Art, Modern -- 20th century.

N6490.O94
The Oxford companion to twentieth-century art/ edited by Harold Osborne. Oxford; Oxford University Press, 1981. x, 656 p.
82-126560   709/.04/00321   0198661193
Art, Modern -- 20th century -- Dictionaries. Artists -- Biography -- Dictionaries.

N6490.P3234
Parry, Pamela Jeffcott.
Contemporary art and artists: an index to reproductions/ compiled by Pamela Jeffcott Parry. Westport, Conn.: Greenwood Press, 1978. xlix, 327 p.
78-057763   709/.04   0313205442
Art, Modern -- 20th century -- Indexes. Artists -- Indexes.

N6490.R4 1960
Read, Herbert Edward, 1893-
Art now; an introduction to the theory of modern painting and sculpture. New York, Pitman [1960] 131 p.
61-019203   709.04
Art -- History -- 20th century. Aesthetics -- Modern -- 20th century.

N6490.R592
Rosenberg, Harold, 1906-1978.
Artworks and packages.   New York, Horizon Press [1969] 232 p.
68-054185   709/.04
Art, Modern -- 20th century. Art -- Technique.

N6490.R77
Rubin, William Stanley.
Dada, Surrealism, and their heritage, by William S. Rubin. New York, Museum of Modern Art; distributed by New York Graphic Society, Greenwich, Conn. [1968] 251 p.
68-017466   709.04
Dadaism. Surrealism. Art, Modern -- 20th century -- Exhibitions.

N6490.S37
Selz, Peter Howard, 1919-
Art nouveau; art and design at the turn of the century, edited by Peter Selz and Mildred Constantine, with articles by Greta Daniel [and others] New York, Museum of Modern Art; [1960, c1959] 192 p.
60-011987   709.04
Art nouveau.

N6490.S7825 2000
Storr, Robert.
Modern art despite modernism/ Robert Storr. New York: Museum of Modern Art: 2000. 247 p.
00-130299   709/.04/00747471   0810962071
Art, Modern -- 20th century -- Exhibitions.

N6490.T365 1995
Taylor, Brandon.
Avant-garde and after: rethinking art now/ Brandon Taylor. New York: H.N. Abrams, c1995. 176 p.
95-079738   709/.04   0810927071
Postmodernism. Art, Modern -- 20th century. Art and society.

N6490.Z365 1996
Zayas, Marius de.
How, when, and why modern art came to New York/ Marius de Zayas; edited by Francis M. Naumann. Cambridge, Mass.: MIT Press, c1996. xiv, 260 p.
95-049910   709/.747/109041   0262041537
Art, Modern -- 20th century -- Marketing. Art patronage -- New York (State) -- New York. Art appreciation -- New York (State) -- New York.

N6494.A66
Morphet, Richard
Encounters: new art from old/ Richard Morphet; introduction by Robert Rosenblum; contributions by Judith Bumpus ... [et al.]. London: National Gallery Co., 2000. 336 p.
00-102773   709/.04/07442132   0300084811
Appropriation (Art) -- Exhibitions. Art, Modern -- 20th century -- Exhibitions. Appropriation (Art) -- Expositions

N6494.A7.A65
Arwas, Victor.
Art deco/ Victor Arwas; [editor, Frank Russell]. New York: Abrams, 1980. 315 p.
80-012363   709/.04/012   0810906910
Art deco. Art, Modern -- 20th century.

N6494.C6.P6 1992
Poggi, Christine, 1953-
In defiance of painting: cubism, futurism, and the invention of collage/ Christine Poggi. New Haven: Yale University Press, c1992. xv, 312 p.
91-037317   709/.04   0300051093
Collage. Art, Modern -- 20th century.

N6494.C6.W35 1992
Waldman, Diane.
Collage, assemblage, and the found object/ Diane Waldman. New York: H.N. Abrams, [1992] 336 p.
92-000287   709/.04   0810931834
Collage. Assemblage (Art) Found objects (Art)

N6494.C8.N4 1966
New York.
Cubism and abstract art, by Alfred H. Barr, Jr. New York, Published for the Museum of Modern Art by Arno Press, 1966 [c1936] 249 p.
66-026123   709.04
Cubism. Art, Abstract.

N6494.C8.R67 1976b
Rosenblum, Robert.
Cubism and twentieth-century art/ Robert Rosenblum. New York: H. N. Abrams, [1976?] 346 p.
80-488131   709/.04/032   0810907674
Cubism. Art, Modern -- 20th century.

N6494.E27.B4 1984
Beardsley, John.
Earthworks and beyond: contemporary art in the landscape/ John Beardsley. New York: Abbeville Press, c1984. 144 p.
83-021424   709/.04/076   089659422X
Earthworks (Art) Avant-garde (Aesthetics) -- 20th century.

N6494.F3.E42
Elderfield, John.
The "wild beasts": Fauvism and its affinities/ John Elderfield. New York: Museum of Modern Art: distributed by Oxford University Press, c1976. 167 p.
76-001491   759.4   087070639X
Fauvism -- Exhibitions. Art, Modern -- 20th century -- Exhibitions.

N6494.M64.G65 1994
Golding, John.
Visions of the modern/ John Golding. Berkeley: University of California Press, 1994. 368 p.
93-041275   709/.04   0520087917
Modernism (Art) Art, Modern -- 20th century.

N6494.M64.M36 1997
Margolin, Victor, 1941-
The struggle for utopia: Rodchenko, Lissitzky, Moholy-Nagy, 1917-1946/ Victor Margolin. Chicago: University of Chicago Press, 1997. xiii, 261 p.
96-034090   709/.04/1   0226505154
Rodchenko, Aleksandr Mikhailovich, -- 1891-1956 -- Philosophy. Lissitzky, El, -- 1890-1941 -- Philosophy. Moholy-Nagy, Laszlo, -- 1895-1946 -- Philosophy. Modernism (Art) Avant-garde (Aesthetics) -- History -- 20th century. Art and society -- History -- 20th century.

N6494.P6.L58 1990
Livingstone, Marco.
Pop art: a continuing history/ Marco Livingstone. New York: H.N. Abrams, 1990. 271 p.
90-000099   709/.04/071   0810937077
Pop art -- History. Art, Modern -- 20th century -- History.

N6494.P66.J67 1996
Josephson, Susan G.
From idolatry to advertising: visual art and contemporary culture/ Susan G. Josephson. Armonk, N.Y.: M.E. Sharpe, c1996. xv, 240 p.
94-045412   701   1563248751
Postmodernism -- Philosophy. Popular culture. Art and technology.

N6494.P7.H37 1993
Harrison, Charles, 1942-
Primitivism, cubism, abstraction: the early twentieth century/ Charles Harrison, Francis Frascina, Gill Perry. New Haven: Yale University Press, in association with the Open University, 1993. 270 p.
92-050988   709/.04/1   0300055153
Primitivism in art. Cubism. Art, Abstract.

N6494.P7.P75 1984
"Primitivism" in 20th century art: affinity of the tribal and the modern/ edited by William Rubin. New York: Museum of Modern Art; c1984. 2 v.
84-060915   709/.04   0870705180
Primitivism in art. Art, Modern -- 20th century.

N6494.R4.F47 1993
Fer, Briony.
Realism, rationalism, surrealism: art between the wars/ Briony Fer, David Batchelor, Paul Wood. New Haven: Yale University Press, in association with the Open University, 1993. 342 p.
92-050987   709/.04/1   0300055188
Realism in art. Constructivism (Art) Surrealism.

N6494.S8.C313
Carra, Massimo, 1922-
Metaphysical art [compiled by] Massimo Carra, with Patrick Waldberg and Ewald Rathke. Translation and historical foreword by Caroline Tisdall. New York, Praeger Publishers [1971] 216 p.
79-116640   750/.1
Surrealism.

N6494.S8.R8
Rubin, William Stanley.
Dada and surrealist art [by] William S. Rubin. New York, H. N. Abrams [1968] 525 p.
68-013064   709/.04
Dadaism. Surrealism.

N6501 History — Special countries

N6501.G64 1994
Goldman, Shifra M.,
Dimensions of the Americas: art and social change in Latin America and the United States/ Shifra M. Goldman. Chicago: University of Chicago Press, 1994. xxiv, 494 p.
94-007458   701/.03/097 20   0226301249
Art, Latin American -- 20th century. Hispanic American art -- 20th century. Art and society -- America -- History -- 20th century.

N6501.I42 1993
Imagery & creativity: ethnoaesthetics and art worlds in the Americas/ edited by Dorothea S. Whitten and Norman E. Whitten, Jr. Tucson: University of Arizona Press, c1993. 377 p.
92-025853   700/.89/97   0816512477
Ethnic art -- America. Ethnic art -- South America.

N6502-6620 History — Special countries — America

N6502.E53 2000
Encyclopedia of Latin American & Caribbean art/ edited by Jane Turner. New York: Grove's Dictionaries, [2000?] xx, 782 p.
99-041595   709/.8/03 21   1884446043
Art, Latin American -- Encyclopedias. Art, Caribbean -- Encyclopedias.

N6502.S367 1999
Scott, John F. 1936-
Latin American art: ancient to modern/ John F. Scott. Gainesville: University Press of Florida, c1999. xxiv, 240 p.
98-046535   709/.8   0813016452
Art, Latin American.

N6502.4.A3 1989
Ades, Dawn.
Art in Latin America: the modern era, 1820-1980/ Dawn Ades; with contributions by Guy Brett, Staton Loomis Catlin, and Rosemary O'Neill. New Haven: Yale University Press, 1989. xxii, 361 p.
89-050603   709/.8/09034   0300045565
Art, Latin American. Art, Modern -- 19th century -- Latin America. Art, Modern -- 20th century -- Latin America.

N6502.5.B3 1989
Baddeley, Oriana, 1954-
Drawing the line: art and cultural identity in contemporary Latin America/ Oriana Baddeley and Valerie Fraser. London; Verso, 1989. viii, 164 p.
89-030197   700/.1/03098   0860912396
Art, Latin American. Art, Modern -- 20th century -- Latin America. Art and society -- Latin America.

N6502.5.B36 2001
Barnitz, Jacqueline.
Twentieth-century art of Latin America/ Jacqueline Barnitz. Austin: University of Texas Press, 2001. 400 p.
99-050871   709/.8/0904   0292708572
Art, Latin American -- 20th century.

N6502.5.B74 1990
Brett, Guy.
Transcontinental: an investigation of reality: nine Latin American artists, Waltercio Caldas .../ Guy Brett; with texts by the artists, Lu Menezes and Paulo Venancio Filho. London; Verso, 1990. 112 p.
90-206918   709/.8/09048   0860915115
Art, Latin American. Art, Modern -- 20th century -- Latin America.

N6502.5.L374 1996
Latin American art in the twentieth century/ edited by Edward J. Sullivan. London: Phaidon Press, [c1996] 352 p.
99-170685   709/.8/0904   0714832103
Art, Latin American. Art, Modern -- 20th century -- Latin America.

N6502.5.L38 1993
Latin American artists of the twentieth century/ edited by Waldo Rasmussen with Fatima Bercht and Elizabeth Ferrer. New York: The Museum of Modern Art, c1993. 424 p.
93-078095   0870704311
Art, Latin American -- Exhibitions. Art, Modern -- 20th century -- Latin America -- Exhibitions.

N6502.5.L83 1993
Lucie-Smith, Edward.
Latin American art of the 20th century/ Edward Lucie-Smith. New York: Thames and Hudson, c1993. 216 p.
92-070861   709/.8/0904   0500202605
Art, Latin American. Art, Modern -- 20th century -- Latin America.

N6502.57.M63.F57 1992
Fletcher, Valerie J.
Crosscurrents of modernism: four Latin American pioneers: Diego Rivera, Joaquin Torres-Garcia, Wifredo Lam, Matta = Intercambios del modernismo: cuatro precursores latinoamericanos: Diego Rivera Valerie Fletcher with essays by Olivier Debroise ... [et al.]; [English translations by James Oles, Margaret Sayers Peden, and Eliot Weinberger; Spanish translations by Carlos Banales and Carlos Tripodi]. Washington, D.C.: Hirshhorn Museum and Sculpture Garden in association with the Smithsonian Institution Press, c1992. 295 p.
92-010029   709/.8/074753   1560982055
Art, Latin American -- Exhibitions. Modernism (Art) -- Latin America -- Exhibitions. Art, Modern -- 20th century -- Latin America -- Exhibitions.

N6503.N67 1995
North American women artists of the twentieth century: a biographical dictionary/ edited by Jules Heller and Nancy G. Heller. New York: Garland, 1995. xxii, 612 p.
94-049710   709/.2/2   0824060490
Women artists -- North America -- Biography -- Dictionaries.

N6505.C7 1994
Craven, Wayne.
American art: history and culture/ Wayne Craven. Madison, Wis.: Brown & Benchmark, c1994. 687 p.
93-071038   709/.73
Art, American.

N6505.D65
Dorra, Henri, 1924-
The American muse. Foreword by Hermann Warner Williams, Jr. New York, Viking Press [1961] 163 p.
61-006664   709.73
Art, American -- History. American literature. Art and literature.

N6505.H35 1994
Haubenstock, Susan H.
Career opportunities in art/ Susan H. Haubenstock and David Joselit. Rev. ed. New York: Facts on File, c1994. xiv, 191 p.
93-043591   702/.3/73 20   0816028907
Art--Vocational guidance -- United States.

N6505.H84 1997
Hughes, Robert, 1938-
American visions: the epic history of art in America/ by Robert Hughes. New York: Alfred A. Knopf, 1997. ix, 635 p.
96-045111   709/.73   0679426272
Art, American -- Themes, motives.

N6505.K56 1992
Kloss, William.
Art in the White House: a nation's pride/ William Kloss; Doreen Bolger ... [et al.]. Washington, D.C.: White House Historical Association in cooperation with the National Geographic Society; New York: Distibuted by H.N. Abrams, c1992. 375 p.
91-068463   708.153   0810939657
Art, European -- Catalogs. Art -- Washington (D.C.) -- Catalogs. Art, American -- Catalogs.

N6505.L37 1960
Larkin, Oliver W.
Art and life in America. New York, Holt, Rinehart and Winston [1966, c1960] xvii, 559 p.
60-006491   709.73
Art -- United States -- History.

N6505.L6 1991
Los Angeles County Museum of Art.
American art: a catalogue of the Los Angeles County Museum of Art collection/ Ilene Susan Fort, Michael Quick. Los Angeles, Calif.: The Museum; c1991. 511 p.
90-013570   759.13/074/79494   0875871550
Art -- California -- Los Angeles -- Catalogs. Art, American -- Catalogs.

N6505.P55
Pierson, William Harvey, 1911-
Arts of the United States, a pictorial survey. William H. Pierson, Jr. and Martha Davidson, editors. New York, McGraw-Hill [1960] x, 452 p.
60-009855   709.73
Art -- United States -- History.

N6505.R8 1982
Rubinstein, Charlotte Streifer.
American women artists: from early Indian times to the present/ Charlotte Streifer Rubinstein. New York, N.Y.: Avon; c1982. x, 560 p.
81-020135   704/.042/0973   0816185352
Women artists -- United States. Indian artists -- United States. Indian women -- North America.

N6505.V66 1982
Von Blum, Paul.
The critical vision: a history of social and political art in the U.S./ Paul Von Blum; with editorial assistance and contributions by Mark Resnick. Boston, MA: South End Press, c1982. xviii, 169 p.
82-061156   709/.73   0896081710
Art, American. Politics in art. Art and society -- United States.

N6505.W57 1991
Wilmerding, John.
American views: essays on American art/ John Wilmerding. Princeton, N.J.: Princeton University Press, 1991. xx, 357 p.
91-004479   759.3   0691040907
Art, American.

N6507.E53 2000
Encyclopedia of American art before 1914/ edited by Jane Turner. New York: Grove's Dictionaries, c2000. xxiii, 688 p.
99-041596   709/.73/03   1884446035
Art, American -- Encyclopedias. Art, Modern -- 18th century -- United States -- Encyclopedias. Art, Modern -- 19th century -- United States -- Encyclopedias.

N6507.G76 2000
Groseclose, Barbara S.
Nineteenth-century American art/ Barbara Groseclose. New York: Oxford University Press, 2000. vi, 234 p.
00-036751   709/.73/09034   0192842250
Art, American -- 19th century.

N6510.A73
The Arts in America: the nineteenth century [by] Wendell D. Garrett [and others] New York, Scribner [1969] xix, 412 p.
78-085279   709/.73
Art, American. Art, Modern -- 19th century -- United States.

N6510.B75 1979
Brooklyn Museum.
The American renaissance, 1876-1917. Brooklyn, N.Y.: Brooklyn Museum; c1979. 232 p.
79-013325   709/.73/074014723   0394508076
Art, American -- Exhibitions. Art, Modern -- 19th century -- United States -- Exhibitions. Art, Modern -- 20th century -- United States -- Exhibitions. United States -- Intellectual life -- 1865-1918.

N6510.B87 1996
Burns, Sarah.
Inventing the modern artist: art and culture in Gilded Age America/ Sarah Burns. New Haven: Yale University Press, c1996. viii, 380 p.
96-005929   701/.03/0973   0300064454
Art, American. Artists -- Psychology. Art and society -- United States -- History -- 19th century.

N6510.F57 1990
Fink, Lois Marie.
American art at the nineteenth-century Paris Salons/ Lois Marie Fink. Washington, D.C.: National Museum of American Art, Smithsonian Institution; Cambridge; New York: Cambridge University Press, 1990. xxiv, 430 p.
89-023885   709/.73/0903407444361   0521384990
Art, Modern -- 19th century -- United States -- Exhibitions. Art, American -- Exhibitions.

N6510.V35 1996
Van Hook, Bailey, 1953-
Angels of art: women and art in American society, 1876-1914/ Bailey Van Hook. University Park, Pa.: Pennsylvania State University Press, c1996. xvi, 287 p.
95-037877   757/.4/097309034   0271015578
Art, American. Art, Modern -- 19th century -- United States. Art, Modern -- 20th century -- United States.

N6512.A586 1982
American artists on art from 1940 to 1980/ edited by Ellen H. Johnson. New York: Harper & Row, c1982. xii, 274 p.
80-008702   700/.973   0064334260
Art, American. Art, Modern -- 20th century -- United States. Happening (Art) -- United States.

N6512.B3 1967
Baur, John I. H. 1909-1987.
Revolution and tradition in modern American art [by] John I. H. Baur. New York, F. A. Praeger [1967] xxii, 170 p.
67-027417   709/.73
Art -- United States. Art, Modern -- 20th century -- United States.

N6512.C597 1999
Corn, Wanda M.
The great American thing: modern art and national identity, 1915-1935/ Wanda M. Corn. Berkeley: University of California Press, c1999. xxiii, 447 p.
99-024604   709/.73/09041   0520210492
Art, American. Art, Modern -- 20th century -- United States. National characteristics, American, in art.

N6512.C854 1994
Cummings, Paul.
Dictionary of contemporary American artists/ Paul Cummings. New York: St. Martin's Press, 1994. x, 786 p.
93-046372   709/.2/273   0312084404
Artists -- United States -- Biography. Art, Modern -- 20th century -- United States.

N6512.E887 1997
Exiles + emigres: the flight of European artists from Hitler/ Stephanie Barron with Sabine Eckmann; contributions by Matthew Affron ... [et al.]. Los Angeles, Calif.: Los Angeles County Museum of Art; c1997. 432 p.
96-078500   704/.03/034073   0810932717
Expatriate artists -- United States -- Exhibitions. Artists -- Europe -- Exhibitions. Art, Modern -- 20th century -- United States -- Exhibitions.

N6512.F57 1991
Fisher, Philip.
Making and effacing art: modern American art in a culture of museums/ Philip Fisher. New York: Oxford University Press, 1991. viii, 267 p.
91-018602   709/.73/0904   0195060466
Art, American. Art, Modern -- 20th century -- United States. Art museum architecture -- United States -- Psychological aspects.

N6512.H355 1999
Haskell, Barbara.
The American century: art & culture, 1900-1950/ Barbara Haskell. New York: Whitney Museum of American Art in association with W.W. Norton, c1999. 408 p.
98-032116   709/.73/0747471   0393047237
Art, American -- Exhibitions. Art, Modern -- 20th century -- United States -- Exhibitions. Arts, American -- Exhibitions.

N6512.H355 1999 Suppl.
Phillips, Lisa.
The American century: art & culture, 1950-2000/ Lisa Phillips. New York: Whitney Museum of American Art in association with W.W. Norton, c1999. 398 p.
99-024969   709/.73/0747471   0393048152
Art, American. Art, Modern -- 20th century -- United States. Arts, American.

N6512.H657 2000
Hopkins, David, 1955-
After modern art: 1945-2000/ David Hopkins. Oxford; Oxford University Press, 2000. 282 p.
00-036750   709/.04   019284234X
Art, American -- 20th century. Art, European -- 20th century.

N6512.L57 1990
Lippard, Lucy R.
A different war: Vietnam in art/ Lucy R. Lippard. Bellingham, Wash.: Whatcom Museum of History and Art; 1990. 131 p.
89-070103　704.9/499597043/07473　0941104435
Vietnamese Conflict, 1961-1975 -- Art and the conflict -- Exhibitions. Art, American -- Exhibitions. Art, Modern -- 20th century -- United States -- Exhibitions.

N6512.M27 1989
Making their mark: women artists move into the mainstream, 1970-85/ Randy Rosen, Chatherine C. Brawer [compilers]. New York: Abbeville Press, c1989. 300 p.
88-022261　704/.042/0973074013　0896599582
Art, American -- Exhibitions. Art, Modern -- 20th century -- United States -- Exhibitions. Women artists -- United States -- Exhibitions.

N6512.M518
Miller, Lynn F.
Lives and works, talks with women artists/ Lynn F. Miller, Sally S. Swenson. Metuchen, N.J.: Scarecrow Press, 1981-1996. v. 1-2
81-009043　709/.2/2　0810814587
Women artists -- United States -- Interviews. Feminism and art -- United States. Art, Modern -- 20th century -- United States.

N6512.M78
Munro, Eleanor C.
Originals: American women artists/ Eleanor Munro. New York: Simon and Schuster, c1979. 528 p.
78-031814　709/.2/2　067123109X
Art, American. Art, Modern -- 20th century -- United States. Women artists -- United States -- Biography.

N6512.N4 1969
Museum of Modern Art (New York, N.Y.)
American realists and magic realists. Edited by Dorothy C. Miller and Alfred H. Barr, Jr., with statements by the artists and an introd. by Lincoln Kirstein. [New York] Published for the Museum of Modern Art by Arno Press, 1969 [c1943] 67 p.
77-086431　760/.0973
Art, American -- Exhibitions. Realism in art -- United States. Surrealism -- United States.

N6512.P27 1984
Painters painting: a candid history of the modern art scene, 1940-1970/ in the words of Josef Albers ... [et. al.]; [compiled by] Emile de Antonio and Mitch Tuchman. New York: Abbeville Press, c1984. 192 p.
83-021526　709/.73　0896594181
Artists -- United States -- Interviews. Modernism (Art) -- United States.

N6512.R63
Rose, Barbara.
American art since 1900; a critical history. New York, F. A. Praeger [1967] 320 p.
67-020743　709/.73
Art, American -- History.

N6512.R64
Rose, Barbara,
Readings in American art since 1900; a documentary survey. New York, F. A. Praeger [1968] xiv, 224 p.
68-016421　709.73
Art, American -- History. Art, Modern -- 20th century -- United States.

N6512.R676 1999
Rosenblum, Robert.
On modern American art: selected essays/ by Robert Rosenblum. New York: Harry N. Abrams, 1999. 384 p.
99-022015　709/.73/09045　0810936836
Art, American. Art, Modern -- 20th century -- United States.

N6512.S255 1988
Sandler, Irving,　1925-
American art of the 1960s/ Irving Sandler. New York: Harper & Row, c1988. xix, 412 p.
87-045662　709/.73　0064385078
Art, American -- Themes, motives. Art, Modern -- 20th century -- United States -- Themes, motives.

N6512.S335 1991
Seitz, William Chapin.
Art in the age of Aquarius, 1955-1970/ William C. Seitz; compiled and edited by Marla Price. Washington: Smithsonian Institution Press, c1992. xviii, 250 p.
90-026271　709/.73/09046　0874748682
Art, American. Art, Modern -- 20th century -- United States. Avant-garde (Aesthetics) -- United States -- History -- 20th century.

N6512.W285 1996
Wagner, Anne Middleton,　1949-
Three artists (three women): modernism and the art of Hesse, Krasner, and O'Keeffe/ Anne Middleton Wagner. Berkeley: University of California Press, c1996. xix, 346 p.
96-014058　709/.2/273　0520206088
O'Keeffe, Georgia, -- 1887-1986. Krasner, Lee, -- 1908- Hesse, Eva, -- 1936-1970. Art, Modern -- 20th century -- United States. Art, American. Women artists -- United States -- Biography -- History and criticism.

N6512.W46
Whitney Museum of American Art.
American art of our century [by] Lloyd Goodrich, director [and] John I. H. Baur, associate director. New York, Praeger [1961] 309 p.
61-015642　708.1471
Art, American. Art -- New York (State) -- New York -- Catalogs. Art, Modern -- 20th century -- United States.

N6512.W532 1999
Whitney Museum of American Art.
Frames of reference: looking at American art, 1900-1950: works from the Whitney Museum of American Art/ Beth Venn and Adam D. Weinberg, editors; with an essay by Kennedy Fraser and contributions by Robert Adams ... [et al.]. New York: The Museum, 1999. 223 p.
99-036420　709/.73/0747471　0874271118
Art, American -- Catalogs. Art, Modern -- 20th century -- United States -- Catalogs. Art -- New York (State) -- New York -- Catalogs.

N6512.5.A2.A27 1984
Abstract painting and sculpture in America, 1927-1944/ edited by John R. Lane and Susan C. Larsen. Pittsburgh: Museum of Art, Carnegie Institute; 1984, c1983. 256 p.
83-003850   759.13/074/013   0810918056
Art, Abstract -- United States -- Exhibitions. Art, American -- Exhibitions. Art, Modern -- 20th century -- United States -- Exhibitions.

N6512.5.A25.A24 1990
Abstract expressionism: creators and critics: an anthology/ edited and with an introduction by Clifford Ross. New York: H.N. Abrams, 1990. 304 p.
89-039710   709/.73/09045   0810919087
Abstract expressionism -- United States. Art, Modern -- 20th century -- United States.

N6512.5.A25.G53 1997
Gibson, Ann Eden, 1944-
Abstract expressionism: other politics/ Ann Eden Gibson. New Haven, CT: Yale University Press, c1997. xxxviii, 248 p.
96-046108   759/.13/09045   0300063393
Abstract expressionism -- United States. Art,Modern -- 20th century -- United States. Artists -- United States -- Psychology.

N6512.5.C64.M67 1994
Morgan, Robert C., 1943-
Conceptual art: an American perspective/ by Robert C. Morgan; with a foreword by Michael Kirby. Jefferson, N.C.: McFarland, 1994. xvii, 198 p.
93-045387   709/.04/075   0899509509
Conceptual art -- United States.

N6512.5.E4.Z87 1995
Zurier, Rebecca.
Metropolitan lives: the Ashcan artists and their New York/ Rebecca Zurier, Robert W. Snyder, Virginia M. Mecklenburg. Washington, D.C.: National Museum of American Art; c1995. 232 p.
95-019609   760/.09747/1074753   0393039013
Ashcan school of art -- Exhibitions. Eight (Group of American artists) -- Exhibitions. Art, Modern -- 20th century -- United States -- Exhibitions.

N6512.5.M5.B35 1988
Baker, Kenneth, 1946-
Minimalism: art of circumstance/ Kenneth Baker. New York: Abbeville Press, c1988. 144 p.
89-163713   709/.73/09045   089659887X
Minimal art -- United States. Art, Modern -- 20th century -- United States.

N6512.5.M63.M63 1993
Modernism in dispute: art since the Forties/ Paul Wood ... [et al.]. New Haven: Yale University Press, in association with the Open University, 1993. 267 p.
93-010674   709/.73/09045   0300055218
Modernism (Art) -- United States. Art, American. Art, Modern -- 20th century -- United States.

N6512.5.M63.P65 2000
Pollock and after: the critical debate/ edited by Frances Frascina. New York: Routledge, 2000.
00-059208   709/.73/0904   0415228662
Modernism (Art) -- United States. Abstract expressionism -- United States. Art, Modern -- 20th century -- United States.

N6512.5.M63.S63 1993
Smith, Terry
Making the modern: industry, art, and design in America/ Terry Smith. Chicago: University of Chicago Press, 1993. xv, 512 p.
92-000935   709/.73/09041   0226763463
Modernism (Art) -- United States. Art, American. Art, Modern -- 20th century -- United States.

N6512.5.P45.G6
Goodyear, Frank Henry, 1944-
Contemporary American realism since 1960/ Frank H. Goodyear, Jr. Boston: New York Graphic Society in association with the Pennsylvania Academy of the Fine Arts, c1981. 255 p.
81-011012   709/.73   0821211269
Photo-realism -- United States. Realism in art -- United States. Art, Modern -- 20th century -- United States.

N6512.5.P6.H36 1992
Hand-painted pop: American art in transition, 1955-62/ exhibition organized by Donna De Salvo and Paul Schimmel; edited by Russell Ferguson; with essays by David Deitcher ... [et al.]. Los Angeles: Museum of Contemporary Art; c1992. 256 p.
92-032102   759.13/09/04507479494   0914357298
Pop art -- United States -- Exhibitions. Art, Modern -- 20th century -- United States -- Exhibitions.

N6512.5.S75
Connor, Celeste, 1961-
Democratic visions: art and theory of the Steiglitz Circle, 1924-1934/ Celeste Connor. Berkeley: University of California Press, c2001. xvi, 236 p.
99-087355   709/.73/09042   0520213548
Stieglitz, Alfred, -- 1864-1946 -- Art patronage. Art, American -- 20th century.

N6525.B6
Bowie, Theodore Robert.
East-West in art; patterns of cultural & aesthetic relationships/ by Theodore Bowie in collaboration with J. Leroy Davidson [and others] With an introduction by Rudolf Wittkower. Bloomington, Indiana University Press [1966] 191 p.
66-012723   709
East and West. Intercultural communication. Art -- History.

N6527.U3 1996
Udall, Sharyn Rohlfsen.
Contested terrain: myth and meanings in Southwest art/ Sharyn R. Udall. Albuquerque: University of New Mexico Press, c1996. 180 p.
95-004386   709/.78   0826316697
Art, American -- Southwest, New -- Themes, motives. Art, Modern -- 20th century -- Southwest, New -- Themes, motives.

N6530.C2 M68 1998
Moure, Nancy Dustin Wall.
California art: 450 years of painting & other media/ Nancy Dustin Wall Moure. Los Angeles: Dustin Publications, 1998. 560 p.
98-233186   709/.794 21   0961462256
Art, American -- California.

N6530.C2.O55 1996
On the edge of America: California modernist art, 1900-1950/ edited by Paul Karlstrom. Berkeley: University of California Press, c1996. xvii, 308 p.
95-035237   709/.794/09041   0520088506
Modernism (Art) -- California. Art, American -- California. Art, Modern -- 20th century -- California.

N6535.N5.N32 1996
Naumann, Francis M.
Making mischief: Dada invades New York/ Francis M. Naumann with Beth Venn; with contributions by Todd Alden ... [et al.]. New York: Whitney Museum of American Art, 1996. 304 p.
96-009890   709/.747/10747471   0874271053
Dadaism -- New York (State) -- New York -- Exhibitions. Art, Modern -- 20th century -- New York (State) -- New York -- Exhibitions.

N6535.T3.C6
Coke, Van Deren, 1921-
Taos and Santa Fe; the artist's environment, 1882-1942. Albuquerque Published by the University of New Mexico Press for the Amon Carter Museum of Western Art, Ft. Worth, Tex. [and] the Art Gallery, University of New Mexico, Albuquerque [1962] 160 p.
63-014924   709.7895
Art, American -- Exhibitions. Art -- New Mexico -- Tao. Art -- New Mexico -- Santa Fe.

N6535.T3.W58 1992
Witt, David L., 1951-
Taos moderns: art of the new/ David L. Witt; foreword by Gerald Nordland; photography by Michael O'Shaughnessy. Santa Pe: Red Crane Books, c1992. xv, 120 p.
92-010213   759.189/53   1878610163
Art, American -- New Mexico -- Taos. Art, Modern -- 20th century -- New Mexico -- Taos. Artists -- New Mexico -- Taos -- Biography.

N6535.W3.F78 1992
Fryd, Vivien Green.
Art & empire: the politics of ethnicity in the United States Capitol, 1815-1860/ Vivien Green Fryd. New Haven: Yale University Press, c1992. x, 273 p.
91-044060   704.9/499735/09753
Art and state -- Washington (D.C.) Allegories. Minorities in art.

N6536.C37 2000
Carter, Alice A.
The Red Rose girls: an uncommon story of art and love/ by Alice A. Carter. New York: H.N. Abrams, 2000. 216 p.
99-039866   759.13   0810944375
Smith, Jessie Willcox, -- 1863-1935. Elliott, Elizabeth Shippen Green. Oakley, Violet, -- 1874- Artists' studios -- Pennsylvania -- Philadelphia Region. Women artists -- United States -- Biography. Lesbian artists -- United States -- Biography.

N6536.C8
Cummings, Paul.
A dictionary of contemporary American artists. New York, St. Martin's Press [1966] xx, 331 p.
65-020815   709.22
Artists -- United States -- Biography -- Dictionaries.

N6536.F5 1965
Fielding, Mantle, 1865-1941.
Mantle Fielding's dictionary of American painters, sculptors, and engravers. With an addendum containing corrections and additional material on the original entries, compiled by James F. Carr. New York, J. F. Carr, 1965. vi, 529 p.
65-027268   709.22
Artists -- United States -- Biography -- Dictionaries.

N6536.W5
Who's who in American art. New York [etc.] R.R. Bowker.
36-027014   709/.22
Artists -- United States -- Biography -- Periodicals.

N6537.A43.H35 1990
Hall, Lee.
Abe Ajay/ by Lee Hall. Seattle: Published for the Academy for Educational Development by the University of Washington Press, c1990. 175 p.
89-016596   709.2   0295968419
Ajay, Abe -- Criticism and interpretation.

N6537.B233.A4 1999
Basquiat, Jean Michel.
Basquiat. Milano: Charta, c1999. lxxi, 205 p.
99-510601   8881582392
Basquiat, Jean Michel -- Exhibitions.

N6537.B52.A4 1995
Wardlaw, Alvia J.
The art of John Biggers: view from the upper room/ by Alvia J. Wardlaw with essays by Edmund Barry Gaither, Alison de Lima Greene, and Robert Farris Thompson. Houston: Museum of Fine Arts, in association with Harry N. Abrams, 1995. 184 p.
94-026005   759.13   0810919567
Biggers, John Thomas, -- 1924- -- Exhibitions. Afro-American mural painting and decoration.

N6537.B53.S48 1993
Shapiro, Michael Edward.
George Caleb Bingham/ Michael Edward Shapiro. New York: H.N. Abrams in association with the National Museum of American Art, Smithsonian Institution, 1993. 159 p.
92-014936   759.13   0810931214
Bingham, George Caleb, -- 1811-1879 -- Criticism and interpretation. West (U.S.) in art.

N6537.B55.A4 1989
Yglesias, Helen.
Isabel Bishop/ Helen Yglesias; foreword by John Russell. New York: Rizzoli, 1989. 180 p.
88-042700   759.13   0847809765
Bishop, Isabel, -- 1902- -- Catalogues raisonnes.

N6537.B75
Chadwick, Whitney.
Amazons in the drawing room: the art of Romaine Brooks/ Whitney Chadwick; with an essay by Joe Lucchesi. Chesterfield, Mass.: Chameleon Books 2000. 128 p.
00-022434   759.13   0520225651
Brooks, Romaine -- Exhibitions.

N6537.B783.A4 1998
Tsujimoto, Karen.
The art of Joan Brown/ Karen Tsujimoto and Jacquelynn Baas; with a foreword by Brenda Richardson. Berkeley: University of California, c1998. xxxv, 272 p.
97-040602   709/.2   0520214684
Brown, Joan, -- 1938- -- Exhibitions.

N6537.C33.A4 1998
Prather, Marla.
Alexander Calder, 1898-1976/ catalogue, Marla Prather; chronology, Alexander S.C. Rower; essay, Arnauld Pierre. Washington: National Gallery of Art; c1998. 367 p.
97-048328   709/.2   0300075189
Calder, Alexander, -- 1898-1976 -- Exhibitions.

N6537.C33.L56 1976
Calder, Alexander, 1898-1976.
Calder's universe/ Jean Lipman; Ruth Wolfe, editorial director. New York: Viking Press in cooperation with the Whitney Museum of American Art, 1976. 351 p.
76-028232   709/.2/4   0670199664
Calder, Alexander, -- 1898-1976.   Artists -- United States -- Biography.

N6537.C35.A4 1998
Cassatt, Mary, 1844-1926.
Mary Cassatt, modern woman/ organized by Judith A. Barter; with contributions by Erica E. Hirshler ... [et al.]. New York: Art Institute of Chicago in association with H.N. Abrams, c1998. 376 p.
98-007306   760/.092   0810940892
Cassatt, Mary, -- 1844-1926 -- Exhibitions. Cassatt, Mary, -- 1844-1926 -- Criticism and interpretation. Impressionism (Art) -- Exhibitions.

N6537.C48.A4 1985
Chicago, Judy, 1939-
The birth project/ by Judy Chicago. Garden City, N.Y.: Doubleday, 1985. 231 p.
84-018783   746/.092/4   0385187106
Chicago, Judy, -- 1939-   Needlework -- United States. Group work in art -- United States.

N6537.C54.S75 1998
Storr, Robert.
Chuck Close/ Robert Storr; with essays by Kirk Varnedoe and Deborah Wye. New York: Museum of Modern Art: c1998. 224 p.
97-075612   759.13   0870700669
Close, Chuck, -- 1940- -- Criticism and interpretation.

N6537.C593 P37 1988
Parry, Ellwood.
The art of Thomas Cole: ambition and imagination/ Ellwood C. Parry, III. Newark: University of Delaware Press, c1988. 419 p.
85-040511   759.13 19   0874132142
Cole, Thomas, 1801-1848. Artists -- United States -- Biography. Hudson River school of landscape painting.

N6537.C6579.A4 1995
John Singleton Copley in America/ Carrie Rebora ... [et al.]; with contributions by Morrison H. Heckscher, Aileen Ribeiro, Marjorie Shelley. New York: Metropolitan Museum of Art: c1995. xv, 348 p.
95-002520   759.13   0870997440
Copley, John Singleton, -- 1738-1815 -- Exhibitions.   Artists and patrons -- United States -- History -- 18th century -- Exhibitions. Group identity in art -- Exhibitions. Social status in art -- Exhibitions. United States -- Biography -- Portraits -- Exhibitions.

N6537.C66.J67
Joseph Cornell/ edited by Kynaston McShine; essays by Dawn Ades ... [et al.]. New York: Museum of Modern Art, c1980. 295 p.
80-084102   709/.2/4   0870702718
Cornell, Joseph -- Addresses, essays, lectures.

N6537.D43.L53 2000
Lieber, Edvard.
Willem de Kooning: reflections in the studio/ Edvard Lieber. New York: H.N. Abrams, 2000. 137 p.
99-056282   709/.2   0810945606
De Kooning, Willem, -- 1904- -- Anecdotes. De Kooning, Willem, -- 1904- -- Friends and associates -- Anecdotes. De Kooning, Willem, -- 1904- -- Pictorial works. Artists -- United States -- Biography.

N6537.D43.W35 1988
Waldman, Diane.
Willem de Kooning/ Diane Waldman. New York: Abrams in association with the National Museum of American Art, Smithsonian Institution, 1988. 156 p.
87-001385   709/.2/4   0810911345
De Kooning, Willem, -- 1904- -- Criticism and interpretation.

N6537.D4464.A4 1996
Hobbs, Susan, 1945-
The art of Thomas Wilmer Dewing: beauty reconfigured/
Susan A. Hobbs with a contribution by Barbara Dayer
Gallati. Washington, DC: Smithsonian Institution Press,
1996. xv, 224 p.
95-049654   759.13   1560986247
Dewing, Thomas Wilmer, -- 1851-1938 -- Exhibitions.

N6537.E3.G6 1982
Goodrich, Lloyd, 1897-
Thomas Eakins/ Lloyd Goodrich. Cambridge, Mass.:
Published for the National Gallery of Art [by] Harvard
University Press, 1982. 2 v.
82-012170   709/.2/4   0674884906
*Eakins, Thomas, -- 1844-1916.   Artists -- United States --
Biography.*

N6537.E3.H65 1992
Homer, William Innes.
Thomas Eakins: his life and art/ William Innes Homer.
New York: Abbeville Press, c1992. 276 p.
92-010163   709/.2   1558592814
*Eakins, Thomas, -- 1844-1916.   Artists -- United States --
Biography.*

N6537.F735
Nochlin, Linda.
Mary Frank: encounters/ curated by Judy Collischan;
essay by Linda Nochlin. Purchase, NY: Neuberger
Museum of Art, Purchase College, State University of
New York; New York: Harry N. Abrams, c2000. 98 p.
00-029317   759.13   0810967235
Frank, Mary, -- 1933- -- Exhibitions.

N6537.G65.S68 1999
Spender, Matthew.
From a high place: a life of Arshile Gorky/ Matthew
Spender. New York: Knopf: 1999. xxiii, 417 p.
99-061595   759.13   0375403787
*Gorky, Arshile, -- 1904-1948.   Artists -- United States --
Biography.*

N6537.G688.A4 1983
Kass, Ray.
Morris Graves, vision of the inner eye/ Ray Kass;
introduction by Theodore F. Wolff. New York: Braziller,
in association with the Phillips Collection, Washington,
D.C., c1983. 174 p.
83-002606   759.13   0807610682
*Graves, Morris, -- 1910- -- Exhibitions. Graves, Morris, --
1910- Artists -- United States -- Biography.*

N6537.G718.A4 1998
Grey, Alex.
The mission of art/ by Alex Grey; foreword by Ken
Wilber. Boston: Shambhala, 1998. xv, 255 p.
98-016930   759.13   1570623961
*Grey, Alex -- Philosophy. Grey, Alex -- Criticism and
interpretation.*

N6537.G9.K36 1999
Kammen, Michael G.
Robert Gwathmey: the life and art of a passionate
observer/ Michael Kammen. Chapel Hill: University of
North Carolina Press, c1999. 240 p.
98-048441   759.13   080782495X
*Gwathmey, Robert, -- 1903-1988.   Artists -- United States --
Biography.*

N6537.H4.A4 1992
Eva Hesse: a retrospective/ exhibition and catalogue
organized by Helen A. Cooper; essays by Maurice Berger
... [et al.]; [edited by Lesley K. Baier]. New Haven: Yale
University Art Gallery: 1992. 253 p.
92-005605   709/.2   0300054890
Hesse, Eva, -- 1936-1970 -- Exhibitions.

N6537.H577.A4 1989
Waldman, Diane.
Jenny Holzer/ Diane Waldman. New York: Solomon R.
Guggenheim Museum: c1989. 116 p.
89-025747   709/.2   0892070684
Holzer, Jenny, -- 1950- -- Exhibitions.

N6537.H58.A4 1995
Cikovsky, Nicolai.
Winslow Homer/ Nicolai Cikovsky, Jr., Franklin Kelly;
with contributions by Judith Walsh and Charles Brock.
Washington: National Gallery of Art; c1995. 420 p.
95-019025   759.13   0894682172
*Homer, Winslow, -- 1836-1910 -- Exhibitions.   Nationalism in
art -- Exhibitions.*

N6537.H6.L48 1995
Levin, Gail, 1948-
Edward Hopper: an intimate biography/ Gail Levin. New
York: Knopf, 1995. xvii, 678 p.
95-002114   760/.092   0394546644
*Hopper, Edward, -- 1882-1967.   Artists -- United States --
Biography.*

N6537.J6.A4 1977
Crichton, Michael, 1942-
Jasper Johns/ by Michael Crichton. New York: Abrams,
in association with the Whitney Museum of American
Art, c1977. 243 p.
77-078150   709/.2/4   0810911612
Johns, Jasper, -- 1930- -- Exhibitions.

N6537.J6.J64 1996
Johnston, Jill.
Jasper Johns: privileged information/ Jill Johnston. New
York, NY: Thames and Hudson, c1996. 335 p.
96-060331   709/.2   0500017360
Johns, Jasper, -- 1930- Artists -- United States -- Biography.

N6537.J6.K6
Johns, Jasper, 1930-
Jasper Johns. Text by Max Kozloff. New York, H. N.
Abrams [1968] 195 p.
67-010589   709/.24
Johns, Jasper, -- 1930-

N6537.K43.A4 1985
Driscoll, John Paul.
John Frederick Kensett, an American master/ John Paul
Driscoll, John K. Howat, with contributions by Dianne
Dwyer, Oswaldo Rodriguez Roque; edited by Susan E.
Strickler. New York: Worcester Art Museum in
association with Norton, c1985. 208 p.
84-029440   759.13   0393019349
Kensett, John Frederick, -- 1816-1872 -- Exhibitions.
Landscape in art -- Exhibitions.

N6537.L45.A4 1989
Jack Levine/ commentary by Jack Levine; introduction
by Milton W. Brown; compiled and edited by Stephen
Robert Frankel. New York: Rizzoli, 1989. 144 p.
88-042699   759.13   0847809773
Levine, Jack, -- 1915- -- Catalogs.

N6537.L46.A4 2000
Sol LeWitt: a retrospective/ edited and with an
introduction by Gary Garrels; with essays by Martin
Friedman ... [et al.]. San Francisco: San Francisco
Museum of Modern Art; c2000. 416 p.
99-057796   709/.2   0918471591
Lewitt, Sol, -- 1928- -- Exhibitions. LeWitt, Sol, -- 1928- --
Exhibitions.

N6537.M37.A4 1990
Fine, Ruth, 1941-
John Marin/ Ruth E. Fine. Washington: National Gallery
of Art; c1990. 312 p.
89-017520   760/.092   1558590153
Marin, John, -- 1870-1953 -- Catalogs.

N6537.M3943
Mathur, Anuradha.
Mississippi floods: designing a shifting landscape/
Anuradha Mathur and Dilip da Cunha. New Haven: Yale
University Press, 2001. xv, 161 p.
00-011101   917.7/02   0300084307
Mathur, Anuradha -- Exhibitions. Cunha, Dilip da --
Exhibitions. Landscape assessment -- Mississippi River Valley.
Mississippi River Valley -- In art -- Exhibitions.

N6537.M6443.A4 1996
Moran, Thomas, 1837-1926.
Thomas Moran, the field sketches, 1856-1923/ Anne
Morand; with an introduction by Joan Carpenter Troccoli.
Norman: University of Oklahoma Press for the Thomas
Gilcrease Institute of American History and Art, Tulsa
c1996. xii, 313 p.
94-049719   759.13   080612704X
Moran, Thomas, -- 1837-1926 -- Themes, motives -- Catalogs.

N6537.M6443.W55 1998
Wilkins, Thurman.
Thomas Moran: artist of the mountains/ by Thurman
Wilkins with the help of Caroline Lawson Hinkley;
foreword by William H. Goetzmann. Norman, Okla.:
University of Oklahoma Press, c1998. xxii, 429 p.
97-035740   760/.092   0806130407
Moran, Thomas, -- 1837-1926.   Artists -- United States --
Biography.

N6537.M66.A4 1989
Staiti, Paul J.
Samuel F.B. Morse/ Paul J. Staiti. Cambridge; Cambridge
University Press, 1989. xxii, 298 p.
88-036918   759.13   0521322189
Morse, Samuel Finley Breese, -- 1791-1872 -- Catalogs.

N6537.M67.C42 1996
Caws, Mary Ann.
Robert Motherwell: what art holds/ Mary Ann Caws.
New York: Columbia University Press, c1996. xxvii,
227 p.
95-020819   759.13   0231096445
Motherwell, Robert -- Criticism and interpretation.   Surrealism
-- United States.

N6537.N36.A4 2000
Hoving, Thomas, 1931-
The art of Dan Namingha/ by Thomas Hoving. New
York: H.N. Abrams, 2000. 160 p.
99-069675   709/.2   0810940507
Namingha, Dan.

N6537.N38.B78 1988
Bruggen, Coosje van.
Bruce Nauman/ Coosje van Bruggen. New York: Rizzoli,
1988. 304 p.
87-042686   700/.92/4   0847808831
Nauman, Bruce, -- 1941- -- Criticism and interpretation.
Conceptual art -- United States.

N6537.N48.A4 1978
Newman, Barnett, 1905-1970.
Barnett Newman/ Harold Rosenberg. New York: Abrams,
1978. 260 p.
77-025433   709/.2/4   0810913607
Newman, Barnett, -- 1905-1970.   Artists -- United States --
Biography.

N6537.O39.A4 2000
Fine, Ruth, 1941-
O'Keeffe on paper/ Ruth E. Fine and Barbara Buhler
Lynes with Elizabeth Glassman and Judith C. Walsh.
Washington, D.C.: National Gallery of Art; [2000] 143 p.
99-089039   759.13   0810966980
O'Keeffe, Georgia, -- 1887-1986 -- Exhibitions.

N6537.O39.H64 1992
Hogrefe, Jeffrey.
O'Keeffe: the life of an American legend/ Jeffrey
Hogrefe. New York: Bantam Books, 1992. xiii, 376 p.
92-002535   759.13   0553081160
O'Keeffe, Georgia, -- 1887-1986.   Artists -- United States --
Biography.

N6537.O39.M477 2001
Messinger, Lisa Mintz.
Georgia O'Keeffe/ Lisa Mintz Messinger. New York,
N.Y.: Thames & Hudson, c2001. 192 p.
00-107990   759.13   0500203407
O'Keeffe, Georgia, -- 1887-1986.   Artists -- United States --
Biography.

N6537.O39.P48 1991
Peters, Sarah Whitaker.
Becoming O'Keeffe: the early years/ Sarah Whitaker Peters. New York: Abbeville Press, c1991. 397 p.
91-000560   759.13   0896599078
O'Keeffe, Georgia, -- 1887-1986.   Artists -- United States -- Biography.

N6537.O39.P65 1988
Pollitzer, Anita, 1894-1975.
A woman on paper: Georgia O'Keeffe/ by Anita Pollitzer; introduction by Kay Boyle. New York: Simon & Schuster, c1988. xxv, 290 p.
88-015643   759.13   067166431X
O'Keeffe, Georgia, -- 1887-1986.   Artists -- United States -- Biography.

N6537.O39.R64 1989
Robinson, Roxana.
Georgia O'Keeffe: a life/ Roxana Robinson. New York: Harper & Row, c1989. x, 639 p.
89-045061   759.13   0060159650
O'Keeffe, Georgia, -- 1887-1986.   Artists -- United States -- Biography.

N6537.P264.A4 1999
Yount, Sylvia.
Maxfield Parrish, 1870-1966/ Sylvia Yount. New York: Harry N. Abrams in association with the Pennsylvania Academy of the Fine Arts, c1999. 160 p.
98-040691   760/.092   0810943670
Parrish, Maxfield, -- 1870-1966 -- Exhibitions.

N6537.P63.A4 2001
Ludman, Joan.
Fairfield Porter: a catalogue raisonne of the paintings, watercolors, and pastels/ Joan Ludman; with essays by Rackstraw Downes, William C. Agee, John T. Spike. New York: Hudson Hills Press, c2001. 396 p.
00-054095   759.13   1555951651
Porter, Fairfield -- Catalogues raisonnes.

N6537.P63.S66 2000
Spring, Justin.
Fairfield Porter: a life in art/ Justin Spring. New Haven: Yale University Press, c2000. xv, 384 p.
99-030563   700/.92   0300076371
Porter, Fairfield.   Artists -- United States -- Biography. Art critics -- United States -- Biography.

N6537.R27.K67 1990
Kotz, Mary Lynn.
Rauschenberg, art and life/ by Mary Lynn Kotz. New York: H.N. Abrams, 1990. 319 p.
90-000217   700/.92   0810937522
Rauschenberg, Robert, -- 1925-   Artists -- United States -- Biography.

N6537.R4.A3 1988
Remington, Frederic, 1861-1909.
Frederic Remington--selected letters/ [edited] by Allen P. Splete and Marilyn D. Splete. New York: Abbeville Press, c1988. xv, 487 p.
86-028786   709/.2/4   089659694X
Remington, Frederic, -- 1861-1909 -- Correspondence.   Artists -- United States -- Correspondence.

N6537.R4.A4 1988
Shapiro, Michael Edward.
Frederic Remington: the masterworks/ [Michael Edward Shapiro, Peter H. Hassrick; with essays by David G. McCullough, Doreen Bolger Burke, John Seelye]. New York: Abrams, 1988. 271 p.
87-023167   709/.2/4   0810915952
Remington, Frederic, -- 1861-1909 -- Criticism and interpretation.

N6537.R4.B26 1989
Ballinger, James K.
Frederic Remington/ James K. Ballinger. New York, N.Y.: Abrams in association with the National Museum of American Art, Smithsonian Institution, 1989. 160 p.
89-000043   709/.2/4   0810915731
Remington, Frederic, -- 1861-1909 -- Criticism and interpretation.

N6537.R4.D57 2001
Dippie, Brian W.
The Frederic Remington Art Museum collection/ by Brian W. Dippie. New York: Frederic Remington Art Museum: 2001. 264 p.
00-049339   709/.2   0810967111
Remington, Frederic, -- 1861-1909 -- Catalogs.   Art -- New York (State) -- Ogdensburg -- Catalogs.   West (U.S.) -- In art -- Catalogs.

N6537.R57.H8 1989
Hunter, Sam, 1923-
Larry Rivers/ by Sam Hunter. New York: Rizzoli, 1989. 358 p.
89-050411   709.2   0847810941
Rivers, Larry, -- 1925- -- Criticism and interpretation.

N6537.R88.H37 1989
Hassrick, Peter H.
Charles M. Russell/ Peter H. Hassrick. New York: Abrams; 1989. 155 p.
88-007391   709/.2/4   0810915715
Russell, Charles M. -- (Charles Marion), -- 1864-1926.   Artists -- United States -- Biography. West (U.S.) in art. Indians of North America -- Pictorial works.

N6537.S338.A4 2000
Schapiro, Meyer, 1904-
Meyer Schapiro: his painting, drawing, and sculpture/ preface by John Russell; introduction by Lillian Milgram Schapiro; texts by Meyer Schapiro; edited by Lillian Milgram Schapiro and Daniel Esterman; photographs by John Bigelow Taylor. New York: H.N. Abrams, 2000. 256 p.
99-038216   709/.2   0810943921
Schapiro, Meyer, -- 1904- -- Contributions in art.   Art, Modern -- 20th century -- United States.

N6537.S34.G68 1999
Gouma-Peterson, Thalia.
Miriam Schapiro: shaping the fragments of art and life/ Thalia Gouma-Peterson; foreword by Linda Nochlin. New York: Harry N. Abrams Publishers, 1999. 160 p.
99-018149   709/.2   0810943778
Schapiro, Miriam, -- 1923-   Artists -- United States -- Biography. Feminism in art.

N6537.S5.G74 1998
Greenfeld, Howard.
Ben Shahn: an artist's life/ Howard Greenfeld. New York: Random House, c1998. 366 p.
97-046748   760/.092   0679419322
Shahn, Ben, -- 1898-1969.   Artists -- United States -- Biography.

N6537.S5.P64 1989
Pohl, Frances K.   1952-
Ben Shahn: New Deal artist in a cold war climate, 1947-1954/ Frances K. Pohl. Austin: University of Texas Press, 1989. x, 237 p.
88-039304   760/.092/4   0292755376
Shahn, Ben, -- 1898-1969 -- Criticism and interpretation. Social problems in art. Politics in art.

N6537.S523.A4 1987a
Troyen, Carol.
Charles Sheeler, paintings and drawings/ by Carol Troyen and Erica E. Hirshler. Boston: Little, Brown, c1987. xii, 225 p.
87-042966   759.13   0878462848
Sheeler, Charles, -- 1883-1965 -- Exhibitions. Sheeler, Charles, -- 1883-1965 -- Criticism and interpretation.

N6537.S616.A4 1982
Fry, Edward F.
David Smith, painter, sculptor, draftsman/ Edward F. Fry and Miranda McClintic. New York: G. Braziller; c1982. 144 p.
82-015446   709/.2/4   0807610569
Smith, David, -- 1906-1965 -- Exhibitions.

N6537.S73.A4 1990
Stella, Joseph, 1877-1946.
Visual poetry: the drawings of Joseph Stella/ [compiled by] Joann Moser. Washington: Published for the National Museum of American Art by the Smithsonian Institution Press, c1990. xviii, 166 p.
89-011520   741.973   0874747384
Stella, Joseph, -- 1877-1946 -- Exhibitions.

N6537.T35.A4 1991
Mosby, Dewey F., 1942-
Henry Ossawa Tanner/ introductory essay and catalogue chapters by Dewey F. Mosby; catalogue entries by Dewey F. Mosby and Darrel Sewell; biographical essay by Rae Alexander-Minter. Philadelphia, PA: Philadelphia Museum of Art; 1991. 307 p.
90-024849   759.13   0847813460
Tanner, Henry Ossawa, -- 1859-1937 -- Exhibitions.

N6537.T5.A4 1989
Duncan, Alastair, 1942-
Masterworks of Louis Comfort Tiffany/ Alastair Duncan, Martin Eidelberg, Neil Harris. New York: Abrams, 1989. 160 p.
89-000422   709/.2/4   0810915375
Tiffany, Louis Comfort, -- 1848-1933 -- Exhibitions.

N6537.T67.D86 1997
Duncan, Michael, 1953-
Joyce Treiman/ Michael Duncan, Theodore F. Wolff. New York: Hudson Hills Press, 1997. 180 p.
97-020203   759.13   1555951414
Treiman, Joyce -- Criticism and interpretation. Treiman, Joyce -- Self-portraits. Human figure in art.

N6537.V43.A4 1979
Vedder, Elihu, 1836-1923.
Perceptions and evocations: the art of Elihu Vedder/ with an introd. by Regina Soria and essays by Joshua C. Taylor, Jane Dillenberger, Richard Murray. Washington: Published for the National Collection of Fine Arts by the Smithsonian Institution Press, 1979. ix, 246 p.
78-009915   709/.2/4   0874749026
Vedder, Elihu, -- 1836-1923 -- Exhibitions.

N6537.W28.A4 2000
Andy Warhol: series and singles: exhibition, Riehen/Basel, 17 Sept.-Dec. 2000/ with essays by Ernst Beyeler ... [et al.]. Riehen/Basel: Fondation Beyeler, 2000. 216 p.
00-111586   760/.092   0300089945
Warhol, Andy, -- 1928- -- Exhibitions.

N6537.W28.B68 1989
Bourdon, David.
Warhol/ David Bourdon. New York: Abrams, 1989. 432 p.
89-000436   700/.92/4   0810917610
Warhol, Andy, -- 1928- Artists -- United States -- Biography.

N6537.W28.D56 1998
Dillenberger, Jane.
The religious art of Andy Warhol/ Jane Daggett Dillenberger. New York: Continuum, c1998. 128 p.
98-008483   709/.2   0826411126
Warhol, Andy, -- 1928- -- Criticism and interpretation. Warhol, Andy, -- 1928- -- Religion.

N6537.W345.A4 1990
Wegman, William.
William Wegman: paintings, drawings, photographs, videotapes/ edited by Martin Kunz; essays by Martin Kunz ... [et al.]; interview with William Wegman by David Ross. New York: Abrams, 1990. 224 p.
90-032650   700/.92   0810939517
Wegman, William -- Exhibitions.

N6537.W4.A4 1984
Curry, David Park.
James McNeill Whistler at the Freer Gallery of Art/ David Park Curry. [Washington]: Freer Gallery of Art, Smithsonian Institution; 1984. 319 p.
83-025525   759.13   0393018474
Whistler, James McNeill, -- 1834-1903 -- Exhibitions.

N6537.W4.B46 1995
Bendix, Deanna Marohn.
Diabolical designs: paintings, interiors, and exhibitions of
James McNeill Whistler/ Deanna Marohn Bendix.
Washington: Smithsonian Institution Press, c1995. xii,
329 p.
94-024957   709/.2   1560984155
*Whistler, James McNeill, -- 1834-1903 -- Criticism and
interpretation.   Aesthetic movement (Art) -- Influence.*

N6537.5.L5 1990
Lippard, Lucy R.
Mixed blessings: new art in a multicultural America/
Lucy R.   Lippard. New York: Pantheon Books, c1990.
viii, 278 p.
89-049400   704/.0693/0973 20   0394577590
*Minority artists -- United States. Intercultural communication --
United States. Ethnic art -- United States.*

N6538.A4 A7 1993
Shared visions: Native American painters and sculptors in
the   twentieth century/ [edited by] Margaret Archuleta
and Rennard Strickland;   essays by Joy L. Gritton, W.
Jackson Rushing. 2nd ed. New York: New Press: c1993.
110 p.
92-050853   704/.0397/0904 20   1565840690
*Indian art -- 20th century -- Exhibitions. Art, American -- 20th
century -- Exhibitions. Indian art -- North America -- 20th
century -- Exhibitions.*

N6538.A4 B7
Broder, Patricia Janis.
American Indian painting & sculpture/ Patricia Janis
Broder. New York: Abbeville Press, c1981. 165 p.
80-066526   750/.8997 19   0896591476
Indian art -- United States. Indian art -- North America.

N6538.A4 H5 1980
Highwater, Jamake.
The sweet grass lives on: fifty contemporary North
American Indian   artists/ Jamake Highwater. 1st ed. New
York: Lippincott & Crowell, c1980. 192 p.
80-007776   709/.2/2   0690019254
*Indian art -- North America -- 20th century. Art, American --
20th century.*

N6538.A4.I2 1994
I stand in the center of the good: interviews with
contemporary Native American artists/   edited   by
Lawrence Abbott. Lincoln: University of Nebraska Press,
c1994. xxii, 310 p.
93-036892   704/.0397073/0904   080321037X
*Indian artists -- United States -- Interviews. Indian art. Art,
Modern -- 20th century -- United States.*

N6538.A83 A83 1994
Asia/America: identities   in   contemporary   Asian
American art/ essays   by Margo Machida, Vishakha N.
Desai, John Kuo Wei Tchen; Margo Machida,   guest
curator. New York, N.Y.: Asia Society Galleries: c1994.
127 p.
93-083676   704/.0395073/0904907473   20
1565840909
Asian American art -- 20th century -- Exhibitions.

N6538.H58 B43 1987
Beardsley, John.
Hispanic art in the United States: thirty contemporary
painters &   sculptors/ John Beardsley, Jane Livingston;
with an essay by Octavio   Paz. Houston: Museum of Fine
Arts; 1987. 260 p.
86-028819   704/.0368073/074013 19   0896596885
Hispanic American art -- 20th century -- Exhibitions.

N6538.H58.H46 1999
Henkes, Robert.
Latin American women artists of the United States: the
works of 33 twentieth-century women/ by Robert Henkes.
Jefferson, N.C.: McFarland, c1999. v, 245 p.
98-043600   704/.042/08968073   0786405198
  *Hispanic American art. Hispanic American women artists --
Psychology. Art, Modern -- 20th century -- United States.*

N6538.J4.B35 1997
Baigell, Matthew.
Jewish-American   artists   and   the   Holocaust/   Matthew
Baigell. New Brunswick, N.J.: Rutgers University Press,
c1997. xi, 138 p.
96-039806   704.9/499405318   0813524040
  *Jewish artists -- United States. Holocaust, Jewish (1939-
1945), in art. Art, American.*

N6538.L3 L38 1988
The Latin American spirit: art and artists in the United
States,   1920-1970: essays/ by Luis R. Cancel ... [et al.].
New York: Bronx Museum of the Arts in association with
Harry N.   343 p.
88-006267   704/.0368073 19   0810924064
*Art, Latin American -- 20th century. Artists -- Latin America.
Artists -- United States.*

N6538.M4 C45 1991
Chicano art: resistance and affirmation, 1965-1985/
edited   by   Richard   Griswold del Castillo, Teresa
McKenna, Yvonne Yarbro-Bejarano. Los Angeles: Wight
Art Gallery, University of California, Los   373 p.
90-025188   704/.0368/7207307479494   20
0943739152
*Mexican American art -- Exhibitions. Politics in art --
Exhibitions. Mexican Americans -- Civil rights.*

N6538.M4 C46 1992
The Chicano codices: encountering art of the Americas/
[edited by   Patricia Draher]. San Francisco: Mexican
Museum, [c1992] 22 p.
92-024171   704/.036872073/07479461   20
188050801X
*Columbus, Christopher -- Influence -- Exhibitions. Mexican
American art -- Exhibitions. Art and history -- United States --
Exhibitions.*

N6538.M4 C664 2002
Contemporary Chicana and Chicano art: artists, works,
culture, and education/ authors, Gary D. Keller ... [et al.].
Tempe, AZ: Bilingual Press/Editorial Bilingue, c2002.
2002-066523   704.03/6872073 21   1931010137
*Mexican American art -- 20th century. Mexican American
artists.*

N6538.M4 G37 1998
Gaspar de Alba, Alicia,
Chicano art inside/outside the master's house: cultural politics and the CARA exhibition/ by Alicia Gaspar de Alba. 1st ed. Austin: University of Texas Press, 1998. xxi, 308 p.
97-011398   704/.0368/72073 21   0292728050
Mexican American art. Politics in art. Mexican American art -- Public opinion. Mexican Americans -- Civil rights.

N6538.M4 Q57
Quirarte, Jacinto,
Mexican American artists. Austin, University of Texas Press [1973] xxv, 149 p.
72-010925   709/.79   0292750064
Mexican American art -- Southwest, New -- 20th century. Mexican American artists -- Southwest, New.

N6538.N5.B525 1989
Black art ancestral legacy: the African impulse in African-American art. Dallas, Tex.: Dallas Museum of Art; c1989. 305 p.
89-023743   704/.0396073/007473   0810931044
Afro-American art -- Exhibitions. Art, Modern -- 20th century -- United States -- Exhibitions.

N6538.N5.D6 1960
Dover, Cedric.
American Negro art. [Greenwich, Conn.] New York Graphic Society [1960] 186 p.
60-051364   709.73
Afro-American art -- United States. Art, American.

N6538.N5.D74
Driskell, David C.
Two centuries of Black American art: [exhibition], Los Angeles County Museum of Art, the High Museum of Art, Atlanta, Museum of Fine Arts, Dallas, the Brooklyn Museum/ David C. Driskell; with catalog notes by Leonard Simon. [Los Angeles]: Los Angeles County Museum of Art; 1976. 221 p.
76-013691   709/.73   0875870708
Afro-American art -- Exhibitions.

N6538.N5.F29
Fax, Elton C.
Black artists of the new generation/ Elton C. Fax; foreword by Romare Bearden. New York: Dodd, Mead, c1977. xiv, 370 p.
77-007053   709/.2/2   0396074340
Afro-American artists -- Biography. Afro-American art. Art, Modern -- 20th century -- United States.

N6538.N5.L39
Lewis, Samella S.
Art: African American/ Samella Lewis. New York: Harcourt Brace Jovanovich, c1978. x, 246 p.
77-078732   704/.0396073   0155034103
Afro-American art. Afro-American artists -- Biography -- History and criticism. Afro-Americans in art.

N6538.N5.L4
Lewis, Samella S.
Black artists on art, [edited by] Samella S. Lewis and Ruth G. Waddy. Los Angeles, Contemporary Crafts Publishers, [1969-   ]
76-097788   709/.22
Afro-American art. Afro-American artists.

N6538.N5.L58 1982
Livingston, Jane.
Black folk art in America, 1930-1980/ by Jane Livingston and John Beardsley with a contribution by Regenia Perry. Jackson: Published for the Corcoran Gallery of Art by the University Press of Mississippi; [s.l.]: Center for the Study of Southern Culture, c1982. 186 p.
81-024072   704/.0396073/074013   0878051589
Afro-American art -- Exhibitions. Primitivism in art -- United States -- Exhibitions. Ethnic art -- United States -- Exhibitions.

N6538.N5.M35 1989
McElroy, Guy C.
African-American artists, 1880-1987: selections from the Evans-Tibbs Collection/ Guy C. McElroy, Richard J. Powell, Sharon F. Patton; introduction by David C. Driskell. Washington, D.C.: Smithsonian Institution Traveling Exhibition Service, in association with University of Washington Press, Seattle, c1989. 125 p.
88-600493   704/.0393073/0074   0295968370
Afro-American art -- Exhibitions. Art, Modern -- 19th century -- United States -- Exhibitions. Art, Modern -- 20th century -- United States -- Exhibitions.

N6538.N5.P68 1999
Powell, Richard J., 1953-
To conserve a legacy: American art from historically Black colleges and universities/ Richard J. Powell, Jock Reynolds; with an introduction by Kinshasha Holman Conwill. Andover, Mass.: Addison Gallery of American Art; 1999. 240 p.
98-050539   704.03/96073/0074   0262161869
Afro-American art -- Exhibitions. Afro-American universities and colleges -- Art collections -- Exhibitions. Art -- Private collections -- Southern States -- Exhibitions.

N6538.N5.T46 1991
Thomison, Dennis, 1937-
The Black artist in America: an index to reproductions/ compiled by Dennis Thomison. Metuchen, N.J.: Scarecrow Press, 1991. lx, 396 p.
91-033050   016.704/0396073   0810825031
Afro-American art -- Indexes.

N6538.N5.V57
Vlach, John Michael, 1948-
The Afro-American tradition in decorative arts/ John Michael Vlach. Cleveland: Cleveland Museum of Art, c1978. xii, 175 p.
77-019326   745/.089/96073   0910386390
Afro-American art -- Exhibitions. Afro-American art -- African influences -- Exhibitions. Afro-American art -- European influences -- Exhibitions.

N6540.N49 2000
Newlands, Anne.
Canadian art: from its beginnings to 2000/ Anne Newlands. Willowdale, Ont.: Firefly Books, 2000. 355 p.
00-455037   709/.71   1552094502
Art, Canadian. Indian art -- Canada.

N6553.C66 1996
Converging cultures: art & identity in Spanish America/ edited by Diana Fane; with essays by Diana Fane ... [et al.]. New York: Harry N. Abrams, 1996. 320 p.
95-021899   709/.72/07474723   0810940302
Art, Mexican -- Exhibitions. Art, Colonial -- Mexico -- Exhibitions. Indian art -- Mexico -- Exhibitions.

N6553.T6813
Toussaint, Manuel, 1890-1955.
Colonial art in Mexico. Translated and edited by Elizabeth Wilder Weismann. Austin, University of Texas Press [1967] xxvi, 493 p.
66-015696   709/.72
Art, Mexican -- History. Art, Colonial -- Mexico -- History.

N6553.W44 1985
Weismann, Elizabeth Wilder, 1908-
Art and time in Mexico: from the Conquest to the Republic/ text by Elizabeth Wilder Weismann; photographs by Judith Hancock Sandoval. New York: Harper & Row, c1985. xviii, 284 p.
84-048202   709/.72   006438506X
Art, Mexican. Art, Colonial -- Mexico.

N6554.C45
Charlot, Jean, 1898-
Mexican art and the Academy of San Carlos, 1785-1915. Foreword by Elizabeth Wilder Weismann. Austin, University of Texas Press [1962] 177 p.
61-013318   709.72
Art, Mexican -- History.

N6555.S3
Schmeckebier, Laurence Eli, 1906-
Modern Mexican art [by] Laurence E. Schmeckebier. Minneapolis, The University of Minnesota Press [c1939] xvii, 190 p.
39-027756   709.72
Painting -- Mexico. Painters, Mexican. Mural painting and decoration.

N6603.C26 1994
Camnitzer, Luis, 1937-
New art of Cuba/ Luis Camnitzer. Austin: University of Texas Press, 1994. xxx, 400 p.
92-043116   709/.7291/09048   0292711492
Art, Cuban. Art, Modern -- 20th century -- Cuba.

N6608.B276.A4 1992
Marshall, Richard, 1947-
Jean-Michel Basquiat/ by Richard Marshall; with essays by Dick Hebdige ... [et al.]. New York: Whitney Museum of American Art: [c1992] 272 p.
92-019045   759.13   0874270812
Basquiat, Jean Michel -- Exhibitions. Basquiat, Jean Michel -- Criticism and interpretation.

N6620.B3913 1992
Bayon, Damian.
History of South American colonial art and architecture: Spanish South America and Brazil/ Damian Bayon and Murillo Marx. New York: Rizzoli, 1992. 442 p.
91-051144   709/.8   0847815552
Architecture, Colonial -- South America. Architecture -- South America. Art, Colonial -- Brazil.

N6750-7233 History — Special countries — Europe

N6750.T58 1998
Toll, Nelly S.
When memory speaks: the Holocaust in art/ Nelly Toll. Westport, Conn.: Praeger, 1998. xviii, 125 p.
97-001746   704.9/499/405318   0275955346
Holocaust, Jewish (1939-1945), in art. Jewish artists -- Europe -- Psychology. World War, 1939-1945 -- Concentration camps -- Europe.

N6754.K38 1995
Kaufmann, Thomas DaCosta.
Court, cloister, and city: the art and culture of Central Europe, 1450-1800/ Thomas DaCosta Kaufmann. Chicago: University of Chicago Press, 1995. 576 p.
95-010237   709/.43/0903   0226427293
Art -- Europe, Central. Architecture -- Europe, Central. Europe, Central -- Civilization.

N6756.C73 1997
Craske, Matthew.
Art in Europe, 1700-1830: a history of the visual arts in an era of unprecedented urban economic growth/ Matthew Craske. Oxford; Oxford University Press, 1997. 320 p.
96-037917   709/.4/09033   0192842463
Art, European. Art, Modern -- 17th-18th centuries -- Europe. Art, Modern -- 19th century -- Europe.

N6757.V38 1999
Vaughan, William, 1943-
Arts of the nineteenth century/ by William Vaughan; introduction, captions, and biographical notes were translated from the French by James Underwood. New York: Abrams, [c1999-   ]
98-003693   709/.034   0810919826
Art, European. Art, Modern -- 19th century -- Europe. Art, American.

N6757.5.A78.H68 1996
Howard, Jeremy.
Art nouveau: international and national styles in Europe/ Jeremy Howard. Manchester; Manchester University Press; 1996. xiv, 240 p.
95-047946   709/.03/49   0719041600
Art nouveau -- Europe. Art, European. Art, Modern -- 19th century -- Europe.

N6758.C68 1990
Cowling, Elizabeth.
On classic ground: Picasso, Leger, de Chirico, and the new classicism, 1910-1930/ Elizabeth Cowling, Jennifer Mundy. London: Tate Gallery, 1990. 264 p.
91-157453   709/.04/107442132   185437043X
Neoclassicism (Art) -- Europe -- Exhibitions. Art, European -- Exhibitions. Art, Modern -- 20th century -- Europe -- Exhibitions.

N6758.M352 1999
Mansbach, Steven A., 1950-
Modern art in Eastern Europe: from the Baltic to the Balkans, ca. 1890-1939/ S.A. Mansbach. Cambridge, UK; Cambridge University Press, 1999. xvi, 384 p.
97-042894   709/.47/0904   0521450853
Art, East European. Art, Modern -- 20th century -- Europe, Eastern.

N6763.D62 1982
Dodwell, C. R.
Anglo-Saxon art: a new perspective/ C.R. Dodwell. Ithaca, N.Y.: Cornell University Press, 1982. x, 353 p.
82-071592   709/.42   0801415160
Art, Anglo-Saxon. Art, Medieval -- England.

N6763.E53 1984
English romanesque art, 1066-1200: Hayward Gallery, London, 5 April-8 July 1984/ [edited by George Zarnecki, Janet Holt and Tristram Holland]. London: Weidenfeld and Nicolson in association with the Arts Council of Great Britain, c1984. 416 p.
84-175635   709/.42/07402165   0297784129
Art, English -- Exhibitions. Art, Medieval -- England -- Exhibitions. Art, Romanesque -- England -- Exhibitions.

N6764.S94 1988
Sweetman, John
The Oriental obsession: Islamic inspiration in British and American art and architecture, 1500-1920/ John Sweetman. Cambridge [Cambridgeshire]; Cambridge University Press, 1988. xviii, 327 p.
86-028383   709/.41   0521329825
Art, British -- Islamic influences. Architecture -- Great Britain -- Islamic influences. Art, American -- Islamic influences.

N6767.R66 1999
Royal Academy of Arts (Great Britain)
Art in the age of Queen Victoria: treasures from the Royal Academy of Arts permanent collection/ edited by Helen Valentine. London: Royal Academy of Arts in association with Yale University Press, New Haven and London, c1999. 167 p.
99-061349   709/.41/07442132   0300079974
Art, Modern -- 19th century -- Great Britain -- Catalogs. Art, Victorian -- Great Britain -- Catalogs. Art -- England -- London -- Catalogs.

N6767.W66 1995
Women in the Victorian art world/ edited by Clarissa Campbell Orr. Manchester; Manchester University Press; c1995. xii, 208 p.
95-171979   704/.042/094109034   0719041228
Women artists -- Great Britain -- History -- 19th century. Women art critics -- Great Britain -- History -- 19th century. Women art collectors -- Great Britain -- History -- 19th century.

N6767.5.P7.W3 1970b
Watkinson, Raymond.
Pre-Raphaelite art and design. Greenwich, Conn., New York Graphic Society [1970] 208 p.
79-120101   709/.42   0821203983
Pre-Raphaelitism

N6767.5.V52.J46 1992
Jenkyns, Richard.
Dignity and decadence: Victorian art and the classical inheritance/ Richard Jenkyns. Cambridge, Mass.: Harvard University Press, 1992. xviii, 363 p.
91-075748   709/.41/09034   0674206258
Art, Victorian -- Great Britain -- Classical influences. Art, British -- Classical influences.

N6784.H35 1999
Harbison, Peter.
The golden age of Irish art: the medieval achievement, 600-1200/ Peter Harbison. New York: Thames and Hudson, 1999. 368 p.
98-061896   709/.415/09021   0500019274
Art, Irish. Art, Medieval -- Ireland.

N6784.H4213 1965b
Henry, Francoise.
Irish art in the early Christian period, to 800 A.D. London, Methuen [1965] xv, 256 p.
68-007707
Art, Irish -- History.

N6797.B57.K4 1971
Keynes, Geoffrey, 1887-
Blake studies: essays on his life and work, by Geoffrey Keynes, Kt. Oxford, Clarendon Press, 1971. xii, 263 p.
72-870938   760/.0924   0198120036
Blake, William, -- 1757-1827. Artists -- Great Britain -- Biography. Poets, English -- 18th century -- Biography. Poets, English -- 19th century -- Biography.

N6797.B758.A4 1995
Alexander, Christine
The art of the Brontes/ Christine Alexander and Jane Sellars. Cambridge; Cambridge University Press, 1995. xxiv, 484 p.
94-004251   759.2   0521432480
Bronte family -- Exhibitions. Authors as artists -- England -- Exhibitions.

N6797.C63.A4 1996
Reynolds, Graham.
The early paintings and drawings of John Constable/ Graham Reynolds. New Haven: Published for the Paul Mellon Centre for Studies in British Art by Yale University Press, 1996. 2 v.
95-038034   759.2   0300063377
Constable, John, -- 1776-1837 -- Catalogs.

N6797.H57.A4 1988a
Hockney, David.
David Hockney: a retrospective/ organized by Maurice Tuchman and Stephanie Barron. Los Angeles, Calif.: Los Angeles County Museum of Art; c1988. 288 p.
87-026146   709/.2/4   0810911671
Hockney, David -- Exhibitions.

N6797.H6.P38 1991
Paulson, Ronald.
Hogarth/ Ronald Paulson. New Brunswick: Rutgers University Press, c1991-c1993. 3 v.
90-024569   760/.092   0813516943
Hogarth, William, -- 1697-1764.   Artists -- England -- Biography.

N6797.M23.C47 1996
Charles Rennie Mackintosh/ edited by Wendy Kaplan. [Glasgow]: Glasgow Museums; c1996. 383 p.
95-047759   709/.2   1558597913
Mackintosh, Charles Rennie, -- 1868-1928 -- Criticism and interpretation.   Arts and crafts movement -- Scotland.

N6797.M5 A4 2001
Kosinski, Dorothy M.
Henry Moore, sculpting the 20th century/ Dorothy M. Kosinski with contributions by Julian Andrews ... [et al.]. [Dallas, Tex.]: Dallas Museum of Art; 2001. 323 p.
00-065687   730/.92   0300089929
Moore, Henry, -- 1898- -- Exhibitions.

N6797.Y4.A76 1998
Arnold, Bruce.
Jack Yeats/ Bruce Arnold. New Haven, CT: Yale University Press, 1998. x, 418 p.
98-019116   759.2/915   0300075499
Yeats, Jack Butler, -- 1871-1957.   Artists -- Ireland -- Biography.

N6808.5.E9.E4613 1989
Egon Schiele and his contemporaries: Austrian painting and drawing from 1900 to 1930 from the Leopold collection, Vienna/ edited by Klaus Albrecht Schroder and Harald Szeemann; with contributions by Antonia Hoerschelmann ... [et al.]. Munich: Prestel; c1989. 295 p.
93-179737   3791309218
Schiele, Egon, -- 1890-1918 -- Exhibitions. Leopold, Rudolf -- Art collections -- Exhibitions. Art, Austrian -- Exhibitions. Art, Modern -- 20th century -- Austria -- Exhibitions. Expressionism (Art) -- Austria -- Exhibitions.

N6811.5.S34.A4 1994
Kallir, Jane.
Egon Schiele/ by Jane Kallir, with an essay by Alessandra Comini. New York: H.N. Abrams; 1994. 192 p.
93-026840   759.36   0810938456
Schiele, Egon, -- 1890-1918 -- Exhibitions.

N6820.5.N93.M36 1991
Mansbach, Steven A., 1950-
Standing in the tempest: painters of the Hungarian avantgarde, 1908-1930/ S.A. Mansbach; with contributions by Richard V. West ... [et al.]. Santa Barbara, Calif.: Santa Barbara Museum of Art; c1991. 240 p.
90-049893   709/.439/1207473   0262132745
Nyolcak (Group of artists) Aktivistak (Group of artists) Avant-garde (Aesthetics) -- Hungary -- History -- 20th century.

N6822.5.M63.K36 1995
Kaplan, Louis, 1960-
Laszlo Moholy-Nagy: biographical writings/ Louis Kaplan. Durham: Duke University Press, c1995. xi, 232 p.
94-040315   709/.2   0822315777
Moholy-Nagy, Laszlo, -- 1895-1946.   Artists -- Hungary -- Biography -- History and criticism. Art, Modern -- 20th century -- Hungary. Deconstruction.

N6834.5.M8.A4 1998
Arwas, Victor.
Alphonse Mucha--the spirit of art nouveau/ Victor Arwas, Jana Brabcova-Orlikova, Anna Dvorak; with an introduction by Ronald F. Lipp and Suzanne Jackson and essays by Quentin Bajac ... [et al.]. Alexandria, Va.: Art Services International, 1998. 344 p.
97-043743   760/.092   0883971232
Mucha, Alphonse Marie, -- 1860-1939 -- Exhibitions. Decoration and ornament -- Art nouveau -- Exhibitions.

N6838.M6.M6 1969
Moholy-Nagy, Sibyl, 1905-
Moholy-Nagy: experiment in totality [by] Sibyl Moholy-Nagy. With an introd. by Walter Gropius. Cambridge, Mass., M.I.T. Press [1969] xvii, 259 p.
69-020265   709/.2/4   026213053X
Moholy-Nagy, Laszlo, -- 1895-1946.

N6843.M5613 2000
Minne-Seve, Viviane.
Romanesque and gothic France: architecture and sculpture/ Viviane Minne-Seve, Herve Kergall; translated from the French by Jack Hawkes and Lory Frankel. New York: H.N. Abrams, 2000. 411 p.
00-038974   709/.44/0902   0810944367
Art, French. Art, Romanesque -- France. Art, Gothic -- France.

N6843.S7
Stoddard, Whitney S.
Monastery and cathedral in France; medieval architecture, sculpture, stained glass, manuscripts, the art of the church treasuries, by Whitney S. Stoddard. Middletown, Conn., Wesleyan University Press [1966] xxi, 412 p.
66-023923   726.0944
Christian art and symbolism -- France -- Medieval, 500-1500. Architecture, Medieval -- France. Church architecture -- France.

N6845.C5913 1998
Cloulas, Ivan.
Treasures of the French Renaissance/ Ivan Cloulas, Michele Bimbenet-Privat; photographs by Serge Chirol; translated from the French by John Goodman. New York: H.N. Abrams, 1998. 304 p.
97-045860   709/.44/09031   0810938839
Art, French. Art, Renaissance -- France. Architecture, Renaissance -- France.

N6846.5.N4.C76 1995
Crow, Thomas E., 1948-
Emulation: making artists for revolutionary France/ Thomas Crow. New Haven: Yale University Press, c1995. 364 p.
94-013225   759.4/09/033   0300060939
David, Jacques Louis, -- 1748-1825 -- Influence. Art, French. France -- History -- Revolution, 1789-1799 -- Art and the revolution. Neoclassicism (Art) -- France.

N6847.G758 2000
The Grove dictionary of art. French artists/ edited by Jane Turner. New York: St. Martin's Press, 2000.
99-089528   709/.2/244.B 21   0312229704
Art, French -- 19th century -- Encyclopedias. Artists -- France -- Encyclopedias.

N6847.G76 2000
The Grove dictionary of art. From Monet to Cézanne: late 19th-century French artists edited by Jane Turner. New York: St. Martin's Press, 2000. xii, 434 p.
99-089532   709/.44/09034   0312229712
Artists -- France -- Dictionaries. Art, French -- Dictionaries. Art, Modern -- 19th century -- France -- Dictionaries.

N6847.K67 1999
Kostenevich, A. G.
French art treasures at the Hermitage: splendid masterpieces, new discoveries/ by Albert Kostenevich. New York: Harry N. Abrams, 1999. 469 p.
99-014103   709/.44/0744721   0810938898
Art, Modern -- 19th century -- France. Art, Modern -- 20th century -- France. Art -- Russia (Federation) -- Saint Petersburg.

N6847.5.P68.L48
Levitine, George.
The dawn of Bohemianism: the Barbu rebellion and primitivism in neoclassical France/ George Levitine. University Park: Pennsylvania State University Press, c1978. xi, 163 p.
77-013892   759.4   0271005270
Painting, French. Primitivism in art -- France. Painting, Modern -- 19th century -- France.

N6847.5.R4.W44
Weisberg, Gabriel P.
The realist tradition: French painting and drawing, 1830-1900/ Gabriel P. Weisberg. Cleveland: Cleveland Museum of Art; c1980. xiii, 346 p.
80-016579   759.4/074/017132   0910386609
Realism in art -- France -- Exhibitions. Art, French -- Exhibitions. Art, Modern -- 19th century -- France -- Exhibitions.

N6850.B64 1995
Boime, Albert.
Art and the French commune: imagining Paris after war and revolution/ by Albert Boime. Princeton, N.J.: Princeton University Press, c1995. xiv, 234 p.
94-005324   701/.03   0691029628
Art -- Political aspects -- France -- Paris. Art and the state -- France -- Paris. Impressionism (Art) -- France -- Paris. Paris (France) -- Intellectual life -- 19th century. Paris (France) -- History -- Commune, 1871.

N6850.M35 1993
Mainardi, Patricia.
The end of the Salon: art and the state in the early Third Republic/ Patricia Mainardi. Cambridge; Cambridge University Press, 1993. xii, 210 p.
92-015566   709/.44/09034   0521432510
Art and state -- France -- History -- 19th century.

N6850.M48 1988
Milner, John, 1946-
The studios of Paris: the capital of art in the late nineteenth century/ John Milner. New Haven: Yale University Press, 1988. vii, 248 p.
87-030044   709/.44/361   0300039905
Art, French -- France -- Paris. Art, Modern -- 19th century -- France -- Paris. Artists' studios -- France -- Paris.

N6850.S56 1989
Silver, Kenneth E.
Esprit de corps: the art of the Parisian avant-garde and the First World War, 1914-1925/ Kenneth E. Silver. Princeton, N.J.: Princeton University Press, c1989. xxiv, 504 p.
89-003735   709/.44/361   0691040524
Avant-garde (Aesthetics) -- France -- Paris -- History -- 20th century. Nationalism and art -- France -- Paris. Painting, French -- France -- Paris.

N6851.S29.R8 1990
Rudolph, Conrad, 1951-
Artistic change at St-Denis: Abbot Suger's program and the early twelfth-century controversy over art/ Conrad Rudolph. Princeton, N.J.: Princeton University Press, c1990. x, 119 p.
89-010606   726/.5/0944362   0691040680
Suger, -- Abbot of Saint Denis, -- 1081-1151 -- Contributions in Gothic art.   Church decoration and ornament -- France -- Saint-Denis -- History -- To 1500. Art, Gothic -- France -- Saint-Denis. Art, French -- France -- Saint-Denis. Saint-Denis (France) -- Buildings, structures, etc.

N6853.B7.Z8713 1988
Zurcher, Bernard.
Georges Braque, life and work/ Bernard Zurcher; translated by Simon Nye. New York: Rizzoli, 1988. 319 p.
88-042710   709/.2/4   0847809862
Braque, Georges, -- 1882-1963.   Artists -- France -- Biography.

N6853.D3.L39 1996
Laughton, Bruce.
Honore Daumier/ Bruce Laughton. New Haven: Yale University Press, c1996. viii, 200 p.
96-021441   760/.092   0300069456
Daumier, Honore, -- 1808-1879.   Artists -- France -- Biography.

N6853.D315.R63 1989
Roberts, Warren, 1933-
Jacques-Louis David, revolutionary artist: art, politics, and the French Revolution/ by Warren Roberts. Chapel Hill: University of North Carolina Press, c1989. xii, 254 p.
88-037320   759.4   0807818453
David, Jacques Louis, -- 1748-1825 -- Criticism and interpretation. David, Jacques Louis, -- 1748-1825 -- Political and social views.   France -- History -- Revolution, 1789-1799 -- Art and the revolution.

N6853.D33.A4 1999
Degas, Edgar, 1834-1917.
Degas and New Orleans: a French impressionist in America/ Gail Feigenbaum; catalogue by Jean Sutherland Boggs; essays by Christopher Benfey ... [et al.]. New Orleans: New Orleans Museum of Art; [Copenhagen]: Ordrupgaard, c1999. xiv, 301 p.
99-070046   0894940724
Degas, Edgar, -- 1834-1917 -- Exhibitions. Degas, Edgar, -- 1834-1917 -- Journeys -- Louisiana -- New Orleans -- Exhibitions. Impressionism (Art) -- France -- Exhibitions. New Orleans (La.) -- Description and travel -- Exhibitions.

N6853.D33.K46 1993
Kendall, Richard.
Degas landscapes/ Richard Kendall. New Haven: Yale University Press in association with the Metropolitan Museum of Art, New York and the Museum of Fine Arts, Houston, c1993. ix, 312 p.
93-011554   760/.092   0300058373
Degas, Edgar, -- 1834-1917 -- Criticism and interpretation. Landscape in art.

N6853.D78.A4 1993
Jean Dubuffet 1943-1963: paintings, sculptures, assemblages: an exhibition / organized by James T. Demetrion; essays by Susan J. Cooke, Jean Planque, and Peter Schjeldahl. Washington, D.C.: Hirshhorn Museum and Sculpture Garden in association with the Smithsonian Institution Press, c1993. 167 p.
93-020414   709/.2   1560982985
Dubuffet, Jean, -- 1901- -- Exhibitions.

N6853.D8.A64 1998
Henderson, Linda Dalrymple, 1948-
Duchamp in context: science and technology in the Large glass and related works/ Linda Dalrymple Henderson. Princeton, N.J.: Princeton University Press, c1998. xxiii, 373 p.
97-041792   709/.2   0691055513
Duchamp, Marcel, -- 1887-1968. -- Bride stripped bare by her bachelors, even. Duchamp, Marcel, -- 1887-1968. -- Criticism and interpretation. Art and science.

N6853.D8.J83 1995
Judovitz, Dalia.
Unpacking Duchamp: art in transit/ Dalia Judovitz. Berkeley: University of California Press, c1995. x, 308 p.
94-026724   709/.2   0520088093
Duchamp, Marcel, -- 1887-1968 -- Criticism and interpretation. Modernism (Art) Postmodernism.

N6853.D8.N39 1999
Naumann, Francis M.
Marcel Duchamp: the art of making art in the age of mechanical reproduction/ Francis M. Naumann. Ghent: Ludion Press; c1999. 331 p.
99-029063   709/.2   0810963345
Duchamp, Marcel, -- 1887-1968 -- Criticism and interpretation. Appropriation (Art) Art -- Reproduction.

N6853.G5.A4 1988
Fletcher, Valerie J.
Alberto Giacometti, 1901-1966/ Valerie J. Fletcher; with essays by Silvio Berthoud and Reinhold Hohl. Washington, D.C.: Published for the Hirshhorn Museum and Sculpture Garden by the Smithsonian Institution Press, c1988. 250 p.
88-042545   709/.2/4   0874744245
Giacometti, Alberto, -- 1901-1966 -- Exhibitions.

N6853.L64.R87 1982
Russell, H. Diane
Claude Lorrain, 1600-1682/ H. Diane Russell. Washington, D.C.: National Gallery of Art, c1982. 480 p.
82-014250   760/.092/4   0894680579
Lorrain, Claude, -- 1600-1682.

N6853.M33.A4 1992
Elderfield, John.
Henri Matisse: a retrospective/ John Elderfield. New York: Museum of Modern Art: c1992. 480 p.
92-081515   709/.2   0810961164
Matisse, Henri, -- 1869-1954 -- Exhibitions.   Women in art -- Exhibitions.

N6853.M33.B65 1998
Bois, Yve Alain.
Matisse and Picasso/ Yve-Alain Bois. New York: Flammarion, 1998.
98-044307   709/.2/2   2080135481
Matisse, Henri, -- 1869-1954 -- Criticism and interpretation. Matisse, Henri, -- 1869-1954 -- Friends and associates. Picasso, Pablo, -- 1881-1973 -- Criticism and interpretation. Artistic collaboration -- France.

N6853.M33.S3513 1984
Schneider, Pierre.
Matisse/ Pierre Schneider; translated by Michael Taylor and Bridget Strevens Romer. New York: Rizzoli, 1984. 752 p.
84-042644   759.4   0847805468
Matisse, Henri, -- 1869-1954.   Artists -- France -- Biography.

N6853.M64.A4 1987
Stuckey, Charles F.
Berthe Morisot, Impressionist/ Charles F. Stuckey and William P. Scott; with the assistance of Suzanne G. Lindsay. New York: Hudson Hills Press: c1987. 228 p.
87-003265   759.4   0933920032
Morisot, Berthe, -- 1841-1895 -- Exhibitions. Morisot, Berthe, -- 1841-1895 -- Influence -- Exhibitions.   Art, French -- Exhibitions. Art, Modern -- 19th century -- France -- Exhibitions. Impressionism (Art) -- France -- Exhibitions.

N6853.P5.A4 1997
Picasso, Pablo, 1881-1973.
Picasso--the early years, 1892-1906/ edited by Marilyn McCully; with contributions from Natasha Staller ... [et al.]. Washington: National Gallery of Art, c1997. 374 p.
96-049663   759.4   0894682687
Picasso, Pablo, -- 1881-1973 -- Exhibitions.

N6853.P5.D2613 1994
Daix, Pierre.
Picasso: life and art/ Pierre Daix; translated by Olivia Emmet. New York, N.Y.: Icon Editions, 1994. xv, 450 p.
90-055530   709/.2   0064309762
Picasso, Pablo, -- 1881-1973.   Artists -- France -- Biography.

N6853.P5.K58 1993
Kleinfelder, Karen L.
The artist, his model, her image, his gaze: Picasso's pursuit of the model/ Karen L. Kleinfelder. Chicago: University of Chicago Press, 1993. xvii, 256 p.
92-012619   709/.2   0226439836
Picasso, Pablo, -- 1881-1973 -- Psychology. Picasso, Pablo, -- 1881-1973 -- Relations with women.   Artists' models -- Psychology.

N6853.P5.L38 1989
Leighten, Patricia Dee, 1946-
Re-ordering the universe: Picasso and anarchism, 1897-1914/ Patricia Leighten. Princeton, N.J.: Princeton University Press, c1989. xvi, 198 p.
88-014065   709/.24   0691040591
Picasso, Pablo, -- 1881-1973 -- Criticism and interpretation. Anarchism in art.

N6853.P5.P519 1996
Picasso and the Spanish tradition/ edited by Jonathan Brown; with contributions by Jonathan Brown ... [et al.]. New Haven: Yale University Press, c1996. xi, 194 p.
96-060716   760/.092   0300064756
Picasso, Pablo, -- 1881-1973 -- Criticism and interpretation. Art, Spanish -- Influence. Identity (Psychology) in art.

N6853.P5.R56 1990
Richardson, John, 1924-
A life of Picasso/ John Richardson with the collaboration of Marilyn McCully. New York: Random House, c1991-1996 v. 1-2
89-042915   709/.2   0394531922
Picasso, Pablo, -- 1881-1973.   Artists -- France -- Biography.

N6853.P5.S33 2000
Schapiro, Meyer, 1904-
The unity of Picasso's art/ Meyer Schapiro. New York: George Braziller, 2000. 199 p.
00-034318   709/.2   0807614793
Picasso, Pablo, -- 1881-1973 -- Criticism and interpretation. Picasso, Pablo, -- 1881-1973. -- Guernica. Einstein, Albert, -- 1879-1955 -- Aesthetics. Cubism.

N6853.P5.S74 1988
Huffington, Arianna Stassinopoulos, 1950-
Picasso: creator and destroyer/ Arianna Stassinopoulos Huffington. New York: Simon and Schuster, c1988. 558 p.
88-011368   709/.2/4   0671454463
Picasso, Pablo, -- 1881-1973.   Artists -- France -- Biography.

N6853.R63.A4 1992
Rodin, Auguste, 1840-1917.
Rodin: Eros and creativity/ edited by Rainer Crone and Siegfried Salzmann; with contributions by Jacques de Caso ... [et al.]. Munich, Germany: Prestel; c1992. 235 p.
92-233153   709/.2   3791311859
Rodin, Auguste, -- 1840-1917 -- Catalogs. Rodin, Auguste, -- 1840-1917 -- Criticism and interpretation. Erotic art -- France -- Catalogs.

N6853.S48
Herbert, Robert L., 1929-
Seurat: drawings and paintings/ Robert L. Herbert. New Haven, CT: Yale University Press, c2001. x, 195 p.
00-043966   759.4   0300071310
Seurat, Georges, -- 1859-1891 -- Criticism and interpretation. Neo-impressionism (Art) -- France.

N6853.T47.S43 1999
Seductive surfaces: the art of Tissot/ edited by Katharine Lochnan. New Haven: Yale University Press, c1999. xvi, 245 p.
99-065333   759.4   0300081847
Tissot, James Jacques Joseph, -- 1836-1902 -- Criticism and interpretation.

N6853.T6.A4 1996
Ives, Colta Feller.
Toulouse-Lautrec in the Metropolitan Museum of Art/ Colta Ives; with a foreword by Philippe de Montebello. New York: The Museum, c1996. 72 p.
96-017722   760/.092   0870998048
Toulouse-Lautrec, Henri de, -- 1864-1901 -- Exhibitions. Art -- New York (State) -- New York -- Exhibitions.

N6853.T6.S93 1999
Sweetman, David, 1943-
Explosive acts: Toulouse-Lautrec, Oscar Wilde, Felix Feneon and the art & anarchy of the fin de siecle/ David Sweetman. New York: Simon & Schuster, c1999. 512 p.
99-059192   760/.092   0684811790
Toulouse-Lautrec, Henri de, -- 1864-1901 -- Criticism and interpretation.

N6853.W38.A4 1984
Grasselli, Margaret Morgan, 1951-
Watteau, 1684-1721/ Margaret Morgan Grasselli and Pierre Rosenberg, with the assistance of Nicole Parmantier. Washington: National Gallery of Art, c1984. 580 p.
84-004918   760/.092/4   0894680749
Watteau, Antoine, -- 1684-1721 -- Exhibitions.

N6861.L513
Lindemann, Gottfried.
History of German art; painting, sculpture, architecture. Translated by Tessa Sayle. New York, Praeger [1971] 228 p.
79-089605   709/.43
Art, German -- History.

N6867.5.M83.M35 1990
Makela, Maria Martha.
The Munich Secession: art and artists in turn-of-the-century Munich/ Maria Makela. Princeton, N.J.: Princeton University Press, c1990. xix, 205 p.
89-036934   709.43/364/09034   0691039828
Art, German -- Germany -- Munich. Art, Modern -- 19th century -- Germany -- Munich. Art, Modern -- 20th century -- Germany -- Munich.

N6868.F74 1990
Art in Germany, 1909-1936: from expressionism to resistance: from the Marvin and Janet Fishman collection/ Reinhold Heller; with a foreword by Eberhard Roters; and contributions by Stephanie T. D'Alessandro ... [et al.]. Munich, Federal Republic of Germany: Prestel, in association with the Milwaukee Art Museum, c1990. 271 p.
90-060653   0944110029
Fishman, Marvin -- Art collections -- Exhibitions. Fishman, Janet -- Art collections -- Exhibitions. Art, German -- Exhibitions. Art, Modern -- 20th century -- Germany -- Exhibitions. Art -- Private collections -- Wisconsin -- Milwaukee -- Exhibitions.

N6868.N38 1957
Museum of Modern Art (New York, N.Y.)
German art of the twentieth century/ by Werner Haftmann, Alfred Hentzen, W.S. Lieberman; edited by A.C. Ritchie. Museum of Modern Art, in collaboration with the City Art Museum of St. Louis, Missouri; distributed by Simon and Schuster 1957. 239 p.
57-011679   709/.43
Art, Modern -- 20th century -- Germany. Art, German -- Exhibitions.

N6868.5.B3.P37
Paret, Peter.
The Berlin Secession: modernism and its enemies in imperial Germany/ Peter Paret. Cambridge, Mass.: Belknap Press of Harvard University Press, 1980. 269 p.
80-015117   709/.431/55   0674067738
Berliner Secession (Group of artists) Modernism (Art) -- Germany. Politics in art. Germany -- History -- William II, 1888-1918.

N6868.5.E9.G37 1993
German expressionism: documents from the end of the Wilhelmine Empire to the rise of national socialism/ edited and annotated by Rose-Carol Washton Long with the assistance of Ida Katherine Rigby and contributions by Stephanie Barron, Rosemarie Haag Bletter, and Peter Chametzky; translations from the German edited by Nancy Roth. New York: G.K. Hall; c1993. xxiv, 349 p.
92-020500   709/.43/09041   0805799540
Expressionism(Art) -- Germany -- Sources. Art, German -- Sources. Art, Modern -- 20th century -- Germany -- Sources.

N6868.5.E9.R6 1989
Robert Gore Rifkind Center for German Expressionist Studies.
German expressionist prints and drawings: the Robert Gore Rifkind Center for German Expressionist Studies. Los Angeles, Calif.: Los Angeles County Museum of Art; c1989. 2 v.
88-007913   760/.0943   3791309595
Art, German -- Catalogs. Expressionism (Art) -- Germany -- Catalogs. Art -- California -- Los Angeles -- Catalogs.

N6868.5.N37.A34 1992
Adam, Peter.
Art of the Third Reich/ Peter Adam. New York: H.N Abrams, 1992. 332 p.
91-025563   709/.43/09043   0810919125
National socialism and art. Art, German. Art, Modern -- 20th century -- Germany.

N6868.5.N37.P4823 2000
Petropoulos, Jonathan.
The Faustian bargain: the art world in Nazi Germany/ Jonathan Petropoulos. New York, N.Y.: Oxford University Press, 2000. xvii, 395 p.
99-033372   709/.43/09043   0195129644
National socialism and art. Art and state -- Germany -- History -- 20th century. Art treasures in war -- Germany. Germany -- Cultural policy -- History -- 20th century.

N6888.B463.S7413 1991
Stachelhaus, Heiner.
Joseph Beuys/ Heiner Stachelhaus; translated by David Britt. New York: Abbeville Press, 1991. 223 p.
90-049991   709/.2   1558591079
Beuys, Joseph.   Artists -- Germany (West) -- Biography.

N6888.B6957 C86 1998
Cuneo, Pia F.
Art and politics in early modern Germany: Jörg Breu the Elder and the fashioning of political identity, ca. 1475-1536/ by Pia F. Cuneo. Leiden; Brill, c1998. vi, 261 p.
98-025296   769.92 21   9004111840
Breu, Jörg, ca. 1480-1537 -- Criticism and interpretation. Politics in art. Art and state -- Germany.

N6888.D8.A4 1988
Rowlands, John, 1931-
The age of Durer and Holbein: German drawings 1400-1550/ John Rowlands; with the assistance of Giulia Bartrum. Cambridge; Cambridge University Press, 1988. 260 p.
88-010836   741.943/074/02142   0521363225
Durer, Albrecht, -- 1471-1528 -- Exhibitions. Holbein, Hans, -- 1497-1543 -- Exhibitions. Art, Late Gothic -- Germany -- Exhibitions. Art, Early Renaissance -- Germany -- Exhibitions. Art, Late Gothic -- Europe, Central -- Exhibitions.

N6888.D8.E57 1991
Eisler, Colin T.
Durer's animals/ Colin Eisler. Washington: Smithsonian Institution Press, c1991. xv, 369 p.
90-021006   760/.092   0874744083
Durer, Albrecht, -- 1471-1528 -- Criticism and interpretation. Animals in art.

N6888.D8.H88 1990
Hutchison, Jane Campbell.
Albrecht Durer: a biography/ by Jane Campbell Hutchison. Princeton, N.J.: Princeton University Press, c1990. xiv, 247 p.
89-028971   760/.092   069103978X
Durer, Albrecht, -- 1471-1528. Artists -- Germany -- Biography.

N6888.G742.G4613
Grosz, George, 1893-1959.
George Grosz: his life and work/ [edited] by Uwe M. Schneede; with contributions by Georg Bussmann and Marina Schneede-Sczesny; translated by Susanne Flatauer. London: G. Fraser, 1979. 182 p.
80-469076   741/.092/4   0860920356
Grosz, George, -- 1893-1959. Artists -- Germany -- Biography.

N6888.K55.F7 1991
Franciscono, Marcel.
Paul Klee: his work and thought/ Marcel Franciscono. Chicago: University of Chicago Press, 1991. x, 395 p.
90-039006   760/.092   0226259900
Klee, Paul, -- 1879-1940 -- Criticism and interpretation.

N6888.K55.J67 1984
Jordan, Jim M.
Paul Klee and cubism/ by Jim M. Jordan. Princeton, N.J.: Princeton University Press, c1984. xxiii, 233 p.
83-013898   760/.092/4   0691040257
Klee, Paul, -- 1879-1940. Cubism.

N6888.K62.A4 1992
Prelinger, Elizabeth.
Kathe Kollwitz/ Elizabeth Prelinger; with essays by Alessandra Comini and Hildegard Bachert. Washington: National Gallery of Art, c1992. 192 p.
91-046307   709/.2   0894681702
Kollwitz, Kathe, -- 1867-1945 -- Exhibitions.

N6913.S53 1995
Siena, Florence, and Padua: art, society, and religion 1280-1400/ edited by Diana Norman. New Haven, Conn.: Yale University Press in association with the Open University, 1995. 2 v.
94-025653   701/.03/094509023   0300061242
Art, Italian. Cities and towns, Medieval -- Italy. Art, Gothic -- Italy.

N6915.I78
Italian art, 1400-1500: sources and documents/ [selected and translated by] Creighton E. Gilbert. Englewood Cliffs, N.J.: Prentice-Hall, c1980. xxviii, 226 p.
79-011069   709/.45   0135079470
Art, Italian. Art, Early Renaissance -- Italy.

N6915.P26 1997
Paoletti, John T.
Art in Renaissance Italy/ John T. Paoletti & Gary M. Radke. Upper Saddle River, NJ: Prentice Hall, c1997. 480 p.
96-018459   709/.45/09024   0810919788
Art, Italian. Art, Renaissance -- Italy.

N6915.S54 1992
Shearman, John K. G.
Only connect--: art and the spectator in the Italian Renaissance/ John Shearman. [Princeton, N.J.]: Princeton University Press, c1992. xvii, 281 p.
91-027246   709/.45/09024   0691099723
Art, Italian. Art, Renaissance -- Italy. Audiences -- Psychology.

N6915.W42 1997
Welch, Evelyn S., 1959-
Art and society in Italy, 1350-1500/ Evelyn Welch. Oxford; Oxford University Press, 1997. 351 p.
96-037916   709/.45/09023   0192842455
Art, Italian. Art, Renaissance -- Italy. Art and society -- Italy.

N6915.W525 1997
Williams, Robert, 1955-
Art, theory, and culture in sixteenth-century Italy: from techne to metatechne/ Robert Williams. Cambridge; Cambridge University Press, 1997. x, 243 p.
96-046389   709/.45/09031   0521495997
Art, Italian. Art, High Renaissance -- Italy. Art, Late Renaissance -- Italy.

N6916.H37 1980
Haskell, Francis, 1928-
Patrons and painters: a study in the relations between Italian art and society in the age of the Baroque/ Francis Haskell. New Haven: Yale University Press, 1980. xviii, 474 p.
80-005213　709/.45　0300025378
Art, Italian. Art, Baroque -- Italy. Art patrons.

N6921.F7.A387 1988
Andres, Glenn M.
The art of Florence/ by Glenn Andres, John M. Hunisak, A. Richard Turner; principal photography by Takashi Okamura. New York: Abbeville Press, c1988. 2 v.
83-006394　709/.45/51　0896594025
Art, Italian -- Italy -- Florence. Art, Renaissance -- Italy -- Florence.

N6921.F7.R47 1999
Rubin, Patricia Lee, 1951-
Renaissance Florence: the art of the 1470s/ Patricia Lee Rubin and Alison Wright; with contributions by Nicholas Penny. London: National Gallery Publications Limited; 1999. 360 p.
99-074591　709/.45/5109024　185709266X
Art, Italian -- Italy -- Florence -- Exhibitions. Art, Renaissance -- Italy -- Florence -- Exhibitions.

N6921.F7.T83 1997
Turner, Richard, 1932-
Renaissance Florence: the invention of a new art/ A. Richard Turner. New York: H.N. Abrams, c1997. 176 p.
96-033309　709/.45/5109024　0810927365
Art, Italian -- Italy -- Florence. Art, Renaissance -- Italy -- Florence.

N6921.F7.W313
Wackernagel, Martin, 1881-
The world of the Florentine Renaissance artist: projects and patrons, workshop and art market/ Martin Wackernagel; translated by Alison Luchs. Princeton, N.J.: Princeton University Press, c1981. xxx, 447 p.
80-039683　709/.45/51　0691039666
Art, Italian -- Italy -- Florence. Art, Renaissance -- Italy -- Florence. Artists -- Italy -- Florence.

N6921.V5.A5913 1999
Art in Venice/ edited by Stefano Zuffi. New York: H.N. Abrams, 1999. 398 p.
99-033480　709/.45/31　0810942046
Art, Italian -- Italy -- Venice -- Catalogs. Art -- Italy -- Venice -- Catalogs.

N6921.V5.B75 1997
Brown, Patricia Fortini, 1936-
Art and life in Renaissance Venice/ Patricia Fortini Brown. New York: Prentice Hall: 1997. 176 p.
96-049514　945/.3105　0810927470
Art, Italian -- Italy -- Venice. Art, Renaissance -- Italy -- Venice. Art patronage -- Italy -- Venice -- History -- 16th century. Venice (Italy) -- Social life and customs.

N6921.V5.H56 1999
Hills, Paul.
Venetian colour: marble, mosaic, painting and glass, 1250-1550/ Paul Hills. New Haven, CT: Yale University Press, c1999. x, 247 p.
99-020880　701/.85/094531　0300081359
Art, Gothic -- Italy -- Venice. Art, Renaissance -- Italy -- Venice. Color in art.

N6921.V5.H8713 1990
Huse, Norbert.
The art of Renaissance Venice: architecture, sculpture, and painting, 1460-1590/ Norbert Huse, Wolfgang Wolters; translated by Edmund Jephcott. Chicago: University of Chicago Press, 1990. v, 382 p.
90-031341　709/.45/3109024　0226361071
Art, Italian -- Italy -- Venice. Art, Renaissance -- Italy -- Venice. Venice (Italy) -- Buildings, structures, etc.

N6923.B5.S37 1991
Scribner, Charles.
Bernini/ by Charles Scribner III. New York: H.N. Abrams, Publishers, 1991. 128 p.
90-046202　709/.2　0810931117
Bernini, Gian Lorenzo, -- 1598-1680. Artists -- Italy -- Biography.

N6923.B9.C55 1961a
Clements, Robert John, 1912-
Michelangelo's theory of art. [New York] New York University Press, [1961] xxxiii, 471 p.
60-014318　701
Michelangelo Buonarroti, -- 1475-1564. Art -- Philosophy. Art, Renaissance.

N6923.B9.G57
Buonarroti, Michel Angelo, 1475-1564.
Michelangelo: paintings, sculptures, architecture, by Ludwig Goldscheider. New York, Phaidon Publishers: distributed by Garden City Books [1953] 228 p.
53-011922　704.91
Michelangelo Buonarroti, 1475-1564 -- Catalogs.

N6923.B9.M59
Morgan, Charles Hill, 1902-
The life of Michelangelo/ by Charles H. Morgan. New York: Reynal, c1960. 253 p.
60-009228　709.45
Michelangelo Buonarroti, -- 1475-1564. Artists -- Italy -- Biography.

N6923.B9.S9 1928
Symonds, John Addington, 1840-1893.
The life of Michelangelo Buonarroti, by John Addington Symonds. New York, The Modern library [1928?]
29-026574
Michelangelo Buonarroti, 1475-1564.

N6923.C638.E39 1997
Ekserdjian, David.
Correggio/ David Ekserdjian. New Haven: Yale University Press, c1997. ix, 334 p.
97-015696　759.5　0300072996
Correggio, -- 1489?-1534 -- Criticism and interpretation.

N6923.L33.B7313 1991
Bramly, Serge, 1949-
Leonardo: discovering the life of Leonardo da Vinci/ Serge Bramly; translated by Sian Reynolds. New York: HarperCollins Publishers, c1991. xvii, 493 p.
90-056356   709/.2   0060160659
Leonardo, -- da Vinci, -- 1452-1519.   Artists -- Italy -- Biography.

N6923.L33.T87 1993
Turner, Richard, 1932-
Inventing Leonardo/ A. Richard Turner. New York: Knopf: 1993. x, 268 p.
92-054879   709/.2   0679415513
Leonardo, -- da Vinci, -- 1452-1519 -- Criticism and interpretation.

N6923.P457.A4 1983
Knox, George.
Piazzetta: a tercentenary exhibition of drawings, prints, and books/ George Knox. Washington: National Gallery of Art, c1983. 258 p.
83-017484   760/.092/4   0894680714
Piazzetta, Giovanni Battista -- Exhibitions.

N6923.P495.W54
Wilton-Ely, John.
The mind and art of Giovanni Battista Piranesi/ John Wilton-Ely. London: Thames and Hudson, c1978. 304 p.
77-092272   769/.92/4   0500091226
Piranesi, Giovanni Battista, -- 1720-1778.   Neoclassicism (Art) -- Italy.

N6923.R597.F73 1994
Franklin, David, 1961-
Rosso in Italy: the Italian career of Rosso Fiorentino/ David Franklin. New Haven: Yale University Press, 1994. x, 326 p.
93-047989   759.5   0300058934
Rosso Fiorentino, -- 1494-1540 -- Criticism and interpretation.

N6923.V32.V37 1998
Vasari's Florence: artists and literati at the Medicean Court/ edited by Philip Jacks. Cambridge; Cambridge University Press, 1998. xvi, 320 p.
96-046902   709/.2   0521580889
Vasari, Giorgio, -- 1511-1574 -- Criticism and interpretation. Medici, House of -- Art patronage.   Art, Italian -- Italy -- Florence. Art, Renaissance -- Italy -- Florence.

N6923.V36.A4 1988
Rearick, William R.
The art of Paolo Veronese, 1528-1588/ W.R. Rearick; with an introductory essay by Terisio Pignatti. Washington: National Gallery of Art; c1988. ix, 212 p.
88-027524   759.5   0894681249
Veronese, -- 1528-1588 -- Exhibitions.

N6925.O813 1969
Osten, Gert von der.
Painting and sculpture in Germany and the Netherlands, 1500 to 1600 [by] Gert von der Osten & Horst Vey; [translated from the German MS. by Mary Hottinger] Harmondsworth, Penguin, 1969. xxii, 403 p.
79-514834   759.3   0140560319
Art, German -- History. Art, Flemish -- History. Art, Dutch -- History.

N6937.F64 1997
Flemish and Dutch painting: from Van Gogh, Ensor, Magritte, and Mondrian to contemporary artists/ edited by Rudi Fuchs and Jan Hoet. New York: Rizzoli, 1997. 359 p.
97-065835   0847820556
Art, Flemish -- Belgium -- Exhibitions. Art, Modern -- 19th century -- Belgium -- Fladers -- Exhibitions. Art, Modern -- 20th century -- Belgium -- Flanders -- Exhibitions.

N6941.D88 1997
Dutch art: an encyclopedia/ edited by Sheila D. Muller; advisory board, Walter S. Gibson ... [et al.]. New York: Garland Pub., 1997. xxx, 489 p.
96-035513   0815300654
Art, Dutch -- Encyclopedias.

N6946.G76 2000
The Grove dictionary of art. Dutch artists/ edited by Jane Turner. New York: St. Martin's Press, 2000.
99-087772   759.9492/09/032 21   0312229720
Art, Dutch -- 17th century -- Encyclopedias. Artists -- Netherlands -- Encyclopedias.

N6953.E82
Escher, M. C. 1898-1972.
The magic of M.C. Escher/ with an introduction by J.L. Locher; designed by Erik The; [translated from the Dutch by Marjolein de Jager]. New York: Harry N. Abrams, 2000.
00-032286   769.92   0810967200
Escher, M. C. -- (Maurits Cornelis), -- 1898-1972 -- Catalogs.

N6953.R4.A4 2001
Rembrandt's women/ [edited by] Julia Lloyd Williams; with contributions from S.A.C. Dudok Van Heel ... [et al.]. New York: Prestel, 2001. 269 p.
2001-090148   3791324985
Rembrandt Harmenszoon van Rijn, -- 1606-1669 -- Exhibitions. Women in art -- Exhibitions.

N6953.R4.A88 1988
Alpers, Svetlana.
Rembrandt's enterprise: the studio and the market/ Svetlana Alpers. Chicago: University of Chicago Press, 1988. xvi, 160 p.
87-016161   759.9492   0226015149
Rembrandt Harmenszoon van Rijn, -- 1606-1669 -- Criticism and interpretation. Rembrandt school. Art, Dutch -- Marketing.

N6953.R4.C48 1990
Chapman, H. Perry, 1954-
Rembrandt's self-portraits: a study in seventeenth-century identity/ H. Perry Chapman. Princeton, N.J.: Princeton University Press, c1990. xix, 189 p.
89-031150　760/.092/4　0691040613
Rembrandt Harmenszoon van Rijn, -- 1606-1669 -- Self-portraits. Identity (Psychology) in art. Identity (Psychology) -- Netherlands.

N6973.R9.H44 1982
Held, Julius Samuel, 1905-
Rubens and his circle: studies/ by Julius S. Held; edited by Anne W. Lowenthal, David Rosand, John Walsh, Jr. Princeton, N.J.: Princeton University Press, c1982. xxiv, 207 p.
80-027441　759.9493　0691039682
Rubens, Peter Paul, -- Sir, -- 1577-1640. Rubens, Peter Paul, -- Sir, -- 1577-1640 -- Influence.

N6973.R9.W48 1987
White, Christopher, 1930-
Peter Paul Rubens: man & artist/ Christopher White. New Haven: Yale University Press, 1987. 310 p.
86-024565　759.9493　0300037783
Rubens, Peter Paul, -- Sir, -- 1577-1640. Artists -- Belgium -- Biography.

N6981.A5413 1969
Alpatov, Mikhail Vladimirovich, 1903-
Russian impact on art [by] Mikhail Alpatov. Edited and with a pref. by Martin L. Wolf. Translated from the Russian by Ivy Litvinov. New York, Greenwood Press, [1969, c1950] xx, 352 p.
75-090461　709/.47　0837121604
Art, Russian -- History. Soviet Union -- Civilization.

N6981.H34 1975
Hamilton, George Heard.
The art and architecture of Russia/ George Heard Hamilton. Harmondsworth [Eng.]; Penguin Books, 1975. xxiv, 342 p.
77-352526　709/.47　0140560068
Art, Russian -- History. Architecture -- Soviet Union -- History.

N6981.K573
Kornilovich, K.
Arts of Russia. Translated from the Russian by James Hogarth. Cleveland, World Pub. Co. [1967-68] 2 v.
67-024469　709/.47
Art, Russian -- History. Architecture -- Soviet Union -- History.

N6981.R52 1963
Rice, Tamara Talbot.
A concise history of Russian art. New York, Praeger [1963] 288 p.
63-016653　709.47
Art, Russian -- History.

N6981.W54
Williams, Robert Chadwell, 1938-
Russian art and American money, 1900-1940/ Robert C. Williams. Cambridge, Mass.: Harvard University Press, 1980. vi, 309 p.
79-016925　382/.45/70947
Art, Russian -- United States. Art -- United States -- Marketing. Art -- Soviet Union -- Marketing. United States -- Commerce -- Soviet Union. Soviet Union -- Commerce -- United States.

N6988.A48 2000
Amazons of the avant-garde: Alexandra Exter ... [et al.]/ edited by John E. Bowlt and Matthew Drutt. New York: Guggenheim Museum; c2000. 365 p.
00-702749　759.7/082/074　0810969246
Women artists -- Russia (Federation) -- Exhibitions. Avant-garde (Aesthetics) -- Russia (Federation) -- History -- 20th century -- Exhibitions. Art, Russian -- Exhibitions.

N6988.A762 1979
Art of the October Revolution/ compiled and introduced by Mikhail Guerman; [translation from the Russian, W. Freeman, D. Saunders, and C. Binns]. New York: Abrams, 1979. 34 p.
77-020741　704.94/9/94708410947　0810906759
Art, Soviet. Art, Modern -- 20th century -- Soviet Union. Socialist realism in art -- Soviet Union. Soviet Union -- History -- Revolution, 1917-1921 -- Art and the Revolution.

N6988.B67 1991
Bown, Matthew Cullerne.
Art under Stalin/ Matthew Cullerne Bown. New York: Holmes & Meier, 1991. 256 p.
91-011281　709/.47/0904　0841912998
Art, Soviet. Socialist realism in art -- Soviet Union. Art, Modern -- 20th century -- Soviet Union.

N6988.I14 1990
Yablonskaya, Miuda
Women artists of Russia's new age, 1900-1935/ M.N. Yablonskaya; edited by Anthony Parton. New York: Rizzoli, 1990. 248 p.
89-042692　704/.042/094709041　0847810909
Constructivism (Art) -- Russian S.F.S.R. Women artists -- Russian S.F.S.R. Art, Russian.

N6988.L56 1990
Lindey, Christine.
Art in the Cold War: from Vladivostok to Kalamazoo, 1945-1962/ Christine Lindey. New York: New Amsterdam Books, 1990. 224 p.
91-189802　1871569192
Socialist realism in art -- Soviet Union. Dissident art -- Soviet Union. Art, Modern -- 20th century -- Soviet Union.

N6988.N47 1977
New art from the Soviet Union: the known and the unknown/ [prepared by] Norton Dodge & Alison Hilton. Washington: Acropolis Books, c1977. 127 p.
77-013442　709/.47　0874912091
Art, Soviet. Dissident art -- Soviet Union. Art, Modern -- 20th century -- Soviet Union.

N6988.R85
Russian avant-garde art: the George Costakis Collection/ general editor, Angelica Zander Rudenstine; introduction by S. Frederick Starr; Collecting art of the avant-garde, by George Costakis. New York: Abrams, 1981. 527 p.
81-001406   709/.47/074   0810915561
Costakis, Georgi -- Art collections. Art, Russian. Art, Modern -- 20th century -- Soviet Union. Avant-garde (Aesthetics) -- Soviet Union.

N6988.S6753 1995
Soviet dissident artists: interviews after Perestroika/ edited by Renee Baigell and Matthew Baigell. New Brunswick, N.J.: Rutgers University Press, c1995. xiv, 405 p.
95-012435   709/.2/247   0813522234
Dissenters, Artistic -- Soviet Union -- Interviews. Art and state -- Soviet Union.

N6988.5.C64.L63 1983
Lodder, Christina, 1948-
Russian constructivism/ Christina Lodder. New Haven: Yale University Press, 1983. viii, 328 p.
83-040002   709/.47   0300027273
Constructivism (Art) -- Soviet Union. Art, Soviet. Art, Modern -- 20th century -- Soviet Union.

N6999.C46.A9 1978
Alexander, Sidney, 1912-
Marc Chagall: a biography/ by Sidney Alexander. New York: Putnam, c1978. 526 p.
77-016526   759.7   0399118942
Chagall, Marc, -- 1887-   Artists -- Russia (Federation) -- Biography.

N6999.G2.H36 2000
Hammer, Martin.
Constructing modernity: the art & career of Naum Gabo/ Martin Hammer & Christina Lodder. New Haven, CT: Yale University Press, c2000. 528 p.
99-024643   730/.92   0300076886
Gabo, Naum, -- 1890- -- Criticism and interpretation.

N6999.K33.A4 1999c
Whitford, Frank.
Kandinsky: watercolours and other works on paper/ Frank Whitford. New York, NY: Thames and Hudson, 1999. 224 p.
99-070842   760/.092
Kandinsky, Wassily, -- 1866-1944 -- Catalogs.

N6999.M34.C7 1991
Crone, Rainer, 1942-
Kazimir Malevich: the climax of disclosure/ Rainer Crone, David Moos. Chicago: University of Chicago Press, 1991. viii, 230 p.
91-010077   759.7   0226120937
Malevich, Kazimir Severinovich, -- 1878-1935 -- Criticism and interpretation.

N6999.R62.A4 1998
Dabrowski, Magdalena.
Aleksandr Rodchenko/ Magdalena Dabrowski, Leah Dickerman, Peter Galassi; with essays by Aleksandr Lavrentev and Varvara Rodchenko. New York, N. Y.: Museum of Modern Art, 1998. 336 p.
98-065575   709/.2   0810961873
Rodchenko, Aleksandr Mikhailovich, -- 1891-1956. Photography, Artistic.

N7006.K4 1987
Kent, Neil.
The triumph of light and nature: Nordic art, 1740-1940/ Neil Kent. New York, N.Y.: Thames and Hudson, 1987. 240 p.
87-050060   759.8   0500234914
Art, Scandinavian. Art, Modern -- Scandinavia.

N7073.M8.T6413 2001
Munch, Edvard, 1863-1944.
Munch in his own words/ Poul Erik Tojner. Munich; Prestel Verlag, c2001. 213 p.
00-110759   3791324942
Munch, Edvard, -- 1863-1944 -- Manuscripts. Munch, Edvard, -- 1863-1944 -- Notebooks, sketchbooks, etc. Munch, Edvard, -- 1863-1944 -- Criticism and interpretation. Artists -- Norway -- Biography -- Correspondence.

N7104.K8
Kubler, George, 1912-
Art and architecture in Spain and Portugal and their American dominions, 1500 to 1800/ George Kubler, Martin Soria. Baltimore: Penguin Books, 1959. xxviii, 445 p.
59-004834   709.46
Architecture -- Spain -- History. Art -- Portugal -- History. Architecture -- Portugal -- History.

N7108.C55 1990
Coad, Emma Dent.
Spanish design and architecture/ Emma Dent Coad. New York: Rizzoli, 1990.
89-028720   745.4/4946/09048   0847811735
Art, Spanish. Art, Modern -- 20th century -- Spain.

N7113.G68.A4 1989
Goya, Francisco, 1746-1828.
Goya and the spirit of enlightenment/ Alfonso E. Perez Sanchez and Eleanor A. Sayre, codirectors of the exhibition; with contributions by Gonzalo Anes ... [et al.]. Boston: Museum of Fine Arts, c1989. cxxviii, 407 p.
88-063605   760/.092   0878463003
Goya, Francisco, -- 1746-1828 -- Exhibitions.

N7113.T3.C63 1990
Combalia Dexeus, Victoria, 1952-
Tapies/ Victoria Combalia Dexeus; [translated by Kenneth Lyons]. New York: Rizzoli, 1990. 128 p.
89-063959   709/.2   0847811972
Tapies, Antoni, -- 1923-

N7193.C5.A4 1982
Hovdenakk, Per.
Christo, complete editions, 1964-1982: catalogue
raisonne and introduction/ by Per Hovdenakk; [editor,
German translation, Jorg Schellmann]. New York, N.Y.:
New York University Press, c1982. 150 p.
82-006468   709/.2/4   0814734170
Christo, -- 1935- -- Catalogs.

N7233.B7.A4 1995
Bach, Friedrich Teja.
Constantin Brancusi, 1876-1957/ Friedrich Teja Bach,
Margit Rowell, Ann Temkin. Philadelphia, Pa.:
Philadelphia Museum of Art; c1995. 406 p.
95-033184   730/.92   0262023954
Brancusi, Constantin, -- 1876-1957 -- Exhibitions.

N7255-7369 History —
Special countries — Asia. The Orient

N7255.P6.S65 2000
Sokol, Stanley S., 1923-
The artists of Poland: a biographical dictionary from the
14th century to the present/ by Stanley S. Sokol; with a
foreword by Sharon F. Kissane. Jefferson, N.C.:
McFarland, c2000. 263 p.
99-052118   709/.2/2438   0786406976
Artists -- Poland -- Biography -- Dictionaries.

N7262.C59 1998
Cleveland Museum of Art.
Masterworks of Asian art/ Michael R. Cunningham ... [et
al.]. Cleveland: Cleveland Museum of Art; 1998. 254 p.
97-045033   709/.5/07477132   0940717433
Art -- Ohio -- Cleveland -- Catalogs. Art, Asian -- Catalogs.

N7277.O378 1998
Ofrat, Gideon.
One hundred years of art in Israel/ Gideon Ofrat;
translated by Peretz Kidron. Boulder, Colo.: Westview
Press, 1998. viii, 392 p.
97-049058   709/.5694/0904   0813333776
Art, Israeli. Art, Modern -- 20th century -- Israel.

N7280.A89 1989
The Arts of Persia/ edited by R.W. Ferrier. New Haven:
Yale University Press, 1989. x, 334 p.
89-031890   709.55   0300039875
Art, Iranian. Art, Islamic -- Iran. Iran -- Antiquities.

N7301.Z49
Zimmer, Heinrich Robert, 1890-1943.
The art of Indian Asia, its mythology and
transformations. Completed and edited by Joseph
Campbell. With photos. by Eliot Elisofon and others.
[New Jersey] Princeton University Press [1960] 2 v.
54-011742   709.54
Art -- India -- History. Art, Indic. Mythology, Hindu.

N7311.A7613 1998
Art of Southeast Asia/ by Maud Girard-Geslan ... [et al.];
preface by Albert le Bonheur; translated from the French
by J.A. Underwood. New York: Harry N. Abrams, Inc.,
1998. 635 p.
97-041442   709/.59   0810919958
Art, Southeast Asian.

N7336.L43 1982
Lee, Sherman E.
A history of Far Eastern art/ Sherman E. Lee. New York:
H.N. Abrams, 1982. 548 p.
81-003603   709/.5   0810910802
Art, East Asian.

N7336.P43 1993
Pearlstein, Elinor L.
Asian art in the Art Institute of Chicago/ Elinor L.
Pearlstein and James T. Ulak with contribution by Naomi
Noble Richard and Debirah Del Gais Muller; preface by
Yutaka Mino. Chicago, Ill.: The Institute, c1993. 152 p.
93-218089   709/.51/074777311   0810919168
*Art -- Illinois -- Chicago -- Catalogs. Art, East Asian --
Catalogs.*

N7340.B64 1993
The British Museum book of Chinese Art/ Jessica
Rawson ... [et al.]; edited by Jessica Rawson. New York:
Thames and Hudson, 1993. 395 p.
92-061337   709/.51   0500277001
Art, Chinese.

N7340.B653
Buhot, Jean.
Chinese and Japanese art, with sections on Korea and
Vietnam. Translated from the French by Remy Inglis
Hall. Edited by Charles McCurdy. Maps by Henri
Jacquinet and Pierre Simonet. Drawings by Claude
Abeille. Garden City, N.Y., Anchor Books [1967] x,
428 p.
67-010368   709/.51
Art, Chinese. Art, Japanese.

N7340.B69
Burling, Judith
Chinese art [by] Judith and Arthur Hart Burling. New
York Bonanza Books [c1953?] 384 p.
53-010705   709.51
Art, Chinese.

N7340.C59 1997
Clunas, Craig.
Art in China/ Craig Clunas. Oxford; Oxford University
Press, 1997. 255 p.
96-047595   709/.51   0192842447
Art, Chinese -- Themes, motives.

N7340.S9
Sullivan, Michael, 1916-
An introduction to Chinese art. Berkeley, University of
California Press, 1961 [c1960] 223 p.
61-003831   709.51
Art, Chinese. Art -- China -- History.

N7343.W38 1995
Watson, William, 1917-
The arts of China to AD 900/ William Watson. New Haven: Yale University Press, c1995. 276 p.
94-049679   709/.51   0300059892
Art, Chinese.

N7345.L35 1988
Laing, Ellen Johnston.
The winking owl: art in the People's Republic of China/ Ellen Johnston Laing. Berkeley: University of California Press, c1988. x, 194 p.
87-012528   709/.51   0520060970
Art, Chinese -- 20th century.

N7345.S79 1996
Sullivan, Michael, 1916-
Art and artists of twentieth-century China/ Michael Sullivan. Berkeley: University of California Press, c1996. xxx, 354 p.
95-025673   709/.51/0904   0520075560
Art, Chinese. Art, Modern -- 20th century -- China.

N7350.K3513
Kat¯o, Sh¯uichi, 1919-
Form, style, tradition: reflections on Japanese art and society/ Shuichi Kato; translated from the Japanese by John Bester. -- Berkeley: University of California Press, [1971] 216 p.
79-129612   709/.52   0520018095
Art and society -- Japan. Art, Japanese.

N7350.M26 1993
Mason, Penelope E., 1935-
History of Japanese art/ Penelope Mason. New York: Abrams, 1993. 431 p.
92-028698   709/.52   0810910853
Art, Japanese.

N7350.W3
Warner, Langdon, 1881-1955.
The enduring art of Japan.   Cambridge, Harvard University Press, 1952. xiii, 113 p.
52-008220   709.52
Art, Japanese -- History.

N7352.L43 1983
Lee, Sherman E.
Reflections of reality in Japanese art/ text by Sherman E. Lee; catalogue by Michael R. Cunningham with James T. Ulak. Cleveland, Ohio: Cleveland Museum of Art; c1983. xii, 292 p.
82-045940   709/.52/074017132   0910386706
Art, Japanese -- Exhibitions. Realism in art -- Japan -- Exhibitions.

N7352.M84 2000
Murase, Miyeko.
Bridge of dreams: the Mary Griggs Burke collection of Japanese art/ Miyeko Murase. New York: Metropolitan Museum of Art; c2000. xiv, 450 p.
99-054465   709/.52/0747471   0870999419
Burke, Mary Griggs -- Art collections -- Exhibitions.   Art, Japanese -- Exhibitions.

N7352.R67
Rosenfield, John M.
Traditions of Japanese art; selections from the Kimiko and John Powers Collection [by] John M. Rosenfield [and] Shujiro Shimada. [Cambridge, Mass.] Fogg Art Museum, Harvard University, 1970. 393 p.
76-133788   709.52   0674901258
Powers, Kimiko -- Art collections. Powers, John -- Art collections. Art, Japanese -- Exhibitions.

N7353.4.J39 1996
Japan's golden age: Momoyama/ Money L. Hickman ... [et al.]. New Haven: Yale University Press in association with Sun & Star 1996 and Dallas Museum of Art, 1996. 320 p.
96-017758   709/.52/0747642812   0300068972
Art, Japanese -- Kamakura-Momoyama periods, 1185-1600 -- Exhibitions.

N7353.5.S656 1998
Singer, Robert T.
Edo, art in Japan 1615-1868/ Robert T. Singer; with John T. Carpenter ... [et al.]. Washington: National Gallery of Art, 1998. 480 p.
98-029138   709/.52/074753   0894682261
Art, Japanese -- Edo period, 1600-1868 -- Exhibitions.

N7360.M31
McCune, Evelyn.
The arts of Korea; an illustrated history.   Tokyo, C.E. Tuttle Co. [1961, c1962] 452 p.
61-011122   709.519
Art, Korean -- History.

N7360.P67 2000
Portal, Jane.
Korea: art and archaeology/ Jane Portal. New York: Thames & Hudson, 2000. 240 p.
99-066554   709/.519   0500282021
Art, Korean. Art, Buddhist.

N7362.A78 1998
Arts of Korea/ editors, Chung Yang-mo, Yi Song-mi, and Kim Hongnam; coordinating editor, Judith G. Smith; contributions by Ahn Hwi-joon ... [et al.]. New York: Metropolitan Museum of Art, 1998.
98-006404   709/.519/0747471   0870998501
Art, Korean -- Exhibitions.

N7369.P35.A4 1993
Paik, Nam June, 1932-
Nam June Paik: video time, video space/ general editors, Toni Stooss and Thomas Kellein. New York: H.N. Abrams, 1993. 147 p.
93-016981   700/.92   0810937298
Paik, Nam June, -- 1932- Video art.

N7380-7399 History —
Special countries — Africa

N7380.B28 1998
Bacquart, Jean-Baptiste.
The tribal arts of Africa/ Jean-Baptiste Bacquart. New York: Thames and Hudson, 1998. 240 p.
98-060234   709/.6   0500018707
Art, African.

N7380.H54 2001
A history of art in Africa/ Monica Blackmun Visona ... [et al.]; introduction by Suzanne Preston Blier; preface by Rowland Abiodun. New York: Harry N. Abrams, 2001. 544 p.
00-022796   709/.6   0810934485
Art, African.

N7380.K36 2000
Kasfir, Sidney Littlefield.
Contemporary African art/ Sidney Littlefield Kasfir. New York, N.Y.: Thames and Hudson, 2000. 224 p.
99-070939   709/.6/09045   0500203288
Art, African. Art, Modern -- 20th century -- Africa.

N7380.L363
Leuzinger, Elsy.
Africa; the art of the Negro peoples. [Translated by Ann E. Keep] New York, McGraw-Hill [1960] 247 p.
60-013819   709.67
Art, Black -- Africa -- History.

N7391.65.B58 1998
Blier, Suzanne Preston.
The royal arts of Africa: the majesty of form/ Suzanne Preston Blier. New York: H.N. Abrams, c1998. 272 p.
97-025456   709/.67   0810927055
Art, Black -- Africa, Sub-Saharan. Ethnic art -- Africa, Sub-Saharan.

N7391.65.C66613 1998
Coquet, Michele.
African royal court art/ Michele Coquet; translated by Jane Marie Todd. Chicago, Ill.: University of Chicago Press, c1998. xi, 181 p.
98-005071   709/.67   0226115755
Art, Black -- Africa, Sub-Saharan. Symbolism in art -- Africa, Sub-Saharan. Art and state -- Africa, Sub-Saharan. Africa, Sub-Saharan -- Kings and rulers -- Art patronage. Africa, Sub-saharan -- Court and courtiers -- Portraits.

N7391.65.V63 1991
Vogel, Susan Mullin.
Africa explores: 20th century African art/ Susan Vogel; assisted by Ima Ebong; contributions by Walter E.A. van Beek ... [et al.]. New York: Center for African Art; c1991. 294 p.
90-026683   709/.67/07473   3791311433
Art, Black -- Africa, Sub-Saharan -- Exhibitions. Art, Modern -- 20th century -- Africa, Sub-Saharan -- Exhibitions.

N7392.W55 1989
Williamson, Sue.
Resistance art in South Africa/ Sue Williamson. New York: St. Martin's Press, 1990, c1989. 159 p.
89-028797   704/.03968/009048   031204142X
Dissident art -- South Africa. Art, Black -- South Africa. Art, Modern -- 20th century -- South Africa.

N7398.C68 1990
Courtney-Clarke, Margaret, 1949-
African canvas: the art of West African women/ photographs and text by Margaret Courtney-Clarke; foreword by Maya Angelou. New York: Rizzoli, 1990. 204 p.
89-024037   709/.66   0847811662
Art, West African -- Pictorial works. Art, Black -- Africa, West -- Pictorial works. Women artists -- Africa, West -- Pictorial works.

N7398.M4913 1992
Meyer, Laure.
Black Africa: masks, sculpture, jewelry/ Laure Meyer; [translation, Helen McPhail ...]. Paris: Terrail, c1992. 224 p.
96-216426   2879390354
Art, Black -- Africa, West.

N7399.I8.S74 1994
Steiner, Christopher Burghard.
African art in transit/ Christopher B. Steiner. Cambridge [England]; Cambridge University Press, 1994. xv, 220 p.
92-047387   382/.457/096668   0521434475
Art, Black -- Economic aspects -- Cote d'Ivoire. Art, Black -- Cote d'Ivoire -- Marketing. Economic anthropology -- Cote d'Ivoire.

N7399.N5.E94 1980
Eyo, Ekpo.
Treasures of ancient Nigeria/ text by Ekpo Eyo and Frank Willett [editor, Rollyn O. Krichbaum; photographer, Dirk Bakker; designer, Betty Binns]. New York: Knopf: distributed by Random House, 1980. xiii, 161 p.
79-003497   730/.09669   0394509757
Art, Nigerian -- Exhibitions.

N7399.N52.Y68 1989
Drewal, Henry John.
Yoruba: nine centuries of African art and thought/ Henry John Drewal and John Pemberton, 3rd with Rowland Abiodun; edited by Allen Wardwell. New York: Center for African Art; c1989. 256 p.
89-022182   730/.089/96333   0945802048
Art and religion -- Nigeria. Yoruba (African people) -- Religion. Art, Yoruba.

N7401-7411 History —
Special countries —
Australasia. Pacific Area

N7401.D73 1988
Dreamings: the art of aboriginal Australia/ Peter Sutton ... [et al.]; editor, Peter Sutton. New York: G. Braziller in association with Asia Society Galleries, 1988. xiii, 266 p.
88-010435   750/.899915   0807612014
Art, Australian aboriginal -- Exhibitions.

N7402.A7.A97 1954
Australia: aboriginal paintings, Arnhem Land/ introduction by Sir Herbert Read. [Greenwich, Conn.]: New York Graphic Society c1954. 14 p.
54-013494   759.994
Painting, Australian (Aboriginal) -- Northern Territory -- Arnhem Land.

N7407.M36.T4 1984
Te Maori: Maori art from New Zealand collections/ edited by Sidney Moko Mead; text by Sidney Moko Mead ... [et al.]; photographs by Athol McCredie. New York: Abrams in association with the American Federation Arts, c1984. 244 p.
83-025725   709/.01/109931074013   0810913445
Art, Maori -- Exhibitions. Art -- Collectors and collecting -- New Zealand -- Exhibitions.

N7410.B8
Buhler, Alfred, 1900-
The art of the South Sea Islands, including Australia and New Zealand, by Alfred Buehler, Terry Barrow [and] Charles P. Mountford. New York, Crown Publishers [1962] 249 p.
62-011806   709.99
Art -- Oceania. Art, Primitive.

N7410.L5
Linton, Ralph, 1893-1953.
Arts of the South Seas, by Ralph Linton and Paul S. Wingert, in collaboration with Rene d'Harnoncourt; color illustrations by Miguel Covarrubias. [New York] The Museum of modern art, distributed by Simon aand Schuster, New York [1946] 199 p.
46-025247   709.9   0405015674
Ethnology -- Oceania. Art, Primitive. Art -- Oceania.

N7411.P3.C63 1997
Cochrane, Susan.
Contemporary art in Papua New Guinea/ Susan Cochrane; with a contribution by Michael A. Mel. Sydney, NSW: Craftsman House; c1997. 167 p.
97-183575   9057032317
Art, Melanesian -- Papua New Guinea. Ethnic art -- Papua New Guinea -- History -- 20th century.

N7417.6 History —
Jewish art — By period

N7417.6.B59 1981
Blatter, Janet.
Art of the Holocaust/ by Janet Blatter and Sybil Milton; historical introduction by Henry Friedlander; preface by Irving Howe. New York: Rutledge Press, c1981. 272 p.
81-005895   741.94   0831704187
Holocaust, Jewish (1939-1945), in art. Art, Jewish.

N7420 General works —
Early works to 1800

N7420.V3 1960
Vasari, Giorgio, 1511-1574.
Vasari on technique; being the introduction to the three arts of design, architecture, sculpture and painting, prefixed to the Lives of the most excellent painters, sculptors, and architects. Now for the first time translated into English by Louisa S. Maclehose. Edited, with introd. & notes, by G. Baldwin Brown. New York, Dover Publications [1960] xxiv, 328 p.
61-000460   702.8   048620717X
Architecture -- Early works to 1800. Sculpture -- Early works to 1800. Painting -- Early works to 1800.

N7425 General works —
1800-   — English

N7425.L88
Lowry, Bates, 1923-
The visual experience; an introduction to art. Englewood Cliffs, N.J., Prentice-Hall [1961?] 272 p.
61-010977   701.18
Art.

N7425.M88
Muehsam, Gerd, 1913-
Guide to basic information sources in the visual arts/ by Gerd Muehsam. Santa Barbara, Calif.: J. Norton Publishers/ABC-Clio, c1978. x, 266 p.
77-017430   707   0874362784
Art -- Sources.

N7425.M9 1967
Munro, Thomas, 1897-
The arts and their interrelations. Cleveland, Press of Western Reserve University [1967] xvi, 587 p.
67-011482   700
Art. Aesthetics.

N7428 General special

N7428.K4
Kepes, Gyorgy, 1906-
The man-made object. New York, G. Braziller [1966] 230 p.
66-013046   701
Creation (Literary, artistic, etc.) Art -- Philosophy. Art -- Technique.

N7428.L56 1983
Lippard, Lucy R.
Overlay: contemporary art and the art of prehistory/ by Lucy R. Lippard. 1st ed. New York: Pantheon Books, c1983. xiv, 266 p.
82-022331   700/.9/04 19   0394711459
Art, Comparative. Art, Modern -- 20th century -- Themes, motives. Art, Prehistoric -- Themes, motives. Art, Prehistoric -- Influence.

N7428.5 General special — Comparative art

N7428.5.B73 1993
Braun, Barbara, 1939-
Pre-Columbian art and the post-Columbian world: ancient American sources of modern art/ Barbara Braun. New York: Harry N. Abrams, c1993. 339 p.
92-029047   709/.04   0810937239
Art, Comparative. Art, Modern -- 20th century. Indian art -- Influence.

N7429 General special — Comparative art — Influences of Oriental, or Islamic art on Western art, and vice versa

N7429.S93 1989
Sullivan, Michael, 1916-
The meeting of Eastern and Western art/ Michael Sullivan. Berkeley: University of California Press, c1989. xxi, 306 p.
88-004788   709   0520059026
Art -- Chinese influences. Art -- Japanese influences. Art, Chinese -- Western influences.

N7429.4 General special — Ethnic art (General)

N7429.4.L83 1994
Lucie-Smith, Edward.
Race, sex, and gender: in contemporary art/ Edward Lucie-Smith. New York: H.N. Abrams, 1994. 224 p.
93-029218   700/.1/03   0810937670
Ethnic art. Minorities in art. Art and society -- History -- 20th century.

N7430 Technique, composition, etc. — General works — 1801-

N7430.A69 1982
Arnheim, Rudolf.
The power of the center: a study of composition in the visual arts/ Rudolf Arnheim. Berkeley: University of California Press, c1982. xii, 227 p.
81-010332   701/.8   0520044266
Composition (Art)

N7430.K47
Kepes, Gyorgy, 1906-
Sign, image, symbol.   New York, G. Braziller [1966] 281 p.
66-013045   701.8
Art -- Technique. Composition (Art) Symbolism in art.

N7430.M62
Moholy-Nagy, Laszlo, 1895-1946.
Vision in motion. Chicago: P. Theobald, [1947] 371 p.
47-004349   701
Art -- Technique. Art and society.

N7430.5 Technique, composition, etc. — General special

N7430.5.C7 1990
Crary, Jonathan.
Techniques of the observer: on vision and modernity in the nineteenth century/ Jonathan Crary. Cambridge, Mass.: MIT Press, c1990. 171 p.
90-006164   701/.15   0262031698
Visual perception. Art, Modern -- 19th century -- Themes, motives. Art and society -- History -- 19th century.

N7430.5.E34 1991
Edgerton, Samuel Y.
The heritage of Giotto's geometry: art and science on the eve of the scientific revolution/ Samuel Y. Edgerton, Jr. Ithaca: Cornell University Press, 1991. x, 319 p.
91-012301   701/.8   0801425735
Giotto, -- 1266?-1337 -- Themes, motives.   Visual perception. Space (Art) Art, Medieval.

N7430.5.S69 1990
Sowers, Robert.
Rethinking the forms of visual expression/ Robert Sowers. Berkeley: University of California Press, c1990. 139 p.
89-034898   701/.15   0520066324
Visual perception. Art -- Psychology. Composition (Art)

N7432.5 Technique, composition, etc. — Styles — Special styles, A-Z

N7432.5.A78.A78 1994
The artist outsider: creativity and the boundaries of culture/ edited by Michael D. Hall and Eugene W. Metcalf, Jr.; with Roger Cardinal. Washington: Smithsonian Institution Press, c1994. xvii, 350 p.
93-084474   700/.1/03   1560983345
Outsider art. Art, Primitive. Art brut.

N7432.5.A78.M34 1996
Maizels, John.
Raw creation: outsider art and beyond/ John Maizels; with an introduction by Roger Cardinal. London: Phaidon Press Limited, 1996. 240 p.
96-198389   0714831492
Outsider art. Art brut. Art, Primitive.

N7432.5.A78.R49 2000
Rhodes, Colin.
Outsider art: spontaneous alternatives/ Colin Rhodes.
New York, N.Y.: Thames & Hudson, 2000. 224 p.
99-065579   709/.04   0500203342
Outsider art. Art brut.

N7432.5.C6.R67 1995
Rosenberg, Martin, 1951-
Raphael and France: the artist as paradigm and symbol/
Martin Rosenberg. University Park, Pa.: Pennsylvania
State University Press, c1995. xii, 226 p.
93-030505   709/.44/0903   0271013001
*Raphael, -- 1483-1520 -- Influence.   Classicism in art --
France. Art, Modern -- France.*

N7433.3 Miscellaneous genres and media, not limited by time period, style, place, or subject matter — Artists' books — General works

N7433.3.A75 1985
Artists' books: a critical anthology and sourcebook/
edited by Joan Lyons. Rochester, N.Y.: Visual Studies
Workshop Press; 269 p.
85-003180   700/.9/04 19   0898220416
Artists' books. Conceptual art.

N7433.3.D78 1995
Drucker, Johanna,
The century of artists' books/ Johanna Drucker. New
York City: Granary Books, 1995. xii, 377 p.
95-079670   702/.8/1 21   1887123016
Artists' books -- History. Art, Modern -- 20th century.

N7433.7 Miscellaneous genres and media, not limited by time period, style, place, or subject matter — Assemblage. Collage. Found objects

N7433.7.R6313 1988
Rodari, Florian.
Collage: pasted, cut, and torn papers/ by Florian Rodari.
Geneva: Skira; 1988. 179 p.
88-006641   702/.8/12   0847809617
Collage -- Technique.

N7433.8 Miscellaneous genres and media, not limited by time period, style, place, or subject matter — Computer art — General works

N7433.8.P7 1984
Prueitt, Melvin L.
Art and the computer/ Melvin L. Prueitt. New York:
McGraw-Hill, c1984. ix, 246 p.
83-024818   760   0070508941
Computer art.

N7438 Popular works

N7438.O82 1952
Ozenfant, Amedee, 1886-
Foundations of modern art. Translation by John Rodker.
New York, Dover Publications [1952] xviii, 348 p.
52-014596   701.17
Art. Art, Modern -- 20th century -- History.

N7445-7445.4 Collected writings (non-serial) — Addresses, essays, lectures, thoughts, and sayings (Collective) — Individual authors

N7445.B546 1968
Berenson, Bernard, 1865-1959.
Seeing and knowing. Greenwich, Conn., New York
Graphic Society [1968] 89 p.
68-013052   701.1
Art -- Addresses, essays, lectures.

N7445.C78 1956
Coomaraswamy, Ananda Kentish, 1877-1947.
Christian and Oriental philosophy of art. New York,
Dover Publications [1956] 146 p.
57-003496   704.91
Art -- Addresses, essays, lectures.

N7445.P22
Panofsky, Erwin, 1892-1968.
Meaning in the visual arts: papers in and on art history.
Garden City, N.Y., Doubleday, 1955. xviii, 362 p.
55-009754   704.91
Art.

N7445.S516
Shahn, Ben, 1898-1969.
The shape of content. Cambridge, Harvard University
Press, 1957. 131 p.
57-012968   704.91
Art -- Addresses, essays, lectures.

N7445.2.M26 1999
Margolis, Joseph, 1924-
What, after all, is a work of art?: lectures in the
philosophy of art/ Joseph Margolis. University Park, Pa.:
Pennsylvania State University Press, c1999. xi, 143 p.
98-041260   701   0271018658
Art -- Philosophy.

N7445.2.P36 1995
Panofsky, Erwin, 1892-1968.
Three essays on style/ Erwin Panofsky; edited by Irving
Lavin; with a memoir by William S. Heckscher.
Cambridge, Mass.: MIT Press, 1995. ix, 245 p.
95-000929   700   0262161516
Art.

N7445.2.R66 1985
Rosenberg, Harold, 1906-1978.
Art & other serious matters/ Harold Rosenberg. Chicago:
University of Chicago Press, 1985. vi, 332 p.
84-008781   709/.04   0226726940
Art -- Addresses, essays, lectures. Art, Modern -- 20th century.
Artists -- United States.

N7454-7476 Art criticism — General special

N7454.K3 1982
Kandinsky, Wassily, 1866-1944.
Kandinsky, complete writings on art/ edited by Kenneth
C. Lindsay and Peter Vergo. Boston, Mass.: G.K. Hall,
c1982. 2 v.
81-012798   700   0805799508
Art, Modern -- 20th century.

N7454.M6.K6 1970
Kostelanetz, Richard,
Moholy-Nagy. New York, Praeger [1970] xviii, 238 p.
70-121715   709/.24

N7476.C37 1987
Carrier, David, 1944-
Artwriting/ David Carrier. Amherst: University of
Massachusetts Press, 1987. xii, 161 p.
86-024995   701/.1/80973   0870235613
Art criticism -- History -- 20th century. Art criticism --
Philosophy.

N7476.W65
Women as interpreters of the visual arts, 1820-1979/
edited by Claire Richter Sherman with Adele M.
Holcomb. Westport, Conn.: Greenwood Press, 1981.
xxiv, 487 p.
80-000785   709/.2/2   0313220565
Women art critics. Women art historians. Women art teachers.

N7477 Art criticism — Popular works on art appreciation

N7477.C645 1999
Cole, Bruce, 1938-
The informed eye: understanding masterpieces of western
art/ Bruce Cole. Chicago: Ivan R. Dee, c1999. xv, 239 p.
99-039154   701/.1   1566632552
Art appreciation.

N7480 Art criticism — Historiography

N7480.A32 1996
Adams, Laurie.
The methodologies of art: an introduction/ Laurie
Schneider Adams. New York, NY: IconEditions, c1996.
xvii, 236 p.
96-010778   701/.18   0064303128
Art -- Historiography. Art -- Methodology.

N7480.E44 1997
Elkins, James, 1955-
Our beautiful, dry, and distant texts: art history as
writing/ James Elkins. University Park, Pa.: Pennsylvania
State University Press, c1997. xvii, 300 p.
96-022842   701/.18   0271016302
Art -- Historiography.

N7483 Art criticism — Biography and criticism of art critics and historians — Individual, A-Z

N7483.B28.G6 1988
Goldberg, Edward L., 1948-
After Vasari: history, art, and patronage in late Medici
Florence/ Edward L. Goldberg. Princeton, N.J.: Princeton
University Press, c1988. xvii, 309 p.
88-022453   709/.45/51   0691040664
Baldinucci, Filippo, -- 1625-1696. Medici, House of -- Art
patronage. Art historians -- Italy -- Biography. Art -- Collectors
and collecting -- Italy -- Florence -- History -- 17th century.

N7483.B4.S25
Samuels, Ernest, 1903-
Bernard Berenson: the making of a connoisseur/ Ernest
Samuels. Cambridge, Mass.: Belknap Press, 1979. xvi,
477 p.
78-026748   709/.2/4   0674067754
Berenson, Bernard, -- 1865-1959. Art critics -- United States --
Biography.

N7483.P3.H64 1984
Holly, Michael Ann.
Panofsky and the foundations of art history/ Michael Ann
Holly. Ithaca, N.Y.: Cornell University Press, 1984.
267 p.
84-045143   709/.2/4   0801416140
Panofsky, Erwin, -- 1892-1968. Art -- Historiography.

N7483.R52.A3 1999
Richardson, John, 1924-
The sorcerer's apprentice: Picasso, Provence, and
Douglas Cooper/ John Richardson. New York: Alfred A.
Knopf, 1999. viii, 318 p.
99-027200   709/.2   0375400338
Richardson, John, -- 1924- Cooper, Douglas, -- 1911- Picasso,
Pablo, -- 1881-1973. Art, Modern -- 20th century -- France --
Provence. Art historians -- United States -- Biography.

N7483.R54.I83 1993
Iversen, Margaret.
Alois Riegl: art history and theory/ Margaret Iversen.
Cambridge, Mass.: MIT Press, c1993. ix, 223 p.
92-026922   709/.2   0262090309
Riegl, Alois, -- 1858-1905 -- Criticism and interpretation. Art -
- Historiography.

N7483.R8.J64 1993
John Ruskin and the Victorian eye/ with essays by Susan
P. Casteras ... [et al.]. New York: Harry N. Abrams;
1993. 223 p.
92-030289   709/.2   0810937662
Ruskin, John, -- 1819-1900 -- Criticism and interpretation.
Perception. Art criticism -- England -- History -- 19th century.

N7483.R8.R87 1984
Ruskin, the critical heritage/ edited by J.L. Bradley.
London; Routledge & K. Paul, 1984. xiii, 436 p.
83-011102   709   0710092865
Ruskin, John, -- 1819-1900 -- Criticism and interpretation. Art criticism -- Great Britain -- History -- 19th century.

N7483.S38.K36 1996
Kammen, Michael G.
The lively arts: Gilbert Seldes and the transformation of cultural criticism in the United States/ Michael Kammen.
New York: Oxford University Press, 1996. x, 495 p.
95-012446   700/.92   0195098684
Seldes, Gilbert, -- 1893-1970. Seldes, Gilbert, -- 1893-1970 -- Influence. Art critics -- United States -- Biography. Arts and society -- United States -- History -- 20th century. Popular culture -- United States.

N7525 Indexes to illustrations (General). Repertoires

N7525.K67
Korwin, Yala H., 1923-
Index to two-dimensional art works/ by Yala H. Korwin.
Metuchen, N.J.: Scarecrow Press, 1981. 2 v.
80-025002   701/.6   0810813815
Art -- Indexes.

N7525.V3 1966
Vance, Lucile E.
Illustration index, by Lucile E. Vance and Esther M. Tracey. New York, Scarecrow Press, 1966. 527 p.
65-013558   011
Pictures -- Indexes.

N7560 Special subjects of art — Choice of subject. Titles. Themes and motives

N7560.E53 1998
Encyclopedia of comparative iconography: themes depicted in works of art/ editor, Helene E. Roberts.
Chicago: Fitzroy Dearborn, 1998. 2 v.
98-163033   704.9/03   1579580092
Art -- Themes, motives -- Encyclopedias.

N7565 Special subjects of art — Iconography. Iconology

N7565.O87 1994
O'Toole, Michael.
The language of displayed art/ Michael O'Toole.
Rutherford: Fairleigh Dickinson University Press, 1994.
xiii, 295 p.
94-013341   701/.4   0838636047
Symbolism in art. Art.

N7570 Special subjects of art — Human figures — General works

N7570.C55
Clark, Kenneth, 1903-
The nude; a study in ideal form. [New York] Pantheon Books [c1956] xxi, 458 p.
56-010423   704.942
Nude in art.

N7570.S38 1969
Selz, Peter Howard, 1919-
New images of man. With statements by the artists. New York, Published for the Museum of Modern Art by Arno Press, [1969] 159 p.
76-086447   704.94/2
Men in art. Art, Modern -- 20th century.

N7575 Special subjects of art — Portraits — General works

N7575.B75 1991
Brilliant, Richard.
Portraiture/ Richard Brilliant. Cambridge, Mass.: Harvard University Press, 1991. 192 p.
91-023513   704.9/42   067469175X
Portraits -- History.

N7593.1 Special subjects of art — Portraits — Medieval and modern

N7593.1.S28 1987
Saunders, Richard H., 1949-
American colonial portraits, 1700-1776/ Richard H. Saunders and Ellen G. Miles. Washington City: Published by the Smithsonian Institution Press for the National Portrait Gallery, 1987. xv, 342 p.
87-600059   704.9/42/09740740153   0874746957
Portraits, American -- Exhibitions. Portraits, Colonial -- United States -- Exhibitions. United States -- Biography -- Portraits.

N7619.5 Special subjects of art — Portraits — Self-portraits

N7619.5.I8.W66 1998
Woods-Marsden, Joanna, 1936-
Renaissance self-portraiture: the visual construction of identity and the social status of the artist/ Joanna Woods-Marsden. New Haven: Yale University Press, c1998. viii, 285 p.
98-007688   704.9/42/094509031   0300075960
Self-portraits, Italian. Portraits, Renaissance -- Italy. Identity (Psychology) in art.

N7630 Special subjects of art —
Humans in art. Human life cycle in art —
Women in art. Feminine beauty (Aesthetics)

N7630.C43 2000
Charnon-Deutsch, Lou.
Fictions of the feminine in the nineteenth-century Spanish press/ Lou Charnon-Deutsch. University Park, PA: Pennsylvania State University Press, c2000. xvi, 307 p.
98-043335   305.4/0946/09034   0271019131
Feminine beauty (Aesthetics) -- Spain -- History -- 19th century. Women in popular culture -- Spain -- History -- 19th century. Women -- Press coverage -- Spain.

N7630.C49 1999
Chicago, Judy, 1939-
Women and art: contested territory/ Judy Chicago and Edward Lucie-Smith. New York: Watson-Guptill Publications, 1999. 192 p.
99-062920   0823058522
Women in art. Artists -- Psychology. Feminist art criticism.

N7640 Special subjects of art —
Humans in art.
Human life cycle in art — Children

N7640.H54 1998
Higonnet, Anne, 1959-
Pictures of innocence: the history and crisis of ideal childhood/ Anne Higonnet. New York, N.Y.: Thames and Hudson, 1998. 256 p.
97-061994   704.9/425   0500018413
Children in art -- Social aspects. Children in art -- History. Photography of children -- Social aspects.

N7660 Special subjects of art —
Nature — Animals. Wildlife

N7660.K55 1971
Klingender, F. D.
Animals in art and thought to the end of the Middle Ages. Edited by Evelyn Antal and John Harthan. Cambridge, Mass., M.I.T. Press [1971] xxviii, 580 p.
77-123254   704.94/32   0262110407
Animals in art. Animals in literature. Animals (Philosophy) -- History.

N7740 Special subjects of art —
Symbolism. Emblematic art —
General works

N7740.C29 1995
Carr-Gomm, Sarah.
The dictionary of symbols in Western art/ Sarah Carr-Gomm New York: Facts on File, 1995. 240 p.
95-017577   704.9/46/03   0816033013
Art -- Dictionaries. Signs and symbols -- Dictionaries.

N7740.H35 1994
Hall, James, 1917-
Illustrated dictionary of symbols in eastern and western art/ James Hall; illustrated by Chris Puleston. New York: IconEditions, c1994. xii, 244 p.
94-036641   704.9/46/03   0064333140
Symbolism in art -- Dictionaries. Art -- Themes, motives -- Dictionaries.

N7760 Special subjects of art —
Mythology. Heroes.
Legends — General works

N7760.P29 1962
Panofsky, Dora.
Pandora's box; the changing aspects of a mythical symbol, by Dora and Erwin Panofsky. New York] Pantheon Books [c1962] xiv, 185 p.
63-001994   704.947
Pandora -- Art.

N7830-8187 Special subjects of art —
Religious art — Christian art

N7830.F37 1959
Ferguson, George Wells, 1899-
Signs & symbols in Christian art. With illus. from paintings of the Renaissance. New York, Oxford University Press [1959] 123 p.
59-004639   704.9482
Christian art and symbolism. Painting, Renaissance.

N7830.M87 1996
Murray, Peter, 1920-
The Oxford companion to Christian art and architecture/ Peter and Linda Murray. Oxford; New York: 1996. xi, 596 p.
96-017840   704.9/482   0198661657
Christian art and symbolism -- Themes, motives.

N7830.S3513 1971b
Schiller, Gertrud.
Iconography of Christian art. Translated by Janet Seligman. Greenwich, Conn., New York Graphic Society [1971-   ]
76-132965   704.948/2   0821203657
Jesus Christ -- Art.

N7831.S9 1970
Swift, Emerson Howland, 1889-
Roman sources of Christian art, by Emerson H. Swift. Westport, Conn., Greenwood Press, [1970, c1951] xx, 248 p.
73-100181   723/.1   0837134307
Christian art and symbolism -- Roman influences.

N7832.B3
Beckwith, John, 1918-
Early Christian and Byzantine art. Harmondsworth, Penguin, 1970. xxv, 211 p.
79-023592   709.02   0140560335
Art, Early Christian. Art, Byzantine.

N7832.H813 1969
Hubert, Jean, 1902-
Europe of the invasions [by] J. Hubert, J. Porcher [and] W. F. Volbach. [Translated by Stuart Gilbert and James Emmons] New York, G. Braziller [1969] xv, 387 p.
75-081858   709.01/5
Art, Early Christian. Art, Medieval. Rome -- History -- Germanic Invasions, 3rd-6th centuries.

N7832.M36 1993
Mathews, Thomas F.
The clash of gods: a reinterpretation of early Christian art/ Thomas F. Mathews. Princeton, N.J.: Princeton University Press, c1993. x, 223 p.
93-019338   709/.02/12   0691033501
Art, Early Christian.

N7832.M47 1988
Milburn, R. L. P. 1907-
Early Christian art and architecture/ Robert Milburn. Berkeley: University of California Press, 1988. xviii, 318 p.
87-040651   709/.02   0520063260
Art, Early Christian. Architecture, Early Christian.

N7832.S26
Schapiro, Meyer, 1904-
Late antique, early Christian and mediaeval art/ Meyer Schapiro. New York: G. Braziller, 1979. xvi, 414 p.
79-013333   709/.02   0807609277
Art, Early Christian. Art, Medieval.

N7832.V63
Volbach, Wolfgang Fritz, 1892-1988.
Early Christian art. Photography by Max Hirmer. [Translated by Christopher Ligota] New York, Abrams [1962] 363 p.
61-008333   709.02
Art, Early Christian. Church architecture -- Europe.

N7850.R67 1996
Ross, Leslie, 1956-
Medieval art: a topical dictionary/ Leslie Ross. Westport, Conn.: Greenwood Press, 1996. xxiv, 292 p.
96-000160   709/.02/03   0313293295
Art, Medieval -- Dictionaries. Christian art and symbolism -- To 500 -- Dictionaries. Christian art and symbolism -- Medieval, 500-1500 -- Dictionaries.

N7908.6.W76 1991
Wroth, William, 1938-
Images of penance, images of mercy: southwestern santos in the late nineteenth century/ by William Wroth; with an introduction to part 2 by Marta Weigle. Norman: Published for Taylor Museum for Southwestern Studies, Colorado Springs Fine Arts Center, by University of Oklahoma Press, c1991. xvii, 196 p.
90-050701   704.9/482   0806123257
Santos (Art) -- Southwest, New -- History -- 19th century. Santos (Art) -- Southwest, New -- Catalogs.

N7949.A1.M3313 1986
Male, Emile, 1862-1954.
Religious art in France: the late Middle Ages: a study of medieval iconography and its sources/ Emile Male; edited by Harry Bober; translated by Marthiel Mathews. Princeton, N.J.: Princeton University Press, c1986. xiii, 597 p.
84-026359   704.9/482/0944   0691099146
Art, French. Art, Medieval -- France. Christian art and symbolism -- Medieval, 500-1500 -- France.

N7949.M313 1958
Male, Emile, 1862-
The Gothic image; religious art in France of the thirteenth century. Translated by Dora Nussey. New York, Harper [1958] 414 p.
58-010152   704.9482
Art -- France -- History. Christian art and symbolism -- Medieval, 500-1500. Art, High Gothic -- France.

N7952.R6.K48 2000
Kessler, Herbert L., 1941-
Rome 1300: on the path of the pilgrim/ Herbert L. Kessler and Johanna Zacharias. New Haven, Conn.; Yale University Press, 2000. 237 p.
99-058270   704.9/482/094563209023   0300081537
Art, Italian -- Italy -- Rome. Christian art and symbolism -- To 500 -- Italy -- Rome. Christian art and symbolism -- Medieval, 500-1500 -- Italy -- Rome. Rome (Italy) -- Church history. Rome (Italy) -- Description and travel. Rome (Italy) -- Buildings, structures, etc.

N8050.M29 2000
MacGregor, Neil, 1946-
Seeing salvation: images of Christ in art/ Neil MacGregor with Erika Langmuir. New Haven: Yale University Press, 2000. 240 p.
00-712288   704.9/4853   0300084781
Jesus Christ -- Art.

N8187.W44 1978
Weitzmann, Kurt, 1904-
The icon: holy images--sixth to fourteenth century/ Kurt Weitzmann. New York: G. Braziller, 1978. 134 p.
78-006495   704.948/2   0807608920
Icons. Icon painting. Votive offerings in art.

N8193-8199 Special subjects of art — Religious art — Non-Christian art

N8193.T5.R47 1991
Rhie, Marylin M.
Wisdom and compassion = Ses rab dan snin rjei rol pa: the sacred art of Tibet/ Marylin M. Rhie, Robert A.F. Thurman; photographs by John Bigelow Taylor. [San Francisco]: Asian Art Museum of San Francisco; 1991. 406 p.
90-046899   704.9/48943923/0951507473   0810939576
Art, Buddhist -- China -- Tibet. Buddhist art and symbolism -- China -- Tibet. Art, Tibetan.

N8193.2.A4.I45
The Image of the Buddha/ Jean Boisselier ... [et al.];
general editor, David L. Snellgrove. London: Serindia
Publications; 1978. 482 p.
78-361874   704.948/9/4363   0906026008
*Gautama Buddha -- Art -- Addresses, essays, lectures.   Art,
Buddhist -- Addresses, essays, lectures.*

N8195.A3.W384 1999
Dehejia, Vidya.
Devi: the great goddess: female divinity in South Asian
art/ Vidya Dehejia; with contributions by Thomas B.
Coburn ... [et al.]. Washington, D.C.: Published by the
Arthur M. Sackler Gallery, Smithsonian Institution in
association with Mapin Publishing, Ahmedabad and
Prestel Verlag, Munich, c1999. 408 p.
98-032426   704.9/489452114/074753   8185822638
*Art, Hindu -- Asia, South -- Exhibitions. Goddesses, Hindu, in
art -- Exhibitions.*

N8195.A4.B58 1993
Blurton, T. Richard.
Hindu art/ T. Richard Blurton. Cambridge, Mass.:
Harvard University Press, 1993. 239 p.
92-011157   704.9/48945   0674391888
Art, Hindu.

N8195.A4.M53 2000
Michell, George.
Hindu art and architecture/ George Michell. New York:
Thames & Hudson, c2000. 224 p.
00-100590   704.9/48945   0500203377
Art, Hindu -- India. Hindu symbolism.

N8199.T3
Little, Stephen, 1954-
Taoism and the arts of China/ Stephen Little with Shawn
Eichman; with essays by Patricia Ebrey ... [et al.].
Chicago: Art Institute of Chicago; c2000. 415 p.
00-034377   704.9/4899514/0951   0520227840
*Art, Taoist -- China -- Exhibitions. Art, Chinese -- Exhibitions.
Taoism -- China -- Exhibitions.*

N8213 Special subjects of art — Landscapes, views, mountains, etc. Places in art — General works

N8213.A53 1999
Andrews, Malcolm.
Landscape and western art/ Malcolm Andrews. Oxford;
Oxford University Press, 1999. vii, 248 p.
00-267839   758/.1/091821   0192100467
*Landscape in art. Landscape -- Philosophy. Nature
(Aesthetics) -- Philosophy.*

N8214.5 Special subjects of art — Landscapes, views, mountains, etc. Places in art — By region or country, A-Z

N8214.5.G7.D36 1993
Daniels, Stephen.
Fields of vision: landscape imagery and national identity
in England and the United States/ Stephen Daniels.
Princeton: Princeton University Press, c1993. x, 257 p.
93-140546   760/.0443642/0942   0691032734
*Landscape in art. Nationalism and art -- England.
Nationalism and art -- United States.*

N8214.5.U6.A47 1980
American light: the luminist movement, 1850-1875:
paintings, drawings, photographs/ [edited by] John
Wilmerding, with contributions by Lisa Fellows Andrus
... [et al.]. Washington, D.C.: National Gallery of Art,
c1980. 330 p.
79-024409   758/.1/09730740153   0064389405
*Luminism (Art) -- Exhibitions. Art, American -- Exhibitions.
Landscape in art -- Exhibitions.*

N8214.5.U6.A53 1993
Anchorage Museum of History and Art.
Painting in the North: Alaskan art in the Anchorage
Museum of History and Art/ Kesler E. Woodward.
Seattle: Anchorage Museum of History and Art: c1993.
159 p.
93-021556   760/.04499798   0295973196
Art, American. Eskimo painting. Eskimo art.

N8214.5.U6.D43 1988
Deak, Gloria-Gilda, 1930-
Picturing America, 1497-1899: prints, maps, and
drawings bearing on the New World discoveries and on
the development of the territory that is now the United
States/ by Gloria Gilda Deak. Princeton, N.J.: Princeton
University Press, c1988. 2 v.
87-038486   760/.0449973   0691039992
*Geographical discoveries in art -- Catalogs. Prints --
Catalogs. Drawing -- Catalogs. America -- Discovery and
exploration -- Maps -- Catalogs. America -- Discovery and
exploration -- Pictorial works -- Catalogs.*

N8214.5.U6.D57 1992
Discovered lands, invented pasts: transforming visions of
the American West/ Jules David Prown ... [et al.]. New
Haven: Yale University Press: c1992. xv, 217 p.
92-053537   760/.0449978   0300057229
*West (U.S.) in art -- Exhibitions. Indians in art -- Exhibitions.
Art, American -- Exhibitions.*

N8214.5.U6.K68 1998
Kovinick, Phil.
An encyclopedia of women artists of the American West/
Phil Kovinick and Marian Yoshiki-Kovinick; foreword
by William H. Goetzmann. Austin: University of Texas
Press, c1998. xxxv, 405 p.
97-003160   704/.042   0292790635
*West (U.S.) -- In art. Women artists -- Biography --
Dictionaries.*

N8214.5.U6.S28 1988
Saunders, Richard H., 1949-
Collecting the West: the C.R. Smith Collection of western American art/ by Richard H. Saunders. Austin: Published for the Archer M. Huntington Art Gallery, College of Fine Arts, the University of Texas at Austin by the University of Texas Press, 1988. 212 p.
87-025526   758/.9978   0292711123
Smith, C. R. -- (Cyrus Rowlett), -- 1899- -- Art collections -- Catalogs. Art, Modern -- 19th century -- Catalogs. Art, Modern -- 20th century -- Catalogs. West (U.S.) in art -- Catalogs.

N8217 Special subjects of art — Other special subjects (alphabetically) — A - Industry

N8217.C63.H64 1978
Hollander, Anne.
Seeing through clothes/ Anne Hollander. New York: Viking Press, 1978. xvi, 504 p.
78-015598   704.9/42   0670631744
Costume in art. Human figure in art. Art -- Psychology.

N8217.G8.K33
Kayser, Wolfgang Johannes, 1906-1960.
The grotesque in art and literature. Translated by Ulrich Weisstein. Bloomington, Indiana University Press [1963] 224 p.
63-009719   700
Grotesque in art. Grotesque in literature.

N8219 Special subjects of art — Other special subjects (alphabetically) — Industry - Love

N8219.L5
Bluhm, Andreas.
Light!: the industrial age 1750-1900: art & science, technology & society/ Andreas Bluhm, Louise Lippincott. New York: Thames & Hudson, 2001. 271 p.
00-105952   704.9/49535   0500510296
Light in art -- Exhibitions. Lighting -- History -- Exhibitions.

N8224 Special subjects of art — Other special subjects (alphabetically) — Med - Mi

N8224.M6.M54 1998
Miller, Jonathan, 1934-
On reflection/ Jonathan Miller; [editor, Valerie Mendes]. London: National Gallery Publications; c1998. 224 p.
98-066560   701/.8   1857092368
Mirrors in art. Reflections. Reflection (Optics) in art.

N8232 Special subjects of art — Other special subjects (alphabetically) — Negroes. Afro-Americans. Blacks

N8232.B57 1990
Boime, Albert.
The art of exclusion: representing Blacks in the nineteenth century/ Albert Boime. Washington: Smithsonian Institution Press, c1990. xvi, 256 p.
89-004213   704.9/499730496073   0874742544
Afro-Americans in art. Art, American. Art, Modern -- 19th century -- United States.

N8232.I46
The Image of the Black in Western art/ foreword by Amadou-Mahtar M'Bow. [Fribourg]: Office du livre, [1976-89] v. 1-2, 4
76-025772   704.94/9/30145196   0688030866
Blacks in art. Art.

N8232.M44 1990
McElroy, Guy C.
Facing history: the Black image in American art, 1710-1940/ Guy C. McElroy; with an essay by Henry Louis Gates, Jr., and contributions by Janet Levine, Francis Martin, Jr., and Claudia Vess; edited by Christopher C. French. San Francisco, CA: Bedford Arts; c1990. 140 p.
89-018007   704.9/499730496073
Afro-Americans in art -- Exhibitions. Art, American -- Exhibitions.

N8236 Special subjects of art — Other special subjects (alphabetically) — Peat - Pray

N8236.P5.E3 1995
Edelman, Murray J. 1919-
From art to politics: how artistic creations shape political conceptions/ Murray Edelman. Chicago: University of Chicago Press, 1995. x, 152 p.
94-018266   701/.03   0226184005
Politics in art. Art.

N8237.8 Special subjects of art — Other special subjects (alphabetically) — Q - R

N8237.8.R3.R34 1988
The Railroad in American art: representations of technological change/ edited by Susan Danly and Leo Marx. Cambridge, Mass.: MIT Press, c1988. 218 p.
86-021037   760/.04496251   0262231263
Railroads in art. Art, American. Art, Modern -- 19th century -- United States.

N8241.5 Special subjects of art —
Other special subjects (alphabetically) —
Sex role

N8241.5.H47 1996
Hersey, George L.
The evolution of allure: sexual selection from the Medici Venus to the Incredible Hulk/ George L. Hersey. Cambridge, Mass.: MIT Press, c1996. xvi, 219 p.
95-038927   700   0262082446
Sex role in art. Art and society.

N8243 Special subjects of art —
Other special subjects (alphabetically) —
Sh - So

N8243.S36.B38 1995
Baxandall, Michael.
Shadows and enlightenment/ Michael Baxandall. New Haven: Yale University Press, c1995. xii, 192 p.
94-040132   701/.8   0300059795
Shades and shadows in art. Visual perception. Art, Modern — 17th-18th centuries.

N8243.S65 D85 1993
Dunitz, Robin J.
Street gallery/ by Robin J. Dunitz. 1st ed. Los Angeles, CA: RJD Enterprises, c1993. viii, 468 p.
92-097162   751.7/3/0979494 20   0963286218
Street art — California — Los Angeles — Guidebooks. Social problems in art. Mural painting and decoration, American — California — Los Angeles — 20th

N8248 Special subjects of art —
Other special subjects (alphabetically) —
Spe - Spo

N8248.S77.L56 1988
Lipsey, Roger, 1942-
An art of our own: the spiritual in twentieth-century art/ Roger Lipsey. Boston: Shambhala; 1988. xxiii, 518 p.
88-018206   701/.08   0877733627
Spirituality in art. Art, Modern — 20th century.

N8354 Art as a profession —
Special classes of persons as artists —
Women

N8354.B67 2000
Borzello, Frances.
A world of our own: women as artists since the Renaissance/ Frances Borzello. New York: Watson-Guptill Publications, c2000. 224 p.
00-103117   0823058743
Women artists.

N8354.C48 1990
Chadwick, Whitney.
Women, art, and society/ Whitney Chadwick. New York, N.Y.: Thames and Hudson, 1990. 383 p.
89-050634   704/.042   0500202419
Women artists — Biography — History and criticism. Feminism and art. Women in art.

N8354.D53 1997
Dictionary of women artists/ editor, Delia Gaze; picture editors, Maja Mihajlovic, Leanda Shrimpton. London; Fitzroy Dearborn Publishers, 1997. 2 v.
97-206872   1884964214
Women artists — Biography — Dictionaries.

N8354.H45 1987
Heller, Nancy.
Women artists: an illustrated history/ Nancy G. Heller. New York: Abbeville Press, c1987. 224 p.
87-000904   704/.042   0896597482
Women artists.

N8354.I58 1996
Inside the visible: an elliptical traverse of 20th century art in, of, and from the feminine/ curated and edited by M. Catherine de Zegher. Cambridge, Mass.: The MIT Press, [1996?] 495 p.
95-047948   704/.042/090407474461   0262540819
Women artists — Exhibitions. Art, Modern — 20th century — Exhibitions.

N8354.M57 1998
Mirror images: women, surrealism, and self-representation/ edited by Whitney Chadwick; essays by Dawn Ades ... [et al.]. Cambridge, Mass.: MIT Press, c1998. xiii, 193 p.
97-046576   704/.042   0262531577
Women artists — Psychology. Self-perception in women. Self-portraits.

N8354.N38 2000
National Museum of Women in the Arts (U.S.)
Women artists: works from the National Museum of Women in the Arts/ Nancy Heller; contributors, Susan Fisher Sterling ... [et al.]. Washington, D.C.: Rizzoli International Publications, 2000. 239 p.
00-101340   704/.042/074753   0847822907
Women artists — Catalogs. Art — Washington (D.C.) — Catalogs.

N8354.P37 1981
Parker, Rozsika.
Old mistresses: women, art, and ideology/ Rozsika Parker, Griselda Pollock. New York: Pantheon Books, c1981. xxi, 184 p.
81-048253   704/.042   0394524306
Women artists. Feminism and art.

N8375 Art critics and historians; historiography

N8375.B46.A15
Berenson, Bernard, 1865-1959.
Bernard Berenson treasury: a selection from the works, unpublished writings, letters, diaries, and journals of the most celebrated humanist and art historian of our times, 1887-1958/ Selected and edited by Hanna Kiel. Introd. by John Walker. Pref. by Nicky Mariano.   Simon and Schuster, 1962. 414 p.
62-014273   927
Berenson, Bernard, — 1865-1959.

N8375.B46.A29
Berenson, Bernard, 1865-1959.
The passionate sightseer; from the diaries, 1947 to 1956.
Pref. by Raymond Mortimer. New York, Simon and
Schuster [1960] 200 p.
60-006799   709.45
Art -- Italy. Italy -- Description and travel.

N8375.B46.A3
Berenson, Bernard, 1865-1959.
Rumor and reflection.   Simon, 1952. 461 p.
52-013219   927
Berenson, Bernard, -- 1865-1959. World War, 1939-1945 --
Personal narratives, Italian. Authors -- Correspondence,
reminiscences, etc.

N8375.B46.M3 1966a
Mariano, Nicky.
Forty years with Berenson/ with an introduction by Sir
Kenneth Clark. Knopf, 1966. 352 p.
66-019387   709.24
Mariano, Nicky. Berenson, Bernard, -- 1865-1959.

N8375.F375.C5
Chisolm, Lawrence W.
Fenollosa: the Far East and American culture.   New
Haven, Yale University Press, 1963. 297 p.
63-017024
Fenollosa, Ernest Francisco, -- 1853-1908.   United States --
Relations -- East Asia. East Asia -- Relations -- United States.

N8380 Art collectors, patrons, etc.

N8380.T3 1948
Taylor, Francis Henry, 1903-1957.
The taste of angels, a history of art collecting from
Rameses to Napoleon. Boston, Little, Brown, 1948. xxx,
661 p.
48-004034   708.051
Art -- Collectors and collecting.

N8560 Examination and conservation of works of art — Preservation. Cleaning. Restoration — General works

N8560.B43 1994
Beck, James H.
Art restoration: the culture, the business, and the scandal/
James Beck with Michael Daley. London: J. Murray,
1994. xiv, 210 p.
94-139915   702/.8/8   0719554306
Art -- Conservation and restoration.

N8600 Economics of art

N8600.C484 1999
Chambers, Karen S.
Artist's resource: the Watson-Guptill guide to academic
programs, artists' colonies and artist-in-residence
programs, conferences, workshops/ Karen S. Chambers.
New York: Watson-Guptill Publications, c1999. 240 p.
00-702736   702/.3/73   0823076571
Art -- Vocational guidance -- Directories. Art -- Economic
aspects -- Directories.

N8600.G69 1994
Grant, Daniel.
The artist's resource handbook/ Daniel Grant. New York:
Allworth Press, c1994. 176 p.
94-070297   706/.8   188055917X
Art -- Economic aspects -- Directories. Art -- Vocational
guidance -- Directories.

N8660 Economics of art — Art dealers — Biography of art dealers

N8660.F383.A2 2000
Feigen, Richard L., 1930-
Tales from the art crypt: the painters, the museums, the
curators, the collectors, the auctions, the art/ Richard
Feigen. New York: Alfred A. Knopf, 2000. x, 296 p.
00-131136   709/.2   039457169X
Feigen, Richard L., -- 1930- Art -- Anecdotes. Art -- Collectors
and collecting. Art dealers -- United States -- Biography.

N8790 Art and the state. Public art — Protection and cultivation of art — Forgeries

N8790.F3 1990
Fake?: the art of deception/ edited by Mark Jones with
Paul Craddock and Nicolas Barker. Berkeley: University
of California Press, 1990. 312 p.
89-052107   707/.4/42142   0520070860
Art -- Forgeries -- Exhibitions.

N8790.F67 1983
The Forger's art: forgery and the philosophy of art/ edited
by Denis Dutton. Berkeley: University of California
Press, c1983. x, 276 p.
82-011029   702/.8/74   0520043413
Art -- Forgeries. Art -- Philosophy.

N8795.3 Art and the state. Public art — Protection and cultivation of art — Theft of works of art

N8795.3.G3.A39 1995
Akinsha, Konstantin.
Beautiful loot: the Soviet plunder of Europe's art
treasures/ Konstantin Akinsha and Grigorii Kozlov, with
Sylvia Hochfield. New York: Random House, c1995. xiii,
301 p.
95-032315   709/.43/09044   0679443894
Art thefts -- Germany -- History -- 20th century. Art treasures
in war. Soviet Union -- Cultural policy.

**N8835-8846 Art and the state. Public art —
Protection and cultivation of art —
Government support of art. Public art**

N8835.C78 1988
Cruikshank, Jeffrey L.
Going public: a field guide to developments in art in public places/ written by Jeffrey L. Cruikshank and Pam Korza; introductions by Richard Andrews and Kathy Halbreich; editor, Pam Korza; contributing editor, Richard Andrews. Amherst, MA: Published by the Arts Extension Service in cooperation 303 p.
87-073446   706/.8 20   0945464002
Public art -- United States -- Handbooks, manuals, etc.

N8835.D57 1990
Dippie, Brian W.
Catlin and his contemporaries: the politics of patronage/ Brian W. Dippie. Lincoln: University of Nebraska Press, c1990. xix, 553 p.
89-004963   759.13   0803216831
Catlin, George, -- 1796-1872 -- Finance, Personal.   Art patronage -- United States -- History -- 19th century. Art and state -- United States.

N8835.D67 1995
Doss, Erika Lee.
Spirit poles and flying pigs: public art and cultural democracy in American communities/ Erika Doss. Washington: Smithsonian Institution Press, c1995. x, 278 p.
94-026010   701/.03   1560984643
Public art -- United States -- Public opinion. Public opinion -- United States.

N8837.B74 2001
Brenson, Michael.
Visionaries and outcasts: the NEA, Congress, and the place of the visual artist in America/ Michael Brenson. New York: New Press: c2001. xii, 157 p.
00-042360   707/.9/73   1565846249
Art, American -- 20th century -- Political aspects. Federal aid to the arts -- United States -- History -- 20th century.

N8838.O25
O'Connor, Francis V.,
Art for the millions; essays from the 1930s by artists and administrators of the WPA Federal Art Project, edited, and with an introd., by Francis V. O'Connor. Greenwich, Conn., New York Graphic Society [1973] 317 p.
78-181347   338.4/7/70973   0821204394
Art, American. Art, Modern -- 20th century -- United States. Federal aid to the arts -- United States.

N8845.S43.R87 1991
Rupp, James M.
Art in Seattle's public places: an illustrated guide/ James M. Rupp; photographs by Mary Randlett. Seattle: University of Washington Press, c1992. 320 p.
90-032846   708.197/772   0295969881
Public art -- Washington (State) -- Seattle -- Guidebooks.

N8846.C6.Y68 1999
Young, John T.
Contemporary public art in China: a photographic tour/ John T. Young. Seattle: University of Washington Press, c1999. xvi, 136 p.
97-047141   709/.51/09045   0295977086
Public art -- China. Art, Chinese -- 20th century. Public art -- China -- Pictorial works.

**N9100 Art and the state. Public art —
Art and war.
Protection of monuments and art works during
wartime. Lost works of art — General works**

N9100.A78 2002
Artful armies, beautiful battles: art and warfare in early modern Europe/ edited by Pia Cuneo. Leiden; Brill, 2002. xii, 266 p.
2001-043354   704.9/4935502 21   9004115889
Art and war. War in art. Art, European -- 16th century. Art, European -- 17th century.

NA Architecture

NA31 Encyclopedias, dictionaries, glossaries, etc.

NA31.B83 1998
Burden, Ernest E., 1934-
Illustrated dictionary of architecture/ Ernest Burden. [New York]: McGraw-Hill, c1998. vii, 261 p.
98-004757   720/.03   0070089884
Architecture -- Dictionaries.

NA31.C44 1995
Ching, Frank, 1943-
A visual dictionary of architecture/ Francis D.K. Ching. New York: Van Nostrand Reinhold, c1995. 319 p.
95-001476   720/.3   0442009046
Architecture -- Dictionaries. Picture dictionaries, English.

NA31.D55 1996
Dictionary of building preservation/ edited by Ward Bucher; Christine Madrid, illustration editor. New York: Preservation Press, J. Wiley, c1996. x, 560 p.
96-019947   720/.3   0471144134
Architecture -- Dictionaries. Building -- Dictionaries. Architecture -- Conservation and restoration.

NA31.E59 1989
Encyclopedia of architecture: design, engineering & construction/ Joseph A. Wilkes, editor-in-chief, Robert T. Packard, associate editor. New York: Wiley, c1988-c1989. 4 v.
87-025222   720/.3   0471633518
Architecture -- Dictionaries.

NA31.H32 1993
Dictionary of architecture & construction/ edited by Cyril M. Harris. New York: McGraw-Hill, c1993. viii, 924 p.
92-043562   720/.3   0070268886
Architecture -- Dictionaries. Building -- Dictionaries.

NA31.S84 1966
Sturgis, Russell, 1836-1909.
A dictionary of architecture and building: biographical, historical, and descriptive, by Russell Sturgis and many architects, painters, engineers, and other expert writers, American and foreign. Detroit, Gale Research Co., 1966. 3 v.
66-026997   720/.3
Architecture -- Bibliography. Architects. Architecture -- Dictionaries.

NA40 Biography (Collective)

NA40.M25 1982
Macmillan encyclopedia of architects/ Adolf K. Placzek, editor in chief. New York: Free Press; c1982. 4 v.
82-017256   720/.92/2   0029250005
Architects -- Biography -- Dictionaries.

NA53 Directories — United States — General

NA53.A37
American architects directory. New York, R.R. Bowker Co.
55-012270   720.69
Architects -- United States -- Directories.

NA105 Architecture and the state — Preservation and restoration of architectural monuments — General works

NA105.W43 1993
Weaver, Martin E., 1938-
Conserving buildings: guide to techniques and materials/ Martin E. Weaver; with F.G. Matero. New York: Wiley, c1993. xiv, 270 p.
91-048263   720/.28/8   0471509450
Buildings -- Conservation and restoration -- Technique. Building materials.

NA200 History — General works

NA200.A45 1960
Allsopp, Bruce.
A general history of architecture from the earliest civilizations to the present day. London, Pitman [1960] xii, 235 p.
60-050700
Architecture--History. [from old catalog]

NA200.A73 1984
Architecture of the Western World/ edited and with an introduction by Michael Raeburn; foreword by Sir Hugh Casson; individual chapters by J.J. Coulton ... [et al.]. New York: Crescent Books: 1984. 304 p.
84-001790   720/.9 19   0517445131
Architecture--History.

NA200.F63 1961
Fletcher, Banister, 1866-1953.
A history of architecture on the comparative method. New York, Scribner, 1961. 1366 p.
61-065079   720.9
Architecture -- History.

NA200.K65 1995
Kostof, Spiro.
A history of architecture: settings and rituals/ Spiro Kostof; revisions by Greg Castillo; original drawings by Richard Tobias. 2nd ed./ revisions by Greg Castillo. New York: Oxford University Press, 1995. 792 p.
94-038787   720/.9 20   0195083784
Architecture--History.

NA202 History — General works — Pictorial works (with little or no text)

NA202.T4 1991
Teague, Edward H., 1952-
World architecture index: a guide to illustrations/ compiled by Edward H. Teague. New York: Greenwood Press, 1991. xix, 447 p.
91-007565   016.72   0313225524
Architecture -- Pictorial works -- Indexes.

NA203 History — General special

NA203.G5 1962
Giedion, S. 1888-1968.
Space, time, and architecture: the growth of a new tradition. Cambridge, Harvard University Press, 1962. xlviii, 778 p.
62-014459   720.9
City planning -- History. Architecture -- History.

NA203.M6 1976
Moholy-Nagy, Sibyl,
Native genius in anonymous architecture in North America/ Sibyl Moholy-Nagy. New York: Schocken Books, 1976, c1957. 190 p.
75-037290   720/.973   0805205128
Vernacular architecture--North America. Architecture--North America.

NA212 History — Ancient architecture — Middle East

NA212.L45 1988
Leick, Gwendolyn, 1951-
A dictionary of ancient Near Eastern architecture/ Gwendolyn Leick; with illustrations by Francis J. Kirk. London; Routledge, 1988. xix, 261 p.
87-023375   722/.5/03   0415002400
Architecture, Ancient -- Middle East -- Dictionaries. Architecture -- Middle East -- Dictionaries. Middle East -- Antiquities -- Dictionaries.

NA215 History — Ancient architecture — Egypt

NA215.A75 1999
Arnold, Dieter, 1936-
Temples of the last pharaohs/ Dieter Arnold. New York:
Oxford University Press, c1999. 373 p.
99-024117   726/.1931   0195126335
Architecture, Ancient -- Egypt. Temples -- Egypt.

NA225 History — Ancient architecture — Persia

NA225.B63 2000
Boardman, John, 1927-
Persia and the West: an archaeological investigation of
the genesis of Achaemenid art/ John Boardman. New
York, N.Y.: Thames & Hudson, 2000. 255 p.
99-066194   722/.52   050005102X
Achaemenid dynasty, -- 559-330 B.C.   Sculpture, Achaemenid.
Architecture, Ancient -- Iran. Iran -- Antiquities.

NA260-335 History — Ancient architecture — Classical. Greek and Roman

NA260.P67 1992
Porphyrios, Demetri.
Classical architecture: the living tradition/ Demetri
Porphyrios. New York: McGraw-Hill, c1992. 155 p.
92-015369   722/.8   0070504784
Architecture, Classical.

NA270.C65 1977
Coulton, J. J.
Ancient Greek architects at work: problems of structure
and design/ J. J. Coulton. Ithaca, N.Y.: Cornell
University Press, 1977. 196 p.
76-044117   722/.8   0801410770
Architecture -- Greece.

NA270.D5 1975b
Dinsmoor, William Bell,
The architecture of ancient Greece: an account of its
historic   development/ William Bell Dinsmoor. 3rd
revised ed. London: Batsford, 1975. xxv, 424 p.
76-376245   722/.8   0713431431
Architecture--Greece--History.

NA270.L36 1996
Lawrence, A. W.
Greek architecture/ A.W. Lawrence. 5th ed./ revised by
R.A. Tomlinson. New Haven: Yale University Press,
c1996. viii, 243 p.
95-053785   722/.8 20   0300064926
Architecture--Greece.

NA270.M34 1964
Martienssen, Rex Distin,
The idea of space in Greek architecture, with special
reference to the Doric temple and its setting. [2d ed.]
Johannesburg, Witwatersrand University Press, 1964
[c1956] xx, 191 p.
66-006819
Architecture, Greek. Temples, Greek. City planning--Greece.

NA270.S3
Scranton, Robert Lorentz, 1912-
Greek architecture. New York, G. Braziller, 1962. 128 p.
62-007532   722.8
Architecture, Greek.

NA275.B413
Berve, Helmut, 1896-
Greek temples, theatres, and shrines/ texts by Helmut
Berve and Gottried Gruben; photos. by Max Hirmer.
H.N. Abrams, 1963. 508 p.
62-019131   722.8
Temples, Greek. Theaters -- Greece. Shrines -- Greece.

NA275.S3 1969
Scully, Vincent Joseph, 1920-
The earth, the temple, and the gods; Greek sacred
architecture [by] Vincent Scully. New York, Praeger
[1969] xxxii, 271 p.
69-015754   726.1/2/08
Temples -- Greece.

NA280.R63 1958
Rodenwaldt, Gerhart, 1886-1945.
The Acropolis. Photographed by Walter Hege. Norman,
University of Oklahoma Press [1958, c1957] 61 p.
58-006859   722.6
Art -- Athens. Athens. -- Acropolis. Architecture -- Athens.

NA300.B63 1978
Boethius, Axel, 1889-1969.
Etruscan and early Roman architecture/ Axel Boethius.
Harmondsworth, Eng.; Penguin Books, 1978. 264 p.
78-001875   722/.7   0140561447
Architecture -- Italy -- Etruria. Architecture -- Rome.

NA310.B6
Boethius, Axel, 1889-
The golden house of Nero: some aspects of Roman
architecture. Ann Arbor: University of Michigan Press,
[1960] 195 p.
57-009137   722.7
*Rome (City) -- Domus Aurea. Architecture, Roman. Cities and
towns -- Rome -- Planning*

NA310.B75
Brown, Frank Edward, 1908-
Roman architecture.   New York, G. Braziller, 1961.
125 p.
61-013688   722.7
Architecture, Roman.

NA310.M2
MacDonald, William Lloyd.
The architecture of the Roman Empire: an introductory
study/ William L. MacDonald. New Haven, Yale
University Press, 1965. v. 1
65-022333   722.7
Architecture, Roman -- History. Architecture -- Rome.

NA310.N28 1968
Nash, Ernest.
Pictorial dictionary of ancient Rome./ by Ernest Nash.
New York: Hacker, 1981. 2 v.
79-091827   0878172653
Architecture -- Rome. Architecture, Roman -- Pictorial works.

NA310.S4
Scherer, Margaret Roseman.
Marvels of ancient Rome/ edited and with a foreword by
Charles Rufus Morey. Phaidon Press, 1955. 430 p.
56-001344   722.6
Architecture -- Italy -- Rome.   Rome (Italy) -- Pictorial works.

NA310.W34
Ward-Perkins, J. B. 1912-
Roman imperial architecture/ J. B. Ward-Perkins.
Harmondsworth, Eng.; Penguin Books, c1981. 532 p.
79-026799   722/.7   0140560459
Architecture, Roman.

NA324.C57 1991
Clarke, John R., 1945-
The houses of Roman Italy, 100 B.C.-A.D. 250: ritual,
space, and decoration/ John R. Clarke. Berkeley:
University of California Press, c1991. xxvii, 411 p.
90-048357   728/.0937   0520072677
*Architecture, Roman -- Italy. Architecture, Domestic -- Italy.
Mural painting and decoration, Roman -- Italy.*

NA327.P6.R53 1988
Richardson, Lawrence.
Pompeii: an architectural history/ L. Richardson, Jr.
Baltimore: Johns Hopkins University Press, c1988.
xxviii, 445 p.
87-017299   722/.7/09377   080183533X
*Architecture -- Italy -- Pompeii (Extinct City)   Pompeii
(Extinct City) -- Buildings, structures, etc.*

NA335.M628.S44 1997
Segal, Arthur.
From function to monument: urban landscapes of Roman
Palestine, Syria, and Provincia Arabia/ Arthur Segal.
Oxford: Oxbow Books; c1997. 184 p.
98-177173   722/.7/09394   1900188139
*Architecture, Roman -- Arabia, Roman. Architecture, Roman -
- Palestine. Architecture, Roman -- Syria.*

NA350 History — Medieval architecture — General works

NA350.H26 1972b
Harvey, John Hooper.
The mediaeval architect [by] John Harvey. New York, St.
Martin's Press [1972] 296 p.
79-190103   723
Architecture, Medieval. Architecture -- Vocational guidance.

NA350.S2
Saalman, Howard.
Medieval architecture; European architecture, 600-1200.
New York, G. Braziller, 1962. 127 p.
62-007530   723.4
Architecture, Medieval.

NA350.S78 1999
Stalley, R. A.
Early medieval architecture/ Roger Stalley. Oxford;
Oxford University Press, 1999. 272 p.
0192100483
*Architecture, Medieval -- Europe, Western. Church
architecture -- Europe, Western.*

NA360-365 History — Medieval architecture — Early Christian

NA360.M3
MacDonald, William Lloyd.
Early Christian & Byzantine architecture. New York, G.
Braziller, 1962. 128 p.
62-007531   723.1
Architecture, Early Christian. Architecture, Byzantine.

NA365.C6 1973
Conant, Kenneth John, 1894-
Carolingian and Romanesque architecture, 800 to 1200/
Kenneth John Conant. Harmondsworth; Penguin, 1973.
xxxix, 345 p.
76-354254   723/.4   0140560130
Architecture, Carolingian. Architecture, Romanesque.

NA370 History — Medieval architecture — Byzantine

NA370.H3 1956
Hamilton, John Arnott.
Byzantine architecture and decoration. With a foreword
by D. Talbot Rice. London, Batsford [1956] viii, 301 p.
57-000499   723.2
*Art, Byzantine. Church architecture, Byzantine. Church
decoration and ornament, Byzantine.*

NA380 History — Medieval architecture — Islamic architecture. Moorish architecture

NA380.A78 1984
Architecture of the Islamic world: its history and social
meaning: with a complete survey of key monuments and
758 illustrations, 112 in color/ texts by Ernst J. Grube ...
[et al.]; edited by George Michell. New York, N.Y.:
Thames and Hudson, 1984, c1978. 288 p.
84-050341   720/.917/671   0500340765
Architecture, Islamic.

NA380.H5 1967
Hill, Derek.
Islamic architecture and its decoration A.D. 800-1500: a
photographic survey by Derek Hill; with an introductory
text by Oleg Grabar. London, Faber, 1967. 95 p.
67-111312   720/.956
*Architecture, Islamic -- History. Decoration and ornament,
Architectural -- History.*

NA380.H58 1977
Hoag, John D.
Islamic architecture/ John D. Hoag. New York: H. N. Abrams, 1977, c1975. 424 p.
76-041805   720/.917/671   0810910101
Architecture, Islamic.

NA380.P43 1996
Petersen, Andrew.
Dictionary of Islamic architecture/ Andrew Petersen. London; Routledge, 1996. 342 p.
96-120478   720/.882971   0415060842
Architecture, Islamic -- Dictionaries.

NA380.C5713 2000
Clevenot, Dominique.
Splendors of Islam: architecture, decoration, and design/ by Dominique Clevenot; photographs by Gerard Degeorge. New York: Vendome Press, 2000.
00-038147   729/.0917/671   0865652147
Architecture, Islamic. Art, Islamic. Islamic art and symbolism.

NA390 History —
Medieval architecture —
Romanesque architecture

NA390.B445 2000
Before and after the end of time: architecture and the year 1000/ Christine Smith ... [et al.]. [New York, NY]: Harvard Design School, c2000 xiv, 106 p.
    0807614939
Richardson, H. H. -- (Henry Hobson), -- 1838-1886. Architecture, Romanesque -- Exhibitions. Art, Romanesque -- Exhibitions. Architecture -- Composition, proportion, etc.

NA390.B813
Busch, Harald, 1904-
Romanesque Europe. With an introd. by R.H.C. Davis. Edited by Harald Busch and Bernd Lohse. With commentaries on the illus. by Helmut Domke. [Translated by Peter Gorge.] New York, Macmillan, 1960 [c1959]
60-003192   723.4
Architecture, Romanesque. Architecture -- Europe.

NA390.C6
Clapham, Alfred William, 1883-1950.
Romanesque architecture in western Europe, by A. W. Clapham. Oxford, The Clarendon press, 1936. xv, 208 p.
36-007537   723.4
Architecture, Romanesque. Church architecture -- Europe.

NA390.R33 1992
Radding, Charles.
Medieval architecture, medieval learning: builders and masters in the age of Romanesque and Gothic/ Charles M. Radding and William W. Clark. New Haven: Yale University Press, c1992. xiii, 166 p.
90-026065   723/.4   0300049188
Architecture, Romanesque. Learning and scholarship -- History -- Medieval, 500-1500. Architecture, Gothic.

NA390.W35 1992
Bizzarro, Tina Waldeier, 1950-
Romanesque architectural criticism: a pre-history/ Tina Waldeier Bizzarro. Cambridge; Cambridge University Press, 1992. vii, 253 p.
91-043494   723/.4   0521410177
Architecture, Romanesque. Architectural criticism -- England. Architectural criticism -- France.

NA440-480 History —
Medieval architecture —
Gothic architecture

NA440.B68
Branner, Robert.
Gothic architecture.   New York, G. Braziller, 1961. 125 p.
61-013690   723.5
Architecture, Gothic.

NA440.B853
Busch, Harald, 1904-
Gothic Europe. With an introduction by Kurt Gerstenberg. Edited by Harald Busch and Bernd Lohse. With commentaries on the illus. by Helmut Domke. [Translated by P. George] London, Batsford [1959]
59-004078   723.5094
Architecture -- Europe. Architecture, Gothic.

NA440.F5 1981
Fitchen, John.
The construction of Gothic cathedrals: a study of medieval vault erection/ by John Fitchen. Chicago: University of Chicago Press, 1981, c1961. xix, 344 p.
80-026291   726/.5143   0226252035
Architecture, Gothic. Christian art and symbolism -- Medieval, 500-1500. Architecture, Medieval.

NA440.J3
Jackson, Thomas Graham, 1835-1924.
Gothic architecture in France, England, and Italy, by Sir Thomas Graham Jackson, bart. Cambridge [Eng.] University Press, 1915. 2 v.
16-003630
Architecture, Gothic.

NA440.P23 1957
Panofsky, Erwin, 1892-1968.
Gothic architecture and scholasticism.   New York, Meridian Books, 1957. 156 p.
57-006681   723.5
Architecture, Gothic. Scholasticism.

NA453.J23
Jantzen, Hans, 1881-
High Gothic; the classic cathedrals of Chartres, Reims, Amiens. Translated from the German by James Palmes. [New York] Pantheon Books [1962] 181 p.
59-011958   726/.6/0944
Art, High Gothic -- France. Architecture, Gothic -- France.

NA480.G7613 1985
Grodecki, Louis,
Gothic architecture/ Louis Grodecki; contributions by Anne Prache and Roland Recht; [translated from the French by I. Mark Paris]. New York: Electa/Rizzoli, 1985, c1978. 221 p.
82-062751   723/.5 19   0847804739
Architecture, Gothic.

NA490 History —
Military architecture —
General works

NA490.T63 1955
Toy, Sidney.
A history of fortification from 3000 B.C. to A.D. 1700. London, Heinemann [1955] 262 p.
55-035812   728.81
Castles. Fortification.

NA500 History —
Modern architecture —
General works

NA500.F75 1992
Frampton, Kenneth.
Modern architecture: a critical history/ Kenneth Frampton. 3rd ed., rev. and enlarged. London: Thames and Hudson, 1992. 376 p.
91-066733   724 20   0500202575
Architecture, Modern--History.

NA500.H5
Hitchcock, Henry Russell, 1903-
Modern architecture: romanticism and reintegration/ Henry-Russell Hitchcock. New York: Payson & Clarke ltd., 1929. xvii, 252 p.
29-025446
Architecture, Modern -- 19th century. Architecture, Modern -- 20th century.

NA500.T3313 1987
Tafuri, Manfredo.
The sphere and the labyrinth: avant-gardes and architecture from Piranesi to the 1970s/ Manfredo Tafuri; translated by Pellegrino d'Acierno and Robert Connolly. Cambridge, Mass.: MIT Press, c1987. 382 p.
86-027703   724   0262200619
Architecture, Modern -- History. Avant-garde (Aesthetics) -- History.

NA510-533 History —
Modern architecture —
Renaissance. 16th century

NA510.L6
Lowry, Bates, 1923-
Renaissance architecture. New York, G. Braziller, 1962. 127 p.
61-013691   724.1
Architecture, Renaissance.

NA510.T56 1993
Thomson, David, 1951-
Renaissance architecture: critics, patrons, luxury/ by David Thomson. Manchester; Manchester University Press c1993. xv, 240 p.
93-016088   724/.12   0719039223
Architecture, Renaissance. Architects and patrons. Architecture and society -- History -- 16th century.

NA520.W5 1965
Wittkower, Rudolf.
Architectural principles in the age of humanism. New York, Random House, [1965, c1962] 173 p.
64-015892   724.945
Architecture -- Italy. Architecture -- Composition, proportion, etc. Architecture, Renaissance.

NA525.C35
Coffin, David R.
The Villa d'Este at Tivoli. Princeton, N.J., Published for the Dept. of Art and Archaeology, 1960. xvi, 186 p.
60-005744   728.84094563
Tivoli, Italy. Villa d'Este.

NA533.W2 1926
Ward, William Henry, 1865-1924.
The architecture of the renaissance in France, New York, C. Scribner's sons: [1926]
28-018475
Renaissance -- France. Gardens. Architecture -- France -- History. France -- History.

NA590 History —
Modern architecture —
Baroque. Rococo

NA590.K3 1966
Kaufmann, Emil, 1891-1953.
Architecture in the Age of Reason; baroque and post-baroque in England, Italy, and France. [Hamden, Conn.] Archon Books, 1966 [c1955] xxvi, 293 p.
66-018643   724.19
Architecture, Baroque.

NA590.M5
Millon, Henry A.
Baroque & rococo architecture. New York, G. Braziller, 1961. 127 p.
61-015492   724.19
Architecture, Baroque. Architecture, Rococo.

NA600 History —
Modern architecture —
Neoclassicism (Greek and Roman revival)

NA600.R94
Rykwert, Joseph, 1926-
The first moderns: the architects of the eighteenth century/ Joseph Rykwert. Cambridge, Mass.: MIT Press, c1980. viii, 585 p.
79-022123   724/.1   0262180901
Neoclassicism (Architecture) Architecture, Modern -- 17th-18th centuries.

NA610 History —
Modern architecture — Gothic revival

NA610.C5 1970
Clark, Kenneth, 1903-
The Gothic revival; an essay in the history of taste [by] Kenneth Clark. New York, Humanities Press, 1970 [c1962] xii, 236 p.
73-014966   720/.942   0391000276
Gothic revival (Architecture) Medievalism -- History. Middle Ages in art.

NA630 History —
Modern architecture — 18th century

NA630.G57
Girouard, Mark, 1931-
Sweetness and light: the Queen Anne movement, 1860-1900/ Mark Girouard. Oxford [Eng.]: Clarendon Press, 1977. xvi, 250 p.
77-030113   724   019817330X
Architecture, Queen Anne. Eclecticism in architecture. Architecture, Modern -- 19th century.

NA642-682 History —
Modern architecture — 19th and 20th centuries

NA642.B413 1971b
Benevolo, Leonardo.
History of modern architecture.   Cambridge, Mass., M.I.T. Press [1971] 2 v.
77-157667   724   0262020807
Architecture, Modern -- 19th century. Architecture, Modern -- 20th century.

NA642.F7 1983
Frampton, Kenneth.
Modern architecture, 1851-1945/ Kenneth Frampton, Yukio Futagawa. New York: Rizzoli, 1983. 465 p.
83-061363   724   0847805069
Architecture, Modern -- 19th century. Architecture, Modern -- 20th century.

NA642.H57
Hitchcock, Henry Russell, 1903-
Modern architecture: romanticism and reintegration. New York, Hacker Art Books, 1970. xvii, 252 p.
73-116356   724   0878170448
Architecture, Modern -- 19th century. Architecture, Modern -- 20th century. Romanticism in architecture.

NA642.R57 1983
Risebero, Bill, 1938-
Modern architecture and design: an alternative history/ Bill Risebero. Cambridge, Mass.: MIT Press, 1983, c1982. 256 p.
82-061310   724   0262181088
Architecture, Modern -- 19th century. Architecture, Modern -- 20th century.

NA645.5.A7.A77 1979
Art nouveau architecture/ edited by Frank Russell. New York: Rizzoli, 1979. 332 p.
78-058703   724.9/1   0847801861
Art nouveau (Architecture) -- Addresses, essays, lectures. Architecture, Modern -- 19th century -- Addresses, essays, lectures.

NA645.5.E25.W37
Watkin, David, 1941-
Morality and architecture: the development of a theme in architectural history and theory from the Gothic revival to the modern movement/ by David Watkin. Oxford [Eng.]: Clarendon Press, 1977. viii, 126 p.
77-006815   724   0198173504
Eclecticism in architecture. Architecture, Modern -- 19th century. Architecture, Modern -- 20th century.

NA680.B25 1980
Banham, Reyner.
Theory and design in the first machine age/ Reyner Banham. Cambridge, Mass.: MIT Press, 1980, c1960. 338 p.
80-000014   724.9/1   0262520583
Architecture, Modern -- 20th century.

NA680.C87 1996
Curtis, William J. R.
Modern architecture since 1900/ William J.R. Curtis. 3rd ed., [rev., expanded, and redesigned]. Upper Saddle River, N.J.: Prentice Hall, [1996] 736 p.
97-120714   0132322730
Architecture, Modern--20th century.

NA680.G7 1965
Gropius, Walter, 1883-1969.
The new architecture and the Bauhaus. Translated from the German by P. Morton Shand, with an introd. by Frank Pick. Cambridge, Mass., M.I.T. Press [1965] 112 p.
65-010279   724.9
Architecture, Modern -- 20th century. Industrial arts -- Study and teaching -- Germany.

NA680.G73
Gropius, Walter, 1883-1969.
Scope of total architecture.   New York, Harper [1955] 185 p.
54-012179
Architecture, Modern -- 20th cent.

NA680.H5 1966
Hitchcock, Henry Russell, 1903-
The international style [by] Henry-Russell Hitchcock and Philip Johnson. With a new foreword and appendix by Henry-Russell Hitchcock. New York, Norton [1966] xiii, 260 p.
66-015312   724.9   0393003116
Architecture. Architecture -- Designs and plans

NA680.J457
Jencks, Charles.
The language of post-modern architecture/ Charles A. Jencks. New York: Rizzoli, 1977. 104 p.
76-062545   724.9   0847800717
Architecture, Modern -- 20th century. Communication in architectural design.

NA680.J63
Johnson, Philip, 1906-
Writings/ Philip Johnson; foreword by Vincent Scully; introd. by Peter Eisenman; commentary by Robert A. M. Stern. New York: Oxford University Press, 1979. 291 p.
77-017482   724.9   0195023781
Architecture, Modern -- 20th century. Architecture.

NA680.K5713 1988
Klotz, Heinrich.
The history of postmodern architecture/ Heinrich Klotz; translated by Radka Donnell. Cambridge, Mass.: MIT Press, c1988. 461 p.
87-003864   724.9/1   0262111233
Architecture, Modern -- 20th century. Architecture, Postmodern.

NA680.N44
New York.
--What is modern architecture? New York: Museum of Modern Art, c1942. 36 p.
43-006952   724.91
Architecture, Modern -- 20th century.

NA680.P374
Peter, John, 1917-
Masters of modern architecture. New York, G. Braziller, 1958. 230 p.
58-011897   724.91
Architecture, Modern -- 20th century. Architects.

NA680.S395
Scully, Vincent Joseph, 1920-
Modern architecture; the architecture of democracy. New York, G. Braziller, 1961. 128 p.
61-013689   724.9
Architecture, Modern -- 20th century.

NA680.S52 1972b
Sharp, Dennis.
A visual history of twentieth-century architecture. [Greenwich, Conn.] New York Graphic Society [1972] 304 p.
78-177906   724.9   0821204254
Architecture, Modern -- 20th century.

NA680.S84 1988
Stern, Robert A. M.
Modern classicism/ Robert A.M. Stern, with Raymond W. Gastil. New York: Rizzoli, 1988. 296 p.
87-043251   724/.6   0847808483
Classicism in architecture. Architecture, Postmodern. Architecture, Modern -- 20th century.

NA680.T2513
Tafuri, Manfredo.
Modern architecture/ Manfredo Tafuri and Francesco Dal Co; translated from the Italian by Robert Erich Wolf. New York: H. N. Abrams, 1979. 448 p.
79-010202   724.9   0810910063
Architecture, Modern -- 19th century. Architecture, Modern -- 20th century. City planning.

NA680.T45 1996
Theorizing a new agenda for architecture: an anthology of architectural theory, 1965-1995/ Kate Nesbitt, editor. New York: Princeton Architectural Press, c1996. 606 p.
95-045968   720/.1   1568980531
Architecture, Modern -- 20th century.

NA680.W7
Wright, Frank Lloyd, 1869-1959.
The future of architecture. New York, Horizon Press, 1953. 326 p.
53-003814   724.91
Architecture, Modern -- 20th century.

NA682.D43.J6 1988
Johnson, Philip, 1906-
Deconstructivist architecture: the Museum of Modern Art, New York/ Philip Johnson and Mark Wigley. Boston: Little, Brown; c1988. 104 p.
88-060826   724/.6   087070298X
Deconstructivism (Architecture) -- Exhibitions. Architecture, Modern -- 20th century -- Exhibitions. Constructivism (Architecture) -- Soviet Union -- Influence -- Exhibitions.

NA682.P67.G49 1996
Ghirardo, Diane Yvonne.
Architecture after modernism/ Diane Ghirardo. New York, N.Y.: Thames and Hudson, 1996. 240 p.
96-060260   724/.6   050020294X
Architecture, Postmodern. Architecture, Modern -- 20th century.

NA682.P67.J4 1990
Jencks, Charles.
The new moderns: from late to neo-modernism/ Charles Jencks. New York: Rizzoli, 1990. 300 p.
89-064021   724/.6   084781212X
Architecture, Postmodern. Deconstructivism (Architecture) Architecture, Modern -- 20th century.

NA682.P67.P6713 1982
Portoghesi, Paolo.
After modern architecture/ Paolo Portoghesi; [translated from the Italian by Meg Shore]. New York: Rizzoli, 1982, c1980. xv, 150 p.
81-051379   724.9/1   0847804089
Architecture, Postmodern. Architecture, Modern -- 20th century.

NA702 History —
Architecture of special countries

NA702.D3
Damaz, Paul F.
Art in Latin American architecture. Pref. by Oscar Niemeyer. New York, Reinhold Pub. Corp. [1963] 232 p.
63-011424   720.98
Architecture -- Latin America. Art, Latin American Art, Modern -- 20th century.

NA702.H5
Hitchcock, Henry Russell, 1903-
Latin American architecture since 1945.   New York, Museum of Modern Art [1955] 203 p.
55-012305   724.91
Architecture -- Latin America. Architecture, Modern -- 20th century. Architecture -- Designs and plans.

NA702.5-913 History —
Architecture of special countries — America

NA702.5.F73 2000
Fraser, Valerie.
Building the new world: studies in the modern architecture of Latin America, 1930-1960/ Valerie Fraser. London; Verso, 2000. vii, 280 p.
2001-274909   720/.98/0904   1859843077
Modern movement (Architecture) -- Latin America.

NA703.N6 1984
Noble, Allen George, 1930-
Wood, brick, and stone: the North American settlement landscape/ Allen G. Noble; drawings by M. Margaret Geib. Amherst: University of Massachusetts Press, 1984. 2 v.
83-024110   728/.097   0870234102
Vernacular architecture -- North America.

NA703.W75 1989
Wright, Sylvia Hart.
Sourcebook of contemporary North American architecture from postwar to postmodern/ Sylvia Hart Wright. New York: Van Nostrand Reinhold, c1989. xv, 200 p.
89-005320   720/.973   0442291906
Architecture -- North America. Architecture, Modern -- 20th century -- North America.

NA705.A5 1978
Andrews, Wayne.
Architecture, ambition, and Americans: a social history of American architecture/ Wayne Andrews. New York: Free Press, c1978. xxx, 332 p.
78-050786   720/.973   0029007704
Architecture -- United States -- History.

NA705.B8
Burchard, John E. 1898-
The architecture of America; a social and cultural history, by John Burchard and Albert Bush-Brown. Boston, Little, Brown [1961] 595 p.
61-005736   720.973
Architecture -- United States -- History.

NA705.F67 1994
Ford, Larry.
Cities and buildings: skyscrapers, skid rows, and suburbs/ Larry R. Ford. Baltimore: Johns Hopkins University Press, c1994. xiii, 304 p.
93-005752   720/.973   0801846463
Architecture -- United States. City planning -- United States.

NA705.G8
Gutheim, Frederick Albert, 1908-
One hundred years of architecture in America, 1857-1957, celebrating the centennial of the American Institute of Architects.   New York, Reinhold Pub. Corp. [1957] 96 p.
57-011223   720.973
Architecture -- United States. Architecture -- Exhibitions.

NA705.H53 1983
Historic America: buildings, structures, and sites/ recorded by the Historic American Buildings Survey and the Historic American Engineering Record; checklist compiled by Alicia Stamm; essays edited by C. Ford Peatross. Washington: Library of Congress: 1983. xvi, 708 p.
83-014422   973   0844404314
Architecture -- United States. Historic buildings -- United States. Historic sites -- United States.

NA705.K64 1987
Kostof, Spiro.
America by design/ Spiro Kostof. New York: Oxford University Press, 1987. x, 388 p.
86-012787   720/.973   0195042832
Architecture -- United States. City planning -- United States. Parks -- United States.

NA705.M78 1967
Mumford, Lewis, 1895-
The South in architecture.   New York, Da Capo Press, 1967. 147 p.
67-027462   720/.975
Jefferson, Thomas, -- 1743-1826. Richardson, H. H. -- (Henry Hobson), -- 1838-1886.   Architecture -- Southern States. Regionalism in architecture -- Southern States.

NA705.P3 1995
Packard, Robert T.
Encyclopedia of American architecture/ Robert T. Packard; Balthazar Korab, illustration editor. New York: McGraw-Hill, c1995. xi, 724 p.
94-013941   720/.973   0070480109
Architecture -- United States -- Dictionaries.

NA705.P5
Pierson, William Harvey, 1911-
American buildings and their architects [by] William H.
Pierson, Jr. Garden City, N.Y., Doubleday, [1970-   ]
79-084361   720/.973
Architecture -- United States. Architects -- United States.

NA705.S36
Scully, Vincent Joseph, 1920-
American architecture and urbanism [by] Vincent Scully.
New York, Praeger [1969] 275 p.
70-076793   720/.973
Architecture -- United States. City planning -- United States.

NA705.S578 1996
Smith, G. E. Kidder 1913-
Source book of American architecture: 500 notable
buildings from the 10th century to the present/ G.E.
Kidder Smith. New York: Princeton Architectural Press,
c1996. 678 p.
95-049186   720/.973   1568980248
Architecture -- United States -- Guidebooks.

NA705.T3 1936
Tallmadge, Thomas Eddy, 1876-1940.
The story of architecture in America, by Thomas E.
Tallmadge ... New York, W.W. Norton & Company, inc.
[c1936]
36-023858   720.973
Architecture -- United States.

NA705.W473
Whiffen, Marcus.
American architecture, 1607-1976/ Marcus Whiffen and
Frederick Koeper. Cambridge, Mass.: MIT Press, c1981.
xv, 495 p.
80-023251   720/.973   0262231050
Architecture -- United States.

NA707.E3
Eberlein, Harold Donaldson.
The architecture of colonial America, by Harold
Donaldson Eberlein; illustrated from photographs by
Mary N. Northend and others. Boston, Little, Brown, and
Company, 1915. xiv, 289 p.
15-022725
Architecture, Colonial. Architecture -- United States.

NA707.H32
Hamlin, Talbot, 1889-1956.
Greek revival architecture in America: being an account
of important trends in American architecture and
American life prior to the war between the states, by
Talbot Hamlin; together with a list of articles on
architecture in some American periodicals prior to 1850
by Sarah Hull Jenkins Simpson Hamlin (1887-1930) and
an introduction by Dean Leopold Arnaud. London,
Oxford university press, 1944. xl, 439 p.
44-000865   724.2735
Architecture -- Bibliography. Architecture -- United States.
Architecture, Greek.

NA707.M63
Morrison, Hugh, 1905-
Early American architecture, from the first colonial
settlements to the national period. New York, Oxford
University Press, 1952. xiv, 619 p.
52-007831   720.973
Architecture -- United States.

NA710.E24
Eaton, Leonard K.
American architecture comes of age; European reaction
to H. H. Richardson and Louis Sullivan [by] Leonard K.
Eaton. Cambridge, Mass., MIT Press [1972] xiii, 256 p.
76-171556   720/.973   0262050102
Richardson, H. H. -- (Henry Hobson), -- 1838-1886. Sullivan,
Louis H., -- 1856-1924.   Architecture -- United States.
Architecture, Modern -- 19th century -- United States.

NA710.M6 1991
Modern architecture in America: visions and revisions/
edited by Richard Guy Wilson and Sidney K. Robinson.
Ames: Iowa State University Press, 1991. xiv, 217 p.
90-034402   720/.973/09034   0813803810
Architecture, Modern -- 19th century -- United States.
Architecture, Modern -- 20th century -- United States.
Architecture -- United States.

NA710.M8 1972
Mumford, Lewis,
Roots of contemporary American architecture; a series of
thirty-seven essays dating from the mid-nineteenth
century to the present. New York, Dover Publications
[1972] xviii, 452 p.
75-171490   720/.973   0486220729
Architecture--United States--19th century. Architecture--
United States--20th century.

NA710.O35 1991
O'Gorman, James F.
Three American architects: Richardson, Sullivan, and
Wright, 1865-1915/ James F. O'Gorman. Chicago:
University of Chicago Press, 1991. xx, 170 p.
90-010957   720/.973/09034   0226620719
Richardson, H. H. -- (Henry Hobson), -- 1838-1886 -- Criticism
and interpretation. Sullivan, Louis H., -- 1856-1924 -- Criticism
and interpretation. Wright, Frank Lloyd, -- 1867-1959 --
Criticism and interpretation. Architecture, Modern -- 19th
century -- United States. Architecture, Modern -- 20th century --
United States. Architecture -- United States.

NA710.R5
The Rise of an American architecture [by] Henry-Russell
Hitchcock [and others] Edited with an introd. and
exhibition notes by Edgar Kaufmann, Jr. New York,
Published in association with the Metropolitan Museum
of Art by Praeger [1970] x, 241 p.
70-116442   720/.973
Architecture -- United States. Architecture, Modern -- 19th
century -- United States. Architecture, Modern -- 20th century.

NA710.V3 1969
Van Brunt, Henry, 1832-1903.
Architecture and society; selected essays of Henry Van Brunt. Edited with an introductory monograph by William A. Coles. Cambridge, Mass., Belknap Press of Harvard University Press, 1969. xvi, 562 p.
69-018028   720
  Architecture, Modern -- 19th century -- United States -- Addresses, essays, lectures. Architecture -- United States -- Addresses, essays, lectures. Architecture and society -- United States -- Addresses, essays, lectures.

NA712.A65
American Institute of Architects.
Mid-century architecture in America; honor awards of the American Institute of Architects, 1949-1961. Foreword by Philip Will, Jr. Edited and with an introd. by Wolf Von Eckardt. Baltimore, Johns Hopkins Press [1961] 254 p.
61-017081   720.973
  Architecture, Modern -- 20th century. Architecture -- United States.

NA712.C65
Condit, Carl W.
The rise of the skyscraper.   [Chicago] University of Chicago Press [1952] 255 p.
52-006468   725.232
  Architecture, Modern. Merchantile buildings. Architecture.

NA717.H36 1995
Hamilton, C. Mark.
Nineteenth-century Mormon architecture and city planning/ C. Mark Hamilton. New York: Oxford University Press, 1995. xvii, 203 p.
94-025270   720/.8/8283   0195075056
  Mormon architecture -- Middle West. Architecture, Modern -- 19th century -- Middle West. Mormon architecture -- Utah.

NA720.L36 1993
Lane, Mills.
Architecture of the Old South/ Mills Lane; special photography by Van Jones Martin. New York: Abbeville Press, 1993. 335 p.
93-001550   720/.975   1558590447
  Architecture -- Southern States. Architecture, Colonial -- Southern States. Architecture, Modern -- 19th century -- Southern States.

NA720.S3 1971
Sanford, Trent Elwood, b. 1897-
The architecture of the Southwest; Indian, Spanish, American.   Westport, Conn., Greenwood Press, [1971, c1950] xii, 312 p.
76-100242   720/.979   0837140129
  Architecture -- Southwest, New.

NA727.P84 1990
Pueblo style and regional architecture/ edited by Nicholas C. Markovich, Wolfgang F.E. Preiser, Fred G. Sturm. New York: Van Nostrand Reinhold, c1990. xv, 348 p.
89-030618   720/.978   0442318960
  Regionalism in architecture -- Southwest, New. Pueblo architecture. Pueblo architecture -- Influence.

NA730.A4.H63 1993
Hoagland, Alison K., 1951-
Buildings of Alaska/ Alison K. Hoagland. New York: Oxford University Press, 1993. xiv, 338 p.
92-046463   720/.9798   0195073630
  Architecture -- Alaska -- Themes, motives.

NA730.C2.K5
Kirker, Harold.
California's architectural frontier; style and tradition in the nineteenth century.   San Marino, Calif., Huntington Library, 1960. xiv, 224 p.
60-011898   720/.9794
  Architecture -- California.

NA730.C2.M3 1975
McCoy, Esther.
Five California architects/ Esther McCoy; chapter on Greene and Greene By Randell L. Makinson. New York: Praeger Publishers, 1975, c1960. vii, 200 p.
74-019818   720/.9794   0275466906
  Architecture -- California. Architects -- California.

NA730.C2.T68 1997
Toward a simpler way of life: the arts & crafts architects of California/ edited by Robert Winter. Berkeley: University of California Press, c1997. 310 p.
96-045103   720/.9794/09034   0520209168
  Architecture -- California. Arts and crafts movement -- California. Architecture, Modern -- 19th century -- California.

NA730.I8.G43 1993
Gebhard, David.
Buildings of Iowa/ David Gebhard, Gerald Mansheim. New York: Oxford University Press, 1993. xx, 565 p.
92-038791   720/.9777   0195061489
  Architecture -- Iowa -- Guidebooks.

NA730.L8.L68 1997
Louisiana buildings, 1720-1940/ the Historic American Buildings Survey; edited by Jessie Poesch and Barbara SoRelle Bacot. Baton Rouge: Louisiana State University Press, c1997. x, 425 p.
96-016959   720/.9763   0807120545
  Architecture -- Louisiana. Decoration and ornament, Architectural -- Louisiana. Historic buildings -- Louisiana.

NA730.M4.C85
Cummings, Abbott Lowell, 1923-
The framed houses of Massachusetts Bay, 1625-1725/ Abbott Lowell Cummings. Cambridge, Mass.: Belknap Press, 1979. xiv, 261 p.
78-008390   728   0674316800
  Wooden-frame houses -- Massachusetts (Colony) Architecture, Modern -- 17th-18th centuries -- Massachusetts (Colony) Architecture, Colonial -- Massachusetts (Colony)

NA730.N32.P376 1995
Marshall, Howard W.
Paradise Valley, Nevada: the people and buildings of an American place/ Howard Wight Marshall. Tucson: University of Arizona Press, c1995. xi, 152 p.
94-026968   720/.9793/54   0816513104
Vernacular architecture -- Nevada -- Paradise Valley -- History -- 19th century. Vernacular architecture -- Nevada -- Paradise Valley -- History -- 20th century. Ranches -- Nevada -- Paradise Valley. Paradise Valley (Nev.) -- History. Paradise Valley (Nev.) -- Social life and customs.

NA730.T5.E26 2000
Echols, Gordon.
Early Texas architecture/ by Gordon Echols. Fort Worth: Texas Christian University Press, c2000. x, 238 p.
99-055193   720/.9764   0875652239
Regionalism in architecture -- Texas. Architecture -- Texas -- 19th century. Architecture -- Texas -- 20th century.

NA730.T5.H46 1993
Henry, Jay C., 1939-
Architecture in Texas, 1895-1945/ Jay C. Henry. Austin: University of Texas Press, 1993. viii, 364 p.
92-028931   720/.9764/09041   0292730721
Architecture, Modern -- 19th century -- Texas. Architecture, Modern -- 20th century -- Texas. Architecture -- Texas.

NA730.V8.M35 1992
The Making of Virginia architecture/ by Charles E. Brownell ... [et al.]. Richmond: Virginia Museum of Fine Arts; c1992. xiii, 457 p.
92-016363   720/.9755   091704634X
Architecture -- Virginia.

NA735.C35.P67 1997
Poston, Jonathan H., 1954-
The buildings of Charleston: a guide to the city's architecte/ Jonathan H. Poston; for the Historic Charleston Foundation. Columbia, S.C.: University of South Carolina Press, c1997. 717 p.
96-037990   720/.9757/915   1570032025
Architecture -- South Carolina -- Charleston. Charleston (S.C.) -- Buildings, structures, etc.

NA735.C4.C6 1964
Condit, Carl W.
Chicago school of architecture: a history of commercial and public building in the Chicago area, 1875-1925/ University of Chicago Press, 1964. 238 p.
64-013287   725.0977311
Architecture -- Chicago. Architecture -- History. Office buildings.

NA735.C4.L37 1993
Larson, George A.
Chicago architecture and design/ George A. Larson, Jay Pridmore; with photography by Hedrich-Blessing. New York: H.N. Abrams, 1993. 256 p.
93-018306   720/.9773/11   0810931923
Architecture -- Illinois -- Chicago. Architecture, Modern -- 19th century -- Illinois -- Chicago. Architecture, Modern -- 20th century -- Illinois -- Chicago. Chicago (Ill.) -- Buildings, structures, etc.

NA735.C4.L49 1997
Lewis, Arnold.
An early encounter with tomorrow: Europeans, Chicago's Loop, and the World's Columbian Exposition/ Arnold Lewis. Urbana: University of Illinois Press, c1997. xv, 353 p.
96-025325   720/.9773/11   0252023056
Eclecticism in architecture -- Illinois -- Chicago. Architecture and society -- Illinois -- Chicago -- History -- 19th century. Chicago (Ill.) -- Buildings, structures, etc.

NA735.C4.T73
Tallmadge, Thomas Eddy, 1876-1940.
Architecture in old Chicago/ by Thomas E. Tallmadge. Chicago, Ill.: The University of Chicago Press [1975,c.1941] xv, 218 p.
41-051761   720.97731
Architecture -- Chicago.

NA735.D2.A4
American Institute of Architects.
The prairie's yield; forces shaping Dallas architecture from 1840 to 1962. New York, Reinhold Pub. Corp. [1962] 72 p.
62-015235
Architecture -- Dallas.

NA735.N5.H8
Huxtable, Ada Louise.
Four walking tours of modern architecture in New York City. [New York] Museum of Modern Art; [c1961] 76 p.
61-011270
Architecture -- New York (N.Y.) Architecture, Modern -- 20th century.

NA735.N5.S727 1999
Stern, Robert A. M.
New York 1880: architecture and urbanism in the gilded age/ Robert A.M. Stern, Thomas Mellins, and David Fishman. New York, N.Y.: Monacelli Press, 1999. 1164 p.
99-017892   720/.9747/109034   1580930271
Eclecticism in architecture -- New York (State) -- New York. Architecture, Modern -- 19th century -- New York (State) -- New York. City planning -- New York (State) -- New York -- History -- 19th century. New York (N.Y.) -- Buildings, structures, etc.

NA735.N5.S73 1983
Stern, Robert A. M.
New York 1900: metropolitan architecture and urbanism, 1890-1915/ by Robert A.M. Stern, Gregory Gilmartin, John Montague Massengale. New York: Rizzoli, 1983. 502 p.
83-042995   720/.9747/1   0847805115
Architecture, Modern -- 19th century -- New York (State) -- New York. Architecture, Modern -- 20th century -- New York (State) -- New York. City planning -- New York (State) -- New York. New York (N.Y.) -- Buildings, structures, etc.

NA735.S44.S43 1991
Seaside: making a town in America/ edited by David
Mohney and Keller Easterling. [New York, N.Y.]:
Princeton Architectural Press, [c1991] 267 p.
91-004302   720/.9759/41   187827144X
*Architecture -- Florida -- Seaside -- Themes, motives. New
towns -- Florida. City planning -- Florida -- Seaside -- History -
- 20th century. Seaside (Fla.) -- Buildings, structures, etc.*

NA735.S45.S53 1994
Shaping Seattle architecture: a historical guide to the
architects/ Jeffrey Karl Ochsner, editor. Seattle:
University of Washington Press in association with the
American Institute of Architects Seattle Chapter and the
Seattle Architectural Foundation, c1994. xlii, 402 p.
94-017618   720/.92/2797772   029597365X
*Architects -- Washington (State) -- Seattle -- Biography.
Architecture -- Washington (State) -- Seattle -- History. Seattle
(Wash.) -- Buildings, structures, etc.*

NA735.W3.A6
American Institute of Architects.
Washington architecture, 1791-1957, prepared by a
committee of the Washington-Metropolitan Chapter,
American Institute of Architects. New York, Reinhold
[1957] 96 p.
57-010358   720.9753
Architecture -- Washington (D.C.)

NA735.W3.T65 1993
Tompkins, Sally Kress.
A quest for grandeur: Charles Moore and the Federal
Triangle/ Sally Kress Tompkins; photographs by Jack E.
Boucher. Washington: Smithsonian Institution Press,
c1993. xxi, 159 p.
92-006574   725/.1/09753   156098161X
*Moore, Charles, -- 1855-1942 -- Influence. Public architecture
-- Washington (D.C.)   Federal Triangle (Washington, D.C.)
Washington (D.C.) -- Buildings, structures, etc.*

NA735.W5.W47 vol. 1
Whiffen, Marcus.
The public buildings of Williamsburg, colonial capital of
Virginia; an architectural history. Williamsburg, Va.,
Colonial Williamsburg [1958] xv, 269 p.
57-013499   724.173
*Architecture, Colonial.   Williamsburg (Va.) -- Public
buildings.*

NA735.W5.W47 vol. 2
Whiffen, Marcus.
The eighteenth-century houses of Williamsburg: a study
of architecture and building in the colonial capital of
Virginia. [S.l.]: pub. by Colonial Williamsburg; distr. by
Holt, 1970. 223 p.
60-013174   728.097554252
*Architecture, Domestic -- Virginia. Architecture, Colonial.
Williamsburg (Va.)*

NA737.G44.A4 1985
Gehry, Frank O., 1929-
Frank Gehry, buildings and projects/ compiled and edited
by Peter Arnell and Ted Bickford; essay by Germano
Celant; text by Mason Andrews; recent work
photographed by Tim Street-Porter. New York: Rizzoli,
1985. xvii, 311 p.
84-042646   720/.92/4   0847805433
*Gehry, Frank O., -- 1929-   Architecture -- United States -- 20th
century.*

NA737.C7.S44 1995
Shand-Tucci, Douglass, 1941-
Ralph Adams Cram: life and architecture/ Douglass
Shand-Tucci. Amherst: University of Massachusetts
Press, [c1995-   ] v. 1
94-011328   720/.92   0870239201
*Cram, Ralph Adams, -- 1863-1942.   Architects -- United States
-- Biography. Gothic revival (Architecture) -- United States.
Avant-garde (Aesthetics) -- Massachusetts -- Boston -- History --
19th century.*

NA737.F8.M2
McHale, John.
R. Buckminster Fuller. New York, G. Braziller, 1962.
127 p.
62-016263   721.46
*Fuller, R. Buckminster -- (Richard Buckminster), -- 1895-
Domes. Architecture, Moderen.*

NA737.F84.A4 1991
Thomas, George E.
Frank Furness: the complete works/ George E. Thomas,
Michael J. Lewis, Jeffrey A. Cohen; introduction by
Robert Venturi. New York, N.Y.: Princeton Architectural
Press, c1991. 385 p.
91-000174   720/.92   1878271040
*Furness, Frank, -- 1839-1912 -- Catalogs.   Architecture,
Modern -- 19th century -- Pennsylvania -- Philadelphia --
Catalogs. Architecture, Modern -- 20th century -- Pennsylvania
-- Philadelphia -- Catalogs. Architecture, Modern -- 19th
century -- United States -- Catalogs. Philadelphia (Pa.) --
Buildings, structures, etc.*

NA737.G44.D35 1998
Dal Co, Francesco, 1945-
Frank O. Gehry: the complete works/ Francesco Dal Co,
Kurt W. Forster; building descriptions by Hadley Arnold.
New York: Monacelli Press, 1998. 614 p.
98-042480   720/.92   1885254636
*Gehry, Frank O., -- 1929-   -- Criticism and interpretation.
Architecture, Postmodern -- United States.*

NA737.G73.A4 1998
Smith, Bruce, 1950-
Greene & Greene: masterworks/ by Bruce Smith;
photography by Alexander Vertikoff. San Francisco:
Chronicle Books, 1998. 240 p.
98-012068   720/.92/2   0811818780
*Architecture, Domestic -- California. Architecture, Modern --
20th century -- California. Arts and crafts movement --
California.*

NA737.G948.G83 1993
Gwathmey Siegel: buildings and projects, 1982-1992/ edited by Brad Collins and Diane Kasprowicz; introduction by Peter Eisenman. New York: Rizzoli, 1993. 336 p.
93-010438   720/.92/2   0847816753
Architectural practice, International. Architecture, Postmodern -- United States.

NA737.H295.G4 1991
Germany, Lisa.
Harwell Hamilton Harris/ by Lisa Germany; foreword by Kenneth Frampton; introduction by Bruno Zevi. Austin: University of Texas Press, 1991. xx, 252 p.
90-044616   720/.92   0292730438
Harris, Harwell Hamilton, -- 1903- -- Criticism and interpretation. Regionalism in architecture -- United States.

NA737.H558.A4 1991
Bruegmann, Robert.
Holabird & Roche, Holabird & Root: an illustrated catalog of works/ by Robert Bruegmann. New York: Garland in cooperation with the Chicago Historical Society, 1991. 3 v.
90-019652   720/.92/2   0824039742
Architecture, Modern -- 19th century -- United States -- Catalogs. Architecture, Modern -- 20th century -- United States -- Catalogs.

NA737.H558.B78 1997
Bruegmann, Robert.
The architects and the city: Holabird & Roche of Chicago, 1880-1918/ Robert Bruegmann. Chicago, Ill.: University of Chicago Press, 1997. xvi, 540 p.
96-022151   720/.92/277311   0226076954
Chicago school of architecture (Movement) Architecture -- Illinois -- Chicago. Chicago (Ill.) -- Buildings, structures, etc.

NA737.H86.B34
Baker, Paul R.
Richard Morris Hunt/ Paul R. Baker. Cambridge, Mass.: MIT Press, c1980. xvi, 588 p.
79-025008   720/.92/4   0262021390
Hunt, Richard Morris, -- 1828-1895. Architects -- United States -- Biography.

NA737.J3.A4 1988
Jacobsen, Hugh Newell.
Hugh Newell Jacobsen, architect/ designed and edited by Massimo Vignelli; photographs by Robert Lautman; introduction by Vincent Scully; text edited by Kevin W. Green. Washington, D.C.: American Institute of Architects Press, c1988. 351 p.
88-011468   720/.92/4   091396297X
Jacobsen, Hugh Newell -- Catalogs. Architecture, Modern -- 20th century -- United States -- Catalogs.

NA737.J47.P54 1997
Piedmont-Palladino, Susan, 1958-
Devil's workshop: 25 years of Jersey Devil architecture/ Susan Piedmont-Palladino and Mark Alden Branch; foreword by Michael Sorkin. New York, N.Y.: Princeton Architectural Press, c1997. xii, 127 p.
97-023411   720/.92/2   1568981139
Architecture, Modern -- 20th century -- United States.

NA737.J6.J3
Jacobus, John M.
Philip Johnson. New York, G. Braziller, 1962. 127 p.
62-016264   720.973
Johnson, Philip, -- 1906-

NA737.J6.S38 1994
Schulze, Franz, 1927-
Philip Johnson: life and work/ by Franz Schulze. New York: A.A. Knopf, 1994. xi, 465 p.
94-000291   720/.92   0394572041
Johnson, Philip, -- 1906- Architects -- United States -- Biography. Architecture, Modern -- 20th century -- United States.

NA737.K32.A2 1991
Kahn, Louis I., 1901-1974.
Louis I. Kahn: writings, lectures, interviews/ introduction and edited by Alessandra Latour. New York: Rizzoli International Publications, 1991. 352 p.
90-050794   720/.92   0847813312
Kahn, Louis I., -- 1901-1974 -- Philosophy. Architecture -- Language.

NA737.K32.S38
Scully, Vincent Joseph, 1920-
Louis I. Kahn. New York, G. Braziller, 1962. 127 p.
62-016265   720.973
Kahn, Louis I., -- 1901-

NA737.L42.V36 1994
Valentine, Maggie, 1949-
The show starts on the sidewalk: an architectural history of the movie theatre, starring S. Charles Lee/ Maggie Valentine. New Haven: Yale University Press, c1994. xiv, 231 p.
93-024977   725/.822/092   0300055277
Lee, S. Charles -- Criticism and interpretation. Motion picture theaters -- United States.

NA737.M435.C37
Cardwell, Kenneth H., 1920-
Bernard Maybeck: artisan, architect, artist/ Kenneth H. Cardwell. Santa Barbara: Peregrine Smith, 1977. 255 p.
77-013773   720/.92/4   0879050225
Maybeck, Bernard R. Architects -- California -- Biography.

NA737.M44.A4 1984
Meier, Richard, 1934-
Richard Meier, architect, 1964/1984/ introduction by Joseph Rykwert. New York: Rizzoli, c1984. 411 p.
83-042911   720/.92/4   0847804968
Meier, Richard, -- 1934- Architecture, Modern -- 20th century -- United States.

NA737.M5.L58 1994
Liscombe, R. W., 1946-
Altogether American: Robert Mills, architect and engineer, 1781-1855/ Rhodri Windsor Liscombe. New York: Oxford University Press, 1994. viii, 372 p.
92-040045   720/.92   019508019X
Mills, Robert, -- 1781-1855. Architects -- United States -- Biography.

NA737.M68.B68 1988
Boutelle, Sara Holmes.
Julia Morgan, architect/ Sara Holmes Boutelle; color photography by Richard Barnes. New York: Abbeville Press, c1988. 271 p.
87-029008 720/.92/4 089659792X
Morgan, Julia, -- 1872-1957. Architects -- California -- Biography. Architecture, Modern -- 20th century -- California. Architecture -- California.

NA737.M85.W66 1996
Wojtowicz, Robert.
Lewis Mumford and American modernism: Eutopian theories for architecture and urban planning/ Robert Wojtowicz. Cambridge; Cambridge University Press, 1996. xii, 224 p.
95-016564 720/.92 0521482151
Mumford, Lewis, -- 1895- -- Criticism and interpretation. Architecture -- United States. Architecture, Modern -- 19th century -- United States. Architecture, Modern -- 20th century -- United States.

NA737.N4.A2 1989
Neutra, Richard Joseph, 1892-1970.
Nature near: late essays of Richard Neutra/ edited by William Marlin; foreword by Norman Cousins. Santa Barbara, Calif.: Capra Press, c1989. xxx, 191 p.
88-007943 720/.92/4 0884962903
Neutra, Richard Joseph, -- 1892-1970 -- Philosophy. Architecture -- Environmental aspects.

NA737.N4.A4 1982
Drexler, Arthur.
The architecture of Richard Neutra: from international style to California modern/ Arthur Drexler and Thomas S. Hines. New York: Museum of Modern Art, c1982. 114 p.
82-081426 720/.92/4 0870705067
Neutra, Richard Joseph, -- 1892-1970 -- Exhibitions. Architecture, Modern -- 20th century -- United States -- Exhibitions.

NA737.N4.H5 1982
Hines, Thomas S.
Richard Neutra and the search for modern architecture: a biography and history/ Thomas S. Hines. New York: Oxford University Press, 1982. 356 p.
81-022530 720/.92/4 0195030281
Neutra, Richard Joseph, -- 1892-1970. Architects -- United States -- Biography. International style (Architecture) -- United States.

NA737.P365.W57 1990
Wiseman, Carter.
I.M. Pei: a profile in American architecture/ Carter Wiseman. New York: H.N. Abrams, 1990. 320 p.
90-030727 720/.92 0810937093
Pei, I. M., -- 1917- Architects -- United States -- Biography.

NA737.P377
Conversations with I.M. Pei: light is the key/ by Gero von Boehm. Munich; Prestel, 2000. 128 p.
00-102989 720.92 3791321765
Pei, I. M., -- 1917- -- Interviews. Architects -- United States -- Interviews Architecture, Modern -- 20th century -- United States.

NA737.P39.A4 1990
Pelli, Cesar.
Cesar Pelli: buildings and projects, 1965-1990/ introduction by Paul Goldberger; essays by Mario Gandelsonas and John Pastier. New York: Rizzoli, 1990. 288 p.
90-034572 720/.92 0847812626
Pelli, Cesar -- Themes, motives. Architecture, Modern -- 20th century -- United States -- Themes, motives.

NA737.P685.T48 2000
Thomas, George E.
William L. Price: arts and crafts to modern design/ George E. Thomas with an introduction by Robert Venturi. New York: Princeton Architectural Press, 2000. xiii, 362 p.
99-050093 720/.92 1568982208
Price, William L., -- 1861-1916. Architects -- United States -- Biography. Architecture, Modern -- 19th century -- United States. Architecture, Modern -- 20th century -- United States.

NA737.R294.R36 1999
Hession, Jane King, 1951-
Ralph Rapson: sixty years of modern design/ Jane King Hession, Rip Rapson, Bruce N. Wright; foreword by William Pedersen. Afton, Minn.: Afton Historical Society Press, c1999. xix, 235 p.
98-053114 720/.92 1890434140
Rapson, Ralph, -- 1914- Architects -- United States -- Biography.

NA737.R5.A4 1982
Ochsner, Jeffrey Karl.
H.H. Richardson, complete architectural works/ Jeffrey Karl Ochsner. Cambridge, MA: MIT Press, c1982. xiii, 466 p.
82-006603 720/.92/4 0262150239
Richardson, H. H. -- (Henry Hobson), -- 1838-1886 -- Catalogs.

NA737.R5.O36 1987
O'Gorman, James F.
H.H. Richardson: architectural forms for an American society/ James F. O'Gorman. Chicago: University of Chicago Press, 1987. xv, 171 p.
86-019223 720/.92/4 0226620697
Richardson, H. H. -- (Henry Hobson), -- 1838-1886 -- Criticism and interpretation. Romanesque revival (Architecture) -- United States.

NA737.S28.S2 1968
Saarinen, Eero, 1910-1961.
Eero Saarinen on his work; a selection of buildings dating from 1947 to 1964 with statements by the architect, edited by Aline B. Saarinen. New Haven, Yale University Press, 1968. 117 p.
68-005268 720/.924

NA737.S3.C5
Christ-Janer, Albert, 1910-1973.
Eliel Saarinen. With a foreword by Alvar Aalto. [Chicago] Univ. of Chicago Press [1948] 153 p.
48-008989
Saarinen, Eliel, -- 1873-1950.

NA737.S35.A4 2001
Schindler, R. M. 1887-1953.
The architecture of R.M. Schindler/ organized by
Elizabeth A.T. Smith and Michael Darling; essays by
Michael Darling ... [et al.]. Los Angeles, Calif.: Museum
of Contemporary Art, Los Angeles; c2001. 284 p.
00-045595   720/.92   0810942232
Schindler, R. M. -- (Rudolph M.), -- 1887-1953 -- Catalogs.
Modern movement (Architecture) -- California -- Catalogs.
Architecture -- California -- 20th century -- Catalogs.

NA737.S35.R213 1988
R.M. Schindler, architect: 1887-1953: a pupil of Otto
Wagner, between international style and space
architecture/ [edited by] August Sarnitz. New York:
Rizzoli, 1988. 224 p.
88-042693   720/.92/4   0847809218
Schindler, R. M. -- (Rudolph M.), -- 1887-1953 -- Criticism and
interpretation. Schindler, R. M. -- (Rudolph M.), -- 1887-1953 --
Catalogs. Architecture, Modern -- 20th century -- United States
-- Catalogs.

NA737.S625.G43 1993
Gebhard, David.
Robert Stacy-Judd: Maya architecture and the creation of
a new style/ text by David Gebhard; photography by
Anthony Peres. Santa Barbara: Capra Press, 1993. 166 p.
92-045278   720/.92   0884963519
Stacy-Judd, Robert -- Criticism and interpretation.   Maya
architecture -- Influence.

NA737.S639.W48 1993
White, Stephen.
Building in the garden: the architecture of Joseph Allen
Stein in India and California/ Stephen White. Delhi;
Oxford University Press, 1993. 383 p.
93-903242   0195629248
Stein, Joseph Allen, -- 1912- -- Criticism and interpretation.
Architecture, Modern -- 20th century -- India. Architecture,
Modern -- 20th century -- California.

NA737.S9.B8
Bush-Brown, Albert.
Louis Sullivan. New York, G. Braziller, 1960. 128 p.
60-013306   720.973
Sullivan, Louis Henri, -- 1856-1924.

NA737.S9.C6
Connely, Willard, 1888-
Louis Sullivan as he lived; the shaping of American
architecture, a biography/ by Willard Connely. New
York, Horizon Press, 1960. 322 p.
60-008160   720.973
Sullivan, Louis H., -- 1856-1924.   Architecture -- United States.

NA737.S9.M6
Morrison, Hugh, 1905-
Louis Sullivan, prophet of modern architecture, by Hugh
Morrison. New York, The Museum of Modern Art and
W. W. Norton & Co., [c1935] xxi, 391 p.
36-027013   927.2
Sullivan, Louis Henry, -- 1856-1924. Adler, Dankmar, -- 1844-
1900. Architecture -- United States.

NA737.T49.T54 1989
Tigerman, Stanley, 1930-
Stanley Tigerman: buildings and projects, 1966-1989/
edited by Sarah Mollman Underhill. New York: Rizzoli,
1989. 288 p.
89-010398   720/.92   084781128X
Tigerman, Stanley, -- 1930- -- Criticism and interpretation.
Architecture, Modern -- 20th century -- United States.

NA737.V45.A84 1989
The Architecture of Robert Venturi/ essays by Vincent
Scully ... [et al.]; edited and with an introduction by
Christopher Mead. Albuquerque: University of New
Mexico Press, c1989. xiii, 115 p.
88-033889   720/.92/4   0826311202
Venturi, Robert -- Criticism and interpretation.   Architecture,
Modern -- 20th century -- United States. Architecture,
Postmodern -- United States.

NA737.W7.A35 1992
Wright, Frank Lloyd, 1867-1959.
Frank Lloyd Wright collected writings/ edited by Bruce
Brooks Pfeiffer; introduction by Kenneth Frampton. New
York: Rizzoli; 1992-1995. 5 v.
91-040987   720   0847815463
Wright, Frank Lloyd, -- 1867-1959 -- Philosophy.

NA737.W7.A48
Wright, Frank Lloyd, 1869-1959.
Writings and buildings/ selected by Edgar Kaufmann and
Ben Raeburn. [New York]: Horizon, [1960] 346 p.
60-008166   0529020572
Wright, Frank Lloyd, -- 1869-1959.   Architecture.

NA737.W7.A87 1993
Alofsin, Anthony.
Frank Lloyd Wright--the lost years, 1910-1922: a study
of influence/ Anthony Alofsin. Chicago: University of
Chicago Press, 1993. ix, 397 p.
92-043355   720/.92   0226013669
Wright, Frank Lloyd, -- 1867-1959 -- Criticism and
interpretation.

NA737.W7.D7
Wright, Frank Lloyd, 1867-1959.
The drawings of Frank Lloyd Wright/ by Arthur Drexler.
New York: Published for the Museum of Modern Art by
Horizon Press, c1962. 320 p.
62-011236   720.973

NA737.W7.E84 1994
Etlin, Richard A.
Frank Lloyd Wright and Le Corbusier: the romantic
legacy/ Richard A. Etlin. Manchester; Manchester
University Press; c1994. xvii, 222 p.
93-012796   720/.92   0719040604
Wright, Frank Lloyd, -- 1867-1959 -- Aesthetics. Le Corbusier, -
- 1887-1965 -- Aesthetics. Architecture, Modern -- 19th century
-- Influence.

NA737.W7.F72 1993
Frank Lloyd Wright: the masterworks/ edited by David
Larkin and Bruce Brooks Pfeiffer; text by Bruce Brooks
Pfeiffer. New York: Rizzoli in association with the Frank
Lloyd Wright Foundation, 1993. 311 p.
93-010434   720/.92   0847817156
*Wright, Frank Lloyd, -- 1867-1959 -- Criticism and
interpretation. Architecture, Modern -- 20th century -- United
States -- Themes, motives.*

NA737.W7.H5 1973
Hitchcock, Henry Russell, 1903-
In the nature of materials, 1887-1941; the buildings of
Frank Lloyd Wright. New foreword and bibliography by
the author. New York, Da Capo Press, 1973 [c1942] xlix,
143 p.
72-075322   720/.92/4   0306712830
Wright, Frank Lloyd, -- 1867-1959.

NA737.W7.J6 1990
Johnson, Donald Leslie.
Frank Lloyd Wright versus America: the 1930s/ Donald
Leslie Johnson. Cambridge, Mass.: MIT Press, c1990. xi,
436 p.
90-030650   720/.92   0262100444
*Wright, Frank Lloyd, -- 1867-1959. Architects -- United States
-- Biography.*

NA737.W7.L37 1991
Laseau, Paul, 1937-
Frank Lloyd Wright: between principle and form/ Paul
Laseau, James Tice. New York: Van Nostrand Reinhold,
c1992. xi, 204 p.
90-027775   720/.92   0442234783
*Wright, Frank Lloyd, -- 1867-1959 -- Criticism and
interpretation. Architecture -- Philosophy.*

NA737.W7.N88 1993
Nute, Kevin, 1958-
Frank Lloyd Wright and Japan: the role of traditional
Japanese art and architecture in the work of Frank Lloyd
Wright/ Kevin Nute. New York: Van Nostrand Reinhold,
c1993. 244 p.
93-025668   720/.92   0442309082
*Wright, Frank Lloyd, -- 1867-1959 -- Criticism and
interpretation. Architecture -- United States -- Japanese
influences.*

NA737.W7.S3
Scully, Vincent Joseph, 1920-
Frank Lloyd Wright. New York, G. Braziller, 1960.
125 p.
60-006075   720.973
Wright, Frank Lloyd, -- 1869-1959.

NA737.W7.S94 1994
Sweeney, Robert L. 1945-
Wright in Hollywood: visions of a new architecture/
Robert L. Sweeney; with a foreword by David G. De
Long. New York, N.Y.: Architectural History
Foundation; c1994. xvii, 271 p.
93-025104   720/.92   026219337X
*Wright, Frank Lloyd, -- 1867-1959 -- Criticism and
interpretation. Modular coordination (Architecture) Concrete
construction. Concrete blocks.*

NA737.Y3.A2 1979
Yamasaki, Minoru, 1912-
A life in architecture/ by Minoru Yamasaki. New York:
Weatherhill, 1979. 195 p.
79-011561   720/.92/4   0834801361
*Yamasaki, Minoru, -- 1912- Architects -- United States --
Biography.*

NA738.N5.A45 1991
African American architects in current practice/ Jack
Travis, editor. [New York, N.Y.]: Princeton Architectural
Press, [c1991] 95 p.
91-025113   720/.89/96073   1878271385
*Afro-American architects -- Employment. Architectural
practice -- United States.*

NA743.C55 1984
Clerk, Nathalie.
Palladian style in Canadian architecture/ Nathalie Clerk.
Ottawa, Ont.: National Historic Parks and Sites Branch,
Parks Canada: Environment Canada; Hull, Quebec,
Canada: Canadian Govt. Pub. Centre, Supply and
Services Canada [distributor], 1984. 154 p.
84-211146   720/.9713   0660115301
*Palladio, Andrea, -- 1508-1580 -- Influence. Architecture,
Colonial -- Canada. Vernacular architecture -- Canada.
Neoclassicism (Architecture) -- Influence.*

NA744.5.G67.B76 1980
Brosseau, Mathilde.
Gothic revival in Canadian architecture/ by Mathilde
Brosseau. Ottawa: Minister of Supply and Services
Canada, [1980] 208 p.
82-109114   720/.971   0660104474
*Gothic revival (Architecture) -- Canada. Architecture --
Canada. Architecture, Modern -- 19th century -- Canada.*

NA744.5.N45.M35 1984
Maitland, Leslie.
Neoclassical architecture in Canada/ Leslie Maitland.
[Ottawa]: National Historic Parks and Sites Branch, Parks
Canada: Environment Canada; Hull, Quebec, Canada:
Canadian Govt. Pub. Centre, Supply and Services Canada
[distributor], 1984. 150 p.
84-221137   720/.971   0660115298
*Neoclassicism (Architecture) -- Canada. Architecture, Modern
-- 19th century -- Canada.*

NA749.B87.C37 1995
Carr, Angela.
Toronto architect Edmund Burke: redefining Canadian
architecture/ Angela Carr. Montreal; McGill-Queen's
University Press, c1995. xiv, 233 p.
00-500223   720/.92   0773512179
*Burke, Edmund, -- 1850-1919. Architects -- Canada --
Biography. Architecture, Modern -- 19th century -- Canada.
Architecture, Modern -- 20th century -- Canada.*

NA749.R37.B37 1983
Barrett, Anthony, 1941-
Francis Rattenbury and British Columbia: architecture and challenge in the Imperial Age/ Anthony A. Barrett & Rhodri Windsor Liscombe. Vancouver: University of British Columbia Press, 1983. xii, 391 p.
84-146737   720/.92/4   0774801786
Rattenbury, Francis Mawson, -- 1867-1935.   Architects -- British Columbia -- Biography. Eclecticism in architecture -- British Columbia.

NA750.Y37 1993
Yampolsky, Mariana, 1925-
The traditional architecture of Mexico/ Mariana Yampolsky; text by Chloe Sayer. New York: Thames and Hudson, 1993. 208 p.
93-060430   720/.972   0500341281
Vernacular architecture -- Mexico.

NA753.K8
Kubler, George, 1912-
Mexican architecture of the sixteenth century.   New Haven, Yale Univ. Press, 1948. 2 v.
48-007149   720.972
Architecture -- Mexico. Architecture, Colonial -- Mexico.

NA755.C413
Cetto, Max L
Modern architecture in Mexico. Arquitectura moderna en Mexico. [Translated from the German into English by D. Q. Stephenson.   Translated from the German into Spanish by Francisco Maigler] New York, Praeger [1961] 224 p.
61-007600   720.972
Architecture -- Mexico. Architecture, Modern -- 20th century.

NA791.C73 1994
Crain, Edward E.
Historic architecture in the Caribbean Islands/ Edward E. Crain. Gainesville: University Press of Florida, c1994. ix, 256 p.
94-003870   720/.9729   0813012937
Architecture -- West Indies. Historic buildings -- West Indies.

NA850.G6
Goodwin, Philip Lippincott, 1885-1958.
Brazil builds; architecture new and old, 1652-1942, by Philip L. Goodwin; photographs by G. E. Kidder Smith. New York, The Museum of modern art, 1943. 198 p.
43-051045   720.981
Architecture -- Brazil.

NA859.N5.P27
Papadaki, Stamo.
Oscar Niemeyer. New York, G. Braziller, 1960. 127 p.
60-013307   720.981
Niemeyer, Oscar, -- 1907-

NA859.N5.P29
Niemeyer, Oscar, 1907-
Oscar Niemeyer: works in progress [by] Stamo Papadaki. New York, Reinhold Pub. Corp. [1956] 192 p.
56-010128   720.81
Architecture -- Brazil. Architecture -- Designs and plans.

NA859.N5.P3
Niemeyer, Oscar, 1907-
The work of Oscar Niemeyer/ [by] Stamo Papadaki; with a foreword by Lucio Costa. [New York]: Reinhold, 1950. 228 p.
50-009965   720.81
Niemeyer, Oscar, -- 1907- Architecture -- Brazil.

NA913.F73 1990
Fraser, Valerie.
The architecture of conquest: building in the Viceroyalty of Peru, 1535-1635/ Valerie Fraser. Cambridge [England]; Cambridge University Press, 1990. xiv, 204 p.
88-036548   720/.985   052134316X
Architecture, Colonial -- Peru (Viceroyalty) Church architecture -- Peru (Viceroyalty)

NA950-1455 History — Architecture of special countries — Europe

NA950.J6 1961
Jordan, Robert Furneaux.
The world of great architecture, from the Greeks to the nineteenth century.   New York, Viking Press [1961] 460 p.
61-008828   720.94
Architecture -- Europe -- History.

NA950.P4 1960
Pevsner, Nikolaus, 1902-
An outline of European architecture. Baltimore, Penguin Books [1960] 740 p.
60-052016   720.94
Architecture -- Europe -- History.

NA956.B47 2000
Bergdoll, Barry.
European architecture 1750-1890/ Barry Bergdoll. New York: Oxford University Press, c2000. vi, 326 p.
00-036747   724/.19   0192842226
Neoclassicism (Architecture) -- Europe. Architecture -- Europe -- 18th century. Architecture -- Europe -- 19th century.

NA956.P413 1983
Perez Gomez, Alberto, 1949-
Architecture and the crisis of modern science/ Alberto Perez-Gomez. Cambridge, Mass.: MIT Press, c1983. x, 400 p.
82-018010   720/.1   0262160919
Architecture -- Philosophy. Architecture, Modern -- 17th-18th centuries -- Europe. Functionalism (Architecture) -- Europe.

NA957.C44 1992
Celik, Zeynep.
Displaying the Orient: architecture of Islam at nineteenth-century world's fairs/ Zeynep Celik. Berkeley: University of California Press, c1992. xv, 245 p.
91-013594   725/.91   0520074947
Exhibition buildings -- Europe -- History -- 19th century. Architecture, Islamic -- United States. Architecture -- United States.

NA957.M5313 1984
Mignot, Claude.
Architecture of the nineteenth century in Europe/ by Claude Mignot; [translated by D.Q. Stephenson]. New York: Rizzoli, 1984. 322 p.
83-043266   724   0847805301
Architecture, Modern -- 19th century -- Europe. Architecture -- Europe.

NA957.Y37 1990
Yarwood, Doreen.
The architecture of Europe/ Doreen Yarwood. Chicago: I.R. Dee, [c1991-   ] v. 4
91-008048   724/.5   0929587650
Architecture, Modern -- 19th century -- Europe. Architecture, Modern -- 20th century -- Europe. Architecture -- Europe.

NA958.B6713 1987
Borsi, Franco.
The monumental era: European architecture and design, 1929-1939/ Franco Borsi; [translated by Pamela Marwood]. New York: Rizzoli, 1987. 207 p.
87-045386   724.9/1   084780805X
Architecture, Modern -- 20th century -- Europe. Eclecticism in architecture -- Europe. International style (Architecture) -- Europe.

NA961.C6 1999
Colvin, Howard Montagu.
Essays in English architectural history/ Howard Colvin. New Haven, Ct.: Published for the Paul Mellon Centre for Studies in British Art by Yale University Press, 1999. viii, 310 p.
98-050532   720/.942   0300070349
Architecture -- Great Britain.

NA961.G5 1953
Gibberd, Frederick.
The architecture of England from Norman times to the present day. London] Architectural Press [1953] 48 p.
65-007614   720.942
Architecture -- England -- History.

NA961.G55 1992
Girouard, Mark, 1931-
Town and country/ Mark Girouard. New Haven: Yale University Press, 1992. 274 p.
92-054168   720/.941   0300051859
Architecture -- England -- Miscellanea. Architecture -- Ireland -- Miscellanea.

NA961.W37 1979
Watkin, David, 1941-
English architecture: a concise history/ David Watkin. New York: Oxford University Press, 1979. 216 p.
79-004409   720/.942   0195201477
Architecture -- England -- History.

NA961.Y3 1967
Yarwood, Doreen.
The architecture of England: from prehistoric times to the present day. London, Batsford, 1967. xvi, 680 p.
68-085154   720/.942
Architecture -- England -- History.

NA963.B66
Bony, Jean.
The English decorated style: Gothic architecture transformed, 1250-1350/ Jean Bony. Ithaca, N.Y.: Cornell University Press, 1979. 315 p.
78-074211   720/.942   0801412439
Architecture -- England. Architecture, Gothic -- Decorated style -- England.

NA963.B76 1968b
Braun, Hugh.
An introduction to English mediaeval architecture. New York, Praeger [1968] 297 p.
68-011982   720.9/42
Architecture -- England. Architecture, Medieval -- England.

NA963.F4 1983
Fernie, E. C.
The architecture of the Anglo-Saxons/ Eric Fernie. New York: Holmes & Meier, 1983. 192 p.
83-012915   720/.941   0841909121
Architecture, Anglo-Saxon. Architecture, Medieval -- England.

NA963.W4 1956
Webb, Geoffrey Fairbank, 1898-
Architecture in Britain: the Middle Ages. [Harmondsworth, Middlesex] Penguin Books [1956] xxi, 234 p.
57-000927   720.942
Architecture -- Great Britain -- History. Architecture, Medieval.

NA964.S85 1977
Summerson, John Newenham, 1904-
Architecture in Britain, 1530 to 1830/ [by] John Summerson. Harmondsworth; Penguin, 1977. 611 p.
79-307193   720/.941   014056103X
Architecture -- Great Britain. Architecture, Renaissance -- Great Britain. Architecture, Baroque -- Great Britain.

NA966.A98 1998
Ayres, James.
Building the Georgian city/ James Ayres. New Haven: Published for the Paul Mellon Centre for Studies in British Art by Yale University Press, c1998. vii, 280 p.
98-007174   720/.941/09033   0300075480
Architecture, Georgian -- Great Britain. Architecture, Modern -- 17th-18th centuries -- Great Britain. Architects and patrons -- Great Britain.

NA966.D37 1980
Davey, Peter.
Architecture of the arts and crafts movement/ Peter Davey. New York: Rizzoli, 1980. 224 p.
80-051623   724/.3   0847803538
Gothic revival (Architecture) -- Great Britain. Gothic revival (Architecture) -- Influence. Arts and crafts movement -- Influence.

NA966.M32
Macaulay, James.
The Gothic revival, 1745-1845/ [by] James Macaulay.
Glasgow: Blackie, 1975. xx, 451 p.
76-364822   720/.9411   0216898927
*Gothic revival (Architecture) -- Great Britain. Architecture --
Great Britain. Architecture, Modern -- 17th-18th centuries --
Great Britain.*

NA966.M68 1995
Mowl, Tim.
Architecture without kings: the rise of Puritan classicism
under Cromwell/ Timothy Mowl & Brian Earnshaw.
Manchester [Eng.]; Manchester University Press: 1995.
xiv, 240 p.
94-043001   720/.942/09032   0719046785
*Jones, Inigo, -- 1573-1652 -- Influence. Cromwell, Oliver, --
1599-1658. Classicism in architecture -- England. Architecture,
Caroline. Architecture -- England.*

NA966.5.G66.M33 1987
McCarthy, Michael J., 1939-
The origins of the Gothic revival/ Michael McCarthy.
New Haven: Published for the Paul Mellon Centre for
Studies in British Art by Yale University Press, 1987. ix,
212 p.
86-028119   720/.942   0300037236
*Gothic revival (Architecture) -- Great Britain. Architecture,
Modern -- 17th-18th centuries -- Great Britain. Architecture,
Modern -- 19th century -- Great Britain.*

NA966.5.N4.S54 2000
Soane, John, 1753-1837.
Sir John Soane: the Royal Academy lectures/ edited with
an introduction by David Watkin. Cambridge; Cambridge
University Press, 2000. viii, 328 p.
99-028761   720   0521770823
Neoclassicism (Architecture) -- England.

NA966.5.N4.S75 1988
Stillman, Damie.
English neo-classical architecture/ Damie Stillman.
London: Zwemmer; c1988. 2 v.
88-060436   720/.941/09033   030200601X
*Neoclassicism (Architecture) -- Great Britain. Architecture,
Modern -- 17th-18th centuries -- Great Britain. Architecture,
Modern -- 19th century -- Great Britain.*

NA967.D59
Dixon, Roger, 1935-
Victorian architecture/ Roger Dixon, Stefan Muthesius.
New York: Oxford University Press, 1978. 288 p.
77-026262   720/.941   0195200489
*Architecture, Victorian -- Great Britain. Architecture -- Great
Britain.*

NA967.F4 1964
Ferriday, Peter,
Victorian architecture. With an introd. by John Betjeman
and contributions by Nikolaus Pevsner [and others]
Philadelphia, Lippincott, 1964 [c1963] 305 p.
64-023474   720.942
*Architecture, Victorian -- England. Architects -- Great
Britain.*

NA967.H55
Hitchcock, Henry Russell, 1903-
Early Victorian architecture in Britain. New Haven, Yale
University Press, 1954. 2 v.
54-005085   724.142081
*Architecture -- Great Britain. Architecture, Victorian -- Great
Britain.*

NA967.R4 1977
Reilly, Paul.
An introduction to Regency architecture/ Paul Reilly. St.
Clair Shores, Mich.: Scholarly Press, 1977. 96 p.
77-153063   720/.942   0403072379
*Architecture, Regency. Decoration and ornament -- Regency
style.*

NA968.N4 1969
Museum of Modern Art (New York, N.Y.)
Modern architecture in England. [New York] Published
for the Museum of Modern Art by Arno Press, 1969.
101 p.
73-086422   720/.942
*Architecture, Modern -- 20th century -- England. Architecture,
Modern -- 20th century -- Exhibitions.*

NA970.H34 1994
Harris, John, 1931-
The Palladian revival: Lord Burlington, his villa and
garden at Chiswick/ John Harris. New Haven: Published
in association with Yale University Press, c1994. vi,
280 p.
93-049024   728.8/09421/82   0300059833
*Burlington, Richard Boyle, -- Earl of, -- 1694-1753 -- Criticism
and interpretation -- Exhibitions. Palladio, Andrea, -- 1508-
1580 -- Influence -- Exhibitions. Classicism in architecture --
England -- London -- Exhibitions. Chiswick (London, England)
-- Buildings, structures, etc. -- Exhibitions. Chiswick House
Garden (Hounslow, London, England) -- Exhibitions.*

NA970.S8 1978
Summerson, John Newenham, 1904-
Georgian London/ John Summerson. Cambridge, Mass.:
MIT Press, 1978. 348 p.
78-053798   720/.9421   0262191733
*Architecture -- England -- London. Architecture, Georgian --
England -- London.*

NA971.M3
Parkinson-Bailey, John J.
Manchester: an architectural history/ John J. Parkinson-
Bailey. New York: Manchester University Press, 2000.
xviii, 386 p.
99-055329   720/.9427/33   0719056063
Architecture -- England -- Manchester -- History.

NA975.C7 1987
Crook, J. Mordaunt 1937-
The dilemma of style: architectural ideas from the
picturesque to the post-modern/ J. Mordaunt Crook.
Chicago: University of Chicago Press, 1987. 348 p.
87-010821   720/.942   0226121194
*Architecture, Modern -- England -- Themes, motives.
Architecture -- England -- Themes, motives. Eclecticism in
architecture -- England.*

NA975.G56 1996
Glendinning, Miles, 1956-
A history of Scottish architecture: from the Renaissance to the present day/ Miles Glendinning, Ranald MacInnes and Aonghus MacKechnis. Edinburgh: Edinburgh University Press, 1996. xiv, 626 p.
97-133666   0748607412
Architecture, Modern -- Scotland.

NA982.C72 1983
Craig, Maurice James.
The architecture of Ireland: from the earliest times to 1880/ Maurice Craig. London: Batsford; 1982 358 p.
83-200312   720/.9415   0713425865
Architecture -- Ireland.

NA988.E17 1872a
Eastlake, Charles L. 1836-1906.
A history of the Gothic revival [by] Charles L. Eastlake; edited with an introduction by J. Mordaunt Crook. Leicester, Leicester U.P., 1970. xviii, 372 p.
70-017391   720/.942   0718550056
Architecture -- England -- History. Gothic revival (Architecture) Medievalism -- England -- History.

NA996.C6 1978
Colvin, Howard Montagu.
A biographical dictionary of British architects, 1600-1840/ Howard Colvin. London: J. Murray, 1978. 1080 p.
78-313391   720/.92/2   0719533287
Architects -- Great Britain -- Biography -- Dictionaries.

NA997.A4.K55 1991
King, David N.
The complete works of Robert and James Adam/ David King. Jordan Hill, Oxford; Butterworth Architecture, 1991. xii, 447 p.
92-140148   720/.92   075061286X
Adam, Robert, -- 1728-1792 -- Criticism and interpretation. Adam, James, -- d. 1794 -- Criticism and interpretation. Neoclassicism (Architecture) -- Great Britain.

NA997.B84.T45
Thompson, Paul Richard, 1935-
William Butterfield [by] Paul Thompson. Cambridge, Mass. M.I.T. Press [1971] xxix, 526 p.
79-169976   720/.924   0710069308
Butterfield, William, -- 1814-1900.

NA997.C5.S58 1996
Sir William Chambers: architect to George III/ edited by John Harris and Michael Snodin. New Haven: Yale University Press in association with the Courtauld Galley, Courtauld Institute of Art, London, c1996. 229 p.
96-021636   720/.92   0300069405
Chambers, William, -- Sir, -- 1726-1796. Architects -- Great Britain -- Biography.

NA997.G6.A4 1999
Godwin, E. W. 1833-1886.
E.W. Godwin: aesthetic movement architect and designer/ Susan Weber Soros, editor; Catherine Arbuthnott ... [et al.]. New Haven: Yale University Press published for the Bard Graduate Center Studies in the Decorative Arts, New York, c1999. 431 p.
99-024645   720/.92   0300080085
Godwin, E. W. -- (Edward William), -- 1833-1886 -- Exhibitions. Architecture, Modern -- 19th century -- Great Britain -- Exhibitions. Aesthetic movement (British art) -- Exhibitions. Interior decoration -- Great Britain -- History -- 19th century -- Exhibitions.

NA997.H3.D6 1980
Downes, Kerry.
Hawksmoor/ Kerry Downes. Cambridge, Mass.: MIT Press, 1980, c1979. xvi, 298 p.
79-090962   720/.92/4   0262040603
Hawksmoor, Nicholas, -- 1661-1736.

NA997.M3.A4 1980
Mackintosh, Charles Rennie, 1868-1928.
Mackintosh architecture: the complete buildings and selected projects/ edited by Jackie Cooper; foreword by David Dunster; introd. by Barbara Bernard. New York: Rizzoli, 1980. 111 p.
80-051133   720/.92/4   0847803309
Mackintosh, Charles Rennie, -- 1868-1928. Eclecticism in architecture -- Great Britain.

NA997.M3.M287 1989
Mackintosh's masterwork: Charles Rennie Mackintosh and the Glasgow School of Art/ William Buchanan ... [et al.]. San Francisco: Chronicle Books, 1989. 224 p.
89-009759   727/.47   0877016631
Mackintosh, Charles Rennie, -- 1868-1928 -- Criticism and interpretation. Art nouveau (Architecture) -- Scotland -- Glasgow. Glasgow (Scotland) -- Buildings, structures, etc.

NA997.N3.A4 1991
Mansbridge, Michael.
John Nash: a complete catalogue/ photographs and text by Michael Mansbridge; introduction by John Summerson. New York: Rizzoli, 1991. 336 p.
90-052872   720/.92   0847813088
Nash, John, -- 1752-1835 -- Catalogs. Eclecticism in architecture -- Great Britain -- Catalogs.

NA997.N3.S85 1980
Summerson, John Newenham, 1904-
The life and work of John Nash, architect/ John Summerson. Cambridge, Mass.: MIT Press, 1980. 217 p.
80-014011   720/.92/4   0262191903
Nash, John, -- 1752-1835. Architects -- England -- Biography.

NA997.P9.A4 1994
Pugin, Augustus Welby Northmore, 1812-1852.
Pugin: a Gothic passion/ edited by Paul Atterbury &
Clive Wainwright. New Haven: Yale University Press in
association with the Victoria & Albert Museum, c1994.
xiii, 310 p.
94-015209   720/.92   0300060122
*Pugin, Augustus Welby Northmore, -- 1812-1852 -- Exhibitions.
Gothic revival (Architecture) -- England -- Exhibitions. Design -
- England -- History -- 19th century.*

NA997.R6.C87 1983
Curl, James Stevens, 1937-
The life and work of Henry Roberts, 1803-1876: the
evangelical conscience and the campaign for model
housing and healthy nations/ James Stevens Curl.
Chichester, Sussex: Phillimore, 1983. xxii, 273 p.
84-123966   720/.92/4   0850334462
*Roberts, Henry, -- 1803-1876.   Architects -- England --
Biography. Architecture, Victorian -- England.*

NA997.R64.S83 1995
Sudjic, Deyan.
The architecture of Richard Rogers/ Deyan Sudjic. New
York: Abrams, 1995. 159 p.
94-072680   720/.92   0810919540
*Rogers, Richard George -- Criticism and interpretation.
Architecture, Modern -- 20th century.*

NA997.S6.G5 1983
Girouard, Mark, 1931-
Robert Smythson & the Elizabethan country house/ Mark
Girouard. New Haven: Yale University Press, 1983. viii,
328 p.
83-050004   720/.92/4   0300031343
*Smythson, Robert, -- 1534 or 5-1614.   Architecture, Elizabethan
-- England. Architecture, Domestic -- England. Country homes -
- England -- History -- 16th century. Great Britain -- History --
Elizabeth, 1558-1603.*

NA997.S7.D37 1999
Darley, Gillian.
John Soane: an accidental romantic/ Gillian Darley. New
Haven: Yale University Press, c1999. x, 358 p.
99-062198   720/.92   0300081650
*Soane, John, -- Sir, -- 1753-1837.   Architects -- England --
Biography.*

NA997.S7.D85 1982
Du Prey, Pierre de la Ruffiniere.
John Soane, the making of an architect/ Pierre de la
Ruffiniere du Prey. Chicago: University of Chicago
Press, 1982. xxiv, 408 p.
81-016453   720/.92/4   0226172988
*Soane, John, -- Sir, -- 1753-1837.   Architects -- England --
Biography. Neoclassicism (Architecture) -- England.*

NA997.S7.S76 1984
Stroud, Dorothy.
Sir John Soane, architect/ Dorothy Stroud. London; Faber
& Faber, 1984. 300 p.
83-011488   720/.92/4   057113050X
Soane, John, -- Sir, -- 1753-1837.

NA997.S7.W38 1996
Watkin, David, 1941-
Sir John Soane: enlightenment thought and the Royal
Academy lectures/ David Watkin. Cambridge; Cambridge
University Press, 1996. xx, 763 p.
95-018311   720/.92   0521440912
*Soane, John, -- Sir, -- 1753-1837.   Architects -- England --
Biography. Neoclassicism (Architecture) -- England.*

NA997.U59.M55 1992
Miller, Mervyn.
Raymond Unwin: garden cities and town planning/
Mervyn Miller. Leicester [England]; Leicester University
Press, 1992. x, 299 p.
91-044165   711/.4/092   0718513630
*Unwin, Raymond, -- Sir, -- 1863-1940.   Architects -- England --
Biography.*

NA997.V3.D68
Downes, Kerry.
Vanbrugh/ by Kerry Downes. London: A. Zwemmer,
c1977. xiv, 291 p.
78-354492   720/.92/4   0302027696
*Vanbrugh, John, -- Sir, -- 1664-1726.   Architects -- England --
Biography. Architecture, Baroque -- England.*

NA997.W38.B6 1989
Bold, John.
John Webb: architectural theory and practice in the
seventeenth century/ John Bold. Oxford: Clarendon
Press; c1989. xix, 192 p.
88-028995   720/.92/4   0198175035
*Webb, John, -- 1611-1672 -- Criticism and interpretation. Webb,
John, -- 1611-1672 -- Catalogs. Architecture, Modern -- 17th-
18th centuries -- England -- Catalogs. Architecture --
Philosophy. Chinese language -- History and criticism.*

NA997.W48.L57
Liscombe, R. W., 1946-
William Wilkins, 1778-1839/ R. W. Liscombe.
Cambridge [Eng.]; Cambridge University Press, 1980. xv,
297 p.
78-073247   720/.92/4   0521225280
*Wilkins, William, -- 1778-1839.   Architects -- England --
Biography. Architecture, Regency -- England.*

NA997.W8.D59 1982
Downes, Kerry.
The architecture of Wren/ Kerry Downes. New York:
Universe Books, 1982. xviii, 139 p.
82-008425   720/.92/4   0876633955
*Wren, Christopher, -- Sir, -- 1632-1723.   Architects -- England
-- Biography.*

NA1011.5.W3.G413 1979
Geretsegger, Heinz.
Otto Wagner 1841-1918: the expanding city, the
beginning of modern architecture/ by Heinz Geretsegger
and Max Peintner; associate author Walter Pichler;
introd. by Richard Neutra; translated by Gerald Onn.
New York: Rizzoli, 1979. 272 p.
78-068493   720/.92/4   0847802175
Wagner, Otto, -- 1841-1918.

NA1011.5.W5.W55 1994
Wijdeveld, Paul.
Ludwig Wittgenstein, architect/ Paul Wijdeveld. Cambridge, Mass.: MIT Press, c1994. 240 p.
93-021602   728.8/092   0262231751
Wittgenstein, Ludwig, -- 1889-1951 -- Criticism and interpretation. Stonborough-Wittgenstein, Margarethe, -- 1882-1958 -- Homes and haunts -- Austria -- Vienna. Architecture -- Philosophy.   Vienna (Austria) -- Buildings, structures, etc.

NA1012.A73 1998
The architecture of historic Hungary/ edited by Dora Wiebenson and Jozsef Sisa; contributions by Pal Lovei ... [et al.]. Cambridge, Mass.: MIT Press, c1998. xxvii, 328 p.
97-036125   720/.9439   0262231921
Architecture -- Hungary -- Themes, motives.

NA1033.P7.S8313 1995
Svacha, Rostislav.
The architecture of new Prague, 1895-1945/ Rostislav Svacha; translated by Alexandra Buchler; photographs by Jan Maly; foreword by Kenneth Frampton; essay by Eric Dluhosch. Cambridge, Mass.: MIT Press, c1995. xxxi, 573 p.
94-046230   720/.94371/209041   0262193582
Architecture, Modern -- 20th century -- Czechoslovakia -- Prague. Architecture -- Czechoslovakia -- Prague.   Prague (Czechoslovaloa) -- Buildings, structures, etc.

NA1046.B75
Braham, Allan.
The architecture of the French Enlightenment/ Allan Braham. Berkeley: University of California Press, c1980. 288 p.
79-003606   720/.944   0520041178
Neoclassicism (Architecture) -- France. Architecture -- France. Architecture, Modern -- 17th-18th centuries -- France.

NA1046.K35 1995
Kalnein, Wend von, 1914-
Architecture in France in the eighteenth century/ Wend von Kalnein; translated from the German by David Britt. New Haven: Yale University Press, 1995. 294 p.
93-049720   720/.944/09033   0300060130
Architecture -- France. Architecture, Modern -- 17th-18th centuries -- France. Architecture, Baroque -- France.

NA1046.5.N4.P513 1991
Picon, Antoine.
French architects and engineers in the Age of Enlightenment/ Antoine Picon; translated by Martin Thom. Cambridge [England]; Cambridge University Press, c1992. xiv, 437 p.
90-023827   720/.944/09033   052138253X
Neoclassicism (Architecture) -- France. Architecture -- Philosophy. Engineering -- Philosophy. France -- Intellectual life -- 18th century.

NA1048.L47 1990
Lesnikowski, Wojciech G.
The new French architecture/ Wojciech Lesnikowski; introduction by Patrice Goulet. New York: Rizzoli, 1990. 223 p.
90-035057   720/.944/09045   0847812243
Architecture, Modern -- 20th century -- France. Architecture -- France.

NA1050.L6713 1988
Loyer, Francois.
Paris nineteenth century: architecture and urbanism/ Francois Loyer; translated by Charles Lynn Clark. New York: Abbeville Press, c1988. 478 p.
88-022269   720/.944/361   0896598853
Architecture, Modern -- 19th century -- France -- Paris. City planning -- France -- Paris -- History -- 19th century.   Paris (France) -- Buildings, structures, etc.

NA1050.V358 1994
Van Zanten, David, 1943-
Building Paris: architectural institutions and the transformation of the French capital, 1830-1870/ David Van Zanten. Cambridge; Cambridge University Press, 1994. xix, 360 p.
93-034299   720/.944/36109034   052139421X
Neoclassicism (Architecture) -- France -- Paris. Architects and patrons -- France -- Paris -- History -- 19th century. City planning -- France -- Paris -- History -- 19th century. Paris (France) -- Buildings, structures, etc.

NA1050.V36 1987
Van Zanten, David, 1943-
Designing Paris: the architecture of Duban, Labrouste, Duc, and Vaudoyer/ David Van Zanten. Cambridge, Mass.: MIT Press, c1987. xvii, 338 p.
87-003994   720/.944/361   0262220318
Neoclassicism (Architecture) -- France -- Paris. Greek revival (Architecture) -- France -- Paris. Architecture, Modern -- 19th century -- France -- Paris. Paris (France) -- Buildings, structures, etc.

NA1053.C43.A4 1998
Taylor, Brian Brace.
Pierre Chareau: designer and architect/ Brian Brace Taylor. Koln; Taschen, c1998. 160 p.
00-295748   3822878871
Chareau, Pierre -- Catalogs.   Architects -- France. Architect-designed furniture -- France. Architecture, Modern -- 20th century -- France.

NA1053.C58.M38 1990
McCormick, Thomas J. 1925-
Charles-Louis Clerisseau and the genesis of neo-classicism/ Thomas J. McCormick. New York, N.Y.: Architectural History Foundation; c1990. xiv, 284 p.
90-031145   720/.92   0262132621
Clerisseau, Charles-Louis, -- 1721-1820.   Architects -- France -- Biography. Neoclassicism (Architecture) -- France.

NA1053.G73.A83 1987
Adam, Peter.
Eileen Gray: architect/designer/ Peter Adam. New York: H.N. Abrams, 1987. 400 p.
87-000998   745.4/4924   0810909960
Gray, Eileen, -- 1878-1976.   Architects -- France -- Biography. Designers -- France -- Biography.

NA1053.G8.F4713 1988
Ferre, Felipe, 1934-
Hector Guimard/ photographs by Felipe Ferre; text by Maurice Rheims; explanatory captions and chronology by Georges Vigne. New York, NY: H.N. Abrams, 1988. 223 p.
86-032232   720/.92/4   0810909731
Guimard, Hector, -- 1867-1942 -- Criticism and interpretation. Art nouveau (Architecture) -- France.

NA1053.J4.A2 1997
Le Corbusier, 1887-1965.
The final testament of Pere Corbu: a translation and interpretation of Mise au point/ by Ivan Zaknic. New Haven: Yale University Press, c1997. x, 180 p.
96-047812   720/.92   0300063539
Le Corbusier, -- 1887-1965 -- Philosophy.

NA1053.J4.A48
Jeanneret-Gris, Charles Edouard, 1887-
Le Corbusier, 1910-60. New York, G. Wittenborn [1960] 334 p.
60-051658   720.9494

NA1053.J4.A49
Jeanneret-Gris, Charles Edouard, 1887-1965.
Le Corbusier, 1910-65. [Edited by] W. Boesiger [and] H. Girsberger. New York, Praeger [1967] 351 p.
67-025150   720/.924

NA1053.J4.B76 1997
Brooks, H. Allen 1925-
Le Corbusier's formative years: Charles-Edouard Jeanneret at La Chaux-de-Fonds/ H. Allen Brooks. Chicago: University of Chicago Press, 1997. xi, 514 p.
96-022865   720/.92   0226075796
Le Corbusier, -- 1887-1965 -- Childhood and youth.   Architects -- France -- Biography. Architects -- Switzerland -- Biography.

NA1053.J4.C5
Choay, Francoise.
Le Corbusier. New York, G. Braziller, 1960. 126 p.
60-006079   720.9494
Le Corbusier, -- 1887-1965.

NA1053.J4.M613
Moos, Stanislaus von.
Le Corbusier, elements of a synthesis/ Stanislaus von Moos. Cambridge, Mass.: MIT Press, c1979. viii, 379 p.
78-025940   720/.92/4   0262220237
Le Corbusier, -- 1887-1965.

NA1053.J4.S44
Sekler, Eduard F.
Le Corbusier at work: the genesis of the Carpenter Center for the Visual Arts/ Eduard F. Sekler, William Curtis; with contributions by Rudolph Arnheim, Barbara Norfleet. Cambridge: Harvard University Press, 1978. ix, 357 p.
77-007315   727/.4/7   0674520599
Le Corbusier, -- 1887-1965.

NA1053.J4.T39 1987
Taylor, Brian Brace.
Le Corbusier, the City of Refuge, Paris 1929/33/ by Brian Brace Taylor; with an introduction by Kenneth Frampton. Chicago: University of Chicago Press, 1987. xiii, 185 p.
87-010946   725/.55/0924   0226791343
Le Corbusier, -- 1887-1965 -- Criticism and interpretation. Asylums -- France -- Paris.   Paris (France) -- Buildings, structures, etc.

NA1053.N68.M67 1998
Morgan, Conway Lloyd.
Jean Nouvel: the elements of architecture/ Conway Lloyd Morgan. New York: Universe Pub., 1998. 238 p.
98-029130   720/.92   0789302268
Nouvel, Jean, -- 1945- -- Criticism and interpretation. Architecture, Modern -- 20th century.

NA1053.V7.E9
Eugene Emmanuel Viollet-le-Duc, 1814-1879. [New York, N.Y.]: Rizzoli, [c1980] 96 p.
81-110823   720/.92/4   0847853136
Viollet-le-Duc, Eugene-Emmanuel, -- 1814-1879.

NA1053.V7.M87 2000
Murphy, Kevin D.
Memory and modernity: Viollet-le-Duc at Vezelay/ Kevin D. Murphy. University Park, Pa.: Pennsylvania State University Press, c2000. xiv, 200 p.
98-041262   726.5/0944/41   027101850X
Viollet-le-Duc, Eugene-Emmanuel, -- 1814-1879 -- Criticism and interpretation.   Catholic church buildings -- Conservation and restoration -- France -- Vezelay.   Vezelay (France) -- Buildings, structures, etc.

NA1065.H57
Hitchcock, Henry Russell, 1903-
German Renaissance architecture/ Henry-Russell Hitchcock. Princeton, N.J.: Princeton University Press, c1981. xxxiv, 379 p.
80-016399   720/.943   0691039593
Architecture, Renaissance -- Germany. Architecture -- Germany.

NA1067.5.N38
Lane, Barbara Miller.
National romanticism and modern architecture in Germany and the Scandinavian countries/ Barbara Miller Lane. Cambridge; Cambridge University Press, 2000. xvi, 416 p.
99-043685   724/.6   0521583098
National romanticism (Architecture) -- Germany. Architecture -- Germany -- 19th century. Architecture -- Germany -- 20th century.

NA1068.F36 1993
Feldmeyer, Gerhard G.
The new German architecture/ Gerhard G. Feldmeyer;
introduction by Manfred Sack; with an essay by Casey
C.M. Mathewson; [translation from the German by Mark
Wilch]. New York: Rizzoli, 1993. 224 p.
92-032826   720/.943/09048   0847816729
*Architecture, Modern -- 20th century -- Germany. Architecture
-- Germany. Architecture and society -- Germany.*

NA1068.L3
Lane, Barbara Miller.
Architecture and politics in Germany, 1918-1945.
Cambridge, Mass., Harvard University Press, 1968.
278 p.
67-022867   720/.943
National socialism and architecture. Architecture -- Germany.

NA1068.N423
Contemporary architecture in Germany. Introd. by Ulrich
Conrads. Text by Werner Marschall. Translated by James
Palmes. New York, Praeger [1962] 231 p.
62-013860   720.943
*Architecture -- Germany (West) Architecture, Modern -- 20th
century.*

NA1068.5.N37.S26 1990
Scobie, Alexander.
Hitler's state architecture: the impact of classical
antiquity/ Alex Scobie. University Park: Published for
College Art Association by the Pennsylvania State
University Press, 1990. xi, 152 p.
89-039018   720/.1/03   0271006919
*Architecture and state -- Germany. National socialism and
architecture.*

NA1088.B4.A827 2000
Anderson, Stanford.
Peter Behrens and a new architecture for the twentieth
century/ Stanford Anderson. Cambridge, Mass.: MIT
Press, c2000. xi, 429 p.
99-049154   720/.92   026201176X
*Behrens, Peter, -- 1868-1940 -- Criticism and interpretation.
Architecture, Modern -- 20th century -- Germany.*

NA1088.G85.I79 1991
Isaacs, Reginald R., 1911-
Gropius: an illustrated biography of the creator of the
Bauhaus/ by Reginald Isaacs. Boston: Little, Brown,
c1991. xix, 344 p.
90-013481   720/.92   0821217534
*Gropius, Walter, -- 1883-1969.   Architects -- Germany --
Biography.*

NA1088.M57.W5 1956
Whittick, Arnold, 1898-
Eric Mendelsohn. London, L. Hill [1956] 219 p.
56-002986   927.2
Mendelsohn, Erich, -- 1887-1953.

NA1088.M65.D7
Drexler, Arthur.
Ludwig Mies van der Rohe. New York, G. Braziller,
1960. 127 p.
60-006077   720.973
Mies van der Rohe, Ludwig, -- 1886-

NA1088.M65.H5
Hilberseimer, Ludwig.
Mies van der Rohe. Chicago, P. Theobald, 1956. 199 p.
56-003870   720.81
Mies van der Rohe, Ludwig, -- 1886-1969.

NA1088.M65.P3
Mies van der Rohe, Ludwig, 1886-1969.
Mies van der Rohe; introduction and notes by Martin
Pawley, with photographs by Yukio Futagawa. London,
Thames & Hudson, 1970. 134 p.
72-554064   720/.924   0500580030

NA1088.M65.S38 1985
Schulze, Franz, 1927-
Mies van der Rohe: a critical biography/ Franz Schulze in
association with the Mies van der Rohe Archive of the
Museum of Modern Art. Chicago: University of Chicago
Press, 1985. xxiii, 355 p.
85-008488   720/.92/4   0226740595
*Mies van der Rohe, Ludwig, -- 1886-1969.   Architects --
Germany -- Biography. Architects -- United States -- Biography.*

NA1088.M65.S54 1985
Spaeth, David A.
Mies van der Rohe/ David Spaeth; pref. by Kenneth
Frampton. New York: Rizzoli, c1985. 205 p.
84-042768   720/.92/4   0847805638
*Mies van der Rohe, Ludwig, -- 1886-1969.   Architecture,
Modern -- 20th century -- Germany. Architecture, Modern --
20th century -- United States.*

NA1088.S24.B58 1995
Blundell-Jones, Peter.
Hans Scharoun/ Peter Blundell Jones. London: Phaidon
Press, 1995. 240 p.
96-142263   720.92   0714828777
*Scharoun, Hans, -- 1893-1972.   Architecture, Modern -- 20th
century. Architectural drawing -- Germany.*

NA1088.S3.A4 1991
Karl Friedrich Schinkel: a universal man/ edited by
Michael Snodin. New Haven: Yale University Press in
association with the Victoria and Albert Museum,
London, 1991. xii, 218 p.
91-050586   720/.92   0300051654
*Schinkel, Karl Friedrich, -- 1781-1841 -- Exhibitions.
Neoclassicism (Architecture) -- Germany -- Exhibitions.*

NA1088.T33.W47 1982
Whyte, Iain Boyd, 1947-
Bruno Taut and the architecture of activism/ Iain Boyd
Whyte. Cambridge [Cambridgeshire]; Cambridge
University Press, 1982. xiii, 280 p.
81-012301   720/.92/4   052123655X
*Taut, Bruno, -- 1880-1938 -- Influence.   Functionalism
(Architecture) -- Germany.*

NA1111.S5
Smith, G. E. Kidder 1913-
Italy builds; its modern architecture and native inheritance. L'Italia costruisce. Photos. by the author. New York, Reinhold [1955] 264 p.
55-006278   724.91
Architecture -- Italy.

NA1115.B813 1985
Burckhardt, Jacob, 1818-1897.
The architecture of the Italian Renaissance/ Jacob Burckhardt; revised and edited by Peter Murray; translated by James Palmes. Chicago: University of Chicago Press, c1985. xxxv, 283 p.
83-018113   720/.945   0226080471
Architecture, Renaissance -- Italy. Architecture -- Italy.

NA1115.H49 1996
Heydenreich, Ludwig Heinrich, 1903-
Architecture in Italy, 1400-1500/ Ludwig H. Heydenreich; revised by Paul Davies; [translated by Mary Hottinger]. New Haven: Yale University Press, 1996. 186 p.
95-036474   720/.945/09024   0300064667
Architecture -- Italy. Architecture, Renaissance -- Italy. Mannerism (Architecture) -- Italy.

NA1115.L666 1995
Lotz, Wolfgang, 1912-
Architecture in Italy, 1500-1600/ Wolfgang Lotz; introduction by Deborah Howard; [translated by Mary Hottinger]. New Haven: Yale University Press, 1995. viii, 205 p.
95-009124   720/.945/09031   0300064683
Architecture, Renaissance -- Italy. Mannerism (Architecture) -- Italy. Architecture -- Italy.

NA1115.M8
Murray, Peter.
The architecture of the Italian Renaissance. New York, Schocken Books [1964, c1963] xviii, 268 p.
64-011469   720.945
Architecture -- Italy. Architecture, Renaissance.

NA1115.W613 1966
Wolfflin, Heinrich, 1864-1945.
Renaissance and baroque. Translated by Kathrin Simon. With an introd. by Peter Murray. Ithaca, N.Y., Cornell University Press [1966] 183 p.
65-022724   724.19
Architecture, Renaissance -- Italy. Architecture, Baroque -- Italy. Architecture, Italian.

NA1118.E86 1990
Etlin, Richard A.
Modernism in Italian architecture, 1890-1940/ Richard A. Etlin. Cambridge, Mass.: MIT Press, c1991. xxiii, 736 p.
90-032983   720/.945/09041   0262050382
Fascism and architecture -- Italy. Architecture, Modern -- 20th century -- Italy. Nationalism and architecture -- Italy.

NA1118.T3413 1989
Tafuri, Manfredo.
History of Italian architecture, 1944-1985/ Manfredo Tafuri; translated by Jessica Levine. Cambridge, Mass.: MIT Press, c1989. ix, 269 p.
88-017482   720/.945   0262200678
Architecture, Modern -- 20th century -- Italy. Architecture -- Italy.

NA1120.B55 1982
Blunt, Anthony, 1907-1983.
Guide to baroque Rome/ Anthony Blunt. London; Granada, 1982. xviii, 317 p.
82-238716   914.5/63204928   0246117621
Architecture, Baroque -- Italy -- Rome -- Guidebooks. Buildings -- Italy -- Rome -- Guidebooks. Rome (Italy) -- Guidebooks. Rome (Italy) -- Buildings, structures, etc. -- Guidebooks.

NA1120.B87 1990
Burroughs, Charles.
From signs to design: environmental process and reform in early Renaissance Rome/ Charles Burroughs. Cambridge, Mass.: MIT Press, c1990. xii, 344 p.
89-013768   307.76/0945/63209024   0262022982
Architecture, Renaissance -- Italy -- Rome. City planning -- Italy -- Rome -- History. Urbanization -- Italy -- Rome -- History. Rome (Italy) -- Buildings, structures, etc.

NA1121.V4 H69 2000
Howard, Deborah.
Venice & the East: the impact of the Islamic world on Venetian architecture, 1100-1500/ Deborah Howard. New Haven: Yale University Press, c2000. xv, 283 p.
00-036486   720/.945/310902   0300085044
Architecture -- Italy -- Venice -- Islamic influences. Venice (Italy) -- Buildings, structures, etc.

NA1121.V4.C65613 1998
Concina, Ennio.
A history of Venetian architecture/ Ennio Concina; translated by Judith Landry. Cambridge; Cambridge University Press, 1998. 356 p.
97-019201   720/.945/31   0521573386
Architecture -- Italy -- Venice. Venice (Italy) -- Buildings, structures, etc.

NA1121.V4.M32
McAndrew, John.
Venetian architecture of the early Renaissance/ John McAndrew. Cambridge, Mass.: MIT Press, c1980. xiii, 599 p.
80-017045   720/.945/31   0262131579
Architecture, Renaissance -- Italy -- Venice. Architecture -- Italy -- Venice. Buildings -- Italy -- Venice. Venice (Italy) -- Buildings, structures, etc.

NA1121.V4.R7 1981
Ruskin, John, 1819-1900.
The stones of Venice/ John Ruskin; edited & introduced by Jan Morris. Boston: Little, Brown, 1981. 239 p.
81-080862   720/.945/31   0316761907
Architecture -- Italy -- Venice.

NA1123.A5.G73 2000
Grafton, Anthony.
Leon Battista Alberti: master builder of the Italian Renaissance/ Anthony Grafton. New York: Hill and Wang, 2000. xi, 417 p.
00-035068   709/.2   0809097524
Alberti, Leon Battista, -- 1404-1472.   Architects -- Italy -- Biography.

NA1123.A5.T38 1998
Tavernor, Robert.
On Alberti and the art of building/ Robert Tavernor. New Haven: Yale University Press, c1998. xii, 278 p.
98-015258   720/.92   0300076150
Alberti, Leon Battista, -- 1404-1472 -- Criticism and interpretation.   Architecture, Renaissance -- Italy. Architects and patrons -- Italy.

NA1123.B8.B3613 1981
Battisti, Eugenio.
Filippo Brunelleschi: the complete work/ Eugenio Battisti; [translated from Italian, Filippo Brunelleschi by Robert Erich Wolf; text revised by Eugenio Battisti and Emily Lane]. New York: Rizzoli, 1981. 400 p.
78-068509   720/.92/4   0847850153
Brunelleschi, Filippo, -- 1377-1446.   Architects -- Italy -- Biography.

NA1123.B8.K5513 1990
Klotz, Heinrich.
Filippo Brunelleschi: the early works and the medieval tradition/ Heinrich Klotz; [translated from the German by Hugh Keith]. New York: Rizzoli, 1990. 175 p.
89-064019   720/.92   0847812111
Brunelleschi, Filippo, -- 1377-1446 -- Criticism and interpretation.   Architecture, Gothic -- Italy -- Influence. Architecture, Medieval -- Influence.

NA1123.B8.S23 1993
Saalman, Howard.
Filippo Brunelleschi: the buildings/ Howard Saalman. University Park, Pa.: Pennsylvania State University Press, 1993. 470 p.
92-046535   720/.92   0271010673
Brunelleschi, Filippo, -- 1377-1446 -- Criticism and interpretation.   Architecture, Renaissance -- Italy -- Florence.

NA1123.B9.A8713 1993
Argan, Giulio Carlo.
Michelangelo architect/ by Giulio Carlo Argan and Bruno Contardi; translated from the Italian by Marion L. Grayson. New York: Harry N. Abrams, 1993. 388 p.
92-038117   720/.92   0810936380
Michelangelo Buonarroti, -- 1475-1564 -- Criticism and interpretation.   Architecture, Renaissance -- Italy.

NA1123.P2.A66
Holberton, Paul.
Palladio's villas: life in the Renaissance countryside/ Paul Holberton. London: Murray, 1990. xiii, 256 p.
90-003232   720/.92/4   0719547822
Palladio, Andrea, -- 1508-1580. Palladio, Andrea, -- 1508-1580 -- Friends and associates.   Architecture, Renaissance -- Italy. Architecture, Domestic -- Italy.

NA1123.P2.B68 1993
Boucher, Bruce.
Andrea Palladio: the architect in his time/ Bruce Boucher; principal photography by Paolo Marton. New York: Abbeville Press, c1994. 336 p.
93-003120   720/.92   1558593810
Palladio, Andrea, -- 1508-1580 -- Criticism and interpretation. Architecture, Renaissance -- Italy.

NA1123.R616.A4 1991
Rossi, Aldo, 1931-
Aldo Rossi: architecture, 1981-1991/ edited by Morris Adjmir; introduction by Diane Ghirardo; text and afterword by Karen Stein; essay by Aldo Rossi. New York, N.Y.: Princeton Architectural Press, c1991. 300 p.
91-027398   720/.92   1878271156
Rossi, Aldo, -- 1931- -- Themes, motives.   Architecture, Postmodern -- Themes, motives.

NA1123.T4.S37 1991
Schumacher, Thomas L.
Surface & symbol: Giuseppe Terragni and the architecture of Italian rationalism/ Thomas L. Schumacher. New York: Princeton Architectural Press, c1991. 295 p.
90-042728   720/.92   0910413592
Terragni, Giuseppe, -- 1904- Architects -- Italy -- Biography. Architecture, Modern -- 20th century -- Italy.

NA1153.B4.A4 1988
Polano, Sergio.
Hendrik Petrus Berlage, complete works/ Sergio Polano; essays by Giovanni Fanelli, Jan de Heer, Vincent van Rossem; [translated by Marie-Helene Agueros and Mayta Munson]. New York: Rizzoli, 1988. 266 p.
87-043252   720/.92   0847809013
Berlage, Hendrik Petrus, -- 1856-1934 -- Catalogues raisonnes. Architecture, Modern -- 19th century -- Netherlands -- Catalogs. Architecture, Modern -- 20th century -- Netherlands -- Catalogs.

NA1173.H6.B613 1991
Borsi, Franco.
Victor Horta/ Franco Borsi, Paolo Portoghesi; foreword by Jean Delhaye; translated from the Italian by Marie-Helene Agueros. New York: Rizzoli, 1991. 413 p.
90-053176   720/.92   0847812901
Horta, Victor, -- baron, -- 1861-1947 -- Criticism and interpretation.   Art nouveau (Architecture) -- Belgium.

NA1181.B72 1993
Brumfield, William Craft, 1944-
A history of Russian architecture/ text and photographs by William Craft Brumfield. Cambridge; Cambridge University Press, 1993. 644 p.
92-029554   720/.947   0521403332
Architecture -- Russia (Federation) -- Themes, motives.

NA1181.V69
Voyce, Arthur
Russian architecture; trends in nationalism and modernism.   New York, Philosophical Library [1948] xxiv, 282 p.
48-006354   720/.947   0837122929
Architecture -- Soviet Union.

NA1187.B78 1991
Brumfield, William Craft, 1944-
The origins of modernism in Russian architecture/ William Craft Brumfield. Berkeley: University of California Press, c1991. xxv, 343 p.
90-034093   720/.947/09041   0520069293
Nationalism and architecture -- Russia (Federation) Architecture, Modern -- 19th century -- Russia (Federation) Architecture, Modern -- 20th century -- Russia (Federation)

NA1188.H84 1994
Hudson, Hugh D.
Blueprints and blood: the Stalinization of Soviet architecture, 1917-1937/ Hugh D. Hudson, Jr. Princeton, N.J.: Princeton University Press, c1994. xviii, 260 p.
93-017638   720/.947/09041   0691033498
Socialist realism and architecture -- Soviet Union. Constructivism (Architecture) -- Soviet Union.

NA1188.K4713 1987
Khan-Magomedov, S.O.
Pioneers of Soviet architecture: the search for new solutions in the 1920s and 1930s/ Selim O. Khan-Magomedov; [translated from the Russian by Alexander Lieven; edited by Catherine Cooke]. New York: Rizzoli, 1987. 618 p.
86-026150   720/.947   0847807444
Architecture, Modern -- 20th century -- Soviet Union -- Themes, motives. Architecture -- Soviet Union -- Themes, motives.

NA1188.T36 1992
Tarkhanov, Alexei.
Architecture of the Stalin era/ Alexei Tarkhanov & Sergei Kavtaradze; designed and compiled by Mikhail Anikst; [translated by Robin and Julia Whitby and James Paver]. New York: Rizzoli, 1992. 192 p.
91-050877   720/.947/0904   0847814734
Socialist realism and architecture -- Soviet Union. Architecture, Modern -- 20th century -- Soviet Union. Architecture -- Soviet Union.

NA1193.N45 1954a
Neuenschwander, Ed. 1924-
Finnish architecture, and Alvar Aalto [by] Ed. and Cl. Neuenschwander. New York, Praeger [1954] 192 p.
54-009527   720.94895
Aalto, Alvar, -- 1898-1976. Architecture -- Finland.

NA1196.S5613 1996
Shvidkovskii, D. O.
St. Petersburg: architecture of the tsars/ photographs by Alexander Orloff; text by Dmitri Shvidkovsky; translated from the French by John Goodman. New York: Abbeville Press Publishers, 1996. 360 p.
96-017849   720/.947/4530903   0789202174
Architecture, Baroque -- Russia (Federation) -- Saint Petersburg. Neoclassicism (Architecture) -- Russia (Federation) -- Saint Petersburg. Architecture -- Russia (Federation) -- Saint Petersburg. Saint Petersburg (Russia) -- Buildings, structures, etc.

NA1199.A2.A43
Aalto, Alvar, 1898-1976.
Alvar Aalto/ [redaktionelle Bearbeitung, Karl Fleig]. Scarsdale, N.Y.: Wittenborn & Co., c1963. 271 p.
63-025167   720.9471
Aalto, Alvar, -- 1898-1976.

NA1201.D66 1992
Donnelly, Marian C.
Architecture in the Scandinavian countries/ Marian C. Donnelly. Cambridge, Mass.: MIT Press, c1992. 401 p.
90-024720   720/.948   0262041189
Architecture -- Scandinavia -- History.

NA1218.M613
Monies, Finn
Wood in architecture. Layout: Gunnar Jensen and Finn Monies. New York, F.W.Dodge Corp., c1961. 107 p.
61-008089   720.9489
Woodwork -- Denmark. Architecture -- Denmark.

NA1288.S6 1957
Smith, G. E. Kidder 1913-
Sweden builds. New York, Reinhold [1957] 270 p.
56-011753   720.9485
Architecture -- Sweden.

NA1301.B4 1939
Bevan, Bernard.
History of Spanish architecture, by Bernard Bevan. London, B.T. Batsford [1938] xvi, 199 p.
39-010655   720.946
Architecture -- Spain. Architecture, Spanish.

NA1303.D63 1989
Dodds, Jerrilynn Denise.
Architecture and ideology in early medieval Spain/ Jerrilynn D. Dodds. University Park: Pennsylvania State University Press, c1990. xiv, 174 p.
88-043437   720/.946/09021   0271006714
Architecture -- Spain. Architecture, Medieval -- Spain. Architecture and society -- Spain.

NA1303.W5
Whitehill, Walter Muir, 1905-
Spanish Romanesque architecture of the eleventh century, by Walter Muir Whitehill. [London] Oxford University Press, 1941. xxix, 307 p.
41-004920   723.46
Architecture, Romanesque. Architecture, Spanish.

NA1306.S5
Sitwell, Sacheverell, 1897-
Spanish baroque art, with buildings in Portugal, Mexico, and other colonies, by Sacheverell Sitwell. [London] Duckworth, 1931. 112 p.
31-031438
Architecture, Baroque. Architecture, Spanish. Church architecture -- Spain.

NA1308.R84 2001
Ruiz Cabrero, Gabriel.
The modern in Spain: architecture after 1948/ Gabriel Ruiz Cabrero. Cambridge, Mass.: MIT Press, 2000. 199 p.
00-056223   720/.946/09045   0262531720
Architecture -- Spain -- 20th century.

NA1308.Z33 1992
Zabalbeascoa, Anatxu.
The new Spanish architecture/ Anatxu Zabalbeascoa; introduction by Peter Buchanan. New York: Rizzoli, 1992. 222 p.
92-002835   720/.946/0904   0847815323
Architecture, Modern -- 20th century -- Spain. Architecture -- Spain.

NA1313.C35.J62 1998
Jodidio, Philip.
Santiago Calatrava/ Philip Jodidio. Koln; Taschen, c1998. 175 p.
00-501026   3822878839
Calatrava, Santiago, -- 1951-   Architecture, Modern -- 20th century.

NA1313.C35.T9723 1999
Tzonis, Alexander.
Santiago Calatrava: the poetics of movement/ Alexander Tzonis. New York: Universe, 1999. 239 p.
99-034196   720/.92   0789303604
Calatrava, Santiago, -- 1951- -- Criticism and interpretation. Architecture, Modern -- 20th century -- Spain. Civil engineering -- Spain -- History -- 20th century.

NA1313.G3.C63 1983
Collins, George Roseborough, 1917-
The designs and drawings of Antonio Gaudi/ George R. Collins, Juan Bassegoda Nonell. Princeton, N.J.: Princeton University Press, c1983. xx, 83 p.
81-008596   720/.92/4   0691039852
Gaudi, Antoni, -- 1852-1926.

NA1313.G3.J4
Gaudi, Antoni, 1852-1926.
Gaudi. Prefacio: Le Corbusier, fotografias: Joaquin Gomis, seleccion y secuencia: J. Prats Valles. Barcelona, Editorial R M [1958] 62 p.
62-067455

NA1313.G3.M273
Gaudi, Antoni, 1852-1926.
Antonio Gaudi, 1852-1926/ Cesar Martinell. [Translated by Peter Simmons. New York: Universe Books, 1960. 16 p.
60-012419   720.946
Gaudi, Antoni, 1852-1926.

NA1348.S55
Smith, G. E. Kidder 1913-
Switzerland builds; its native and modern achitecture. Photos. by the author. New York, A. Bonnier [1950] 234 p.
50-058202   720.9494
Architecture -- Switzerland. Architecture -- Designs and plans.

NA1353.B67.A4 1987
Botta, Mario, 1943-
Mario Botta, architecture, 1960-1985/ [edited by] Francesco Dal Co; contributions by Mercedes Daguerre, Sergio Polano, Mirko Zardini. Milan: Electa; 1987, c1985. 287 p.
87-009618   720/.92/4   0847808386
Botta, Mario, -- 1943- -- Catalogs. Botta, Mario, -- 1943- -- Criticism and interpretation. Architecture -- Switzerland -- Catalogs. Architecture, Modern -- 20th century -- Switzerland -- Catalogs.

NA1353.S45.M36 1996
Mallgrave, Harry Francis.
Gottfried Semper: architect of the nineteenth century: a personal and intellectual biography/ Harry Francis Mallgrave. New Haven, CT: Yale University Press, 1996. viii, 443 p.
95-047561   720/.92   0300066244
Semper, Gottfried, -- 1803-1879.   Architects -- Switzerland -- Biography.

NA1455.F5.P66 1992
Poole, Scott.
The new Finnish architecture/ Scott Poole; introduction by Colin St. John Wilson. New York: Rizzoli, 1992. 219 p.
91-012431   720/.94897/0904   0847813169
Architecture -- Finland. Architecture, Modern -- 20th century -- Finland.

NA1455.F53.A2314 1999
Aalto, Alvar, 1898-1976.
Alvar Aalto: toward a human modernism/ edited by Winfried Nerdinger; with essays by Friedrich Achleitner ... [et al.]. Munich; Prestel, c1999. 168 p.
99-018300   720/.92   3791320491
Aalto, Alvar, -- 1898-1976 -- Criticism and interpretation. Architecture, Modern -- 20th century -- Finland.

NA1455.F53.A233 1998
Alvar Aalto in his own words/ edited, with introduction by Goran Schildt. New York: Rizzoli, 1998.
97-031230   720/.92   0847820807
Aalto, Alvar, -- 1898-1976 -- Philosophy.

NA1455.F53.A255
Pearson, Paul David, 1936-
Alvar Aalto and the international style/ by Paul David Pearson. New York: Whitney Library of Design, 1978. 240 p.
77-020029   720/.92/4   0823070239
Aalto, Alvar, -- 1898-1976.   International style (Architecture)

NA1455.S563.P643613 1997
Prelovsek, Damjan.
Joze Plecnik, 1872-1957: architectura perennis/ Damjan Prelovsek; translated from the German by Patricia Crampton and Eileen Martin. New Haven: Yale University Press, 1997. 332 p.
96-048899   720/.92   0300069537
Plecnik, Joze, -- 1872-1957 -- Criticism and interpretation. Architecture, Modern -- 20th century.

NA1460-1555 History —
Architecture of special countries —
Asia. The Orient

NA1460.S44 1989
Serageldin, Ismail, 1944-
Space for freedom: the search for architectural excellence in Muslim societies/ by Ismail Serageldin. [Geneva, Switzerland]: Aga Khan Award for Architecture; c1989. 304 p.
89-214662   720/.917/671   0408500492
Architecture -- Islamic countries. Architecture, Modern -- 20th century -- Islamic countries. Architecture -- Conservation and restoration -- Islamic countries.

NA1478.J4.K767 1994
Kroyanker, David.
Jerusalem architecture/ David Kroyanker; introduction by Teddy Kollek. New York: Vendome Press in association with the Jerusalem Institute for Israel Studies: Distributed in the USA and Canada by Rizzoli International Publications through St. Martin's Press, [1994] 210 p.
94-012430   720/.95694/42   0865651477
Architecture -- Jerusalem. City planning -- Jerusalem -- History. Jerusalem -- Buildings, structures, etc.

NA1480.P6
Pope, Arthur Upham, 1881-1969.
Persian architecture; the triumph of form and color. New York, G. Braziller [1965] 288 p.
65-010275   720.955
Architecture -- Iran -- History. Architecture, Islamic -- Iran.

NA1483.W5
Wilber, Donald Newton.
The architecture of Islamic Iran; the Il Khanid period, by Donald N. Wilber. New York, Greenwood Press, [1969, c1955] xi, 208 p.
72-088972   720.9/55   0837125049
Architecture -- Iran. Architecture, Islamic -- Iran.

NA1486.K5.O43 1987
O'Kane, Bernard.
Timurid architecture in Khurasan/ Bernard O'Kane. Costa Mesa, Calif., U.S.A.: Mazda Publishers in association with Undena Publications, 1987. xv, 418 p.
85-043494   722/.52   0939214350
Architecture, Timurid -- Iran -- Khurasan. Architecture, Islamic -- Iran -- Khurasan. Architecture -- Iran -- Khurasan. Khurasan (Iran) -- Antiquities. Iran -- Antiquities.

NA1501.C58 1998
Cooper, Ilay.
Traditional buildings of India/ Ilay Cooper, Barry Dawson. New York: Thames and Hudson, c1998. 192 p.
97-061642   720/.954   0500341613
Architecture -- India. Vernacular architecture -- India.

NA1501.F4 1910
Fergusson, James, 1808-1886.
History of Indian and Eastern architecture, by the late James Fergusson. Rev. and edited, with additions [on] Indian architecture, by James Burgess and Eastern architecture by R. Phene Spiers. Delhi, Munshiram Manoharlal [1967] 2 v.
67-006740
Architecture, Oriental. Architecture -- India.

NA1502.M46 1989
Metcalf, Thomas R., 1934-
An imperial vision: Indian architecture and Britain's raj/ Thomas R. Metcalf. Berkeley: University of California Press, c1989. xiv, 302 p.
87-035485   722/.44   0520062353
Architecture, British -- India. Architecture, British -- India -- British influences. India -- History -- British occupation, 1765-1947.

NA1504.L36 1997
Lang, Jon T.
Architecture and independence: the search for identity-- India 1880 to 1980/ Jon Lang, Madhavi Desai, Miki Desai. Delhi; Oxford University Press, 1997. xix, 347 p.
97-914012   720/.954/0904   0195639006
Architecture, Modern -- 20th century -- India.

NA1510.D67.C87 1988
Curtis, William J. R.
Balkrishna Doshi: an architecture for India/ William J.R. Curtis; [editor, Carmen Kagal]. New York: Rizzoli, 1988. 191 p.
87-043269   720/.92   0847809374
Doshi, Balkrishna V. -- Criticism and interpretation. Architecture, Modern -- 20th century -- India.

NA1510.8.H56.B47 1997
Bernier, Ronald M.
Himalayan architecture/ Ronald M. Bernier; with a foreword by Dalai Lama. Madison: Fairleigh Dickinson University Press; c1997. 196 p.
95-035280   720/.95496   0838636020
Architecture -- Himalaya Mountains Region. Vernacular architecture -- Himalaya Mountains Region.

NA1525.8.Y43 P69 1999
Powell, Robert, 1942-
Rethinking the skyscraper: the complete architecture of Ken Yeang/ Robert Powell. New York: Whitney Library of Design, 1999. 208 p.
99-062059   0823045536
Yeang, Ken, -- 1948- -- Criticism and interpretation. Skyscrapers -- Malaysia. Plants in architecture -- Malaysia.

NA1526.D39 1994
Dawson, Barry.
The traditional architecture of Indonesia/ Barry Dawson, John Gillow. New York: Thames and Hudson, 1994. 192 p.
94-060282   720/.9598   050034132X
Vernacular architecture -- Indonesia. Architecture -- Indonesia.

NA1540.L536 1984
Liang, Ssu-cheng, 1901-
A pictorial history of Chinese architecture: a study of the development of its structural system and the evolution of its types/ Liang Ssu-cheng; edited by Wilma Fairbank. Cambridge, Mass.: MIT Press, c1984. xxiv, 200 p.
83-025607   720/.951   0262121034
Architecture -- China.

NA1540.L57 1989
Liu, Laurence G.
Chinese architecture/ Laurence G. Liu. New York: Rizzoli, 1989. 297 p.
89-042686   720/.951   0847810828
Architecture -- China.

NA1543.5.J813 1998
Ju, Ching-hua, 1928-
Palace architecture/ Ru Jinghua, Peng Hualiang; [translated by Zang Erzhong ... et al.]. Wien; Springer-Verlag, c1998. 193 p.
98-010802   728.8/2/0951   3211829903
Palaces -- China. Architecture -- China -- Ming-Ching dynasties, 1368-1912.

NA1550.N4
New York.
The architecture of Japan, by Arthur Drexler. New York [1955] 286 p.
55-005987   720.952
Architecture -- Japan.

NA1550.O813
Ota, Hirotaro, 1912-
Traditional Japanese architecture and gardens. Edited by Ota Hirotaro. [Tokyo] Kokusai Bunka Shinkokai [1972] xv, 305 p.
73-165531   720/.952
Architecture -- Japan. Gardens, Japanese -- Japan. Gardens -- Japan.

NA1550.S49 1999
Shelton, Barrie, 1944-
Learning from the Japanese city: West meets East in urban design/ Barrie Shelton. London; E & FN Spon, 1999. xiii, 210 p.
98-048053   711/.4/0952   0419223509
Architecture -- Japan -- Themes, motives. Architecture and society -- Japan. Architecture and history -- Japan.

NA1553.K58
Kirby, John B.
From castle to teahouse; Japanese architecture of the Momoyama period. Tokyo, C. E. Tuttle Co. [1962] xv, 222 p.
62-009361   720.952
Architecture -- Japan -- History.

NA1554.5.S74 1987
Stewart, David B.
The making of a modern Japanese architecture: 1868 to the present/ David B. Stewart. Tokyo; Kodansha International, c1987. 304 p.
87-081685   720/.952/0904   0870118447
Architecture -- Japan -- 1868- Architecture -- Japan -- 19th century. Architecture -- Japan -- 20th century.

NA1555.E44 1991
Emerging Japanese architects of the 1990s/ edited by Jackie Kestenbaum. New York: Columbia University Press, c1991. 121 p.
90-042111   720/.952/09045
Architecture -- Japan -- 20th century. Architects -- Japan -- Psychology.

NA1557-1599 History — Architecture of special countries — Africa

NA1557.K9.I83 1960
Ishimoto, Yasuhiro, 1921-
Katsura: tradition and creation in Japanese architecture. Architecture in Japan/ Walter Gropius. Tradition and creation in Japanese architecture/ Kenzo Tange; photographs, Yasuhiro Ishimoto. New Haven: Yale University Press, 1960. vi, 36 p.
60-051016   720.952
Architecture -- Japan.

NA1559.A5.A4 1989
Ando, Tadao, 1941-
Tadao Ando: the Yale studio & current works/ introduction by Kenneth Frampton; essays by Tadao Ando, George T. Kunihiro, Peter Eisenman. New York: Rizzoli, 1989. 143 p.
88-043423   720/.92   084781033X
Ando, Tadao, -- 1941- -- Themes, motives. Architecture -- Japan -- 20th century -- Themes, motives. Architecture -- Study and teaching -- Connecticut -- New Haven.

NA1559.I79.A4 1998
Isozaki, Arata.
Arata Isozaki: four decades of architecture/ preface by Richard Koshalek; essay by David B. Stewart. New York: Universe Pub.; 1998. 235 p.
98-034095   720/.92   0789302306
Isozaki, Arata -- Exhibitions.

NA1559.M8.B64 1996
Bognar, Botond, 1944-
Togo Murano: master architect of Japan/ by Botond Bognar; with an introduction by Fumihiko Maki. New York: Rizzoli International Publications, c1996. 160 p.
95-046479   720/.92   084781887X
Murano, Togo, -- 1891- -- Criticism and interpretation. Architecture -- 20th century -- Japan.

NA1559.T33.B6
Boyd, Robin.
Kenzo Tange. New York, G. Braziller, 1962. 125 p.
62-016267   720.952
Tange, Kenzo, -- 1913- Architecture, Moderen -- 20th century.

NA1559.T35.A4 1999
Taniguchi, Yoshio, 1937-
The architecture of Yoshio Taniguchi/ Yoshio Taniguchi.
New York: Harry N. Abrams, 1999. 282 p.
98-074033   720/.92   0810919974
*Taniguchi, Yoshio, -- 1937- -- Catalogs. Architecture, Modern
-- 20th century -- Japan -- Catalogs.*

NA1580.E44 1997
Elleh, Nnamdi.
African architecture: evolution and transformation/
Nnamdi Elleh. New York: McGraw-Hill, c1997. xvii,
382 p.
96-013634   0070215065
*Ethnic architecture -- Africa. Vernacular architecture --
Africa.*

NA1590.K813
Kultermann, Udo.
New architecture in Africa. Translated from the German
by Ernst Flesch. New York, Universe Books 1963 180 p.
63-012537   720.96
Architecture -- Africa. Architecture, Modern -- 20th century.

NA1590.2.M44.W75 1991
Wright, Gwendolyn.
The politics of design in French colonial urbanism/
Gwendolyn Wright. Chicago: University of Chicago
Press, c1991. viii, 389 p.
90-045063   720/.1/03   0226908461
*Architecture, French -- Morocco. City planning -- Morocco.
Architecture, French -- Indochina. France -- Colonies --
Administration.*

NA1591.6.S82.S284 1995
Greenlaw, Jean-Pierre.
The coral buildings of Suakin: Islamic architecture,
planning, design and domestic arrangements in a red sea
port/ Jean-Pierre Greenlaw; foreword by Mansour Khalid.
London; Kegan Paul International; c1995. 132 p.
94-007372   720/.9625   0710304897
*Architecture, Turkish -- Sudan -- Sawakin. Architecture,
Islamic -- Sudan -- Sawakin. Architecture -- Sudan -- Sawakin.
Sawakin (Sudan) -- Buildings, structures, etc.*

NA1598.B68 1996
Bourdier, Jean-Paul.
Drawn from African dwellings/ Jean-Paul Bourdier and
Trinh T. Minh-ha. Bloomington, Ind.: Indiana University
Press, c1996. xiii, 308 p.
95-035891   728/.0966   0253330432
*Vernacular architecture -- Africa, West. Symbolism in
architecture -- Africa, West. Housing, Rural -- Africa, West.*

NA1599.L4.B4 1988
Belcher, Max.
A land and life remembered: Americo-Liberian folk
architecture/ photographs by Max Belcher; text by Svend
E. Holsoe and Bernard L. Herman; afterword by Rodger
P. Kingston. Athens: University of Georgia Press; c1988.
xii, 176 p.
88-020531   720/.9666/2074014482   0820310859
*Architecture -- Liberia -- Exhibitions. Vernacular architecture
-- Liberia -- Exhibitions. Architecture -- Southern States --
Influence -- Exhibitions. Liberia -- Civilization -- History -- 19th
century -- Exhibitions.*

NA1605 History —
Architecture of special countries —
Australasia. Pacific Area

NA1605.A5.A4 1982
Taylor, Jennifer, 1935-
John Andrews: architecture, a performing art/ Jennifer
Taylor & John Andrews. New York: Oxford University
Press, 1982. 176 p.
78-013466   720/.92/4   0195505573
Andrews, John, -- 1933-

NA1605.S4.A4 1992
Frampton, Kenneth.
Harry Seidler: four decades of architecture/ Kenneth
Frampton, Philip Drew. London; Thames and Hudson,
1992. 431 p.
92-080804   720/.92   0500978387
*Seidler, Harry, -- 1923- -- Catalogues raisonnes. Architecture,
Modern -- 20th century -- Catalogs.*

NA1995 Architecture as a profession

NA1995.S27 1983
Saint, Andrew.
The image of the architect/ Andrew Saint. New Haven:
Yale University Press, 1983. xi, 180 p.
82-048909   720/.68   0300030134
Architecture -- Vocational guidance. Architectural practice.

NA1996 Business management for architects

NA1996.C84 1991
Cuff, Dana, 1953-
Architecture: the story of practice/ Dana Cuff.
Cambridge, Mass.: MIT Press, c1991. xi, 306 p.
90-042960   720/.68   0262031752
*Architectural practice -- United States. Architects -- United
States -- Interviews. Architecture and society -- United States.*

NA1996.L37 1993
Larson, Magali Sarfatti.
Behind the postmodern facade: architectural change in late twentieth-century America/ Magali Sarfatti Larson. Berkeley: University of California Press, c1993. xviii, 319 p.
92-025694   720/.68   0520081358
Architectural practice -- United States. Architectural services marketing -- United States. Architecture -- United States -- Technological innovations.

NA1996.R33 1996
Reconstructing architecture: critical discourses and social practices/ Thomas A. Dutton and Lian Hurst Mann, editors. Minneapolis, Minn.: University of Minnesota Press, c1996. vii, 329 p.
96-022384   720/.1/03   0816628084
Architectural practice -- Decision making. Architecture and society -- History -- 20th century. Architecture, Postmodern -- Social aspects.

NA1996.W48 1990
Williamson, Roxanne, 1928-
American architects and the mechanics of fame/ Roxanne Kuter Williamson. Austin: University of Texas Press, 1991. 286 p.
90-035729   720/.973   0292751214
Architects -- Selection and appointment -- United States. Architects and patrons -- United States. Architectural services marketing -- United States.

NA1996.W64 1999
Woods, Mary N., 1950-
From craft to profession: the practice of architecture in nineteenth-century America/ Mary N. Woods. Berkeley: University of California Press, c1999. xvi, 265 p.
98-041510   720/.23/73   0520214943
Architectural practice -- United States -- History -- 19th century.

NA1997 Women architects

NA1997.A32 2000
Adams, Annmarie.
Designing women: gender and the architectural profession/ Annmarie Adams and Peta Tancred. Toronto: University of Toronto Press, c2000. xiii, 190 p.
00-709111   720/.82/0971   0802044174
Women architects -- Canada.

NA1997.A73 2001
The architect: women in contemporary architecture. New York: Watson-Guptill; 2001. 184 p.
00-110045   0823016528
Women architects -- Biography. Architects -- Biography. Architecture, Modern -- 20th century.

NA1997.A74 1989
Architecture: a place for women/ Ellen Perry Berkeley, editor, Matilda McQuaid, associate editor. Washington: Smithsonian Institution Press, c1989. xxxiii, 277 p.
88-029299   720/.88042   0874742315
Women architects -- United States -- Employment. Women architects -- United States -- Psychology.

NA1997.W65
Women in American architecture: a historic and contemporary perspective: a publication and exhibition organized by the Architectural League of New York through its Archive of Women in Architecture edited by Susana Torre. New York: Whitney Library of Design, 1977. 224 p.
76-054960   720/.973   0823074854
Women architects -- United States -- Addresses, essays, lectures.

NA2127 Study and teaching. Research — Special countries

NA2127.S66.M37 1999
Marty, Myron A.
Frank Lloyd Wright's Taliesin Fellowship/ Myron A. Marty, Shirley L. Marty. Kirksville, Mo.: Thomas Jefferson University Press, c1999. xxi, 312 p.
99-034910   720/.7/077576   0943549744
Wright, Frank Lloyd, -- 1867-1959 -- Friends and associates -- Interviews. Wright, Olgivanna Lloyd -- Friends and associates -- Interviews. Architecture -- Study and teaching -- Arizona -- Scottsdale. Architecture -- Study and teaching -- Wisconsin -- Spring Green. Architects -- United States -- Interviews.

NA2310 Study and teaching. Research — Special schools — Europe. By country and school, A-Z

NA2310.F8.E33 1982
The Beaux-arts and nineteenth-century French architecture/ edited by Robin Middleton. Cambridge, Mass.: MIT Press, 1982. 280 p.
81-082327   720/.7/1144361   0262131730
Architecture -- Study and teaching -- France. Architecture -- France. Architecture, Modern -- 19th century -- France.

NA2310.I8.A448 1991
Yegul, Fikret K., 1941-
Gentlemen of instinct and breeding: architecture at the American Academy in Rome, 1894-1940/ Fikret K. Yegul. New York: Oxford University Press, 1991. xii, 242 p.
90-032097   720/.071/145632   019506349X
Architecture -- Study and teaching -- Italy -- Rome. Art, American -- Italy -- Rome. Architectural rendering -- Italy -- Rome.

NA2335 Competitions — General and international

NA2335.H34 1988
Haan, Hilde de, 1949-
Architects in competition: international architectural competi[ti]ons of the last 200 years/ Hilde de Haan and Ids Haagsma; with essays by Dennis Sharp and Kenneth Frampton. London; Thames and Hudson, 1988. 219 p.
87-050250   720/.79   0500341036
Architecture -- Competitions.

**NA2440 Exhibitions. By place —
Local — United States.
By city and gallery or other place
of exhibition, A-Z**

NA2440.N47.M873 1971
Cooper Union for the Advancement of Science and Art.
Education of an architect: a point of view. An exhibition by the Cooper Union School of Art & Architecture at the Museum of Modern Art, New York City, November 1971. New York, [1971] 323 p.
74-184158   720/.71/17471
Architecture -- Exhibitions. Architecture -- Study and teaching -- New York (State) -- New York.

NA2500 General works —
Theory. Philosophy

NA2500.A42 1991
Agrest, Diana.
Architecture from without: theoretical framings for a critical practice/ Diana I. Agrest. Cambridge, Mass.: MIT Press, c1991. ix, 203 p.
90-035114   720/.1   0262011158
Symbolism in architecture.

NA2500.C45
Chang, Amos Ih Tiao.
The existence of intangible content in architectonic form based upon the practicality of Laotzu's philosophy, by Amos Ih Tiao Chang. Princeton [Princeton University Press] 1956. 72 p.
56-006543   720.1
Lao-tzu. Lao-tzu. -- Tao te ching. Architecture. Taoism.

NA2500.D75 1997
Dripps, R. D.
The first house: myth, paradigm, and the task of architecture/ R.D. Dripps. Cambridge, Mass.: MIT Press, c1997. xii, 154 p.
97-008889   720/.1   0262041634
Architecture -- Philosophy. Architecture and society.

NA2500.F73 1990
Frascari, Marco.
Monsters of architecture: anthropomorphism in architectural theory/ Marco Frascari. Savage, Md.: Rowman & Littlefield, c1991. xi, 140 p.
90-033555   720/.1   084767648X
Architecture -- Philosophy. Symbolism in architecture.

NA2500.H375 1997
Harries, Karsten.
The ethical function of architecture/ Karsten Harries. Cambridge, Mass.: MIT Press, c1997. xiii, 403 p.
96-008639   723/.1/04   0262082527
Architecture -- Philosophy. Architecture -- Moral and ethical aspects.

NA2500.K7513 1994
Kruft, Hanno-Walter.
A history of architectural theory: from Vitruvius to the present/ Hanno-Walter Kruft; translated by Ronald Taylor, Elsie Callander, and Antony Wood. London: Zwemmer; c1994. 706 p.
93-050746   720/.1   1568980019
Architecture -- Philosophy. Architecture -- Historiography.

NA2500.R68 1993
Roth, Leland M.
Understanding architecture: its elements, history, and meaning/ Leland M. Roth. New York, NY: Icon Editions, c1993. xxxi, 542 p.
88-045540   720/.1   0064384934
Architecture. Architecture -- History.

NA2500.S4 1924
Scott, Geoffrey, 1885-1929.
The architecture of humanism; a study in the history of taste. Garden City, N.Y., Doubleday, 1954. 197 p.
54-014934   720.1
Architecture. Aesthetics.

NA2500.S43
Scruton, Roger.
The aesthetics of architecture/ Roger Scruton. Princeton, N.J.: Princeton University Press, c1979. x, 302 p.
79-084026   720/.1   0691039488
Architecture -- Aesthetics.

NA2500.S47 1994
Shepheard, Paul.
What is architecture?: an essay on landscapes, buildings, and machines/ Paul Shepheard. Cambridge, Mass.: MIT Press, c1994. viii, 131 p.
93-030168   720   0262193418
Architecture.

NA2500.Z413
Zevi, Bruno, 1918-
Architecture as space; how to look at architecture. Edited by Joseph A. Barry; translated by Milton Gendel. New York, Horizon Press [1957] 288 p.
57-007362   720
Space (Architecture)

NA2515-2517 General works —
General treatises — Early works to 1800

NA2515.A32 1955
Alberti, Leon Battista, 1404-1472.
Ten books on architecture. Translated into Italian by Cosimo Bartoli and into English by James Leoni; edited by Joseph Rykwert. London, A. Tiranti, 1955.
55-012712   720
Architecture -- Early works to 1800.

NA2515.A3513 1988
Alberti, Leon Battista, 1404-1472.
On the art of building in ten books/ Leon Battista Alberti; translated by Joseph Rykwert, Neil Leach, and Robert Tavernor. Cambridge, Mass.: MIT Press, c1988. xxiii, 442 p.
87-026271   720   0262010992
Architecture -- Early works to 1800.

NA2515.P253 1997
Palladio, Andrea, 1508-1580.
The four books on architecture/ Andrea Palladio; translated by Robert Tavernor and Richard Schofield. Cambridge, Mass.: MIT Press, c1997. xxxv, 436 p.
96-036406   720   0262161621
Architecture -- Early works to 1800.

NA2515.V6135 1999
Vitruvius Pollio.
Vitruvius: ten books on architecture/ translation by Ingrid D. Rowland; commentary and illustrations by Thomas Noble Howe; with additional commentary by Ingrid D. Rowland and Michael J. Dewar. New York: Cambridge University Press, 1999. xvi, 333 p.
98-011716   720   0521553644
Architecture -- Early works to 1800.

NA2517.S5 1970
Serlio, Sebastiano, 1475-1554.
The book of architecture by Sebastiano Serlio, London, 1611. Introd. by A. E. Santaniello. New York, B. Blom, 1970. 1 v.
68-056509   720
Architecture -- Early works to 1800.

NA2520 General works —
General treatises — 1800-

NA2520.J4 1970
Jeanneret-Gris, Charles Edouard, 1887-1965.
Towards a new architecture, by Le Corbusier. Translated from the French by Frederick Etchells. -- New York: Praeger, [1970] 269 p.
76-092371   720
Architecture.

NA2520.V813 1959
Viollet-le-Duc, Eugene-Emmanuel, 1814-1879.
Discourses on architecture. Translated from the French by Benjamin Bucknall. New York, Grove Press [1959] 2 v.
59-006254
Architecture.

NA2520.W85
Wright, Frank Lloyd, 1867-1959.
Frank Lloyd Wright on architecture; selected writings 1894-1940, edited with an introduction by Frederick Gutheim. New York, Duell, Sloan and Pearce, 1941. xviii, 275 p.
41-011296   720.81
Wright, Frank Lloyd, -- 1867-1959. Architecture.

NA2540 General works —
General special

NA2540.O44
Olgyay, Victor, 1910-
Design with climate: bioclimatic approach to architectural regionalism. Some chapters based on cooperative research with Aladar Olgyay. Princeton, N.J., Princeton University Press, 1963. v, 190 p.
61-007423   729
Architecture and climate.

NA2540.5 General works —
Site planning

NA2540.5.L43 1993
Leatherbarrow, David.
The roots of architectural invention: site, enclosure, materials/ David Leatherbarrow. Cambridge [England]; Cambridge University Press, 1993. xviii, 242 p.
92-038508   720/.1   0521442656
Building sites -- Planning. Architectural design. Building materials.

NA2542.35 Architecture in relation
to special subjects —
Environmental aspects of architecture

NA2542.35.C77 1995
Crowe, Norman.
Nature and the idea of a man-made world: an investigation into the evolutionary roots of form and order in the built environment/ Norman Crowe. Cambridge, Mass.: MIT Press, c1995. xx, 270 p.
94-045594   720/.47   0262032228
Architecture -- Environmental aspects. Nature -- Effect of human beings on.

NA2542.35.D88 1993
Dwelling, seeing, and designing: toward a phenomenological ecology/ edite by David Seamon. Albany: State University of New York Press, c1993. xviii, 363 p.
91-043854   720/.1
Architecture -- Environmental aspects. Phenomenology.

NA2542.35.E575 1996
Environmental design: an introduction for architects and engineers/ edited by Randall Thomas. London; E & FN Spon, 1996. xiv, 225 p.
95-071097   0419199306
Architecture -- Environmental aspects. Environmental engineering. City planning.

NA2542.35.L36 1994
Lang, Jon T.
Urban design: the American experience/ Jon Lang. New York: Van Nostrand Reinhold, c1994. xiii, 509 p.
93-015893   720/.47   0442013604
Architecture -- Environmental aspects -- United States. Architecture and society -- United States. City planning -- United States.

NA2542.35.S63 1997
Slessor, Catherine.
Eco-tech: sustainable architecture and high technology/ Catherine Slessor; photographs by John Linden. New York: Thames and Hudson, 1997. 192 p.
97-060233   0500341575
Architecture -- Environmental aspects. Architecture -- Technological innovations. Architecture, Modern -- 20th century.

NA2542.36 Architecture in relation to special subjects — Sustainable architecture

NA2542.36.H34 2001
Hagan, Susannah.
Taking shape: a new contract between architecture and nature/ Susannah Hagan. Oxford; Architectural Press, 2001.
2001-022073   720/.47   0750649488
Sustainable architecture. Architecture -- Aesthetics. Architecture and society.

NA2542.4 Architecture in relation to special subjects — Human factors and architecture

NA2542.4.A68 1989
Architects' people/ edited by Russell Ellis and Dana Cuff. New York: Oxford University Press, 1989. xix, 291 p.
88-025409   720/.1/03   0195054954
Architecture -- Human factors. Architecture and society.

NA2542.4.K38 1994
Katz, Peter, 1954-
The new urbanism: toward an architecture of community/ Peter Katz; afterword by Vincent Scully; essays by Todd Bressi ... [et al.]. New York: McGraw-Hill, c1994. xlii, 245 p.
92-047474   720/.1/03   0070338892
Architecture -- Human factors -- United States. Architects and community -- United States. Architecture -- Human factors -- Canada.

NA2543 Architecture in relation to special subjects — Architecture in relation to other subjects, A-Z

NA2543.H55.C67 1991
Constancy and change in architecture/ edited by Malcolm Quantrill and Bruce Webb. College Station: Texas A&M University Press, c1991. xviii, 149 p.
90-023669   720/.1   0890964726
Architecture and history. Architecture and society.

NA2543.S6.B76
Buildings and society: essays on the social development of the built environment/ edited by Anthony D. King. London; Routledge & Kegan Paul, 1980. ix, 318 p.
80-040938   720/.1/03   0710006160
Architecture and society -- Addresses, essays, lectures. Architecture -- Environmental aspects -- Addresses, essays, lectures.

NA2543.S6.H48 1999
Herzog, Lawrence A.
From Aztec to high tech: architecture and landscape across the Mexico-United States border/ Lawrence A. Herzog. Baltimore, Md.: Johns Hopkins University Press, 1999. xiv, 241 p.
98-030340   720/.972/1   0801860091
Architecture and society -- Mexico, North. Architecture -- Mexico, North -- Influence. Architecture and society -- Southwest, New. Mexico, North -- Relations -- Southwest, New. Southwest, New -- Relations -- Mexico, North.

NA2543.S6.K87 1991
Kurokawa, Kisho, 1934-
Intercultural architecture: the philosophy of symbiosis/ Kisho Kurokawa. Washington, D.C.: American Institute of Architects Press, c1991. 208 p.
92-127562   720/.1/0309045   1558350357
Architecture and society -- History -- 20th century. Symbiosis (Psychology)

NA2543.S6.S9
Sullivan, Louis H., 1856-1924.
The testament of stone; themes of idealism and indignation from the writings of Louis Sullivan. Edited, with an introd., by Maurice English. [Evanston, Ill.] Northwestern University Press, 1963. xxvii, 227 p.
63-015297   720.1
Architecture and society.

NA2543.S6.W525 1999
Willis, Daniel, 1957-
The emerald city and other essays on the architectural imagination/ Daniel Willis. New York: Princeton Architectural Press, 1999. xvi, 301 p.
98-048641   720/.1   1568981740
Architecture and society. Architecture -- Philosophy.

NA2543.W65.B48 1995
Betsky, Aaron.
Building sex: men, women, architecture, and the construction of sexuality/ Aaron Betsky. New York: William Morrow, c1995. xix, 236 p.
94-034019   720/.82   0688131670
Architecture and women. Architecture and society.

NA2543.W65.W45 1992
Weisman, Leslie.
Discrimination by design: a feminist critique of the man-made environment/ Leslie Kanes Weisman. Urbana: University of Illinois Press, c1992. x, 190 p.
91-016024   720/.82   0252018494
Architecture and women -- United States.

NA2550 Works for general readers

NA2550.R313 1962
Rasmussen, Steen Eiler, 1898-
Experiencing architecture. [Translation from Danish by Eve Wendt. Cambridge [Mass.] M.I.T. Press, Massachusetts Institute of Technology, 1962. 245 p.
62-021637 720
Architecture.

NA2550.R7
Ruskin, John, 1819-1900.
The poetry of architecture: or, The architecture of the nations of Europe considered in its association with natural scenery and national character. With illustrations by the author. Sunnyside, G. Allen, 1893. xii, 261 p.
11-028000 720/.94
Architecture.

NA2560 Addresses, essays, lectures — Collections

NA2560.L413 1981
Le Corbusier, 1887-1965.
The ideas of Le Corbusier on architecture and urban planning/ texts edited and presented by Jacques Guiton; translation by Margaret Guiton. New York: G. Braziller, 1981. 127 p.
80-070993 720 0807610046
Architecture. City planning.

NA2563 Addresses, essays, lectures — Single papers

NA2563.S8 1998
Summerson, John Newenham, 1904-
Heavenly mansions and other essays on architecture/ John Summerson; [with a foreword by Kent Bloomer]. New York: Norton, c1998. xviii, 253 p.
98-038745 720 0393318575
Architecture.

NA2599.5 Architectural criticism — General works

NA2599.5.B6613 1979b
Bonta, Juan Pablo.
Architecture and its interpretation: a study of expressive systems in architecture/ Juan Pablo Bonta. New York: Rizzoli, 1979. 271 p.
79-064574 720/.01 084780237X
Architectural criticism.

NA2599.5.S38 1995
Schwarzer, Mitchell.
German architectural theory and the search for modern identity/ Mitchell Schwarzer. Cambridge; Cambridge University Press, 1995. xiv, 364 p.
94-046427 720/.1 0521481503
Architectural criticism -- Austria -- History -- 19th century. Architects -- Austria -- Psychology. Architectural criticism -- Germany -- History -- 19th century.

NA2700 Architectural drawing — General works — 1801-

NA2700.L26 1991
Lacy, Bill.
100 contemporary architects: drawings & sketches/ selected by Bill Lacy. New York: H.N. Abrams, 1991. 272 p.
91-010155 720/.22/222 0810936615
Architectural drawing -- 20th century -- Themes, motives.

NA2700.M38 1983
Masterpieces of architectural drawing/ edited by Helen Powell and David Leatherbarrow. New York: Abbeville Press, 1983, c1982. 192 p.
82-022643 720/.22/2 0896593266
Architectural drawing.

NA2700.R52 1994
Robbins, Edward, 1944-
Why architects draw/ Edward Robbins; interviews with Edward Cullinan ... [et al.]. Cambridge, Mass.: MIT Press, c1994. 315 p.
93-039911 720/.28/4 0262181576
Architectural drawing. Architectural design. Architects -- Interviews.

NA2706 Architectural drawing — By region or country, A-Z

NA2706.A9.W47 1989
Whyte, Iain Boyd, 1947-
Three architects from the master class of Otto Wagner: Emil Hoppe, Marcel Kammerer, Otto Schonthal/ Iain Boyd Whyte. Cambridge, Mass.: MIT Press, c1989. 240 p.
88-063733 720/.9436/1309041 0262231425
Wagner, Otto, -- 1841-1918 -- Influence. Hoppe, Emil, -- d. 1957 -- Criticism and interpretation. Kammerer, Marcel, -- d. 1969 -- Criticism and interpretation. Architectural studios -- Austria -- Vienna. Art nouveau (Architecture) -- Austria -- Vienna. Architectural drawing -- 19th century -- Austria -- Vienna.

NA2706.S6.A73 1990
Architectural drawings of the Russian avant-garde/ essay by Catherine Cooke. New York: Museum of Modern Art: c1990. 143 p.
90-061320 720/.22/247090410747471 0870705563
Constructivism (Architecture) -- Soviet Union -- Exhibitions. Avant-garde (Aesthetics) -- Soviet Union -- History -- 20th century -- Exhibitions. Architectural drawing -- Russia (Federation) -- Moscow -- Exhibitions.

NA2707 Architectural drawing — Special artists, A-Z

NA2707.G37.A4 1951
Garnier, Tony, 1869-1948.
Tony Garnier, 1869-1948. [France]: Comite des amis de Tony Garnier, [1951]
85-223218   720/.22/2
Garnier, Tony, -- 1869-1948.   Architectural drawing -- 20th century -- France.

NA2707.L37.A4 1994
Latrobe, Benjamin Henry, 1764-1820.
The architectural drawings of Benjamin Henry Latrobe/ Jeffrey A. Cohen and Charles E. Brownell. New Haven: Published for the Maryland Historical Society and the American Philosophical Society by Yale University Press, 1994. 2 v.
94-003121   720/.22/22   0300061005
Latrobe, Benjamin Henry, -- 1764-1820 -- Catalogs. Architectural drawing -- 18th century -- United States -- Catalogs. Architectural drawing -- 19th century -- United States -- Catalogs. Architectural drawing -- 18th century -- England -- Catalogs.

NA2707.S28.M48 1995
Meyer, Esther da Costa, 1947-
The work of Antonio Sant'Elia: retreat into the future/ Esther da Costa Meyer. New Haven: Yale University Press, c1995. x, 249 p.
94-039125   720/.92   0300043090
Sant'Elia, Antonio, -- 1888-1916 -- Criticism and interpretation. Futurism (Architecture)

NA2707.S3.A4 1988
Albertini, Bianca.
Carlo Scarpa: architecture in details/ Bianca Albertini, Sandro Bagnoli; foreword by Stefan Buzas; introduction by Maria Antonietta Crippa; English translation by Donald Mills. Cambridge, Mass.: MIT Press, 1988. ix, 226 p.
88-012713   720/.92   0262011077
Scarpa, Carlo, -- 1906-1978 -- Notebooks, sketchbooks, etc.

NA2707.S94.A4 2000
Twombly, Robert C.
Louis Sullivan: the poetry of architecture/ Robert Twombly, Narciso G. Menocal. New York: W.W. Norton, c2000. 439 p.
00-020746   720/.92   0393048233
Sullivan, Louis, -- 1856-1924 -- Catalogs. Sullivan, Louis, -- 1856-1924 -- Philosophy.

NA2707.W34.A4 1987
Wagner, Otto, 1841-1918.
Sketches, projects, and executed buildings/ Otto Wagner; with an introduction by Peter Haiko. New York: Rizzoli, 1987. 261 p.
87-045546   720/.22/2   084780853X
Wagner, Otto, -- 1841-1918.   Architectural drawing -- 19th century -- Austria. Architectural drawing -- 20th century -- Austria. Art nouveau (Architecture) -- Austria -- Vienna -- Designs and plans.

NA2707.W74.A4 1990
Pfeiffer, Bruce Brooks.
Frank Lloyd Wright drawings: masterworks from the Frank Lloyd Wright Archives/ by Bruce Brooks Pfeiffer. New York: Abrams, c1990. 303 p.
89-017820   720/.22/22   0810917734
Wright, Frank Lloyd, -- 1867-1959.   Architectural drawing -- United States.

NA2728 Data processing. Computer-aided design

NA2728.R34 1987
Radford, Antony.
CADD made easy: a comprehensive guide for architects and designers/ Antony Radford, Garry Stevens. New York: McGraw-Hill, c1987. x, 354 p.
86-018017   720/.28/5   0070510946
Architectural design -- Data processing. Architectural practice -- Data processing. Computer-aided design.

NA2750 Architectural design — General works

NA2750.A64 1991
Anthony, Kathryn H.
Design juries on trial: the renaissance of the design studio/ Kathryn H. Anthony. New York: Van Nostrand Reinhold, c1991. xviii, 257 p.
91-000723   729/.079   0442002351
Architectural design -- Evaluation. Architectural design -- Awards. Communication in architectural design.

NA2750.A65 1990
Antoniades, Anthony C.
Poetics of architecture: theory of design/ Anthony C. Antoniades. New York: Van Nostrand Reinhold, c1990. xiv, 303 p.
89-036617   720/.1   0442239904
Architectural design.

NA2750.B46 1996
Berlage, Hendrik Petrus, 1856-1934.
Hendrik Petrus Berlage: thoughts on style, 1886-1909/ introduction by Iain Boyd Whyte; translation by Iain Boyd Whyte and Wim de Wit. Santa Monica, CA: Getty Center for the History of Art and the Humanities, c1996. 331 p.
95-014641   720/.1   0892363339
Communication in architectural design. Modernism (Art) -- Influence. Symbolism in architecture.

NA2750.B864 1995
Burden, Ernest E., 1934-
Elements of architectural design: a visual resource/ Ernest Burden. New York: Van Nostrand Reinhold, c1995. viii, 278 p.
93-029677   721   0442013396
Architectural design.

NA2750.M58 1990
Mitchell, William J. 1944-
The logic of architecture: design, computation, and cognition/ William J. Mitchell. Cambridge, Mass.: MIT Press, c1990. x, 292 p.
88-027201   720/.1   0262132389
Architectural design. Computer-aided design. Visual perception.

NA2760 Architectural design — Composition. Proportion

NA2760.A74
Arnheim, Rudolf.
The dynamics of architectural form: based on the 1975 Mary Duke Biddle lectures at the Cooper Union/ Rudolf Arnheim. Berkeley: University of California Press, c1977. vi, 289 p.
76-019955   729   0520033051
Architecture -- Composition, proportion, etc. Architecture -- Psychological aspects. Visual perception.

NA2760.M365 1990
Mark, Robert.
Light, wind, and structure: the mystery of the master builders/ Robert Mark. New York: McGraw-Hill Pub. Co., c1990. xvii, 209 p.
89-034736   721   0070404038
Architecture -- Composition, proportion, etc. Structural engineering. Technological innovations.

NA2760.V46 1977
Venturi, Robert.
Complexity and contradiction in architecture/ Robert Venturi; with an introd. by Vincent Scully. New York: Museum of Modern Art; 1977. 132 p.
77-077289   720/.1   0870702815
Architecture -- Composition, proportion, etc.

NA2765 Architectural design — Composition. Proportion — Space

NA2765.M66
Moore, Charles Willard, 1925-
Dimensions: space, shape & scale in architecture/ Charles Moore, Gerald Allen. New York: Architectural Record Books, c1976. viii, 183 p.
76-028406   729   0070023360
Space (Architecture) Architecture -- Composition, proportion, etc. Visual perception.

NA2765.W39 1995
Weber, Ralf.
On the aesthetics of architecture: a psychological approach to the structure and the order of perceived architectural space/ Ralf Weber. Aldershot; Brookfield, USA: c1995. xiv, 279 p.
95-075555   720/.1   185628977X
Space (Architecture) -- Psychological aspects. Architecture -- Aesthetics.

NA2793 Architectural design — Remodeling buildings for other use (General)

NA2793.P69 1999
Powell, Ken, 1947-
Architecture reborn: converting old buildings for new uses/ Kenneth Powell. New York: Rizzoli, 1999. 256 p.
98-075136   720/.28/6   0847821811
Buildings -- Remodeling for other use. Architecture -- Conservation and restoration. Buildings -- Repair and reconstruction.

NA2800 Architectural acoustics

NA2800.A68
Architectural acoustics/ edited by Thomas D. Northwood. Stroudsburg, Pa.: Dowden, Hutchinson & Ross; c1977. xv, 428 p.
76-054182   729/.29   0879332573
Architectural acoustics -- Addresses, essays, lectures.

NA2800.B36 1993
Barron, Michael.
Auditorium acoustics and architectural design/ Michael Barron. London; E & FN Spon, 1993. xv, 443 p.
92-038096   729/.29/0941   0442316232
Architectural acoustics. Music-halls -- Great Britain. Music-halls.

NA2800.C713 1982
Cremer, Lothar, 1905-
Principles and applications of room acoustics/ Lothar Cremer and Helmut A. Muller; translated by Theodore J. Schultz. London; Applied Science; c1982. 2 v.
84-119658   729/.29   0853341133
Architectural acoustics.

NA2800.R36 1988
Rettinger, Michael, 1905-
Handbook of architectural acoustics and noise control: a manual for architects and engineers/ Michael Rettinger. Blue Ridge Summit, PA: TAB Professional and Reference Books, c1988. 247 p.
88-008558   729/.29   0830626867
Architectural acoustics. Noise control. Soundproofing.

NA2815 Orders of architecture — Works since 1800

NA2815.R95 1996
Rykwert, Joseph, 1926-
The dancing column: on order in architecture/ Joseph Rykwert. Cambridge, Mass.: MIT Press, c1996. xviii, 598 p.
95-035555   721/.36   0262181703
Architecture -- Orders. Columns, Doric. Columns, Ionic.

NA2840 Architectural details, motives, etc. — General and miscellaneous

NA2840.F67 1990
Ford, Edward R.
The details of modern architecture/ Edward R. Ford.
Cambridge, Mass.: MIT Press, c1990-c1996. 2 v.
89-031772   724/.5   026206121X
Architecture -- Details. Architecture, Modern -- 19th century.
Architecture, Modern -- 20th century.

NA2890 Architectural details, motives, etc. — Domes

NA2890.S6
Smith, E. Baldwin 1888-1956.
The dome, a study in the history of ideas.   Princeton,
Princeton University Press, 1950. ix, 164 p.
50-008444   721.46
Domes.

NA2940 Architectural details, motives, etc. — Walls — General works

NA2940.U58 2000
Unwin, Simon, 1952-
An architecture notebook: wall/ Simon Unwin. New
York: Routledge, 2000.
00-055337   721/.2   0415228735
Walls -- Psychological aspects. Space (Architecture)

NA3503-3511 Architectural decoration — Special countries

NA3503.S68
Southworth, Susan.
Ornamental ironwork: an illustrated guide to its design,
history & use in American architecture/ by Susan and
Michael Southworth; photos. by Charles C. Withers.
Boston: D. R. Godine, 1978. 202 p.
77-094111   739/.4773   0879232331
Architectural ironwork -- United States. Decoration and
ornament, Architectural -- United States.

NA3503.7.B32 1981
Badger, Daniel D.
Badger's Illustrated catalogue of cast-iron architecture/ by
Daniel D. Badger; with a new introduction by Margot
Gayle. New York: Dover Publications, c1981. xvii, 35 p.
81-068875   721/.0447141   0486242234
Cast-iron fronts (Architecture) -- United States -- Catalogs.
Architectural ironwork -- United States -- History -- 19th
century -- Catalogs.

NA3507.D37 1989
Darling, Sharon S.
Teco: art pottery of the Prairie School/ Sharon S. Darling
with a contribution by Richard Zakin. Erie, Pa.: Erie Art
Museum, c1989. 191 p.
89-084291   738.3/09773/22   0961662328
Terra-cotta -- Middle West. Decoration and ornament,
Architectural -- Middle West. Prairie school (Architecture) --
Middle West.

NA3511.N48.T86 1997
Tunick, Susan.
Terra-cotta skyline: New York's architectural ornament/
Susan Tunick; contemporary photographs by Peter
Mauss. New York: Princeton Architectural Press, 1997.
xv, 160 p.
96-052343   729/.5   1568981058
Architectural terra-cotta -- New York (State) -- New York.
Decoration and ornament, Architectural -- New York (State) --
New York. New York (N.Y.) -- Buildings, structures, etc.

NA3542 Architectural decoration — Special countries — Europe

NA3542.B4 1983
Beard, Geoffrey W.
Stucco and decorative plasterwork in Europe/ Geoffrey
Beard. New York: Harper & Row, c1983. 224 p.
82-049006   729/.5   0064303837
Stucco -- Europe. Plasterwork, Decorative -- Europe.

NA3576 Architectural decoration — Special countries — Asia. The Orient

NA3576.A1.A45 1991
Allen, Margaret Prosser, 1913-
Ornament in Indian architecture/ Margaret Prosser Allen.
Newark: University of Delaware Press; [1991] 504 p.
89-040766   720/.954   0874133998
Decoration and ornament, Architectural -- India -- Themes,
motives.

NA3750 Architectural decoration — Mosaic. Tesselated work. Terrazzo work — General works

NA3750.R6713 1970
Rossi, Ferdinando.
Mosaics, a survey of their history and techniques [by]
Ferdinando Rossi. [Translated from the Italian by David
Ross] New York, Praeger [1970] 200 p.
72-089606   729/.7
Mosaics. Marquetry. Carving (Art industries)

NA4140 Special classes of buildings — Classed by material — Glass

NA4140.G57 1993
Glass in building: a guide to modern architectural glass performance: Pilkington/ David Button ... [et al.]; editors, David Button and Brian Pye. Oxford, England; Butterworth Architecture, 1993. xi, 372 p.
92-017060   721/.04496   0750605901
Glass construction.

NA4160 Special classes of buildings — Classed by form — Other special forms (not A-Z)

NA4160.D73 1979
Drew, Philip, 1943-
Tensile architecture/ Philip Drew. Boulder, Colo.: Westview Press, 1979. xxii, 237 p.
79-007357   720   0891585508
Tensile architecture.

NA4195-4473 Special classes of buildings — Classed by use — Public buildings — National, state, municipal, etc. Government buildings

NA4195.V35 1992
Vale, Lawrence J., 1959-
Architecture, power, and national identity/ Lawrence J. Vale. New Haven: Yale University Press, c1992. x, 338 p.
91-024557   725/.11   0300049587
Capitols.

NA4205.C7
Craig, Lois A.
The Federal presence: architecture, politics, and symbols in United States government building/ Lois Craig and the staff of the Federal Architecture Project. Cambridge, Mass.: MIT Press, c1978. xv, 580 p.
78-015366   725/.1/0973   0262030578
Public buildings -- United States. Architecture and state -- United States.

NA4287.L6.P67 1995
Port, M. H.
Imperial London: civil government building in London 1850-1915/ M.H. Port. New Haven: Published for the Paul Mellon Centre for Studies in British Art by Yale University Press, 1995. 344 p.
94-010254   725/.1/0942109034   0300059779
Public buildings -- England -- London. Public architecture -- England -- London. Eclecticism in architecture -- England -- London. London (England) -- Buildings, structures, etc.

NA4431.A47 1984
Lebovich, William L.
America's city halls/ William L. Lebovich; Historic American Buildings Survey. Washington, D.C.: Preservation Press, c1984. 223 p.
83-021310   725/.13/0973   0891331158
City halls -- United States. Historic buildings -- United States.

NA4473.C48
Lounsbury, Carl.
From statehouse to courthouse: an architectural history of South Carolina's colonial capitol and Charleston County courthouse/ Carl R. Lounsbury. Columbia, S.C.: University of South Carolina Press, c2001. x, 113 p.
00-010292   725/.15/09757915   1570033781
Architecture -- Conservation and restoration -- South Carolina -- Charleston. Architecture, Colonial -- South Carolina -- Charleston. Charleston (S.C.) -- Buildings, structures, etc.

NA4600-6046 Special classes of buildings — Classed by use — Public buildings — Religious buildings. Religious architecture

NA4600.B37 1996
Barrie, Thomas.
Spiritual path, sacred place: myth, ritual, and meaning in architecture/ Thomas Barrie. Boston: Shambhala, 1996. x, 284 p.
95-035552   726/.5   1570620059
Church architecture.

NA4670.B55 1989
Bloom, Jonathan
Minaret, symbol of Islam/ Jonathan Bloom. Oxford: Published by Oxford University Press for the Board of the Faculty of Oriental Studies, University of Oxford, c1989. 216 p.
88-155903   726/.2   0197280137
Minarets. Islamic art and symbolism.

NA4670.M67 1994
The mosque: history, architectural development & regional diversity/ edited by Martin Frishman and Hasan-Uddin Khan; texts by Mohammad Al-Asad ...[et al.] New York: Thames and Hudson, c1994. 288 p.
94-060347   726/.2   0500341338
Mosques. Architecture, Islamic.

NA4670.P47 1994
Pereira, Jose, 1931-
Islamic sacred architecture: a stylistic history/ Jose Pereira. New Delhi: Books & Books, 1994. ix, 379 p.
94-902212   8185016372
Architecture, Islamic -- History. Mosques. Mausoleums.

NA4817.K7 1986
Krautheimer, Richard, 1897-
Early Christian and Byzantine architecture/ Richard Krautheimer. Harmondsworth, Middlesex, England; Penguin, 1986. 556 p.
90-146104   726   0140561684
Architecture, Early Christian. Architecture, Byzantine. Church architecture -- History.

NA4817.W55 1990
White, L. Michael.
Building God's house in the Roman world: architectural adaptation among pagans, Jews, and Christians/ L. Michael White. Baltimore, Md.: Johns Hopkins University Press, c1990. xv, 211 p.
89-032588   726/.5/093709015   0801839068
Architecture, Early Christian. Basilicas. Temples, Roman.

NA4830.G5313 1983
Gimpel, Jean.
The cathedral builders/ by Jean Gimpel; translated by Teresa Waugh. New York: Grove Press, 1983. 127 p.
82-048042   726/.6/094   039452893X
Cathedrals. Architecture, Medieval. Christian art and symbolism -- Medieval, 500-1500.

NA4830.I2713 1998
Icher, Francois.
Building the great cathedrals/ Francois Icher; translated from the French by Anthony Zielonka. New York: Harry N. Abrams, c1998. 200 p.
98-025867   726.6/094/0902   0810940175
Cathedrals -- History.

NA4830.S5 1962
Simson, Otto Georg von, 1912-
The Gothic cathedral; origins of Gothic architecture and the medieval concept of order.   New York] Pantheon Books [1962] xxiii, 278 p.
63-002039   726.6
Architecture, Gothic. Cathedrals.

NA5205.W55 1997
Williams, Peter W.
Houses of God: region, religion, and architecture in the United States/ Peter W. Williams. Urbana: University of Illinois Press, c1997. xv, 321 p.
96-025358   726/.5/0973   0252019067
Church architecture -- United States. Liturgy and architecture -- United States. Synagogue architecture -- United States.

NA5210.I83 1999
Ivey, Paul Eli,
Prayers in stone: Christian Science architecture in the United   States, 1894-1930/ Paul Eli Ivey. Urbana: University of Illinois Press, c1999. xvii, 227 p.
98-025358   726.5/895 21   0252024451
Christian Science church buildings -- United States. Architecture -- United States -- 19th century. Architecture -- United States -- 20th century.

NA5230.N6.T74 1993
Treib, Marc.
Sanctuaries of Spanish New Mexico/ Marc Treib; drawings by Dorothee Imbert; foreword by J.B. Jackson. Berkeley: University of California Press, c1993. xvi, 352 p.
93-007058   726/.5/09789   0520064208
Church architecture -- New Mexico. Architecture, Spanish colonial -- New Mexico.

NA5235.O258.S58 1996
Siry, Joseph, 1956-
Unity Temple: Frank Lloyd Wright and architecture for liberal religion/ Joseph M. Siry. Cambridge [England]; Cambridge University Press, 1996. xvi, 365 p.
95-020194   726/.5/092   0521495423
Wright, Frank Lloyd, -- 1867-1959 -- Criticism and interpretation.   Oak Park (Ill.) -- Buildings, structures, etc.

NA5453.C35 1998
Calkins, Robert G.
Medieval architecture in Western Europe: from A.D. 300 to 1500/ Robert G. Calkins. New York: Oxford University Press, 1998. x, 342 p.
97-008135   726.5/09/02   0195112415
Church architecture -- Europe, Western. Architecture, Medieval -- Europe, Western.

NA5453.W55 1990
Wilson, Christopher, 1948-
The Gothic cathedral: the architecture of the great church, 1130-1530, with 220 illustrations/ Christopher Wilson. New York, N.Y. (500 5th Ave., New York): Thames and Hudson, 1990. 304 p.
89-050544   726/.6/0940902
Cathedrals -- Europe. Architecture, Gothic -- Europe. Architecture, Medieval -- Europe.

NA5461.B3 1960
Batsford, Harry.
The cathedrals of England [by] Harry Batsford [and] Charles Fry. London, Batsford [1960] 224 p.
61-000680   726.60942
Cathedrals -- England. Church architecture -- England.

NA5461.P48 1985
Pevsner, Nikolaus, 1902-
The cathedrals of England/ by Nikolaus Pevsner and Priscilla Metcalf, with contributions by various hands. Harmondsworth, Middlesex, England; Viking, 1985. 2 v.
84-051886   726/.6/0942   0670801259
Cathedrals -- England. Church decoration and ornament -- England.

NA5463.F4 1984
Fergusson, Peter, 1934-
Architecture of solitude: Cistercian abbeys in twelfth-century England/ Peter Fergusson. Princeton, N.J.: Princeton University Press, c1984. xxv, 188 p.
83-043072   726/.7/0942   0691040249
Architecture, Medieval -- England. Cistercian architecture -- England. Abbeys -- England.

NA5543.H8 1961
Hurlimann, Martin, 1897-
French cathedrals. [Text by] Jean Bony. 199 photos. by Martin Hurlimann. Descriptive notes by Peter Meyer New York, Viking Press [1961] 311 p.
61-008827
Architecture, Gothic Cathedrals -- France

NA5544.E8
Evans, Joan, 1893-
Monastic architecture in France, from the Renaissance to the Revolution. Cambridge (Eng.) University Press, 1964. xiii, 186 p.
64-002430   726.70944
Monasteries -- France. Architecture -- France -- History

NA5550.N7.T4
Temko, Allan.
Notre-Dame of Paris. New York, Viking Press, 1955. viii, 341 p.
55-009643   726.6 726.5*
Notre-Dame de Paris (Cathedral)

NA5551.C5.B8613 1996
Burckhardt, Titus.
Chartres and the birth of the cathedral/ by Titus Burckhardt; translated from the German by William Stoddart; foreword by Keith Critchlow. Bloomington, Ind.: World Wisdom Books, c1996. 135 p.
95-032639   726/.6/094451   0941532216
Architecture, Gothic -- France -- Chartres. Chartres (France) -- Buildings, structures, etc.

NA5563.B3 1956
Baum, Julius, 1882-
German cathedrals. With an introduction by Julius Baum. Photographs by Helga Schmidt-Glassner. New York, Vanguard Press [1956] 63 p.
57-002247   726.5
Cathedrals -- Germany. Church architecture -- Germany.

NA5573.H37 1983
Harries, Karsten.
The Bavarian rococo church: between faith and aestheticism/ Karsten Harries. New Haven [Conn.]: Yale University Press, c1983. xv, 282 p.
82-011168   726/.5/09433   0300027206
Church architecture -- Germany -- Bavaria. Architecture, Rococo -- Germany -- Bavaria.

NA5620.O7.C66 1980
Connors, Joseph
Borromini and the Roman oratory: style and society/ Joseph Connors. New York: Architectural History Foundation; c1980. xiv, 375 p.
80-016111   726/.4   0262030713
Borromini, Francesco, -- 1599-1667. Architecture, Baroque -- Italy -- Rome (City) Oratorians.

NA5621.F7
King, Ross.
Brunelleschi's dome: the story of the great cathedral in Florence/ Ross King. New York: Walker & Co., 2000. 194 p.
00-043316   726.6/0945/51   0802713661
Brunelleschi, Filippo, -- 1377-1446. Domes -- Italy -- Florence -- Design and construction. Florence (Italy) -- Buildings, structures, etc.

NA5811.G7.R6
Rosenthal, Earl E.
The Cathedral of Granada; a study in the Spanish Renaissance. Princeton, N.J., Princeton University Press, 1961. xiii, 235 p.
61-006908   726.6094682
Catedral de Granada.

NA5870.A9.K33
Kahler, Heinz.
Hagia Sophia. With a chapter on the mosaics by Cyril Mango. Translated by Ellyn Childs. New York, Praeger [1967] 74 p.
67-029605   726/.5/094961
Mosaics -- Turkey -- Istanbul.

NA5870.A9.M28 1988
Mainstone, R. J. 1923-
Hagia Sophia: architecture, structure, and liturgy of Justinian's great church/ Rowland J. Mainstone. New York, N.Y.: Thames and Hudson, 1988. 288 p.
86-050969   726/.6/09563   0500340986
Architecture, Byzantine -- Turkey -- Istanbul. Church architecture -- Turkey -- Istanbul. Liturgy and architecture -- Turkey -- Istanbul. Istanbul (Turkey) -- Buildings, structures, etc.

NA5870.I7.M3
Mathews, Thomas F.
The early churches of Constantinople: architecture and liturgy [by] Thomas F. Mathews. University Park, Pennsylvania State University Press [1971] xviii, 194 p.
78-111972   726/.5/094961   0271001089
Architecture, Byzantine -- Turkey -- Istanbul. Church architecture -- Istanbul. Liturgy and architecture -- Turkey -- Istanbul. Istanbul (Turkey) -- Buildings, structures, etc.

NA5991.G6 1988
Golombek, Lisa.
The Timurid architecture of Iran and Turan/ Lisa Golombek and Donald Wilber; with contributions by Terry Allen ... [et al.]. Princeton, N.J.: Princeton University Press, [c1988-   ] v. 1
87-002305   720/.955   0691035873
Architecture, Timurid -- Asia, Central. Architecture, Islamic -- Asia, Central. Architecture -- Asia, Central. Asia, Central -- Antiquities. Iran -- Antiquities.

NA5997.5.I84.G73 1990
Grabar, Oleg.
The great mosque of Isfahan/ Oleg Grabar. New York: New York University Press, 1990. x, 141 p.
89-003213   726/.2/095595   0814730272
Architecture, Islamic -- Iran -- Isfahan. Isfahan (Iran) -- Buildings, structures, etc.

NA6001.E53 1983
Encyclopaedia of Indian temple architecture/ edited by Michael W. Meister; coordinated by M.A. Dhaky. New Delhi: American Institute of Indian Studies; 1983-1996 v. 1
82-050173   726/.14/0954   0195615379
Temples -- India. Architecture -- Details.

NA6001.L613
Louis-Frederic.
The art of India; temples and sculpture. Introd. by Jean Naudou. [Translated from the French by Eva M. Hooykaas and A. H. Christie] New York, H. N. Abrams [1960] 464 p.
59-012873   726.10954
Temples -- India. Sculpture -- India.

NA6002.K72 1976
Kramrisch, Stella, 1898-
The Hindu temple/ by Stella Kramrisch; photographs by Raymond Burnier. Delhi: Motilal Banarsidass, 1976. 2 v.
77-911201   726/.1/45
Temples, Hindu.

NA6002.S8313 1998
Stierlin, Henri.
Hindu India: from Khajuraho to the temple city of Madurai/ Henri Stierlin; photos, Anne and Henri Stierlin [; English translation, Chris Miller]. Koln; Taschen, c1998. 237 p.
00-500527   726/.145/0954   3822876496
Temples, Hindu -- India. Temples, Jaina -- India. Architecture, Hindu -- India.

NA6002.W5 1982
Williams, Joanna Gottfried, 1939-
The art of Gupta India: empire and province/ Joanna Gottfried Williams. Princeton, N.J.: Princeton University Press, c1982. xxvi, 209 p.
81-013783   722/.44   0691039887
Architecture, Gupta. Temples, Hindu. Sculpture, Gupta.

NA6008.A33.R66 1989
Romance of the Taj Mahal/ Pratapaditya Pal ... [et al.]. London: Thames and Hudson; c1989. 256 p.
89-050548   726/.8/09542   0500235562
Shahjahan, -- Emperor of India, -- ca. 1592-1666 -- Art patronage -- Exhibitions. Taj Mahal (Agra, India) -- Exhibitions. Art, Mogul -- Exhibitions. Art, Islamic -- India -- Exhibitions.

NA6046.L5.S74 1997
Steinhardt, Nancy Shatzman.
Liao architecture/ Nancy Shatzman Steinhardt. Honolulu: University of Hawaii Press, c1997. xv, 497 p.
97-003096   726/.7843/095182   0824818431
Monasteries, Buddhist -- China -- Liao River Region. Building, Wooden -- China -- Liao River Region. Sepulchral monuments -- China -- Liao River Region.

NA6120-6165 Special classes of buildings — Classed by use — Public buildings — Cemetery architecture

NA6120.C65 1991
Colvin, Howard Montagu.
Architecture and the after-life/ Howard Colvin. New Haven: Yale University Press, 1991. xi, 418 p.
91-006768   726/.8/094   0300050984
Mausoleums. Martyria. Sepulchral monuments.

NA6139.F4 1990
Fedak, Janos, 1946-
Monumental tombs of the Hellenistic age: a study of selected tombs from the pre-classical to the early imperial era/ Janos Fedak. Toronto; University of Toronto Press, c1990. xii, 498 p.
91-157623   726/.8/0938   080202694X
Tombs -- Mediterranean Region. Architecture, Hellenistic -- Mediterranean Region. Architecture -- Mediterranean Region.

NA6165.D75 1993
Driskel, Michael Paul.
As befits a legend: building a tomb for Napoleon, 1840-1861/ Michael Paul Driskel. Kent, Ohio: Kent State University Press, c1993. xviii, 251 p.
93-012099   726/.8/0944361   0873384849
Napoleon -- I, -- Emperor of the French, -- 1769-1821 -- Tomb. Visconti, Louis, -- 1791-1853 -- Criticism and interpretation. Sepulchral monuments -- France -- Public opinion. Public opinion -- France. Art and state -- France -- History -- 19th century. Paris (France) -- Buildings, structures, etc.

NA6212-6233 Special classes of buildings — Classed by use — Public buildings — Commercial buildings

NA6212.K78 1998
Kruty, Paul Samuel.
Frank Lloyd Wright and Midway Gardens/ Paul Kruty. Urbana: University of Illinois Press, c1998. xx, 262 p.
97-004830   720/.92   0252023668
Wright, Frank Lloyd, -- 1867-1959 -- Criticism and interpretation. Commercial buildings -- Illinois -- Chicago -- History -- 19th century. Lost architecture -- Illinois -- Chicago. Chicago (Ill.) -- Buildings, structures, etc.

NA6218.G4313 1983
Geist, Johann Friedrich, 1936-
Arcades, the history of a building type/ Johann Friedrich Geist. Cambridge, Mass.: MIT Press, c1983. viii, 596 p.
82-010014   725/.21   0262070820
Arcades. Architecture, Modern -- 19th century.

NA6230.H89 1984
Huxtable, Ada Louise.
The tall building artistically reconsidered: the search for a skyscraper style/ Ada Louise Huxtable. New York: Pantheon Books, c1984. 128 p.
84-042664   725/.2   0394537734
Skyscrapers.

NA6230.M513 1995
Mierop, Caroline.
Skyscrapers: higher and higher/ Caroline Mierop; preface, Paul Goldberger; in collaboration with Georges Binder and with the participation of the Council on Tall Buildings and Urban Habitat; [translation, John Hellon]. Paris: NORMA, c1995. 222 p.
     2909283208
Architecture, Modern -- 20th century. Skyscrapers. Architecture, Modern -- 19th century.

NA6232.L36 1996
Landau, Sarah Bradford, 1935-
Rise of the New York skyscraper, 1865-1913/ Sarah Bradford Landau & Carl W. Condit. New Haven: Yale University Press, 1996. xvi, 478 p.
95-034061   720/.483/097471   0300064446
Skyscrapers -- New York (State) -- New York -- History. New York (N.Y.) -- Buildings, structures, etc.

NA6232.S5 1990
The Sky's the limit: a century of Chicago skyscrapers/ edited by Pauline A. Saliga; introduction by John Zukowsky; contributions by Jane H. Clarke, Pauline A. Saliga, and John Zukowsky. New York: Rizzoli, 1990. 304 p.
89-043565   720/.483/0977311   0847811794
Skyscrapers -- Illinois -- Chicago. Architecture, Modern -- 19th century -- Illinois -- Chicago. Architecture, Modern -- 20th century -- Illinois -- Chicago. Chicago (Ill.) -- Buildings, structures, etc.

NA6233.B3.P7
Wright, Frank Lloyd, 1867-1959.
The story of the Tower: the tree that escaped the crowded forest/ Frank Lloyd Wright. New York: Horizon Press, c1956. 130 p.
56-007826   725.232
Wright, Frank Lloyd, -- 1867-1959.   Bartlesville (Okla.) -- Buildings, structures, etc.

NA6233.C4.C387 1988
Siry, Joseph, 1956-
Carson Pirie Scott: Louis Sullivan and the Chicago department store/ Joseph Siry. Chicago: University of Chicago Press, 1988. viii, 290 p.
87-034003   725/.21/0924   0226761363
Sullivan, Louis H., -- 1856-1924 -- Criticism and interpretation. Architecture -- Illinois -- Chicago. Architecture, Modern -- 20th century -- Illinois -- Chicago. Skyscrapers -- Illinois -- Chicago. Chicago (Ill.) -- Buildings, structures, etc.

NA6233.C4.C466 2001
Solomonson, Katherine, 1956-
The Chicago Tribune Tower competition: skyscraper design and cultural change in the 1920s/ Katherine Solomonson. New York: Cambridge University Press, c2001. xiii, 370 p.
00-040356   725/.23/0977311   0521590566
Skyscrapers -- Illinois -- Chicago -- Designs and plans.

NA6233.N5.W673 1999
Darton, Eric.
Divided we stand: a biography of New York's World Trade Center/ Eric Darton. New York: Basic Books, c1999. x, 241 p.
99-032069   725/.23/097471   0465017010
Skyscrapers -- New York (State) -- New York. City planning -- New York (State) -- New York. New York (N.Y.) -- Buildings, structures, etc.

NA6233.N5.W674 1999
Gillespie, Angus K., 1942-
Twin towers: the life of New York City's World Trade Center/ Angus Kress Gillespie. New Brunswick, N.J.: Rutgers University Press, c1999. xvi, 263 p.
99-015068   725/.23/097471   0813527422
Skyscrapers -- New York (State) -- New York. City planning -- New York (State) -- New York. New York (N.Y.) -- Buildings, structures, etc.

NA6313 Special classes of buildings — Classed by use — Public buildings — Transportation and storage buildings

NA6313.N4.B45 2000
Belle, John.
Grand Central: gateway to a million lives/ John Belle and Maxine R. Leighton. New York: Norton, c2000. vii, 230 p.
98-051419   725/.31/097471   0393047652
Railroad stations -- Conservation and restoration -- New York (State) -- New York. New York (N.Y.) -- Buildings, structures, etc. -- Conservation and restoration.

NA6313.N4.G72 1982
Grand Central Terminal: city within the city/ Deborah Nevins, general editor; with a foreword by Jacqueline Kennedy Onassis; essays by Deborah Nevins ... [et al.]. [New York]: Municipal Art Society of New York, c1982. 145 p.
82-081177   725/.31/097471   0960689222
Public buildings -- Conservation and restoration -- New York (State) -- New York.

NA6402-6403 Special classes of buildings — Classed by use — Public buildings — Industrial architecture. Factories, mills, etc.

NA6402.B4713 2000
Bergeron, Louis, 1929-
Industry, architecture, and engineering: American ingenuity, 1750-1950/ by Louis Bergeron and Maria Teresa Maiullari-Pontois; foreword by Eric DeLony; translated by Jane Marie Todd. New York: Harry N. Abrams, 2000. 287 p.
00-025279   609/.73
Industrial engineering -- United States. Architecture -- United States.

NA6403.G3.J44 1995
Jefferies, Matthew.
Politics and culture in Wilhelmine Germany: the case of industrial architecture/ Matthew Jefferies. Oxford; Berg Publishers, 1995. xiii, 318 p.
95-034402   725/.4/0103094309034   0854969454
Architecture, Industrial -- Germany -- History -- 19th century. Architecture, Industrial -- Germany -- History -- 20th century. Architecture and state -- Germany.

NA6602 Special classes of buildings — Classed by use — Public buildings — Education buildings

NA6602.A76.L66 1999
Loomis, John A., 1951-
Revolution of forms: Cuba's forgotten art schools/ John A. Loomis; foreword by Gerardo Mosquera. New York: Princeton Architectural Press, c1999. xxxiii, 186 p.
98-025831   727/.47/09729124   1568981570
Porro, Ricardo, -- 1925- Garatti, Vittorio, -- 1927- Gottardi, Roberto, -- 1927- Architecture -- Political aspects -- Cuba -- Havana. Architecture, Modern -- 20th century -- Cuba. Art schools -- Cuba -- Havana. Cubanacan (Havana, Cuba) -- Buildings, structures, etc.

NA6695 Special classes of buildings — Classed by use — Public buildings — Museum architecture

NA6695.D38 1990
Davis, Douglas, 1933-
The museum transformed: design and culture in the post-Pompidou age/ Douglas Davis. New York: Abbeville Press, c1990. 238 p.
89-018227   727/.7/0103   1558590641
Art museum architecture. Architecture and society. Architecture, Modern -- 20th century.

NA6695.L68 1989
Loud, Patricia Cummings.
The art museums of Louis I. Kahn/ Patricia Cummings Loud; foreword by Michael P. Mezzatesta. Durham: Published by Duke University Press in association with Duke University Museum of Art, 1989. 303 p.
89-051072   728/.7/092   0822309890
Kahn, Louis I., -- 1901-1974 -- Exhibitions. Kahn, Louis I., -- 1901-1974 -- Criticism and interpretation. Art museum architecture -- United States -- Exhibitions. Architecture, Modern -- 20th century -- United States -- Exhibitions.

NA6695.N49 1998
Newhouse, Victoria.
Towards a new museum/ Victoria Newhouse. New York: Monacelli Press, 1998. 288 p.
98-004584   727/.7/09045   1885254601
Art museum architecture. Architecture, Modern -- 20th century.

NA6821-6840 Special classes of buildings — Classed by use — Public buildings — Theaters. Opera houses. Music halls

NA6821.I94
Izenour, George C.
Theater design/ by George C. Izenour; with two essays on the room acoustics of multiple-use by Vern O. Knudsen and Robert B. Newman; foreword by Alois M. Nagler. New York: McGraw-Hill, c1977. xxxiii, 631 p.
76-056258   725/.822   0070320861
Theater architecture.

NA6821.M83
Mullin, Donald C.
The development of the playhouse; a survey of theatre architecture from the Renaissance to the present [by] Donald C. Mullin. Berkeley, University of California Press, 1970. xvi, 197 p.
77-084532   725/.822   0520013913
Theater architecture -- History.

NA6840.F72.P379 1991
Mead, Christopher Curtis.
Charles Garnier's Paris opera: architectural empathy and the renaissance of French classicism/ Christopher Curtis Mead. New York, N.Y.: Architectural History Foundation; c1991. 343 p.
91-014366   725/.822/092   0262132753
Garnier, Charles, -- 1825-1898 -- Criticism and interpretation. Architecture, Modern -- 19th century -- France -- Paris. Neoclassicism (Architecture) -- France -- Paris. Paris (France) -- Buildings, structures, etc.

NA6840.G7.O76 1988
Orrell, John.
The human stage: English theatre design, 1567-1640/ John Orrell. Cambridge [England]; Cambridge University Press, 1988. xix, 292 p.
87-031158   725/.822/0942   0521308593
Theater architecture -- England. Architecture, Renaissance -- England. Architecture, Modern -- 17th-18th centuries -- England.

NA6880.5-7860 Special classes of buildings — Classed by use — Public buildings — Convention facilities, coliseums, lecture halls, etc.

NA6880.5.U62.M335 1999
Mollenhoff, David V.
Frank Lloyd Wright's Monona Terrace: the enduring power of a civic vision/ David V. Mollenhoff and Mary Jane Hamilton. Madison: University of Wisconsin Press, c1999. xii, 323 p.
98-029148   725/.13/092   0299155005
Wright, Frank Lloyd, -- 1867-1959 -- Criticism and interpretation. Convention facilities -- Wisconsin -- Madison. Madison (Wis.) -- Buildings, structures, etc.

NA7125.S5513 1992
Shimomura, Junichi, 1952-
Art nouveau architecture: residential masterpieces, 1892-1911/ Junichi Shimomura. San Francisco: Cadence Books, 1992. 180 p.
91-023220   728/.09/034   0929279824
Art nouveau (Architecture) Architecture, Domestic. Architecture, Modern -- 19th century.

NA7126.S48
Sherwood, Roger.
Modern housing prototypes/ Roger Sherwood. Cambridge, Mass.: Harvard University Press, c1978. x, 167 p.
78-015508   728.3/1/0222   0674579410
Architecture, Domestic -- Designs and plans. Architecture, Modern -- 20th century -- Designs and plans.

NA7205.B33 1994
Baker, John Milnes, 1932-
American house styles: a concise guide/ John Milnes
Baker. New York: W.W. Norton, c1994. 190 p.
92-042937　728/.37/0973　0393034216
Architecture, Domestic -- United States -- Themes, motives.

NA7205.M35 1984
McAlester, Virginia, 1943-
A field guide to American houses/ by Virginia and Lee
McAlester; with drawings by Lauren Jarrett, and model
house drawings by Juan Rodriguez-Arnaiz. New York:
Knopf, 1984. xv, 525 p.
82-048740　728/.0973　0394739698
Architecture, Domestic -- United States -- Guidebooks.
United States -- Guidebooks.

NA7205.M36 1994
McAlester, Virginia, 1943-
Great American houses and their architectural styles/
Virginia and Lee McAlester; photographs by Alex
McLean; drawings by Larry Boerder; floor plans by Carol
Boerder-Snyder. New York: Abbeville Press, c1994.
348 p.
94-011055　728.8/0973　1558597506
Architecture, Domestic -- United States -- Themes, motives.
Interior decoration -- United States -- Themes, motives.

NA7207.C85 1994
Culbertson, Margaret.
American house designs: an index to popular and trade
periodicals, 1850-1915/ compiled by Margaret
Culbertson. Westport, Conn.: Greenwood Press, 1994.
xiv, 326 p.
94-030280　016.728/022/2　0313292027
Architecture, Domestic -- United States -- Designs and plans -
- Periodicals -- Indexes. Architecture, Modern -- 19th century --
United States -- Designs and plans -- Periodicals -- Indexes.
Architecture, Modern -- 20th century -- United States -- Designs
and plans -- Periodicals -- Indexes.

NA7207.R68 1999
Roth, Leland M.
Shingle styles: innovation and tradition in American
architecture 1874 to 1982/ photography by Bret Morgan;
text by Leland M. Roth. New York: H.N. Abrams, 1999.
240 p.
99-014102　728/.0973　0810944774
Architecture, Domestic -- Shingle style. Architecture, Modern
-- 19th century -- United States. Architecture, Modern -- 20th
century -- United States.

NA7207.S38 1971
Scully, Vincent Joseph, 1920-
The shingle style and the stick style: architectural theory
and design from Richardson to the origins of Wright/ by
Vincent J. Scully, Jr. New Haven: Yale University Press,
1971. lix, 184 p.
70-140539　728.3/7/0973　0300014341
Architecture, Domestic -- Shingle style -- United States.
Architecture, Domestic -- Stick style -- United States.
Architecture, Domestic -- United States.

NA7207.W55 1998
White, Samuel G.
The houses of McKim, Mead & White/ Samuel G. White;
photographs by Jonathan Wallen. New York: Rizzoli,
1998. 252 p.
98-005673　728/.0973/09034　0847820718
Architecture, Domestic -- United States. Eclecticism in
architecture -- United States. Architecture, Modern -- 19th
century -- United states.

NA7208.W68
Wright, Frank Lloyd, 1867-1959.
The natural house. New York, Horizon Press, 1954.
223 p.
54-012278　728.081
Architecture, Domestic -- United States. Architecture, Modern
-- 20th century -- United States. Architecture, Domestic --
Designs and plans.

NA7218.L44 1999
Legler, Dixie.
Prairie style: house and gardens by Frank Lloyd Wright
and the Prairie School/ Dixie Legler, Christian Korab.
New York: Stewart, Tabori & Chang, 1999. 207 p.
99-015471　728/.37/09730904　1556709315
Wright, Frank Lloyd, -- 1867-1959.　Prairie School
(Architecture) Architecture, Domestic -- Middle West.

NA7235.C22.S353
Bay area houses/ edited by Sally Woodbridge; introd. by
David Gebhard; photos. by Morley Baer, Roger
Sturtevant, and others; architectural drawings by
Randolph Meadors and Floyd Campbell. New York:
Oxford University Press, 1976. 329 p.
76-009261　728/.09794/6　0195020847
Architecture, Domestic -- California -- San Francisco Bay
Area.

NA7235.C22.S684 1989
Blueprints for modern living: history and legacy of the
case study houses/ exhibition organized by Elizabeth A.T.
Smith; essays by Esther McCoy ... [et al.]. Los Angeles:
Museum of Contemporary Art; c1989. 256 p.
89-013206　728/.37/09794907479494
Architecture, Domestic -- California, Southern -- Case studies
-- Exhibitions. International style (Architecture) -- California,
Southern -- Case studies -- Exhibitions. Housing, Single family -
- California, Southern -- Case studies -- Exhibitions.

NA7235.N5.G87 1992
Guter, Robert P.
Building by the book: pattern book architecture in New
Jersey/ Robert P. Guter, Janet W. Foster; photographs by
Jim DelGiudice. New Brunswick, N.J.: Rutgers
University Press, c1992. xv, 260 p.
92-006516　728/.37/09749　0813518482
Architecture, Domestic -- New Jersey -- Designs and plans.

NA7235.T4.C85 1999
Culbertson, Margaret.
Texas houses built by the book: the use of published designs, 1850-1925/ Margaret Culbertson. College Station, Tex.: Texas A&M University Press, c1999. xviii, 129 p.
98-042584   728/.09764/09034   0890968632
Architecture, Domestic -- Texas. Architecture, Modern -- 19th century -- Texas. Architecture, Modern -- 20th century -- Texas.

NA7238.B3.H38 1999
Hayward, Mary Ellen.
The Baltimore rowhouse/ Mary Ellen Hayward and Charles Belfoure; foreword by James Marston Fitch. New York: Princeton Architectural Press, 1999. xii, 211 p.
99-014573   728/.312/097526   1568981775
Row houses -- Maryland -- Baltimore. Architecture, Domestic -- Maryland -- Baltimore.

NA7238.L6
Smith, Kathryn, 1945-
Schindler House/ Kathryn Smith; new photography by Grant Mudford. New York: Harry N. Abrams, 2001. 88 p.
00-057619   728/.092   0810929856
Schindler, R. M. -- (Rudolph M.), -- 1887-1953 -- Criticism and interpretation. Schindler, R. M. -- (Rudolph M.), -- 1887-1953 -- Homes and haunts -- California -- Los Angeles. Wright, Frank Lloyd, -- 1867-1959 -- Influence. Modern movement (Architecture) -- California -- Los Angeles.   Los Angeles (Calif.) -- Buildings, structures, etc.

NA7238.P25
Hewitt, Mark A.
Gustav Stickley's Craftsman Farms: the quest for an arts and crafts utopia/ Mark Alan Hewitt. [Syracuse, N.Y.]: Syracuse University Press, 2001. xviii, 248 p.
00-050511   728/.092   0815606893
Stickley, Gustav, -- 1858-1942 -- Homes and haunts -- New Jersey -- Parsippany. Stickley, Gustav, -- 1858-1942 -- Criticism and interpretation. Arts and crafts movement -- New Jersey -- Parsippany. Log buildings -- New Jersey -- Parsippany. Furniture, Mission -- New Jersey -- Parsippany. Craftsman Farms (Parsippany, N.J.) Parsippany (N.J.) -- Buildings, structures, etc.

NA7238.P5.M58 1992
Mother's house: the evolution of Vanna Venturi's house in Chestnut Hill/ edited and introducted by Frederic Schwartz; preface by Aldo Rossi; with essays by Vincent Scully and Robert Venturi. New York: Rizzoli, c1992. 224 p.
92-005315   728/.372/092   0847811417
Venturi, Robert -- Criticism and interpretation. Eclecticism in architecture -- Pennsylvania -- Chestnut Hill (Philadelphia) Philadelphia (Pa.) -- Buildings, structures, etc. Chestnut Hill (Philadelphia, Pa.) -- Buildings, structures, etc.

NA7239.G83
Gwathmey Siegel houses/ foreword, Robert Siegel; preface, Robert A.M. Stern; introduction Paul Goldberger; edited by Brad Collins. New York: Monacelli Press, 2000. 464 p.
99-046640   728/.372/097309045   1580930158
Architect-designed houses -- United States. Architecture, Domestic -- United States. Architecture -- United States -- 20th century.

NA7274.L5913 1999
Llanes, Llilian.
The houses of Old Cuba/ Llilian Llanes; photography by Jean-Luc de Laguarigue. New York: Thames and Hudson, 1999. 199 p.
99-070935   728/.097291   0500019533
Architecture, Domestic -- Cuba. Architecture, Colonial -- Cuba. Color in architecture -- Cuba.

NA7328.B83 1971
Brunskill, R. W.
Illustrated handbook of vernacular architecture [by] R. W. Brunskill. New York, Universe Books [1971, c1970] 229 p.
71-134757   728/.0942   0876631383
Vernacular architecture -- Great Britain.

NA7328.J44 2000
Jeremiah, David.
Architecture and design for the family in twentieth-century Britain, 1900-1970/ David Jeremiah. New York: Manchester University Press, 2000. viii, 229 p.
00-021949   728/.0941/0904   0719049288
Architecture, Domestic -- England. Architecture -- England -- 20th century. Interior decoration -- England -- History -- 20th century.

NA7328.L66 1993
Long, Helen C., 1958-
The Edwardian house: the middle-class home in Britain, 1880-1914/ Helen C. Long. Manchester; Manchester University Press; c1993. xv, 208 p.
93-014634   728/.0942/09034   071903728X
Architecture, Domestic -- Great Britain. Architecture, Edwardian -- Great Britain. Interior decoration -- Great Britain -- History -- 19th century. Great Britain -- Social life and customs.

NA7328.M8713
Muthesius, Hermann, 1861-1927.
The English house/ by Hermann Muthesius; edited with an introd. by Dennis Sharp; and a pref. by Julius Posener; translated by Janet Seligman. New York: Rizzoli, 1979. xxii, 246 p.
78-068490   728/.0942   0847802191
Architecture, Domestic -- England. Architecture, Modern -- 19th century -- England. Dwellings -- England.

NA7424.6.A1.S94 1991
Szabo, Albert.
Afghanistan: an atlas of indigenous domestic architecture/ by Albert Szabo and Thomas J. Barfield; foreword by Eduard F. Sekler. Austin: University of Texas Press, 1991. xxiv, 264 p.
90-012528   728/.09581   0292704194
Architecture, Domestic -- Afghanistan. Vernacular architecture -- Afghanistan.

NA7448.G6 1992
Golany, Gideon.
Chinese earth-sheltered dwellings: indigenous lessons for modern urban design/ Gideon S. Golany. Honolulu: University of Hawaii Press, c1992. xix, 178 p.
91-021496   728/.0473/0951   0824813693
Earth sheltered houses -- China.

NA7451.U3313 1990
Ueda, Atsushi, 1930-
The inner harmony of the Japanese house/ Atsushi Ueda; with an introduction by Gunter Nitschke; [translation ... by Stephen Suloway]. Tokyo; Kodansha International, 1990. 199 p.
90-004310   728/.0952   0870119346
Architecture, Domestic -- Japan. Room layout (Dwellings) -- Japan. Shoji screens -- Japan.

NA7461.A1.P78 1995
Prussin, Labelle.
African nomadic architecture: space, place, and gender/ Labelle Prussin. Washington: Smithsonian Institution Press: c1995. xxii, 245 p.
94-043109   728
Tents -- Africa, Northeast. Architecture, Domestic -- Africa, Northeast. Vernacular architecture -- Africa, Northeast.

NA7468.6.L4.V36 1998
Van Wyk, Gary.
African painted houses: Basotho dwellings of Southern Africa/ Gary N. van Wyk. New York: Harry N. Abrams, 1998. 168 p.
97-036230   728/.096885   0810919907
Sotho (African people) -- Dwellings. Color in architecture -- Lesotho. Architecture and society -- Lesotho.

NA7540.D38 1995
Davis, Sam.
The architecture of affordable housing/ Sam Davis. Berkeley: University of California Press, c1995. ix, 208 p.
94-007469   728/.1/0973   0520087585
Architecture, Domestic -- United States. Public housing -- United States. Architecture, Domestic -- California.

NA7561.H4 1990
Hewitt, Mark A.
The architect & the American country house, 1890-1940/ Mark Alan Hewitt; architectural photographs by Richard Cheek. New Haven: Yale University Press, c1990. xiii, 312 p.
89-077575   728.8/0973   0300047401
Country homes -- United States. Architects and patrons -- United States. United States -- Social life and customs -- 20th century.

NA7562.G5 1979
Girouard, Mark, 1931-
The Victorian country house/ Mark Girouard. New Haven: Yale University Press, 1979. vii, 467 p.
79-064077   728.8/3/0942   0300023901
Country homes -- Great Britain -- History -- 19th century. Manors -- Great Britain -- History -- 19th century. Architecture, Victorian -- Great Britain.

NA7570.K56 1984
King, Anthony D.
The bungalow: the production of a global culture/ Anthony D. King. London; Routledge & Kegan Paul, 1984. xviii, 310 p.
83-013778   728.3/73   0710095384
Bungalows. Architecture and society.

NA7571.K44 1993
Kelly, Barbara M.
Expanding the American dream: building and rebuilding Levittown/ Barbara M. Kelly; [with a foreword by Willliam R. Taylor]. Albany: State University of New York Press, c1993. xi, 284 p.
91-046676   307.3/3616/09747245   0791412873
Suburban homes -- New York (State) -- Levittown. Planned communities -- New York (State) -- Levittown. Architects and housing developers -- New York (State) -- Levittown.

NA7571.S54 1999
Smeins, Linda E.
Building an American identity: pattern book homes and communities, 1870-1900/ Linda E. Smeins. Walnut Creek, CA: AltaMira Press, c1999. 335 p.
98-040127   728/.0973/09034   0761989625
Suburban homes -- United States. Eclecticism in architecture -- United States. Nationalism and architecture -- United States.

NA7594.G6 1989
Goy, Richard J. 1947-
Venetian vernacular architecture: traditional housing in the Venetian lagoon/ Richard J. Goy. Cambridge; Cambridge University Press, 1989. xxi, 360 p.
88-018155   728/.0945/31   0521345812
Architecture, Domestic -- Italy -- Venice. Vernacular architecture -- Italy -- Venice. Venice (Italy) -- Buildings, structures, etc.

NA7610.A58 1982
American country houses of the Gilded Age (Sheldon's "Artistic country-seats")/ new text by Arnold Lewis. New York: Dover Publications, 1982. xx, 104 p.
81-017384   048624301X
Country homes -- United States -- Pictorial works. Country homes -- United States -- Designs and plans. Architecture, Modern -- 19th century -- United States -- Pictorial works.

NA7620.H8
Hussey, Christopher, 1899-
English country houses.   London, Country Life, ltd. 1955-1958. 3 v.
55-003901
Architecture, Domestic -- England.   England -- Historic houses, etc.

NA7620.W55 2000
Wilson, Richard.
Creating paradise: the building of the English country house, 1660-1880/ Richard Wilson and Alan Mackley. London; Hambledon and London, 2000. xviii, 428 p.
2001-515123   728.80942   1852852526
Manors -- England -- History. Mansions -- England -- History. Country homes -- England -- History. Great Britain -- Social life and customs -- History.

NA7740.K55 1993
Klingensmith, Samuel John.
The utility of splendor: ceremony, social life, and architecture at the court of Bavaria, 1600-1800/ Samuel John Klingensmith; edited for publication by Christian F. Otto and Mark Ashton. Chicago: University of Chicago Press, c1993. xx, 315 p.
93-017138   725/.17/09433   0226443302
Palaces -- Germany -- Bavaria. Architecture, Modern -- 17th-18th centuries -- Germany -- Bavaria. Bavaria (Germany) -- Kings and rulers -- Dwellings. Bavaria (Germany) -- Court and courtiers. Bavaria (Germany) -- Social life and customs.

NA7755.C6
Coffin, David R.
The villa in the life of Renaissance Rome/ David R. Coffin. Princeton, N.J.: Princeton University Press, c1979. xx, 385 p.
78-009049   945/.632/05   0691039429
Palaces -- Italy -- Rome. Architecture, Renaissance -- Italy -- Rome. Palaces -- Italy -- Rome Region. Rome (Italy) -- Social life and customs. Rome Region (Italy) -- Social life and customs. Rome (Italy) -- Buildings, structures, etc.

NA7860.H34 1993
Hawes, Elizabeth, 1940-
New York, New York: how the apartment house transformed the life of the city (1869-1930)/ Elizabeth Hawes. New York: Knopf, 1993. xv, 285 p.
92-054796   728/.314/09747109041   0679409653
Apartment houses -- New York (State) -- New York. Architecture, Modern -- 19th century -- New York (State) -- New York. Architecture, Modern -- 20th century -- New York (State) -- New York. New York (N.Y.) -- Buildings, structures, etc.

NA8208.5-8230 Special classes of buildings — Classed by use — Farm architecture

NA8208.5.M36 1988
McMurry, Sally Ann, 1954-
Families and farmhouses in nineteenth-century America: vernacular design and social change/ Sally McMurry. New York: Oxford University Press, 1988. xiii, 261 p.
87-024787   728/.67/0973   0195044754
Farmhouses -- United States. Vernacular architecture -- United States. Architecture, Modern -- 19th century -- United States.

NA8230.B27 1995
Barns of the Midwest/ edited by Allen G. Noble and Hubert G.H. Wilhelm. Athens, Ohio: Ohio University Press, c1995. xi, 295 p.
94-044659   728/.922/0977   0821411152
Barns -- Middle West -- History. Vernacular architecture -- Middle West.

NA8230.E5 1992
Ensminger, Robert F., 1927-
The Pennsylvania barn: its origin, evolution, and distribution in North America/ Robert F. Ensminger. Baltimore: Johns Hopkins University Press, 1992. xvii, 238 p.
91-039897   728/.922/0973   0801843049
Barns -- Pennsylvania -- History.

NA8230.N63 1995
Noble, Allen George, 1930-
The old barn book: a field guide to North American barns and other farm structures/ Allen G. Noble and Richard K. Cleek; with illustrations by M. Margaret Geib. New Brunswick, N.J.: Rutgers University Press, c1995. xii, 222 p.
94-041300   728/.922/0973   0813521726
Barns -- United States. Barns -- Canada. Farm buildings -- United States.

NA8360 Special classes of buildings — Classed by use — Minor buildings, outbuildings, gates, fences, etc.

NA8360.C86 2000
Cunningham, Anne S., 1946-
Crystal palaces: garden conservatories of the United States/ Anne S. Cunningham. New York: Princeton Architectural Press, c2000. xiii, 178 p.
00-008825   728/.924/0973   1568982429
Conservatories -- United States.

NA8450 Special classes of buildings — Classed by use — Ornamental buildings for parks and gardens

NA8450.C58
Connolly, Cyril, 1903-1974.
Les pavillons; French pavilions of the eighteenth century [by] Cyril Connolly & Jerome Zerbe. New York, Macmillan, 1962. 205 p.
62-008761
Pavilions. Architecture, Domestic -- France.

NA8450.D35 1995
Dams, Bernd H.
Pleasure pavilions and follies in the gardens of the ancien regime/ Bernd H. Dams & Andrew Zega; foreword by Charles Ryskamp. Paris; Flammarion, c1995. 190 p.
97-177521   2080135619
Pavilions -- France. Follies (Architecture) -- France.

NA8460 Special classes of buildings — Classed by use — Follies

NA8460.S2813 1988
Saudan, Michel, 1930-
From folly to follies: discovering the world of gardens/ pictures and text by Michel Saudan and Sylvia Saudan-Skira; introduction by Francois Crouzet. New York: Abbeville Press, c1988. ix, 237 p.
87-011438   728/.9   0896597784
Follies (Architecture) -- Europe -- Themes, motives.

NA9030 Aesthetics of cities.
City planning and beautifying — General works — 1870-1944

NA9030.G4 1968b
Geddes, Patrick, 1854-1932.
Cities in evolution: an introduction to the town planning movement and to the study of civics. London, Benn, 1968. xxxv, 409 p.
72-365406   711/.4   0510431216
City planning -- History. Cities and towns.

NA9030.G6
Goodman, Percival.
Communitas: means of livelihood and ways of life, by Percival Goodman and Paul Goodman. Chicago, Ill., The University of Chicago press [1947] x, 141 p.
47-003439   711.4
Cities and towns -- Planning -- 1945-

NA9030.G7
Gropius, Walter, 1883-1969.
Rebuilding our communities ... Chicago, P. Theobald, 1945. 61 p.
46-025089   711.4
City planning. Architecture, Domestic.

NA9030.J45 1961
Jellicoe, Geoffrey Alan, 1900-
Motopia; a study in the evolution of urban landscape/ G. A. Jellicoe. New York, Praeger, 1961. 165 p.
61-007040   711.4
City planning.

NA9030.M48
Meyerson, Martin.
Face of the metropolis, by Martin Meyerson, with Jaqueline Tyrwhitt, Brian Falk, Patricia Sekler. Sponsored by ACTION, the National Council for Good Cities. New York, Random House [1963] 249 p.
61-013841   711.4
City planning. Architecture, Modern -- 20th century.

NA9030.S2
Saarinen, Eliel, 1873-1950.
The city, its growth, its decay, its future [by] Eliel Saarinen. New York, Reinhold publishing corporation [1943]
43-009034   711.6
City planning. Cities and towns -- Growth.

NA9030.S613 1965
Sitte, Camillo, 1843-1903.
City planning according to artistic principles. Translated from the German by George R. Collins and Christiane Crasemann Collins. New York, Random House [1965] xvii, 205 p.
64-017102   711/.4/01
City planning.

NA9031 Aesthetics of cities.
City planning and beautifying — General works — 1945-

NA9031.A38 1987
Alexander, Christopher.
A new theory of urban design/ Christopher Alexander ... [et al.]. New York: Oxford University Press, 1987. 251 p.
85-025854   711/.4/01   0195037537
City planning -- California -- San Francisco -- Simulation methods. City planning -- Philosophy.

NA9031.B69 1998
Bosselmann, Peter.
Representation of places: reality and realism in city design/ Peter Bosselmann. Berkeley: University of California Press, c1998. xiv, 228 p.
97-000081   711/.4   0520206584
City planning. Communication in architectural design.

NA9031.B72 1994
Boyer, M. Christine.
The city of collective memory: its historical imagery and architectural entertainments/ M. Christine Boyer. Cambridge, Mass.: MIT Press, c1994. x, 560 p.
94-010041   711/.4   0262023717
City planning -- Psychological aspects. Architecture -- Aesthetics. Urban beautification.

NA9031.S65
Spreiregen, Paul D.
Urban design: the architecture of towns and cities, written and illustrated by Paul D. Spreiregen. New York, McGraw-Hill [1965] xi, 243 p.
65-025520   711.4
City planning.

NA9040 Aesthetics of cities.
City planning and beautifying — General works — Addresses, essays, lectures

NA9040.B73
Breese, Gerald William.
An approach to urban planning/ edited by Gerald Breese and Dorothy E. Whiteman. Princeton: Princeton University Press, 1953. 147 p.
52-013142   711
City planning.

NA9050 Aesthetics of cities.
City planning and beautifying — General special

NA9050.B22
Bacon, Edmund N.
Design of cities [by] Edmund N. Bacon. New York, Viking Press [1967] 296 p.
66-023826   711/.4/09
City planning. Space (Architecture) Harmony (Aesthetics)

NA9050.W75 1945
Wright, Frank Lloyd, 1867-1959.
When democracy builds/ Frank Lloyd Wright. Chicago: University of Chicago Press, 1945. x, 130 p.
45-003051   711.1
City planning -- United States Architecture. Social problems

NA9052 Aesthetics of cities.
City planning and beautifying —
Special topics — Beautifications

NA9052.S5813 1979
Sitte, Camillo, 1843-1903.
The art of building cities: city building according to its artistic fundamentals/ by Camillo Sitte; translated by Charles T. Stewart. Westport, Conn.: Hyperion Press, 1979, c1945. xi, 128 p.
78-014144   711/.4   0883558173
Urban beautification. Art, Municipal.

NA9053 Aesthetics of cities.
City planning and beautifying —
Special topics — Others, A-Z

NA9053.B58.B55 1999
Blau, Eve.
The architecture of Red Vienna, 1919-1934/ Eve Blau. Cambridge, Mass: MIT Press, c1999. xvii, 509 p.
98-025675   720/.9436/1309042   0262024519
City blocks -- Austria -- Vienna. Public housing -- Austria -- Vienna. Architecture -- Government policy -- Austria -- Vienna.

NA9053.C57.C66 1992
The Company town: architecture and society in the early industrial age/ edited by John S. Garner. New York: Oxford University Press, 1992. 245 p.
91-035627   307.76/7/09034   0195070275
Company town architecture -- History -- 19th century.

NA9053.M43.B36
Banham, Reyner.
Megastructure: urban futures of the recent past/ [by] Reyner Banham. London: Thames and Hudson, 1976. 224 p.
78-307289   720   0500340684
Megastructures. City planning.

NA9053.N4.F75 1988
Friedman, David, 1943 Aug. 15-
Florentine new towns: urban design in the late Middle Ages/ David Friedman. New York, N.Y.: Architectural History Foundation; c1988. x, 373 p.
88-006289   711/.4/094551   0262061139
New towns -- Italy -- Florence Region. Cities and towns, Medieval -- Italy -- Florence Region. City planning -- Italy -- Florence Region.

NA9053.S4.L44 1988
Leeuwen, Thomas A. P. van.
The skyward trend of thought: the metaphysics of the American skyscraper/ Thomas A.P. van Leeuwen. Cambridge, Mass.: MIT Press, 1988, c1986. viii, 176 p.
88-000870   725/.2
Skyscrapers -- United States. Architecture, Modern -- 20th century -- United States.

NA9053.S6.B76 1990
Broadbent, Geoffrey.
Emerging concepts in urban space design/ Geoffrey Broadbent. London; Van Nostrand Reinhold (International), 1990. ix, 380 p.
89-024950   711/.4   0747600252
Space (Architecture) City planning. Architecture -- Environmental aspects.

NA9053.S7.R8
Rudofsky, Bernard, 1905-
Streets for people; a primer for Americans. Photos. by the author. Garden City, N.Y., Doubleday [1969] 351 p.
76-078735   711/.74
Urban beautification. Streets.

NA9053.S7.S82 1994
Streets: critical perspectives on public space/ edited by Zeynep Celik, Diane Favro, Richard Ingersoll. Berkeley: University of California Press, c1994. vii, 294 p.
93-042658   711/.4   0520085507
Streets -- History. City planning -- History.

NA9070 Aesthetics of cities.
City planning and beautifying —
Public squares and promenades — General works

NA9070.C49 1998
Cleary, Richard Louis .
The place royale and urban design in the ancient regime/ Richard L. Cleary. New York: Cambridge University Press, 1998.
98-003572   711/.55   0521572681
Plazas -- France. Architecture, Modern -- 17th-18th centuries -- France. Architecture and state -- France -- History -- 17th century.

NA9070.T73 1997
Trachtenberg, Marvin.
Dominion of the eye: urbanism, art, and power in early modern Florence/ Marvin Trachtenberg. Cambridge; Cambridge University Press, 1997. xx, 358 p.
96-041192   711/.55/4551   0521555027
Plazas -- Italy -- Florence. City planning -- Italy -- Florence. Architecture, Medieval -- Italy -- Florence. Florence (Italy) -- Buildings, structures, etc.

**NA9085 Aesthetics of cities.
City planning and beautifying —
Biography — Individual, A-Z**

NA9085.L96.A4 1990
Lynch, Kevin, 1918-
City sense and city design: writings and projects of Kevin Lynch/ edited by Tridib Banerjee and Michael Southworth. Cambridge, Mass.: MIT Press, c1990. ix, 853 p.
89-038350   711/.4/092   0262121433
Lynch, Kevin, -- 1918- -- Philosophy. City planning -- United States -- History -- 20th century. City planning -- History -- 20th century.

**NA9090 Aesthetics of cities.
City planning and beautifying —
History — General works**

NA9090.H54 1958
Hiorns, Frederick R.
Town-building in history; an outline review of conditions, influences, ideas, and methods affecting "planned " towns through five thousand years. New York, Criterion Books [1958] 443 p.
58-006724   711.09
Cities and towns -- History. Cities and towns -- Planning -- Great Britain. Cities and towns -- Planning -- History. Great Britain -- History.

NA9090.J413 1929a
Le Corbusier, 1887-1965.
The city of to-morrow and its planning, by Le Corbusier. Translated from the 8th French ed. of Urbanisme by Frederick Etchells. Cambridge, Mass., M.I.T. Press [1971, c1929] xv, 301 p.
78-148855   711/.4   0262120410
City planning.

NA9090.M58
Moholy-Nagy, Sibyl, 1905-
Matrix of man; an illustrated history of urban environment [by] Sibyl Moholy-Nagy. New York, Praeger [1968] 317 p.
68-011320   711/.4/09
City planning -- History. Urban ecology.

NA9090.R313
Rasmussen, Steen Eiler, 1898-
Towns and buildings: described in drawings and words. Cambridge, Mass., M.I.T. Press [1969, c1951] viii, 203 p.
69-013127   711/.4/09
City planning -- History. Architecture -- History.

**NA9094-9095 Aesthetics of cities.
City planning and beautifying —
History — Modern**

NA9094.A713
Argan, Giulio Carlo.
The Renaissance city [by] Giulio C. Argan. [Translated by Susan Edna Bassnett] New York, G. Braziller [1970, c1969] 128 p.
70-090409   711/.4
City planning. Architecture, Renaissance.

NA9094.8.L6913 1983
Loyer, Francois.
Architecture of the industrial age, 1789-1914/ Francois Loyer; [translated from the French by R.F.M. Dexter]. Geneva, Switzerland: Skira, c1983. 319 p.
83-042959   711/.4/094   0847805018
City planning -- History -- 19th century. Urbanization -- History. Industrialization -- History.

NA9095.U74 1992
Urban landscapes: international perspectives/ edited by J.W.R. Whitehand and P.J. Larkham. London; Routledge, 1992. xvii, 333 p.
92-012622   711/.4/09   0415070740
City planning -- History -- 20th century. Architecture -- Environmental aspects.

**NA9105-9265 Aesthetics of cities.
City planning and beautifying —
Special countries and cities**

NA9105.A87 1989
Attoe, Wayne.
American urban architecture: catalysts in the design of cities/ Wayne Attoe and Donn Logan. Berkeley: University of California Press, c1989. xv, 190 p.
88-014395   711/.4/0973   0520061527
City planning -- United States. Architecture -- United States.

NA9105.D4 1964aa
Who designs America? The American Civilization Conference at Princeton, edited for the American Civilization Program by Laurence B. Holland. Papers by Susanne K. Langer [and others] Garden City, N.Y., Anchor Books [1966] 357 p.
66-017453   711.40973
City planning -- United States -- Addresses, essays, lectures. Architecture -- United States -- Addresses, essays, lectures.

NA9105.G37 1996
Garvin, Alexander.
The American city: what works, what doesn't/ Alexander Garvin. New York: McGraw-Hill, c1996. xiv, 477 p.
95-030375   711/.4/0973   0070229198
City planning -- United States -- Case studies.

NA9105.T85
Tunnard, Christopher.
The city of man. New York, Scribner, 1953. 424 p.
53-011226   711
Cities and towns -- Planning -- United States.

NA9108.L9
Lynch, Kevin, 1918-
The image of the city. Cambridge [Mass.] Technology Press, 1960. 194 p.
60-007362   711.40973
City planning -- United States.

NA9108.T82
Tunnard, Christopher.
Man-made America: chaos or control? An inquiry into selected problems of design in the urbanized landscape, by Christopher Tunnard and Boris Pushkarev in association with Geoffrey Baker [and others] With drawings by Philip Lin and Vladimir Pozharsky and photos. by John Reed and Charles R. Schulze. New Haven, Yale University Press, 1963. xii, 479 p.
62-016243   711.30973
Architecture -- Environmental aspects -- United States. Urban beautification -- United States. Architecture -- Conservation and restoration -- United States.

NA9127.C4.B48 1991
Bluestone, Daniel M.
Constructing Chicago/ Daniel Bluestone. New Haven: Yale University Press, c1991. 235 p.
91-014675   711/.4/097731109034   0300048483
City planning -- Illinois -- Chicago -- History -- 19th century. Urban beautification -- Illinois -- Chicago -- History -- 19th century. Architects and patrons -- Illinois -- Chicago. Chicago (Ill.) -- Buildings, structures, etc.

NA9127.S3.S3
Scott, Mel, 1906-
The San Francisco Bay area; a metropolis in perspective. Berkeley, University of California Press, 1959. ix, 333 p.
59-012537   711.4097946
Regional planning -- San Francisco Bay region.   San Francisco Bay region.

NA9183.B7213 1988
Braunfels, Wolfgang.
Urban design in Western Europe: regime and architecture, 900-1900/ Wolfgang Braunfels; translated by Kenneth J. Northcott. Chicago: University of Chicago Press, 1988. xiii, 407 p.
87-030060   711/.4/094   0226071782
City planning -- Europe -- History. Architecture -- Europe -- History.

NA9183.S525 1999
Shaping the great city: modern architecture in Central Europe, 1890-1937/ edited by Eve Blau and Monika Platzer; in association with the Bundesministerium fur Unterricht und Kulturelle Angelegenheiten, Vienna ... [et al.]; with contributions by Friedrich Achleitner ... [et al.]. Munich; Prestel, c1999. 271 p.
99-067782   711/.4/094309041   379132151X
City planning -- Europe, Central -- History -- 20th century. City planning -- Europe, Central -- History -- 19th century. Architecture, Modern -- 20th century -- Europe, Central.

NA9185.A795
Ashworth, William.
The genesis of modern British town planning; a study in economic and social history of the nineteenth and twentieth centuries. London, Routledge & Paul [1954] xii, 259 p.
54-001614   711
City planning -- Great Britain.

NA9200.B4.B35 1990
Balfour, Alan
Berlin: the politics of order, 1737-1989/ Alan Balfour. New York: Rizzoli, 1990. 269 p.
90-034705   720/.1/03   0847812715
City planning -- Germany -- Berlin. Architecture and state -- Germany -- Berlin. Neoclassicism (Architecture) -- Germany -- Berlin.

NA9201.W85 1976
Wycherley, R. E.
How the Greeks built cities/ by R.E. Wycherley. New York: Norton, 1976, c1962. xxi, 235 p.
76-010762   711/.4/0938   0393008142
City planning -- Greece. Architecture -- Greece.

NA9202.A8.B37 2000
Bastea, Eleni.
The creation of modern Athens: planning the myth/ Eleni Bastea. New York, NY: Cambridge University Press, c2000. xix, 280 p.
99-010717   711/.4/094951209034   0521641209
City planning -- Greece -- Athens -- History -- 19th century. Nationalism and architecture -- Greece -- Athens. Athens (Greece) -- Buildings, structures, etc.

NA9245.N4.L3
Lampl, Paul.
Cities and planning in the ancient Near East. New York, Braziller [1968] 128 p.
68-024699   711/.4/093
City planning -- Middle East.

NA9265.S8 1990
Steinhardt, Nancy Shatzman.
Chinese imperial city planning/ Nancy Shatzman Steinhardt. Honolulu: University of Hawaii Press, c1990. xi, 228 p.
89-020541   711/.4/0951   0824812441
City planning -- China -- History.

**NA9330 Aesthetics of cities.
City planning and beautifying —
Ornamental structures
(Monuments, arches, fountains, etc.) —
War memorials. National cemeteries**

NA9330.G4.Y68 2000
Young, James Edward.
At memory's edge: after-images of the Holocaust in contemporary art and architecture/ James E. Young. New Haven: Yale University Press, 2000. 248 p.
00-100482   704.9/499405318   0300080328
   Holocaust, Jewish (1939-1945), and architecture -- Germany. Symbolism and architecture -- Germany. Deconstructivism (Architecture) -- Germany.

**NA9348-9355 Aesthetics of cities.
City planning and beautifying —
Ornamental structures
(Monuments, arches, fountains, etc.) —
Monuments**

NA9348.M6.M46 1989
Mexican monuments: strange encounters/ conceived and coordinated by Helen Escobedo with photographs by Paolo Gori and essays by Nestor Garcia Canclini ... [et al.]. New York: Abbeville Press, c1989. 251 p.
88-036694   730/.972   089659906X
   Monuments -- Mexico. Memorials -- Mexico.

NA9355.L6
Bayley, Stephen.
The Albert Memorial: the monument in its social and architectural context/ Stephen Bayley. London: Scolar, 1981. 160 p.
82-111123   725/.94/0942132   0859675947
Albert, -- Prince Consort of Victoria, Queen of Great Britain, -- 1819-1861 -- Monuments. Albert Memorial (London, England) Gothic revival (Architecture) -- Great Britain. Gothic revival (Art) -- Great Britain.

**NA9370 Aesthetics of cities.
City planning and beautifying —
Ornamental structures
(Monuments, arches, fountains, etc.) —
Memorial and triumphal arches**

NA9370.R6.B43b
Berenson, Bernard, 1865-1959.
The Arch of Constantine; or, The decline of form. New York, Macmillan Company, 1954. 80 p.
55-001152   729.336
   Human figure in art. Sculpture, Roman. Rome (Italy) -- Arco di Costantino.

NB Sculpture

NB36 Indexes to sculpture

NB36.C55
Clapp, Jane.
Sculpture index. Metuchen, N.J., Scarecrow Press, 1970 [c1970-7] 2 v. in 3.
79-009538   730/.16   081080249X
   Sculpture -- Indexes.

NB60 History —
General works

NB60.C5
Chase, George Henry, 1874-1952.
A history of sculpture, by George Henry Chase...and Chandler Rathfon Post. New York, Harper & brothers [c1925] 582 p.
25-003621
   Sculpture -- History.

NB60.H5
Hibbard, Howard, 1928-
Masterpieces of western sculpture: from medieval to modern/ Howard Hibbard. New York: Harper & Row, [1977] 239 p.
77-002416   735   0060118784
   Sculpture, Modern -- Catalogs. Sculpture, Medieval -- Catalogs.

NB60.R36 1997
Rawson, Philip S.
Sculpture/ Philip Rawson. Philadelphia: University of Pennsylvania Press, c1997. xi, 162 p.
96-028432   731/.028   0812282582
   Sculpture.

NB85-86 History —
Ancient sculpture — Classical

NB85.B37 1999
Barkan, Leonard.
Unearthing the past: archaeology and aesthetics in the making of Renaissance culture/ Leonard Barkan. New Haven: Yale University Press, c1999. xxxiii, 428 p.
99-024893   709/.02/4   0300076770
   Sculpture, Classical. Sculpture, Classical -- Reproduction. Art, Renaissance -- Classical influences.

NB86.V47 1981
Vermeule, Cornelius Clarkson, 1925-
Greek and Roman sculpture in America: masterpieces in public collections in the United States and Canada/ Cornelius C. Vermeule. Malibu, Calif.: The J. Paul Getty Museum; c1981. ix, 406 p.
81-003057   733/.074/013   0520043243
   Sculpture, Classical -- United States.

NB90-94 History —
Ancient sculpture — Greek

NB90.B48 1961
Bieber, Margarete, b. 1879.
The sculpture of the Hellenistic Age.   New York,
Columbia University Press [1961] xi, 259 p.
61-066470   733.3
Sculpture, Greek.

NB90.C26
Carpenter, Rhys, 1889-
Greek sculpture, a critical review. [Chicago] University
of Chicago Press [1960] xiv, 275 p.
60-014233   733.3
Sculpture, Greek.

NB90.R54 1970
Richter, Gisela Marie Augusta, 1882-
The sculpture and sculptors of the Greeks, by Gisela M.
A. Richter. New Haven, Yale University Press, 1970. xvi,
317 p.
70-099838   733/.3   0300012810
Sculpture, Greek. Sculptors -- Greece.

NB90.R56
Ridgway, Brunilde Sismondo, 1929-
The archaic style in Greek sculpture/ by Brunilde
Sismondo Ridgway. Princeton, N.J.: Princeton University
Press, c1977. xix, 336 p.
76-019655   733/.3   0691039208
Sculpture, Greek.

NB90.R57
Ridgway, Brunilde Sismondo, 1929-
The severe style in Greek sculpture.   Princeton, N.J.,
Princeton University Press, 1970. xviii, 155 p.
77-113008   733/.3   0691038694
Sculpture, Greek.

NB91.A7.L27 2000
Lagerlof, Margaretha Rossholm, 1943-
The sculptures of the Parthenon: aesthetics and
interpretation/ Margaretha Rossholm Lagerlof. New
Haven, CT: Yale University Press, c2000. viii, 204 p.
99-047026   733/.3/09385   0300073917
Sculpture, Greek -- Greece -- Athens.

NB94.S63 1991
Smith, R. R. R.
Hellenistic sculpture: a handbook/ R.R.R. Smith. New
York, N.Y.: Thames and Hudson, 1991. 287 p.
90-063385   733/.3   0500202494
Sculpture, Hellenistic -- Themes, motives.

NB115 History —
Ancient sculpture — Italian

NB115.K57 1992
Kleiner, Diana E. E.
Roman sculpture/ Diana E.E. Kleiner. New Haven: Yale
University Press, c1992. xii, 477 p.
91-046265   733/.5   0300046316
Sculpture, Roman.

NB135-140 History —
Ancient sculpture —
Special materials of ancient sculpture
other than stone

NB135.M38 1996
Mattusch, Carol C.
Classical bronzes: the art and craft of Greek and Roman
statuary/ Carol C. Mattusch. Ithaca: Cornell University
Press, 1996. xvii, 241 p.
95-036843   733   0801431824
Bronze sculpture, Classical. Bronze figurines, Classical.

NB140.M38 1988
Mattusch, Carol C.
Greek bronze statuary: from the beginnings through the
fifth century B.C./ Carol C. Mattusch. Ithaca, N.Y.:
Cornell University Press, 1988. xviii, 246 p.
88-047737   733/.3   0801421489
Bronze sculpture, Greek. Bronzes, Greek.

NB163 History — Ancient sculpture —
Special subjects of ancient sculpture

NB163.V62.C575 1995
Havelock, Christine Mitchell.
The Aphrodite of Knidos and her successors: a historical
review of the female nude in Greek art/ Christine
Mitchell Havelock. Ann Arbor: University of Michigan
Press, c1995. xii, 158 p.
94-039539   730/.92   047210585X
*Praxiteles, -- 4th cent. B.C. -- Aphrodite of Cnidus. Aphrodite
(Greek deity) -- Art. Marble sculpture, Greek. Female nude in
art.*

NB170 History —
Medieval sculpture

NB170.D813 1990
Duby, Georges.
Sculpture: the great art of the Middle Ages from the fifth
to the fifteenth century/ by Georges Duby, Xavier Barral i
Altet, Sophie Guillot de Suduiraut. New York:
Skira/Rizzoli, 1990. 318 p.
90-053149   734   0847812855
Sculpture, Medieval.

NB170.S213
Salvini, Roberto.
Medieval sculpture.   Greenwich, Conn., New York
Graphic Society [1970, c1969] 368 p.
68-012365   734
Sculpture, Medieval.

NB175 History —
Medieval sculpture — Romanesque

NB175.H39
Hearn, M. F. 1938-
Romanesque sculpture: the revival of monumental stone sculpture in the eleventh and twelfth centuries/ M. F. Hearn. Ithaca, N.Y.: Cornell University Press, 1981. 240 p.
80-014383   734/.24   0801412870
Sculpture, Romanesque. Sculpture, Medieval.

NB175.S28 1977b
Schapiro, Meyer, 1904-
Romanesque art/ Meyer Schapiro. New York: G. Braziller, 1977. ix, 368 p.
76-011842   709/.02/1   080760853X
Sculpture, Romanesque -- Addresses, essays, lectures. Art, Romanesque -- Addresses, essays, lectures.

NB180 History —
Medieval sculpture — Gothic

NB180.W55 1995
Williamson, Paul, 1954-
Gothic sculpture, 1140-1300/ Paul Williamson. New Haven: Yale University Press, c1995. ix, 301 p.
94-049678   734/.25   0300063385
Sculpture, Gothic.

NB197.3-198 History —
Modern sculpture — 19th and 20th centuries

NB197.3.J36 1985
Janson, H. W. 1913-
19th-century sculpture/ H.W. Janson; [editor, Phyllis Freeman; designer Bob McKee]. New York: Abrams, 1985. 288 p.
84-012508   735/.22   0810913690
Sculpture, Modern -- 19th century.

NB198.B84
Burnham, Jack, 1931-
Beyond modern sculpture; the effects of science and technology on the sculpture of this century. New York, G. Braziller [1968] x, 402 p.
68-016106   735/.29
Sculpture, Modern -- 20th century. Sculpture -- Technique.

NB198.L83 1987
Lucie-Smith, Edward.
Sculpture since 1945/ Edward Lucie-Smith. New York: Universe, 1987. 160 p.
87-013584   735/.23   0876636652
Sculpture, Modern -- 20th century -- Themes, motives.

NB198.R4
Read, Herbert Edward, 1893-1968.
A concise history of modern sculpture [by] Herbert Read. New York, Praeger [1964] 310 p.
64-019789   735/.23
Sculpture, Modern -- 20th century -- History.

NB198.S355 1992
Senie, Harriet.
Contemporary public sculpture: tradition, transformation, and controversy/ Harriet F. Senie. New York: Oxford University Press, 1992. viii, 276 p.
91-033760   735/.235   0195073185
Public sculpture. Sculpture, Modern -- 20th century.

NB205-210 History —
Special countries

NB205.T86
200 years of American sculpture/ Tom Armstrong ... [et al.]. [Boston]: D. R. Godine, c1976. 350 p.
76-001762   730/.973/07401471   0879231858
Sculpture, American -- Exhibitions. Neoclassicism (Art) -- United States -- Exhibitions. Sculpture, Modern -- 19th century -- United States -- Exhibitions.

NB210.G3 1968
Gardner, Albert Ten Eyck.
Yankee stonecutters; the first American school of sculpture, 1800-1850.   Freeport, N.Y., Books for Libraries Press [1968, c1945] 84 p.
68-058790   730/.922
Sculpture, American -- History. Sculpture, Modern -- 19th century -- United States. Sculptors, American.

NB210.M48 1999
Metropolitan Museum of Art (New York, N.Y.)
American sculpture in the Metropolitan Museum of Art/ edited by Thayer Tolles; catalogue by Lauretta Dimmick, Donna J. Hassler, Thayer Tolles; photographs by Jerry L. Thompson. New York: The Museum, [c1999-   ] v. 1
99-024636   730/.973/0747471   0870999141
Sculpture, Modern -- 19th century -- United States -- Catalogs. Sculpture, Modern -- 20th century -- United States -- Catalogs. Sculpture -- New York (State) -- New York -- Catalogs.

NB210.R49 1993
Reynolds, Donald M.
Masters of American sculpture: the figurative tradition from the American renaissance to the millennium/ Donald Martin Reynolds. New York: Abbeville Press, c1993. 275 p.
93-024578   730/.0973/0904   1558592768
Sculpture, American. Human figure in art. Sculpture, Modern -- 19th century -- United States.

NB212-439 History —
Special countries —
America

NB212.D39 2000
Day, Holliday T.
Crossroads of American sculpture: David Smith, George Rickey, John Chamberlain, Robert Indiana, William T. Wiley, Bruce Nauman/ Holliday T.   Day; with contributions by Dore Ashton and Lena Vigna. Indianapolis, Ind.: Indianapolis Museum of Art, c2000. 252 p.
00-009526   730/.973/07477252 21   0936260726
Sculpture, American -- 20th century -- Exhibitions.

NB235.N5.B64 1989
Bogart, Michele Helene, 1952-
Public sculpture and the civic ideal in New York City, 1890-1930/ Michele H. Bogart. Chicago: University of Chicago Press, c1989. xvi, 390 p.
88-021815   730/.9747/1   0226063097
Public sculpture -- New York (State) -- New York -- Themes, motives. Art patronage -- New York (State) -- New York.

NB236.R8 1990
Rubinstein, Charlotte Streifer.
American women sculptors: a history of women working in three dimensions/ Charlotte Streifer Rubinstein. Boston, MA: G.K. Hall, 1990. xv, 638 p.
89-026846   730/.82   0816187320
Women sculptors -- United States -- Biography. Sculpture, American.

NB237.B65.A2 1998
Bourgeois, Louise, 1911-
Destruction of the father reconstruction of the father: writings and interviews, 1923-1997/ Louise Bourgeois; edited and with texts by Marie-Laure Bernadac and Hans-Ulrich Obrist. Cambridge, Mass.: MIT Press in association with Violette Editions, 1998. 384 p.
97-043132   730/.92   0262522462
Bourgeois, Louise, -- 1911- Bourgeois, Louise, -- 1911- -- Interviews. Sculptors -- United States -- Biography. Sculptors -- United States -- Interviews.

NB237.B65.A4 1994
Bourgeois, Louise, 1911-
Louise Bourgeois: the locus of memory, works 1982-1993/ Charlotta Kotik, Terrie Sultan, Christian Leigh. New York: H.N. Abrams, c1994. 144 p.
93-028375   709/.2   0810931273
Bourgeois, Louise, -- 1911- -- Exhibitions. Bourgeois, Louise, -- 1911- -- Criticism and interpretation.

NB237.B65.B47 1995
Bernadac, Marie-Laure.
Louise Bourgeois/ Marie-Laure Bernadac. Paris: Flammarion, c1995. 191 p.
95-205689   2080121847
Bourgeois, Louise, -- 1911- -- Criticism and interpretation.

NB237.C46.S46 1999
Selz, Peter Howard, 1919-
Barbara Chase-Riboud, sculptor/ essays by Peter Selz and Anthony F. Janson. New York: Harry N. Abrams, c1999. 143 p.
99-014101   730/.92   0810941074
Chase-Riboud, Barbara -- Criticism and interpretation.

NB237.G8.W7
Wright, Nathalia.
Horatio Greenough, the first American sculptor.   Univ. of Pa. Pr., 1963.
62-011261   927.3
Greenough, Horatio. Sculptors, American.

NB237.H42.A4 1989
Barrette, Bill.
Eva Hesse: sculpture: catalogue raisonne/ by Bill Barrette. New York: Timken Publishers, 1989. 274 p.
88-022440   730/.92/4   0943221021
Hesse, Eva, -- 1936-1970 -- Catalogues raisonnes.

NB237.H6.S53 1991
Sherwood, Dolly.
Harriet Hosmer, American sculptor, 1830-1908/ Dolly Sherwood. Columbia: University of Missouri Press, c1991. xiii, 378 p.
91-015632   730/.92   0826207669
Hosmer, Harriet Goodhue, -- 1830-1908.   Sculptors -- United States -- Biography.

NB237.J48 A4 1994
Man on fire: Luis Jiménez = El hombre en llamas/ [foreword, Ellen Landis; introduction, James Moore; contributing authors, Rudolfo Anaya ... et al.; Spanish translations, Margarita B. Montalvo]. Albuquerque, N.M.: The Albuquerque Museum, c1994. ix, 189 p.
93-073295   730/.92 20   0826315518
Jimenez, Luis, 1940- -- Exhibitions. Artist's preparatory studies -- United States -- Exhibitions.

NB237.M3.A4 1989
Rand, Harry.
Paul-Manship/ Harry Rand. Washington: Published for the National Museum of American Art by the Smithsonian Institution Press, c1989. 214 p.
88-015594   730/.92/4   0874748348
Manship, Paul, -- 1885-1966 -- Exhibitions.

NB237.N6.A4 1989
Grove, Nancy.
Isamu Noguchi: portrait sculpture/ by Nancy Grove. Washington City: Published by the Smithsonian Institution Press for the National Portrait Gallery, 1989. xvi, 123 p.
89-005861   730/.92/4   0874744776
Noguchi, Isamu, -- 1904- -- Exhibitions.   Portrait sculpture, American -- Exhibitions. Portrait sculpture -- 20th century -- United States -- Exhibitions.

NB237.N6.A86 1994
Altshuler, Bruce.
Isamu Noguchi/ Bruce Altshuler. New York: Abbeville Press, c1994. 127 p.
93-036608   709/.2   1558597549
Noguchi, Isamu, -- 1904- -- Criticism and interpretation.

NB237.N6.H86
Hunter, Sam, 1923-
Isamu Noguchi/ text by Sam Hunter. New York: Abbeville Press, [1978] 334 p.
78-005288   730/.92/4   0896590038
Noguchi, Isamu, -- 1904- Sculptors -- United States -- Biography.

NB237.R5.R67
Rickey, George
George Rickey/ Nan Rosenthal. New York: H. N. Abrams, 1977. 220 p.
76-020569   730/.92/4   0810904330
Rickey, George.

NB237.S46.A77 1987
Public art, public controversy: the Tilted Arc on trial/ [edited by Sherrill Jordan ... et al.]. New York, N.Y.: American Council for the Arts, c1987. x, 198 p.
87-018741   730/.92/4   091540057X
Serra, Richard, -- 1939- -- Tilted arc.   Steel sculpture, American. Public sculpture -- United States -- Public opinion. Public opinion -- United States.

NB237.S567.G7
Smith, David, 1906-1965.
David Smith. Text and photos. by the author. Edited by Cleve Gray. New York, Holt, Rinehart, and Winston [1968] 176 p.
68-018582   730/.924
Smith, David, 1906-1965.

NB237.S567.M27 1983
Marcus, Stanley E., 1926-
David Smith, the sculptor and his work/ Stanley E. Marcus. Ithaca, N.Y.: Cornell University Press, 1983. 207 p.
83-045148   730/.92/4   0801415101
Smith, David, -- 1906-1965.

NB253.W4 1971
Weismann, Elizabeth (Wilder) 1908-
Mexico in sculpture, 1521-1821.   Westport, Conn., Greenwood Press, [1971, c1950] 226 p.
75-095137   730/.972   0837125308
Sculpture -- Mexico.

NB439.M3.A4 1991
Grove, Nancy.
Magical mixtures--Marisol portrait sculpture/ Nancy Grove. Washington, D.C.: Published by the Smithsonian Institution Press for the National Portrait Gallery, c1991. 96 p.
90-050892   709/.2   1560980427
Marisol, -- 1930- -- Exhibitions.

NB458-955 History —
Special countries — Europe

NB458.E45
Elsen, Albert Edward, 1927-
Modern European sculpture, 1918-1945: unknown beings and other realities/ Albert E. Elsen. New York: G. Braziller in association with the Albright-Knox Art Gallery, Buffalo, N.Y., c1979. 192 p.
78-027519   735/.23   0807609218
Sculpture, European -- Exhibitions. Sculpture, Modern -- 20th century -- Europe -- Exhibitions. Avant-garde (Aesthetics) -- Europe -- Exhibitions.

NB463.S8
Stone, Lawrence.
Sculpture in Britain: the Middle Ages.   [Baltimore] Penguin Books [1955] xxi, 297 p.
55-003485   735.42
Sculpture, Medieval. Sculpture -- Great Britain.

NB467.R4 1982
Read, Benedict.
Victorian sculpture/ Benedict Read. New Haven: Published for Paul Mellon Centre for Studies in British Art by Yale University Press, 1982. x, 414 p.
81-070483   730/.941   0300025068
Sculpture, British. Sculpture, Victorian -- Great Britain. Sculpture, Modern -- 19th century -- Great Britain.

NB467.5.N48.B42 1983
Beattie, Susan.
The new sculpture/ Susan Beattie. New Haven: Published for the Paul Mellon Centre for Studies in British Art by Yale University Press, 1983. 272 p.
83-042876   730/.942   0300028601
New sculpture (Art movement) -- Great Britain. Sculpture, British. Sculpture, Modern -- 19th century -- Great Britain.

NB497.C35.W3 1982
Waldman, Diane.
Anthony Caro/ by Diane Waldman. New York: Abbeville Press, c1982. 232 p.
81-067311   730/.92/4   0896592308
Caro, Anthony, -- 1924- Sculptors -- Great Britain -- Biography.

NB497.E6.B8
Buckle, Richard.
Jacob Epstein, sculptor.   Cleveland, World Pub. Co. [c1963] 448 p.
63-011957
Epstein, Jacob, -- Sir, -- 1880-1959.

NB497.G64
Goldsworthy, Andy, 1956-
Time/ Andy Goldsworthy; chronology by Terry Friedman. New York: Harry N. Abrams, 2000. 202 p.
2001-267862   730/.92   0810944820
Goldsworthy, Andy, -- 1956- -- Catalogs. Goldsworthy, Andy, -- 1956- -- Diaries. Outdoor sculpture -- Catalogs.

NB497.M6.A35 1967
Moore, Henry, 1898-
Henry Moore on sculpture; a collection of the sculptor's writings and spoken words edited, with an introd., by Philip James. New York, Viking Press [1967] 293 p.
66-020426   730
Moore, Henry, -- 1898- -- Philosophy.

NB497.M6.F52
Moore, Henry, 1898-
Henry Moore: sculpture and environment/ photos. and text by David Finn; foreword by Kenneth Clark; commentaries by Henry Moore. New York: H. N. Abrams, 1976. 490 p.
76-012588   730/.92/4   0810913135
Moore, Henry, -- 1898-

NB497.M6.N43
Neumann, Erich.
The archetypal world of Henry Moore. Translated from the German by R. F. C. Hull. [New York] Pantheon Books [1959] 138 p.
58-008988   730.942
Moore, Henry, -- 1898-

NB543.S31413 1973
Sauerlander, Willibald.
Gothic sculpture in France, 1140-1270. Translated by Janet Sondheimer. Photos. by Max Hirmer. New York, H. N. Abrams [1973, c1972] 527 p.
76-160223   731/.88/20944   0810901471
   Sculpture, Gothic -- France. Sculpture, French.

NB553.A7.A4 1980
Museum of Modern Art (New York, N.Y.)
Arp/ edited with an introd. by James Thrall Soby; articles by Jean Hans Arp ... [et.al]. New York: Museum of Modern Art, New York; distributed by Doubleday c1958. 126 p.
58-013761   709/.2/4
Arp, Jean, -- 1887-1966 -- Exhibitions.

NB553.G35.P6 1970
Pound, Ezra, 1885-1972.
Gaudier-Brzeska, a memoir [by] Ezra Pound. New York, New Directions Pub. Corp., [1970] 147 p.
78-107490   730/.924
Gaudier-Brzeska, Henri, -- 1891-1915.

NB553.P45.P42
Penrose, Roland,
The sculpture of Picasso. Chronology by Alicia Legg. New York, Museum of Modern Art [1967] 231 p.
67-029395   730/.924
Picasso, Pablo, -- 1881-1973.

NB553.R7.B88 1993
Butler, Ruth, 1931-
Rodin: the shape of genius/ Ruth Butler. New Haven: Yale University Press, c1993. xv, 591 p.
92-043552   730/.92   0300054009
Rodin, Auguste, -- 1840-1917.   Sculptors -- France -- Biography.

NB553.R7.G78 1987
Grunfeld, Frederic V.
Rodin: a biography/ Frederic V. Grunfeld. New York: Holt, c1987. xii, 738 p.
87-000258   730/.92/4   0805002790
Rodin, Auguste, -- 1840-1917.   Sculptors -- France -- Biography.

NB568.5.E9.G47 1983
German expressionist sculpture/ organized by Stephanie Barron. Los Angeles, CA: Los Angeles County Museum of Art, [1983] 224 p.
83-013552   730/.943/074   0875871151
   Sculpture, German -- Exhibitions. Expressionism (Art) -- Germany -- Exhibitions. Sculpture, Modern -- 20th century -- Germany -- Exhibitions.

NB588.R5.A4 1999
Riemenschneider, Tilman, d. 1531.
Tilman Riemenschneider: master sculptor of the late Middle Ages/ Julien Chapuis; with contributions by Michael Baxandall ... [et al.]. Washington: National Gallery of Art, Washington; c1999. 352 p.
99-025450   730/.92   0300081626
Riemenschneider, Tilman, -- d. 1531 -- Exhibitions.

NB620.M66 1989
Montagu, Jennifer.
Roman baroque sculpture: the industry of art/ Jennifer Montagu. New Haven: Yale University Press, 1989. xi, 244 p.
88-030482   730/.945/632   0300043929
   Sculpture, Italian -- Italy -- Rome. Sculpture, Baroque -- Italy -- Rome. Sculpture -- Italy -- Rome -- Study and teaching.

NB623.A44.M66 1985
Montagu, Jennifer.
Alessandro Algardi/ Jennifer Montagu. New Haven: Published in association with the J. Paul Getty Trust by Yale University Press, 1985. 2 v.
84-052244   730/.92/4   0300031734
Algardi, Alessandro, -- 1598-1654 -- Criticism and interpretation. Algardi, Alessandro, -- 1598-1654 -- Catalogs.

NB623.B9.B2413 1982
Baldini, Umberto.
The sculpture of Michelangelo/ Umberto Baldini; photographs by Liberto Perugi; [translated by Clare Coope]. New York: Rizzoli, 1982, c1981. 299 p.
82-060032   730/.92/4   084780447X
Michelangelo Buonarroti, -- 1475-1564.

NB623.D7.P59213 1993
Poeschke, Joachim.
Donatello and his world: sculpture of the Italian Renaissance/ Joachim Poeschke; photographs by Albert Hirmer and Irmgard Ernstmeier-Hirmer; translated from the German by Russell Stockman. New York: H.N. Abrams, 1993. 496 p.
92-038115   730/.92   0810932113
Donatello, -- 1386?-1466 -- Criticism and interpretation. Sculpture, Italian. Sculpture, Renaissance -- Italy.

NB623.G465.A4 1987
Avery, Charles.
Giambologna: the complete sculpture/ Charles Avery; principal photographs by David Finn. Mt. Kisco, N.Y.: Moyer Bell, c1987. 288 p.
87-015227   730/.92/4   0918825393
Giambologna, -- 1529-1608 -- Catalogues raisonnes. Sculpture, Italian -- Catalogs. Sculpture -- 16th century -- Italy -- Catalogs. Mannerism (Art) -- Italy -- Catalogs.

NB623.R72.P66 1980
Pope-Hennessy, John Wyndham, 1913-
Luca della Robbia/ John Pope-Hennessy. Ithaca, N.Y.: Cornell University Press, 1980. 288 p.
79-013566   730/.92/4   0801412560
Robbia, Luca della, -- 1400?-1482.

NB623.V5.B88 1997
Butterfield, Andrew, 1959-
The sculptures of Andrea del Verrocchio/ Andrew Butterfield. New Haven: Yale University Press, c1997. 262 p.
97-013650   730/.92   0300071949
Verrocchio, Andrea del, -- 1435?-1488 -- Criticism and interpretation.   Sculpture, Renaissance -- Italy -- Themes, motives.

NB813.G6.W57
Withers, Josephine.
Julio Gonzalez: sculpture in iron/ Josephine Withers. New York: New York University Press, c1978. xv, 181 p.
76-026798   730/.92/4   0814791719
Gonzalez, Julio, -- 1876-1942.   Sculptors -- Spain -- Biography.

NB933.B7.S52 1989
Shanes, Eric.
Constantin Brancusi/ Eric Shanes. New York: Abbeville Press, c1989. 128 p.
88-007359   730/.92/4   0896599299
Brancusi, Constantin, -- 1876-1957 -- Criticism and interpretation.

NB955.P63.A2337 1994
Rose, Barbara.
Magdalena Abakanowicz/ Barbara Rose. New York: Harry N. Abrams, 1994. 224 p.
93-026843   709/.2   0810919478
Abakanowicz, Magdalena -- Criticism and interpretation. Fiberwork -- Poland.

NB1000-1053 History — Special countries — Asia. The Orient

NB1000.P34
Pal, Pratapaditya.
The sensuous immortals: a selection of sculptures from the Pan-Asian collection/ Pratapaditya Pal. Los Angeles: Los Angeles County Museum of Art; [1977] 264 p.
77-002619   732/.4/074019494   0875870791
Sculpture -- South Asia -- Exhibitions. Sculpture -- Asia, Southeastern -- Exhibitions.

NB1007.S67.K7
Kramrisch, Stella, 1898-
The presence of Siva/ Stella Kramrisch; photography by Praful C. Patel. Princeton, N.J.: Princeton University Press, c1981. x, 514 p.
80-008558   704.9/48945211   069103964X
Siva (Hindu deity) -- Art. Sculpture, Hindu -- India -- Elephanta Island. Cave temples -- India -- Elephanta Island. Ellora Caves (India)

NB1026.F6 1990
Fontein, Jan.
The sculpture of Indonesia/ Jan Fontein; with essays by R. Soekmono, Edi Sedyawati. Washington, D.C.: National Gallery of Art; c1990. 312 p.
89-013678   730/.9598/07473   0894681419
Sculpture, Indonesian -- Exhibitions.

NB1053.W34
Watson, William, 1917-
The sculpture of Japan, from the fifth to the fifteenth century. New York, Viking [1960] 216 p.
60-000910   730.952
Sculpture, Japanese. Art, Buddhist.

NB1080-1097 History — Special countries — Africa

NB1080.T76
Trowell, Kathleen Margaret.
Classical African sculpture [by] Margaret Trowell. New York, Praeger [1964] 103 p.
64-023110   730.96
Sculpture, African. Sculpture, Primitive.

NB1091.65.S54 1987
Sieber, Roy, 1923-
African art in the cycle of life/ Roy Sieber and Roslyn Adele Walker. Washington, D.C.: Published for the National Museum of African Art by the Smithsonian Press, c1987. 155 p.
87-020493   732/.2/0967074153   0874748216
Sculpture, African -- Exhibitions. Sculpture, Primitive -- Africa, Sub-Saharan -- Exhibitions. Art and society -- Africa, Sub-Saharan -- Exhibitions.

NB1097.W4.W5 1967b
Willett, Frank.
Ife in the history of West African sculpture. New York, McGraw-Hill [1967] 232 p.
67-014151   732/.2/096692
Sculpture, Primitive. Sculpture -- Ife.

NB1137 General works — Relation to other arts. Sculpture and architecture

NB1137.M37
Martin, F. David, 1920-
Sculpture and enlivened space: aesthetics and history/ F. David Martin. Lexington, Ky.: University Press of Kentucky, c1981. 276 p.
79-004006   730/.1   0813113865
Sculpture -- Philosophy. Painting -- Philosophy.

NB1140 General works — Treatises. Compends — 1801-

NB1140.H6
Hoffman, Malvina, 1887-1966.
Sculpture inside and out [by] Malvina Hoffman. New York, W. W. Norton & company [c1939] 330 p.
39-027322   730
Sculpture. Sculpture -- Technique.

NB1140.R4
Read, Herbert Edward, 1893-1968.
The art of sculpture. [New York] Pantheon Books [1956] xxxi, 152 p.
56-010426   730
Sculpture.

NB1140.W57 1977b
Wittkower, Rudolf.
Sculpture: processes and principles/ Rudolf Wittkower.
New York: Harper & Row, c1977. 288 p.
77-000258   730   0064300919
Sculpture.

NB1170 Technique

NB1170.A63 1983
Andrews, Oliver.
Living materials: a sculptor's handbook/ Oliver Andrews.
Berkeley: University of California Press, c1983. xii,
348 p.
77-071057   731/.2   0520034473
Sculpture -- Technique. Modeling.

NB1170.R5
Rich, Jack C., 1914-
The materials and methods of sculpture. New York,
Oxford Univ. Press, 1947. xxi, 416 p.
47-011263   731
Sculpture -- Technique. Artists' materials.

NB1202 Sculpture materials

NB1202.P46 1993
Penny, Nicholas, 1949-
The materials of sculpture/ Nicholas Penny. New Haven:
Yale University Press, 1993. ix, 318 p.
93-003574   730/.028   0300055544
Sculpture materials.

NB1210 Sculpture in special materials —
Stone — Special types, A-Z

NB1210.M3.K3 1990
Kasson, Joy S.
Marble queens and captives: women in nineteenth-
century American sculpture/ Joy S. Kasson. New Haven:
Yale University Press, c1990. xviii, 293 p.
89-077342   730/.973/09034   0300045964
*Marble sculpture, American. Marble sculpture -- 19th century
-- United States. Women in art.*

NB1220 Sculpture in special materials —
Metals

NB1220.C65 2000
Collischan, Judy.
Welded sculpture of the twentieth century/ Judy
Collischan. New York: Hudson Hills Press in association
with the Neuberger Museum of Art, Purchase, New York;
[Lanham, MD]: Distributed by National Book Network,
c2000. 139 p.
99-053999   735/.23   1555951678
Welded sculpture -- 20th century.

NB1220.P5 1993
Picasso and the age of iron/ curated by Carmen Gimenez;
essays by Dore Ashton, Francisco Calvo Serraller. New
York, N.Y.: Guggenheim Museum, 1993. 331 p.
93-213832   735/.23/00747471   0892071036
*Picasso, Pablo, -- 1881-1973 -- Influence -- Exhibitions. Metal
sculpture -- Exhibitions. Art, Modern -- 20th century --
Exhibitions. Sculpture, Modern -- 20th century -- Exhibitions.*

NB1255 Sculpture in special materials —
Wood. Driftwood — Special. By country, A-Z

NB1255.G3.B39
Baxandall, Michael.
The limewood sculptors of Renaissance Germany/
Michael Baxandall. New Haven: Yale University Press,
1980. xx, 420 p.
79-023258   730/.943   0300024231
*Wood sculpture, Renaissance -- Germany. Wood sculpture,
German.*

NB1296.2 Sculpture - Special forms —
Portrait sculpture.
Group portraits — By period

NB1296.2.A75 1996
Arnold, Dorothea.
The royal women of Amarna: images of beauty from
ancient Egypt/ Dorothea Arnold with contributions by
James P. Allen and L. Green. New York: Metropolitan
Museum of Art: c1996. xxi, 169 p.
96-034517   732/.8/0747471   0870998161
*Amenhotep -- III, -- King of Egypt -- Family -- Art --
Exhibitions. Portrait sculpture, Ancient -- Egypt -- Tell el-
Amarna -- Exhibitions. Portrait sculpture, Egyptian -- Egypt --
Tell el-Amarna -- Exhibitions. Queens -- Egypt -- Tell el-
Amarna -- Portraits -- Exhibitions.*

NB1296.2.R87 1989
Russmann, Edna R.
Egyptian sculpture: Cairo and Luxor/ by Edna R.
Russmann; photographs by David Finn. Austin:
University of Texas Press, 1989. xi, 230 p.
89-005315   732/.8   029270402X
*Portrait sculpture, Egyptian -- Egypt -- Cairo. Portrait
sculpture, Ancient -- Egypt -- Cairo. Portrait sculpture,
Egyptian -- Egypt -- Luxor.*

NB1296.2.S63 1988
Spanel, Donald, 1952-
Through ancient eyes: Egyptian portraiture: an exhibition
organized for the Birmingham Museum of Art,
Birmingham, Alabama, April 21-July 31, 1988/ by
Donald Spanel. Birmingham, Ala.: The Museum; c1988.
xiii, 159 p.
88-007325   732/.8
*Portrait sculpture, Egyptian -- Exhibitions. Portrait sculpture,
Ancient -- Egypt -- Exhibitions.*

NB1820 Sculpture - Special forms — Sepulchral monuments — Effigies

NB1820.M72 2000
Morganstern, Anne McGee, 1936-
Gothic tombs of kinship in France, the low countries, and England/ Anne McGee Morganstern; with an appendix on the heraldry of the Crouchback tomb in Westminster Abbey by John A. Goodall. University Park, Pa.: Pennsylvania State University Press, c2000. xix, 252 p.
98-041261   731/.76/0940902   0271018593
Effigies -- France. Sepulchral monuments, Gothic -- France. Effigies -- Europe, Northern.

NB1880 Sculpture - Special forms — Sepulchral monuments — Stone monuments, tablets, etc

NB1880.C6.P68 1991
Powers, Martin Joseph, 1949-
Art & political expression in early China/ Martin J. Powers. New Haven: Yale University Press, c1991. xiv, 438 p.
90-020341   732/.71   0300047673
Sepulchral monuments -- Political aspects -- China -- History. Sculpture, Chinese -- Chin-Han dynasties, 221 B.C.-220 A.D.

NB1910 Special subjects — Religious subjects — General works

NB1910.B57 1995
Blier, Suzanne Preston.
African vodun: art, psychology, and power/ Suzanne Preston Blier. Chicago: University of Chicago Press, 1995. xi, 476 p.
94-002180   730/.09668   0226058581
Sculpture, Black -- Benin. Sculpture, Primitive -- Benin. Sculpture -- Benin.

NB1912 Special subjects — Religious subjects — Special, A-Z

NB1912.H55.D38 1997
Davis, Richard H.
Lives of Indian images/ Richard H. Davis. Princeton, NJ: Princeton University Press, c1997. xiii, 331 p.
96-022196   730/.954   069102622X
Gods, Hindu, in art. Sculpture, Hindu. Art and anthropology -- India.

NB1930 Special subjects — Humans — General works

NB1930.F59 1998
Flynn, Tom, 1956-
The body in three dimensions/ Tom Flynn. New York City: Harry N. Abrams, Inc., c1998. 176 p.
97-034767   731/.82   0810927160
Human figure in art.

NC Drawing. Design. Illustration

NC45 Collective biography

NC45.W5
Who's who in graphic art.   Zurich: Amstutz & Herdeg Graphis Press, [1962-   ]
62-051802
Artists -- Directories. Artists -- Biography. Graphic arts -- Bio-bibliography.

NC70 History of drawing — Medieval

NC70.D7 1998
Drawing, 1400-1600: invention and innovation/ edited by Stuart Currie. Aldershot, Hants, England; Ashgate, c1998. xxii, 237 p.
97-033668   741/.09/024   1859283640
Drawing, Gothic. Drawing, Renaissance. Drawing, Baroque.

NC80 History of drawing — Modern

NC80.R6
Rosenberg, Jakob, 1893-
Great draughtsmen from Pisanello to Picasso. Cambridge, Harvard University Press, 1959. xxvi, 142 p.
59-007661   741.94
Drawing. Drawing -- History. Artists.

NC108-287 History of drawing — Special countries

NC108.Z87 1988
Zurier, Rebecca.
Art for the Masses: a radical magazine and its graphics, 1911-1917/ Rebecca Zurier; with an introd. by Leslie Fishbein, and artists' biographies by Elise K. Kenney and Earl Davis. Philadelphia: Temple University Press, 1988. xviii, 216 p.
87-010033   760/.0973   0877225133
Drawing, American. Drawing -- 20th century -- United States. Social problems in art.

NC139.B45.A4 1990
Adams, Henry, 1949-
Thomas Hart Benton: drawing from life/ Henry Adams. New York: Abbeville Press, c1990. 207 p.
89-037316   741.973   1558590110
Benton, Thomas Hart, -- 1889-1975 -- Exhibitions.

NC139.C32.A2 1989
Cadmus, Paul, 1904-
The drawings of Paul Cadmus/ introduction by Guy
Davenport. New York: Rizzoli, 1989. 144 p.
89-042957   741.973   0847811441
Cadmus, Paul, -- 1904-   Human figure in art. Nude in art.

NC139.J58.S5 1984
Shapiro, David, 1947-
Jasper Johns drawings, 1954-1984/ text by David
Shapiro; project director, David Whitney; editor,
Christopher Sweet. New York: Abrams, 1984. 211 p.
83-025775   741/.092/4   0810911566
Johns, Jasper, -- 1930-

NC139.K27
Kahn, Wolf, 1927-
Wolf Kahn pastels/ by Wolf Kahn; with an introduction
by Barbara Novak. New York: Harry N. Abrams, 2000.
00-022801   741.2/35   0810967073
Kahn, Wolf, -- 1927- Landscape in art.

NC139.K37.A4 1999
Bois, Yve Alain.
Ellsworth Kelly: the early drawings, 1948-1955/ Yve-
Alain Bois. Cambridge, Mass.: Harvard University Art
Museums; 1999. 263 p.
98-053905   741.973   1891771094
Kelly, Ellsworth, -- 1923- -- Exhibitions.

NC139.P6.A4 1992
Cernuschi, Claude, 1961-
Jackson Pollock, "psychoanalytic" drawings/ Claude
Cernuschi; foreword by Michael P. Mezzatesta. Durham:
Duke University Press in association with the Duke
University Museum of Art, 1992. ix, 143 p.
91-039716   741.973   0822312506
*Pollock, Jackson, -- 1912-1956 -- Exhibitions.   Psychoanalysis
and art -- Exhibitions.*

NC139.R56.A4 1979
Rivers, Larry, 1925-
Drawings and digressions/ by Larry Rivers with Carol
Brightman. New York: C.N. Potter: 1979. 263 p.
79-004614   741.9/73   0517534304
Rivers, Larry, -- 1925-

NC228.B47 2000
Bermingham, Ann.
Learning to draw: studies in the cultural history of a
polite and useful art/ Ann Bermingham. New Haven, CT:
Published for the Paul Mellon Centre for Studies in
British Art by Yale University Press, c2000. xv, 304 p.
99-059794   306.4/7   0300080395
  *Drawing, English -- Social aspects. Art, Amateur -- England --
History.*

NC242.B3.C36 1998
Calloway, Stephen.
Aubrey Beardsley/ Stephen Calloway. New York, N.Y.:
Harry N. Abrams, 1998. 224 p.
97-027611   741/.092   0810940094
*Beardsley, Aubrey, -- 1872-1898 -- Criticism and interpretation.
Erotic drawing -- England.*

NC242.B3.F55 1987
Fletcher, Ian.
Aubrey Beardsley/ by Ian Fletcher. Boston: Twayne
Publishers, c1987. 206 p.
87-016464   741.6/092/4   0805769587
*Beardsley, Aubrey, -- 1872-1898 -- Criticism and interpretation.
Drawing, English. Drawing -- 19th century -- England.*

NC242.B3.S66 1995
Snodgrass, Chris.
Aubrey Beardsley, dandy of the grotesque/ Chris
Snodgrass. New York: Oxford University Press, 1995.
xix, 338 p.
94-018473   741/.092   0195090624
*Beardsley, Aubrey, -- 1872-1898 -- Criticism and interpretation.
Grotesque in art.*

NC242.C46.M34 1990
McCorduck, Pamela, 1940-
Aaron's code: meta-art, artificial intelligence, and the
work of Harold Cohen/ Pamela McCorduck. New York:
W.H. Freeman, c1991. xvi, 225 p.
90-036940   760   0716721732
*Cohen, Harold, -- 1928- -- Criticism and interpretation.
Computer drawing -- Themes, motives.*

NC242.G3.A4 1970
Hayes, John T.
The drawings of Thomas Gainsborough/ John Hayes.
New Haven: Published for the Paul Mellon Centre for
Studies in British Art by Yale University Press, 1971,
c1970. 2 v.
78-140108   741/.092/4   0300014252
Gainsborough, Thomas, -- 1727-1788 -- Catalogs.

NC242.T3 . S3
Sarzano, Frances.
Sir John Tenniel. London, Art and Technics, 1948. 96 p.
48-003330   741.91
Tenniel, John, -- Sir, -- 1820-1914.

NC245.S34.N4313 1989
Nebehay, Christian Michael, 1909-
Egon Schiele sketchbooks/ Christian M. Nebehay. New
York: Rizzoli, 1989. 374 p.
89-042970   700/.92   0847811336
Schiele, Egon, -- 1890-1918 -- Criticism and interpretation.

NC248.M55.A4 1999
Jean-Francois Millet: drawn into the light/ Alexandra R.
Murphy ... [et al.]. New Haven, CT: Yale University
Press, 1999. 137 p.
99-011142   741.944   0300079257
Millet, Jean Francois, -- 1814-1875 -- Exhibitions.

NC248.P64.A4 1995
Clayton, Martin, 1967-
Poussin: works on paper: drawings from the collection of
Her Majesty Queen Elizabeth II/ Martin Clayton. New
York: Thames and Hudson, 1995. 208 p.
94-061097   741.944   050023700X
*Poussin, Nicolas, -- 1594?-1665 -- Exhibitions. Elizabeth, -- II, -
- Queen of Great Britain, -- 1926- -- Art collections --
Exhibitions.   Drawing -- Private collections -- England --
Windsor (Berkshire) -- Exhibitions.*

NC248.R58.E4
Elsen, Albert Edward, 1927-
The drawings of Rodin [by] Albert Elsen [and] J. Kirk T.
Varnedoe. With additional contributions by Victoria
Thorson and Elisabeth Chase Geissbuhler. New York,
Praeger Publishers [1972, c1971] 191 p.
76-159409   741.9/44
Rodin, Auguste, -- 1840-1917.

NC257.B8.H57 1988
Hirst, Michael.
Michelangelo and his drawings/ Michael Hirst. New
Haven: Yale University Press, c1988. xvi, 132 p.
88-050431   741/.092/4   0300043910
*Michelangelo Buonarroti, -- 1475-1564 -- Criticism and
interpretation. Michelangelo Buonarroti, -- 1475-1564 --
Themes, motives.*

NC257.L56.A4 1997
Lippi, Filippino, d. 1504.
The drawings of Filippino Lippi and his circle/ George R.
Goldner, Carmen C. Bambach; [with] Alessandro Cecchi
... [et al.]. New York: Metropolitan Museum of Art:
c1997. xii, 406 p.
97-028294   741.945   0870998285
*Lippi, Filippino, -- d. 1504 -- Exhibitions. Lippi, Filippino, -- d.
1504 -- Influencce -- Exhibitions. Drawing -- 15th century --
Italy -- Exhibitions.*

NC257.T5.A4 1996e
Tiepolo, Giovanni Battista, 1696-1770.
Domenico Tiepolo, master draftsman/ curated by
Adelheid M. Gealt, George Know. Bloomington: Indiana
University Press, c1996. 253 p.
97-002504   741.945   025333330X
Tiepolo, Giovanni Battista, -- 1696-1770 -- Exhibitions.

NC263.G56.W6513 1987
Wolk, Johannes van der.
The Seven sketchbooks of Vincent van Gogh/ Johannes
van der Wolk; translated from the Dutch by Claudia
Swan. New York: H.N. Abrams, 1987. 320 p.
87-001351   741.9492   0810917319
*Gogh, Vincent van, -- 1853-1890 -- Criticism and interpretation.
Gogh, Vincent van, -- 1853-1890 -- Notebooks, sketchbooks, etc.
Drawing, Dutch. Drawing -- 19th century -- Netherlands.
Artists' preparatory studies -- Netherlands.*

NC287.G65
Bareau, Juliet Wilson.
Goya: drawings from his private albums/ Juliet Wilson-
Bareau; with an essay by Tom Lubbock. London:
Hayward Gallery in association with Lund Humphries,
2001. 206 p.
00-112061   741.946   0853318042
*Goya, Francisco, -- 1746-1828 -- Exhibitions. Goya, Francisco,
-- 1746-1828 -- Notebooks, sketchbooks, etc. -- Exhibitions.*

NC703 General works —
Theory of design

NC703.K58 1952
Klee, Paul, 1879-1940.
Pedagogical sketchbook/ Paul Klee; [introd. and
translation by Sibyl Moholy-Nagy] New York: F.A.
Praeger, c1953. 60 p.
52-013103   745.42
Composition (Art) Design.

NC703.S35
Scott, Robert Gillam.
Design fundamentals. New York, McGraw-Hill, 1951.
ix, 199 p.
51-009565   745.4
Design. Proportion (Art)

NC715 General works —
General special

NC715.R7
Rosenberg, Jakob, 1893-
On quality in art; criteria of excellence, past and present.
[Princeton, N.J.] Princeton University Press [1967] xxiv,
264 p.
67-022342   701/.1/8
Art criticism. Drawing.

NC735 Technique —
Studies for artists

NC735.W36
Watrous, James, 1908-
The craft of old-master drawings/ James Watrous.
Madison, Wis.: University of Wisconsin Press, 1957.
170 p.
56-009307   741
Drawing -- Study and teaching. Drawing -- History. Drawing.

NC750 Technique —
Perspective — 1801-

NC750.E44 1994
Elkins, James, 1955-
The poetics of perspective/ James Elkins. Ithaca: Cornell
University Press, 1994. xv, 324 p.
94-016310   701/.82   0801427967
Perspective. Space perception. Aesthetics.

NC750.P2313 1991
Panofsky, Erwin, 1892-1968.
Perspective as symbolic form/ Erwin Panofsky; translated
by Christopher S. Wood. New York: Zone Books; 1991.
196 p.
91-010716   701/.82   0942299523
Perspective.

NC760 Special subjects (Technique, history and collections) — Art anatomy

NC760.G67 1991
Goldfinger, Eliot.
Human anatomy for artists: the elements of form/ by Eliot Goldfinger. New York: Oxford University Press, 1991. xiii, 348 p.
91-002891   702/.8   0195052064
Anatomy, Artistic. Human figure in art.

NC760.S32 1957
Schider, Fritz, 1846-1907.
An atlas of anatomy for artists. Rev. by M. Auerbach and translated by Bernard Wolf. New bibliography by Adolf Placzek. Additional illus. from the old masters and historical sources. With a new section on hands selected by Heidi Lenssen. [New York] Dover Publications [c1957] 1 v.
58-003622   743.4
Anatomy, Artistic. Human anatomy -- Atlases.

NC780 Special subjects (Technique, history and collections) — Art anatomy — Animal and wildlife anatomy and drawing

NC780.E62 1956
Ellenberger, Wilhelm, 1848-1929.
An atlas of animal anatomy for artists, by W. Ellenberger, H. Baum, and H. Dittrich. New York, Dover Publications, 1956. 153 p.
56-014001   743.6
Animal painting and illustration. Anatomy, Artistic.

NC960 Drawing for reproduction — Illustration

NC960.B62 1969b
Bland, David.
A history of book illustration; the illuminated manuscript and the printed book. Berkeley, University of California Press, 1969. 459 p.
69-012472   745.6/7
Illustration of books -- History. Illumination of books and manuscripts -- History.

NC960.B7
The artist & the book, 1860-1960, in western Europe and the United States. Boston, Museum of Fine Arts; [1961] 232 p.
61-013493   741.64
Illustrated books -- Exhibitions.

NC961.63 Drawing for reproduction — Illustration — Directories

NC961.63.C37 1989
Castagno, John, 1930-
Artists as illustrators: an international directory with signatures and monograms, 1800 -- the present/ by John Castagno. Metuchen, N.J.: Scarecrow Press, 1989. xvii, 625 p.
88-034832   741.6/092/2   0810821680
Illustrators -- Directories. Illustrators -- Autographs -- Facsimiles. Artists' marks.

NC963 Drawing for reproduction — Illustration — Special styles, A-Z

NC963.S87.H8 1988
Hubert, Renee Riese, 1916-
Surrealism and the book/ Renee Riese Hubert. Berkeley: University of California Press, c1988. xvii, 358 p.
86-016099   741.64/09/04   0520057198
Surrealism -- Themes, motives. Illustration of books -- 20th century -- Themes, motives. Narrative art -- Themes, motives.

NC965 Drawing for reproduction — Illustration of children's books — General works

NC965.M34 1992
Marantz, Sylvia S.
Artists of the page: interviews with children's book illustrators/ by Sylvia Marantz, Kenneth Marantz. Jefferson, N.C.: McFarland, c1992. xvi, 255 p.
91-050951   741.6/42/0922 20   0899507018
Illustrators -- Interviews. Illustrated children's books. Illustration of books -- 20th century.

NC965.M59
Miller, Bertha E. Mahony.
Illustrators of children's books, 1744-1945, compiled by Bertha E. Mahony, Louise Payson Latimer [and] Beulah Folmsbee. Boston, Horn Book, 1947. xvi, 527 p.
47-031264   741/.092/2
Illustrators. Children's literature -- Illustrations. Illustration of books.

NC975.5 Illustration in special countries — United States — Special illustrators, A-Z

NC975.5.H65.T38 1992
Tatham, David.
Winslow Homer and the illustrated book/ David Tatham. Syracuse, N.Y.: Syracuse University Press, 1992. xiv, 348 p.
91-013534   741.6/4/092   0815625502
Homer, Winslow, -- 1836-1910 -- Criticism and interpretation. Illustration of books -- 19th century -- United States.

NC997.L54-R27 Commercial art.
Advertising art — General works

NC997.L54 1992
Livingston, Alan.
The Thames and Hudson encyclopaedia of graphic design and designers/ Alan and Isabella Livingston. New York, N.Y.: Thames and Hudson, 1992. 215 p.
92-070862   741.6/03   0500202591
Graphic arts -- Dictionaries. Commercial art -- Dictionaries. Designers -- Biography -- Dictionaries.

NC997.R27 1993
Rand, Paul, 1914-
Design, form, and chaos/ Paul Rand. New Haven: Yale University Press, 1993. xii, 218 p.
92-062277   741.6   0300055536
Commercial art. Design.

NC998 Commercial art. Advertising art — History — General works

NC998.H65 1994
Hollis, Richard.
Graphic design: a concise history/ Richard Hollis. New York: Thames and Hudson, 1994. 224 p.
93-060431   741.6/09   0500202702
Graphic arts -- History. Commercial art -- History.

NC998.4 Commercial art. Advertising art — History — By period

NC998.4.G667 2001
Graphic design history/ edited by Steven Heller and Georgette Balance. New York: Allworth Press, c2001. 341 p.
2001-022588   741.6/09/04   1581150946
Commercial art -- 20th century -- History. Commercial artists -- Biography.

NC998.5-998.6 Commercial art. Advertising art — History — By region or country

NC998.5.A1.G65 1989
Graphic design in America: a visual language history/ foreword, Caroline Hightower; introduction, Mildred Friedman; essays, Joseph Giovannini ... [et al.]; interviews, Steven Heller. Minneapolis: Walker Art Center; 1989. 264 p.
89-000445   741.6/0973/074   0810910365
Commercial art -- United States -- Exhibitions. Graphic arts -- United States -- Exhibitions.

NC998.6.F72.P374 1988
The Graphic arts and French society, 1871-1914/ edited by Phillip Dennis Cate; essays by Phillip Dennis Cate [... et al.]. New Brunswick, [N.J.]: Rutgers University Press: c1988. viii, 195 p.
87-016274   741.6/0944/361   0813512786
Graphic arts -- France -- Paris -- History -- 19th century. Graphic arts -- France -- Paris -- History -- 20th century. Prints, French -- France -- Paris. Paris (France) -- Intellectual life.

NC998.6.J3.F73 1996
Fraser, James, 1933-
Japanese modern: graphic design between the wars/ [text by] James Fraser, [edited by] Steven Heller, [art direction] Seymour Chwast. San Francisco, CA: Chronicle Books, c1996. 131 p.
95-021550   741.6/0952/09042   0811805093
Commercial art -- Japan. Modernism (Art) -- Japan.

NC999 Commercial art. Advertising art — Directories

NC999.D57
Directory/ Graphic Artists Guild. New York, N.Y.: The Guild, 1984. 4 v.
81-080062   741.6/025/73
Commercial artists -- United States -- Directories.

NC999.E825 1999
Evans, Poppy,
Graphic designer's ultimate resource directory/ Poppy Evans. Cincinnati, Ohio: North Light Books, c1999. 192 p.
98-032411   741.6/029/473 21   089134912X
Commercial art -- United States -- Directories. Graphic arts -- United States -- Directories. Graphic arts equipment industry -- United States -- Directories.

NC1001.6 Commercial art. Advertising art — Economics of commercial art

NC1001.6.G7 1997
Graphic Artists Guild handbook: pricing & ethical guidelines. 9th ed. New York, NY: The Guild; xi, 313 p.
98-183613   741.6/068/8 21   0932102093
Graphic arts -- United States -- Marketing. Artists -- Professional ethics -- United States. Artists -- Legal status, laws, etc. -- United States.

NC1002 Commercial art.
Advertising art — Special topics, A-Z

NC1002.L47.L87 1996
Lupton, Ellen.
Letters from the avant-garde: modern graphic design/ Ellen Lupton and Elaine Lustig Cohen. New York: Princeton Architectural Press, 1996. 95 p.
96-028655   741.6   1568980523
Letterheads -- History -- 20th century. Stationery -- History -- 20th century. Business announcements -- History -- 20th century.

NC1055-1115 Books of reproductions of drawings

NC1055.L5.P58
Leonardo, da Vinci, 1452-1519.
The drawings of Leonardo da Vinci/ with an introduction and notes by A. E. Popham. New York: Reynal & Hitchcock, [1945] 172 p.
45-010204   741.91
Leonardo, -- da Vinci, -- 1452-1519.

NC1075.S47.S6
Shahn, Ben, 1898-1969.
Ben Shahn: his graphic art. Text by James Thrall Soby. New York, G. Braziller, 1957. 139 p.
57-012840   741.91

NC1115.B316
Beardsley, Aubrey, 1872-1898.
The best of Beardsley, collected and ed. by R.A. Walker. London, Bodley Head [1948] 21 p.
49-002062   741.91

NC1280 Printed ephemera.
Imagerie populaire — General works

NC1280.R52 2001
Rickards, Maurice, 1919-
The encyclopedia of ephemera/ Maurice Rickards. New York: Routledge, 2000. x, 402 p.
00-062569   769.5/03   0415926483
Printed ephemera -- Dictionaries. Printed ephemera -- Collectors and collecting.

NC1325 Caricature.
Pictorial humor and satire — History — General works

NC1325.W67 1999
The world encyclopedia of cartoons/ Maurice Horn, editor. Philadelphia: Chelsea House, 1999. 945 p.
98-037201   741.5/03   0791048551
Caricatures and cartoons. Comic books, strips, etc. Wit and humor, Pictorial.

NC1355 Caricature.
Pictorial humor and satire — History — Modern

NC1355.B28513
A History of the comic strip, by Pierre Couperie [and others] Translated from the French by Eilleen B. Hennessy. New York, Crown Publishers [1968] 256 p.
68-020471   741.5/09
Comic books, strips, etc. -- History and criticism.

NC1425-1429 Caricature.
Pictorial humor and satire — History — Special countries

NC1425.S54 1994
Sheppard, Alice, 1945-
Cartooning for suffrage/ Alice Sheppard; introduction by Elisabeth Israels Perry. Albuquerque: University of New Mexico Press, c1994. xxviii, 276 p.
93-010570   741.5/082   0826314589
Women -- Suffrage -- Caricatures and cartoons. Women cartoonists -- United States -- Psychology. Cartooning -- United States -- History -- 19th century.

NC1426.R3 1998
Reaves, Wendy Wick, 1950-
Celebrity caricature in America/ Wendy Wick Reaves; Pie Friendly, research assistant. New Haven: National Portrait Gallery, Smithsonian Institution, in association with Yale University Press, c1998. xiii, 306 p.
97-046906   741.5/074/753   0300074638
American wit and humor, Pictorial -- New York (State) -- New York -- History -- 20th century -- Exhibitions. Celebrities -- United States -- Caricatures and cartoons -- Exhibitions.

NC1428.N427
The New Yorker twenty-fifth anniversary album, 1925-1950. New York, Harper [1951] 1 v.
51-013315   741.5
American wit and humor, Pictorial.

NC1429.M428.A2 1971
Mauldin, Bill, 1921-
The brass ring [by] Bill Mauldin. New York, Norton [1971] 275 p.
78-152671   741/.0924   0393074633
Mauldin, Bill, -- 1921-

NC1429.N3.K4
Keller, Morton.
The art and politics of Thomas Nast. New York, Oxford University Press, 1968. vii, 353 p.
68-019762   817/.4
Nast, Thomas, -- 1840-1902.

NC1429.T48
Thurber, James, 1894-1961.
Men, women, and dogs, a book of drawings, with a preface by Dorothy Parker. New York, Harcourt, Brace [1943] x, 211 p.
43-017507

NC1765 Caricature.
Pictorial humor and satire —
Animated films — General works

NC1765.B4213 1994
Bendazzi, Giannalberto.
Cartoons: one hundred years of cinema animation/ by
Giannalberto Bendazzi; [translated by Anna Taraboletti-
Segre]. Bloomington, Ind.: Indiana University Press,
c1994. xxiii, 514 p.
94-029075   791.43/3   0253311683
Animated films -- History and criticism.

NC1766 Caricature.
Pictorial humor and satire —
Animated films — By country, A-Z

NC1766.J3.N37 2001
Napier, Susan Jolliffe.
Anime from Akira to Princess Mononoke: experiencing
contemporary Japanese animation/ Susan J. Napier. New
York: Palgrave, 2001. viii, 311 p.
00-051473   791.43/3   0312238622
Animated films -- Japan.

NC1766.U5.L46 1999
Lenburg, Jeff.
The encyclopedia of animated cartoons/ Jeff Lenburg;
foreword by June Foray. New York: Facts on File, c1999.
xv, 576 p.
98-046100   791.43/3   0816038317
Animated films -- United States -- History and criticism.

NC1766.U5.S66 1993
Smoodin, Eric Loren.
Animating culture: Hollywood cartoons from the sound
era/ Eric Smoodin. New Brunswick, N.J.: Rutgers
University Press, c1993. xvi, 216 p.
92-032891   791.43/3   0813519489
Animated films -- United States -- History and criticism.
Animated films -- Political aspects -- United States.

NC1766.U52.D58 1981
Thomas, Frank, 1912-
Disney animation: the illusion of life/ Frank Thomas and
Ollie Johnston. New York: Abbeville Press, c1981.
575 p.
81-012699   741.5/8/0979494   0896592324
Animated films -- United States -- History and criticism.

NC1766.U52.D5927 1997
Watts, Steven, 1952-
The Magic Kingdom: Walt Disney and the American way
of life/ Steven Watts. Boston: Houghton Mifflin, 1997.
xvii, 526 p.
97-018301   791.43/092   0395835879
Disney, Walt, -- 1901-1966.   Animators -- United States --
Biography.

NC1766.U52.W3737 1988
Schneider, Steve.
That's all folks!: the art of Warner Bros. animation/ Steve
Schneider; foreword by Ray Bradbury. New York: H.
Holt, c1988. 252 p.
88-081823   741.5/8/0979493   0805008896
Animated films -- United States -- History and criticism.

NC1766.5 Caricature.
Pictorial humor and satire —
Animated films — Special topics, A-Z

NC1766.5.A35.S26 1997
Sampson, Henry T., 1934-
That's enough, folks: Black images in animated cartoons,
1900-1960/ Henry T. Sampson. Lanham, Md.: Scarecrow
Press, 1998. viii, 249 p.
96-049987   791.43/6520396073   081083250X
Animated films -- United States -- History and criticism. Afro-
Americans in motion pictures.

NC1766.5.C45.C64 1997
Cohen, Karl F.
Forbidden animation: censored cartoons and blacklisted
animators in America/ by Karl F. Cohen. Jefferson, N.C.:
McFarland & Co., c1997. 230 p.
97-023882   791.43/3   0786403950
Animated films -- Censorship -- United States. Animators --
United States -- Biography.

NC1806.8 Posters — History — Modern

NC1806.8.M87 1988
Museum of Modern Art (New York, N.Y.)
The modern poster/ Stuart Wrede. New York: Museum of
Modern Art; c1988. 263 p.
88-060744   741.67/4/090407401471   0870705709
Posters -- 20th century -- Exhibitions.

NC1807 Posters —
Special countries, A-Z

NC1807.S65.W48 1988
White, Stephen, 1945-
The Bolshevik poster/ Stephen White. New Haven: Yale
University Press, 1988. vii, 152 p.
88-014275   741.67/4/0947   0300043392
Posters, Soviet. Posters -- 20th century -- Soviet Union.

NC1807.U5.D46 1987
DeNoon, Christopher.
Posters of the WPA/ Christopher DeNoon; introduction,
Francis V. O'Connor. Los Angeles: Wheatley Press, in
association with the University of Washington Press,
Seattle, c1987. 175 p.
87-050519   741.67/4/0973   0295965436
Posters, American -- Catalogs. Posters -- 20th century --
United States -- Catalogs.

NC1807.U5.H49 1998
Heyman, Therese Thau.
Posters American style/ Therese Thau Heyman. New York: National Museum of American, Smithsonian Institution in association with H.N. Abrams, c1998. 191 p.
97-038050　741.6/74/0973074753　0810937492
Posters, American -- Exhibitions. Posters -- 19th century -- United States -- Exhibitions. Posters -- 20th century -- United States -- Exhibitions.

NC1815 Posters — General special

NC1815.A33 1984
Ades, Dawn.
The 20th-century poster: design of the avant-garde/ by Dawn Ades with contributions by Robert Brown ... [et al.]; Mildred Friedman, editor. New York: Abbeville Press, 1984. 215 p.
83-073420　741.67/4/0904　0896594335
Posters -- 20th century -- Themes, motives.

NC1850 Posters — Posters by special artists

NC1850.T6.J83
Toulouse-Lautrec, Henri de, 1864-1901.
The posters of Toulouse-Lautrec. [Text by] Edouard Julien. Translated from the French by Daphne Woodward. Monte-Carlo, A. Sauret; 1951. 101 p.
51-008340　741.67
Posters.

NC1883 Book jackets. Phonorecord jackets — Special countries, A-Z

NC1883.U6.H45 1995
Heller, Steven.
Jackets required/ Steven Heller, Seymour Chwast. San Francisco: Chronicle Books, c1995. 143 p.
94-013260　741.6/4/097309041　0811803961
Book jackets -- United States -- History -- 20th century -- Themes, motives. Book jackets -- United States -- Design.

ND Painting

ND35 Biography — Collective — 1801-

ND35.B413
Berckelaers, Ferdinand Louis, 1901-
Dictionary of abstract painting, New York, Tudor Pub. Co. [1957] 304 p.
58-001975
Painters -- Dictionaries. Art, Abstract. Painting -- History.

ND38 Biography — Collective — Women painters

ND38.G73 1979
Greer, Germaine, 1939-
The obstacle race: the fortunes of women painters and their work/ Germaine Greer. New York: Farrar, Straus, Giroux, 1979. 373 p.
79-017026　759　0374224129
Women painters -- Biography. Painting -- History.

ND40 Catalogues raisonnés (General)

ND40.W75 1991
Wright, Christopher, 1945-
The world's master paintings: from the early Renaissance to the present day: a comprehensive listing of works by 1,300 painters and a complete guide to their locations worldwide/ compiled by Christopher Wright. London; Routledge, 1992. 2 v.
91-031694　750/.74　0415022401
Painting -- Catalogs. Painters -- Catalogs.

ND45 Other general catalogs of paintings. Indexes to paintings

ND45.M6
Monro, Isabel Stevenson.
Index to reproductions of European paintings; a guide to pictures in more than three hundred books, by Isabel Stevenson Monro and Kate M. Monro. New York, Wilson, 1956. 668 p.
55-006803　016.759
Painting -- Indexes.

ND50 History — General works

ND50.B396 1999
Beckett, Wendy.
Sister Wendy's 1000 masterpieces/ Sister Wendy Beckett; contributing consultant, Patricia Wright. New York: DK Pub., 1999. 512 p.
99-020355　759　0789446030
Painting -- History. Art appreciation.

ND50.E2 1960
Eastlake, Charles Lock, Sir.
Methods and materials of painting of the great schools and masters. Dover, 1960. 2 v.
61-000459　751.4
Painting -- Technique. Painting -- History.

ND50.R6 1951a
Robb, David Metheny, 1903-
The Harper history of painting: the occidental tradition, by David M. Robb. New York, Harper [1951] 1006 p.
51-007191　750.9
Painting -- History.

ND75 History — Ancient — Egyptian

ND75.M4
Mekhitarian, Arpag.
Egyptian painting. Translated by Stuart Gilbert. [New York] Skira [1954] 164 p.
54-011064   759.932   0847801616
Painting, Egyptian.

ND120 History — Ancient — Classical

ND120.M25
Maiuri, Amedeo, 1886-1963.
Roman painting. Translated by Stuart Gilbert. Geneva Skira; Distributed by World Pub. Co. [1953] 158 p.
53-008293   751.73
Painting, Roman. Mural painting and decoration, Roman. Painting, Greco-Roman.

ND140 History — Medieval — General works

ND140.B4 1971
Berenson, Bernard, 1865-1959.
Studies in medieval painting. New York, Da Capo Press, 1971 [c1930] xxii, 148 p.
73-153884   759.02   0306702924
Painting, Medieval. Illumination of books and manuscripts, Medieval.

ND140.D85
Dupont, Jacques.
Gothic painting. Translated by Stuart Gilbert. Geneva Skira [1954] 215 p.
54-007294   750.902
Painting, Gothic.

ND140.G683
Grabar, Andre, 1896-
Romanesque painting from the eleventh to the thirteenth century: Mural painting, by Andre Grabar.   Book illumination, by Carl Nordenfalk. [Translated by Stuart Gilbert. New York] Skira [1958] 229 p.
58-008335   750.902
Painting, Romanesque. Painting, Romanesque.

ND140.G7
Grabar, Andre, 1896-
Early medieval painting from the fourth to the eleventh century: Mosaics and mural painting, by Andre Grabar. Book illumination, by Carl Nordenfalk. Translated by Stuart Gilbert. [New York] Skira [1957] 241 p.
57-011641   750.902
Painting, Medieval.

ND141 History — Medieval — General special

ND141.B85 1970
Bunim, Miriam (Schild) 1912-
Space in medieval painting and the forerunners of perspective. New York, AMS Press [1970, c1940] xviii, 261 p.
70-121231   751.4   0404012299
Perspective. Painting, Medieval.

ND142 History — Medieval — Byzantine

ND142.G7
Grabar, Andre, 1896-
Byzantine painting; historical and critical study. Translated by Stuart Gilbert. Geneva Skira [1953] 200 p.
53-011064   755.3
Christian art and symbolism. Mural painting and decoration. Mosaics.

ND170-196 History — Modern — By century

ND170.D86 1999
Dunkerton, Jill.
Durer to Veronese: sixteenth-century paintings in the National Gallery/ Jill Dunkerton, Susan Foister, and Nicholas Penny. New Haven, Conn.: Yale University Press; c1999. xi, 317 p.
99-025852   759.03/074/42132   0300072201
Painting -- 16th century -- Europe. Painting -- England -- London. Painting, European.

ND170.H3 1991
Hall, Marcia B.
Color and meaning: practice and theory in Renaissance painting/ Marcia B. Hall. Cambridge; Cambridge University Press, 1992. xiv, 274 p.
91-018934   759.03   0521392225
Painting, Renaissance.

ND170.V43
Venturi, Lionello, 1885-1961.
The sixteenth century, from Leonardo to El Greco. Text by Lionello Venturi. Translated by Stuart Gilbert. [New York] Skira [1956] 283 p.
56-009860   750.903
Painting, Renaissance -- History. Painting -- 16th century.

ND180.D8 1951a
Dupont, Jacques.
The seventeenth century; the new developments in art from Caravaggio to Vermeer. Text by Jacques Dupont and Francois Mathey. Translated by S.J.C. Harrison. Geneva, Skira [1951] 135 p.
52-043278   750.903
Painting -- History. Painting. Painters.

ND190.N57 1977b
Norman, Geraldine.
Nineteenth-century painters and painting: a dictionary/ Geraldine Norman. Berkeley: University of California Press, 1977. 240 p.
76-024594   759.05   0520033280
Painters -- Biography -- Dictionaries. Painting, Modern -- 19th century -- Dictionaries.

ND190.R39
Raynal, Maurice.
The nineteenth century; new sources of emotion from Goya to Gauguin. Translated by James Emmons. Geneva, Skira [1951] 147 p.
51-014572   750.903
Painting, Modern -- 19th century. Painting. Painters.

ND192.I4.R83 1999
Rubin, James Henry.
Impressionism/ James H. Rubin. London: Phaidon, 1999. 447 p.
99-494999   0714838268
Impressionism (Art) Impressionism (Art) -- France. Painting, French.

ND192.I4.W67 1990
World Impressionism: the international movement, 1860-1920/ edited by Norma Broude. New York: H.N. Abrams, c1990. 424 p.
90-000218   759.05/4   0810917742
Impressionism (Art) Painting, Modern -- 19th century. Painting, Modern -- 20th century.

ND195.H323 1965
Haftmann, Werner.
Painting in the twentieth century. New York, Praeger [1965] 2 v.
65-025066   759.06
Painting, Modern -- 20th century. Painters.

ND195.R4 1969
Read, Herbert Edward, 1893-1968.
A concise history of modern painting. New York, Praeger [1969, c1968] 380 p.
70-005526   759.06
Painting, Modern -- 20th century.

ND196.C8.G6 1968
Golding, John.
Cubism: a history and an analysis, 1907-1914. London, Faber, 1968. 208 p.
76-368417   759.06
Cubism. Painting, Modern -- 20th century.

ND196.R4
Prendeville, Brendan.
Realism in 20th century painting/ Brendan Prendeville. New York, N.Y.: Thames & Hudson, c2000. 224 p.
99-069883   759.06   0500203369
Realism in art. Painting, Modern -- 20th century.

ND198 History — Islamic painting

ND198.A7 1965
Arnold, Thomas Walker, 1864-1930.
Painting in Islam; a study of the place of pictorial art in Muslim culture. With a new introd. by B. W. Robinson. New York, Dover Publications [1965] xviii, 159 p.
65-012451   759.956
Civilization, Islamic. Painting, Islamic. Illumination of books and manuscripts.

ND205-457 History — Special countries

ND205.B8 1965
Burroughs, Alan, 1897-1965.
Limners and likenesses; three centuries of American paintings. New York, Russell & Russell, 1965 [c1936] ix, 246 p.
65-018793   759.13
Painting, American -- History.

ND205.D298 1991
Detroit Institute of Arts.
American paintings in the Detroit Institute of Arts/ introduction by Nancy Rivard Shaw; essays by Mary Black ... [et al.]. New York: Hudson Hills Press: c1991-c1997. v. 1-2
90-085027   759.13/074/77434   1555950442
Painting -- Michigan -- Detroit -- Catalogs. Painting, American -- Catalogs.

ND205.M57
Monro, Isabel Stevenson.
Index to reproductions of American paintings; a guide to pictures occurring in more than eight hundred books, by Isabel Stevenson Monro and Kate M. Monro. New York, H.W. Wilson Co., 1948. 731 p.
48-009663   759.13
Painting. Painting, American. Painters, American.

ND205.N373 1980
Metropolitan Museum of Art (New York, N.Y.)
American paintings in the Metropolitan Museum of Art/ edited by Kathleen Luhrs. New York: The Museum in association with Princeton University Press, 1980-c1994. v. 1-3
80-081074   759.13/074/01471   0870992449
Painting -- New York (State) -- New York -- Catalogs. Painting, American -- Catalogs.

ND205.P74
Prown, Jules David.
American painting; from its beginnings to the Armory Show. Introd. by John Walker. [Geneva] Skira [distributed in the U.S. by World Pub. Co., Cleveland, [1969] 144 p.
70-080455   759.13
Painting, American. Painters -- United States.

ND205.R53 1965
Richardson, Edgar Preston, 1902-
Painting in America, from 1502 to the present [by] E. P. Richardson. New York, Crowell [1965] xiii, 456 p.
65-023777   759.13
Painting, American -- History.

ND205.T5
Three hundred years of American painting, by Alexander Eliot, art editor of Time. With an introd. by John Walker. New York, Time Inc., 1957. x, 318 p.
57-004528   759.13
Painting -- United States -- History. Painting, American.

ND205.5.P74.A43
American folk painters of three centuries/ Jean Lipman, Tom Armstrong, editors. New York: Hudson Hills Press: trade distribution by Simon & Schuster, c1980. 233 p.
79-021212   759.13/074/01471   0933920059
Painting, American -- Exhibitions. Primitivism in art -- United States -- Exhibitions.

ND207.A678 1992
American icons: transatlantic perspectives on eighteenth- and nineteenth-century American art/ edited by Thomas W. Gaehtgens and Heinz Ickstadt. Santa Monica, Calif.: Getty Center for the History of Art and Humanities, c1992. 360 p.
92-022423   759.13   0892362464
Painting, American. Painting, Modern -- 17th-18th century -- United States. Painting, Modern -- 19th century -- United States.

ND207.F55 1967
Flexner, James Thomas, 1908-
America's old masters. New York, Dover Publications [1967] 365 p.
67-016702   759.13
West, Benjamin, -- 1738-1820. Copley, John Singleton, -- 1737-1815 Peale, Charles Willson, -- 1741-1827. Painters.

ND210.A724 1999
America: the New World in 19th-century painting/ edited by Stephan Koja; with contributions by Nicolai Cikovsky, Jr. ... [et al.]. Munich; Prestel, c1999. 296 p.
99-027114   759.13/09/03407443613   3791320882
Painting, American -- Exhibitions. Painting, Modern -- 19th century -- United States -- Exhibitions. United States -- In art -- Exhibitions.

ND210.F65 1990
Foshay, Ella M., 1948-
Mr. Luman Reed's picture gallery: a pioneer collection of American art/ Ella M. Foshay; introduction by Wayne Craven; catalogue by Timothy Anglin Burgard. New York: Abrams in association with the New-York Historical Society, 1990. 228 p.
90-032371   759.14/074/7471   0810937514
Reed, Luman, -- d. 1836 -- Art collections -- Catalogs. Painting, Modern -- 19th century -- United States -- Catalogs. Painting, European -- Catalogs. Painting, American -- Catalogs.

ND210.L83 1994
Lubin, David M.
Picturing a nation: art and social change in nineteenth-century America/ David M. Lubin. New Haven: Yale University Press, c1994. xvii, 364 p.
93-019392   759.13/09/034   0300057326
Painting, American. Painting, Modern -- 19th century -- United States. United States -- Social life and customs -- 19th century -- Pictorial works.

ND210.N68 1969
Novak, Barbara.
American painting of the nineteenth century; realism, idealism, and the American experience. New York, Praeger [1969] 350 p.
77-076792   759.13
Painting, American -- History. Painting, Modern -- 19th century -- United States.

ND210.P27 1989
Paris 1889: American artists at the Universal Exposition/ Annette Blaugrund; with essays by Annette Blaugrund ... [et al.]. Philadelphia: Pennsylvania Academy of the Fine Arts; 1989. 304 p.
89-003898   759.13/074/74   0943836123
Painting, American -- Exhibitions. Painting, Modern -- 19th century -- United States -- Exhibitions.

ND210.P96 1996
Pyne, Kathleen A., 1949-
Art and the higher life: painting and evolutionary thought in late nineteenth-century America/ Kathleen Pyne. Austin: University of Texas Press, 1996. xvi, 416 p.
95-043964   759.13/09/034
Painting, American. Painting, Modern -- 19th century -- United States. Evolution (Biology) -- Philosophy.

ND210.5.I4.G474 1984
Gerdts, William H.
American impressionism/ William H. Gerdts. New York: Abbeville Press, c1984. 336 p.
84-006365   759.13   0896594513
Impressionism (Art) -- United States. Painting, American. Painting, Modern -- 19th century -- United States.

ND210.5.I4.G476 1991
Gerdts, William H.
Masterworks of American impressionism: exhibition catalogue/ by William H. Gerdts. New York: H. N. Abrams; 1991. 163 p.
90-046961   759.13/09/03407449478   0810936143
Painting, American -- Exhibitions. Painting, Modern -- 19th century -- United States -- Exhibitions. Painting, Modern -- 20th century -- United States -- Exhibitions.

ND210.5.I4.H53 1991
Hiesinger, Ulrich W., 1943-
Impressionism in America: the Ten American Painters/ Ulrich W. Hiesinger. Munich: Prestel; c1991. 255 p.
92-120587   759.147/1/0747471   3791311425
Painting, American -- Exhibitions. Impressionism (Art) -- United States -- Exhibitions. Painting, Modern -- 20th century -- United States -- Exhibitions.

ND210.5.I4.W456 1994
Weinberg, H. Barbara 1942-
American impressionism and realism: the painting of modern life, 1885-1915/ H. Barbara Weinberg, Doreen Bolger, David Park Curry; with the assistance of N. Mishoe Brennecke. New York: Metropolitan Museum of Art: c1994. xiii, 384 p.
94-002762   759.13/09/0340747471   0870997009
Impressionism (Art) -- United States -- Exhibitions. Painting, American -- Exhibitions. Painting, Modern -- 19th century -- United States -- Exhibitions.

ND210.5.P7.L56 1942
Lipman, Jean, 1909-
American primitive painting. London, Oxford Univ. Press, 1942. 158 p.
42-014277   759.13
Primitivism in art -- United States. Painting, American. Painting, Modern -- 19th century -- United States.

ND212.A4465 1989
Abstraction, geometry, painting: selected geometric abstract painting in America since 1945/ organized by Michael Auping; and with an essay. New York: H.N. Abrams in with Albright-Knox Art Gallery, 1989. 232 p.
88-039709   759.13/074/74   0810910276
Painting, Abstract -- United States -- Exhibitions. Painting, Modern -- 20th century -- United States -- Exhibitions.

ND212.B74
Brown, Milton Wolf, 1911-
American painting, from the Armory show to the depression/ by Milton W. Brown. Princeton: Princeton University Press, 1970, c1955, xii, 243 p.
53-010147   759.13   0691038686
Painting, American -- 20th century.

ND212.G36
Geldzahler, Henry.
American painting in the twentieth century. New York, Metropolitan Museum of Art; distributed by New York Graphic Society, Greenwich, Conn. [1965] 236 p.
65-016668   759.13
Painting, American. Painting, Modern -- 20th century -- United States.

ND212.G47 1990
Gerdts, William H.
Art across America: two centuries of regional painting, 1710-1920/ William H. Gerdts. New York: Abbeville Press, c1990. 3 v.
90-000598   759.13   1558590331
Painting, American. Painting, Modern -- 20th century -- United States. Regionalism in art.

ND212.H46 1991
Henkes, Robert.
American women painters of the 1930s and 1940s: the lives and work of ten artists/ by Robert Henkes. Jefferson, N.C.: McFarland, c1991. xv, 236 p.
90-053708   759.13/082   0899504744
Women painters -- United States -- Biography. Painting, American. Painting, Modern -- 20th century -- United States.

ND212.T5
Time-Life Books.
American painting, 1900-1970, by the editors of Time-Life Books. New York [c1970] 192 p.
72-131017   759.13
Painting, American. Painting, Modern -- 20th century -- United States.

ND212.5.A25.A22 1987
Abstract expressionism: the critical developments/ organized by Michael Auping; with essays by Michael Auping ... [et al.]; and an interview with Lawrence Alloway. New York: H.N. Abrams in association with Albright-Knox Art Gallery, 1987. 302 p.
86-032071   759.13/074/014797   0810918668
Abstract expressionism -- United States -- Exhibitions. Painting, American -- Exhibitions. Painting, Modern -- 20th century -- United States -- Exhibitions.

ND212.5.A25.H63 1981
Hobbs, Robert Carleton, 1946-
Abstract expressionism, the formative years/ by Robert Carleton Hobbs and Gail Levin. Ithaca: Cornell University Press, 1981, c1978. 140 p.
80-069992   759.13   0801413656
Abstract expressionism -- United States -- Exhibitions. Painting, American -- Exhibitions. Painting, Modern -- 20th century -- United States -- Exhibitions.

ND212.5.A25.L45 1993
Leja, Michael, 1951-
Reframing abstract expressionism: subjectivity and painting in the 1940s/ Michael Leja. New Haven, CT: Yale University Press, c1993. viii, 392 p.
92-032992   759.147/1/09044   0300044615
Pollock, Jackson, -- 1912-1956 -- Criticism and interpretation. Painting, Modern -- 20th century -- United States. Subjectivity in art. Abstract expressionism -- United States.

ND212.5.A25.S2 1970
Sandler, Irving, 1925-
The triumph of American painting; a history of abstract expressionism. New York, Praeger Publishers [1970] xv, 301 p.
75-124607   759.13
Abstract expressionism -- United States -- History.

ND212.5.P67.T83 1982
Tsujimoto, Karen.
Images of America: precisionist painting and modern photography/ Karen Tsujimoto. Seattle: Published for the San Francisco Museum of Modern Art by University of Washington Press, c1982. 248 p.
82-002586   759.13/074/013   0295959355
Precisionism -- United States -- Exhibitions. Painting, Modern -- 20th century -- United States -- Exhibitions. Photography -- United States -- Exhibitions.

ND212.5.R4.W36 1989
Ward, John L. 1938-
American realist painting, 1945-1980/ by John L. Ward.
Ann Arbor, Mich.: UMI Research Press, c1989. xiv,
431 p.
88-022639   759.13   0835718670
Painting, American. Painting, Modern -- 20th century --
United States. Realism in art -- United States.

ND212.5.S9.L48 1978
Levin, Gail, 1948-
Synchromism and American color abstraction, 1910-
1925/ Gail Levin. New York: G. Braziller, c1978. 144 p.
77-021051   759.13   0807608823
Synchromism (Art) -- United States. Painting, American.
Painting, Abstract -- United States.

ND212.5.T34.P67 1999
Porter, Dean A.
Taos artists and their patrons, 1898-1950/ Dean A. Porter,
Teresa Hayes Ebie, Suzan Campbell; with contributions
by Elizabeth Cunningham ... [et al.]; general editor,
Suzan Campbell. Notre Dame, Ind.: Snite Museum of
Art; c1999. 400 p.
98-052976   709/.789/53   0826321097
Taos school of art. Art patronage -- New Mexico -- Taos. West
(U.S.) in art.

ND225.I53 1995
Independent spirits: women painters of the American
West, 1890-1945/ Patricia Trenton, editor; with essays by
Sandra D'Emilio ... et al.]. Berkeley: Autry Museum of
Western Heritage in association with the University of
California Press, c1995. xiii, 304 p.
95-017367   759.18/082   0520202023
Painting, American -- Exhibitions. Painting, Modern -- 19th
century -- West (U.S.) -- Exhibitions. Painting, Modern -- 20th
century -- West (U.S.) -- Exhibitions.

ND235.S27.L36 1996
Landauer, Susan.
The San Francisco school of abstract expressionism/
Susan Landauer; with an introduction by Dore Ashton.
Berkeley: University of California Press; c1996. xxiii,
271 p.
94-047988   759.194/61/09045   0520086104
Painting, American -- California -- San Francisco. Painting,
Modern -- 20th century -- California -- San Francisco. Abstract
expressionism -- California -- San Francisco.

ND237.A4.A4 1979
Gerdts, William H.
"A man of genius": the art of Washington Allston (1779-
1843)/ by William H. Gerdts & Theodore E. Stebbins, Jr.
Boston: Museum of Fine Arts, c1979. 255 p.
79-056222   759.13   0878461469
Allston, Washington, -- 1779-1843 -- Exhibitions.

ND237.A4.A64 1988
Bjelajac, David.
Millennial desire and the apocalyptic vision of
Washington Allston/ David Bjelajac. Washington, D.C.:
Smithsonian Institution Press, c1988. xiv, 226 p.
87-026619   759.13   0874742641
Allston, Washington, -- 1779-1843. -- Belshazzar's feast.
Belshazzar -- Art. Allston, Washington, -- 1779-1843 --
Criticism and interpretation. Symbolism in art -- United States.
Painting, American. Painting, Modern -- 19th century -- United
States.

ND237.A85.H6 2001
Hobbs, Robert Carleton, 1946-
Milton Avery: the late paintings/ Robert Hobbs. New
York: Harry N. Abrams, 2001. 112 p.
00-068928   759.13   0810942747
Avery, Milton, -- 1885-1965 -- Exhibitions. Avery, Milton, --
1885-1965 -- Criticism and interpretation.

ND237.B45.A4 1992
The Paintings of George Bellows/ Michael Quick ... [et
al.]; with an introduction by John Wilmerding. Fort
Worth, Tex.: Amon Carter Museum; c1992. vii, 261 p.
91-026691   759.13   0883600684
Bellows, George, -- 1882-1925 -- Exhibitions.

ND237.B45.D6 1991
Doezema, Marianne, 1950-
George Bellows and urban America/ Marianne Doezema.
New Haven: Yale University Press, c1992. viii, 244 p.
91-019375   759.13   0300050437
Bellows, George, -- 1882-1925 -- Criticism and interpretation.
United States in art. Cities and towns in art.

ND237.B47.A28
Benton, Thomas Hart, 1889-1975.
An American in art; a professional and technical
autobiography.   Lawrence, University Press of Kansas
[1969] 197 p.
69-016060   759.13
Benton, Thomas Hart, -- 1889-1975. Artists -- Biography.

ND237.B47.A3 1968
Benton, Thomas Hart, 1889-1975.
An artist in America. Columbia, University of Missouri
Press [1968] xxii, 369 p.
68-020096   759.13
Benton, Thomas Hart, -- 1889-1975.   Artists -- Biography.
United States -- Description and travel.

ND237.B47.B3 1975
Benton, Thomas Hart, 1889-1975.
Thomas Hart Benton/ text by Matthew Baigell. New
York: H. N. Abrams: distributed by New American
Library, c1975. 159 p.
75-027668   759.13   0810920557
Benton, Thomas Hart, -- 1889-1975.

ND237.B47.D67 1991
Doss, Erika Lee.
Benton, Pollock, and the politics of modernism: from regionalism to abstract expressionism/ Erika Doss. Chicago: University of Chicago Press, c1991. xvi, 445 p.
91-018541   759.13   0226159426
Benton, Thomas Hart, -- 1889-1975 -- Criticism and interpretation. Pollock, Jackson. -- 1912-1956 -- Criticism and interpretation. Regionalism in art -- United States. Abstract expressionism -- United States. Modernism (Art) -- Political aspects -- United States -- History -- 20th century.

ND237.B585.A4 1991
Anderson, Nancy K.
Albert Bierstadt: art & enterprise/ Nancy K. Anderson, Linda S. Ferber; with a contribution by Helena E. Wright. New York: Hudson Hills Press in association with the Brooklyn Museum, c1990. 327 p.
90-039692   759.13   1555950590
Bierstadt, Albert, -- 1830-1902 -- Exhibitions.   West (U.S.) in art -- Exhibitions.

ND237.B59.M3
McDermott, John Francis, 1902-
George Caleb Bingham, river portraitist.   Norman, University of Oklahoma Press [1959] xxviii, 454 p.
59-013474   759.13
Bingham, George Caleb, -- 1811-1879.

ND237.B59.R37 1991
Rash, Nancy, 1940-
The painting and politics of George Caleb Bingham/ Nancy Rash. New Haven: Yale University Press, c1991. x, 286 p.
90-036010   759.13   0300047312
Bingham, George Caleb, -- 1811-1879 -- Criticism and interpretation. Bingham, George Caleb, -- 1811-1879 -- Political and social views.

ND237.C3.P65 1998
Pollock, Griselda.
Mary Cassatt: painter of modern women/ Griselda Pollock. London: Thames & Hudson, 1998. 224 p.
98-060039   759.13   0500203172
Cassatt, Mary, -- 1844-1926 -- Criticism and interpretation. Women in art. Impressionism (Art)

ND237.C3.S9
Sweet, Frederick Arnold.
Miss Mary Cassatt, impressionist from Pennsylvania Sweet, Frederick Arnold. Norman University of Oklahoma Press 1966. xx, 242 p.
66-013423   759.1
Cassatt, Mary, 1844-1926.

ND237.C35.M3 1959
McCracken, Harold, 1894-
George Catlin and the old frontier.   New York, Dial Press, 1959. 216 p.
59-009434   759.13
Catlin, George, -- 1796-1872.   Indians of North America -- West (U.S.) -- Pictorial works. Frontier and pioneer life -- West (U.S.) -- Pictorial works.

ND237.C35.T78 1979
Truettner, William H.
The natural man observed: a study of Catlin's Indian gallery/ William H. Truettner. Washington: Smithsonian Institution Press, 1979. 323 p.
78-015152   759.13   0874749182
Catlin, George, -- 1796-1872.   Painters -- United States -- Biography. Indians of North America -- Pictorial works. West (U.S.) in art.

ND237.C48.G36 1995
Gallati, Barbara Dayer.
William Merritt Chase/ Barbara Dayer Gallati. New York: Harry N. Abrams in association with the National Museum of American Art, Smithsonian Institution, 1995. 143 p.
94-003487   759.13   0810940299
Chase, William Merritt, -- 1849-1916 -- Criticism and interpretation.   Realism in art -- United States.

ND237.C492.A28
Chicago, Judy, 1939-
Through the flower: my struggle as a woman artist/ by Judy Chicago; with an introd. by Anais Nin. Garden City, N.Y.: Doubleday, 1975. xi, 226 p.
74-012680   759.13   0385097824
Chicago, Judy, -- 1939- Painters -- United States -- Biography.

ND237.C52.K45 1988
Kelly, Franklin.
Frederic Edwin Church and the national landscape/ Franklin Kelly. Washington, D.C.: Smithsonian Institution Press, c1988. 179 p.
88-004605   759.13   0874745926
Church, Frederick Edwin, -- 1826-1900.   Landscape painting, American. Landscape painting -- 19th century -- United States.

ND237.C6.A4 1990
Powell, Earl A.
Thomas Cole/ Earl A. Powell. New York: H.N. Abrams, 1990. 144 p.
90-000121   759.13   0810931583
Cole, Thomas, -- 1801-1848 -- Criticism and interpretation. Hudson River school of landscape painting.

ND237.C8.M67 1994
Morgan, H. Wayne
Kenyon Cox: 1856-1919: a life in American art/ H. Wayne Morgan. Kent, Ohio: Kent State University Press, c1994. xii, 290 p.
93-033967   759.13   0873384857
Cox, Kenyon, -- 1856-1919.   Painters -- United States -- Biography. Art critics -- United States -- Biography.

ND237.C88.A4 1998
Junker, Patricia A.
John Steuart Curry: inventing the Middle West/ Patricia Junker; with contributions by Henry Adams ... [et al.]. New York: Hudson Hills Press, 1998. 252 p.
97-049621   759.13   1555951392
Curry, John Steuart, -- 1897-1946 -- Exhibitions.   Regionalism in art -- United States -- Exhibitions.   Middle West -- In art -- Exhibitions.

ND237.C884.A4 1999
Curtis, Philip C.
American dreamer: the art of Philip C. Curtis/ essays by
Whitney Chadwick ... [et al.]; foreword by James K.
Ballinger. New York: Hudson Hills Press in association
with Phoenix Art Museum, c1999. 179 p.
99-034201   759.13   155595166X
Curtis, Philip C. -- Themes, motives.

ND237.D334.A4 1994
Prather, Marla.
Willem de Kooning: paintings/ essays by David
Sylvester, Richard Shiff; catalogue by Marla Prather.
Washington: National Gallery of Art; c1994. 231 p.
93-048522   759.13   0300060114
De Kooning, Willem, -- 1904- -- Exhibitions. De Kooning,
Willem, -- 1904-

ND237.D465.N67 1987
Nordland, Gerald.
Richard Diebenkorn/ Gerald Nordland. New York:
Rizzoli, 1987. 248 p.
87-042688   759.13   084780870X
Diebenkorn, Richard, -- 1922- -- Criticism and interpretation.
Painting, American. Painting, Modern -- 20th century -- United
States.

ND237.E15.P6
Porter, Fairfield.
Thomas Eakins. New York, G. Braziller, 1959. 127 p.
59-012225   759.13
Eakins, Thomas, -- 1844-1916.

ND237.E15.T56 1993
Thomas Eakins/ general editor, John Wilmerding.
Washington, DC: Smithsonian Institution Press, 1993.
212 p.
93-085709   759.13   1560983132
Eakins, Thomas, -- 1844-1916 -- Criticism and interpretation.
Eakins, Thomas, -- 1844-1916 -- Appreciation.   Painting,
Modern -- 19th century -- United States -- History and criticism.
Painting, Modern -- 20th century -- United States -- History and
criticism. Photography -- United States.

ND237.E7.K87 2000
Kuspit, Donald B. 1935-
Jimmy Ernst/ text by Donald Kuspit; introduction by Kurt
Vonnegut with contributions by Louis Simpson ... [et al.].
New York: Hudson Hills, 2000. 166 p.
00-040910   759.13   1555951910
Ernst, Jimmy, -- 1920- -- Criticism and interpretation. Ernst,
Jimmy, -- 1920- -- Interviews.

ND237.E75.A4 1978
Estes, Richard, 1932-
Richard Estes: the urban landscape/ essay by John
Canaday; catalogue and interview by John Arthur.
Boston: Museum of Fine Arts: New York Graphic
Society, c1978. 69 p.
78-059702   759.13   0878461264
Estes, Richard, -- 1932- -- Exhibitions. Cities and towns in art
-- Exhibitions. Painters -- United States -- Interviews.

ND237.E8.T39 1987
Taylor, Kendall.
Philip Evergood: never separate from the heart/ Kendall
Taylor. Lewisburg, Pa.: Bucknell University Press;
c1987. 210 p.
86-047724   759.13   0838751113
Evergood, Philip, -- 1901-1973.   Painters -- United States --
Biography.

ND237.F6728.D57 1999
Dispenza, Joseph, 1942-
The magical realism of Alyce Frank/ by Joseph Dispenza.
[Santa Fe, N.M.]: New Mexico Magazine, c1999. 95 p.
99-074037   759.13   0937206571
Frank, Alyce, -- 1932- -- Catalogs.   Landscape in art --
Catalogs. Magic realism (Art) -- Catalogs. New Mexico -- In
art -- Catalogs.

ND237.F675.A4 1989
Carmean, E. A.
Helen Frankenthaler: a paintings retrospective/ E.A.
Carmean, Jr. New York: Abrams, 1989. iv, 113 p.
88-039301   759.13   0810911795
Frankenthaler, Helen, -- 1928- -- Exhibitions.

ND237.F75
Frieseke, Frederick C. 1874-1939.
Frederick Carl Frieseke: the evolution of an American
impressionist/ guest curator, Nicholas Kilmer; catalogue
and exhibition coordinator, Linda McWhorter; essays by
Nicholas Kilmer ... [et al.]. Savannah, GA: Telfair
Museum of Art; 2001. 218 p.
00-066593   759.13   0691089221
Frieseke, Frederick C. -- (Frederick Carl), -- 1874-1939 --
Exhibitions. Impressionism (Art) -- United States -- Catalogs.

ND237.G32
Rieder, William.
A charmed couple: the art and life of Walter and Matilda
Gay/ William Rieder. New York: Harry N. Abrams,
2000. 239 p.
00-026627   759.13   0810945614
Gay, Walter, -- 1856-1937. Gay, Matilda, -- b. 1855. Painters --
United States -- Biography. Painters' spouses -- United States --
Biography. Expatriate painters -- France -- Biography.

ND237.G614.A4 1994
The pictographs of Adolph Gottlieb/ essays by Lawrence
Alloway ... [et al.]. New York: Hudson Hills Press in
association with Adolph & Esther Gottlieb Foundation,
c1994. 143 p.
94-021579   759.13   1555951147
Gottlieb, Adolph, -- 1903-1974 -- Exhibitions.

ND237.G8 A82 1990
Ashton, Dore.
A critical study of Philip Guston/ by Dore Ashton.
Berkeley: University of California Press, [1990] xvii,
216 p.
89-020505   759.13 20   0520069323
Guston, Philip, 1913- -- Criticism and interpretation.

ND237.G82.N67 1995
North, Percy, 1945-
Bernhard Gutmann: an American impressionist, 1869-1936/ by Percy North; preface by William H. Gerdts; Christian title, Bernhard Gutmann Collection, curator. New York: Abbeville Press, c1995. 199 p.
95-015263   759.13   1558596119
Gutmann, Bernhard, -- 1869-1936 -- Criticism and interpretation.

ND237.H315.A4 1992
William M. Harnett/ edited by Doreen Bolger, Marc Simpson, and John Wilmerding, with the assistance of Thayer Tolles Mickel. Fort Worth: Amon Carter Museum; 1992. 333 p.
91-026675   759.13   0883600692
Harnett, William Michael, -- 1848-1892 -- Criticism and interpretation. Harnett, William Michael, -- 1848-1892 -- Exhibitions.

ND237.H3434.M38 1990
Mattison, Robert Saltonstall.
Grace Hartigan: a painter's world/ Robert Saltonstall Mattison. New York: Hudson Hills Press: c1990. 156 p.
90-080947   759.13   1555950418
Hartigan, Grace -- Criticism and interpretation. Abstract expressionism -- United States.

ND237.H3435.R63 1995
Robertson, Bruce, 1955-
Marsden Hartley/ Bruce Robertson. New York: Abrams in association with the National Museum of American Art, Smithsonian Institution, 1995. 144 p.
93-046820   759.13   0810934167
Hartley, Marsden, -- 1877-1943. Painters -- United States -- Biography.

ND237.H39.A4 1999
Stebbins, Theodore E.
Martin Johnson Heade/ Theodore E. Stebbins, Jr.; with contributions by Janet L. Comey, Karen E. Quinn, Jim Wright. Boston: Museum of Fine Arts, c1999. 197 p.
99-060202   759.13   0300081693
Heade, Martin Johnson, -- 1819-1904 -- Exhibitions.

ND237.H58.W44 1999
Weekley, Carolyn J.
The kingdoms of Edward Hicks/ by Carolyn J. Weekley; with the assistance of Laura Pass Barry. Williamsburg, Va.: Colonial Williamsburg Foundation, 1999. xvi, 254 p.
98-033231   759.13   0879352051
Hicks, Edward, -- 1780-1849 -- Criticism and interpretation.

ND237.H584.P67 1991
Porter, Dean A.
Victor Higgins: an American master/ Dean A. Porter. Salt Lake City: Peregrine Smith Books, 1991. 304 p.
90-049993   759.13   0879053623
Higgins, Victor, -- 1884-1949. Painters -- New Mexico -- Biography.

ND237.H667.F7513 1998
Friedel, Helmut.
Hans Hofmann/ by Helmut Friedel and Tina Dickey. New York: Hudson Hills Press, 1998. 124 p.
98-018456   759.13   1555951546
Hofmann, Hans, -- 1880-1966 -- Criticism and interpretation. Abstract expressionism -- United States.

ND237.H66948
Brown, Steven C.
Sun dogs & eagle down: the Indian paintings of Bill Holm/ by Steven C. Brown; chronology & bibliography by Lloyd J. Averill; captions by Bill Holm. Seattle, Wash.: University of Washington Press; c2000. x, 198 p.
00-021618   759.13   029597947X
Holm, Bill, -- 1925- -- Criticism and interpretation. Indians in art. Indians of North America -- Pictorial works.

ND237.H7.A4 1988
Simpson, Marc.
Winslow Homer: paintings of the Civil War/ Marc Simpson with contributions by Nicolai Cikovsky, Jr. ... [et al.]. San Francisco: Fine Arts Museums of San Francisco: c1988. 283 p.
88-080734   759.13   0884010600
Homer, Winslow, -- 1836-1910 -- Exhibitions. United States -- History -- Civil War, 1861-1865 -- Art and the war -- Exhibitions.

ND237.H7.A4 1988a
Wood, Peter H., 1943-
Winslow Homer's images of Blacks: the Civil War and Reconstruction years/ Peter H. Wood, Karen C.C. Dalton; introduction by Richard J. Powell. Austin: Menil Collection: c1988. 144 p.
88-026629   759.13   0292790473
Homer, Winslow, -- 1836-1910 -- Exhibitions. Afro-Americans in art -- Exhibitions. Afro-Americans -- History -- 1863-1877 -- Pictorial works -- Exhibitions.

ND237.H7.A4 1990
Robertson, Bruce, 1955-
Reckoning with Winslow Homer: his late paintings and their influence/ Bruce Robertson. [Cleveland, Ohio]: Published by the Cleveland Museum of Art in cooperation with Indiana University Press; Bloomington: Distributed by Indiana University Press, c1990. xvi, 196 p.
90-031989   759.13   0940717026
Homer, Winslow, -- 1836-1910 -- Exhibitions. Homer, Winslow, -- 1836-1910- -- Influence -- Exhibitions.

ND237.H7.A4 1990b
Homer, Winslow, 1836-1910.
Winslow Homer in the 1890s: Prout's Neck observed/ essays by Philip C. Beam ... [et al.]. New York: Hudson Hills Press, c1990. 154 p.
90-080948   759.13   1555950426
Homer, Winslow, -- 1836-1910 -- Exhibitions. Homer, Winslow, -- 1836-1910 -- Homes and haunts -- Maine -- Prouts Neck. Prouts Neck (Me.) in art -- Exhibitions.

ND237.H7.A4 2001
Conrads, Margaret C., 1955-
Winslow Homer and the critics: forging a national art in the 1870s/ Margaret C. Conrads. Princeton, N.J.: Princeton University Press in association with the Nelson-Atkins Museum of Art, c2001. xi, 252 p.
00-064257 759.13 0691070997
Homer, Winslow, -- 1836-1910 -- Exhibitions. Homer, Winslow, -- 1836-1910 -- Criticism and interpretation. Art criticism -- United States -- History -- 19th century.

ND237.H7.G3
Gardner, Albert Ten Eyck.
Winslow Homer, American artist: his world and his work. New York, C. N. Potter [c1961] 262 p.
61-011762 759.13
Homer, Winslow, -- 1836-1910.

ND237.H75.A4 1980
Hopper, Edward, 1882-1967.
Edward Hopper: the art and the artist/ Gail Levin. New York: Norton: 1980. xv, 299 p.
79-027958 759.13 039301374X
Hopper, Edward, -- 1882-1967 -- Exhibitions.

ND237.H75.G6 1971
Hopper, Edward, 1882-1967.
Edward Hopper. Text by Lloyd Goodrich. New York, H. N. Abrams [1971] 306 p.
78-101620 759.13 0810901870
Hopper, Edward, -- 1882-1967.

ND237.I5.C54 1993
Cikovsky, Nicolai.
George Inness/ Nicolai Cikovsky, Jr. New York: H.N. Abrams; c1993. 143 p.
93-018308 759.13 0810934620
Innes, George, -- 1825-1894 -- Criticism and interpretation.

ND237.J7.A4 1999
Carbone, Teresa A.
Eastman Johnson: painting America/ Teresa A. Carbone [and] Patricia Hills; with contributions by Jane Weiss, Sarah Burns, Anne C. Rose; edited by Teresa A. Carbone. New York: Brooklyn Museum of Art, in association with Rizzoli International Publications, c1999. 272 p.
99-014456 759.13 0847822141
Johnson, Eastman, -- 1824-1906 -- Exhibitions.

ND237.J73.P69 1991
Powell, Richard J., 1953-
Homecoming: the art and life of William H. Johnson/ Richard J. Powell; introduction by Martin Puryear. Washington, D.C.: National Museum of American Art, Smithsonian Institution; Cambridge; New York: Cambridge University Press, c1991. xxiii, 255 p.
91-052670 759.13 0847814211
Johnson, William H., -- 1901-1970. Afro-American painters -- Biography.

ND237.K677.A4 1983
Rose, Barbara.
Lee Krasner: a retrospective/ Barbara Rose. Houston: Museum of Fine Arts; c1983. 184 p.
83-062554 759.13 087070415X
Krasner, Lee, -- 1908- -- Exhibitions. Krasner, Lee, -- 1908- -- Criticism and interpretation. Abstract expressionism -- United States -- Exhibitions. Painting, Modern -- 20th century -- United States -- Exhibitions.

ND237.K677.H63 1993
Hobbs, Robert Carleton, 1946-
Lee Krasner/ Robert Hobbs. New York: Abbeville Press, 1993. 127 p.
93-004141 759.13 1558596518
Krasner, Lee, -- 1908- -- Criticism and interpretation. Abstract expressionism -- United States.

ND237.L27.A4 1988
Wilmerding, John.
Paintings by Fitz Hugh Lane/ John Wilmerding; with contributions by Elizabeth Garrity Ellis ... [et al.]. Washington: National Gallery of Art; c1988. 163 p.
88-005086 759.13 0894681176
Lane, Fitz Hugh, -- 1804-1865 -- Exhibitions. Landscape painting, American -- Exhibitions. Landscape painting -- 19th century -- United States -- Exhibitions. Luminism (Art) -- Exhibitions.

ND237.L29.J23 1993
Jacob Lawrence: the migration series/ edited by Elizabeth Hutton Turner; introduction by Henry Louis Gates, Jr.; essays by Lonnie G. Bunch ... [et. al.]. Washington, D.C.: Rappahannock Press, 1993. 172 p.
93-001402 759.13 0963612905
Lawrence, Jacob, -- 1917- -- Criticism and interpretation. Afro-Americans in art.

ND237.L29.O94 2000
Over the line: the art and life of Jacob Lawrence/ edited with an introduction by Peter T. Nesbett, Michelle DuBois; essays by Patricia Hills ... [et al.]. Seattle, WA: University of Washington Press in association with Jacob Lawrence Catalogue Raisonné Project, c2000. 285 p.
00-056409 759.13 029597964X
Lawrence, Jacob, -- 1917- -- Criticism and interpretation. Painters -- United states -- Biography. Afro-American painters -- Biography.

ND237.L627.A74 1988
Tomkins, Calvin, 1925-
Roy Lichtenstein: mural with blue brushstroke/ essay by Calvin Tomkins; photographs and interview by Bob Adelman. New York: H.N. Abrams, 1988, c1987. 128 p.
87-072175 759.13 0810912961
Lichtenstein, Roy, -- 1923- -- Mural with blue brushstroke. Mural painting and decoration -- 20th century -- New York (State) -- New York. Mural painting and decoration, American. New York (N.Y.) -- Buildings, structures, etc.

ND237.M24.G7
Marin, John, 1870-1953.
John Marin. Edited by Cleve Gray. New York, Holt, Rinehart and Winston [1970] 176 p.
77-102144 759.13 0030841518

ND237.M58.B47 1988
Bernstock, Judith E., 1946-
Joan Mitchell/ by Judith E. Bernstock. New York: Hudson Hills Press in association with the Herbert F. Johnson Museum of Art, Cornell University: Distributed in the U.S. by Rizzoli, c1988. 227 p.
87-035376   759.13   0933920814
Mitchell, Joan, -- 1926- -- Criticism and interpretation. Abstract expressionism -- United States. Painting, American. Painting, Modern -- 20th century -- United States.

ND237.M715.K56 1992
Kinsey, Joni.
Thomas Moran and the surveying of the American West/ Joni Louise Kinsey. Washington: Smithsonian Institution Press, c1992. x, 237 p.
91-023705   759.13   1560981709
Moran, Thomas, -- 1837-1926 -- Criticism and interpretation. West (U.S.) in art.

ND237.M75.L3
Larkin, Oliver W.
Samuel F. B. Morse and American democratic art. Boston, Little, Brown, 1954. viii, 215 p.
54-008284   927.5
Morse, Samuel Finley Breese, -- 1791-1872.   Art -- United States. -- History.

ND237.M78.A22
Moses, 1860-1961.
Grandma Moses: my life's history. Edited by Otto Kallir. New York] Harper [1952] xi, 140 p.
51-011940   927.5
Moses, -- Grandma, -- 1860-1961.   Artists -- Biography.

ND237.M78.A4 2001
Kallir, Jane.
Grandma Moses in the 21st century/ Jane Kallir; with contributions by Roger Cardinal ... [et al.]. Alexandria, VA: Art Services International, 2001. 263 p.
00-038990   759.13   088397133X
Moses, -- Grandma, -- 1860-1961 -- Exhibitions.   Primitivism in art -- United States -- Exhibitions.

ND237.M852.A35 1992
Motherwell, Robert.
The collected writings of Robert Motherwell/ edited by Stephanie Terenzio. New York: Oxford University Press, 1992. xxvii, 325 p.
92-013639   709/.04   0195077008
Motherwell, Robert -- Philosophy.   Art. Art, Modern -- 20th century.

ND237.M895.V35 1998
Vaill, Amanda.
Everybody was so young: Gerald and Sara Murphy, a lost generation love story/ Amanda Vaill. Boston: Houghton Mifflin Co., 1998. viii, 470 p.
97-049149   759.13   0395652413
Murphy, Gerald, -- 1888-1964. Murphy, Sara.   Painters -- United States -- Biography. Painters' spouses -- United States -- Biography. Expatriate painters -- France -- Biography.

ND237.N43.B45 1991
Belcher, Gerald L., 1941-
Collecting souls, gathering dust: the struggles of two American artists, Alice Neel and Rhoda Medary/ Gerald L. Belcher and Margaret L. Belcher. New York: Paragon House, 1991. xi, 304 p.
90-038684   759.13   1557783365
Neel, Alice, -- 1900- -- Criticism and interpretation. Medary, Rhoda, -- d. 1981 -- Criticism and interpretation. Women painters -- United States -- Biography -- History and criticism. Feminism and art -- United States.

ND237.O5.E43 1991
Eldredge, Charles C.
Georgia O'Keeffe/ Charles C. Eldredge. New York: H.N. Abrams in association with the National Museum of American Art, Smithsonian Institution, 1991. 160 p.
90-048459   759.13   0810936577
O'Keeffe, Georgia, -- 1887-1986 -- Criticism and interpretation.

ND237.O5.L96 1989
Lynes, Barbara Buhler, 1942-
O'Keeffe, Stieglitz and the critics, 1916-1929/ by Barbara Buhler Lynes. Ann Arbor, Mich.: UMI Research Press, c1989. x, 376 p.
89-033444   759.13   0835719308
O'Keeffe, Georgia, -- 1887-1986 -- Criticism and interpretation. Stieglitz, Alfred, -- 1864-1946 -- Influence. Stieglitz, Alfred, -- 1864-1946 -- Relations with women. Art criticism -- United States -- History -- 20th century.

ND237.P1668
Allmon, Warren D.
Rock of ages, sands of time/ paintings by Barbara Page; text by Warren Allmon; foreword by Rosamond Wolff Purcell. Chicago: University of Chicago Press, c2001. xxiv, 347 p.
00-048848   759.13   0226644790
Page, Barbara -- Catalaogs.   Fossils in art -- Catalogs.

ND237.P269.A4 1996
The Peale family: creation of a legacy, 1770-1870/ Lillian B. Miller, editor. New York: Abbeville Press, c1996. 319 p.
96-013975   759.13   0789202069
Peale family -- Exhibitions.   Painting, American -- Exhibitions. Painting, Modern -- 17th-18th century -- United States -- Exhibitions. Painting, Modern -- 19th century -- United States -- Exhibitions.

ND237.P27.N48 1990
New perspectives on Charles Willson Peale: a 250th anniversary celebration/ Lillian B. Miller and David C. Ward, editors. Pittsburgh, Pa.: Published for the Smithsonian Institution by the University of Pittsburgh Press, c1991. xviii, 317 p.
90-039185   759.13   0822936607
Peale, Charles Willson, -- 1741-1827 -- Criticism and interpretation.

ND237.P29.N46 2001
Nemerov, Alexander.
The body of Raphaelle Peale: still life and selfhood, 1812-1824/ Alexander Nemerov. Berkeley: University of California Press, c2001. xiv, 260 p.
00-037407   759.13   0520224981
Peale, Raphaelle, -- 1774-1825 -- Criticism and interpretation. Human figure in art. Still-life painting, American. Still-life painting -- 19th century -- United States.

ND237.P375.A4 1990
Martindale, Meredith.
Lilla Cabot Perry: an American impressionist/ Meredith Martindale, with the assistance of Pamela Moffat; including an essay by Nancy Mowll Mathews. Washington, D.C.: National Museum of Women in the Arts, 1990. 164 p.
90-061820   759.13   0940979144
Perry, Lilla Cabot -- Exhibitions. Impressionism (Art) -- United States -- Exhibitions.

ND237.P472.S35 1994
Schimmel, Julie, 1941-
Bert Geer Phillips and the Taos art colony/ Julie Schimmel, Robert R. White. Albuquerque: University of New Mexico, c1994. xxv, 352 p.
93-005082   759.13   0826314449
Phillips, Bert Geer, -- 1868-1956 -- Criticism and interpretation. Phillips, Bert Geer, -- 1868-1956 -- Catalogues raisonnes. Taos school of art.

ND237.P73.A4 1998
Varnedoe, Kirk, 1946-
Jackson Pollock/ Kirk Varnedoe, with Pepe Karmel. New York: Museum of Modern Art; c1998. 336 p.
98-067140   759.13   0870700685
Pollock, Jackson, -- 1912-1956 -- Exhibitions.

ND237.P73.L36 1989
Landau, Ellen G.
Jackson Pollock/ Ellen G. Landau. New York: Abrams, 1989. 283 p.
89-000241   759.13   0810937026
Pollock, Jackson, -- 1912-1956 -- Criticism and interpretation. Abstract expressionism -- United States.

ND237.P73 N34 1989
Naifeh, Steven W.,
Jackson Pollock: an American saga/ by Steven Naifeh and Gregory White Smith. 1st ed. New York, N.Y.: C.N. Potter: 934 p.
88-032387   759.13.B 19   0517560844
Pollock, Jackson, 1912-1956. Painters -- United States -- Biography.

ND237.R72484.S55 1991
Simon, Joan, 1949-
Susan Rothenberg/ by Joan Simon. New York: H.N. Abrams, 1991. 205 p.
91-008278   759.13   0810937530
Rothenberg, Susan, -- 1945- -- Criticism and interpretation.

ND237.R725.A4 1998
Rothko, Mark, 1903-1970.
Mark Rothko: the works on canvas: catalogue raisonne/ David Anfam. New Haven: Yale University Press; c1998. 708 p.
98-025970   759.13   0300074891
Rothko, Mark, -- 1903-1970 -- Catalogues raisonnes.

ND237.R725 A93 1996
Ashton, Dore.
About Rothko/ Dore Ashton. New York: Da Capo Press, 1996. 225 p.
95-052293   759.13 B 20   0306807041
Rothko, Mark, 1903-1970. Painters -- United States -- Biography.

ND237.R725.C5 1989
Chave, Anna.
Mark Rothko: subjects in abstraction/ Anna C. Chave. New Haven: Yale University Press, c1989. 229 p.
88-016881   759.13   0300041780
Rothko, Mark, -- 1903-1970 -- Criticism and interpretation.

ND237.R7254.F63 1998
Flam, Jack D.
Judith Rothschild: an artist's search/ by Jack Flam. New York: Hudson Hills Press, 1998. 168 p.
98-004695   759.13   1555951503
Rothschild, Judith. Painters -- United States -- Biography.

ND237.R754.A4 1990
Kushner, Marilyn S., 1948-
Morgan Russell/ by Marilyn S. Kushner; introduction by William C. Agee. New York: Hudson Hills Press in association with the Montclair Art Museum: Distributed in the U.S., its territories and possessions ... by Rizzoli International Publications, c1990. 221 p.
90-004013   759.13   1555950469
Russell, Morgan, -- 1886-1953 -- Exhibitions. Synchromism (Art) -- United States -- Exhibitions.

ND237.R8.A4 1989
Broun, Elizabeth.
Albert Pinkham Ryder/ Elizabeth Broun; with catalogue by Eleanor L. Jones ... [et al.]. Washington: Published for the National Museum of American Art by the Smithsonian Institution Press, c1989. viii, 344 p.
89-600053   759.13   0874743281
Ryder, Albert Pinkham, -- 1847-1917 -- Exhibitions.

ND237.R8.H66 1989
Homer, William Innes.
Albert Pinkham Ryder, painter of dreams/ by William Innes Homer and Lloyd Good-rich. New York: Abrams, 1989. 256 p.
89-000227   759.13   0810915995
Ryder, Albert Pinkham, -- 1847-1917 -- Criticism and interpretation.

ND237.S3.A4 1998
Ormond, Richard.
John Singer Sargent: complete paintings/ Richard Ormond, Elaine Kilmurray. New Haven: Published for the Paul Mellon Centre for Studies in British Art by Yale University Press, [c1998-   ] v. 1
97-027380   759.13   0300072457
Sargent, John Singer, -- 1856-1925 -- Catalogues raisonnes.

ND237.S3.A4 1998a
Sargent, John Singer, 1856-1925.
John Singer Sargent/ edited by Elaine Kilmurray and Richard Ormond. Princeton: Princeton University Press, 1998. 285 p.
98-067170   759.13   069100434X
Sargent, John Singer, -- 1856-1925 -- Exhibitions.

ND237.S3.A77 1999
Promey, Sally M., 1953-
Painting religion in public: John Singer Sargent's Triumph of religion at the Boston Public Library/ Sally M. Promey. Princeton, N.J.: Princeton University Press, c1999. x, 365 p.
99-012158   759.13   0691015651
Sargent, John Singer, -- 1856-1925. -- Triumph of religion. Mural painting and decoration -- Massachusetts -- Boston. Protestantism in art.

ND237.S3.F334 2000
Fairbrother, Trevor J.
John Singer Sargent: the sensualist/ Trevor Fairbrother. Seattle, Wash.: Seattle Art Museum: c2000. 226 p.
00-057405   759.13   0300087446
Sargent, John Singer, -- 1856-1925 -- Criticism and interpretation.

ND237.S3.O7 1970b
Ormond, Richard.
John Singer Sargent: paintings, drawings, watercolors. New York, Harper & Row [1970] 264 p.
76-114743   759.13
Sargent, John Singer, -- 1856-1925.

ND237.S3.R3 1982
Ratcliff, Carter.
John Singer Sargent/ by Carter Ratcliff. New York: Abbeville Press, 1982. 256 p.
82-006779   759.13   089659307X
Sargent, John Singer, -- 1856-1925.

ND237.S43715.T58 1997
Titterton, Robert J.
Julian Scott: artist of the Civil War and Native America: with 97 illustrations/ Robert J. Titterton. Jefferson, N.C.: McFarland & Co., c1997. ix, 315 p.
96-036436   759.13   0786402725
Scott, Julian, -- 1846-1901.   Painters -- United States -- Biography. Indians of North America -- Pictorial works. United States -- History -- Civil War, 1861-1865 -- Art and the war.

ND237.S465.A4 1998
Chevlowe, Susan.
Common man, mythic vision: the paintings of Ben Shahn/ Susan Chevlowe; with contributions by Diana L. Linden ... [et al.]. Princeton, N.J.: Princeton University Press, c1998. xvi, 194 p.
98-024384   759.13   0691004064
Shahn, Ben, -- 1898-1969 -- Exhibitions.

ND237.S47.L8 1991
Lucic, Karen, 1950-
Charles Sheeler and the cult of the machine/ Karen Lucic. Cambridge, Mass.: Harvard University Press, 1991. 167 p.
90-028893   759.13   0674111109
Sheeler, Charles, -- 1883-1965 -- Criticism and interpretation. Precisionism -- United States. Machines in art.

ND237.S57.L68 1995
Loughery, John.
John Sloan: painter and rebel/ John Loughery. New York: H. Holt, 1995. xxiii, 438 p.
94-039986   759.13   0805028781
Sloan, John, -- 1871-1951.   Painters -- United States -- Biography. Art and society -- New York (State) -- New York -- History -- 20th century. New York (N.Y.) -- Intellectual life -- 20th century.

ND237.S685.J3
Jaffe, Irma B.
Joseph Stella [by] Irma B. Jaffe. Cambridge, Mass., Harvard University Press, 1970. xviii, 262 p.
71-082294   759.13   0674483650
Stella, Joseph, -- 1877-1946.

ND237.S75.B66 1995
Bloemink, Barbara J.
The life and art of Florine Stettheimer/ Barbara J. Bloemink. New Haven: Yale University Press, c1995. xv, 303 p.
95-030528   759.13   0300063407
Stettheimer, Florine, -- 1871-1944.   Painters -- United States -- Biography.

ND237.S78.A4 1979
Still, Clyfford, 1904-
Clyfford Still/ edited by John P. O'Neill. New York: Metropolitan Museum of Art: distributed by H. N Abrams, c1979. 222 p.
79-019696   759.13   0870992139
Still, Clyfford, -- 1904- -- Exhibitions.

ND237.T8.A32 1970
Trumbull, John, 1756-1843.
The autobiography of Colonel John Trumbull, patriot-artist, 1756-1843. Edited by Theodore Sizer. New York, Kennedy Graphics, 1970 [c1953] xxiii, 404 p.
79-116912   759.13   0306712423
Trumbull, John, -- 1756-1843.

ND237.T85.P48 1999
Peters, Lisa N.
John Henry Twachtman: an American impressionist/ Lisa N. Peters. Atlanta, Ga.: High Museum of Art; c1999. 191 p.
99-019402   759.13   1555951783
Twachtman, John Henry, -- 1853-1902 -- Criticism and interpretation. Impressionism (Art) -- United States.

ND237.W45.A86
Alberts, Robert C.
Benjamin West: a biography/ Robert C. Alberts. Boston: Houghton Mifflin, 1978. xvi, 525 p.
78-017241   759.13   0395262895
West, Benjamin, -- 1738-1820. Painters -- United States -- Biography.

ND237.W6.A4 1980
Young, Andrew McLaren.
The paintings of James McNeill Whistler/ Andrew McLaren Young, Margaret MacDonald, Robin Spencer, with the assistance of Hamish Miles. New Haven: Published for the Paul Mellon Centre for Studies in British Art by Yale University Press, 1980. 2 v.
80-005214   759.13   0300023847
Whistler, James McNeill, -- 1834-1903 -- Catalogs.

ND237.W6.P7
Prideaux, Tom.
The world of Whistler, 1834-1903, by Tom Prideaux and the editors of Time-Life Books. New York, Time-Life Books [1970] 191 p.
70-116437   759.13
Whistler, James McNeill, -- 1834-1903.

ND237.W6.S83
Sutton, Denys.
James McNeill Whistler; paintings, etchings, pastels & watercolours. [London] Phaidon Press [1966] 197 p.
66-008772   759.13
Whistler, James McNeill, -- 1834-1903.

ND237.W624.J36 1989
Janson, Anthony F.
Worthington Whittredge/ Anthony F. Janson. Cambridge; Cambridge University Press, 1989. xx, 250 p.
89-015778   759.13
Whittredge, Worthington, -- 1820-1910 -- Criticism and interpretation. Hudson River school of landscape painting.

ND237.W93.M4 1996
Meryman, Richard, 1926-
Andrew Wyeth: a secret life/ Richard Meryman. New York, NY: HarperCollins, c1996. 447 p.
96-016816   759.13   0060171138
Wyeth, Andrew, -- 1917- Painters -- United States -- Biography.

ND237.W93.S95
Wyeth, Andrew, 1917-
Andrew Wyeth. Introd. by David McCord. Selection by Frederick A. Sweet. Boston, Museum of Fine Arts [1970] 224 p.
76-127419   759.13

ND237.W94.A3
Wyeth, N. C. 1882-1945.
The Wyeths; the letters of N. C. Wyeth, 1901-1945. Edited by Betsy James Wyeth. Boston, Gambit, 1971. xii, 858 p.
73-137021   759.13   087645046X
Wyeth, N. C. -- (Newell Convers), -- 1882-1945. Wyeth family.

ND237.W94.M53 1998
Michaelis, David.
N.C. Wyeth: a biography/ by David Michaelis. New York: Alfred Knopf, 1998. x, 555 p.
98-006143   759.13   0679426264
Wyeth, N. C. -- (Newell Convers), -- 1882-1945. Painters -- United states -- Biography.

ND238.A4 H53
Highwater, Jamake.
Song from the earth: American Indian painting/ Jamake Highwater. 1st ed. Boston: New York Graphic Society: published by Little, Brown, viii, 212 p.
75-037201   759.13   0821206982
Indian painting -- North America.

ND238.A4.S48 1988
Seymour, Tryntje Van Ness.
When the rainbow touches down: the artists and stories behind the Apache, Navajo, Rio Grande Pueblo, and Hopi paintings in the William and Leslie Van Ness Denman Collection/ by Tryntje Van Ness Seymour. Phoenix, Ariz.: Heard Museum; c1988. xv, 377 p.
87-082906   750/.8997073/074019177   0934351015
Denman, William, -- 1872-1959 -- Art collections -- Exhibitions. Denman, Leslie -- Art collections -- Exhibitions. Indian painting -- Southwest, New -- Exhibitions. Indian art -- Southwest, New -- Pictorial works -- Exhibitions. Painting -- Private collections -- United States -- Exhibitions.

ND249.K3.H3
Kane, Paul, 1810-1871.
Paul Kane's frontier; including Wanderings of an artist among the Indians of North America, by Paul Kane. Edited with a biographical introd. and a catalogue raisonne by J. Russell Harper. Austin, Published for the Amon Carter Museum, Fort Worth, and the National Gallery of Canada by the University of Texas Press [1971] xviii, 350 p.
79-146522   759.11   0292701101
Indians of North America -- Pictorial works. Frontier and pioneer life in art.

ND254.W54 1996
Widdifield, Stacie G.,
The embodiment of the national in late nineteenth-century Mexican painting/ Stacie G. Widdifield. Tucson: University of Arizona Press, c1996. xvi, 213 p.
96-004447   759.972/09/034 20   0816515611
Painting, Mexican -- 19th century. Nationalism in art.

ND259.K33.A2 1995
Kahlo, Frida.
The diary of Frida Kahlo: an intimate self-portrait/
introduction by Carlos Fuentes; essay and commentaries
by Sarah M. Lowe. New York: H.N. Abrams; c1995.
295 p.
94-045994   759.972   0810932210
Kahlo, Frida -- Diaries.   Painters -- Mexico -- Diaries.
Surrealism -- Mexico.

ND259.O7.A9 2001
Anreus, Alejandro.
Orozco in gringoland: the years in New York/ Alejandro
Anreus. Albuquerque: University of New Mexico Press,
c2001. xii, 180 p.
00-009645   759.972   0826320678
Orozco, Jose Clemente, -- 1883-1949 -- Criticism and
interpretation.

ND259.R5.C66 1997
Craven, David, 1951-
Diego Rivera: as epic modernist/ by David Craven. New
York: G.K. Hall, 1997. xiii, 251 p.
97-024321   759.972   0816105375
Rivera, Diego, -- 1886-1957 -- Criticism and interpretation.

ND259.R5.H28 1999
Hamill, Pete, 1935-
Diego Rivera/ Pete Hamill. New York: Harry N. Abrams,
1999. 207 p.
99-028100   759.972   0810932342
Rivera, Diego, -- 1886-1957. Painters -- Mexico -- Biography.

ND259.T3.A4 1982
Tamayo, Rufino, 1899-
Rufino Tamayo/ texts by Octavio Paz, Jacques Lassaigne;
[translation by Kenneth Lyons]. New York: Rizzoli,
1982. 299 p.
82-050504   759.972   0847804550
Tamayo, Rufino, -- 1899-

ND450.L3
Lassaigne, Jacques, 1910-
The fifteenth century, from Van Eyck to Botticelli. Text
by Jacques Lassaigne and Giulio Carlo Argan. Translated
by Stuart Gilbert. [New York] Skira [1955] 235 p.
55-010592   750.94
Painting -- Europe -- History.

ND457.W45 1992
Weisberg, Gabriel P.
Beyond impressionism: the naturalist impulse/ Gabriel P.
Weisberg. New York: H.N. Abrams, 1992. 303 p.
92-006749   759.05/3   0810919222
Naturalism in art. Painting, European. Painting, Modern --
19th century -- Europe.

ND467-1101 History —
Special countries — Europe

ND467.G3 1966
Gaunt, William, 1900-
The pre-Raphaelite dream/ by William Gaunt. New York:
Schocken Books, 1966. 294 p.
66-014869   759.2
Painters -- Great Britain. English poetry. English poetry --
19th century -- History and criticism.

ND467.L36 1999
Lambourne, Lionel.
Victorian painting/ Lionel Lambourne. London: Phaidon
Press, 1999. 512 p.
00-361504   759.2/09/034   0714837768
Painting, Victorian. Painting, Modern -- 19th century -- Great
Britain.

ND467.5.I46.M38 1989
McConkey, Kenneth.
British impressionism/ Kenneth McConkey. New York:
Abrams, 1989. 160 p.
89-000084   759.2   0810912368
Impressionism (Art) -- Great Britain. Painting, British.
Painting, Modern -- 19th century -- Great Britain.

ND467.5.P7.C37 1990
Casteras, Susan P.
English Pre-Raphaelitism and its reception in America in
the nineteenth century/ Susan P. Casteras. Rutherford
[N.J.]: Fairleigh Dickinson University Press; c1990.
209 p.
87-046421   759.2   0838633285
Pre-Raphaelitism -- England -- Public opinion. Painting,
English -- Public opinion. Painting, Modern -- 19th century --
England -- Public opinion.

ND467.5.V52.G55 1990
Gillett, Paula, 1934-
Worlds of art: painters in Victorian society/ Paula Gillett.
New Brunswick: Rutgers University Press, c1990. xiii,
299 p.
89-030373   759.2   0813514592
Painting, British. Painting, Victorian -- Great Britain.
Feminism and art -- Great Britain. Great Britain -- Civilization
-- 19th century.

ND497.B16.P46 1997
Peppiatt, Michael.
Francis Bacon: anatomy of an enigma/ Michael Peppiatt.
New York: Farrar, Straus and Giroux, 1997. xviii, 366 p.
97-007554   759.2   0374104948
Bacon, Francis, -- 1909-   Painters -- Great Britain --
Biography.

ND497.B16.S93 2000
Sylvester, David.
Looking back at Francis Bacon/ David Sylvester. New
York: Thames & Hudson, 2000. 272 p.
99-069757   759.2   0500019940
Bacon, Francis, -- 1909- -- Criticism and interpretation.

ND497.B44.S62 1983
Spalding, Frances.
Vanessa Bell/ Frances Spalding. New Haven: Ticknor &
Fields, 1983. xvi, 399 p.
83-004967   759.2   089919205X
Bell, Vanessa, -- 1879-1961.   Painting, English. Painting,
Modern -- 20th century -- England. Women painters -- England
-- Biography.

ND497.B6.B42
Blunt, Anthony, 1907-
The art of William Blake.   New York, Columbia
University Press, 1959. ix, 122 p.
59-012399   759.2
Blake, William, -- 1757-1827.

ND497.B63.A4 1991
Noon, Patrick J.
Richard Parkes Bonington--on the pleasure of painting/
Patrick Noon. New Haven: Yale Center for British Art,
1991. 315 p.
91-065083   760/.092   0300051085
Bonington, Richard Parkes, -- 1801-1828 -- Exhibitions.

ND497.B73.B46 1998
Bendiner, Kenneth, 1947-
The art of Ford Madox Brown/ Kenneth Bendiner.
University Park, Pa.: Pennsylvania State University
Press, c1998. xviii, 204 p.
96-031023   959.2   0271016566
Brown, Ford Madox, -- 1821-1893 -- Criticism and
interpretation.

ND497.C375.G47 1989
Gerzina, Gretchen.
Carrington: a life/ Gretchen Holbrook Gerzina. New
York: Norton, 1989. xxiv, 342 p.
88-037330   759.2   0393026981
Carrington, Dora de Houghton, -- 1893-1932.   Painters --
England -- Biography. Bloomsbury group.

ND497.G2.H383 1982
Hayes, John T.
The landscape paintings of Thomas Gainsborough: a
critical text and catalogue raisonne/ John Hayes. Ithaca,
N.Y.: Cornell University Press, 1982. 2 v.
82-070753   759.2   0801415284
Gainsborough, Thomas, -- 1727-1788.

ND497.G68.T87 1987
Turnbaugh, Douglas Blair.
Duncan Grant and the Bloomsbury Group/ by Douglas
Blair Turnbaugh. Secaucus, N.J.: L. Stuart, c1987. 119 p.
87-017998   759.2   0818404426
Grant, Duncan, -- 1885-1978. Grant, Duncan, -- 1885-1978 --
Friends and associates.   Painters -- England -- Biography.
Painting, English. Painting, Modern -- 20th century -- England.

ND497.H7.M6 1969
Moore, Robert Etheridge, 1920-
Hogarth's literary relationships.   New York, Octagon
Books, 1969 [c1948] viii, 202 p.
70-076001   759.2
Hogarth, William, -- 1697-1764. Fielding, Henry, -- 1707-1754.
Art and literature. English literature -- 18th century -- History
and criticism.

ND497.H7.Q4 1955
Quennell, Peter, 1905-
Hogarth's progress. London: Collins, 1955. 318 p.
55-003679
Hogarth, William, -- 1697-1764.

ND497.L6.A4 1996
Frederic, Lord Leighton: eminent Victorian artist/
Stephen Jones ... [et al.]. New York: H.N. Abrams; 1996.
256 p.
95-040906   759.2   0810935783
Leighton of Stretton, Frederic Leighton, -- Baron, -- 1830-1896
-- Exhibitions.

ND497.R4.W3 1973
Reynolds, Joshua, 1723-1792.
Reynolds [by] Ellis Waterhouse. [New York] Phaidon;
distributed by Praeger, [1973] 192 p.
78-158100   759.2   0714815195
Reynolds, Joshua, -- Sir, -- 1723-1792.

ND497.T8.A4 1997
Rodner, William S., 1948-
J.M.W. Turner: romantic painter of the industrial
revolution/ William S. Rodner. Berkeley: University of
California Press, c1997. xiv, 222 p.
97-011127   759.2   0520204794
Turner, J. M. W. -- (Joseph Mallord William), -- 1775-1851 --
Themes, motives.   Industrial revolution in art.   Great Britain --
In art.

ND497.T8.H56 1993
Hill, David, 1953-
Turner on the Thames: river journeys in the year 1805/
David Hill. New Haven: Yale University Press, c1993. x,
182 p.
92-045911   759.2   0300053894
Turner, J. M. W. -- (Joseph Mallord William), -- 1775-1851 --
Criticism and interpretation. Turner, J. M. W. -- (Joseph
Mallord William), -- 1775-1851 -- Notebooks, sketchbooks, etc.
Thames River (England) in art.

ND497.T8.N5 1990
Nicholson, Kathleen Dukeley.
Turner's classical landscapes: myth and meaning/
Kathleen Nicholson. Princeton, N.J.: Princeton
University Press, c1990. xv, 302 p.
89-028301   759.2   069104080X
Turner, J. M. W. -- (Joseph Mallord William), -- 1775-1851 --
Criticism and interpretation.   Landscape in art. Romanticism in
art -- England. Mythology, Classical, in art.

ND546.C66
Conisbee, Philip.
Painting in eighteenth-century France/ Philip Conisbee. Ithaca, N.Y.: Cornell University Press, 1981. 223 p.
81-066151   759.4   0801414245
   Painting, French. Painting, Modern -- 17th-18th centuries -- France.

ND547.K683 1995
Kostenevich, A. G.
Hidden treasures revealed: impressionist masterpieces and other important French paintings preserved by the State Hermitage Museum, St. Petersburg/ Albert Kostenevich. New York: Ministry of Culture of the Russian Federation, The State Hermitage Museum, St. Petersburg in association with H.N. Abrams, 1995. 292 p.
94-073477   0810934329
   Painting, Modern -- 19th century -- France -- Exhibitions. Painting, Modern -- 20th century -- France -- Exhibitions. Painting -- Russia (Federation) -- Saint Petersburg -- Exhibitions.

ND547.L54 1969
Leymarie, Jean.
Impressionism; biographical and critical study. Translated from the French by James Emmons. Geneva Skira; Distributed in the United States by the World Pub. Co., Cleveland, 1969, c1955 2 v.
77-010349   759.05
   Impressionism (Art) -- France. Painting, French. Painters -- France.

ND547.5.I4.B76 1991
Broude, Norma.
Impressionism: a feminist reading: the gendering of art, science, and nature in the nineteenth century/ Norma Broude. New York: Rizzoli, 1991. 192 p.
91-010846   759.05/4   0847813975
   Impressionism (Art) -- France. Painting, Modern -- 19th century -- France. Feminism and art -- France.

ND547.5.I4.G69 1993
Great French paintings from the Barnes Foundation: Impressionist, Post-impressionist, and Early Modern. New York: Knopf; 1993. xvii, 318 p.
92-029654   759.4/09/03407474812   0679409637
   Wattenmaker, Richard J. Post-impressionism (Art) -- France -- Catalogs. Painting, Modern -- 19th century -- France -- Catalogs. Modernism (Art) -- France -- Catalogs.

ND547.5.I4.I4472 1991
Impressionism/ David Bomford ... [et al.]; with contributions by Raymond White and Louise Williams. London: National Gallery, in association with Yale University Press, c1990. 227 p.
90-071601   759.4/09/03407442132   0300050356
   Painting, French -- Exhibitions. Painting, Modern -- 19th century -- France -- Exhibitions. Impressionism (Art) -- France -- Exhibitions.

ND547.5.I4.I495 1998
Impressionists in winter: effets de neige/ Charles S. Moffett ... [et al.]. Washington, D.C.: Phillips Collection in collaboration with Philip Wilson Publishers, 1998. 240 p.
98-008265   758/.1/0944074753   0856674958
   Impressionism (Art) -- France -- Exhibitions. Painting, French -- Exhibitions. Snow in art -- Exhibitions.

ND547.5.I4.M37 1995
Medina, Joyce, 1953-
Cezanne and modernism: the poetics of painting/ Joyce Medina. Albany, NY: State University of New York Press, c1995. x, 250 p.
94-031716   759.4/09/034   0791422313
Cezanne, Paul, -- 1839-1906 -- Criticism and interpretation. Modernism (Art) -- France. Painting, Modern -- 19th century -- France. Impressionism (Art) -- France.

ND547.5.I4.M64 1993
Modernity and modernism: French painting in the nineteenth century/ Francis Frascina ... [et. al.]. New Haven: Yale University Press, in association with the Open University, c1993. 297 p.
92-035017   759.4/09/034   0300055137
   Painting, French. Impressionism (Art) -- France. Modernism (Art) -- France.

ND548.P39 1995
Perry, Gillian.
Women artists and the Parisian avant-garde: modernism and feminine art, 1900 to the late 1920s/ Gill Perry. Manchester [England]; Manchester University Press; 1995. xiv, 186 p.
94-042772   759.4/361/082   0719041643
   Painting, French. Painting, Modern -- 20th century -- France -- Paris. Women painters -- France -- Paris.

ND548.5.F3.H4 1992
Herbert, James D., 1959-
Fauve painting: the making of cultural politics/ James D. Herbert. New Haven: Yale University Press, 1992. 224 p.
92-001286   759.4/09/041   0300050682
   Fauvism -- France. Painting, French. Painting, Modern -- 20th century -- France.

ND550.H66 2001
Homburg, Cornelia.
Vincent Van Gogh and the painters of the petit boulevard/ Cornelia Homburg; with essays by Elizabeth C. Childs, John House, Richard Thomson, and a chronology by Lynn DuBard. [St. Louis, Mo.]: Saint Louis Art Musuem in association with Rizzoli, c2001. 255 p.
2001-269294   0847823326
   Painting, French -- France -- Paris -- Exhibitions. Painting, Modern -- 19th century -- France -- Paris -- Exhibitions.

ND551.G5.G47 1993
Gerdts, William H.
Monet's Giverny: an impressionist colony/ William H. Gerdts. New York: Abbeville Press, c1993. 256 p.
93-007379   709/.44/24   1558593861
   Inpressionism (Art) -- France -- Giverny. Artist colonies -- France -- Giverny. Impressionist artists -- France -- Giverny. Giverny (France) -- Social life and customs -- 19th century.

ND553.B23.W43 1999
Weber, Nicholas Fox, 1947-
Balthus: a biography/ Nicholas Fox Weber. New York:
Knopf, 1999. 644 p.
99-028422   760/.092   0679407375
Balthus, -- 1908- Painters -- France -- Biography.

ND553.B6.A9
Ashton, Dore.
Rosa Bonheur: a life and a legend/ text by Dore Ashton;
illustrations and captions by Denise Browne Hare. New
York: Viking, 1981. xiii, 206 p.
80-036749   759.4   0670608130
Bonheur, Rosa, -- 1822-1899. Painters -- France -- Biography.

ND553.B6.K613 1997
Klumpke, Anna, 1856-1942.
Rosa Bonheur: the artist's (auto)biography/ Anna
Klumpke; translated by Gretchen van Slyke. Ann Arbor:
University of Michigan Press, c1997. xxxviii, 295 p.
97-020701   759.4   0472108255
*Bonheur, Rosa, -- 1822-1899. Animal painters -- France --
Biography.*

ND553.B86.A4 1997
Golding, John.
Braque: the late works/ John Golding, Sophie Bowness,
Isabelle Monod-Fontaine. New Haven: Yale University
Press, c1997. ix, 134 p.
96-051627   759.4   0300071590
Braque, Georges, -- 1882-1963 -- Exhibitions.

ND553.C243.V37 1987
Varnedoe, Kirk, 1946-
Gustave Caillebotte/ Kirk Varnedoe. New Haven: Yale
University Press, 1987. vi, 220 p.
87-050644   759.4   0300037228
*Caillebotte, Gustave, -- 1848-1894 -- Criticism and
interpretation.*

ND553.C33.A4 1988
Gowing, Lawrence.
Cezanne, the early years, 1859-1872/ catalogue by
Lawrence Gowing; with contributions by Gotz Adriani ...
[et al.]; edited by Mary Anne Stevens. New York:
Abrams, 1988. 226 p.
88-003510   759.4   0810910489
*Cezanne, Paul, -- 1839-1906 -- Exhibitions. Painting, French -
- Exhibitions. Painting, Modern -- 19th century -- France --
Exhibitions.*

ND553.C33.C3 1995
Callow, Philip.
Lost earth: a life of Cezanne/ Philip Callow. Chicago:
Ivan R. Dee, 1995. xiii, 395 p.
95-010065   759.4   1566630843
Cezanne, Paul, -- 1839-1906. Painters -- France -- Biography.

ND553.C33.L5 1969b
Lindsay, Jack, 1900-
Cezanne; his life and art. [Greenwich, Conn.] New York
Graphic Society [1969] viii, 360 p.
76-077230   759.4   0821203401
Cezanne, Paul, -- 1839-1906.

ND553.C4.A413 1979
Rosenberg, Pierre.
Chardin, 1699-1779: a special exhibition organized by
the Reunion des Musees Nationaux, Paris, the Cleveland
Museum of Art, and Museum of Fine Arts, Boston/ Pierre
Rosenberg; catalog translated by Emilie P. Kadish and
Ursula Korneitchouk; edited by Sally W. Goodfellow.
Cleveland: Cleveland Museum of Art, c1979. 423 p.
78-074107   759.4   091038648X
Chardin, Jean Baptiste Simeon, -- 1699-1779 -- Exhibitions.

ND553.C4.R5613 1996
Roland Michel, Marianne.
Chardin/ Marianne Roland Michel. New York: Abrams,
c1996. 293 p.
95-044780   759.4   0810940418
*Chardin, Jean Baptiste Simeon, -- 1699-1779. Painters --
France -- Biography.*

ND553.C8.A4 1996
Tinterow, Gary.
Corot/ Gary Tinterow, Michael Pantazzi, Vincent
Pomarede. New York: Metropolitan Museum of Art:
c1996. xvi, 479 p.
96-006768   759.4   0870997696
Corot, Jean Baptiste Camille, -- 1796-1875 -- Exhibitions.

ND553.C8.G245 1991
Galassi, Peter.
Corot in Italy: open-air painting and the classical-
landscape tradition/ Peter Galassi. New Haven, Conn.:
Yale University Press, c1991. viii, 258 p.
90-043790   759.4   0300049579
*Corot, Jean-Baptiste-Camille, -- 1796-1875 -- Criticism and
interpretation. Corot, Jean-Baptiste-Camille, -- 1796-1875 --
Journeys -- Italy.   Italy -- Description and travel. Italy -- In
art.*

ND553.C9.F28 1993
Faunce, Sarah.
Gustave Courbet/ by Sarah Faunce. New York: H.N.
Abrams, 1993. 126 p.
92-021998   759.4   0810931826
Courbet, Gustave, -- 1819-1877 -- Criticism and interpretation.

ND553.C9.F74 1990
Fried, Michael.
Courbet's realism/ Michael Fried. Chicago: University of
Chicago Press, 1990. xviii, 378 p.
89-035432   759.4   0226262146
*Courbet, Gustave, -- 1819-1877 -- Criticism and interpretation.
Realism in art -- France.*

ND553.C9.H47 1991
Herding, Klaus.
Courbet: to venture independence/ Klaus Herding;
translated by John William Gabriel. New Haven: Yale
University Press, c1991. viii, 269 p.
90-026292   759.4   0300037449
*Courbet, Gustave, -- 1819-1877 -- Psychology.   Autonomy
(Psychology)*

ND553.C9565.B64
Boime, Albert.
Thomas Couture and the eclectic vision/ Albert Boime.
New Haven: Yale University Press, 1980. xxii, 683 p.
79-023507   759.4   0300021585
Couture, Thomas, -- 1815-1879.   Eclecticism in art -- France.
Painters -- France -- Biography.

ND553.D25.L44 1999
Lee, Simon, 1924-
David/ Simon Lee. London: Phaidon, 1999. 351 p.
99-233997   0714838047
David, Jacques Louis, -- 1748-1825. David, Jacques Louis, --
1748-1825 -- Criticism and interpretation.   Neoclassicism (Art)
-- France. Painters -- France -- Biography.

ND553.D3.M38 1984
McMullen, Roy.
Degas: his life, times, and work/ Roy McMullen. Boston:
Houghton Mifflin, 1984. viii, 517 p.
84-000677   709/.2/4   0395276039
Degas, Edgar, -- 1834-1917.   Painters -- France -- Biography.

ND553.D33.A4 1981
Johnson, Lee,
The paintings of Eugene Delacroix: a critical catalogue,
1816-1831/ Lee Johnson. Oxford: Clarendon Press, 1981-
1989. v. 1-6
80-040988   759.4   0198173148
Delacroix, Eugene, -- 1798-1863 -- Catalogs.

ND553.D33.H36 1995
Hannoosh, Michele, 1954-
Painting and the Journal of Eugene Delacroix/ Michele
Hannoosh. Princeton, N.J.: Princeton University Press,
1995. xix, 221 p.
94-025302   759.4   0691043949
Delacroix, Eugene, -- 1798-1863 -- Psychology. Delacroix,
Eugene, -- 1798-1863. -- Journal. Ut pictura poesis (Aesthetics)

ND553.D33.J5713 1998
Jobert, Barthelemy.
Delacroix/ Barthelemy Jobert. Princeton, N.J.: Princeton
University Press, 1998. 335 p.
98-024954   759.4   0691004188
Delacroix, Eugene, -- 1798-1863 -- Criticism and interpretation.

ND553.D774.C313 1971
Cabanne, Pierre.
Dialogues with Marcel Duchamp. Translated from the
French by Ron Padgett. New York, Viking Press [1971]
136 p.
77-083255   759.4   0670240176
Duchamp, Marcel, -- 1887-1968.

ND553.D774.S3
Schwarz, Arturo, 1924-
The complete works of Marcel Duchamp. New York, H.
N. Abrams [1969] xxi, 630 p.
69-011987   709/.24
Duchamp, Marcel, -- 1887-1968.

ND553.F7.A88 1988
Ashton, Dore.
Fragonard in the universe of painting/ Dore Ashton.
Washington, D.C.: Smithsonian Institution Press, c1988.
256 p.
87-043110   759.4   0874742080
Fragonard, Jean-Honore, -- 1732-1806 -- Criticism and
interpretation.   Painting, French. Painting, Modern -- 17th-
18th centuries -- France.

ND553.F7.M38 1993
Massengale, Jean Montague.
Jean-Honore Fragonard/ text by Jean Montague
Massengale. New York: H.N. Abrams, 1993. 128 p.
92-021996   759.4   0810933136
Fragonard, Jean-Honore, -- 1732-1806.   Painters -- France --
Biography.

ND553.F7.S53 1990
Sheriff, Mary D.
Fragonard: art and eroticism/ Mary D. Sheriff. Chicago:
University of Chicago Press, 1990. xiv, 253 p.
89-004783   759.4   0226752739
Fragonard, Jean-Honore, -- 1732-1806 -- Criticism and
interpretation. Erotic art -- France.

ND553.G27.A4813 1978
Gauguin, Paul, 1848-1903.
The writings of a savage/ Paul Gauguin; edited by Daniel
Guerin; with an introduction by Wayne Andersen;
translated by Eleanor Levieux. New York: Viking Press,
1978. xxxix, 304 p.
76-053574   759.4   0670791733
Gauguin, Paul, -- 1848-1903 -- Correspondence. Gauguin, Paul,
-- 1848-1903 -- Written works.   Painters -- France --
Correspondence.

ND553.G27.A74 1971
Andersen, Wayne V.
Gauguin's paradise lost [by] Wayne Andersen. With the
assistance of Barbara Klein. New York, Viking Press
[1971] xii, 371 p.
72-135347   759.4   0670335932
Gauguin, Paul, -- 1848-1903.

ND553.G27.G53 1993
Gibson, Michael, 1929-
Paul Gauguin/ Michael Gibson. New York: Rizzoli, 1993.
128 p.
92-041547   759.4   0847817377
Gauguin, Paul, -- 1848-1903 -- Criticism and interpretation.
Post-impressionism (Art) -- France.

ND553.G27.H33 1955
Hanson, Lawrence.
Noble savage; the life of Paul Gauguin, by Lawrence and
Elisabeth Hanson. New York, Random House [1955,
c1954] 299 p.
55-005792   927.5
Gauguin, Paul, -- 1848-1903.

ND553.G27.J58 2000
Jirat-Wasiutynski, Vojtech.
Technique and meaning in the paintings of Paul Gauguin/ Vojtech Jirat-Wasiutynski, H. Travers Newton, Jr. Cambridge; Cambridge University Press, 2000. xv, 286 p.
99-014193   759.4
Gauguin, Paul, -- 1848-1903 -- Criticism and interpretation. Painting -- Technique.

ND553.G45.E317 1983
Eitner, Lorenz.
Gericault, his life and work/ Lorenz E.A. Eitner. London: Orbis Pub., c1983. 376 p.
81-068742   760/.092/4   0801414687
Gericault, Theodore, -- 1791-1824.   Painters -- France -- Biography.

ND553.L28.A4 1996
Conisbee, Philip.
Georges de La Tour and his world/ Philip Conisbee; essays by Jean-Pierre Cuzin ... [et al.]; technical essays by Claire Barry ... [et al.]. Washington: National Gallery of Art, c1996. 319 p.
96-026801   759.4   0300069480
La Tour, Georges du Mesnil de, -- 1593-1652 -- Exhibitions. La Tour, Georges du Mesnil, -- 1593-1652 -- Psychology.

ND553.M3.A4 2000
Mauner, George L., 1931-
Manet: the still-life paintings/ by George Mauner with an essay by Henri Loyrette. New York: H. N. Abrams in association with the American Federation of Arts, 2000. 198 p.
00-042009   759.4   0810943913
Manet, Edouard, -- 1832-1883 -- Exhibitions.   Still-life painting, French -- Exhibitions.

ND553.M3.F75 1996
Fried, Michael.
Manet's modernism, or, The face of painting in the 1860s/ Michael Fried. Chicago: University of Chicago Press, 1996. xxviii, 647 p.
95-014461   759.4   0226262162
Manet, Edouard, -- 1832-1883 -- Criticism and interpretation. Painting, French. Painting, Modern -- 19th century -- France.

ND553.M3.L63 2001
Locke, Nancy, 1963-
Manet and the family romance/ Nancy Locke. Princeton, N.J.: Princeton University Press, c2001. viii, 223 p.
00-064265   759.4   0691050600
Manet, Edouard, -- 1832-1883 -- Criticism and interpretation. Manet, Edouard, -- 1832-1883 -- Psychology. Family in art.

ND553.M37.A35 1995
Matisse, Henri, 1869-1954.
Matisse on art/ [edited by] Jack Flam. Berkeley: University of California Press, c1995. xviii, 322 p.
95-007226   701   0520200373
Matisse, Henri, -- 1869-1954 -- Aesthetics.   Art.

ND553.M37.A64 1993
Flam, Jack D.
Matisse: the Dance/ Jack Flam. Washington [D.C.]: National Gallery of Art, c1993. 87 p.
93-015991   759.4   0894681974
Matisse, Henri, -- 1869-1954. -- Dance. Matisse, Henri, -- 1869-1954 -- Criticism and interpretation.   Mural painting and decoration, French -- Pennsylvania -- Merion.

ND553.M37.B34 1966
Barr, Alfred Hamilton, 1902-
Matisse, his art and his public, by Alfred H. Barr, Jr. [New York] Published for the Museum of Modern Art by Arno Press, 1966 [c1951] 591 p.
66-026118   759.4
Matisse, Henri, -- 1869-1954.

ND553.M7.A4 1978
Monet, Claude, 1840-1926.
Monet's years at Giverny: beyond Impressionism. New York: Metropolitan Museum of Art, c1978. 180 p.
78-000328   759.4   0870991744
Monet, Claude, -- 1840-1926 -- Exhibitions. Monet, Claude, -- 1840-1926 -- Homes and haunts -- France -- Giverny. Post-impressionism (Art) -- France -- Exhibitions. Impressionism (Art) -- France -- Exhibitions.

ND553.M7.A4 1995b
Stuckey, Charles F.
Claude Monet: 1840-1926/ Charles F. Stuckey; with the assistance of Sophia Shaw. New York: Thames and Hudson; c1995. 282 p.
94-061569   759.4   0865591342
Monet, Claude, -- 1840-1926 -- Exhibitions.   Impressionism (Art) -- France -- Exhibitions.

ND553.M7.A4 1997
Pissarro, Joachim.
Monet and the Mediterranean/ Joachim Pissarro. New York: Rizzoli in association with the Kimbell Art Museum, Forth Worth, Texas, 1997. 191 p.
96-035758   759.4   0847817830
Monet, Claude, -- 1840-1926 -- Exhibitions.   Western Mediterranean in art -- Exhibitions.

ND553.M7.A4 1999
Champa, Kermit Swiler.
Monet & Bazille: a collaboration/ essays by Kermit Swiler Champa and Dianne W. Pitman; edited by David A. Brenneman. Atlanta, Ga.: High Museum of Art; 1999. 107 p.
98-031450   759.4   0810963841
Monet, Claude, -- 1840-1926 -- Exhibitions. Bazille, Frederic, -- 1841-1870 -- Exhibitions.   Artistic collaboration -- France -- Exhibitions.

ND553.M7.H43 1994
Herbert, Robert L., 1929-
Monet on the Normandy coast: tourism and painting, 1867-1886/ Robert L. Herbert. New Haven: Yale University Press, c1994. xvii, 149 p.
94-013913   759.4   0300059736
Monet, Claude, -- 1840-1926 -- Criticism and interpretation. Tourist trade and art -- France -- Normandy. Normandy (France) in art.

ND553.M7.S7 1992
Spate, Virginia.
Claude Monet: life and work, with over 300 illustrations, 135 in colour/ Virginia Spate. New York: Rizzoli, 1992. 348 p.
92-050137   759.4   0847815714
Monet, Claude, -- 1840-1926.   Painters -- France -- Biography.

ND553.M7.T79 1995
Tucker, Paul Hayes, 1950-
Claude Monet: life and art/ Paul Hayes Tucker. New Haven: Yale University Press, c1995. ix, 250 p.
94-040130   759.4   0300062982
Monet, Claude, -- 1840-1926 -- Criticism and interpretation.

ND553.M7.T83 1989
Tucker, Paul Hayes, 1950-
Monet in the '90s: the series paintings/ Paul Hayes Tucker. Boston: Museum of Fine Arts; c1989. xvi, 307 p.
89-063207   759.4   0300046596
Monet, Claude, -- 1840-1926 -- Criticism and interpretation.

ND553.M88.H5 1990
Higonnet, Anne, 1959-
Berthe Morisot/ Anne Higonnet. New York, N.Y.: Harper & Row, 1990. xiii, 240 p.
89-045669   759.4   0060162325
Morisot, Berthe, -- 1841-1895.   Artists -- France -- Biography.

ND553.M88.H53 1992
Higonnet, Anne, 1959-
Berthe Morisot's images of women/ Anne Higonnet. Cambridge, Mass.: Harvard University Press, 1992. 311 p.
91-029966   759.4   0674067983
Morisot, Berthe, -- 1841-1895 -- Criticism and interpretation. Women in art.

ND553.P5.A4 1994
Freeman, Judi.
Picasso and the weeping women: the years of Marie-Therese Walter & Dora Maar/ Judi Freeman. Los Angeles, Calif.: Los Angeles County Museum of Art; c1994. 215 p.
93-038179   709/.2   0847818004
Picasso, Pablo, -- 1881-1973 -- Exhibitions. Walter, Marie-Therese, -- 1909-1977. Maar, Dora. Women in art -- Exhibitions. Artists' models -- France -- Biography.

ND553.P5.A4 1998
Picasso, Pablo, 1881-1973.
Picasso and the war years, 1937-1945/ [organized by the Fine Arts Museums of San Francisco, in collaboration with the Solomon R. Guggenheim Museum, New York]; Steven A. Nash, editor with Robert Rosenblum; contributions by Brigitte Baer ... [et al.] New York, N.Y.: Thames and Hudson; 1998. 256 p.
98-060335   759.4   0500092745
Picasso, Pablo, -- 1881-1973 -- Exhibitions.   War in art.

ND553.P5.A66 1988b
Chipp, Herschel Browning.
Picasso's Guernica: history, transformations, meanings/ Herschel B. Chipp; with a chapter by Javier Tusell. Berkeley: University of California Press, c1988. xii, 261 p.
87-030893   759.4   0520060431
Picasso, Pablo, -- 1881-1973. -- Guernica. Picasso, Pablo, -- 1881-1973 -- Criticism and interpretation. Painting, French. Painting, Modern -- 20th century -- France. Spain -- History -- Civil War, 1936-1939 -- Art and the war.

ND553.P5.P477
Picasso in perspective/ edited by Gert Schiff. Englewood Cliffs, N.J.: Prentice-Hall, c1976. viii, 184 p.
76-040110   759.4   0136758010
Picasso, Pablo, -- 1881-1973.

ND553.P5.S76
Stein, Gertrude, 1874-1946.
Gertrude Stein on Picasso. Edited by Edward Burns. Afterword by Leon Katz and Edward Burns. Published in cooperation with the Museum of Modern Art. New York, Liveright [1970] 122 p.
78-131273   759.6   087140513X
Picasso, Pablo, -- 1881-1973.   Painters -- France -- Biography.

ND553.P55.A4 1992
Brettell, Richard R.
The impressionist and the city: Pissarro's series paintings/ Richard R. Brettell and Joachim Pissarro; edited by MaryAnne Stevens. New Haven: Yale University Press, c1992. liii, 230 p.
92-050580   759.4   0300053509
Pissarro, Camille, -- 1830-1903 -- Exhibitions.   Cities and towns in art -- Exhibitions.

ND553.P55.P488 1993
Pissarro, Joachim.
Camille Pissarro/ Joachim Pissarro. New York: H.N. Abrams, 1993. 309 p.
93-012280   759.4   0810937247
Pissarro, Camille, -- 1830-1903 -- Criticism and interpretation.

ND553.P55.S53
Shikes, Ralph E.
Pissarro, his life and work/ by Ralph E. Shikes and Paula Harper; [designed by Abe Lerner]. New York: Horizon Press, c1980. 362 p.
79-056132   759.4   0818001283
Pissarro, Camille, -- 1830-1903.   Painters -- France -- Biography.

ND553.P8.A4 1995
Verdi, Richard.
Nicolas Poussin, 1594-1665/ Richard Verdi; with an essay by Pierre Rosenberg. London: Zwemmer in association with the Royal Academy of Arts, c1995. 336 p.
95-219504   759.4   0302006478
Poussin, Nicolas, -- 1594?-1665 -- Exhibitions.

ND553.P8.B64
Blunt, Anthony, 1907-1983.
Nicolas Poussin. New York, Bollingen Foundation; distributed by Pantheon Books, [1967]
66-016237 759.4
Poussin, Nicolas, -- 1594?-1665.

ND553.P8.C35 1993
Carrier, David, 1944-
Poussin's paintings: a study in art-historical methodology/ David Carrier. University Park, Pa.: Pennsylvania State University Press, c1993. xviii, 276 p.
91-026026 759.4 0271008164
Poussin, Nicolas, -- 1594?-1665 -- Criticism and interpretation. Classicism in art -- France.

ND553.P8.O24 1988
Oberhuber, Konrad.
Poussin, the early years in Rome: the origins of French classicism/ by Konrad Oberhuber; foreword by Edmund P. Pillsbury. New York: Hudson Hills Press; c1988. 367 p.
88-009173 759.4
Poussin, Nicolas, -- 1594?-1665 -- Criticism and interpretation. Poussin, Nicolas, -- 1594?-1665 -- Homes and haunts -- Italy -- Rome. Classicism in art -- France.

ND553.R35.H6
Hobbs, Richard.
Odilon Redon/ Richard Hobbs. London: Studio Vista, 1977. 192 p.
77-365881 760/.092/4 0289706157
Redon, Odilon, -- 1840-1916. Painters -- France -- Biography.

ND553.R45.A73 1997
House, John, 1945-
Pierre-Auguste Renoir: La promenade/ John House. Los Angeles, Calif.: J. Paul Getty Museum, c1997. 88 p.
97-021894 759.4 0892363657
Renoir, Auguste, -- 1841-1919. -- Promenade. Renoir, Auguste, -- 1841-1919 -- Criticism and interpretation. Impressionism (Art) -- France.

ND553.R67.A4 1985
Henri Rousseau: essays/ by Roger Shattuck ... [et al.; translations from the French by Richard Miller]. New York: Museum of Modern Art; 1985. 269 p.
84-061967 759.4 0870705644
Rousseau, Henri Julien Felix, -- 1844-1910 -- Exhibitions. Primitivism in art -- France -- Exhibitions.

ND553.S5.A4 1991
Herbert, Robert L., 1929-
Georges Seurat, 1859-1891/ Robert L. Herbert [with] Francoise Cachin ... [et al.]. New York: Metropolitan Museum of Art: c1991. x, 450 p.
91-017309 759.4 0870996185
Seurat, Georges, -- 1859-1891 -- Exhibitions.

ND553.S5.C643 1988
Courthion, Pierre.
Georges Seurat/ Pierre Courthion; [translated by Norbert Guterman]. New York: H.N. Abrams, 1988. 128 p.
87-073460 759.4 0810915197
Seurat, Georges, -- 1859-1891. Painting, French. Painting, Modern -- 19th century -- France. Post-impressionism (Art) -- France.

ND553.S5.R4 1946
Rewald, John.
Georges Seurat. New York, Wittenborn & company, 1946. xx, 125 p.
46-005269 927.5
Seurat, Georges, -- 1859-1891.

ND553.S52.S65 1997
Smith, Paul, 1956-
Seurat and the avant-garde/ Paul Smith. New Haven: Yale University Press, c1997. x, 211 p.
96-034527 759.4 0300070020
Seurat, Georges, -- 1859-1891 -- Criticism and interpretation. Symbolism (Art movement) -- Influence. Avant-garde (Aesthetics) -- France -- History -- 19th century -- Language.

ND553.S62.A83 1992
Alfred Sisley/ edited by MaryAnne Stevens; with contributions by Isabelle Cahn ... [et al]. London: Royal Academy of Arts; 1992. 300 p.
92-050345 0300052448
Sisley, Alfred, -- 1839-1899 -- Criticism and interpretation.

ND553.S7 F72
Wheeler, Monroe, 1899-
Soutine. [New York] Published for the Museum of Modern Art by Arno Press, 1966 [c1950] 115 p.
66-026125
Soutine, Haim, -- 1894-1943.

ND553.T7.A4 1987
Adriani, Gotz, 1940-
Toulouse-Lautrec/ Gotz Adriani. New York, N.Y.: Thames and Hudson, 1987. 336 p.
87-050249 759.4 0500091803
Toulouse-Lautrec, Henri de, -- 1864-1901 -- Exhibitions. Painting, French -- Exhibitions. Painting, Modern -- 19th century -- France -- Exhibitions.

ND553.T7.H39 1997
Heller, Reinhold.
Toulouse-Lautrec: the soul of Montmartre/ Reinhold Heller. Munich; Prestel; c1997. 118 p.
97-003739 759.4 3791317393
Toulouse-Lautrec, Henri de, -- 1864-1901 -- Criticism and interpretation. Paris (France) -- Intellectual life -- 19th century. Montmartre (Paris, France) -- Intellectual life.

ND553.V9.G76 1993
Groom, Gloria Lynn.
Edouard Vuillard: painter-decorator: patrons and projects, 1892-1912/ Gloria Groom. New Haven: Yale University Press, c1993. viii, 260 p.
93-029680 759.4 0300055552
Vuillard, Edouard, -- 1868-1940 -- Themes, motives. Artists and patrons -- France. Interior architecture -- France.

ND553.V9.N4 1969
Museum of Modern Art (New York, N.Y.)
Edouard Vuillard, by Andrew Carnduff Ritchie. The Museum of Modern Art, New York, in collaboration with the Cleveland Museum of Art. [New York] Published for the Museum of Modern Art by Arno Press, 1969 [c1954] 104 p.
79-086445   759.4
Vuillard, Edouard, -- 1868-1940.

ND553.W3 P65 2000
Plax, Julie Anne.
Watteau and the cultural politics of eighteenth-century France/ Julie Anne Plax. Cambridge; Cambridge University Press, 2000. xii, 260 p.
99-037851   759.4 21   052164268X
Watteau, Antoine, 1684-1721 -- Criticism and interpretation. Watteau, Antoine, 1684-1721 -- Themes, motives.

ND553.W3.P66 1984b
Posner, Donald.
Antoine Watteau/ Donald Posner. Ithaca, N.Y.: Cornell University Press, 1984. 300 p.
83-045154   759.4   0801415713
Watteau, Antoine, -- 1684-1721.   Painters -- France -- Biography. Genre painting -- 18th century -- France.

ND565.B413
Benesch, Otto, 1896-1964.
German painting, from Durer to Holbein. Text by Otto Benesch [translated from the German by H. S. B. Harrison.] Geneva Skira; distributed in the U.S. by the World Pub. Co., Cleveland, [1966] 197 p.
66-022489   759.3
Painting, German -- History. Painting, Renaissance -- Germany.

ND567.5.R6.V38 1980
Vaughan, William, 1943-
German romantic painting/ William Vaughan. New Haven, Conn.: Yale University Press, 1980. 260 p.
80-013170   759.3   0300023871
Romanticism in art -- Germany. Painting, German. Painting, Modern -- 19th century -- Germany.

ND568.5.E9.S45
Selz, Peter Howard, 1919-
German expressionist painting. Berkeley, University of California Press, 1957. xx, 379 p.
57-010501   759.915
Expressionism (Art) -- Germany. Painting, Modern -- 20th century -- Germany. Painting, German.

ND588.A4.W63 1993
Wood, Christopher S.
Albrecht Altdorfer and the origins of landscape/ Christopher S. Wood. Chicago: University of Chicago Press, c1993. 323 p.
93-013123   759.3   0226906019
Altdorfer, Albrecht, -- ca. 1480-1538 -- Criticism and interpretation. Landscape painting, Renaissance -- Germany.

ND588.B37.S4 1996
Selz, Peter Howard, 1919-
Max Beckmann/ Peter Selz. New York: Abbeville Press, 1996. 127 p.
95-042055   759.3   1558598898
Beckmann, Max, -- 1884-1950 -- Criticism and interpretation. New objectivity (Art) -- Germany.

ND588.C8.A4 1978
Friedlander, Max J., 1867-1958.
The paintings of Lucas Cranach/ Max J. Friedlander & Jakob Rosenberg; [catalogue translated by Heinz Norden; introd. translated by Ronald Taylor.] Ithaca, N.Y.: Cornell University Press, c1978. 202 p.
77-018410   759.3   0801410614
Cranach, Lucas, -- 1472-1553 -- Catalogs.

ND588.D9.P28 1955
Panofsky, Erwin, 1892-1968.
The life and art of Albrecht Durer. Princeton, N. J., Princeton University Press, 1955. xxxii, 317 p.
55-006248   927.5   0691003033
Durer, Albrecht, -- 1471-1528.

ND588.F75.H629 2000
Hofmann, Werner, 1924-
Caspar David Friedrich/ Werner Hofmann. London: Thames & Hudson, 2000. 304 p.
00-101621   0500092958
Friedrich, Caspar David, -- 1774-1840 -- Criticism and interpretation. Romanticism in art.

ND588.F75.K64 1990
Koerner, Joseph Leo.
Caspar David Friedrich and the subject of landscape/ Joseph Leo Koerner. New Haven: Yale University Press, 1990. 256 p.
90-070526   759.3   0300049269
Friedrich, Caspar David, -- 1774-1840 -- Criticism and interpretation.   Landscape in art. Romanticism in art -- Germany.

ND588.H7.A4 1985
Rowlands, John, 1931-
Holbein: the paintings of Hans Holbein the Younger/ John Rowlands. Oxford: Phaidon, 1985. 288 p.
85-118106   759.3   0714823589
Holbein, Hans, -- 1497-1543 -- Catalogs. Holbein, Hans, -- 1497-1543 -- Criticism and interpretation.

ND588.K464.A4 1987a
Rosenthal, Mark
Anselm Kiefer/ by Mark Rosenthal; organized by A. James Speyer, Mark Rosenthal. Chicago: Art Institute of Chicago; 1987. 171 p.
87-029007   759.3   0876330715
Kiefer, Anselm, -- 1945- -- Exhibitions.   Painting, German -- Germany (West) -- Exhibitions. Painting, Modern -- 20th century -- Germany (West) -- Exhibitions. Artists' books -- Germany (West) -- Exhibitions.

ND588.K464.G55 1990
Gilmour, John, 1939-
Fire on the earth: Anselm Kiefer and the postmodern world/ John C. Gilmour. Philadelphia: Temple University Press, 1990. xvi, 214 p.
89-020137 759.3 0877226903
Kiefer, Anselm, -- 1945- -- Criticism and interpretation. Postmodernism.

ND588.K5.S26
San Lazzaro, Gualtieri di.
Klee; a study of his life and work. Translated from the Italian by Stuart Hood. New York, Praeger [1957] 304 p.
57-011232 927.5
Klee, Paul, -- 1879-1940.

ND588.P46.Y38 1993
Yau, John, 1950-
A.R. Penck/ text by John Yau. New York: H.N. Abrams, 1993. 127 p.
92-043358 759.3 0810937255
Penck, A. R., -- 1939- -- Criticism and interpretation. Figurative painting, German.

ND588.R48.A4 1988b
Nasgaard, Roald.
Gerhard Richter paintings/ by Roald Nasgaard; with an essay by I. Michael Danoff and an interview with Gerhard Richter by Benjamin H. Buchloh; edited by Terry A. Neff. New York, N.Y.: Thames and Hudson, 1988. 160 p.
87-051302 759.3 0500014426
Richter, Gerhard, -- 1932- -- Exhibitions.

ND613.M25 1997
Maginnis, Hayden B. J.
Painting in the age of Giotto: a historical reevaluation/ Hayden B.J. Maginnis. University Park, Pa.: Pennsylvania State University Press, c1997. xviii, 217 p.
96-011306 759.5/09/023 0271015993
Painting, Italian. Painting, Gothic -- Italy. Painting, Renaissance -- Italy.

ND613.O3213
Oertel, Robert.
Early Italian painting to 1400. New York, Praeger [1968, c1966] 376 p.
68-013133 759.5
Painting, Italian -- History. Painting, Medieval -- Italy.

ND615.F66 1971
Freedberg, S. J. 1914-
Painting in Italy, 1500 to 1600 [by] S. J. Freedberg. Harmondsworth, Penguin Books [1971, c1970] xix, 554 p.
78-027513 759.5 0140560351
Painting, Italian. Painting, Renaissance -- Italy. Mannerism (Art) -- Italy.

ND615.F67
Freedberg, S. J. 1914-
Painting of the high Renaissance in Rome and Florence. Cambridge, Harvard University Press, 1961. 2 v.
61-007390 759.5
Painting -- Italy -- Rome -- History. Painting -- Italy -- Florence -- History. Painting, Italian.

ND616.5.B3.F56 1997
Finaldi, Gabriele.
Discovering the Italian baroque: the Denis Mahon collection/ Gabriele Finaldi and Michael Kitson; with contributions by Christopher Brown, Humphrey Wine and Denis Mahon. London: National Gallery Publications, 1997. 192 p.
96-071403 759.046 1857091779
Mahon, Denis -- Art collections -- Exhibitions. Painting, Italian -- Exhibitions. Painting, Baroque -- Italy -- Exhibitions. Painting -- Private collections -- England -- Exhibitions.

ND617.5.M3.B65 1993
Boime, Albert.
The art of the Macchia and the Risorgimento: representing culture and nationalism in nineteenth-century Italy/ Albert Boime. Chicago: University of Chicago Press, 1993. xxi, 338 p.
92-017169 759.5/51/09034 0226063305
Macchiaioli. Painting, Modern -- 19th century -- Italy. Art and society -- Italy.

ND617.5.M3.B7 1987
Broude, Norma.
The Macchiaioli: Italian painters of the nineteenth century/ Norma Broude. New Haven: Yale University Press, c1987. xxiii, 324 p.
86-028270 759.5/51 0300035470
Macchiaioli. Painting, Italian -- Italy -- Tuscany. Painting, Modern -- 19th century -- Italy -- Tuscany.

ND621.S6.M34 2001
Maginnis, Hayden B. J.
The world of the early Sienese painter/ Hayden B.J. Maginnis; with a translation of the Sienese Breve dell'Arte del pittori by Gabriele Erasmi. University Park, Pa.: Pennsylvania State University Press, 2000. 310 p.
99-035892 759.5/58 0271020040
Painters -- Italy -- Siena -- Historiography. Siena (Italy) -- History -- Rule of the Nine, 1287-1355.

ND621.V5.H77 1995
Humfrey, Peter, 1947-
Painting in Renaissance Venice/ Peter Humfrey. New Haven: Yale University Press, c1995. vii, 320 p.
94-035348 759.5/31/09024 0300062478
Painting, Italian -- Italy -- Venice. Painting, Renaissance -- Italy -- Venice.

ND621.V5.S83 1970
Steer, John, 1928-
A concise history of Venetian painting. New York, Praeger [1970] 216 p.
70-099495 759.5
Painting, Italian -- Italy -- Venice.

ND622.V4
Venturi, Lionello, 1885-1961.
Italian painting ... Critical studies by Lionello Venturi.
Historical surveys by Rosabianca Skira-Venturi.
Translated by Stuart Gilbert. Geneva, A. Skira [1950-52]
3 v.
50-011049   759.5
  Painters -- Italy. Painting, Italian.

ND623.A5395.P4 1992
Perlingieri, Ilya Sandra.
Sofonisba Anguissola: the first great woman artist of the
Renaissance/ Ilya Sandra Perlingieri. New York: Rizzoli,
1992. 223 p.
91-038245   759.5   0847815447
*Anguissola, Sofonisba, -- ca. 1532 or 3-1625. Painters -- Italy -
- Biography. Painting, Renaissance -- Italy.*

ND623.B39.G64 1989
Goffen, Rona, 1944-
Giovanni Bellini/ Rona Goffen. New Haven: Yale
University Press, c1989. ix, 347 p.
89-033263   759.5   0300043341
Bellini, Giovanni, -- d.1516 -- Criticism and interpretation.

ND623.B7.L53 1978b
Lightbown, R. W.
Sandro Botticelli/ Ronald Lightbown. Berkeley:
University of California Press, c1978. 2 v.
76-046237   759.5   0520033728
*Botticelli, Sandro, -- 1444 or 5-1510.   Painters -- Italy --
Biography.*

ND623.B9.A43
Buonarroti, Michel Angelo, 1475-1564.
The complete work of Michelangelo. New York, Reynal
[1965] 597 p.
66-003040   709.24
Michelangelo Buonarroti, -- 1475-1564.

ND623.B9.A69 1998a
Barnes, Bernadine Ann.
Michelangelo's Last Judgment: the Renaissance response/
Bernadine Barnes. Berkeley: University of California
Press, c1998. xix, 171 p.
97-000082   759.5   0520205499
*Michelangelo Buonarroti, -- 1475-1564. -- Last Judgment.
Michelangelo Buonarroti, -- 1475-1564. -- Criticism and
interpretation. Judgment Day in art.*

ND623.B9.D453 1996
De Vecchi, Pierluigi.
Michelangelo: the Vatican frescoes/ Pierluigi De Vecchi;
with an essay on the restoration by Gianluigi Colalucci.
New York: Abbeville Press Pub., c1996. 271 p.
96-034725   759.5   0789202328
*Michelangelo Buonarroti, -- 1475-1564 -- Criticism and
interpretation.   Mural painting and decoration, Italian --
Vatican City. Mural painting and decoration, Renaissance --
Vatican City.*

ND623.B9.O74 1989
Oremland, Jerome D.
Michelangelo's Sistine ceiling: a psychoanalytic study of
creativity/ Jerome D. Oremland. Madison, Conn.:
International Universities Press, c1989. xvii, 322 p.
88-012257   759.5   0823633640
*Michelangelo Buonarroti, -- 1475-1564 -- Criticism and
interpretation.   Psychoanalysis and art. Mural painting and
decoration, Renaissance -- Vatican City -- Themes, motives.*

ND623.C2.L49 1982b
Links, J. G.
Canaletto/ J.G. Links. Ithaca, N.Y.: Cornell University
Press, 1982. 239 p.
82-070752   759.5   0801415322
Canaletto, -- 1697-1768. Painters -- Italy -- Biography.

ND623.C26.G53 1995
Gilbert, Creighton.
Caravaggio and his two cardinals/ Creighton E. Gilbert.
University Park, Pa.: Pennsylvania State University
Press, c1995. xiii, 322 p.
93-044381   759.5   0271013125
*Caravaggio, Michelangelo Merisi da, -- 1573-1610 -- Criticism
and interpretation. Jesus Christ -- Art. John, -- the Baptist, Saint
-- Art. Mannerism (Art) -- Italy -- Rome. Art patronage -- Italy --
Rome -- History -- 16th century.*

ND623.C26.H44 1983
Hibbard, Howard, 1928-
Caravaggio/ Howard Hibbard. New York: Harper & Row,
c1983. xii, 404 p.
78-002145   759.5   0064333221
Caravaggio, Michelangelo Merisi da, -- 1573-1610.

ND623.C26.L36 1999
Langdon, Helen.
Caravaggio: a life/ Helen Langdon. New York: Farrar,
Straus and Giroux, 1999. xi, 436 p.
98-051195   0374118949
*Caravaggio, Michelangelo Merisi da, -- 1573-1610. Painters --
Italy -- Biography.*

ND623.C26.R62 2000
Robb, Peter.
M: the man who became Caravaggio/ Peter Robb. New
York: Henry Holt, 2000. 570 p.
99-043576   759.5   0805063560
*Caravaggio, Michelangelo Merisi da, -- 1573-1610. Painters --
Italy -- Biography.*

ND623.C3.S513 1994
Sgarbi, Vittorio.
Carpaccio/ Vittorio Sgarbi; translated from the Italian by
Jay Hyams. New York: Abbeville Press, [1994?] 271 p.
94-039743   759.5   0789200007
*Carpaccio, Vittore, -- 1455?-1525? -- Criticism and
interpretation. Carpaccio, Vittore, -- 1455?-1525? -- Catalogs.*

ND623.C47.H67
Horster, Marita.
Andrea del Castagno: complete edition with a critical catalogue/ Marita Horster. Ithaca, N.Y.: Cornell University Press, 1980. 224 p.
79-006028   759.5   0801413168
Castagno, Andrea del, -- 1423-1457.   Painters -- Italy -- Biography.

ND623.F5.A4 1997
Spike, John T.
Fra Angelico/ John T. Spike. New York: Abbeville Press, c1996. 280 p.
96-051128   759.5   0789203227
Angelico, -- fra, -- ca. 1400-1455 -- Catalogs.

ND623.F5.D5313 1995
Didi-Huberman, Georges.
Fra Angelico: dissemblance & figuration/ Georges Didi-Huberman; translated by Jane Marie Todd. Chicago: University of Chicago Press, 1995. xiv, 274 p.
94-032177   759.5   0226148130
Angelico, -- fra, -- ca. 1400-1455 -- Criticism and interpretation. Human figure in art. Symbolism in art.

ND623.F5.H66 1993
Hood, William, 1940-
Fra Angelico at San Marco/ William Hood. New Haven: Yale University Press, 1993. xv, 338 p.
92-014504   759.5   0300057342
Angelico, -- fra, -- ca. 1400-1455 -- Criticism and interpretation. Monasticism and religious orders in art. Spirituality in art.

ND623.G35.C45 1982
Christiansen, Keith.
Gentile da Fabriano/ Keith Christiansen. Ithaca, N.Y.: Cornell University Press, 1982. ix, 193 p.
80-070584   759.5   0801413605
Gentile, -- da Fabriano, -- ca. 1370-1427. Painters -- Italy -- Biography.

ND623.G364.B58 1998
Bissell, R. Ward.
Artemisia Gentileschi and the authority of art: critical reading and catalogue raisonne/ R. Ward Bissell. University Park, Pa.: Pennsylvania State University Press, 1998. xxiv, 446 p.
97-048437   759.5   0271017872
Gentileschi, Artemisia, -- ca. 1597-ca. 1651 -- Criticism and interpretation. Gentileschi, Artemisia, -- ca. 1597-ca. 1651 -- Catalogues raisonnes.

ND623.G364.G368 2001
Garrard, Mary D.
Artemisia Gentileschi around 1622: the shaping and reshaping of an artistic identity/ Mary D. Garrard. Berkeley: University of California Press, c2001. xxii, 179 p.
00-056385   759.5   0520224264
Gentileschi, Artemisia, -- 1593-1652 or 3 -- Criticism and interpretation.

ND623.G364.G37 1989
Garrard, Mary D.
Artemisia Gentileschi: the image of the female hero in Italian Baroque art/ by Mary D. Garrard. Princeton, N.J.: Princeton University Press, c1989. xxv, 607 p.
88-009881   759.5   0691040508
Gentileschi, Artemisia, -- ca. 1597-ca. 1651 -- Criticism and interpretation. Women heroes in art. Painting, Italian. Painting, Baroque -- Italy.

ND623.G4.C33 2000
Cadogan, Jeanne K.
Domenico Ghirlandaio: artist and artisan/ Jean K. Cadogan. New Haven, CT: Yale University Press, c2000. xi, 425 p.
00-040830   759.5   0300087209
Ghirlandaio, Domenico, -- 1449-1494 -- Criticism and interpretation. Ghirlandaio, Domenico, -- 1449-1494 -- Catalogues raisonnes.

ND623.G5.A8913 1997
Anderson, Jaynie.
Giorgione: the painter of "poetic brevity"/ Jaynie Anderson. New York: Flammarion, c1997.
97-033012   759.5   2080136445
Giorgione, -- 1477-1511 -- Criticism and interpretation. Giorgione, -- 1477-1511 -- Catalogues raisonnes.

ND623.G5.P5613 1999
Pignatti, Terisio, 1920-
Giorgione/ Terisio Pignatti, Filippo Pedrocco. New York: Rizzoli, 1999. 224 p.
99-014405   759.5   0847822028
Giorgione, -- 1477-1511.

ND623.G6.G58 1988
Goffen, Rona, 1944-
Spirituality in conflict: Saint Francis and Giotto's Bardi Chapel/ Rona Goffen. University Park: Pennsylvania State University Press, c1988. xvii, 142 p.
87-029233   759.5   0271006218
Giotto, -- 1266?-1337 -- Criticism and interpretation. Francis of Assisi, -- Saint, -- 1182-1226 -- Art. Mural painting and decoration, Gothic -- Italy -- Florence. Mural painting and decoration, Italian -- Italy -- Florence.

ND623.G8.A86 1996
Ahl, Diane Cole, 1949-
Benozzo Gozzoli/ Diane Cole Ahl. New Haven: Yale University Press, c1996. vii, 340 p.
96-060714   759.5   0300066996
Benozzo, -- di Lese, -- 1420-1497 -- Criticism and interpretation. Benozzo, -- di Lese, -- 1420-1497 -- Catalogues raisonnes.

ND623.L5.A15 1970b
Leonardo, da Vinci, 1452-1519.
The notebooks of Leonardo da Vinci. Compiled and edited from the original manuscripts by Jean Paul Richter. New York, Dover Publications [1970] 2 v.
72-104981   709   0486225720
Leonardo, -- da Vinci, -- 1452-1519 -- Notebooks, sketchbooks, etc.

ND623.L5.B78 1998
Brown, David Alan, 1942-
Leonardo da Vinci: origins of a genius/ David Alan Brown. New Haven: Yale University Press, c1998. vii, 240 p.
98-015164   759.5   0300072465
Leonardo, -- da Vinci, -- 1452-1519 -- Criticism and interpretation.

ND623.L5.M32413 2000
Marani, Pietro C.
Leonardo da Vinci--the complete paintings/ Pietro C. Marani; appendices edited by Pietro C. Marani and Edoardo Villata. New York City: Abrams, 2000. 384 p.
00-027556   759.5   0810935813
Leonardo, -- da Vinci, -- 1452-1519 -- Criticism and interpretation.

ND623.L5.V25
Vallentin, Antonina, 1893-1957.
Leonardo da Vinci; the tragic pursuit of perfection [by] Antonina Vallentin, translated by E. W. Dickes. New York, The Viking press, 1938. xii, 561 p.
38-028996   927.5
Leonardo, -- da Vinci, -- 1452-1519.

ND623.L58.F88 1955
Freud, Sigmund, 1856-1939.
Leonardo da Vinci: a study in psychosexuality/ by Sigmund Freud; authorized translation by A.A. Brill. New York: Vintage Books, [1955?] c1947 xxxviii, 122 p.
55-008302
Leonardo, -- da Vinci, -- 1452-1519.

ND623.L7.H65 1999
Holmes, Megan, 1959-
Fra Filippo Lippi the Carmelite painter/ Megan Holmes. New Haven, Conn.: Yale University Press, c1999. ix, 301 p.
99-014918   759.5   0300081049
Lippi, Filippo, -- ca. 1406-1469 -- Criticism and interpretation. Painting, Renaissance -- Italy.

ND623.L77.E35 1989
Eisenberg, Marvin, 1922-
Lorenzo Monaco/ Marvin Eisenberg. Princeton, N.J.: Princeton University Press, c1989. xxii, 242 p.
88-019559   759.5   0691040427
Lorenzo, -- Monaco, -- 1370 or 71-1425 -- Criticism and interpretation. Lorenzo, -- Monaco, -- 1370 or 71-1425 -- Catalogues raisonnes.

ND623.L8.A4 1997
Brown, David Alan, 1942-
Lorenzo Lotto: rediscovered master of the Renaissance/ David Alan Brown, Peter Humfrey, Mauro Lucco; with contributions by Augusto Gentili ... [et al.]. Washington: National Gallery of Art; c1997. 237 p.
97-026418   759.5   0894682571
Lotto, Lorenzo, -- 1480?-1556? -- Exhibitions.

ND623.M3.G7 1992
Greenstein, Jack Matthew.
Mantegna and painting as historical narrative/ Jack M. Greenstein. Chicago: University of Chicago Press, 1992. xiv, 301 p.
91-032451   759.5   0226307077
Mantegna, Andrea, -- 1431-1506 -- Criticism and interpretation. Jesus Christ -- Art. History in art.

ND623.P255.G68 1994
Gould, Cecil Hilton Monk, 1918-
Parmigianino/ Cecil Gould. New York: Abbeville Press, c1994. 216 p.
94-039742   760/.092   1558598928
Parmigianino, -- 1503-1540 -- Criticism and interpretation. Parmigianino, -- 1503-1540 -- Catalogs. Mannerism (Art) -- Italy.

ND623.P4.A4 1997
Pietro Perugino: master of the Italian Renaissance/ Joseph Antenucci Becherer, with contributions by Katherine R. Smith Abbott ... [et al.]. New York, N.Y.: Rizzoli International; 1997. xxi, 317 p.
97-033981   0847820769
Perugino, -- ca. 1450-1523 -- Exhibitions. Perugino, -- ca. 1450-1523 -- Criticism and interpretation.

ND623.P548.L54 1992
Lightbown, R. W.
Piero della Francesca/ Ronald Lightbown. New York: Abbeville Press, c1992. 308 p.
91-040577   759.5   1558591680
Piero, -- della Francesca, -- 1416?-1492 -- Criticism and interpretation.

ND623.R2.A76 1997
Raphael's "School of Athens"/ edited by Marcia Hall. Cambridge; Cambridge University Press, 1997. xii, 182 p.
96-019745   759.5   0521444470
Raphael, -- 1483-1520. -- School of Athens. Raphael, -- 1483-1520 -- Criticism and interpretation.

ND623.R2.P677
Pope-Hennessy, John Wyndham, 1913-
Raphael [by] John Pope-Hennessy. [New York] New York University Press [c1970] 303 p.
70-088138   759.5   081470476X
Raphael, -- 1483-1520.

ND623.R7.S45 1995
Scott, Jonathan, 1940-
Salvator Rosa: his life and times/ Jonathan Scott. New Haven: Yale University Press, c1995. ix, 259 p.
95-007225   700/.92   0300064160
Rosa, Salvatore, -- 1615-1673. Artists -- Italy -- Biography.

ND623.S45.A2 1995
Severini, Gino, 1883-1966.
The life of a painter: the autobiography of Gino Severini/ translated by Jennifer Franchina. Princeton, N.J.: Princeton University Press, c1995. xv, 310 p.
95-022065   759.5   0691044198
Severini, Gino, -- 1883-1966. Painters -- Italy -- Biography.

ND623.T5.A84 1994
Alpers, Svetlana.
Tiepolo and the pictorial intelligence/ Svetlana Alpers, Michael Baxandall. New Haven: Yale University Press, c1994. ix, 186 p.
94-013926   759.5   0300059787
Tiepolo, Giovanni Battista, -- 1696-1770 -- Criticism and interpretation.

ND623.T7.A65 2000
Meilman, Patricia, 1947-
Titian and the altarpiece in Renaissance Venice/ Patricia Meilman. Cambridge; Cambridge University Press, 2000. xvi, 260 p.
98-051718   759.5   0521640954
Titian, -- ca. 1488-1576. -- Death of St. Peter Martyr. Peter, -- the Apostle, Saint -- Art. Altarpieces, Renaissance -- Italy -- Venice.

ND623.T7.G56 1997
Goffen, Rona, 1944-
Titian's women/ Rona Goffen. New Haven: Yale University Press, c1997. ix, 342 p.
97-007650   0300068468
Titian, -- ca. 1488-1576 -- Criticism and interpretation. Women in art.

ND623.T7.P32 1969
Panofsky, Erwin, 1892-1968.
Problems in Titian, mostly iconographic. [New York] New York University Press [1969] xv, 208 p.
68-016828   759.5   0714813257
Titian, -- ca. 1488-1576.

ND635.W64 1989
Wolfthal, Diane.
The beginnings of Netherlandish canvas painting, 1400-1530/ Diane Wolfthal. Cambridge, CB; Cambridge University Press, 1989. xiv, 252 p.
88-001492   759.9493/1   0521342597
Painting, Flemish. Painting, Gothic -- Belgium. Painting, Renaissance -- Belgium.

ND641.W5 1955a
Wilenski, Reginald Howard, 1877-
Dutch painting/ by R.H. Wilenski. London: Faber and Faber, [1955] 211 p.
56-000776
Painting, Dutch. Painters.

ND644.L42
Leymarie, Jean.
Dutch painting. Skira, 1956.
56-009861   759.9492
Painting, Dutch. Painters -- Netherlands. Painting, Dutch.

ND646.D767 1999
Dutch classicism in seventeenth-century painting/ Albert Blankert ... [et al.]. Rotterdam: NAi Publishers, c1999. 351 p.
00-296130   759.9492/09/032074434164   9056621211
Painting, Dutch -- Exhibitions. Painting, Modern -- 17th-18th centuries -- Netherlands -- Exhibitions. Classicism in art -- Netherlands -- Exhibitions.

ND646.S495 1995
Slive, Seymour, 1920-
Dutch painting 1600-1800/ Seymour Slive. New Haven, Conn.: Yale University Press, c1995. vi, 378 p.
95-014215   759.9492/09/032   0300064187
Painting, Dutch. Painting, Modern -- 17th-18th centuries -- Netherlands.

ND651.U88.S67 1997
Spicer, Joaneath A.
Masters of light: Dutch painters in Utrecht during the golden age/ Joaneath A. Spicer with Lynn Federle Orr; with essays by Marten Jan Bok ... [et al.]. Baltimore: Walters Art Gallery; 1997. 480 p.
97-061810   0884010937
Painting, Dutch -- Netherlands -- Utrecht -- Exhibitions. Painting, Modern -- 17th-18th centuries -- Netherlands -- Utrecht -- Exhibitions. Utrecht (Netherlands) -- Intellectual life -- Exhibitions.

ND653.B75.W513
Winkelmann-Rhein, Gertraude.
The paintings and drawings of Jan 'Flower' Bruegel. New York, H. N. Abrams [1969, c1968] 88 p.
69-012479   760/.0924
Bruegel, Jan, -- 1568-1625.

ND653.G7.A26 1959
Gogh, Vincent van, 1853-1890.
Complete letters, with reproductions of all the drawings in the correspondence. Greenwich, Conn., New York Graphic Society [1959] 3 v.
58-006726   [759.9492] 927.5
Artists -- Correspondence, reminiscences, etc.

ND653.G7.A4 1998
Kendall, Richard.
Van Gogh's van Goghs: masterpieces from the Van Gogh Museum, Amsterdam/ Richard Kendall with contributions by John Leighton and Sjraar van Heugten. Washington: National Gallery of Art; c1998. 160 p.
98-021871   759.9492   0810963663
Gogh, Vincent van, -- 1853-1890 -- Exhibitions. Painting -- Netherlands -- Amsterdam -- Exhibitions.

ND653.G7.A43 1946
Gogh, Vincent van, 1853-1890.
Dear Theo; the autobiography of Vincent van Gogh. Edited by Irving Stone. Garden City, New York, Doubleday & company, inc., 1946 [c1937]
46-004152   927.5
Gogh, Vincent van, -- 1853-1890. Artists -- Correspondence, reminiscences, etc.

ND653.G7.H255 1982
Hammacher, Abraham Marie, 1897-
Van Gogh, a documentary biography/ A.M. Hammacher, Renilde Hammacher. New York: Macmillan, 1982. 240 p.
82-007224   759.9492   0025477102
Gogh, Vincent van, -- 1853-1890. Painters -- Netherlands -- Biography.

ND653.G7.H79413 1990
Hulsker, Jan.
Vincent and Theo van Gogh: a dual biography/ Jan Hulsker; James M. Miller, editor. Ann Arbor: Fuller Publications, c1990. xv, 470 p.
89-028907   759.9492   0940537052
Gogh, Vincent van, -- 1853-1890. Gogh, Theo van, -- 1857-1891. Painters -- Netherlands -- Biography. Art dealers -- Netherlands -- Biography.

ND653.G7.T67453 1969
Tralbaut, Marc Edo.
Vincent van Gogh [by] Marc Edo Tralbaut. New York, Viking Press [1969] 350 p.
76-087251   759.9492   0670742783
Gogh, Vincent van, -- 1853-1890.   Painters -- Netherlands -- Biography.

ND653.G7.Z458 1997
Zemel, Carol M.
Van Gogh's progress: Utopia, modernity, and late-nineteenth-century art/ Carol Zemel. Berkeley: University of California Press, c1997. xxii, 316 p.
96-004850   759.9492   0520088492
Gogh, Vincent van, -- 1853-1890 -- Criticism and interpretation. Gogh, Vincent van, -- 1853-1890 -- Philosophy. Utopias.

ND653.G7H275
Hanson, Lawrence.
Passionate pilgrim: the life of Vincent Van Gogh. Random, c1955. 300 p.
55-008162   927.5
Van Gogh, Vincent   Artists -- Biography.

ND653.H75.A4 1998
Sutton, Peter C.
Pieter de Hooch, 1629-1684/ Peter C. Sutton. Hartford, Conn.: Dulwich Picture Gallery, Wadsworth Atheneum: c1998. 183 p.
98-026337   759.9492   0300077572
Hooch, Pieter de -- Exhibitions.

ND653.L73.A4 1993
Leyster, Judith, 1609-1660.
Judith Leyster: a Dutch master and her world/ project directors, James A. Welu, Pieter Biesboer; contributors, Pieter Biesboer ... [et al.]. [Worcester, England]: Worcester Art Museum; c1993. 391 p.
93-012478   759.9492   0300055641
Leyster, Judith, -- 1609-1660 -- Exhibitions.

ND653.M76.B4
Berckelaers, Ferdinand Louis, 1901-
Piet Mondrian, life and work [by] Michel Seuphor [pseud.]. Amsterdam, Contact [1957?] 443 p.
57-028732   927.5
Mondriaan, Pieter Cornelis, 1872-1944.

ND653.R4.A4 1999a
Rembrandt Harmenszoon van Rijn, 1606-1669.
Rembrandt by himself/ edited by Christopher White and Quentin Buvelot; essays, Ernst van de Wetering, Volker Manuth, and Marieke de Winkel; catalogue, Edwin Buijsen ... [et al]. London: National Gallery Publications Ltd.; c1999. 272 p.
99-070647   759.9492   0300077890
Rembrandt Harmenszoon van Rijn, -- 1606-1669 -- Self-portraits. Rembrandt Harmenszoon van Rijn, -- 1606-1669 -- Criticism and interpretation.

ND653.R4.A7 1982
Haverkamp Begemann, Egbert.
Rembrandt, the Nightwatch/ E. Haverkamp-Begemann. Princeton, N.J.: Princeton University Press, c1982. xv, 138 p.
81-047921   759.9492   0691039917
Rembrandt Harmenszoon van Rijn, -- 1606-1669. -- Night watch.

ND653.R4.A73 1994
Bailey, Anthony.
Responses to Rembrandt/ Anthony Bailey. New York, NY: Timken Publishers, c1994. xiv, 140 p.
93-015042   759.9492   0943221188
Rembrandt Harmenszoon van Rijn, -- 1606-1669. -- Polish rider. Rembrandt Harmenszoon van Rijn, -- 1606-1669 -- Criticism and interpretation. Painting, Dutch -- Expertising. Painting, Dutch -- Historiography. Painting, Dutch -- Attribution.

ND653.R4.S24 1999
Schama, Simon.
Rembrandt's eyes/ Simon Schama. New York: Alfred A. Knopf, 1999. xi, 750 p.
99-019971   759.9492   067940256X
Rembrandt Harmenszoon van Rijn, -- 1606-1669. Rubens, Peter Paul, -- Sir, -- 1577-1640 -- Influence. Painters -- Netherlands -- Biography.

ND653.R95.W35 1991
Walford, E. John, 1945-
Jacob van Ruisdael and the perception of landscape/ E. John Walford. New Haven: Yale University Press, 1991. xii, 243 p.
91-013525   759.9492   0300049943
Ruisdael, Jacob van, -- 1628 or 9-1682 -- Criticism and interpretation. Landscape painting -- Netherlands -- History -- 19th century.

ND653.V5.A4 1995
Vermeer, Johannes, 1632-1675.
Johannes Vermeer/ [curators, Frederik J. Duparc and Arthur K. Wheelock, Jr.]. Washington: National Gallery of Art; c1995. 229 p.
95-023917   759.9492   0300065582
Vermeer, Johannes, -- 1632-1675 -- Exhibitions.

ND653.V5.A9313 1994
Arasse, Daniel.
Vermeer, faith in painting/ Daniel Arasse; translated by Terry Grabar. Princeton, N.J.: Princeton University Press, c1994. xiii, 136 p.
93-033549   759.9492   0691033625
Vermeer, Johannes, -- 1632-1675 -- Criticism and interpretation.   Spirituality in art.

ND653.V5.M65 1989
Montias, John Michael, 1928-
Vermeer and his milieu: a web of social history/ John Michael Montias. Princeton, N.J.: Princeton University Press, c1989. xx, 407 p.
88-030685   759.9492   0691040516
Vermeer, Johannes, -- 1632-1675.   Painters -- Netherlands -- Biography.

ND653.V5.W48 1995
Wheelock, Arthur K.
Vermeer & the art of painting/ Arthur K. Wheelock, Jr. New Haven: Yale University Press, c1995. x, 205 p.
94-040119   759.9492   0300062397
Vermeer, Johannes, -- 1632-1675 -- Criticism and interpretation. Vermeer, Johannes, -- 1632-1675 -- Themes, motives.

ND665.L33
Lassaigne, Jacques, 1910-
Flemish painting. Text by Jacques Lassaigne. [Translated by Stuart Gilbert. New York] A. Skira [1957-   ]
57-011640   759.9493
Painting, Flemish.

ND669.F5.M47 1998
Metropolitan Museum of Art (New York, N.Y.)
From Van Eyck to Bruegel: early Netherlandish paintings in the Metropolitan Museum of Art/ edited by Maryan W. Ainsworth and Keith Christiansen; with contributions by Maryan W. Ainsworth ... [et al.]. New York: Metropolitan Museum of Art: c1998. xi, 452 p.
98-022196   759.9493/074/7471   0870998706
Panel painting -- 15th century -- Flanders -- Exhibitions. Panel painting -- 16th century -- Flanders -- Exhibitions. Panel painting -- New York (State) -- New York -- Exhibitions.

ND673.B73.G47 1977b
Gibson, Walter S.
Bruegel/ Walter S. Gibson. New York: Oxford University Press, 1977. 216 p.
76-056922   760/.092/4   0195199537
Bruegel, Pieter, -- ca. 1525-1569.

ND673.C312.U68 1990
Upton, Joel M. 1940-
Petrus Christus: his place in Fifteenth-Century Flemish painting/ Joel M. Upton. University Park: Pennsylvania State University Press, c1990. xv, 130 p.
88-043440   759.9493   0271006722
Christus, Petrus, -- ca. 1410-1472 or 3 -- Criticism and interpretation.   Panel painting -- 15th century -- Flanders. Art patronage -- Flanders.

ND673.D9.A4 1999a
Brown, Christopher, 1948-
Van Dyck, 1599-1641/ Christopher Brown, Hans Vlieghe; with contributions from Frans Baudouin ... [et al.]. New York: Rizzoli, 1999. 359 p.
98-068686   759.9493   084782196X
Van Dyck, Anthony, -- Sir, -- 1599-1641 -- Exhibitions.

ND673.D9.B57 2000
Blake, Robin.
Anthony Van Dyck: a life, 1599-1641/ Robin Blake. Chicago, Ill.: Ivan R. Dee, 2000. xii, 435 p.
99-058351   759.9493   156663282X
Van Dyck, Anthony, -- Sir, -- 1599-1641.   Painters -- Belgium -- Biography.

ND673.E6.H313
Haesaerts, Paul, 1901-
Ensor. Pref. by Jean Cassou. [Translated from the French by Norbert Guterman] New York, Abrams 1957. 100 p.
58-009032   759.9493
Ensor, James, -- 1860-1949.   Artists, Belgian.

ND673.E9A8413 2001
Albus, Anita, 1942-
The art of arts: rediscovering painting/ Anita Albus; translated by Michael Robertson. New York: Alfred A. Knopf, 2000. x, 386 p.
00-020320   750/.1   0375400990
Eyck, Jan van, -- 1390-1440 -- Contributions in oil painting. Painting, Renaissance -- Europe, Northern. Visual perception. Color in art.

ND673.E9.W44 1994
Hall, Edwin.
The Arnolfini betrothal: medieval marriage and the enigma of Van Eyck's double portrait/ Edwin Hall. Berkeley: University of California Press, c1994. xxi, 180 p.
93-034947   759.9493   0520212215
Eyck, Jan van, -- 1390-1440. -- Wedding portrait of Giovanni Arnolfi and Keanne Cenami.   Panel painting -- 15th century -- Expertising -- Flanders. Marriage customs and rites, Medieval.

ND673.M35.A4 1998
Magritte, Rene, 1898-1967.
Magritte, 1898-1967/ edited by Gisele Ollinger-Zinque and Frederik Leen. Ghent: Ludion Press; [c1998] 335 p.
98-156454   759.9493   0810963590
Magritte, Rene, -- 1898-1967 -- Exhibitions.

ND673.M35.G3 1970
Gablik, Suzi.
Magritte. Greenwich, Conn., New York Graphic Society [1970] 208 p.
77-125894   759.9493   0500490031
Magritte, Rene, -- 1898-1967.

ND673.R9.M766 1989
Muller, Jeffrey M., 1948-
Rubens: the artist as collector/ Jeffrey M. Muller.
Princeton, N.J.: Princeton University Press, c1989. xv,
185 p.
88-016984   709/.2/4   0691040648
*Rubens, Peter Paul, -- Sir, -- 1577-1640 -- Art collections. Art
-- Private collections -- Belgium -- Antwerp.*

ND681.M6 1979a
Gosudarstvennaia Tretiakovskaia galereia.
The Tretyakov Gallery, Moscow: Russian painting/
[introduced by V. Volodarsky; notes by M. Epstein ... et
al.; translated by B. Meyerovich]. New York: H. N.
Abrams; c1979. 326 p.
79-051258   759.7/074/07312   0810916576
   *Painting -- Russia (Federation) -- Moscow -- Catalogs.
Painting, Russian -- Catalogs.*

ND687.5.R4.V34
Valkenier, Elizabeth Kridl.
Russian realist art: the state and society: the
Peredvizhniki and their tradition/ by Elizabeth Valkenier.
Ann Arbor: Ardis, c1977. xv, 251 p.
77-151042   759.7   0882332643
   *Peredvizhniki (Society) Realism in art -- Russia. Painting,
Modern -- 19th century -- Russia.*

ND688.B75 1998
Bown, Matthew Cullerne.
Socialist realist painting/ Matthew Cullerne Bown. New
Haven: Yale University Press, c1998. xviii, 506 p.
97-028079   759.7/09/04   0300068441
   *Socialist realism in art -- Soviet Union. Painting, Soviet.
Painting, Modern -- 20th century -- Soviet Union.*

ND699.C5.B33 1998
Baal-Teshuva, Jacob.
Marc Chagall, 1887-1985/ Jacob Baal-Teshuva. Koln;
Taschen, c1998. 279 p.
00-500990   709/.2   3822882712
*Chagall, Marc, -- 1887- -- Criticism and interpretation.
Painting, French. Painting, Modern -- 20th century.*

ND699.K3.A4 1979
Kandinsky, Wassily, 1866-1944.
Kandinsky/ by Hans K. Roethel, in collaboration with
Jean K. Benjamin. New York: Hudson Hills Press, c1979.
172 p.
79-012966   759.7   0933920008
Kandinsky, Wassily, -- 1866-1944.

ND699.K3.L66
Long, Rose-Carol Washton.
Kandinsky, the development of an abstract style/ Rose-
Carol Washton Long. Oxford: Clarendon Press; 1980.
xxvi, 201 p.
79-041130   759.7   0198173113
Kandinsky, Wassily, -- 1866-1944. Painting, Abstract.

ND699.K3.M47 1997
Messer, Thomas M.
Vasily Kandinsky/ Thomas M. Messer. New York: H.N.
Abrams, 1997. 128 p.
96-037573   759.47   0810912287
*Kandinsky, Wassily, -- 1866-1944 -- Criticism and
interpretation.*

ND699.K3.W42 1995
Weiss, Peg, 1932-
Kandinsky and Old Russia: the artist as ethnographer and
shaman/ Peg Weiss. New Haven: Yale University Press,
c1995. xx, 291 p.
94-026210   759.7   0300056478
*Kandinsky, Wassily, -- 1866-1944 -- Criticism and
interpretation. Folklore -- Russia (Federation) Shamanism --
Russia (Federation)*

ND699.K3.W43
Weiss, Peg, 1932-
Kandinsky in Munich: the formative Jugendstil years/ by
Peg Weiss. Princeton, N.J.: Princeton University Press,
c1979. xxi, 268 p.
78-051203   759.7   0691039348
*Kandinsky, Wassily, -- 1866-1944. Art nouveau -- Germany --
Munich.*

ND699.K88.S78 1989
Stupples, Peter.
Pavel Kuznetsov: his life and art/ Peter Stupples.
Cambridge [England]; Cambridge University Press, 1989.
xix, 370 p.
89-000994   759.7   0521364884
*Kuznetsov, Pavel Varfolomeevich, -- 1878-1968. Painters --
Russia (Federation) -- Biography.*

ND699.R4.V3 1990
Valkenier, Elizabeth Kridl.
Ilya Repin and the world of Russian art/ by Elizabeth
Kridl Valkenier. New York: Columbia University Press,
c1990. xiv, 248 p.
89-039557   759.7   0231069642
*Repin, Ilia Efimovich, -- 1844-1930. Painters -- Russia
(Federation) -- Biography. Realism in art -- Russia (Federation)*

ND699.R6.D43 1989
Decter, Jacqueline.
Nicholas Roerich: the life and art of a Russian master/
Jacqueline Decter with the Nicholas Roerich Museum.
Rochester, Vt.: Park Street Press; c1989. 224 p.
89-031663   759.7   0892811560
*Rerikh, Nikolai Konstantinovich, -- 1874-1947 -- Criticism and
interpretation.*

ND717.5.R65.M66 1993
Monrad, Kasper.
The golden age of Danish painting/ catalogue by Kasper
Monrad; essays by Philip Conisbee ... [et al.]. New York:
Hudson Hills Press in association with Los Angeles
County Museum of Art; [Lanham, Md.]: c1993. 237 p.
93-017552   759.89/09/03407479494   155595085X
   *Painting, Danish -- Exhibitions. Romanticism in art --
Denmark -- Exhibitions. Painting, Modern -- 19th century --
Denmark -- Exhibitions.*

ND773.M8.H43 1984
Heller, Reinhold.
Munch: his life and work/ Reinhold Heller. Chicago: University of Chicago Press, 1984. 240 p.
83-024098   759.81   0226326438
Munch, Edvard, -- 1863-1944.   Painters -- Norway -- Biography.

ND801.P85
Post, Chandler Rathfon, 1881-1959.
A history of Spanish painting, by Chandler Rathfon Post. Cambridge, Mass., Harvard University Press, 1930-66. 14 v. in 20.
30-007776   759.6
Painting, Spanish -- History.

ND804.B74 1991
Brown, Jonathan, 1939-
The Golden Age of painting in Spain/ Jonathan Brown. New Haven: Yale University Press, 1991. ix, 330 p.
90-012564   759.6/09/03   0300047606
Painting, Spanish. Painting, Modern -- Spain.

ND806.B76
Brown, Jonathan, 1939-
Images and ideas in seventeenth-century Spanish painting/ Jonathan Brown. Princeton, N.J.: Princeton University Press, c1978. viii, 168 p.
78-052485   759.6   0691039410
Painting, Modern -- 17th-18th centuries -- Spain. Art and society -- Spain -- History -- 17th century. Painting, Baroque -- Spain.

ND813.D3.A4 2000
Dali, Salvador, 1904-
Dali's optical illusions/ edited by Dawn Ades. Hartford, Conn.: Wadsworth Atheneum Museum of Art; c2000. 195 p.
99-038348   709/.2   0300081774
Dali, Salvador, -- 1904- -- Exhibitions.   Optical illusions in art -- Exhibitions. Visual perception -- Exhibitions.

ND813.D3.D4413
Dali, Salvador, 1904-
Salvador Dali. Text by Robert Descharnes. Translated by Eleanor R. Morse. New York, Abrams [1976] 175 p.
74-004257   759.6   0810902222
Dali, Salvador, -- 1904- Painters -- Spain -- Biography.

ND813.G7.C56 2001
Ciofalo, John J., 1957-
The self-portraits of Francisco Goya/ John J. Ciofalo. Cambridge; Cambridge University Press, 2001. xiii, 240 p.
00-027756   759.6   0521771366
Goya, Francisco, -- 1746-1828 -- Self-portraits.

ND813.G7.G324
Gassier, Pierre.
Goya; [biographical and critical study. Translated by James Emmons. New York] Skira [1955?] 139 p.
55-010594   927.5
Goya, Francisco, -- 1746-1828.

ND813.G7.G53
Glendinning, Nigel, 1929-
Goya and his critics/ Nigel Glendinning. New Haven: Yale University Press, 1977. xii, 340 p.
76-049693   759.6   0300020112
Goya, Francisco, -- 1746-1828.

ND813.G7.L564 1983
Licht, Fred, 1928-
Goya, the origins of the modern temper in art/ Fred Licht. New York: Harper & Row, 1983, c1979. 288 p.
82-048152   759.6   0064301230
Goya, Francisco, -- 1746-1828.

ND813.G75.K313 1969b
Kahnweiler, Daniel Henry, 1884-
Juan Gris; his life and work. Translated by Douglas Cooper. New York, H. N. Abrams [1969, c1946] 347 p.
69-011532   759.6
Gris, Juan, -- 1887-1927.

ND813.G75.N4
Museum of Modern Art (New York, N.Y.)
Juan Gris,   1958.
58-008632   927.5
Gris, Juan. Painters, Spanish.

ND813.M5.S9 1969
Sweeney, James Johnson, 1900-
Joan Miro.   New York, Published for the Museum of Modern Art by Arno Press, 1969 [c1941] 87 p.
78-086434   759.6
Miro, Joan, -- 1893-

ND813.T4.B7
Theotocopuli, Dominico, d. 1614.
El Greco (Domenicos Theotocopoulos) Text by Leo Bronstein. -- New York: H. N. Abrams, 1950. 126 p.
50-012757   759.6
Greco, 1541?-1614 -- Catalogs.

ND813.T4.W4
Wethey, Harold E. 1902-1984.
El Greco and his school.   Princeton, N.J., Princeton University Press, 1962. 2 v.
61-007427   759.6
Greco, -- 1541?-1614.   Artists -- Italy.

ND813.V4.B893 1998
Brown, Jonathan, 1939-
Velazquez: the technique of genius/ Jonathan Brown and Carmen Garrido; with special photography by Carmen Garrido. New Haven: Yale University Press, c1998. 215 p.
98-019941   759.6   0300072937
Velazquez, Diego, -- 1599-1660 -- Criticism and interpretation.

ND813.V4.H37 1982
Harris, Enriqueta.
Velazquez/ Enriqueta Harris. Ithaca, N.Y.: Cornell University Press, 1982. 240 p.
82-070748   759.6   0801415268
Velazquez, Diego, -- 1599-1660.   Painters -- Spain -- Biography.

ND813.V4.L627 1968b
Lopez-Rey, Jose
Velazquez' work and world   Greenwich, Conn., New York Graphic Society [1968] 172 p.
70-005436
Velazquez, Diego, -- 1599-1660

ND813.V4.M35 1988
McKim-Smith, Gridley, 1943-
Examining Velazquez/ Gridley McKim-Smith, Greta Andersen-Bergdoll, Richard Newman; with technical photography by Andrew Davidhazy. New Haven: Yale University Press, c1988. xii, 162 p.
87-031872   759.6   0300036159
Velazquez, Diego, -- 1599-1660 -- Criticism and interpretation. Painting, Spanish -- Expertising.

ND980.G72 1977
Gray, Basil, 1904-
Persian painting.   [New York] Skira; distributed by World Pub. Co., Cleveland, 1961, [1961] 191 p.
61-010169   759.955
Illumination of books and manuscripts -- Iran. Painting -- Iran.

ND1002.R32
Randhawa, Mohindar Singh, 1909-
Indian painting; the scene, themes, and legends [by] Mohinder Singh Randhawa and John Kenneth Galbraith. Boston, Houghton Mifflin, 1968. xiii, 142 p.
66-019836
Painting, Indic -- History.

ND1005.U5
Unesco.
Ceylon: paintings from temple, shrine and rock. Pref. [by] W. G. Archer, introd. [by] S. Paranavitana. [Greenwich, Conn.] New York Graphic Society [1957] 29 p.
57-059245   759.954
Art, Buddhist. Paintings, Sinhalese. Art, Buddhist.

ND1021.S26813 2000
Santi Leksukhum.
Temples of gold: seven centuries of Thai Buddhist paintings/ by Santi Leksukhum; photographs by Gilles Mermet; translated from the French by Kenneth D. Whitehead. New York: George Braziller, 2000. 263 p.
00-033717   755/.943/09593 21   0807614769
Painting, Thai. Painting, Buddhist -- Thailand.

ND1040.R6 1959
Rowley, George.
Principles of Chinese painting. Princeton, N.J., Princeton University Press, 1959. 85 p.
60-000325   759.951
Painting, Chinese.

ND1040.S47 1982
Silbergeld, Jerome.
Chinese painting style: media, methods, and principles of form/ Jerome Silbergeld. Seattle: University of Washington Press, c1982. xi, 68 p.
81-021837   751.42/51   0295958960
Painting, Chinese. Painting -- Technique.

ND1040.T48 1997
Three thousand years of Chinese painting/ Richard M. Barnhart ... [et al.]. New Haven: Yale University Press; c1997. 402 p.
97-011152   759.951   0300070136
Painting, Chinese.

ND1043.3.C3
Cahill, James, 1926-
An index of early Chinese painters and paintings: Tang, Sung, and Yuan/ by James Cahill, incorporating the work of Osvald Siren and Ellen Johnston Laing. Berkeley: University of California Press, c1980. x, 391 p.
77-085755   759.951/016   0520035763
Painting, Chinese -- Tang-Five dynasties, 618-960 -- Indexes. Painting, Chinese -- Sung-Yuan dynasties, 960-1368 -- Indexes.

ND1043.5.C34
Cahill, James, 1926-
The compelling image: nature and style in seventeenth-century Chinese painting/ James Cahill. Cambridge, Mass.: Harvard University Press, 1982. 250 p.
81-001272   759.951   0674152808
Painting, Chinese -- Ming-Ching dynasties, 1368-1912. Painting, Modern -- 17th-18th centuries -- China. Painting, Chinese -- Foreign influences.

ND1043.5.C35 1994
Cahill, James, 1926-
The painter's practice: how artists lived and worked in traditional China/ James Cahill. New York: Columbia University Press, c1994. xi, 187 p.
93-008790   305.9/75/0951   0231081804
Painting, Chinese -- Ming-Ching dynasties, 1368-1912. Painters -- China -- Social conditions. Painters -- China -- Economic conditions.

ND1045.F66 2001
Fong, Wen.
Between two cultures: late-nineteenth- and twentieth-century Chinese paintings from the Robert H. Ellsworth collection in the Metropolitan Museum of Art/ Wen C. Fong. New York: Metropolitan Museum of Art; c2001. xi, 286 p.
00-068727   759.951/074/7471   0870999842
Ellsworth, Robert Hatfield, -- 1929- -- Art collections -- Catalogs.   Painting -- New York (State) -- New York -- Catalogs. Painting, Chinese -- 20th century -- Catalogs. Painting, Chinese -- Ming-Qing dynasties, 1368-1912 -- Catalogs.

ND1049.C53.A4 1990
Wang, Fang-yu, 1913-
Master of the lotus garden: the life and art of Bada Shanren, 1626-1705/ Wang Fangyu, Richard M. Barnhart; Judith G. Smith, editor. New Haven, Conn.: Yale University Art Gallery: c1990. 299 p.
90-070036   759.951   0300049331
Chu, Ta, -- 1626-ca. 1705 -- Exhibitions.

ND1050.A41
Akiyama, Terukazu, 1918-
Japanese painting. [Geneva?] Skira; [1961] 216 p.
61-015270   759.952   0847801314
Painting, Japanese -- History. Paintings, Japanese.

ND1053.U5
Unesco.
Japan: ancient Buddhist paintings. Pref. [by] Serge Elisseeff. Introd. [by] Takaaki Matsushita. [Greenwich, Conn.] New York Graphic Society [1959] 21 p.
59-001730   759.952
Paintings, Japanese. Art, Buddhist.

ND1101.M37 1999
McCulloch, Susan.
Contemporary aboriginal art: a guide to the rebirth of an ancient culture/ Susan McCulloch. Honolulu: University of Hawaii Press, 1999. 240 p.
99-034262   704.03/9915   0824822684
Painting, Australian aboriginal. Painting, Modern -- 20th century -- Australia.

ND1130 General works — Early works to 1800

ND1130.L47213 1989
Leonardo, da Vinci, 1452-1519.
Leonardo on painting: an anthology of writings/ by Leonardo da Vinci with a selection of documents relating to his career as an artist; edited by Martin Kemp; selected and translated by Martin Kemp and Margaret Walker. New Haven: Yale University Press, 1989. viii, 328 p.
88-051825   750   0300045425
Painting -- Early works to 1800.

ND1135 General works — 1800-

ND1135.E44 1999
Elkins, James, 1955-
What painting is: how to think about oil painting, using the language of alchemy/ James Elkins. New York: Routledge, 1999. x, 246 p.
98-014702   750/.1/8   0415921139
Painting.

ND1140 General works — General special

ND1140.B45 1999
Bell, Julian, 1952-
What is painting?: representation and modern art/ Julian Bell. New York: Thames and Hudson, 1999. 256 p.
98-061188   750/.1   0500281017
Painting -- Philosophy. Painting, Modern.

ND1140.B59 1990
Bois, Yve Alain.
Painting as model/ Yve-Alain Bois. Cambridge, Mass.: MIT Press, c1990. xxx, 327 p.
89-078293   750/.1   0262023067
Painting -- Philosophy.

ND1140.W78 1987
Wollheim, Richard, 1923-
Painting as an art/ Richard Wollheim. Princeton, N.J.: Princeton University Press, c1987. 384 p.
87-003222   750/.1/9   0691099642
Painting -- Psychological aspects. Visual perception. Painting -- Philosophy.

ND1143 General works — Popular works — Appreciation of painting

ND1143.F69
Freedman, Leonard,
Looking at modern painting [by] Gibson A. Danes [and others] New York, Norton [1961] 140 p.
61-009154   759.06
Painting. Art, Modern -- 20th century.

ND1145 General works — Popular works — Famous pictures described and interpreted

ND1145.K5 1948
Kimball, Fiske, 1888-1955.
Great paintings in America; one hundred and one masterpieces in color, selected and interpreted by Fiske Kimball and Lionello Venturi. New York, Coward-McCann [1948] 216 p.
48-010923   759
Painting -- United States.

ND1145.V4
Venturi, Lionello, 1885-1961.
Painting and painters; how to look at a picture, from Giotto to Chagall. New York, Scribner [1945] xx, 250 p.
45-035033   759
Painting. Painters.

ND1150 General works — Essays, lectures, etc.

ND1150.G5 1957
Gilson, Etienne, 1884-1978.
Painting and reality. [New York] Pantheon Books [1957] xxiv, 367 p.
57-011125   750.4
Painting -- Addresses, essays, lectures. Art -- Philosophy. Reality.

ND1170 Painting in relation to other subjects, A-Z

ND1170.C7 1958
Craven, Thomas, 1889-
A treasury of art masterpieces, from the Renaissance to the present day. New York, Simon and Schuster, 1958. xvi, 327 p.
58-004024   759
Painting. Painters.

ND1260-1265 Technique. Styles. Materials and methods

ND1260.H463 1958
Herberts, Kurt.
The complete book of artists' techniques. New York, Praeger [1958] 351 p.
58-012424   751.4
Painting -- Technique. Art -- Technique.

ND1265.L52
Leymarie, Jean.
Fauvism: biographical and critical study. Translated by James Emmons. [New York] Skira [1959] 163 p.
59-007255   759.06
Fauvism -- France. Painting, French. Painting, Modern -- 20th century -- France.

ND1265.R4 1961
Rewald, John, 1912-
The history of impressionism. New York, Museum of Modern Art [1961] 662 p.
61-007684   759.05
Impressionism (Art) Art, Modern -- 19th century -- History.

ND1265.R5
Richter, Hans, 1888-1976.
Dada: art and anti-art. New York, McGraw-Hill [1965] 246 p.
65-019077   709.04
Dadaism.

ND1309-1319 Special subjects of painting — Portraits. Group portraits. Self-portraits — History

ND1309.B47 1999
Berger, Harry.
Fictions of the pose: Rembrandt against the Italian Renaissance/ Harry Berger, Jr. Stanford, Calif.: Stanford University Press, c2000. xxi, 624 p.
99-039775   757   0804733236
Rembrandt Harmenszoon van Rijn, -- 1606-1669 -- Self-portraits. Portrait painting -- Psychological aspects -- History.

ND1313.2.C36 1990
Campbell, Lorne.
Renaissance portraits: European portrait-painting in the 14th, 15th, and 16th centuries/ Lorne Campbell. New Haven, CT: Yale University Press, 1990. xiii, 290 p.
89-022686   757/.094/09024   0300046758
Portrait painting, Renaissance -- Europe. Portrait painting, European.

ND1316.5.J65 1999
Johnston, Sona.
The faces of impressionism: portraits from American collections/ Sona Johnston with the assistance of Susan Bollendorf; essay by John House. New York: Rizzoli, 1999.
99-023337   757/.0944/07475271   0847822109
Portrait painting, French -- Exhibitions. Portrait painting -- 19th century -- France -- Exhibitions. Impressionism (Art) -- France -- Exhibitions.

ND1319.R4513 1999
Riegl, Alois, 1858-1905.
The group portraiture of Holland/ Alois Riegl; introduction by Wolfgang Kemp; translations by Evelyn M. Kain and David Britt. Los Angeles, CA: Getty Research Center for the History of Art and the Humanities, 1999. 412 p.
99-026062   757/.6/09492   089236548X
Portraits, Group -- Netherlands. Portrait painting, Dutch. Portrait painting -- 16th century -- Netherlands.

ND1329 Special subjects of painting — Portraits. Group portraits. Self-portraits — Biography of portrait painters

ND1329.B4.B43 1997
Beckett, Wendy.
Max Beckmann and the self/ Wendy Beckett. Munich; Prestel, c1997. 119 p.
97-003597   759.3   3791317377
Beckmann, Max, -- 1884-1950 -- Self-portraits. Beckmann, Max, -- 1884-1950 -- Criticism and interpretation.

ND1329.C54.A4 1995a
Guare, John.
Chuck Close: life and work, 1988-1995/ text by John Guare. New York, N.Y.: Thames and Hudson in association with Yarrow Press, 1995. 125 p.
95-060602   759.13   0500092532
Close, Chuck, -- 1940-   Physically handicapped artists -- United States. Artists -- Portraits.

ND1329.D93.A4 1994
Moir, Alfred.
Anthony van Dyck/ text by Alfred Moir. New York: H.N. Abrams, 1994. 128 p.
94-008419   759.9493   0810939177
Van Dyck, Anthony, -- Sir, -- 1599-1641 -- Catalogs. Europe -- Biography -- Portraits -- Catalogs.

ND1329.I53.A4 1999
Ingres, Jean-Auguste-Dominique, 1780-1867.
Portraits by Ingres: image of an epoch/ edited by Gary Tinterow and Philip Conisbee; drawings entries by Hans Naef; with contributions by Philip Conisbee ... [et al.]. New York: Metropolitan Museum of Art: c1999. xii, 596 p.
98-048508   759.4   0870998900
Ingres, Jean-Auguste-Dominique, -- 1780-1867 -- Exhibitions.

ND1329.N36.A9 1998
Allara, Pamela.
Pictures of people: Alice Neel's American portrait gallery/ by Pamela Allara. Hanover, NH: University Press of New England [for] Brandeis University Press, 1998. xix, 338 p.
97-018403   759.13   0874518377
Neel, Alice, -- 1900- -- Criticism and interpretation.   United States -- Biography -- Portraits.

ND1329.R65.C76 2000
Cross, David A., 1951-
A striking likeness: the life of George Romney/ David Cross. Aldershot; Ashgate, c2000. xiv, 258 p.
98-053571   759.2   1840146710
Romney, George, -- 1734-1802.   Portrait painters -- England -- Biography.

ND1329.S63.S28 1995
Saunders, Richard H., 1949-
John Smibert: colonial America's first portrait painter/ Richard H. Saunders. New Haven: Yale University Press, c1995. xii, 280 p.
94-042682   759.13   0300042582
Smibert, John, -- 1688-1751. Smibert, John, -- 1688-1751 -- Catalogues raisonnes.   Portrait painters -- United States -- Biography.

ND1329.V53.S54 1996
Sheriff, Mary D.
The exceptional woman: Elisabeth Vigee-Lebrun and the cultural politics of art/ Mary D. Sheriff. Chicago: University of Chicago Press, 1996. xiv, 353 p.
95-016654   759.4   0226752755
Vigee-Lebrun, Louise-Elisabeth, -- 1755-1842 -- Criticism and interpretation.   Women painters -- France -- Psychology. Artists and patrons -- France -- History -- 18th century.

ND1329.3 Special subjects of painting — Portraits. Group portraits. Self-portraits — Special subjects, A-Z

ND1329.3.A77
Self-portraits by women painters/ Liana De Girolami Cheney, Alicia Craig Faxon, Kathleen Lucey Russo. Aldershot, Hants, England; Ashgate, c2000. xxvi, 267 p.
98-053155   757/.4   1859284248
Women painters -- Psychology. Self-perception in women. Self-portraits.

ND1337 Special subjects of painting — Portrait miniatures. Miniature painting — History

ND1337.I5.K68 1997
Kossak, Steven.
Indian court painting, 16th-19th century/ Steven Kossak. New York: Metropolitan Museum of Art: c1997. ix, 142 p.
96-053500   751.7/7/09540747471   0870997823
Miniature painting, Indic -- India -- Exhibitions.

ND1351.5-1366.7 Special subjects of painting — Landscape painting — History

ND1351.5.A49 1987
American paradise: the world of the Hudson River school/ introduction by John K. Howat. New York: Metropolitan Museum of Art: 1987. xvii, 347 p.
87-015417   758/.1/097473   0870994964
Hudson River school of landscape painting. Landscape painting, American. Landscape painting -- 19th century -- United States.

ND1351.5.B47
Bermingham, Peter.
American art in the Barbizon mood/ Peter Bermingham. Washington: Published for the National Collection of Fine Arts by the Smithsonian Institution Press, 1975. 191 p.
74-026664   758/.1/0973
Landscape painting, American -- Exhibitions. Barbizon school -- Influence.

ND1351.5.B65 1991
Boime, Albert.
The magisterial gaze: manifest destiny and American landscape painting, c. 1830-1865/ Albert Boime. Washington: Smithsonian Institution Press, c1991. xi, 188 p.
90-027719   758/.1/097309034   1560980958
Landscape painting, American. Landscape painting -- 19th century -- United States. Messianism, Political -- United States -- Influence.

ND1351.5.H27 1998
Harvey, Eleanor Jones.
The painted sketch: American impressions from nature, 1830-1880/ by Eleanor Jones Harvey. [Dallas, Tex.]: Dallas Museum of Art in association with H.N. Abrams, c1998. 299 p.
98-002960   758/.173/07473   0810963647
Oil sketches -- United States -- Exhibitions. Landscape painting, American -- Exhibitions. Landscape painting -- 19th century -- United States -- Exhibitions.

ND1351.5.M53 1993
Miller, Angela L.
The empire of the eye: landscape representation and American cultural politics, 1825-1875/ Angela Miller. Ithaca: Cornell University Press, 1993. xii, 298 p.
92-037226   758/.173/097309034   0801428300
Landscape painting, American. Landscape painting -- 19th century -- United States. Nationalism and art -- United States.

ND1351.5.N68
Novak, Barbara.
Nature and culture: American landscape and painting, 1825-1875/ Barbara Novak. New York: Oxford University Press, 1980. x, 323 p.
79-010131   758/.1/0973   0195026063
Landscape painting, American. Landscape painting -- 19th century -- United States.

ND1351.5.W56 1994
Wilmerding, John.
The artist's Mount Desert: American painters on the Maine Coast/ John Wilmerding. Princeton, N.J.: Princeton University Press, c1994. 195 p.
93-043453   758/.174145   0691034583
Mount Desert (Me.) in art. Landscape painting, American. Landscape painting -- 19th century -- United States.

ND1351.6.A78 1989
Arthur, John, 1939-
Spirit of place: contemporary landscape painting & the American tradition/ John Arthur. Boston: Bulfinch Press, c1989. 159 p.
89-030353   758/.1/0973   0821217070
Landscape painting, American. Landscape painting -- 20th century -- United States.

ND1353.4.C66 1996
Conisbee, Philip.
In the light of Italy: Corot and early open-air painting/ Philip Conisbee, Sarah Faunce, Jeremy Strick; with Peter Galassi, guest curator. Washington: National Gallery of Art; c1996. 288 p.
95-047753   758/.145/09407473   0300067941
Corot, Jean-Baptiste-Camille, -- 1796-1875 -- Exhibitions. Landscape painting, European -- Exhibitions. Landscape painting -- 18th century -- Europe -- Exhibitions. Landscape painting -- 19th century -- Europe -- Exhibitions. Italy -- In art -- Exhibitions.

ND1354.4.B34 1993
Baetjer, Katharine.
Glorious nature: British landscape painting, 1750-1850/ catalogue, Katharine Baetjer; essays, Michael Rosenthal ... [et al.]. New York: Hudson Hills Press; c1993. 271 p.
93-017550   758/.142/094207478883   1555950922
Landscape painting, British -- Exhibitions. Landscape painting -- 18th century -- Great Britain -- Exhibitions. Landscape painting -- 19th century -- Great Britain -- Exhibitions.

ND1354.4.P39 1993
Payne, Christiana.
Toil and plenty: images of the agricultural landscape in England, 1780-1890/ Christiana Payne. New Haven: Yale University Press, c1993. xi, 219 p.
93-013885   758/.142/09420747468   0300057733
Landscape painting, English -- Exhibitions. Landscape painting -- 18th century -- England -- Exhibitions. Landscape painting -- 19th century -- England -- Exhibitions.

ND1354.5.S72 2001
Staley, Allen.
The Pre-Raphaelite landscape/ Allen Staley. New Haven: Published for the Paul Mellon Centre for Studies in British Art by Yale University Press, c2001. 272 p.
00-110195   758/.1/094209034   0300084080
Landscape painting, English -- 19th century. Pre-Raphaelitism -- England.

ND1356.5.D39 1984
A Day in the country: impressionism and the French landscape/ Los Angeles County Museum of Art [and] the Art Institute of Chicago [and] Reunion des musees nationaux; [edited by Andrea P.A. Belloli]. Los Angeles, Calif.: Los Angeles County Museum of Art, 1984. 375 p.
84-003885   758/.144/0944074   0875871186
Landscape painting, French -- Exhibitions. Landscape painting -- 19th century -- France -- Exhibitions. Impressionism (Art) -- France -- Exhibitions.

ND1359.S8
Stechow, Wolfgang, 1896-1974.
Dutch landscape painting of the seventeenth century. [London] Phaidon [1966] ix, 494 p.
66-002795   759.9492
Landscape painting, Dutch. Landscape painting -- Technique.

ND1359.2.G5 1989
Gibson, Walter S.
Mirror of the earth: the world landscape in sixteenth-century Flemish painting/ Walter S. Gibson. Princeton, N.J.: Princeton University Press, c1989. xxiii, 156 p.
88-029308   758/.1/094931   0691040540
Landscape painting, Flemish. Landscape painting -- 16th century -- Flanders. Earth in art.

ND1359.3.S88 1987
Sutton, Peter C.
Masters of 17th-century Dutch landscape painting/ Peter C. Sutton, with contributions by Albert Blankert ... [et al.]; this exhibition was organized by Peter C. Sutton and P.J.J. van Thiel. Boston: Museum of Fine Arts, 1987. xv, 563 p.
87-043078   758/.1/09492074   0812281055
Landscape painting, Dutch -- Exhibitions. Landscape painting -- 17th century -- Netherlands -- Exhibitions.

ND1361.5.G87 1998
Gunnarsson, Torsten.
Nordic landscape painting in the nineteenth century/ Torsten Gunnarsson; translated by Nancy Adler. New Haven: Yale University Press, c1998. ix, 293 p.
98-024071   758/.1/094809034   0300070411
Landscape painting, Scandinavian. Landscape painting -- 19th century -- Scandinavia.

ND1366.7.S93
Sullivan, Michael, 1916-
The birth of landscape painting in China. Berkeley, University of California Press, [1962-   ]
60-016863   758/.1/0951   0520035585
Landscape painting, Chinese. Symbolism in art -- China.

ND1366.7.S94
Sullivan, Michael, 1916-
Symbols of eternity: the art of landscape painting in China/ Michael Sullivan. Stanford, Calif.: Stanford University Press, 1979. xiii, 205 p.
78-065393   758/.1/0951   0804710252
Landscape painting, Chinese.

ND1390 Special subjects of painting — Still life — General works

ND1390.E2313 1998
Ebert-Schifferer, S.
Still life: a history/ Sybille Ebert-Schifferer. New York: Abrams, 1998. 420 p.
98-003888   758/.4   0810941902
Still-life painting -- History. Nature (Aesthetics)

ND1403 Special subjects of painting — Plants. Trees. Flowers. Fruit — Special countries

ND1403.N43.T39 1995
Taylor, Paul, 1963-
Dutch flower painting, 1600-1720/ Paul Taylor. New Haven: Yale University Press, c1995. viii, 227 p.
94-040131   758/.42/0949209032   0300053908
Flowers in art. Still-life painting, Dutch. Still-life painting -- 17th century -- Netherlands.

ND1432 Special subjects of painting — Other subjects — Religious

ND1432.E85.D78 1999
Drury, John, 1936-
Painting the word: Christian pictures and their meanings/ John Drury. New Haven, Conn.: Yale University Press; 1999. xv, 201 p.
99-025840   246   0300077777
Jesus Christ -- Art.   Christian art and symbolism -- Medieval, 500-1500 -- Europe. Christian art and symbolism -- Modern period, 1500- -- Europe. Painting, European.

ND1432.E85.F74 1980
Friedmann, Herbert, 1900-1987.
A bestiary for Saint Jerome: animal symbolism in European religious art/ Herbert Friedmann. Washington: Smithsonian Institution Press, 1980. 378 p.
79-607804   704.94/6   0874744466
Jerome, -- Saint, -- d. 419 or 20 -- Art.   Christian art and symbolism. Christian saints in art. Painting, European.

ND1432.M45 A78 2001
Art and faith in Mexico: the nineteenth-century retablo tradition/ edited by Elizabeth Netto Calil Zarur and Charles Muir Lovell. Albuquerque: University of New Mexico Press, c2001. 359 p.
00-011009   755/.2/097207478961   0826323251
Painting, Mexican -- 19th century -- Exhibitions. Folk art -- Mexico -- Exhibitions. Votive offerings -- Mexico -- Exhibitions.

ND1432.M46.D87 1995
Durand, Jorge.
Miracles on the border: retablos of Mexican migrants to the United States/ Jorge Durand & Douglas S. Massey; with photographs by the authors. Tucson: University of Arizona Press, c1995. xvi, 216 p.
94-032080   755/.2   0816514712
Painting, Mexican. Christian art and symbolism -- Modern period, 1500- -- Mexico. Votive offerings in art -- Mexico.

ND1441-1441.5 Special subjects of painting — Other subjects — Historical

ND1441.R43 1995
Redefining American history painting/ edited by Patricia M. Burnham, Lucretia Hoover Giese. Cambridge; Cambridge University Press, 1995. xvii, 409 p.
95-002402   758/.9973   052146059X
History in art. Narrative painting, American.

ND1441.5.T76 2000
Troccoli, Joan Carpenter.
Painters and the American West: the Anschutz collection/ Joan Carpenter Troccoli; with the assistance of Marlene Chambers and Jane Comstock and an essay by Sarah Anschutz Hunt. Denver, Colo.: Denver Art Museum; c2000. 218 p.
00-030329   758.9978/007478883   0300087225
Anschutz, Philip -- Art collections -- Exhibitions.   Painting, American -- 20th century -- Exhibitions. Painting, American -- 19th century -- Exhibitions. Painting -- Private collections -- Colorado -- Denver -- Exhibitions. West (U.S.) -- In art -- Exhibitions.

ND1441.5.G47 1988
Gerdts, William H.
Grand illusions: history painting in America/ William H. Gerdts and Mark Thistlethwaite. Fort Worth, Tex.: Amon Carter Museum, 1988. 174 p.
87-025394   759.13   0883600560
Narrative painting, American -- Themes, motives. Narrative painting -- 19th century -- United States -- Themes, motives. Narrative painting, American -- European influences.

ND1451.5-1452 Special subjects of painting — Other subjects — Genre

ND1451.5.J64 1991
Johns, Elizabeth, 1937-
American genre painting: the politics of everyday life/ Elizabeth Johns. New Haven: Yale University Press, c1991. xvi, 250 p.
91-009613   754/.0973/09034   0300050194
Genre painting, American. Genre painting -- 19th century -- United States. United States in art.

ND1452.I8.B76 1988
Brown, Patricia Fortini, 1936-
Venetian narrative painting in the age of Carpaccio/ Patricia Fortini Brown. New Haven: Yale University Press, 1988. 310 p.
87-010669   759.5/31   0300040253
Carpaccio, Vittore, -- 1455?-1525? -- Themes, motives. Bellini, Gentile, -- d. 1507 -- Themes, motives. Narrative painting, Italian -- Italy -- Venice -- Themes, motives. Narrative painting, Renaissance -- Italy -- Venice -- Themes, motives. Art and society -- Italy -- Venice.

ND1452.N43.M37 1984
Masters of seventeenth-century Dutch genre painting: Philadelphia Museum of Art, March 18 to May 13, 1984, Gemaldegalerie, Staatliche Museen Preussischer Kulturbesitz, Berlin (West), June 8 to Augu [edited by Jane Iandola Watkins]. Philadelphia: Philadelphia Museum of Art, 1984. lxxxviii, 397 p.
84-005798   754/.09492/074   0812279514
Genre painting, Dutch -- Exhibitions. Genre painting -- 17th century -- Netherlands -- Exhibitions.

ND1457 Special subjects of painting — Other subjects — Calligraphy as painting

ND1457.J32.L63 1998
Seo, Audrey Yoshiko.
The art of twentieth-century Zen: paintings and calligraphy by Japanese masters/ Audrey Yoshiko Seo, with Stephen Addiss; with a chapter by Matthew Welch. Boston: Shambhala, 1998. xii, 220 p.
98-022210   755/.94327/0952   1570623589
Painting, Zen -- Japan -- Exhibitions. Calligraphy, Zen -- Japan -- Exhibitions. Painting, Japanese -- 20th century -- Exhibitions.

ND1460 Special subjects of painting — Other subjects — Miscellaneous, A-Z

ND1460.A74.R44 1997
Reeves, Eileen Adair.
Painting the heavens: art and science in the age of Galileo/ Eileen Reeves. Princeton, N.J.: Princeton University Press, c1997. x, 310 p.
96-051631   758/.952/094   0691043981
Astronomy in art. Painting, European. Painting, Modern -- 17th-18th centuries -- Europe.

ND1460.G37
Strong, Roy C.
The artist & the garden/ Roy Strong. New Haven: Published for the Paul Mellon Centre for Studies in British Art by Yale University Press, c2000. 288 p.
00-035922   758/.9635   0300085206
Gardens in art. Painting, English. Painting, Modern -- England.

ND1460.W65.N63 1999
Nochlin, Linda.
Representing women/ Linda Nochlin. New York: Thames and Hudson, 1999. 272 p.
98-061187   757/.4/09034   0500019045
Women in art. Painting, Modern -- 19th century. Painting, Modern -- 20th century.

ND1475 Painting technique and styles — Technique — Composition

ND1475.D86 1991
Dunning, William V., 1933-
Changing images of pictorial space: a history of spatial illusion in painting/ William V. Dunning. Syracuse: Syracuse University Press, 1991. xi, 254 p.
90-010211   750/.1/8   0815625057
Composition (Art) Space (Art) Painting -- Technique.

ND1475.K46 1990
Kemp, Martin.
The science of art: optical themes in western art from Brunelleschi to Seurat/ Martin Kemp. New Haven: Yale University Press, 1990. viii, 375 p.
88-033767   750/.1/8   0300043376
Painting -- Technique. Composition (Art) Perspective.

ND1500 Painting materials and methods — General. Technical manuals for artists

ND1500.M3 1982
Mayer, Ralph, 1895-
The artist's handbook of materials and techniques/ by Ralph Mayer. New York: Viking Press, 1981. xv, 733 p.
81-050514   750/.28   0670136662
Painting -- Technique. Artists' materials.

ND1500.T5 1956
Thompson, Daniel Varney, 1902-
The materials and techniques of medieval painting. With a foreword by Bernard Berenson. New York, Dover Publications [1956] 239 p.
57-004711   751
Pigments. Painting, Medieval. Painting -- Technique.

ND1510 Painting materials and methods — Pigments

ND1510.A77 1986
Artists' pigments: a handbook of their history and characteristics/ Robert L. Feller, editor. Washington: National Gallery of Art, c1986-c1997. v. 1-3
85-028349   751.2   0894680862
Pigments. Artists' materials.

ND1635 Examination and conservation of paintings — Technical examination: Expertising, x-ray, micrography, etc.

ND1635.K57 2000
Kirsh, Andrea.
Seeing through paintings: physical examination in art historical studies/ Andrea Kirsh and Rustin S. Levenson. New Haven: Yale University Press, 2000. 328 p.
99-051835   751.6/2   0300080468
Painting -- Expertising. Painting, European. Painting, American.

ND1837-2071 Watercolor painting — History — Special countries

ND1837.W94.A4 1998
Venn, Beth.
Unknown terrain: the landscapes of Andrew Wyeth/ Beth Venn and Adam D. Weinberg; with a contribution by Michael Kammen. New York: Whitney Museum of American Art: c1998. 223 p.
98-010230   759.13   0874271169
Wyeth, Andrew, -- 1917- -- Exhibitions. Landscape in art -- Exhibitions.

ND1839.D85.K48 1993
Ketner, Joseph D.
The emergence of the African-American artist: Robert S.
Duncanson, 1821-1872/ Joseph D. Ketner. Columbia:
University of Missouri Press, c1993. x, 235 p.
92-021542   759.13   0826208800
Duncanson, Robert S., -- 1821-1872. Afro-American painters --
Biography. Landscape painters -- United States -- Biography.

ND1839.E2.H6
Hoopes, Donelson F.
Eakins watercolors, by Donelson F. Hoopes. New York,
Watson-Guptill [1971] 87 p.
78-152785   759.13   0823015904
Eakins, Thomas, -- 1844-1916.

ND1839.M84.A4 1980
Clark, Carol, 1947-
Thomas Moran: watercolors of the American West: text
and catalogue raisonne/ by Carol Clark. Austin:
Published for the Amon Carter Museum of Western Art
by the University of Texas Press, c1980. 180 p.
80-013459   759.13   0292750595
Moran, Thomas, -- 1837-1926 -- Exhibitions.   West (U.S.) in art
-- Exhibitions.

ND1839.S33 A4 2001
Gerdts, William H.
Alice Schille/ William H. Gerdts. New York: Hudson
Hills Press; c2001. 216 p.
00-054094   759.13   1555951813
Schille, Alice, -- 1869-1955 -- Catalogs.

ND1954.D8.K5713 1988
Koreny, Fritz.
Albrecht Durer and the animal and plant studies of the
Renaissance/ Fritz Koreny; [translation from the German
by Pamela Marwood and Yehuda Shapiro]. Boston:
Little, Brown, c1988. 278 p.
87-029737   759.3   0821216244
Durer, Albrecht, -- 1471-1528 -- Themes, motives.   Watercolor
painting, German. Watercolor painting, Renaissance --
Germany. Animals in art.

ND2071.A328 1989
Addiss, Stephen, 1935-
The art of Zen: paintings and calligraphy by Japanese
monks, 1600-1925/ Stephen Addiss. New York: H.N.
Abrams, 1989. 223 p.
88-027499   759.952   0810918862
Painting, Zen. Calligraphy, Zen. Buddhist art and symbolism -
- Japan.

ND2608-2880 Mural painting —
Special countries

ND2608.B36 1984
Barnett, Alan W.
Community murals: the people's art/ Alan W. Barnett.
Philadelphia: Art Alliance Press; 516 p.
82-045464   751.7/3/0973 19   0845347314
Street art -- United States. Mural painting and decoration,
American -- 20th century.

ND2608.H84 1989
Hurlburt, Laurance P., 1937-
The Mexican muralists in the United States/ Laurance P.
Hurlburt; foreword by David W. Scott. Albuquerque:
University of New Mexico Press, c1989. xv, 320 p.
88-030000   759.13   0826311342
Orozco , Jose Clemente, -- 1883-1949 -- Criticism and
interpretation. Rivera, Diego, -- 1886-1957 -- Criticism and
interpretation. Siqueiros, David Alfaro -- Criticism and
interpretation. Mural painting and decoration, Mexican --
United States. Mural painting and decoration -- 20th century --
United States. Politics in art.

ND2635.C2 S56 1993
Signs from the heart: California Chicano murals/ edited
with an introduction by Eva Sperling Cockcroft and
Holly Barnet-Sánchez. Venice, Calif.: Social and Public
Art Resource Center; 116 p.
93-017526   751.7/3/08968720794 20   0826314481
Street art -- California. Mexican American mural painting and
decoration -- California -- 20th Mexican Americans --
California -- Politics and government -- Pictorial

ND2638.S26 D74 1991
Drescher, Tim.
San Francisco murals: community creates its muse, 1914-
1990/ Timothy W. Drescher. St. Paul: Pogo Press, c1991.
104 p.
90-062366   751.7/3/097946 20   0961776773
Mural painting and decoration, American -- California -- San
Francisco Street art -- California -- San Francisco -- Catalogs.

ND2644.F63 1998
Folgarait, Leonard.
Mural painting and social revolution in Mexico, 1920-
1940: art of the new order/ Leonard Folgarait.
Cambridge; Cambridge University Press, 1998. xiv,
256 p.
97-032154   751.7/3/097209041   0521581478
Orozco, Jose Clemente, -- 1883-1949 -- Criticism and
interpretation. Rivera, Diego, -- 1886-1957 -- Criticism and
interpretation. Siqueiros, David Alfaro -- Criticism and
interpretation. Mural painting and decoration, Mexican. Art and
revolution -- Mexico. Mural painting and decoration -- Mexico -
- History -- 20th century.

ND2755.L38 1990
Lavin, Marilyn Aronberg.
The place of narrative: mural decoration in Italian
churches, 431-1600/ Marilyn Aronberg Lavin. Chicago:
University of Chicago Press, c1990. xx, 406 p.
89-049474   751.7/3/0945   0226469565
Mural painting and decoration, Italian -- Themes, motives.
Mural painting and decoration, Medieval -- Italy -- Themes,
motives. Mural painting and decoration, Renaissance -- Italy --
Themes, motives.

ND2755.M4
Meiss, Millard.
The great age of fresco: discoveries, recoveries and
survivals. London, Phaidon, 1970. 251 p.
72-591489   751.7/3/0945   0714814083
Mural painting and decoration, Medieval -- Italy. Mural
painting and decoration, Renaissance -- Italy. Mural painting
and decoration, Italian.

ND2756.T9.B6 1980
Borsook, Eve.
The mural painters of Tuscany: from Cimabue to Andrea del Sarto/ by Eve Borsook. Oxford: Clarendon Press; c1980. lvii, 158 p.
78-040645   751.7/3/09455   0198173016
Mural painting and decoration, Italian -- Italy -- Tuscany. Mural painting and decoration, Gothic -- Italy -- Tuscany. Mural painting and decoration, Renaissance -- Italy -- Tuscany.

ND2757.F5.B313 1992
Baldini, Umberto.
The Brancacci Chapel/ Umberto Baldini, Ornella Casazza. New York: Abrams, 1992. 380 p.
91-044033   751.6/2/094551   0810931206
Mural painting and decoration, Renaissance -- Italy -- Florence. Mural painting and decoration, Italian -- Italy -- Florence.

ND2757.R6.S38 1991
Scott, John Beldon, 1946-
Images of nepotism: the painted ceilings of Palazzo Barberini/ John Beldon Scott. Princeton, N.J.: Princeton University Press, c1991. xiii, 243 p.
89-024313   751.7/3/0945632   0691040753
Urban -- VIII, -- Pope, -- 1568-1644 -- Art patronage. Allegories. Authority in art. Ceilings -- Italy -- Rome.

ND2779.U5
Unesco.
Norway: paintings from the stave churches. Pref. [by] Roar Hauglid; introd. [by] Louis Grodecki. [Greenwich, Conn.] New York Graphic Society, [c1955] 24 p.
56-000279   751.73
Mural painting and decoration -- Norway. Decoration and ornament -- Norway. Christian art and symbolism.

ND2809.U5
Unesco.
Yugoslavia: mediaeval frescoes. Pref. [by] David Talbot Rice; introd. [by] Svetozar Radojcic. [Greenwich, Conn.] New York Graphic Society [1955] 29 p.
55-003680   751.73
Mural painting and decoration. Decoration and ornament -- Yugoslavia.

ND2819.C92.L974 1991
Carr, Annemarie Weyl.
A Byzantine masterpiece recovered, the thirteenth-century murals of Lysi, Cyprus/ Annemarie Weyl Carr, Laurence J. Morrocco; introduction by Bertrand Davezac. Austin, Tex.: University of Texas Press: c1991. 157 p.
90-019435   751.7/3/095645   0292781172
Mural painting and decoration, Byzantine -- Cyprus -- Lysi. Mural painting and decoration, Byzantine -- Conservation and restoration -- Cyprus -- Lysi.

ND2829.A4.B44 1998
Behl, Benoy K., 1956-
The Ajanta Caves: artistic wonder of ancient Buddhist India/ text and photographs by Benoy K. Behl; with additional notes on the Jataka stories by Sangitika Nigam; foreword by Milo C. Beach. New York: Harry N. Abrams, 1998. 256 p.
97-032237   751.7/3/095484   0810919834
Gautama Buddha -- Art. Mural painting and decoration, Indic -- India -- Ajanta. Mural painting and decoration, Buddhist -- India -- Ajanta. Cave temples, Buddhist -- India -- Ajanta. Ajanta Caves (India)

ND2880.C6613 2000
Comment, Bernard, 1960-
The painted panorama/ Bernard Comment; [translated from the French by Anne-Marie Glasheen]. New York: H.N. Abrams, 2000. 272 p.
99-073779   751.7/4/09034   0810943654
Panoramas -- History -- 19th century.

ND2889 Illuminating of manuscripts and books — Dictionaries

ND2889.B76 1994
Brown, Michelle
Understanding illuminated manuscripts: a guide to technical terms/ Michelle P. Brown. Malibu, Calif.: J. Paul Getty Museum in association with the British Library, c1994. 127 p.
93-042239   745.6/7/0940902   0892362170
Illumination of books and manuscripts -- Dictionaries.

ND2890 Illuminating of manuscripts and books — Biographical dictionaries

ND2890.B83
Bradley, John William, 1830-1916.
A dictionary of miniaturists, illuminators, calligraphers, and copyists, with references to their works, and notices of their patrons, from the establishment of Christianity to the eighteenth centur New York, B. Franklin [1958] 3 v.
61-035160   703
Artists -- Dictionaries. Calligraphers. Copyists.

ND2900 Illuminating of manuscripts and books — History — General works

ND2900.W4 1970
Weitzmann, Kurt, 1904-
Illustrations in roll and codex; a study of the origin and method of text illustration. Princeton [N.J.] Princeton University Press, 1970. x, 261 p.
70-022791   096.1   0691038651
Illumination of books and manuscripts -- History.

ND2920-2950 Illuminating of manuscripts and books — History — Medieval

ND2920.A44 1992
Alexander, J. J. G.
Medieval illuminators and their methods of work/ Jonathan J.G. Alexander. New Haven: Yale University Press, 1992. vii, 214 p.
92-005576   745.6/7/0940902   0300056893
Illumination of books and manuscripts, Medieval. Illumination of books and manuscripts -- Technique.

ND2930.W42
Weitzmann, Kurt, 1904-
Late antique and early Christian book illumination/ Kurt Weitzmann. New York: G. Braziller, 1977. 126 p.
76-016444   745.6/7/09495   0807608300
Illumination of books and manuscripts, Early Christian.

ND2930.W43
Weitzmann, Kurt, 1904-
Studies in classical and Byzantine manuscript illumination. Edited by Herbert L. Kessler. With an introd. by Hugo Buchthal. Chicago, University of Chicago Press [1971] xxii, 346 p.
77-116381   745/.6/7   0226892468
Illumination of books and manuscripts, Byzantine -- History.

ND2940.N67
Nordenfalk, Carl Adam Johan, 1907-
Celtic and Anglo-Saxon painting: book illumination in the British Isles, 600-800/ Carl Nordenfalk. New York: G. Braziller, 1977. 124 p.
76-016443   745.6/7/0941   0807608254
Illumination of books and manuscripts, Celtic. Illumination of books and manuscripts, Anglo-Saxon. Illumination of books and manuscripts, Medieval -- Great Britain.

ND2950.C37
Carolingian painting/ introduction by Florentine Mutherich; provenances and commentaries by Joachim E. Gaehde. New York: G. Braziller, 1976. 126 p.
76-015908   745.6/7/094   0807608513
Illumination of books and manuscripts, Carolingian. Illumination of books and manuscripts, Medieval.

ND3128-3241 Illuminating of manuscripts and books — History — Special countries

ND3128.M67
Morgan, Nigel J.
The golden age of English manuscript painting, 1200-1500/ Richard Marks and Nigel Morgan. New York: G. Braziller, c1981. 119 p.
80-012985   745.6/7/0942   0807609714
Illumination of books and manuscripts, English. Illumination of books and manuscripts, Gothic -- England.

ND3147.A8813
Avril, Francois.
Manuscript painting at the court of France: the fourteenth century, 1310-1380/ Francois Avril; [translated from the French by Ursule Molinaro, with the assistance of Bruce Benderson]. New York: G. Braziller, 1978. 118 p.
77-078721   745.6/7/0944   0807608785
Illumination of books and manuscripts, French. Illumination of books and manuscripts, Gothic -- France. France -- Court and courtiers.

ND3161.F7.P35 1994
Painting and illumination in early Renaissance Florence, 1300-1450/ Laurence B. Kanter ... [et al.]. New York: Metropolitan Museum of Art: c1994. x, 394 p.
94-029418   745.6/7/0945510747471   0870997254
Illumination of books and manuscripts, Italian -- Italy -- Florence -- Exhibitions. Illumination of books and manuscripts, Renaissance -- Italy -- Florence -- Exhibitions.

ND3167.G65 1990
The Golden age of Dutch manuscript painting/ introduction by James H. Marrow; catalogue essays by Henri L.M. Defoer, Anne S. Korteweg, Wilhelmina C.M. Wustefeld. New York, N.Y.: George Braziller, 1990. 318 p.
89-085967   745.6/7/0949230747471
Illumination of books and manuscripts, Dutch -- Exhibitions. Illumination of books and manuscripts, Gothic -- Netherlands -- Exhibitions.

ND3199.W54
Williams, John, 1928 Feb. 25-
Early Spanish manuscript illumination/ John Williams. New York: G. Braziller, 1977. 117 p.
77-004042   745.6/7/0946   0807608661
Illumination of books and manuscripts, Spanish. Illumination of books and manuscripts, Medieval -- Spain.

ND3241.S68 1992
Soudavar, Abolala.
Art of the Persian courts: selections from the Art and History Trust Collection/ Abolala Soudavar; with a contribution by Milo Cleveland Beach. New York: Rizzoli, c1992. 423 p.
92-028278   745.6/7/09550747641411   0847816605
Illumination of books and manuscripts, Islamic -- Iran -- Catalogs. Illumination of books and manuscripts -- Texas -- Houston -- Catalogs. Illumination of books and manuscripts, Iranian -- Catalogs.

ND3310 Illuminating of manuscripts and books — General works — Treatises since 1800

ND3310.B32 1979
Backhouse, Janet.
The illuminated manuscript/ Janet Backhouse. Oxford: Phaidon, 1979. 80 p.
78-073502   745.6/7   0714819697
Illumination of books and manuscripts.

ND3327 Illuminating of manuscripts and books — Special techniques, A-Z

ND3327.G54.W55 2000
Whitley, Kathleen P.
The gilded page: the history and technique of manuscript gilding/ Kathleen P. Whitley. New Castle, DE: Oak Knoll Press; 2000. xiii, 222 p.
98-007123   745.6/7   1884718582
Gilding -- Technique. Illumination of books and manuscripts -- Technique.

ND3359-3380.4 Illuminating of manuscripts and books — Histories and reproductions of special illuminated works — Special works

ND3359.U82.C65 2000
Cohen, Adam S.
The Uta Codex: art, philosophy, and reform in eleventh-century Germany/ Adam S. Cohen. University Park: Pennnsylvania State University Press, c2000. 276 p.
99-040189   745.6/7/094334709021   027101959X
Illumination of books and manuscripts, Ottonian -- Germany -- Regensburg. Illumination of books and manuscripts, Medieval -- Germany -- Regensburg. Christian art and symbolism -- Medieval, 500-1500 -- Germany -- Regensburg.

ND3363.A1.W54 1997
Wieck, Roger S.
Painted prayers: the book of hours in medieval and Renaissance art/ Roger S. Wieck. New York: George Braziller, 1997. 144 p.
96-036927   242/.094/0902   0807614181
Books of hours -- Texts. Books of hours -- Illustrations. Illumination of books and manuscripts, Medieval.

ND3363.B5.T713 1969b
The Tres riches heures of Jean, Duke of Berry. Musee Conde, Chantilly. Introd. and legends by Jean Longnon and Raymond Cazelles. Pref. by Millard Meiss. [Translated from the French by Victoria Benedict] New York, G. Braziller [1969]
70-079776   745.6/7/0944
Books of hours -- Illustrations. Illumination of books and manuscripts, Gothic -- France. Illumination of books and manuscripts, French.

ND3363.C3.P55 1966
The Hours of Catherine of Cleves. Introd. and commentaries by John Plummer. New York, G. Braziller [1966] 359 p.
66-023096   096.1
Illumination of books and manuscripts, Dutch.

ND3380.4.R65.H36 1990
Hamburger, Jeffrey F., 1957-
The Rothschild canticles: art and mysticism in Flanders and the Rhineland circa 1300/ Jeffrey F. Hamburger. New Haven: Yale University Press, c1990. xii, 336 p.
90-034551   745.6/7/094428   0300043082
Illumination of books and manuscripts, Gothic -- Flanders. Illumination of books and manuscripts, German -- Germany -- Rhineland. Illumination of books and manuscripts, Medieval -- Germany -- Rhineland.

NE Print media

NE400 Printmaking and engraving — History of printmaking — General

NE400.G74 1996
Griffiths, Antony.
Prints and printmaking: an introduction to the history and techniques/ Antony Griffiths. Berkeley: University of California Press, c1996. 160 p.
96-012571   760/.28   0520207149
Prints -- Technique.

NE400.H66 1963
Hind, Arthur Mayger, 1880-1957.
A history of engraving & etching from the 15th century to the year 1914; being the 3d and fully rev. ed. of A short history of engraving and etching. New York, Dover Publications [1963] xviii, 487 p.
63-005658   765.09
Engraving -- History. Etching -- History.

NE400.H79 1996
Hults, Linda C.
The print in the western world: an introductory history/ Linda C. Hults. Madison, Wis.: University of Wisconsin Press, c1996. xx, 948 p.
95-007231   769.9   0299137007
Prints -- History.

NE400.P58 2000
Platzker, David, 1965-
Hard pressed: 600 years of prints and process/ David Platzker and Elizabeth Wyckoff. New York: Hudson Hill Press, 2000. 126 p.
00-040935   769.9   1555951929
Prints -- Technique -- History.

NE400.P77 1981
Prints: history of an art/ Michel Melot ... [et al.; part 1 translated from the French by Helga Harrison and Dennis Corbyn] Geneva: Skira; c1981. 278 p.
81-051310   769.9   0847803929
Prints -- History.

NE430-491 Printmaking and engraving — History of printmaking — Modern

NE430.I85 1969
Ivins, William Mills, 1881-1961.
Prints and visual communication. New York, Da Capo Press, 1969. xxv, 190 p.
68-031583   769/.9
Prints -- History. Photomechanical processes.

NE441.5.R44.L35 1994
Landau, David, 1950-
The Renaissance print, 1470-1550/ David Landau and Peter Parshall. New Haven: Yale University Press, 1994. xii, 433 p.
93-005682   769.94/09/024   0300057393
Prints, Renaissance. Prints -- 15th century. Prints -- 16th century.

NE491.P76
Printed art: a view of two decades/ Riva Castleman. New York, N.Y.: Museum of Modern Art, c1980. 144 p.
79-056089   769.9/046/07401471   0870705318
Prints -- 20th century -- Exhibitions.

NE507-771 Printmaking and engraving — History of printmaking — Special countries

NE507.A87 1988
Aspects of American printmaking, 1800-1950/ edited by James F. O'Gorman. Syracuse, N.Y.: Syracuse University Press, 1988. x, 245 p.
88-002291   769.973   0815624271
Prints, American -- Congresses. Prints -- 19th century -- United States -- Congresses. Prints -- 20th century -- United States -- Congresses.

NE507.W37 1984
Watrous, James, 1908-
American printmaking: a century of American printmaking, 1880-1980/ James Watrous. Madison, Wis.: University of Wisconsin Press, 1984. x, 334 p.
83-016956   769.973   0299096807
Prints, American. Prints -- 19th century -- United States. Prints -- 20th century -- United States.

NE507.W53 1993
Williams, Lynn Barstis, 1946-
American printmakers, 1880-1945: an index to reproductions and biocritical information/ compiled by Lynn Barstis Williams. Metuchen, N.J.: Scarecrow Press, 1993. xxxvi, 441 p.
93-041591   016.76992/273   0810827867
Prints, American -- Indexes. Prints -- 19th century -- United States -- Indexes. Prints -- 20th century -- United States -- Indexes.

NE508.B76 1999
Bryce, Betty Kelly, 1942-
American printmakers, 1946-1996: an index to reproductions and biocritical information/ Betty Kelly Bryce. Lanham, Md.: Scarecrow Press, 1999. xxxiv, 570 p.
98-043773   016.76992/273   081083586X
Prints, American -- Indexes. Prints -- 20th century -- United States -- Indexes. Printmakers -- United States -- Indexes.

NE508.C38 1991
Castleman, Riva.
Seven master printmakers: innovations in the eighties, from the Lilja collection/ Riva Castleman. New York: Museum of Modern Art: c1991. 119 p.
91-060021   769.92/273/074747   0870701940
Prints, American -- Themes, motives -- Exhibitions. Prints -- 20th century -- United States -- Themes, motives -- Exhibitions.

NE508.C86 1992
Cunningham, Eldon L., 1956-
Printmaking: a primary form of expression/ Eldon L. (E.C.) Cunningham. Niwot, Colo.: University Press of Colorado, c1992. ix, 186 p.
92-001151   769.92/273   0870812475
Prints, American. Prints -- 20th century -- United States. Printmakers -- United States -- Biography -- History and criticism.

NE508.F54 1987
Field, Richard S.
A graphic muse: prints by contemporary American women/ Richard S. Field, Ruth E. Fine. New York: Hudson Hills Press in association with the Mount Holyoke College Art Museum, c1987. 163 p.
87-012806   769/.088042   0933920792
Prints, American -- United States -- Exhibitions. Prints -- 20th century -- United States -- Exhibitions. Women artists -- United States -- Exhibitions.

NE508.J63
Johnson, Una E.
American prints and printmakers: a chronicle of over 400 artists and their prints from 1900 to the present/ Una E. Johnson. Garden City, N.Y.: Doubleday, 1980. xviii, 266 p.
79-008931   769.92/2   0385149212
Prints, American. Prints -- 20th century -- United States. Printmakers -- United States.

NE508.P69 1995
Printmaking in America: collaborative prints and presses, 1960-1990/ Trudy V. Hansen ... [et al.]. New York: H.N. Abrams in association with Mary and Leigh Block Gallery, Northwestern University, 1995. 248 p.
94-025246   769.973/074/7731   0810937433
Prints, American -- Exhibitions. Prints -- 20th century -- United States -- Exhibitions. Group work in art -- United States -- Exhibitions.

NE535.N6.A33 1991
Adams, Clinton, 1918-
Printmaking in New Mexico, 1880-1990/ Clinton Adams. Albuquerque: University of New Mexico Press, c1991. ix, 167 p.
90-047752   769.9789   0826313078
Prints, American -- New Mexico. Prints -- 19th century -- New Mexico. Prints -- 20th century -- New Mexico.

NE538.M33.C65 1999
Colescott, Warrington, 1921-
Progressive printmakers: Wisconsin artists and the print renaissance/ Warrington Colescott, Arthur Hove. Madison, Wis.: University of Wisconsin Press, c1999. 221 p.
98-051818   769.9775/83   0299161102
Prints, American -- Wisconsin -- Madison. Prints -- 20th century -- Wisconsin -- Madison.

NE539.B3.A4 1984
Fern, Alan Maxwell, 1930-
The complete prints of Leonard Baskin: a catalogue raisonne 1948-1983/ by Alan Fern and Judith O'Sullivan; introduction by Ted Hughes. Boston: Little, Brown, c1984. 304 p.
84-000860   769.92/4   0821215620
Baskin, Leonard, -- 1922- -- Catalogs.

NE539.C3.A4 1979
Breeskin, Adelyn Dohme, 1896-
Mary Cassatt: a catalogue raisonne of the graphic work/ Adelyn Dohme Breeskin. Washington: Smithsonian Institution Press, 1979. 189 p.
78-022472   769/.92/4   0874742846
Cassatt, Mary, -- 1844-1926 -- Catalogs.

NE539.C3.A4 1989
Mathews, Nancy Mowll.
Mary Cassatt: the color prints/ Nancy Mowll Mathews and Barbara Stern Shapiro. New York: H.N. Abrams; 1989. 207 p.
88-008107   769.92/4   0810910497
Cassatt, Mary, -- 1844-1926 -- Exhibitions.

NE539.D44.A4 1987
Lumsdaine, Joycelyn Pang.
The prints of Adolf Dehn: a catalogue raisonne/ compiled by Joycelyn Pang Lumsdaine and Thomas O'Sullivan; with essays by Richard W. Cox and Clinton Adams. St. Paul: Minnesota Historical Society Press, 1987. viii, 268 p.
87-007776   769.92/4   0873512030
Dehn, Adolf, -- 1895-1968 -- Catalogs.   Prints, American -- Catalogs. Prints -- 20th century -- United States -- Catalogs.

NE539.D5.A4 1977
Dine, Jim, 1935-
Jim Dine prints, 1970-1977. New York: Published in association with the Williams College artist-in-residence program by Harper & Row, c1977. 134 p.
77-003758   769/.92/4   0064300838
Dine, Jim, -- 1935- -- Exhibitions.

NE539.F68.A4 1993
Fine, Ruth, 1941-
Helen Frankenthaler: prints/ Ruth E. Fine. Washington: National Gallery of Art; c1993. 159 p.
92-043980   769.92   0894681915
Frankenthaler, Helen, -- 1928- -- Exhibitions.

NE539.G74
Knestrick, Walter.
Red Grooms: the graphic work/ introduction and catalogue by Walter Knestrick; essay by Vincent Katz. New York: Harry N. Abrams, 2001.
00-056555   769.92   0810967332
Grooms, Red -- Catalogs.

NE539.H65.A4 1979
Hopper, Edward, 1882-1967.
Edward Hopper, the complete prints/ [compiled by] Gail Levin. New York: Norton, c1979. 89 p.
79-013567   769/.92/4   0393012751
Hopper, Edward, -- 1882-1967 -- Catalogs.

NE539.J57.A4 1987
Foirades/Fizzles: echo and allusion in the art of Jasper Johns. [Los Angeles]: Grunwald Center for the Graphic Arts: c1987. 322 p.
87-015012   769.92/4   0943739004
Johns, Jasper, -- 1930- -- Exhibitions. Beckett, Samuel, -- 1906- -- Foirades -- Illustrations -- Exhibitions. Prints, American -- Exhibitions. Prints -- 20th century -- United States -- Exhibitions.

NE539.M23.A4 1992
Lewison, Jeremy.
Brice Marden: prints, 1961-1991: a catalogue raisonne/ Jeremy Lewison. London: Tate Gallery, 1992. 175 p.
93-172129   769.92   185437091X
Marden, Brice, -- 1938- -- Exhibitions.

NE539.M67.A4 1990
Terenzio, Stephanie C.
The prints of Robert Motherwell/ Stephanie Terenzio; catalogue raisonne, 1943-1990 by Dorothy C. Belknap. New York: Hudson Hills Press in association with the American Federation of Arts: Distributed in the U.S. by Rizzoli, c1991. 380 p.
90-081566   769.92   0933920962
Motherwell, Robert -- Catalogues raisonnes.

NE539.S72.A4 1983
Axsom, Richard H., 1943-
The prints of Frank Stella: a catalogue raisonne, 1967-1982/ by Richard H. Axsom; with the assistance of Phylis Floyd and Matthew Rohn; foreword by Evan M. Maurer. New York: Hudson Hills Press; c1983. 192 p.
82-015729   769.92/4   0933920407
Stella, Frank -- Catalogs.

NE546.P6.A4 1979
Posada's Mexico/ edited by Ron Tyler. Washington: Library of Congress: for sale by the Supt. of Docs., U.S. Govt. Print. Off., 1979. xii, 315 p.
79-022460   769/.92/4   0844403156
Posada, Jose Guadalupe, -- 1852-1913 -- Exhibitions.   Prints, Mexican -- Exhibitions. Mexico in art -- Exhibitions.

NE546.P6.B47 1972
Posada, Jose Guadalupe, 1852-1913.
Posada's popular Mexican prints; 273 cuts, by Jose Guadalupe Posada. Selected and edited, with an introd. and commentary, by Roberto Berdecio and Stanley Appelbaum. New York, Dover Publications [1972] xxi, 156 p.
77-178994   769/.92/4   0486228541
Posada, Jose Guadalupe, -- 1852-1913.   Mexico in art.

NE625.6.S8.S87 1997
Surrealist prints/ edited by Gilbert Kaplan; essays, Timothy Baum, Riva Castleman, Robert Rainwater. New York: Distributed by Harry N. Abrams, 1997. 155 p.
96-052626   769.94/074/79494   0810963396
Kaplan, Gilbert E. -- Art collections -- Exhibitions. Prints, European -- Exhibitions. Prints -- 20th century -- Europe -- Exhibitions. Surrealism -- Europe -- Exhibitions.

NE642.B5.W5
Wingfield Digby, George Frederick, 1911-
Symbol and image in William Blake. Oxford, Clarendon Press, 1957. xx, 143 p.
58-000298   769.2
Blake, William, -- 1757-1827. Blake, William, -- 1757-1827. -- For the sexes: The gates of Paradise. Symbolism in art.

NE642.H6.A4 1970
Hogarth, William, 1697-1764.
Hogarth's graphic works/ compiled and with a commentary by Ronald Paulson. New Haven: Yale University Press, 1970. 2 v.
79-118892   769/.92/4
Hogarth, William, -- 1697-1764. Hogarth, William, -- 1697-1764 -- Catalogues raisonnes.

NE642.S52
Bromberg, Ruth.
Walter Sickert, prints: a catalogue raisonne/ Ruth Bromberg. New Haven: Published for the Paul Mellon Centre for Studies in British Art by Yale University Press, c2000. 312 p.
99-059502   769.92   0300081618
Sickert, Walter, -- 1860-1942 -- Catalogues raisonnes.

NE642.S6.D64 1999
D'Oench, Ellen.
Copper into gold: prints by John Raphael Smith (1752-1812)/ Ellen G. D'Oench. New Haven, CT: Yale University Press, 1999. xiv, 300 p.
98-089216   769.92   0300076304
Smith, John Raphael, -- 1752-1812 -- Criticism and interpretation. Smith, John Raphael, -- 1752-1812 -- Catalogues raisonnes.

NE642.T9.H47 1990
Herrmann, Luke.
Turner prints: the engraved work of J.M.W. Turner/ Luke Herrmann. New York: New York University Press, 1990. 288 p.
90-005989   769.92   0814734723
Turner, J. M. W. -- (Joseph Mallord William), -- 1775-1851 -- Criticism and interpretation.

NE647.2.S73 1992
Stewart, Philip.
Engraven desire: Eros, image & text in the French eighteenth century/ by Philip Stewart. Durham: Duke University Press, 1992. xiv, 380 p.
91-012735   769.944/09/033   0822311771
Engraving, French -- Themes, motives. Engraving -- 18th century -- France -- Themes, motives. French literature -- Illustrations.

NE647.6.I4.M4413 1996
Melot, Michel.
The impressionist print/ Michel Melot; translated from the French by Caroline Beamish. New Haven: Yale University Press, c1996. 296 p.
95-050606   769.944/09/034   0300067925
Prints, French. Impressionism (Art) -- France. Prints -- 19th century -- France.

NE650.B58.H6
Braque, Georges, 1882-1963.
Georges Braque: his graphic work. Introd. by Werner Hofmann. New York, H. N. Abrams [1961] xxxiii, 86 p.
61-015293   759.4

NE650.D45.A4 1984
Reed, Sue Welsh.
Edgar Degas: the painter as printmaker/ Sue Welsh Reed and Barbara Stern Shapiro; with contributions by Clifford S. Ackley and Roy L. Perkinson; essay by Douglas Druick and Peter Zegers. Boston: Museum of Fine Arts, c1984. lxxii, 272 p.
84-061859   769.92/4   0878462430
Degas, Edgar, -- 1834-1917 -- Exhibitions.

NE650.G5.L8
Giacometti, Alberto, 1901-1966.
Giacometti: the complete graphics and 15 drawings, by Herbert C. Lust. Introd. by John Lloyd Taylor. New York, Tudor Pub. Co. [1970] 224 p.
73-114205   769/.924   0814804101

NE650.T68.A4 1988
Adriani, Gotz, 1940-
Toulouse-Lautrec: the complete graphic works: a catalogue raisonne: the Gerstenberg collection/ Gotz Adriani; [translated from the German by Eileen Martin]. New York, N.Y.: Thames and Hudson, 1988. 432 p.
88-050223   769.92   0500091889
Toulouse-Lautrec, Henri de, -- 1864-1901 -- Catalogues raisonnes. Gerstenberg, Otto, -- 1848-1935 -- Art collections -- Catalogs. Prints -- Private collections -- Germany -- Berlin -- Catalogs.

NE654.D9.B63
Durer, Albrecht, 1471-1528.
Albrecht Durer: master printmaker [by] Dept. of Prints & Drawings Boston, Museum of Fine Arts [c1971] xxiv, 295 p.
77-183708

NE659.L56 2000
Lincoln, Evelyn.
The invention of the Italian Renaissance printmaker/ Evelyn Lincoln. New Haven: Yale University Press, c2000. viii, 207 p.
99-087337   769.945/09/031   0300080417
Mantegna, Andrea, -- 1431-1506. Beccafumi, Domenico, -- 1486-1551. Scultori, Diana, -- ca. 1545-ca. 1590. Prints -- 16th century -- Italy. Prints, Italian. Prints, Renaissance -- Italy.

NE667.2.A25
Ackley, Clifford S.
Printmaking in the age of Rembrandt: [exhibition catalogue]/ Clifford S. Ackley. Boston: Museum of Fine Arts, [c1981] xlviii, 316 p.
80-084002   769.9492/074/014461   0878461965
Prints, Dutch -- Exhibitions. Prints -- 17th century -- Netherlands -- Exhibitions.

NE771.C48
Chibbett, David G.
The history of Japanese printing and book illustration/ David Chibbett. Tokyo; Kodansha International; 1977. 264 p.
76-009362   769/.952   0870112880
Prints, Japanese -- Japan. Illustration of books -- Japan. Printing -- Japan -- History.

**NE850 Printmaking and engraving —
General works. Treatises — 1851-**

NE850.S23
Saff, Donald, 1937-
Printmaking: history and process/ Donald Saff, Deli Sacilotto. New York: Holt, Rinehart and Winston, c1978. xii, 436 p.
76-054995   760/.2/8   0030421063
Prints -- Technique.

NE940-950 Printmaking and engraving — Collections of prints in book form

NE940.S3
Sachs, Paul J. 1878-1965.
Modern prints & drawings; a guide to a better understanding of modern draughtsmanship. Selected and with an explanatory text by Paul J. Sachs. New York, Knopf [1954] 261 p.
54-006137   769
Prints. Drawing.

NE950.C7
Craven, Thomas, 1889-
A treasury of American prints; a selection of one hundred etchings and lithographs by the foremost living American artists, edited by Thomas Craven. New York, Simon and Schuster [c1939] 100 p.
39-027722   769
Prints, American. Prints -- 20th century -- United States.

NE950.Z5
Zigrosser, Carl, 1891-
The expressionists; a survey of their graphic art. New York, G. Braziller, 1957. 37 p.
57-001608   769.084
Expressionism (Art) Prints -- 20th century -- Germany. Printmakers.

**NE954.3 Printmaking and engraving —
Special subjects — Landscapes. Views**

NE954.3.N4.G53 2000
Gibson, Walter S.
Pleasant places: the rustic landscape from Bruegel to Ruisdael/ Walter S. Gibson. Berkeley: University of California Press, c2000. xxviii, 291 p.
99-029336   769/.436492/09492   0520216989
Landscape prints, Dutch -- Netherlands -- Haarlem. Landscape prints -- 17th century -- Netherlands -- Haarlem. Netherlands -- In art.

NE954.3.N4.L48 1994
Levesque, Catherine, 1955-
Journey through landscape in seventeenth-century Holland: the Haarlem print series and Dutch identity/ Catherine Levesque. University Park, Pa.: Pennsylvania State University Press, c1994. xxii, 169 p.
94-008293   769/.43649235   0271010495
Landscape prints, Dutch -- Netherlands -- Haarlem. Landscape prints -- 17th century -- Netherlands -- Haarlem. Netherlands in art.

**NE958.3 Printmaking and engraving —
Special subjects — Religious prints**

NE958.3.G3.M68 1989
Moxey, Keith P. F., 1943-
Peasants, warriors, and wives: popular imagery in the Reformation/ Keith Moxey. Chicago: University of Chicago Press, 1989. xiv, 165 p.
88-037668   769/.4994332   0226543919
Printed ephemera -- Germany -- Nuremberg -- History -- 16th century. Wood-engraving, German -- Germany -- Nuremberg. Wood-engraving -- 16th century -- Germany -- Nuremberg.

**NE962 Printmaking and engraving —
Special subjects — Other subjects, A-Z**

NE962.W48.T96 1994
Tyler, Ronnie C., 1941-
Prints of the West/ Ron Tyler. Golden, Colo.: Fulcrum Pub., c1994. viii, 197 p.
93-050794   769/.49978   1555911749
Prints, American. Prints -- 19th century -- United States. Prints -- 20th century -- United States.

NE962.W65.R87 1990
Russell, H. Diane
Eva/Ave: woman in Renaissance and Baroque prints/ H. Diane Russell with Bernadine Barnes. Washington: National Gallery of Art; c1990. 238 p.
90-015521   769/.424/094074753   0894681575
Prints, Renaissance -- Exhibitions. Prints, Baroque -- Exhibitions. Women in art -- Exhibitions.

**NE1030 Wood engraving. Woodcuts. Xylography.
Block printing — History.
Collections of wood engravings (in book form) —
General works**

NE1030.H55 1963
Hind, Arthur Mayger, 1880-1957.
An introduction to a history of woodcut, with a detailed survey of work done in the fifteenth century. New York, Dover Publications [1963] 2 v.
63-005621   761.209
Illustrated books -- 15th and 16th centuries -- Bibliography. Wood-engraving -- History. Illustrated books -- 15th and 16th centuries.

**NE1205-1212 Wood engraving. Woodcuts.
Xylography. Block printing —
Wood engravers (Lives and works) —
Special artists**

NE1205.D9.A3 1963
Durer, Albrecht, 1471-1528.
The complete woodcuts of Albrecht Durer. Edited by Willi Kurth. With an introd. by Campbell Dodgson. [German text translated by Silvia M. Welsh] New York, Dover Publications [1963] 44 p.
63-017929   769.943

NE1205.D9.K5
Durer, Albrecht, 1471-1528.
Complete engravings, etchings, and woodcuts. [Text by] Karl-Adolf Knappe. New York, H.N. Abrams [1965] lviii, 385 p.
65-012092   769.943

NE1212.B5.A45 1962
Bewick, Thomas, 1753-1828.
1800 woodcuts by Thomas Bewick and his school. With an introd. by Robert Hutchinson. New York, Dover Publications [1962] xiv, 247 p.
62-051830   769/.942   0486207668
Bewick, Thomas, -- 1753-1828.   Wood-engraving. Engraving -- Specimens.

**NE1310 Wood engraving. Woodcuts. Xylography.
Block printing —
Japanese colored wood engravings.
Ukiyoe prints — General works**

NE1310.M48
Michener, James A. 1907-
Japanese prints; from the early masters to the modern, by James A. Michener, with notes on the prints by Richard Lane. With the cooperation of the Honolulu Academy of Arts. Tokyo, C. E. Tuttle Co. [1959] 287 p.
59-010410   769.952
Color prints, Japanese.

**NE1321-1322 Wood engraving. Woodcuts.
Xylography. Block printing —
Japanese colored wood engravings.
Ukiyoe prints — History**

NE1321.W47
Whitford, Frank.
Japanese prints and Western painters/ Frank Whitford. New York: Macmillan, 1977. 264 p.
76-045182   769/.952   002627180X
Ukiyoe -- History. Color prints, Japanese -- History. Prints, European -- Japanese influences.

NE1321.8.K487 1989
Keyes, Roger S.
The male journey in Japanese prints/ Roger S. Keyes. Berkeley: University of California Press, c1989. xxx, 189 p.
88-022736   769/.423/0952074019467   0520065123
Ukiyoe -- Exhibitions. Color prints, Japanese -- Edo period, 1600-1868 -- Exhibitions. Wood-engraving, Japanese -- Edo period, 1600-1868 -- Exhibitions.

NE1321.8.L36 1978
Lane, Richard, 1926-
Images from the floating world: the Japanese print: including an illustrated dictionary of ukiyo-e/ Richard Lane. New York: Putnam, c1978. 364 p.
78-053445   769/.952   0399121935
Ukiyoe. Color prints, Japanese -- Edo period, 1600-1868. Color prints, Japanese -- Meiji period, 1868-1912. Japan -- Social life and customs -- Pictorial works.

NE1322.M48 2000
Merritt, Helen.
Woodblock kuchi-e prints: reflections of Meiji culture/ Helen Merritt, Nanako Yamada. Honolulu: University of Hawai'i Press, c2000. xii, 284 p.
99-032145   769.952/09/034   0824820738
Color prints, Japanese -- Meiji period, 1868-1912. Illustration of books -- Japan -- Meiji period, 1868-1912. Frontispiece.

**NE1325 Wood engraving. Woodcuts. Xylography.
Block printing —
Japanese colored wood engravings.
Ukiyoe prints — Special artists, A-Z**

NE1325.A5.A4 2001
Faulkner, Rupert.
Hiroshige fan prints/ Rupert Faulkner. London: V&A Publications; 2001. 160 p.
00-107864   0810965763
Ando, Hiroshige, -- 1797-1858.   Fans -- Japan. Painted fans -- Japan.

**NE1815 Metal engraving. Copper, steel, etc. —
Mezzotint engraving — General works**

NE1815.W38 1990
Wax, Carol, 1953-
The mezzotint: history and technique/ by Carol Wax.
New York: H.N. Abrams, 1990. 296 p.
89-018123   766/.2/09   0810936038
Mezzotint engraving -- Technique.

**NE1860 Metal engraving. Copper, steel, etc. —
Color prints
(General or produced by metal engraving alone)
— Special publishers, printers, etc., A-Z**

NE1860.N4.A32 1962
Fine art reproductions of old & modern masters.   New
York Graphic Society, 1961. 444 p.
61-018343   759.0838
Color prints -- Catalogs.

**NE2012-2054.5 Etching and aquatint — History.
Collections of etchings in book form —
Special countries**

NE2012.W45.L6 1984
Lochnan, Katharine Jordan.
The etchings of James McNeill Whistler/ Katharine A.
Lochnan. New Haven: Published in association with the
Art Gallery of Ontario by Yale University Press, 1984. xi,
308 p.
84-040185   769.92/4   0300032757
*Whistler, James McNeill, -- 1834-1903.   Etchers -- United
States -- Biography.*

NE2047.6.G34.H39 1972
Hayes, John T.
Gainsborough as printmaker/ John Hayes. New Haven:
Published for the Paul Mellon Centre for Studies in
British Art by Yale University Press, 1972, c1971. xx,
114 p.
79-179475   769/.92/4   0300015615
Gainsborough, Thomas, -- 1727-1788.

NE2054.5.R4.A4 2000
Hinterding, Erik.
Rembrandt the printmaker/ Erik Hinterding, Ger Luijten,
and Martin Royalton-Kisch; with contributions by Marijn
Schapelhouman, Peter Schatborn, and Ernst van de
Wetering. London: British Museum Press; 2000. 384 p.
2001-320110   769.92   071412625X
Rembrandt Harmenszoon van Rijn, -- 1606-1669 -- Exhibitions.

NE2054.5.R4.W44 1999
White, Christopher, 1930-
Rembrandt as an etcher: a study of the artist at work/
Christopher White. New Haven, Conn.: Yale University
Press, c1999. xi, 284 p.
98-047322   769.92   0300079532
*Rembrandt Harmenszoon van Rijn, -- 1606-1669 -- Criticism
and interpretation.*

**NE2243 Monotype (Printmaking) —
History — 17th-19th centuries**

NE2243.P34
The Painterly print: monotypes from the seventeenth to
the twentieth century; [exhibition] The Metropolitan
Museum of Art, May 1-June 29, 1980, Museum of Fine
Arts, Boston ...   New York: Metropolitan Museum of
Art, c1980. xiii, 259 p.
80-010441   769/.074/014461   0870992236
Monotype (Engraving) -- Exhibitions.

**NE2245 Monotype (Printmaking) —
By region or country, A-Z**

NE2245.U54.M67 1997
Moser, Joann.
Singular impressions: the monotype in America/ Joann
Moser. Washington: Published for the National Museum
of American Art by the Smithsonian Institution Press,
c1997. x, 212 p.
96-039416   769.973   1560987375
Monotype (Engraving), American.

**NE2295 Lithography — History.
Collections in book form — General works**

NE2295.L37 1988
Lasting impressions: lithography as art/ edited by Pat
Gilmour. Philadelphia: University of Pennsylvania Press,
1988. 416 p.
88-001304   763/.09   0812281268
Lithography -- History. Lithography, American.

**NE2349.5 Lithography — History.
Collections in book form — Special countries**

NE2349.5.B66.A4 1989
Bonnard, Pierre, 1867-1947.
Pierre Bonnard, the graphic art/ Colta Ives, Helen
Giambruni, Sasha M. Newman. New York: Metropolitan
Museum of Art: c1989. xii, 260 p.
89-012847   769.92   0810931001
Bonnard, Pierre, -- 1867-1947 -- Exhibitions.

**NE2415 Lithography — Biography —
Special lithographers**

NE2415.C7.P43
Peters, Harry Twyford, 1881-1948.
Currier & Ives, printmakers to the American people, by
Harry T. Peters. Garden City, N.Y., Doubleday, Doran &
co., inc., 1942.
42-024944   763
*Lithography, American. Lithography -- 19th century -- United
States.*

NE2415.M8.L5
Munch, Edvard, 1863-1944.
Edvard Munch, a selection of his prints from American collections [by] William S. Lieberman. New York, Museum of Modern Art; distributed by Simon and Schuster, [1957] 39 p.
57-007371   769.2
Lithographs, Norwegian -- Exhibitions. Engravings, Norwegian -- Exhibitions. Wood-engravings, Norwegian -- Exhibitions.

NE2425 Lithography — General works — Since 1850

NE2425.L5713 1983
Lithography: 200 years of art, history, & technique/ Domenico Porzio, general editor, with the collaboration of Rosalba and Marcello Tabanelli; essays by Jean Adhemar ... [et al.]; translated from the Italian by Geoffrey Culverwell. New York: H.N. Abrams, 1983. 280 p.
83-003691   763   0810912821
Lithography.

NE2451 Lithography — Collections in book form

NE2451.T64
Toulouse-Lautrec, Henri de, 1864-1901.
Toulouse-Lautrec: his complete lithographs and dry-points/ by Jean Adhemar. H. N. Abrams, 1965. 370 p.
65-021831   769.924
Toulouse-Lautrec, Henri de, -- 1864-1901.

NK Decorative arts. Applied arts. Decoration and ornament

NK27 Collected writings — Individual authors

NK27.H47 2000
Herbert, Robert L., 1929-
Nature's workshop: Renoir's writings on the decorative arts/ Robert L. Herbert. New Haven, CT: Yale University Press, c2000. xiv, 278 p.
99-020881   745   0300081367
Renoir, Auguste, -- 1841-1919 -- Written works. Renoir, Auguste, -- 1841-1919 -- Knowledge -- Decorative arts. Decorative arts.

NK30 Dictionaries

NK30.M38 2000
Materials & techniques in the decorative arts: an illustrated dictionary/ edited by Lucy Trench. Chicago: University of Chicago Press, 2000. ix, 572 p.
00-029865   745/.028   0226812006
Decorative arts -- Dictionaries.

NK460 Museums, galleries, etc. — United States. By city and museum, A-Z

NK460.W3.R467 1998
Renwick Gallery.
Skilled work: American craft in the Renwick Gallery, National Museum of American Art, Smithsonian Institution. Washington, D.C.: Smithsonian Institution Press, c1998. 191 p.
97-032357   745/.0973/074753   1560988312
Decorative arts -- United States -- Catalogs. Decorative arts -- Washington (D.C.) -- Catalogs.

NK535 Private collections — United States — Special. By collector, A-Z

NK535.C68.E88 1998
The extraordinary in the ordinary: textiles and objects from the collections of Lloyd Cotsen and the Neutrogena Corporation: works in cloth, ceramic, wood, metal, straw, and paper from cultures th edited by Mary Hunt Kahlenberg; photography by Pat Pollard. New York: Harry Abrams in association with the Museum of International Folk Art, Museum of New Mexico, 1998. 280 p.
98-010601   745/.074789/56   0810913968
Cotsen, Lloyd E. -- Art collections -- Exhibitions. Decorative arts -- Private collections -- New Mexico -- Santa Fe -- Exhibitions. Decorative arts -- New Mexico -- Santa Fe -- Exhibitions. Decorative arts -- Exhibitions.

NK600 History — General works

NK600.L8 1984
Lucie-Smith, Edward.
The story of craft: the craftsman's role in society/ Edward Lucie-Smith. New York: Van Nostrand Reinhold, 1984, c1981. 288 p.
83-006516   745/.09   0442259107
Decorative arts -- History. Decorative arts -- Social aspects. Arts and crafts movement -- Social aspects.

NK607 History —
Folk and decorative art of ethnic or religious groups not limited to one country — General works

NK607.G5 1989
Glassie, Henry H.
The spirit of folk art: the Girard Collection at the Museum of International Folk Art/ Henry Glassie; color photography by Michel Monteaux; black-and-white photography and drawings by Henry Glassie. New York: Abrams in association with the Museum of New Mexico, Santa Fe, 1989. 276 p.
88-021854 745/.074/018956 0810915227
Girard, Alexander -- Art collections -- Exhibitions. Folk art -- Exhibitions.

NK670-680 History — Ancient — Classical

NK670.F76 1993
From pasture to polis: art in the age of Homer/ Museum of Art and Archaeology, University of Missouri-Columbia; edited by Susan Langdon; with an essay by Jeffrey M. Hurwit. Columbia: University of Missouri Press, c1993. xiii, 250 p.
93-024787 709/.38/07473 0826209289
Decorative arts, Ancient -- Greece -- Exhibitions. Greece -- History -- Geometric period, ca. 900-700 B.C. -- Exhibitions.

NK680.R65
Roman crafts/ edited by Donald Strong & David Brown. New York: New York University Press, 1976. 256 p.
76-028589 0814778011
Decorative arts. Handicraft -- Rome.

NK775.5 History — Modern — 19th century

NK775.5.A7
Art Nouveau: 1890-1914/ edited by Paul Greenhalgh. London: Victoria and Albert Museum; 2000. 496 p.
00-028027 709/.03/4907442134 0894682792
Decoration and ornament -- Art nouveau -- Exhibitions. Decorative arts -- England -- London -- Exhibitions. Decorative arts -- History -- 19th century -- Exhibitions.

NK805-1073.5 History — Special countries

NK805.C65 1965
Comstock, Helen,
The concise encyclopedia of American antiques. New York, Hawthorn Books [1965] 848 p.
65-009391 745.10973
Decorative arts -- United States. Art, American. Antiques -- Dictionaries.

NK805.D48 1979
Dewhurst, C. Kurt.
Artists in aprons: folk art by American women/ C. Kurt Dewhurst, Betty MacDowell, Marsha MacDowell. New York: Dutton, c1979. xviii, 202 p.
78-055945 745/.0973 0525058575
Folk art -- United States. Women artists -- United States. Folk artists -- Hungary.

NK805.F56 1990
Five star folk art: one hundred American masterpieces/ Jean Lipman ... [et al.]. New York: H.N. Abrams in association with the Museum of American Folk Art, 1990. 176 p.
90-000120 745/.0973 0810933020
Folk art -- United States.

NK805.H67
Hornung, Clarence Pearson.
Treasury of American design; a pictorial survey of popular folk arts based upon watercolor renderings in the Index of American Design, at the National Gallery of Art, by Clarence P. Hornung. Foreword by J. Carter Brown. Introd. by Holger Cahill. New York, H. N. Abrams [1972] 2 v.
76-142742 745/.0973 0810905167
Decorative arts -- United States. Decoration and ornament -- United States.

NK805.N35 1990
National Museum of American Art (U.S.)
Made with passion/ Lynda Roscoe Hartigan, with contributions by Andrew L. Connors, Elizabeth Tisdel Holmstead, and Tonia L. Horton. Washington: Published for the National Museum of American Art by the Smithsonian Institution Press, c1990. xv, 240 p.
90-009622 745/.0973/074753 0874742935
Hemphill, Herbert Waide -- Art collections -- Exhibitions. Folk art -- Private collections -- Washington (D.C.) -- Exhibitions. Folk art -- United States -- Exhibitions.

NK808.E46 1987
The Eloquent object: the evolution of American art in craft media since 1945/ edited by Marcia Manhart and Tom Manhart; coordinating editor, Carol Haralson. Tulsa: Philbrook Museum of Art; c1987. 289 p.
87-050325 745/.0973 0866590064
Decorative arts -- United States -- History -- 20th century.

NK808.R6 1990
Rosenak, Chuck.
Museum of American Folk Art encyclopedia of twentieth-century American folk art and artists/ Chuck and Jan Rosenak; contributors, Robert Bishop, Barbara Cate, Lee Kogan. New York: Abbeville Press, c1990. 416 p.
90-043923 709/.2/2730904 1558590412
Folk art -- United States -- History -- 20th century -- Dictionaries. Folk artists -- United States -- Biography -- Dictionaries.

NK835.N5 G38 1994
Gavin, Robin Farwell.
Traditional arts of Spanish New Mexico: the Hispanic Heritage Wing at the Museum of International Folk Art/ by Robin Farwell Gavin. Santa Fe: Museum of New Mexico Press, c1994. viii, 96 p.
93-048863   0890132585
Decorative arts, Spanish colonial -- New Mexico -- Catalogs. Hispanic American decorative arts -- New Mexico -- Catalogs. Decorative arts -- New Mexico -- Santa Fe -- Catalogs.

NK835.P4.L5 1963
Lichten, Frances.
Folk art of rural Pennsylvania. New York, Scribner [1963, c1946] xiv, 276 p.
63-004600
Folk art -- Pennsylvania. Decorative arts -- Pennsylvania.

NK928.R56 1984
Rococo: art and design in Hogarth's England: 16 May-30 September 1984, the Victoria and Albert Museum. [London]: Trefoil Books: [c1984] 333 p.
85-165949   709/.42/07402134   086294046X
Decorative arts, Rococo -- England -- Exhibitions. Decorative arts -- England -- History -- 18th century -- Exhibitions. Art, Rococo -- England -- Exhibitions.

NK947.T76 1991
Troy, Nancy J.
Modernism and the decorative arts in France: art Nouveau to Le Corbusier/ Nancy J. Troy. New Haven: Yale University Press, c1991. xx, 300 p.
90-040881   745/.0944/09041   0300045549
Decorative arts -- France -- History -- 19th century. Decorative arts -- France -- History -- 20th century. Modernism (Art) -- France.

NK951.C35
Campbell, Joan, 1929-
The German Werkbund: the politics of reform in the applied arts/ by Joan Campbell. Princeton, N.J.: Princeton University Press, c1978. xii, 350 p.
77-071974   745/.06/243   0691052506
Decorative arts -- Germany.

NK975.R35 1990
Razina, T. M.
Folk art in the Soviet Union/ Tatyana Razina, Natalia Cherkasova, Alexander Kantsedikas; [translated from the Russian by Ruslan Smirnov]. New York: Harry N. Abrams; 1990. 459 p.
86-026497   745/.0947   0810909448
Folk art -- Soviet Union.

NK979.Z313
Zahle, Erik, 1898-
A treasury of Scandinavian design; [the standard authority on Scandinavian-designed furniture, textiles, glass, ceramics, and metal] New York, Golden Press [c1961] 299 p.
63-009343   745.0948
Decorative arts -- Scandinavia. Decorative arts -- Finland.

NK1047.B37 1993
Barnard, Nicholas.
Arts and crafts of India/ Nicholas Barnard; photographs by Robyn Beeche. London: Conran Octopus, 1993. 192 p.
94-177617   745/.0954   1850295042
Decorative arts -- India. Handicraft -- India.

NK1051.6.B3.G53 1997
Glassie, Henry H.
Art and life in Bangladesh/ Henry Glassie; photography, drawings, and design by the author. Bloomington: Indiana University Press, 1997. 511 p.
96-006518   745/.095492   0253332915
Folk art -- Bangladesh. Bangladesh -- Social life and customs.

NK1068.S596 1995
So, Jenny F.
Traders and raiders on China's northern frontier/ Jenny F. So and Emma C. Bunker. Seattle: Arthur M. Sackler Gallery, Smithsonian Institution, in association with University of Washington Press, c1995. 203 p.
95-018910   745/.0931   0295974737
Decorative arts -- China -- History -- To 221 B.C. Decorative arts -- China -- History -- Chin-Han dynasties, 221 B.C.-220 A.D.

NK1073.5.K52
Kim, Chewon, 1909-
Treasures of Korean art; 2000 years of ceramics, sculpture, and jeweled arts. Text by Chewon Kim and Won-Yong Kim. New York, H. N. Abrams [1966] xv, 283 p.
66-023402   709.519
Art objects, Korean. Pottery -- Korea. Art, Buddhist -- Korea.

NK1141 Arts and crafts movement — History — United States

NK1141.A78 1993
The arts and crafts movement in California: living the good life/ [edited by] Kenneth R. Trapp; with essays by Leslie Greene Bowman ... [et al.]. Oakland, Calif.: Oakland Museum; c1993. 328 p.
92-028352   745/.09794/09034   1558593934
Arts and crafts movement -- California -- History -- 19th century. Arts and crafts movement -- California -- History -- 20th century.

NK1141.B64 1990
Bowman, Leslie Greene.
American arts & crafts: virtue in design/ Leslie Greene Bowman. Los Angeles, Calif.: Los Angeles County Museum of Art; c1990. 255 p.
90-038064   745/.0973/07479494   0821218247
Palevsky, Max -- Art collections -- Exhibitions. Evans, Jodie -- Art collections -- Exhibitions. Arts and crafts movement -- United States -- Exhibitions. Decorative arts -- United States -- History -- 19th century -- Exhibitions. Decorative arts -- Private collections -- California -- Los Angeles -- Exhibitions.

NK1141.C55 1972
Clark, Robert Judson.
The arts and crafts movement in America, 1876-1916; an exhibition organized by the Art Museum, Princeton University and the Art Institute of Chicago. Edited by Robert Judson Clark. With texts by the editor and others. [Princeton, N.J.] distributed by Princeton University Press [1972] 190 p.
72-077734   745/.0973/074013   069103883X
Decorative arts -- United States -- Exhibitions. Arts and crafts movement.

NK1141.I33 1993
The Ideal home 1900-1920: the history of twentieth-century American craft/ Janet Kardon, editor; with essays by Eileen Boris ... [et al.]. New York: H.N. Abrams in association with the American Craft, 1993. 304 p.
93-003121   745/.0973/09041   0810934671
Arts and crafts movement -- United States. Decorative arts -- United States -- History -- 20th century. Interior decoration -- United States -- History -- 20th century.

NK1165 Decoration and ornament.
Design — Dictionaries

NK1165.E48 1997
Encyclopedia of interior design/ editor, Joanna Banham; picture editor, Leanda Shrimpton. London; Fitzroy Dearborn Publishers, c1997. 2 v.
97-149314   1884964192
Interior decoration -- Encyclopedias. Interior decoration -- History -- Encyclopedias.

NK1175 Decoration and ornament.
Design — History — General works

NK1175.A8
Aslin, Elizabeth.
The aesthetic movement; prelude to Art nouveau. New York, Praeger [1969] 192 p.
76-084860   709/.03
Arts and crafts movement -- Great Britain. Aesthetic movement (British art)

NK1382-1396 Decoration and ornament.
Design — History — Modern

NK1382.M63.D86 1998
Duncan, Alastair, 1942-
Modernism: modernist design 1880-1940: the Norwest collection, Norwest Corporation, Minneapolis/ text by Alastair Duncan. Woodbridge, Suffolk, England: Antique Collectors' Club, c1998. 275 p.
00-701294   745/.09/041074776579   1851492747
Design -- History -- 19th century. Design -- History -- 20th century. Decorative arts -- History -- 19th century.

NK1390.B3 1988
Battersby, Martin.
The decorative Thirties.   New York, Walker [1971] 208 p.
70-159516   745.4/442   0802703534
Decorative arts -- History -- 20th century. Decoration and ornament -- History -- 20th century.

NK1390.D67 1990
Dormer, Peter.
The meanings of modern design: towards the twenty-first century/ Peter Dormer. New York, N.Y.: Thames and Hudson, 1990. 192 p.
89-051583   745.4/442   0500235708
Design -- History -- 20th century -- Economic aspects. Design, Industrial -- History -- 20th century -- Economic aspects.

NK1390.H44 1993
Hiesinger, Kathryn B., 1943-
Landmarks of twentieth-century design: an illustrated handbook/ by Kathryn B. Hiesinger and George H. Marcus. New York: Abbeville Press, c1993. 431 p.
93-000180   745.4/442   1558592792
Design -- History -- 20th century -- Themes, motives. Design, Industrial -- History -- 20th century -- Themes, motives.

NK1390.J85 1993
Julier, Guy.
The Thames and Hudson encyclopaedia of 20th century design and designers/ Guy Julier. New York, N.Y.: Thames and Hudson, 1993. 216 p.
93-060123   745.4/442/03   0500202699
Design -- History -- 20th century -- Dictionaries. Designers -- Biography -- Dictionaries.

NK1390.M54 1990
Miller, R. Craig.
Modern design in the Metropolitan Museum of Art, 1890-1990/ R. Craig Miller; photographs by Mark Darley. New York: The Museum: 1990. xiii, 312 p.
90-006293   745/.09/040747471   0870995987
Design -- History -- 20th century.

NK1390.P53 1990
Pile, John F.
Dictionary of 20th-century design/ John Pile. New York: Facts on File, c1990. viii, 312 p.
89-077863   745.4/442/03   0816018111
Design -- History -- 20th century -- Dictionaries.

NK1390.W59 1997
Woodham, Jonathan M.
Twentieth century design/ Jonathan M. Woodham. Oxford; Oxford University Press, 1997. 288 p.
96-047594   745.2/09/04   0192842471
Design -- History -- 20th century.

NK1394.D47 1991
Design 1935-1965: what modern was: selections from the Liliane and David M. Stewart Collection/ edited by Martin Eidelberg; essay by Paul Johnson; contributors, Kate Carmel ... [et al.]. Montreal: Musee des arts decoratifs de Montreal; 1991. 424 p.
90-046962   745/.09/0407471428   0810932059
Stewart, David M. -- Art collections -- Exhibitions. Stewart, Liliane -- Art collections -- Exhibitions. Decorative arts -- History -- 20th century -- Exhibitions. Decoration and ornament -- International style -- Exhibitions. Decorative arts -- Private collections -- Quebec (Province) -- Montreal -- Exhibitions.

NK1396.P66.C65 1989
Collins, Michael, 1950-
Post-modern design/ Michael Collins & Andreas Papadakis. New York: Rizzoli, 1989. 288 p.
89-061361   745.4/442   0847811360
   Design -- History -- 20th century. Postmodernism.

NK1396.P66.D47 1988
Design after modernism: beyond the object/ edited by John Thackara. New York, N.Y.: Thames and Hudson, 1988. 240 p.
87-051020   745.4/442   0500234833
   Design -- History -- 20th century. Postmodernism.

NK1403.5-1457 Decoration and ornament. Design — History — Special countries

NK1403.5.H4 1992
Heckscher, Morrison H.
American rococo, 1750-1775: elegance in ornament/ Morrison H. Heckscher, Leslie Greene Bowman. New York: Metropolitan Museum of Art; c1992. xv, 288 p.
91-029595   745.4/4974/090330747471   0870996304
   Decoration and ornament, Rococo -- United States -- Exhibitions. Decoration and ornament -- United States -- History -- 18th century -- Exhibitions.

NK1404.J65 2000
Johnson, J. Stewart.
American modern, 1925-1940: design for a new age/ by J. Stewart Johnson. New York: Harry N. Abrams, Inc. in association with the American Federation of Arts, 2000. 192 p.
99-053254   745/.0973/0747471   0810942089
   Decorative arts -- New York (State) -- New York -- Exhibitions. Decorative arts -- United States -- History -- 20th century -- Exhibitions.

NK1404.P85 1988
Pulos, Arthur J.
The American design adventure, 1940-1975/ Arthur J. Pulos. Cambridge, Mass.: MIT Press, c1988. vii, 446 p.
87-026266   745.2/0973   0262161060
   Design, Industrial -- United States -- History -- 20th century.

NK1412.E18.K57 1995
Kirkham, Pat.
Charles and Ray Eames: designers of the twentieth century/ Pat Kirkham. Cambridge, Mass.: MIT Press, c1995. x, 486 p.
94-024920   745.4/4922   0262111993
Eames, Charles. Eames, Ray. Designers -- United States -- Biography.

NK1412.N45.A24 1995
Abercrombie, Stanley.
George Nelson: the design of modern design/ Stanley Abercrombie; foreword by Ettore Sottsass, Jr.; appendixes compiled by Judith Nasatir. Cambridge, Mass.: MIT Press, c1995. xx, 353 p.
94-013536   745.4/492   0262011425
Nelson, George, -- 1908-   Designers -- United States -- Biography.

NK1443.A1.G47 1994
Gere, Charlotte.
Nineteenth-century design from Pugin to Mackintosh/ Charlotte Gere and Michael Whiteway. New York: Abrams, 1994. 312 p.
93-005092   745.4/441   0810936720
   Design -- Great Britain -- History -- 19th century. Design -- Great Britain -- History -- 20th century. Design -- United States -- History -- 19th century.

NK1449.A1.G76 2001
Groom, Gloria Lynn.
Beyond the easel: decorative paintings by Bonnard, Vuillard, Denis, and Roussel, 1890-1930/ by Gloria Groom; with an essay by Nicolas Watkins and contributions by Jennifer Paoletti and Therese Barruel. Chicago: Art Institute of Chicago; c2001. xiii, 289 p.
00-043970   759.4/074/7471   0300089252
   Decoration and ornament -- France -- History -- 19th century -- Exhibitions. Decoration and ornament -- France -- History -- 20th century -- Exhibitions. Symbolism in art -- France -- Exhibitions.

NK1457.S35 1982
Scandinavian modern design, 1880-1980/ Cooper-Hewitt Museum; David Revere McFadden, general editor. New York: Abrams, 1982. 287 p.
82-008899   745.4/4948   0810916436
   Design -- Scandinavia -- History -- 19th century -- Exhibitions. Design -- Scandinavia -- History -- 20th century -- Exhibitions.

NK1505 Decoration and ornament. Design — Theory of ornament and design

NK1505.A38 2000
Albers, Anni.
Anni Albers: selected writings on design/ edited and with an introduction by Brenda Danilowitz; foreword by Nicholas Fox Weber. Hanover: University Press of New England, c2000. xiii, 79 p.
00-010582   701/.8   0819564478
   Design -- Philosophy. Decoration and ornament -- Philosophy.

NK1535 Decoration and ornament. Design — Collections of designs — Special artists, A-Z

NK1535.E25.N48 1989
Neuhart, John.
Eames design: the work of the Office of Charles and Ray Eames/ John Neuhart, Marilyn Neuhart, Ray Eames. New York: H.N. Abrams, 1989. 456 p.
89-000169   745.4/4922   0810908794
Design -- United States -- History -- 20th century.

NK1535.E25.W67 1997
The work of Charles and Ray Eames: a legacy of invention/ essays by Donald Albrecht ... [et al.]. New York: Harry N. Abrams in association with the Library of Congress and the Vitra Design Museum, 1997. 205 p.
97-004086   745.4/4922   0810917998
Eames, Charles -- Criticism and interpretation. Eames, Ray -- Criticism and interpretation. Design -- United States -- History -- 20th century.

NK1535.M86.T3613 1987
Tanchis, Aldo, 1955-
Bruno Munari: design as art/ Aldo Tanchis; [translated from the Italian by Huw Evans]. Cambridge, Mass.: MIT Press, 1987, c1986. 137 p.
87-015272   709/.2/4   0262200651
Munari, Bruno -- Criticism and interpretation. Design -- Italy -- History -- 20th century.

NK2003-2049 Interior decoration. House decoration — History and styles — Special countries

NK2003.S9
Sweeney, John A. H.
The treasure house of early American rooms. Photos. by Gilbert Ask. Introd. by Henry Francis du Pont. New York, Viking Press [1963] 179 p.
63-015585   747.213
Furniture. Decorative arts -- United States. Interior decoration -- United States.

NK2043.G45 1989
Gere, Charlotte.
Nineteenth-century decoration: the art of the interior/ Charlotte Gere. New York: H.N. Abrams, 1989. 408 p.
89-000158   747.2/048   0810913828
Interior decoration -- Great Britain -- History -- 19th century. Decoration and ornament -- Great Britain -- History -- 19th century. Decoration and ornament, Architectural -- Great Britain -- History -- 19th century.

NK2049.P37.S33 1995
Scott, Katie, 1958-
The rococo interior: decoration and social spaces in early eighteenth-century Paris/ Katie Scott. New Haven: Yale University Press, c1995. ix, 342 p.
95-011085   747/.888/094436109033   0300045824
Interior decoration -- France -- Paris -- History -- 18th century. Decoration and ornament, Rococo -- France -- Paris.

NK2110 Interior decoration. House decoration — General works — 1850-

NK2110.P55 1988
Pile, John F.
Interior design/ by John F. Pile. New York: H.N. Abrams, 1988. 541 p.
87-001179   729   0810911213
Interior decoration.

NK2110.W5 1978
Wharton, Edith, 1862-1937.
The decoration of houses/ Edith Wharton and Ogden Codman, Jr.; introductory notes by John Barrington Bayley and William A. Coles. New York: Norton, 1978. xlix, 204 p.
78-017020   747/.8/8   0393044688
Interior decoration.

NK2205 Furniture — Dictionaries. Encyclopedias

NK2205.D5 2001
Dictionary of furniture/ [edited by] Charles Boyce. New York: Facts on File, c2001. xxii, 376 p.
00-035334   749/.03   0816042292
Furniture -- Dictionaries.

NK2270 Furniture — History — General works

NK2270.B63 1969
Boger, Louise Ade.
The complete guide to furniture styles.   New York, Scribner [1969] xii, 500 p.
73-085267   749.2
Furniture -- Styles.

NK2270.L82 1979
Lucie-Smith, Edward.
Furniture: a concise history/ Edward Lucie-Smith. New York: Oxford University Press, 1979. 216 p.
79-004393   749.2   0195201450
Furniture -- History.

NK2395 Furniture — History — Modern

NK2395.H34 1989
Habegger, Jerryll, 1944-
Sourcebook of modern furniture/ Jerryll Habegger, Joseph H. Osman. New York, N.Y.: Van Nostrand Reinhold, c1989. xxiii, 469 p.
88-010895   749.2/049   0442232764
Furniture -- History -- 20th century -- Catalogs. Architect-designed furniture -- History -- 20th century -- Catalogs. Furniture designers -- Catalogs.

NK2406-2685 Furniture — History — Special countries

NK2406.C58
Comstock, Helen.
American furniture: seventeenth, eighteenth, and nineteenth century styles/ Helen Comstock. New York: Bonanza, [1962] 336 p.
62-018074   749.211
Furniture, American -- History.

NK2406.G74 1996
Greene, Jeffrey P.
American furniture of the 18th century/ Jeffrey P. Greene. Newtown, CT: Taunton Press, c1996. 311 p.
96-012859   749/.213/09033   1561581046
Furniture -- United States -- History -- 18th century. Furniture -- United States -- History -- 19th century.

NK2407.B43 1998
Becksvoort, Christian.
The Shaker legacy: perspectives on an enduring furniture style/ Christian Becksvoort; photographs by John Sheldon. Newtown, Conn.: Taunton Press, c1998. 233 p.
98-006987   749.213/088/288   1561582182
Skaker furniture.

NK2407.R54 1993
Rieman, Timothy D.
The complete book of Shaker furniture/ Timothy D. Rieman, Jean M. Burks. New York: H.N. Abrams, 1993. 400 p.
92-047357   749.213/08/8288   0810938413
Shaker furniture.

NK2438.W37
Monkman, Betty C.
The White House: its historic furnishings and first families/ by Betty C. Monkman; principal photography by Bruce White. Washington, D.C.: White House Historical Association; c2000. 320 p.
00-027085   917.5304/41   0789206242
Furniture -- United States -- Washington, D.C. -- History.

NK2439.H43.A4 1994
Herter Brothers: furniture and interiors for a gilded age/ Katherine S. Howe ... [et. al.]. New York: Harry N. Abrams in association with the Museum of Fine Arts, Houston, c1994. 272 p.
94-070768   749.213   0810934264
Furniture -- United States -- History -- 19th century -- Exhibitions. Interior decoration -- United States -- History -- 19th century -- Exhibitions.

NK2685.75.S53
Sieber, Roy, 1923-
African furniture and household objects/ Roy Sieber. Bloomington: Indiana University Press, c1980. 279 p.
79-005340   749.2/967/074013   0253119278
Furniture -- Africa, Sub-Saharan -- Exhibitions. House furnishings -- Africa, Sub-Saharan -- Exhibitions.

NK2715 Furniture — Special articles of furniture — Chairs. Miniature chairs

NK2715.K36 1976
Kane, Patricia E.
300 years of American seating furniture: chairs and beds from the Mabel Brady Garvan and other collections at Yale University/ Patricia E. Kane. Boston: New York Graphic Society, c1976. 319 p.
78-017892   749/.3   0821206788
Chairs -- United States -- Catalogs. Beds -- United States -- Catalogs.

NK2883 Rugs. Carpets — Other countries

NK2883.R67 1983
Rostov, Charles I.
Chinese carpets/ by Charles I. Rostov and Jia Guanyan, with Li Linpan and Zhang H.Z. New York: Abrams, 1983. 223 p.
83-003836   746.7/51   0810907852
Rugs -- China.

NK3049 Tapestries. Wall hangings — History — Special countries

NK3049.B3.B44 1987
Bernstein, David J.
The mystery of the Bayeux tapestry/ David J. Bernstein. Chicago: University of Chicago Press, 1987, c1986. 272 p.
86-030864   746.3942   0226044009
Bayeux tapestry. Hastings, Battle of, 1066, in art. Great Britain -- History -- William I, 1066-1087 -- Historiography.

NK3049.U5.N43 1976
Cloisters (Museum)
The unicorn tapestries/ Margaret B. Freeman, Curator Emeritus, The Cloisters. New York: Metropolitan Museum of Art: distributed by Dutton, 1976. 244 p.
76-002466   746.3/94   0870991477
Tapestry, Medieval -- France. Tapestry, Gothic -- France. Hunt of the unicorn (Tapestries)

NK3400 Wallpapers — History — General works

NK3400.P37 1994
The papered wall: history, pattern, technique/ edited by Lesley Hoskins. New York: Abrams, 1994. 256 p.
94-010915   676/.2848/09   0810937301
Wallpaper -- History. Wallpaper -- Themes, motives. Wallpaper -- Technique.

NK3610-3620 Other arts and art industries — Alphabets. Calligraphy. Initials — Roman

NK3610.K46 1999
Kendrick, Laura.
Animating the letter: the figurative embodiment of writing from late antiquity to the Renaissance/ Laura Kendrick. Columbus, Ohio: Ohio State University Press, c1999. ix, 326 p.
99-019159   302.2/244/0902   0814208223
Initials. Illumination of books and manuscripts, Medieval.

NK3620.M56 1980
Modern scribes and lettering artists.   New York: Taplinger Pub. Co., 1980. 160 p.
80-050362   745.6/197/09047   0800852974
Calligraphy. Lettering.

NK3634 Other arts and art industries — Alphabets. Calligraphy. Initials — Non-Roman

NK3634.A2.K73 1991
Kraus, Richard Curt.
Brushes with power: modern politics and the Chinese art of calligraphy/ Richard Curt Kraus. Berkeley: University of California Press, c1991. xii, 208 p.
90-023590   745.6/19951   0520072855
Calligraphy, Chinese -- Political aspects.   China -- Cultural policy.

NK3780-4166 Other arts and art industries — Ceramics — History

NK3780.C37 1992
Ceramics of the world: from 4000 B.C. to the present/ general editors, Lorenzo Camusso and Sandro Bortone. New York: H.N. Abrams, Inc., 1992. 399 p.
91-029808   738/.09   0810931753
Pottery -- History. Porcelain -- History.

NK3780.C663 1999
Cooper, Emmanuel.
Ten thousand years of pottery/ Emmanuel Cooper Philadelphia: University of Pennsylvania Press, 1999. 352 p.
99-049100   738/.09   0812235541
Pottery -- History.

NK3780.M86 1998
Munsterberg, Hugo, 1916-
World ceramics: from prehistoric to modern times/ Hugo and Marjorie Munsterberg. New York: Penguin Studio Books, c1998. 191 p.
98-018836   738/.09
Pottery -- History. Porcelain -- History.

NK3780.R53 1987
Rice, Prudence M.
Pottery analysis: a sourcebook/ Prudence M. Rice. Chicago: University of Chicago Press, c1987. xxiv, 559 p.
86-024958   738   0226711188
Pottery -- History. Pottery -- Expertising. Pottery -- Analysis.

NK3780.V56 1999
Vincentelli, Moira.
Women and ceramics: gendered vessels/ Moira Vincentelli. New York: Manchester University Press, 1999.
99-043120   738/.082   0719038391
Pottery -- History. Women potters.

NK3840.S65 1991
Sparkes, Brian A.
Greek pottery: an introduction/ Brian A. Sparkes. Manchester; Manchester University Press; c1991. xii, 186 p.
91-017266   666/.3938   0719022363
Pottery, Greek.

NK3930.P4 2000b
Peterson, Susan, 1925-
Contemporary ceramics/ Susan Peterson. New York: Watson-Guptill Publications, 2000. 176 p.
00-100543   738/.09/045   0823009378
Art pottery -- 20th century -- Pictorial works. Ceramic sculpture -- 20th century -- Pictorial works.

NK4005.E94 1989
Everson Museum of Art.
American ceramics: the collection of Everson Museum of Art/ edited by Barbara Perry. New York: Rizzoli; 1989. 400 p.
88-031282   738/.0973/074014766   0847810259
Pottery -- New York (State) -- Syracuse -- Catalogs. Porcelain, American -- Catalogs. Porcelain -- New York (State) -- Syracuse -- Catalogs.

NK4005.L48 1988
Levin, Elaine.
The history of American ceramics, 1607 to the present: from pipkins and bean pots to contemporary forms/ by Elaine Levin. New York: H.N. Abrams, c1988. 351 p.
88-003332   738/.0973   0810911728
Pottery, American.

NK4007.C56 1987
Clark, Garth, 1947-
American ceramics, 1876 to the present/ Garth Clark. New York: Abbeville Press, c1987. 351 p.
87-001177   738/.0973   0896597431
Pottery, American. Pottery -- 19th century -- United States. Pottery -- 20th century -- United States.

NK4008.C47 1981
Ceramic sculpture: six artists/ Richard Marshall and Suzanne Foley. New York: Whitney Museum of American Art; c1981. 144 p.
81-014703   730/.0973/07401471   0874270359
Ceramic sculpture -- California -- Exhibitions. Pottery -- 20th century -- California -- Exhibitions.

NK4008.L67 1990
Los Angeles County Museum of Art.
Clay today: contemporary ceramists and their work: a catalogue of the Howard and Gwen Laurie Smits Collection at the Los Angeles County Museum of Art/ Martha Drexler Lynn. Los Angeles, Calif.: The Museum; c1990. 239 p.
89-013731   730/.0973/07479494   0877017565
Smits, Howard -- Art collections -- Catalogs. Smits, Gwen Laurie -- Art collections -- Catalogs. Ceramic sculpture -- 20th century -- United States -- Catalogs. Ceramic sculpture -- 20th century -- England -- Catalogs. Ceramic sculpture -- Private collections -- California -- Los Angeles -- Catalogs.

NK4165.M39 1976b
Medley, Margaret.
The Chinese potter: a practical history of Chinese ceramics/ Margaret Medley. New York: Scribner, c1976. 288 p.
76-006023   738/.0951   0684146843
Pottery, Chinese -- History. Porcelain, Chinese -- History.

NK4165.V3 1991
Vainker, S. J.
Chinese pottery and porcelain: from prehistory to the present/ S.J. Vainker. New York: George Braziller, 1991. 240 p.
90-024330   738/.0951   080761260X
Pottery, Chinese. Porcelain, Chinese.

NK4166.T95.M56
Mino, Yutaka.
Freedom of clay and brush through seven centuries in northern China: Tzu-chou type wares, 960-1600 A.D.: Indianapolis Museum of Art, November 17, 1980-January 18, 1981, China House Gallery, New Yo Yutaka Mino; catalogue with the assistance of Katherine R. Tsiang. Indianapolis: Indianapolis Museum of Art; c1980. 264 p.
80-008642   738.3/7   0253131707
Tzu ware -- Exhibitions. Pottery, Chinese -- Sung-Yuan dynasties, 960-1368 -- Exhibitions. Pottery, Chinese -- Ming-Ching dynasties, 1368-1912 -- Exhibitions.

NK4210 Other arts and art industries — Ceramics — Individual potters, families, and firms, A-Z

NK4210.B5.A4 1998
Carney, Margaret, 1949-
Charles Fergus Binns: the father of American studio ceramics: including a catalogue raisonne/ Margaret Carney; with essays by Paul Evans, Susan Strong, Richard Zakin. New York: Hudson Hills Press, c1998. 254 p.
97-046898   738/.092   1555951449
Binns, Charles Fergus, -- 1857-1934 -- Exhibitions. Art pottery -- New York (State) -- Exhibitions.

NK4210.M42.R44 1987
Reed, Cleota.
Henry Chapman Mercer and the Moravian Pottery and Tile Works/ Cleota Reed. Philadelphia: University of Pennsylvania Press, c1987. xxv, 255 p.
87-018941   738/.092/4   0812280768
Mercer, Henry Chapman, -- 1856-1930. Pottery, American. Pottery -- 20th century -- United States. Tiles -- United States -- History -- 20th century.

NK4210.O42.C5 1989
Clark, Garth, 1947-
The mad potter of Biloxi: the art & life of George E. Ohr/ Garth Clark, Robert A. Ellison, Jr., Eugene Hecht; photography by John White; special consultant, Martin Shack. New York: Abbeville Press, c1989. 192 p.
89-006978   738/.092   0896599272
Ohr, George E., -- 1857-1918 -- Criticism and interpretation. Pottery, American -- Mississippi -- Biloxi.

NK4210.S367.A4 1993
Lynn, Martha Drexler.
The clay art of Adrian Saxe/ Martha Drexler Lynn with a contribution by Jim Collins. Los Angeles: Los Angeles County Museum of Art, c1993. 160 p.
93-005654   730/.092   0500092389
Saxe, Adrian Anthony, -- 1943- -- Exhibitions. Ceramic sculpture -- 20th century -- California -- Exhibitions.

NK4215 Other arts and art industries — Ceramics — Potters' marks

NK4215.C46 1965
Chaffers, William, 1811-1892.
Marks & monograms on European and oriental pottery and porcelain. The British section edited by Geoffrey A. Godden. The European and oriental sections edited by Frederick Litchfield & R. L. Hobson. London, W. Reeves [1965] 2 v.
66-038182   738.0278
Pottery -- History. Pottery, Oriental. Porcelain -- History.

NK4360 Other arts and art industries — Ceramics — Stoneware (Grès de Flandres, Steinzeug, Steingut)

NK4360.R45
Rhodes, Daniel, 1911-
Stoneware & porcelain; the art of high-fired pottery. Philadelphia, Chilton Co., Book Division [1959] 217 p.
59-015040   738.14
Stoneware. Porcelain.

NK4605.5 Other arts and art industries — Ceramics — Decoration of pottery

NK4605.5.U63.C482 1996a
Sexual politics: Judy Chicago's Dinner party in feminist art history/ Amelia Jones, editor; with essays by Laura Cottingham ... [et al.]. [Los Angeles, CA]: UCLA at the Armand Hammer Museum of Art and Cultural Center in association with University of California Press, Berkeley, c1996. 264 p.
95-050772   709/.2   0520205650
Chicago, Judy, -- 1939- -- Dinner party -- Exhibitions. China painting -- United States -- Exhibitions. Needlework -- United States -- Exhibitions. Women in art -- Exhibitions.

NK4645-4695 Other arts and art industries — Ceramics — Special objects

NK4645.A69
Arias, Paolo Enrico.
A history of 1000 years of Greek vase painting. Text and notes by P.E. Arias. Photos, by Max Hirmer. [Translated and rev. by B. Shefton] New York, H.N. Abrams [1962] 410 p.
61-013857   738.382
Vases, Greek. Vase-painting, Greek.

NK4645.L66 1991
Looking at Greek vases/ edited by Tom Rasmussen and Nigel Spivey. Cambridge [England]; Cambridge University Press, 1991. xvii, 282 p.
90-002568   738.3/82/0938   052137524X
Vases, Greek.

NK4645.S47 1994
Shapiro, H. A. 1949-
Myth into art: poet and painter in classical Greece/ H.A. Shapiro. London; Routledge, 1994. xx, 196 p.
93-002262   738.3/82/0938   0415067928
Vase-painting, Greek. Mythology, Greek, in art. Ut pictura poesis (Aesthetics)

NK4670.7.A78.M5313 1996
Barry, Mike, 1948-
Design and color in Islamic architecture: eight centuries of the tile-maker's art/ photographs by Roland and Sabrina Michaud; text by Michael Barry. New York: Vendome Press, 1996. 315 p.
96-013602   738.6/0917/671   0865659753
Decoration and ornament, Architectural -- Asia. Architecture, Islamic -- Asia. Color in architecture -- Asia.

NK4695.T33.C58 2000
China and glass in America, 1880-1980: from tabletop to TV tray/ Charles L. Venable ... [et al.]; photography by Tom Jenkins. Dallas, Tex.: Dallas Museum of Art; c2000. 496 p.
99-059422   738/.074/7642812   0810966921
Ceramic tableware -- United States -- History -- 19th century -- Exhibitions. Ceramic tableware -- United States -- History -- 20th century -- Exhibitions. Ceramic tableware -- Social aspects -- United States -- History -- 19th century -- Exhibitions.

NK4998.5 Other arts and art industries — Enamel — Congresses. Yearbooks

NK4998.5.S6 1998
Speel, Erika.
Dictionary of enamelling/ Erika Speel. Brookfield, Vt.: Ashgate, c1998. xvi, 152 p.
97-023088   738.4   1859282725
Enamel and enameling -- Dictionaries.

NK5102 Other arts and art industries — Glass — Museums

NK5102.C65
Corning Museum of Glass.
The Corning Museum of Glass: a decade of glass collecting, 1990-1999/ by David Whitehouse. Corning, N.Y.: The Museum; c2000. 128 p.
99-085943   748/.074/74783   0810967103
Glassware -- New York (State) -- Corning -- Catalogs.

NK5106 Other arts and art industries — Glass — History

NK5106.G54 1991
Glass, 5,000 years/ edited by Hugh Tait. New York: H.N. Abrams, c1991. 256 p.
91-010629   748.29   0810933616
Glassware -- History.

NK5112 Other arts and art industries — Glass — United States

NK5112.C64
Steuben Glass, inc.
Poetry in crystal; interpretations in crystal of thirty-one new poems by contemporary American poets. New York, [1963] 86 p.
63-012592   748.2913
Glassware, American. American poetry -- 20th century.

NK5344 Other arts and art industries — Glass — Stained glass. Glass painting

NK5344.C3.C38
Caviness, Madeline Harrison, 1938-
The early stained glass of Canterbury Cathedral, circa 1175-1220/ Madeline Harrison Caviness. Princeton, N.J.: Princeton University Press, c1977. xix, 190 p.
77-010419   748.5/922/34   0691039275
Glass painting and staining, Gothic -- England -- Canterbury. Glass painting and staining -- England -- Canterbury. Christian art and symbolism -- Medieval, 500-1500.

NK5698 Other arts and art industries — Glyptic arts — Gems (Engraved stones)

NK5698.F3.S66 1979b
Snowman, A. Kenneth 1919-
Carl Faberge: goldsmith to the Imperial Court of Russia/ A. Kenneth Snowman. New York: Viking Press, c1979. 160 p.
79-063369   739.2/092/4   0670204862
Faberge, Peter Carl, -- 1846-1920.

NK5850 Other arts and art industries — Glyptic arts — Ivory carving. Ivories

NK5850.I9 1987
Ivory: an international history and illustrated survey. New York: Abrams, 1987. 352 p.
86-032126   736/.62/09   0810911183
Ivories -- History.

NK7106.4-7398 Other arts and art industries — Metalwork — Gold and silver. Plate. Jewelry

NK7106.4.S38.S39 1999
Scythian gold: treasures from ancient Ukraine/ Ellen D. Reeder, editor; with essays by Esther Jacobson ... [et al.]. New York: Harry Abrams in association with the Walters Art Gallery and the San Antonio Museum of Art, 1999. 352 p.
99-014769   739.2/273951/07473   0810944766
Goldwork -- Ukraine -- Kiev -- Exhibitions. Goldwork, Scythian -- Exhibitions. Decoration and ornament -- Animal forms -- Exhibitions.

NK7106.4.T45.A53 1998
Ancient gold: the wealth of the Thracians: treasures from the Republic of Bulgaria/ Ivan Marazov, general editor; with essays by Alexander Fol ... [et al.]; and photographs by Ivo Hadjimishev. New York: Harry N. Abrams, in association with the Trust for Museum Exhibitions, in cooperation with the Ministry of Culture of the Republic of Bulgaria, c1998. 256 p.
97-036226   739.2/0939/807473   0810919923
Goldwork, Thracian -- Exhibitions. Silverwork, Thracian -- Exhibitions. Bulgaria -- Antiquities -- Exhibitions.

NK7143.G55 1990
Glanville, Philippa.
Women silversmiths, 1685-1845: works from the collection of the National Museum of Women in the Arts/ Philippa Glanville, Jennifer Faulds Goldsborough. New York, N.Y.: Thame and Hudson, 1990. 176 p.
89-051744   739.2/3741/082   0500235783
Silverwork -- Great Britain -- History -- 19th century -- Exhibitions. Silverwork -- Ireland -- History -- 18th century -- Exhibitions. Silverwork -- Ireland -- History -- 19th century -- Exhibitions.

NK7303.3.W55 1994
Williams, Dyfri.
Greek gold: jewelry of the classical world/ Dyfri Williams and Jack Ogden. New York: Abrams, 1994. 256 p.
94-000108   739.2/2738/074   0810933888
Jewelry -- England -- London -- Exhibitions. Gold jewelry, Ancient -- Greece -- Exhibitions. Jewelry -- Russia (Federation) -- Saint Petersburg -- Exhibitions.

NK7398.F355.A4 1999
Purcell, Katherine.
Falize: a dynasty of jewelers/ Katherine Purcell. London; Thames and Hudson, c1999. 320 p.
99-070848   0500019118
Falize family.   Jewelry -- France -- History -- 20th century. Jewelry -- France -- History -- 19th century.

NK7398.F37
Loring, John.
Paulding Farnham: Tiffany's lost genius/ by John Loring. New York: H.N. Abrams, 2000. 151 p.
00-022807   739.27/092   0810935112
Farnham, Paulding, -- 1859-1927 -- Criticism and interpretation.   Jewelry -- United States -- Design -- History.

NK7983.22 Other arts and art industries — Metalwork — Bronzes. Gilt bronzes

NK7983.22.N48 1980
Metropolitan Museum of Art (New York, N.Y.)
The great bronze age of China: an exhibition from the People's Republic of China/ edited by Wen Fong; introductory essays by Ma Chengyuan ... [et al.]; catalogue by Robert W. Bagley, Jenny F. So, Maxwell K. Hearn. New York: Metropolitan Museum of Art, c1980. xv, 386 p.
79-027616   730/.0951/074013   0870992260
Bronzes, Chinese -- To 221 B.C. -- Exhibitions. Bronzes, Chinese -- Chin-Han dynasties, 221 B.C.-220 A.D. -- Exhibitions. Terra-cotta sculpture, Chinese -- Chin-Han dynasties, 221 B.C.-220 A.D. -- Exhibitions.

NK8804 Other arts and art industries — Textile arts and art needlework — General. Collectors' manuals

NK8804.B5
Birrell, Verla Leone, 1903-
The textile arts, a handbook of fabric structure and design processes: ancient and modern weaving, braiding, printing, and other textile techniques. New York, Harper [1959] 514 p.
58-008363   746
Textile fabrics.

NK8806 Other arts and art industries — Textile arts and art needlework — History

NK8806.T45 1993
Textiles, 5,000 years: an international history and illustrated survey/ edited by Jennifer Harris. New York: H.N. Abrams, 1993. 320 p.
93-016980   746/.09   0810938758
Textile fabrics -- History.

NK8898 Other arts and art industries — Textile arts and art needlework — Special artists, A-Z

NK8898.M67.P37 1983
Parry, Linda.
William Morris textiles/ Linda Parry. New York: Viking Press, c1983. 192 p.
82-070184   747.22   0670770752
Morris, William, -- 1834-1896 -- Contributions in decorative arts. Textile fabrics -- England -- History -- 19th century.

NK8950 Other arts and art industries — Textile arts and art needlework — Woven fabrics

NK8950.B47.W46 1993
Weltge-Wortmann, Sigrid.
Women's work: textile art from the Bauhaus/ Sigrid Wortmann Weltge. San Francisco: Chronicle Books, 1993. 208 p.
93-019064   746/.082   0811804666
Women textile designers -- Germany -- Berlin -- Biography -- History and criticism. Textile fabrics -- Germany -- Berlin -- History -- 20th century.

NK8998-9212 Other arts and art industries — Textile arts and art needlework — Needlework

NK8998.L3.A2 1998
Larsen, Jack Lenor.
Jack Lenor Larsen: a weaver's memoir/ by Jack Lenor Larsen. New York: H.N. Abrams, 1998. 160 p.
98-012989   745.4/4/92   0810935899
Larsen, Jack Lenor. Men weavers -- United States -- Biography.

NK9104.H68 1991
Houck, Carter.
The quilt encyclopedia illustrated/ by Carter Houck; foreword by Robert Bishop and Elizabeth Warren. New York: H.N. Abrams in association with the Museum of American Folk Art, 1991. 192 p.
90-046201   746.9/7/03   0810934574
Quilts -- Dictionaries.

NK9112.F698 1990
Fox, Sandi.
Wrapped in glory: figurative quilts & bedcovers, 1700-1900/ Sandi Fox. New York: Thames and Hudson; 1990. 167 p.
90-070394   746.9/7/097307479494   050001499X
Quilts -- United States -- Exhibitions. Quilts -- England -- Exhibitions. Coverlets -- United States -- Exhibitions.

NK9198.R56.A4 1998
Dancing at the Louvre: Faith Ringgold's French collection and other story quilts/ Dan Cameron ... [et al.]; New Museum of Contemporary Art, New York. Berkeley, Calif.: University of California Press, c1998. ix, 167 p.
97-031079   746.46/092   0520214293
Ringgold, Faith -- Exhibitions. Afro-American quilts -- Exhibitions.

NK9212.S64 1991
Smith, Barbara Lee.
Celebrating the stitch: contemporary embroidery of North America/ Barbara Lee Smith. Newtown, CT: Taunton Press, c1991. x, 230 p.
91-008961   746.44/0973/09045   094239139X
Embroidery -- United States -- History -- 20th century -- Themes, motives. Embroidery -- Canada -- History -- 20th century -- Themes, motives.

NK9500 Other arts and art industries — Textile arts and art needlework — Textile decoration

NK9500.M45 1991
Meller, Susan.
Textile designs: two hundred years of European and American patterns for printed fabrics organized by motif, style, color, layout, and period/ Susan Meller, Joost Elffers; photographs by Ted Croner. New York: Harry N. Abrams, 1991. 464 p.
90-048073   746.6/2041   0810938537
Textile design -- Themes, motives. Textile printing.

NK9500.S87 1993
The Surface designer's art: contemporary fabric printers, painters, and dyers/ introduction by Katherine Westphal. Asheville, N.C., U.S.A.: Lark Books, 1993. 176 p.
92-042334   746.6   0937274674
Textile design -- History -- 20th century. Textile fabrics -- History -- 20th century. Textile designers -- Philosophy.

NK9798 Other arts and art industries — Woodwork — Wood carving

NK9798.T65.A93 1998
Ardery, Julia S., 1953-
The temptation: Edgar Tolson and the genesis of twentieth-century folk art/ Julia S. Ardery. Chapel Hill: University of North Carolina Press, c1998. x, 353 p.
97-023897   736/.4/092   080782397X
Tolson, Edgar, -- 1904-1984. Wood-carvers -- Kentucky -- Biography. Folk artists -- Kentucky -- Biography. Folk art -- United States -- History -- 20th century.

NX Arts in general

NX22 Societies. Councils —
United States — General

NX22.C46 1998
A century of arts & letters: the history of the National
Institute of Arts & Letters and the American Academy of
Arts & Letters as told, decade by decade, by eleven
members/ Louis Auchincloss ... [et al.]; John Updike,
editor. New York: Columbia University Press, c1998. xii,
346 p.
97-040940   700/.6/073   0231102488
*National Institute of Arts and Letters (U.S.) -- History. American
Academy and Institute of Arts and Letters -- History.*

NX60 Collected writings —
Several authors

NX60.L33
The Language of images/ edited by W. J. T. Mitchell.
Chicago: University of Chicago Press, c1980. 307 p.
80-005225   700   0226532151
   Arts.

NX65 Collected writings —
Individual authors

NX65.B37 1982
Barthes, Roland.
A Barthes reader/ edited, and with an introd. by Susan
Sontag. New York: Hill and Wang, c1982. xxxviii, 495 p.
80-026762   700   0809028158
   Arts -- Addresses, essays, lectures.

NX65.B696 1978
Bronowski, Jacob, 1908-1974.
The visionary eye: essays in the arts, literature, and
science/ J. Bronowski; selected and edited by Piero E.
Ariotti in collaboration with Rita Bronowski. Cambridge,
Mass.: MIT Press, c1978. x, 185 p.
78-018163   700   0262021293
   *Arts -- Addresses, essays, lectures. Science and the arts --
Addresses, essays, lectures. Imagination -- Addresses, essays,
lectures.*

NX110 Directories — United States

NX110.A767 2000
Artists communities: a directory of residences in the
United States that offer time and space for creativity/
introduction by Stanley Kunitz; edited by Tricia Snell;
Alliance of Artists' Communities. New York: Allworth
Press, c2000. xxxiii, 219 p.
99-058837   700.973   158115044X
   Artist colonies -- United States -- Directories.

NX165 Psychology of the arts and
the artist

NX165.A79
The Arts and cognition/ edited by David Perkins and
Barbara Leondar. Baltimore: Johns Hopkins University
Press, c1977. viii, 341 p.
76-017237   700/.1   0801818435
   Arts -- Psychological aspects. Cognition -- Psychology.

NX165.B35 1998
Belgrad, Daniel.
The culture of spontaneity: improvisation and the arts in
postwar America/ Daniel Belgrad. Chicago: University of
Chicago Press, 1998. xii, 343 p.
97-029793   700/.1/030973   0226041883
   *Improvisation in art. Arts, American. Arts, Modern -- 20th
century -- United States.*

NX165.L4513 1997
Levi-Strauss, Claude.
Look, listen, read/ Claude Levi Strauss; translated by
Brian C.J. Singer. New York: BasicBooks, c1997. v,
202 p.
96-051629   700/.1/9   0465068804
   Arts -- Psychological aspects. Artists -- Psychology.

NX165.W5 1982
Winner, Ellen.
Invented worlds: the psychology of the arts/ Ellen
Winner. Cambridge, Mass.: Harvard University Press,
1982. xvi, 431 p.
82-001020   700/.1/9   0674463609
   Arts -- Psychological aspects.

NX170 Interrelationships among the arts
in general — General works

NX170.M58 1994
Mitchell, W. J. Thomas, 1942-
Picture theory: essays on verbal and visual
representation/ W.J.T. Mitchell. Chicago: University of
Chicago Press, 1994. xv, 445 p.
93-034057   700/.1   0226532313
   Ut pictura poesis (Aesthetics) Arts, Modern. Postmodernism.

NX180 The arts in relation to other
subjects, A-Z

NX180.A77.S83 1994
The Subversive imagination: artists, society, and
responsibility/ edited by Carol Becker. New York:
Routledge, 1994. xx, 258 p.
93-036230   700/.1/03   0415905915
   Artists and community. Artists -- Psychology.

NX180.F4.B63 1994
Blair, Karen J.
The torchbearers: women and their amateur arts associations in America, 1890-1930/ Karen J. Blair. Bloomington: Indiana University Press, c1994. x, 259 p.
93-000485   700/.1/03   0253311926
Feminism and the arts -- United States -- History -- 19th century. Feminism and the arts -- United States -- History -- 20th century. Women -- United States -- Societies and clubs.

NX180.F4.L38 1984
Lauter, Estella, 1940-
Women as mythmakers: poetry and visual art by twentieth-century women/ Estella Lauter. Bloomington: Indiana University Press, c1984. xvii, 267 p.
83-048636   700/.88042   0253366062
Feminism and the arts. Women artists. Women poets.

NX180.F4.M37 1991
McCormick, Richard W., 1951-
Politics of the self: feminism and the postmodern in West German literature and film/ Richard W. McCormick. Princeton, N.J.: Princeton University Press, 1991. xii, 262 p.
90-047160   830.9/1/09045   0691068518
Feminism and the arts -- Germany (West) Postmodernism -- Germany (West)

NX180.M3.C37 1998
Carroll, Noel
A philosophy of mass art/ Noel Carroll. Oxford: Clarendon Press; 1998. xii, 425 p.
97-025934   700/.1/03   0198711298
Mass media and the arts. Popular culture.

NX180.S6.B56 1989
Blau, Judith R., 1942-
The shape of culture: a study of contemporary cultural patterns in the United States/ Judith R. Blau. Cambridge; Cambridge University Press, 1989. xii, 207 p.
89-000981   700/.1/030973   0521370981
Arts and society -- United States -- History -- 20th century. Popular culture -- United States.

NX180.S6.D58 2000
Dissanayake, Ellen.
Art and intimacy: how the arts began/ Ellen Dissanayake. Seattle, Wa: University of Washington Press, c2000. xvii, 265 p.
99-037639   701/.15   0295979119
Arts and society. Intimacy (Psychology)

NX180.S6.H3413 1982
Hauser, Arnold, 1892-1978.
The sociology of art/ Arnold Hauser; translated by Kenneth J. Northcott. Chicago: University of Chicago Press, 1982. xxi, 776 p.
81-013098   700/.1/03   0226319490
Arts and society.

NX180.S6.H5 1983
Hillier, Bevis, 1940-
The style of the century, 1900-1980/ Bevis Hillier. New York: Dutton, 1983. 239 p.
83-071008   700/.9/04   0525933018
Popular culture -- History -- 20th century. Arts, Modern -- 20th century. Civilization, Modern -- 20th century.

NX180.S6.K32 1993
Kalaidjian, Walter B., 1952-
American culture between the wars: revisionary modernism & postmodern critique/ Walter Kalaidjian. New York: Columbia University Press, c1993. xvi, 316 p.
93-015213   700/.1/03097309041   0231082789
Arts and society -- United States -- History -- 20th century. Feminism and the arts -- United States. Afro-American arts.

NX180.S6.K36 1989
Kaplan, Max, 1911-
The arts: a social perspective/ Max Kaplan. Rutherford, N.J.: Fairleigh Dickinson University Press, c1989.
88-046153   700/.1/03   0838633552
Arts and society.

NX212 Performance in the arts

NX212.B57 1998
Birringer, Johannes H.
Media & performance: along the border/ Johannes Birringer. Baltimore: Johns Hopkins Univesity Press, 1998. xxv, 381 p.
98-012702   700/.9/04   0801858518
Arts, Modern -- 20th century. Performance. Postmodernism.

NX303 Study and teaching. Research — History — Special countries

NX303.A724 1990
Artistic intelligences: implications for education/ edited by William J. Moody. New York: Teachers College Press, c1990. xii, 195 p.
90-042042   700/.7/073   0807730505
Arts -- Study and teaching -- United States -- Congresses. Students -- Intelligence levels -- United States -- Congresses. Creative thinking -- Congresses.

NX303.P52
Peterson's professional degree programs in the visual and performing arts. Princeton, NJ: Peterson's, [c1995-   ] 7 v.
95-660580   700/.71/173
Arts -- Study and teaching (Higher) -- United States -- Periodicals. Universities and colleges -- United States -- Directories -- Periodicals.

NX447.5 History of the arts — Chronological lists

NX447.5.B76 1994
Brownstone, David M.
Timelines of the arts and literature/ David Brownstone and Irene Franck. New York, NY: HarperCollins, c1994. vi, 711 p.
93-011603   700/.2/02   0062700693
Arts -- Chronology.

NX449.7-458 History of the arts — By period — Modern

NX449.7.G68.B76 1999
Brooks, Chris.
The Gothic revival/ Chris Brooks. London [England]: Phaidon Press, 1999. 447 p.
00-362452   700/.41   0714834807
Gothic revival (Art) Arts, Modern.

NX450.5.H8 1990
Hulse, Clark, 1947-
The rule of art: literature and painting in the Renaissance/ Clark Hulse. Chicago: University of Chicago Press, c1990. xv, 215 p.
89-039546   700/.9/024   0226360520
Arts, Renaissance.

NX450.5.P37 1980
Pater, Walter, 1839-1894.
The Renaissance: studies in art and poetry: the 1893 text/ Walter Pater; edited, with textual and explanatory notes, by Donald L. Hill. Berkeley: University of California Press, c1980. xxv, 489 p.
76-024582   700/.94   0520033256
Arts, Renaissance.

NX454.A8 1991
Ashton, Dore.
A fable of modern art/ Dore Ashton. Berkeley: University of California Press, c1991. 128 p.
90-020992   700/.9/04 20   0520073010
Balzac, Honoré de, 1799-1850. Le chef-d'œuvre inconnu -- Influence. Arts, Modern -- 19th century. Arts, Modern -- 20th century. Nature (Aesthetics)

NX456.A76 1991
The Arts: a history of expression in the 20th century/ edited by Ronald Tamplin. Oxford; Oxford University Press, 1991. 256 p.
90-052898   700/.9/04   0195208528
Arts, Modern -- 20th century -- History.

NX456.C3213 1992
Calabrese, Omar.
Neo-Baroque: a sign of the times/ Omar Calabrese; translated by Charles Lambert; with a foreword by Umberto Eco. Princeton, N.J.: Princeton University Press, c1992. xiv, 227 p.
91-044179   700/.9/04   0691031711
Arts, Modern -- 20th century -- Themes, motives. Arts, Modern -- 20th century -- Philosophy.

NX456.C534 1998
Chronology of twentieth-century history. edited by Frank N. Magill. Chicago Fitzroy Dearborn, 1998. 2 v.
98-192491   700/.9/04 21   1884964664
Arts, Modern -- 20th century. Arts and society -- History -- 20th century. Arts, Modern -- 20th century -- Chronology. Arts and society -- History -- 20th century -- Chronology.

NX456.M65 1991
Modernity and mass culture/ edited by James Naremore and Patrick Brantlinger. Bloomington: Indiana University Press, c1991. vi, 278 p.
90-041881   700/.1/030904   0253206278
Arts, Modern -- 20th century. Arts and society -- History -- 20th century.

NX456.O92 1997
Outsider art: contesting boundaries in contemporary culture/ edited by Vera L. Zolberg and Joni Maya Cherbo. Cambridge; Cambridge University Press, 1997. xiv, 218 p.
96-052184   700/.9/045   0521581117
Arts, Modern -- 20th century. Arts and society -- History -- 20th century. Outsider art.

NX456.P613
Poggioli, Renato, 1907-1963.
The theory of the avant-garde. Translated from the Italian by Gerald Fitzgerald. Cambridge, Mass., Belknap Press of Harvard University Press, 1968. xvii, 250 p.
68-017630   709.04
Arts -- History. Avant-garde (Aesthetics)

NX456.R59 1996
Robertson, Jack.
Twentieth-century artists on art: an index to writings, statements, and interviews by artists, architects, and designers/ Jack S. Robertson. New York: G.K. Hall; c1996. xvi, 834 p.
95-033700   016.7/0092/2   0816190593
Artists -- Indexes. Artists -- Interviews -- Indexes. Arts, Modern -- 20th century -- Indexes.

NX456.W66 1993
Wollen, Peter.
Raiding the icebox: reflections on twentieth-century culture/ Peter Wollen. Bloomington: Indiana University Press, c1993. viii, 222 p.
92-044592   700/.9/04   0253365872
Arts, Modern -- 20th century. Arts and society -- History -- 20th century. Culture.

NX456.5.D3.C75 1996
Crisis and the arts: the history of Dada/ Stephen C. Foster, editor. New York: G.K. Hall; [c1996-] v. 1-2
96-026622   700/.9/042   0816173540
Dadaism -- History. Arts, Modern -- 20th century -- History.

NX456.5.P66.A74 1984
Art after modernism: rethinking representation/ edited and with an introduction by Brian Wallis; foreword by Marcia Tucker. New York: New Museum of Contemporary Art; 1984. xviii, 461 p.
84-022708   700/.9/04   0879235632
Postmodernism -- Addresses, essays, lectures. Arts, Modern -- 20th century -- Addresses, essays, lectures.

NX456.5.P66.J46 1987
Jencks, Charles.
Post-modernism: the new classicism in art and architecture/ Charles Jencks. New York: Rizzoli, 1987. 360 p.
87-009481   700/.9/04   0847808351
Arts, Modern -- 20th century. Postmodernism.

NX456.5.P66.W66 1999
Woods, Tim.
Beginning postmodernism/ Tim Woods. Manchester; Manchester University Press, 1999.
99-048812   149/.97   0719052106
Postmodernism. Arts, Modern -- 20th century.

NX456.5.P7.T67 1990
Torgovnick, Marianna, 1949-
Gone primitive: savage intellects, modern lives/ Marianna Torgovnick. Chicago: University of Chicago Press, 1990. xi, 328 p.
89-020375   700   0226808319
Primitivism in art. Arts, Modern -- 20th century. Arts -- Psychological aspects.

NX456.5.S8.S92 1998
Surrealist women: an international anthology/ edited with introductions by Penelope Rosemont. Austin: University of Texas Press, 1998. lx, 516 p.
97-035357   700/.41163/082   029277088X
Surrealism. Arts, Modern -- 20th century. Women artists -- Psychology.

NX458.B87
Butler, Christopher.
After the wake: an essay on the contemporary avant-garde/ Christopher Butler. Oxford: Clarendon Press; 1980. xi, 177 p.
79-041663   700/.9/04   0198157665
Avant-garde (Aesthetics) Arts, Modern -- 20th century.

NX458.D38 1977
Davis, Douglas, 1933-
Artculture: essays on the post-modern/ Douglas Davis; introd. by Irving Sandler. New York: Harper & Row, c1977. xii, 176 p.
76-027504   700/.9/04   0064310000
Arts, Modern -- 20th century. Avant-garde (Aesthetics)

NX458.V58 1998
The visual culture reader/ edited, with introductions by Nicholas Mirzoeff. London; Routledge, 1998. xvi, 530 p.
99-188035   306.47 21   0415141346
Arts, Modern -- 20th century. Popular culture. Visual communication.

NX503-589 History of the arts — Special countries

NX503.A49 1993
American cultural leaders: from colonial times to the present/ Justin Harmon ... [et al.]; editors, Amy Lewis, Paula McGuire; consulting editors, Robert J. Clark, Richard M. Ludwig, Peter Westergaard. Santa Barbara, Calif.: ABC-CLIO, c1993. xviii, 550 p.
93-036284   700/.92/273   0874366739
Arts, American. Arts, Modern -- United States. Artists -- United States -- Biography -- Dictionaries.

NX503.7.C66 2000
Conron, John.
American picturesque/ John Conron. University Park, PA: Pennsylvania State University Press, c2000. xxiii, 363 p.
98-051056   700/.973/09034   0271019204
Arts, American. Arts, Modern -- 19th century -- United States. Picturesque, The.

NX503.7.E355 2000
Edwards, Holly.
Noble dreams, wicked pleasures: orientalism in America, 1870-1930/ Holly Edwards; with essays by Brian T. Allen ... [et al.]. Princeton, N.J.: Princeton University Press, 2000.
00-036685   704.9/4995   0691050031
Arts, American -- 19th century -- Exhibitions. Arts, American -- 20th century -- Exhibitions. Orientalism in art -- United States -- Exhibitions.

NX503.7.C64 1985
The Colonial revival in America/ edited by Alan Axelrod. New York: Norton, c1985. x, 377 p.
84-001092   700/.973   039301942X
Colonial revival (Art). Arts, Modern -- 19th century -- United States.

NX503.7.C78 1993
Crunden, Robert Morse.
American salons: encounters with European modernism, 1885-1917/ Robert M. Crunden. New York: Oxford University Press, 1993. xv, 493 p.
91-026718   700/.973/09034   0195065697
Modernism (Art) -- United States. Arts, American. Arts, Modern -- 19th century -- United States.

NX503.7.V36 1989
Vance, William L.
America's Rome/ William L. Vance. New Haven: Yale University Press, c1989. 2 v.
88-020737   700/.973   0300036701
Arts, American -- Italian influences. Arts, Modern -- 19th century -- United States. Arts, Modern -- 20th century -- United States. Rome (Italy) -- In art. Rome (Italy) -- Intellectual life -- 19th century. Rome (Italy) -- Intellectual life -- 20th century.

NX504.A87 1992
Ashton, Dore.
The New York school: a cultural reckoning/ by Dore Ashton. Berkeley: University of California Press, [1992] x, 246 p.
92-011669   700/.9747/10904 20   0520081064
New York school of art. Arts, American -- 20th century.

NX504.A89 1992
Auslander, Philip, 1956-
Presence and resistance: postmodernism and cultural politics in contemporary American performance/ Philip Auslander. Ann Arbor: University of Michigan Press, c1992. viii, 206 p.
92-026051   700/.973/09048   0472102990
Performance art -- United States. Arts and society -- United States -- History -- 20th century. Postmodernism -- United States.

NX504.C78 2000
Crunden, Robert Morse.
Body & soul: the making of American modernism/ Robert M. Crunden. New York: Basic Books, c2000. xvii, 475 p.
99-048435   700/.973/09041   0465014844
Arts, American -- 20th century. Modernism (Art) -- United States.

NX504.H36 1984
Haskell, Barbara.
Blam! the explosion of pop, minimalism, and performance, 1958-1964/ Barbara Haskell; with an essay on the American independent cinema by John G. Hanhardt. New York: Whitney Museum of American Art in association with W.W. Norton & Co., c1984. 160 p.
84-007304   700/.973/07401471   0874270006
Arts, American -- Exhibitions. Avant-garde (Aesthetics) -- United States -- History -- 20th century -- Exhibitions.

NX504.M44 1991
Melosh, Barbara.
Engendering culture: manhood and womanhood in New Deal public art and theater/ Barbara Melosh. Washington: Smithsonian Institution Press, c1991. xiii, 297 p.
90-009948   700/.973/09043   0874747201
Men in art. Women in art. Social realism.

NX504.M584 2000
A modern mosaic: art and modernism in the United States/ edited by Townsend Ludington; assistant editors, Thomas Fahy & Sarah P. Reuning. Chapel Hill: University of North Carolina Press, c2000. 439 p.
00-064843   709/.73/09041   0807825786
Modernism (Art) -- United States. Arts, American -- 20th century. Popular culture -- United States -- History -- 20th century.

NX504.P65 1991
Polcari, Stephen.
Abstract Expressionism and the modern experience/ Stephen Polcari. Cambridge [England]; Cambridge University Press, 1991. xxiii, 408 p.
90-049472   700/.973/0904   0521404533
Abstract expressionism -- United States. Arts, Modern -- 20th century -- United States.

NX504.S29 1989
Sayre, Henry M., 1948-
The object of performance: the American avant-garde since 1970/ Henry M. Sayre. Chicago: University of Chicago Press, 1989. xvi, 308 p.
88-027481   700/.973   0226735575
Performance art -- United States. Avant-garde (Aesthetics) -- United States -- History -- 20th century.

NX504.S57 1992
Siporin, Steve.
American folk masters: the National Heritage Fellows/ Steve Siporin; color photography by Michel Monteaux. New York: H.N. Abrams; 1992. 256 p.
91-040510   745/.092/273   0810919176
Folk artists -- United States -- Biography. Ethnic arts -- United States -- History -- 20th century.

NX504.W38 1991
Watson, Steven.
Strange bedfellows: the first American avant-garde/ Steven Watson. New York: Abbeville Press, c1991. 439 p.
90-047476   700/.973/09041   0896599345
Avant-garde (Aesthetics) -- United States -- History -- 20th century. Arts, American. Arts and society -- United States -- History -- 20th century.

NX509.A1
Wehr, Wesley, 1929-
The eighth lively art: conversations with painters, poets, musicians & the wicked witch of the west/ Wesley Wehr. Seattle: University of Washington Press, c2000. ix, 301 p.
00-021017   700/.9795   0295979569
Wehr, Wesley, -- 1929- -- Friends and associates. Artists -- Northwest, Pacific. Arts, American -- Northwest, Pacific -- 20th century.

NX510.C2
Reading California: art, image, and identity, 1900-2000/ edited by Stephanie Barron, Sheri Bernstein, Ilene Susan Fort; preface by Stephanie Barron. Los Angeles: Los Angeles County Museum of Art; c2000. 415 p.
00-055971   306.4/7/09794   0520227662
Arts, American -- California -- 20th century. California -- In art.

NX510.N43
Montano, Mary Caroline.
Tradiciones nuevomexicanas: Hispano arts and culture of New Mexico/ Mary Montano. Albuquerque: the University of New Mexico Press, c2001. viii, 374 p.
00-011474   700/.9789   0826321364
Arts, American -- New Mexico.

NX511.C45.A78 1996b
Art in Chicago, 1945-1995/ organized by Lynne Warren; essays by Jeff Abell ... [et al.]; with contributions from Monique Meloche and Dominic Molon. New York, N.Y.: Thames and Hudson; 1996. 312 p.
96-060369   050023728X
Arts, American -- Illinois -- Chicago -- Exhibitions. Arts, Modern -- 20th century -- Illinois -- Chicago -- Exhibitions. Arts and society -- Illinois -- Chicago -- History -- 20th century -- Exhibitions.

NX511.N4.B26 1993
Banes, Sally.
Greenwich Village 1963: avant-garde performance and
the effervescent body/ Sally Banes. Durham: Duke
University Press, 1993. ix, 308 p.
93-018393   700/.9747/1   082231357X
*Arts, American -- New York (State) -- New York. Arts, Modern
-- 20th century -- New York (State) -- New York. Popular culture
-- New York (State) -- New York.*

NX511.N4.L48 1981
Lewis, David L., 1936-
When Harlem was in vogue/ David Levering Lewis. New
York: Knopf: 1981. xiv, 381 p.
80-002704   700/.899607307471   0394495721
*Afro-American arts -- New York (State) -- New York. Arts,
Modern -- 20th century -- New York (State) -- New York. Harlem
Renaissance. Harlem (New York, N.Y.) -- Intellectual life -- 20th
century.*

NX511.N4.S38 1999
Scott, William B., 1945-
New York modern: the arts and the city/ William B. Scott
and Peter M. Rutkoff. Baltimore: Johns Hopkins
University Press, 1999. xx, 448 p.
98-041864   700/.9747/10904   0801859980
*Arts, American -- New York (State) -- New York. Arts, Modern
-- 20th century -- New York (State) -- New York. New York
(N.Y.) -- Social life and customs -- 20th century.*

NX512.G66
Gomez-Pena, Guillermo.
Dangerous border crossers: the artist talks back/
Guillermo Gomez-Pena. London; Routledge, 2000. xvii,
285 p.
99-052962   709/.2   0415182379
Gomez-Pena, Guillermo. Performance art -- United States.

NX512.M67.B47 1989
Berger, Maurice.
Labyrinths: Robert Morris, minimalism, and the 1960s/
Maurice Berger. New York: Harper & Row, c1989. xvi,
175 p.
88-037606   700/.92/4   0064303845
*Morris, Robert, -- 1931- -- Criticism and interpretation.
Minimal art -- United States. Arts and society -- United States.*

NX512.W37.P66 1996
Pop out: Queer Warhol/ edited by Jennifer Doyle,
Jonathan Flatley & Jose Esteban Munoz. Durham: Duke
University Press, 1996. viii, 280 p.
95-035410   700/.92   082231732X
*Warhol, Andy, -- 1928- -- Criticism and interpretation. Warhol,
Andy, -- 1928- -- Sexual behavior. Gay artists in popular
culture -- United States.*

NX512.3.A35.T95 1992
Tyler, Bruce Michael, 1948-
From Harlem to Hollywood: the struggle for racial and
cultural democracy, 1920-1943/ Bruce M. Tyler. New
York: Garland, 1992. xiv, 243 p.
91-042174   700/.89/96073   0815308140
*Afro-American arts. Harlem Renaissance. Afro-Americans --
Social conditions -- To 1964. Harlem (New York, N.Y.) --
Intellectual life -- 20th century.*

NX512.3.A83 C74 1999
Yellow light: the flowering of Asian American arts/
edited by Amy Ling. Philadelphia, PA: Temple
University Press, c1999. ix, 374 p.
98-029511   700/.92/3951073 B 21   1566398177
Asian American arts -- 20th century.

NX512.3.N5.B8 1972
Butcher, Margaret (Just) 1913-
The Negro in American culture, based on materials left
by Alain Locke. New York, Knopf, 1972 [c1971] x,
313 p.
74-038321   700/.8996073   0394479432
Afro-American arts.

NX512.3.N5.H8
Huggins, Nathan Irvin, 1927-
Harlem renaissance. New York, Oxford University Press,
1971. xi, 343 p.
70-159646   700/.97471   0195014561
*Afro-American arts -- New York (State) -- New York. Arts,
Modern -- 20th century -- New York (State) -- New York. Harlem
Renaissance. Harlem (New York, N.Y.) -- Intellectual life -- 20th
century.*

NX542.B88 1994
Butler, Christopher.
Early modernism: literature music and painting in
Europe, 1900-1916/ Christopher Butler. Oxford:
Clarendon Press, 1994. xviii, 318 p.
93-026945   700/.94/09041   0198117469
*Modernism (Art) -- Europe. Arts, European. Arts, Modern --
20th century -- Europe.*

NX542.L46 1998
Lemke, Sieglinde.
Primitivist modernism: black culture and the origins of
transatlantic modernism/ Sieglinde Lemke. Oxford;
Oxford University Press, 1998. 183 p.
97-001352   700/.4112/08996   019510403X
*Modernism (Art) -- Europe. Arts, European. Modernism (Art)
-- United States.*

NX543.C36 1988
The Cambridge guide to the arts in Britain/ edited by
Boris Ford. Cambridge [England]; Cambridge University
Press, 1988-1991. 9 v.
87-011671   700/.941
Arts, British.

NX543.C38 2000
Caws, Mary Ann.
Bloomsbury and France: art and friends/ Mary Ann Caws
and Sarah Bird Wright; with a preface by Michael
Holroyd. New York: Oxford University Press, 2000.
xviii, 430 p.
98-054638   820.9/00912   0195117522
*Bloomsbury group. Artists -- Great Britain -- Biography.
France -- Relations -- Great Britain. Great Britain -- Relations -
- France.*

NX543.S73 1994
Stansky, Peter.
London's burning: life, death, and art in the second World War/ Peter Stansky and William Abrahams. Stanford, Calif.: Stanford University Press, 1994. xiii, 201 p.
93-086764　700/.942/09044　0804723400
　Arts, British. Arts, Modern -- 20th century -- Great Britain. World War, 1939-1945 -- Art and the war.

NX544.A1.E18 2000
Early modern visual culture: representation, race, empire in Renaissance England/ edited by Peter Erickson and Clark Hulse. Philadelphia: University of Pennsylvania Press, c2000. 403 p.
00-039287　700/.942/09031　0812235592
　Arts, English. Renaissance -- England.

NX547.6.R67.R53 1983
Riede, David G.
Dante Gabriel Rossetti and the limits of Victorian vision/ David G. Riede. Ithaca: Cornell University Press, 1983. 288 p.
82-022099　821/.8　0801415527
Rossetti, Dante Gabriel, -- 1828-1882. Rossetti, Dante Gabriel, -- 1828-1882 -- Criticism and interpretation.

NX550.A1.G63 1987
Gordon, Donald E.
Expressionism: art and idea/ Donald E. Gordon. New Haven: Yale University Press, c1987. xvii, 263 p.
86-009188　709/.04/042　0300033109
　Expressionism (Art) -- Germany. Arts, Modern -- 20th century -- Germany. Expressionism (Art) -- Influence.

NX550.A1.S2913 1988
Schrader, Barbel.
The "golden" twenties: art and literature in the Wiemar Republic/ Barbel Schrader, Jurgen Schebera. New Haven: Yale University Press, 1988. 271 p.
87-050845　700/.943　0300041446
　Arts, German. Arts, Modern -- 20th century -- Germany. Arts and society -- Germany -- History -- 20th century. Germany -- History -- 1918-1933. Germany -- Intellectual life -- 20th century.

NX552.Z9.M533 1990
Barolsky, Paul, 1941-
Michelangelo's nose: a myth and its maker/ Paul Barolsky. University Park: Pennsylvania State University Press, c1990. xx, 169 p.
89-028363　700/.92　0271006951
Michelangelo Buonarroti, -- 1475-1564 -- Criticism and interpretation. Michelangelo Buonarroti, -- 1475-1564 -- Psychology. Arts, Renaissance -- Italy.

NX556.A1.A74 1983
Art and culture in nineteenth-century Russia/ edited by Theofanis George Stavrou. Bloomington: Indiana University Press, c1983. xix, 268 p.
81-048634　700/.947　0253310512
　Arts, Russian. Arts, Modern -- 19th century -- Russia. Arts and society -- Russia -- History -- 19th century.

NX556.A1.S66 1995
Soviet hieroglyphics: visual culture in late twentieth-century Russia/ edited by Nancy Condee. Bloomington: Indiana University Press; 1995. xxv, 179 p.
94-022839　700/.1/03094709049　025331402X
　Arts, Soviet. Arts and society -- Soviet Union. Arts, Russian.

NX556.Z9.L376 1993
Parton, Anthony.
Mikhail Larionov and the Russian avant-garde/ Anthony Parton. Princeton, N.J.: Princeton University Press, c1993. xxiv, 254 p.
92-020814　700/.92　0691036039
Larionov, Mikhail Fedorovich, -- 1881-1964 -- Criticism and interpretation. Avant-garde (Aesthetics) -- Russia (Federation) -- History -- 20th century.

NX583.A1.T48 1983
Theories of the arts in China/ edited by Susan Bush and Christian Murck. Princeton, N.J.: Princeton University Press, c1983. xxvi, 447 p.
83-042551　700/.1　0691040206
　Arts, Chinese -- Congresses.

NX589.T72
The Traditional artist in African societies. Warren L. d'Azevedo, editor. Bloomington, Indiana University Press [1973] xxi, 454 p.
79-160126　700/.966　0253399017
　Arts, Black -- Africa, West.

NX600 History of the arts —
Special movements, A-Z

NX600.F8.M37 1972
Marinetti, Filippo Tommaso, 1876-1944.
Marinetti, selected writings. Edited, and with an introd., by R. W. Flint. Translated by R. W. Flint and Arthur A. Coppotelli. New York, Farrar, Straus and Giroux [1972] 366 p.
71-189338　700/.9/04　0374202907
　Futurism (Art)

NX600.S9.A95 1980
The Autobiography of surrealism/ edited by Marcel Jean. New York: Viking Press, 1980. xxiii, 472 p.
76-046637　700/.9/04　0670142352
　Surrealism. Arts, Modern -- 20th century.

NX600.S9.L5
Lippard, Lucy R.,
Surrealists on art. Edited by Lucy R. Lippard. Englewood Cliffs, N.J., Prentice-Hall [1970] x, 213 p.
78-104858　709/.04　0138780900
　Surrealism.

NX600.S95.M3813 1990
Mathieu, Pierre-Louis.
The symbolist generation, 1870-1910/ Pierre-Louis Mathieu. New York: Skira: 1990. 219 p.
89-043610　700　0847812189
　Symbolism (Art movement) Arts, Modern -- 19th century. Arts, Modern -- 20th century.

NX634 Economics of the arts

NX634.C68 1998
Cowen, Tyler.
In praise of commercial culture/ Tyler Cowen. Cambridge, Mass.: Harvard University Press, 1998. ix, 278 p.
97-040445   700/.68/8   0674445910
Arts -- Marketing. Arts -- Economic aspects. Arts and society.

NX640 Criticism in the arts — General works

NX640.M55 1992
Miller, J. Hillis 1928-
Illustration/ J. Hillis Miller. Cambridge, Mass.: Harvard University Press, 1992. 168 p.
91-028136   700/.1   0674443578
Arts. Deconstruction. Art criticism -- History -- 20th century.

NX640.5 Criticism in the arts — Biography of arts critics — Individual, A-Z

NX640.5.F46.H35 1988
Halperin, Joan U.
Felix Feneon, aesthete & anarchist in fin-de-siecle Paris/ Joan Ungersma Halperin; foreword by Germaine Bree. New Haven: Yale University Press, c1988. xviii, 425 p.
88-009649   700/.92/4   0300043007
Feneon, Felix, -- 1861-1944.   Art critics -- France -- Biography. Art critics -- France -- Political activity. Arts, French -- France -- Paris.

NX650 Special subjects or topics, A-Z

NX650.E85.M33 1995
MacKenzie, John M.
Orientalism: history, theory, and the arts/ John M. MacKenzie. Manchester; Manchester University Press; c1995. xxii, 232 p.
94-043434   700   0719018617
Orientalism in art. Arts, Modern.

NX650.L32.S53 1997
Shindo, Charles J.
Dust bowl migrants in the American imagination/ Charles J. Shindo. Lawrence: University Press of Kansas, c1997. xv, 252 p.
96-032301   700/.1/030973   0700608109
Migrant agricultural laborers in art. Arts, American. Arts, Modern -- 20th century -- United States. California -- Rural conditions. Great Plains -- Rural conditions.

NX650.M9.R45 1993
Reid, Jane Davidson, 1918-
The Oxford guide to classical mythology in the arts, 1300-1990s/ Jane Davidson Reid; with the assistance of Chris Rohmann. New York: Oxford University Press, 1993. 2 v.
92-035374   700   0195049985
Mythology, Classical, in art -- Catalogs. Arts, Modern -- Catalogs.

NX650.P6.B88 1995
But is it art?: the spirit of art as activism/ edited by Nina Felshin. Seattle: Bay Press, c1995. 412 p.
94-036846   700/.1/03   0941920291
Arts -- Political aspects. Politics in art. Social problems in art.

NX650.P6.M36 1995
Mapping the terrain: new genre public art/ edited by Suzanne Lacy. Seattle, Wash.: Bay Press, c1995. 293 p.
94-035417   700/.1/03   0941920305
Arts -- Political aspects. Politics in art. Social problems in art.

NX650.P6.P47 1993
Phelan, Peggy.
Unmarked: the politics of performance/ Peggy Phelan. London; Routledge, 1993. xi, 207 p.
92-007895   700/.1/03   0415068215
Arts -- Political aspects. Politics in art. Feminism and the arts.

NX650.S68.K25 1999
Kahn, Douglas, 1951-
Noise, water, meat: a history of sound in the arts/ Douglas Kahn. Cambridge, Mass.: MIT Press, 1999. ix, 455 p.
98-051886   700   0262112434
Sound in art. Arts, Modern -- 20th century.

NX652 Characters, persons, classes of persons, and ethnic groups — By name of character, person, class of persons, or ethnic group, A-Z

NX652.A37.G83 1997
Gubar, Susan, 1944-
Racechanges: white skin, black face in American culture/ Susan Gubar. New York: Oxford University Press, 1997. xxiii, 327 p.
96-028151   305.8/00973   0195110021
Afro-Americans in popular culture. Blackface entertainers -- United States -- History -- 20th century. Arts, Modern -- 20th century -- United States.

NX652.A37.I43 1988
Images of Blacks in American culture: a reference guide to information sources/ edited by Jessie Carney Smith; foreword by Nikki Giovanni. New York: Greenwood Press, 1988. xvii, 390 p.
87-024964   700   0313248443
Afro-Americans in art. Arts, American.

NX652.G38 I5 1995
In a different light: visual culture, sexual identity, queer practice / edited by Nayland Blake, Lawrence Rinder, Amy Scholder. San Francisco: City Lights Books, c1995. x, 351 p.
94-049371   700/.8/664 20   087286300X
Gay artists -- United States -- Psychology. Gay artists in popular culture -- United States. Lesbian artists -- United States -- Psychology. Lesbian artists in popular culture -- United States. Arts, American. Art and society -- United States.

NX653 Special geographic areas and places as subjects, A-Z

NX653.A35.N413 1992
Nederveen Pieterse, Jan.
White on black: images of Africa and Blacks in Western popular culture/ Jan Nederveen Pieterse. New Haven: Yale University Press, 1992. 259 p.
91-041603   700   0300050208
  Africa in art. Blacks in art. Arts -- Themes, motives.

NX653.S68.D4 1987
The Desert is no lady: southwestern landscapes in women's writing and art/ edited by Vera Norwood and Janice Monk. New Haven: Yale University Press, c1987. xii, 281 p.
86-028265   700/.88042   0300036884
  Southwest, New, in art. Arts, American -- Southwest, New. Arts, Modern -- 20th century -- Southwest, New.

NX701.2 Patronage of the arts — Biography of arts patrons — Individual, A-Z

NX701.2.M43
Kent, D. V.
Cosimo de' Medici and the Florentine Renaissance: the patron's oeuvre/ Dale Kent. New Haven: Yale University Press, c2000. xiii, 537 p.
00-031038   945/.5105/092   0300081286
Medici, Cosimo de', -- 1389-1464 -- Art patronage. Arts, Italian -- Italy -- Florence. Arts, Renaissance -- Italy -- Florence. Florence (Italy) -- Social life and customs.

NX705.5 Patronage of the arts — Special regions or countries, A-Z

NX705.5.U6.C38 2000
Caves, Richard E.
Creative industries: contracts between art and commerce/ Richard E. Caves. Cambridge, Mass.; Harvard University Press, 2000. ix, 454 p.
99-086569   338.4/77/00973   0674001648
  Arts -- Economic aspects -- United States -- History -- 20th century.

NX705.5.U6.M86 2000
Munson, Lynne, 1968-
Exhibitionism: art in an era of intolerance/ Lynne Munson. Chicago: Ivan R. Dee, 2000. 237 p.
00-043107   701/.03/0973   1566633249
  Art patronage -- United States -- History -- 20th century. Postmodernism -- Influence.

NX730-735 Patronage of the arts — Governmental patronage — Special countries

NX730.P79 1992
Public policy and the aesthetic interest: critical essays on defining cultural and educational relations/ edited by Ralph A. Smith and Ronald Berman. Urbana: University of Illinois Press, c1992. xii, 283 p.
91-027335   700/.1/03   0252018990
Art and state -- United States. Arts -- Scholarships, fellowships, etc. -- United States. Art patronage -- United States. United States -- Cultural policy.

NX735.B54 1988
Biddle, Livingston, 1918-
Our government and the arts: a perspective from the inside/ Livingston Biddle; foreword by Isaac Stern. New York, N.Y.: ACA Books, c1988. xii, 539 p.
88-006168   353.0085/4   0915400677
National Endowment for the Arts -- History.

NX735.D79 1992
Dubin, Steven C.
Arresting images: impolitic art and uncivil actions/ Steven C. Dubin. London; Routledge, 1992. x, 374 p.
92-005776   700/.1/03   0415904358
  Arts -- United States -- Censorship. Art patronage -- United States. Art and state -- United States.

NX735.L48 1997
Levy, Alan Howard.
Government and the arts: debates over federal support of the arts in America from George Washington to Jesse Helms/ Alan Howard Levy. Lanham, Md.: University Press of America, c1997. xi, 147 p.
96-052505   700/.973   0761806741
  Federal aid to the arts -- United States. Art patronage -- United States.

NX735.P83 1991
Public money and the muse: essays on government funding for the arts/ Stephen Benedict, editor. New York: W.W. Norton, c1991. 288 p.
91-009348   353/.0085/4   0393030156
  Federal aid to the arts -- United States.

NX765 Administration of the arts. Administrators. Arts boards — Special countries — United States

NX765.S78 1989
Stolper, Carolyn L.
Successful fundraising for arts and cultural organizations/ by Carolyn L. Stolper & Karen Brooks Hopkins. Phoenix, AZ.: Oryx Press, 1989. xiv, 193 p.
88-038482   700/.68/1   0897745647
  Arts publicity -- United States -- Handbooks, manuals, etc. Arts fund raising -- United States -- Handbooks, manuals, etc.

**NX800 Arts centers. Arts facilities —
Special countries — United States**

NX800.A78 1987
Art in action: American art centers and the New Deal/
edited by John Franklin White. Metuchen, N.J.:
Scarecrow Press, 1987. vii, 187 p.
87-016500   700/.973   0810820072
*Art centers -- United States. Federal aid to the arts -- United
States -- History -- 20th century. New Deal, 1933-1939. United
States -- Politics and government -- 1933-1945.*

INDEXES

Metting, Fred. ML394.M5 2001

Meyer, Esther da Costa. NA2707.S28.M48 1995

Meyer, Laure. N7398.M4913 1992

Meyer, Leonard B. ML430.5.M5 1989, ML3800.M63, ML3800.M633

Meyerbeer, Giacomo. ML410.M61.A3 1999, ML410.M61.A4 1989

Meyerson, Martin. NA9030.M48

Michaelis, David. ND237.W94.M53 1998

Michell, George. N8195.A4.M53 2000

Michener, James A. NE1310.M48

Mickelsen, William C. ML430.M5

Mierop, Caroline. NA6230.M513 1995

Mies van der Rohe, Ludwig. NA1088.M65.P3

Mignot, Claude. NA957.M5313 1984

Milbrath, Constance. N351.M54 1998

Milburn, R. L. P. N7832.M47 1988

Milhaud, Darius. ML410.M674.A32 1970

Miller, Angela L. ND1351.5.M53 1993

Miller, Bertha E. Mahony. NC965.M59

Miller, J. Hillis. NX640.M55 1992

Miller, Jonathan. N8224.M6.M54 1998

Miller, Leta E. ML410.H2066.M55 1998

Miller, Lynn F. N6512.M518

Miller, Mervyn. NA997.U59.M55 1992

Miller, Philip Lieson. ML54.6.M5 R5 1973

Miller, R. Craig. NK1390.M54 1990

Miller, Richard. MT121.S38.M55 1999, MT820.M599 1996, MT820.M5995 2000, MT820.M6 1993, MT823.M55, MT823.M55 1997, MT825.M646 1986

Millington, Barry. ML410.W1 M58 1999

Millon, Henry A. NA590.M5

Milner, John. N6850.M48 1988

Milnes, Gerald. ML3551.7.W4.M55 1999

Minne-Seve, Viviane. N6843.M5613 2000

Mino, Yutaka. NK4166.T95.M56

Minor, Vernon Hyde. N380.M556 1994

Mitchell, Donald. ML410.M23.M48 1986

Mitchell, W. J. Thomas. NX170.M58 1994

Mitchell, William J. ML55.M49, NA2750.M58 1990

Mixter, Keith E. ML113.M59 1996

Moholy-Nagy, Laszlo. N7430.M62

Moholy-Nagy, Sibyl. N6838.M6.M6 1969, NA203.M6 1976, NA9090.M58

Moir, Alfred. ND1329.D93.A4 1994

Moldenhauer, Hans. ML410.W33.M55 1979

Mollenhoff, David V. NA6880.5.U62.M335 1999

Monet, Claude. ND553.M7.A4 1978

Monies, Finn. NA1218.M613

Monkman, Betty C. NK2438.W37

Monrad, Kasper. ND717.5.R65.M66 1993

Monro, Isabel Stevenson. ND45.M6, ND205.M57

Monson, Ingrid T. ML3506.M64 1996

Montagu, Jennifer. NB620.M66 1989, NB623.A44.M66 1985

Montagu, Jeremy. ML465.M65

Montano, Mary Caroline. NX510.N43

Monteverdi, Claudio. ML410.M77.A4 1995

Montias, John Michael. ND653.V5.M65 1989

Moody, Bill. ML3506.M66 1993

Moore, Allan F. ML421.B4.M66 1997

Moore, Charles Willard. NA2765.M66

Moore, F. Richard. MT723.M6 1990

Moore, Gerald. ML410.S4.M65, ML417.M85.A3 1979, MT68.M6 1984

Moore, Henry. NB497.M6.A35 1967, NB497.M6.F52

Moore, Jerrold Northrop. ML410.E41 M65 1984

Moore, Robert Etheridge. ND497.H7.M6 1969

Moore, Robin. ML3486.C8.M66 1997

Moortgat, Anton. N5370.M6613

Moos, Stanislaus von. NA1053.J4.M613

Moran, Thomas. N6537.M6443.A4 1996

Mordden, Ethan. ML410.R6315.M7 1992, ML1705.M67

Morey, Carl. ML120.C2.M67 1997

Morey, Charles Rufus. N5970.M6

Morgan, Charles Hill. N6923.B9.M59

Morgan, Conway Lloyd. NA1053.N68.M67 1998

Morgan, H. Wayne. ND237.C8.M67 1994

Morgan, Nigel J. ND3128.M67

Morgan, Robert C. N6512.5.C64.M67 1994

Morgan, Robert P. ML197.M675 1990

Morganstern, Anne McGee. NB1820.M72 2000

Morley, Thomas. MT6.M86 1953

Morphet, Richard. N6494.A66

Morris, Gareth. MT340.M73 1991

Morrison, Craig. ML3535.M67 1996

Morrison, Hugh. NA707.M63, NA737.S9.M6

Mosby, Dewey F. N6537.T35.A4 1991

Moser, Joann. NE2245.U54.M67 1997

Moses. ND237.M78.A22

Motherwell, Robert. ND237.M852.A35 1992

Moure, Nancy Dustin Wall. N6530.C2 M68 1998

Mowl, Tim. NA966.M68 1995

Moxey, Keith P. F. NE958.3.G3.M68 1989

Mozart, Leopold. MT262.M93 1951

Mozart, Wolfgang Amadeus. ML49.M83 M42 1991, ML410.M9 A187 1990, ML410.M9 A4 2000

Muehsam, Gerd. N7425.M88

Muller, Jeffrey M. ND673.R9.M766 1989

Mullin, Donald C. NA6821.M83

Mumford, Lewis. NA705.M78 1967, NA710.M8 1972

Munch, Charles. ML422.M9 A32 1978

American century: art & culture, 1900-1950, The / N6512.H355 1999

American century: art & culture, 1950-2000, The / N6512.H355 1999 Suppl.

American ceramics: the collection of Everson Museum of Art / NK4005.E94 1989

American ceramics, 1876 to the present / NK4007.C56 1987

American city: what works, what doesn't, The / NA9105.G37 1996

American colonial portraits, 1700-1776 / N7593.1.S28 1987

American composers: dialogues on contemporary music / ML390.S942 1991

American country houses of the Gilded Age (Sheldon's "Artistic country-seats") / NA7610.A58 1982

American cultural leaders: from colonial times to the present / NX503.A49 1993

American culture between the wars: revisionary modernism & postmodern critique / NX180.S6.K32 1993

American design adventure, 1940-1975, The / NK1404.P85 1988

American dreamer: the art of Philip C. Curtis / ND237.C884.A4 1999

American experimental music, 1890-1940 / ML200.5.N55 1990

American film music: major composers, techniques, trends, 1915-1990 / ML2075.D33 1990

American folk masters: the National Heritage Fellows / NX504.S57 1992

American folk music and left-wing politics, 1927-1957 / ML3918.F65

American folk painters of three centuries / ND205.5.P74.A43

American furniture: seventeenth, eighteenth, and nineteenth century styles / NK2406.C58

American furniture of the 18th century / NK2406.G74 1996

American genre painting: the politics of everyday life / ND1451.5.J64 1991

American house designs: an index to popular and trade periodicals, 1850-1915 / NA7207.C85 1994

American house styles: a concise guide / NA7205.B33 1994

American icons: transatlantic perspectives on eighteenth- and nineteenth-century American art / ND207.A678 1992

American impressionism / ND210.5.I4.G474 1984

American impressionism and realism: the painting of modern life, 1885-1915 / ND210.5.I4.W456 1994

American in art; a professional and technical autobiography, An / ND237.B47.A28

American Indian painting & sculpture / N6538.A4 B7

American light: the luminist movement, 1850-1875: paintings, drawings, photographs / N8214.5.U6.A47 1980

American modern, 1925-1940: design for a new age / NK1404.J65 2000

American muse, The / N6505.D65

American music in the twentieth century / ML200.5.G36 1997

American music librarianship: a biographical and historical survey / ML111.B77 1990

American musical comedy: from Adonis to Dreamgirls / ML1711.B66 1982

American musical landscape, The / ML200.C68 1993

American musical revue: from The passing show to Sugar babies / ML1711.B665 1985

American musical theatre: a chronicle / ML1711.B67 2001

American musical theatre song encyclopedia, The / ML102.M88.H59 1995

American musicians: fifty-six portraits in jazz / ML395.B34 1986

American musicians II: seventy-two portraits in jazz / ML395.B36 1996

American Negro art / N6538.N5.D6 1960

American opera / ML1711.K56 2001

American painting in the twentieth century / ND212.G36

American painting of the nineteenth century; realism, idealism, and the American experience / ND210.N68 1969

American painting, 1900-1970 / ND212.T5

American painting, from the Armory show to the depression / ND212.B74

American painting; from its beginnings to the Armory Show / ND205.P74

American paintings in the Detroit Institute of Arts / ND205.D298 1991

American paintings in the Metropolitan Museum of Art / ND205.N373 1980

American paradise: the world of the Hudson River school / ND1351.5.A49 1987

American picturesque / NX503.7.C66 2000

American popular ballad of the golden era, 1924-1950, The / ML3477.F67 1995

American popular music: new approaches to the twentieth century / ML3477.A42 2001

American popular music business in the 20th century / ML200.S263 1991

American primitive painting / ND210.5.P7.L56 1942

American printmakers, 1880-1945: an index to reproductions and biocritical information / NE507.W53 1993

American printmakers, 1946-1996: an index to reproductions and biocritical information / NE508.B76 1999

American printmaking: a century of American printmaking, 1880-1980 / NE507.W37 1984

American prints and printmakers: a chronicle of over 400 artists and their prints from 1900 to the present / NE508.J63

American realist painting, 1945-1980 / ND212.5.R4.W36 1989

American realists and magic realists / N6512.N4 1969

American renaissance, 1876-1917, The / N6510.B75 1979

American rococo, 1750-1775: elegance in ornament / NK1403.5.H4 1992

American salons: encounters with European modernism, 1885-1917 / NX503.7.C78 1993

American sculpture in the Metropolitan Museum of Art / NB210.M48 1999

American song: the complete musical theatre companion / ML128.M78.B6 1996

American urban architecture: catalysts in the design of cities / NA9105.A87 1989

American views: essays on American art / N6505.W57 1991

American visions: the epic history of art in America / N6505.H84 1997

Architecture after modernism / NA682.P67.G49 1996

Architecture and design for the family in twentieth-century Britain, 1900-1970 / NA7328.J44 2000

Architecture and ideology in early medieval Spain / NA1303.D63 1989

Architecture and independence: the search for identity--India 1880 to 1980 / NA1504.L36 1997

Architecture and its interpretation: a study of expressive systems in architecture / NA2599.5.B6613 1979b

Architecture and politics in Germany, 1918-1945 / NA1068.L3

Architecture and society; selected essays of Henry Van Brunt / NA710.V3 1969

Architecture and the after-life / NA6120.C65 1991

Architecture and the crisis of modern science / NA956.P413 1983

Architecture as space; how to look at architecture / NA2500.Z413

Architecture from without: theoretical framings for a critical practice / NA2500.A42 1991

Architecture in Britain, 1530 to 1830 / NA964.S85 1977

Architecture in Britain: the Middle Ages / NA963.W4 1956

Architecture in France in the eighteenth century / NA1046.K35 1995

Architecture in Italy, 1400-1500 / NA1115.H49 1996

Architecture in Italy, 1500-1600 / NA1115.L666 1995

Architecture in old Chicago / NA735.C4.T73

Architecture in Texas, 1895-1945 / NA730.T5.H46 1993

Architecture in the Age of Reason; baroque and post-baroque in England, Italy, and France / NA590.K3 1966

Architecture in the Scandinavian countries / NA1201.D66 1992

Architecture notebook: wall, An / NA2940.U58 2000

Architecture of affordable housing, The / NA7540.D38 1995

Architecture of America; a social and cultural history, The / NA705.B8

Architecture of ancient Greece: an account of its historic development, The / NA270.D5 1975b

Architecture of colonial America, The / NA707.E3

Architecture of conquest: building in the Viceroyalty of Peru, 1535-1635, The / NA913.F73 1990

Architecture of England from Norman times to the present day, The / NA961.G5 1953

Architecture of England: from prehistoric times to the present day, The / NA961.Y3 1967

Architecture of Europe, The / NA957.Y37 1990

Architecture of historic Hungary, The / NA1012.A73 1998

Architecture of humanism; a study in the history of taste, The / NA2500.S4 1924

Architecture of Ireland: from the earliest times to 1880, The / NA982.C72 1983

Architecture of Islamic Iran; the Il Khanid period, The / NA1483.W5

Architecture of Japan, The / NA1550.N4

Architecture of -ew Prague, 1895-1945, The / NA1033.P7.S8313 1995

Architecture of R.M. Schindler, The / NA737.S35.A4 2001

Architecture of Red Vienna, 1919-1934, The / NA9053.B58.B55 1999

Architecture of Richard Neutra: from international style to California modern, The / NA737.N4.A4 1982

Architecture of Richard Rogers, The / NA997.R64.S83 1995

Architecture of Robert Venturi, The / NA737.V45.A84 1989

Architecture of solitude: Cistercian abbeys in twelfth-century England / NA5463.F4 1984

Architecture of the Anglo-Saxons, The / NA963.F4 1983

Architecture of the arts and crafts movement / NA966.D37 1980

Architecture of the French Enlightenment, The / NA1046.B75

Architecture of the industrial age, 1789-1914 / NA9094.8.L6913 1983

Architecture of the Islamic world: its history and social meaning: with a complete survey of key monuments and 758 illustrations, 112 in color / NA380.A78 1984

Architecture of the Italian Renaissance, The / NA1115.B813 1985

Architecture of the Italian Renaissance, The / NA1115.M8

Architecture of the nineteenth century in Europe / NA957.M5313 1984

Architecture of the Old South / NA720.L36 1993

Architecture of the renaissance in France, The / NA533.W2 1926

Architecture of the Roman Empire: an introductory study, The / NA310.M2

Architecture of the Southwest; Indian, Spanish, American, The / NA720.S3 1971

Architecture of the Stalin era / NA1188.T36 1992

Architecture of the Western World / NA200.A73 1984

Architecture of Wren, The / NA997.W8.D59 1982

Architecture of Yoshio Taniguchi, The / NA1559.T35.A4 1999

Architecture reborn: converting old buildings for new uses / NA2793.P69 1999

Architecture without kings: the rise of Puritan classicism under Cromwell / NA966.M68 1995

Architecture, ambition, and Americans: a social history of American architecture / NA705.A5 1978

Architecture, power, and national identity / NA4195.V35 1992

Arnold Schoenberg companion, The / ML410.S283.A745 1998

Arnold Schoenberg-- the composer as Jew / ML410.S283.R55 1990

Arnolfini betrothal: medieval marriage and the enigma of Van Eyck's double portrait, The / ND673.E9.W44 1994

Arp / NB553.A7.A4 1980

Arresting images: impolitic art and uncivil actions / NX735.D79 1992

Art & empire: the politics of ethnicity in the United States Capitol, 1815-1860 / N6535.W3.F78 1992

Art & music of John Lennon, The / ML420.L38.R6 1991

Art & other serious matters / N7445.2.R66 1985

Art & physics: parallel visions in space, time, and light / N70.S48 1991

Art & political expression in early China / NB1880.C6.P68 1991

Art: African American / N6538.N5.L39

Art across America: a comprehensive guide to American art museums and exhibition galleries / N510.A777 2000

Brahms, his life and work / ML410.B8 G42 1982

Brahms, the four symphonies / ML410.B8.F75 1996

Brahms's vocal duets and quartets with piano: a guide with full texts and translations / MT115.B73 S7 1998

Brahms--the vocal music / ML410.B8.B38 1995

Brancacci Chapel, The / ND2757.F5.B313 1992

Braque: the late works / ND553.B86.A4 1997

Brass bibliography: sources on the history, literature, pedagogy, performance, and acoustics of brass instruments / ML128.W5.F3 1990

Brass instruments: their history and development / ML933.B33 1978

Brass music of black composers: a bibliography / ML128.W5.H62 1996

Brass performance and pedagogy / MT418.J64 2002

Brass ring, The / NC1429.M428.A2 1971

Brazil builds; architecture new and old, 1652-1942 / NA850.G6

Brazilian popular music & globalization / ML3487.B7.B76 2001

Breakout: profiles in African rhythm / ML3502.5.S73 1992

Brice Marden: prints, 1961-1991: a catalogue raisonne / NE539.M23.A4 1992

Bridge of dreams: the Mary Griggs Burke collection of Japanese art / N7352.M84 2000

Bringing opera to life; operatic acting and stage direction / ML1700.G738 B7

British brass band: a musical and social history, The / ML1331.1.B75 2000

British impressionism / ND467.5.I46.M38 1989

British Museum book of Chinese Art, The / N7340.B64 1993

Britten / ML410.B853 K45 2001

Broadway musical: collaboration in commerce and art, The / ML1711.8.N3.R67 1993

Broadway song companion: an annotated guide to musical theatre literature by voice type and song style, The / ML128.M78.D48 1998

Brother Ray: Ray Charles' own story / ML420.C46 A3 1992

Bruce Nauman / N6537.N38.B78 1988

Bruckner / ML410.B88 W26 1996

Bruegel / ND673.B73.G47 1977b

Brunelleschi's dome: the story of the great cathedral in Florence / NA5621.F7

Bruno Munari: design as art / NK1535.M86.T3613 1987

Bruno Taut and the architecture of activism / NA1088.T33.W47 1982

Bruno Walter: a world elsewhere / ML422.W27 R93 2001

Brushes with power: modern politics and the Chinese art of calligraphy / NK3634.A2.K73 1991

Building an American identity: pattern book homes and communities, 1870-1900 / NA7571.S54 1999

Building by the book: pattern book architecture in New Jersey / NA7235.N5.G87 1992

Building God's house in the Roman world: architectural adaptation among pagans, Jews, and Christians / NA4817.W55 1990

Building in the garden: the architecture of Joseph Allen Stein in India and California / NA737.S639.W48 1993

Building Paris: architectural institutions and the transformation of the French capital, 1830-1870 / NA1050.V358 1994

Building sex: men, women, architecture, and the construction of sexuality / NA2543.W65.B48 1995

Building the Georgian city / NA966.A98 1998

Building the great cathedrals / NA4830.I2713 1998

Building the new world: studies in the modern architecture of Latin America, 1930-1960 / NA702.5.F73 2000

Buildings and society: essays on the social development of the built environment / NA2543.S6.B76

Buildings of Alaska / NA730.A4.H63 1993

Buildings of Charleston: a guide to the city's architect, The / NA735.C35.P67 1997

Buildings of Iowa / NA730.I8.G43 1993

Bungalow: the production of a global culture, The / NA7570.K56 1984

But is it art?: the spirit of art as activism / NX650.P6.B88 1995

Byzantine architecture and decoration / NA370.H3 1956

Byzantine masterpiece recovered, the thirteenth-century murals of Lysi, Cyprus, A / ND2819.C92.L974 1991

Byzantine painting; historical and critical study / ND142.G7

Byzantium: from antiquity to the Renaissance / N6250.M33 1998

C. Hubert H. Parry: his life and music / ML410.P173.D5 1992

CADD made easy: a comprehensive guide for architects and designers / NA2728.R34 1987

Cadenza: a musical career / ML422.L38.A3

Calder's universe / N6537.C33.L56 1976

California art: 450 years of painting & other media / N6530.C2 M68 1998

California soul: music of African Americans in the West / ML3479.C37 1998

California's architectural frontier; style and tradition in the nineteenth century / NA730.C2.K5

Call to assembly: the autobiography of a musical storyteller, A / ML419.R84 A3 1991

Callas at Juilliard: the master classes / MT820.C17 1987

Cambridge companion to Bach, The / ML410.B13.C36 1997

Cambridge companion to Bartok, The / ML410.B26.C35 2001

Cambridge companion to Beethoven, The / ML410.B4.C24 2000

Cambridge companion to Berg, The / ML410.B47.C38 1997

Cambridge companion to Berlioz, The / ML410.B5.C27 2000

Cambridge companion to Brahms, The / ML410.B8 C36 1999

Cambridge companion to Chopin, The / ML410.C54.C2 1992

Cambridge companion to Ravel, The / ML410.R23.C36 2000

Cambridge companion to Schubert, The / ML410.S3.C18 1997

Cambridge companion to singing, The / ML1460.C28 2000

Cambridge companion to the clarinet, The / ML945.C36 1995

Cambridge companion to the organ, The / ML550.C35 1998

Cambridge companion to the piano, The / ML650.C3 1998

Cambridge companion to the recorder, The / ML990.R4 C35 1995

Cambridge companion to the saxophone, The / ML975.C36 1998

Life of Mozart, The / ML410.M9 R847 1998

Life of Musorgsky, The / ML410.M97 E42 1999

Life of Picasso, A / N6853.P5.R56 1990

Life of Richard Strauss, The / ML410.S93.G53 1999

Life of Schubert, The / ML410.S3 G53 2000

Life of Verdi, The / ML410.V4.R74 2000

Life of Webern, The / ML410.W33.B32 1998

Light!: the industrial age 1750-1900: art & science, technology & society / N8219.L5

Light, wind, and structure: the mystery of the master builders / NA2760.M365 1990

Lilla Cabot Perry: an American impressionist / ND237.P375.A4 1990

Limewood sculptors of Renaissance Germany, The / NB1255.G3.B39

Limners and likenesses; three centuries of American paintings / ND205.B8 1965

Listen / MT6.K365 2000

Listen to the music: a self-guided tour through the orchestral repertoire / MT125.K72 1988

Listening composer, The / ML410.P2925.A3 1990

Listening in Paris: a cultural history / ML270.J64 1995

Listening out loud: becoming a composer / MT40.S98 1988

Listening to movies: the film lover's guide to film music / ML2075.K37 1994

Listening to salsa: gender, Latin popular music, and Puerto Rican cultures / ML3535.5.A63 1998

Liszt / ML410.L7 W35 2000

Literary lorgnette: attending opera in imperial Russia, The / ML1737.B83 2000

Literature of American music III, 1983-1992 / ML120.U5 M135 1996

Literature of American music in books and folk music collections: a fully annotated bibliography, The / ML120.U5 H7

Literature of American music in books and folk music collections. a fully annotated bibliography, The / ML120.U5.H7 Suppl. 1

Literature of jazz: a critical guide, The / ML128.J3.K45 1980

Literature of music bibliography: an account of the writings on the history of music printing & publishing, The / ML112.K765 1992

Literature of rock, The / ML128.R6.H6

Lithography: 200 years of art, history, & technique / NE2425.L5713 1983

Lively arts: Gilbert Seldes and the transformation of cultural criticism in the United States, The / N7483.S38.K36 1996

Lives and works, talks with women artists / N6512.M518

Lives of Indian images / NB1912.H55.D38 1997

Lives of the great 20th-century artists / N6489.L83 1999

Lives of the great composers, The / ML390.S393 1997

Living materials: a sculptor's handbook / NB1170.A63 1983

Logic of architecture: design, computation, and cognition, The / NA2750.M58 1990

London's burning: life, death, and art in the second World War / NX543.S73 1994

Long steel rail: the railroad in American folksong / ML3551.C57

Look, listen, read / NX165.L4513 1997

Looking at Greek vases / NK4645.L66 1991

Looking at modern painting / ND1143.F69

Looking back at Francis Bacon / ND497.B16.S93 2000

Lorenz Hart: a poet on Broadway / ML423.H32.N6 1994

Lorenzo Lotto: rediscovered master of the Renaissance / ND623.L8.A4 1997

Lorenzo Monaco / ND623.L77.E35 1989

Loretta Lynn: Coal miner's daughter / ML420.L947.A3

Lost chords: white musicians and their contribution to jazz, 1915-1945 / ML3508.S85 1999

Lost earth: a life of Cezanne / ND553.C33.C3 1995

Lotte Lehmann, a life in opera & song / ML420.L33.G6 1988

Lou Harrison: composing a world / ML410.H2066.M55 1998

Louis Armstrong: a cultural legacy / ML141.N4.A76 1994

Louis Armstrong companion: eight decades of commentary, The / ML419.A75.L68 1999

Louis Armstrong, in his own words: selected writings / ML419.A75.A3 1999

Louis Armstrong--a self-portrait. The interview by Richard Meryman / ML419.A75.A7

Louis I. Kahn: writings, lectures, interviews / NA737.K32.A2 1991

Louis I. Kahn / NA737.K32.S38

Louis Sullivan: the poetry of architecture / NA2707.S94.A4 2000

Louis Sullivan as he lived; the shaping of American architecture, a biography / NA737.S9.C6

Louis Sullivan, prophet of modern architecture / NA737.S9.M6

Louis Sullivan / NA737.S9.B8

Louise Bourgeois / NB237.B65.B47 1995

Louise Bourgeois: the locus of memory, works 1982-1993 / NB237.B65.A4 1994

Louisiana buildings, 1720-1940 / NA730.L8.L68 1997

Love and theft: blackface minstrelsy and the American working class / ML1711.L67 1993

Luca della Robbia / NB623.R72.P66 1980

Ludwig Mies van der Rohe / NA1088.M65.D7

Ludwig van Beethoven: approaches to his music / ML410.B4.D213 1991

Ludwig Wittgenstein, architect / NA1011.5.W5.W55 1994

Luigi Dallapiccola / ML410.D138.V6 1977

Lush life; a biography of Billy Strayhorn / ML410.S9325.H35 1996

Lutoslawski and his music / ML410.L965.S8

M: the man who became Caravaggio / ND623.C26.R62 2000

Mabel Mercer: a life / ML420.M388.H4 1987

Macchiaioli: Italian painters of the nineteenth century, The / ND617.5.M3.B7 1987

Machaut's Mass: an introduction / ML410.G966.L3 1990

Mackintosh architecture: the complete buildings and selected projects / NA997.M3.A4 1980

My heart belongs / ML420.M332.A3

My life / ML410.W1.W146 1983

My life / ML420.P52.A3 1990

My life and music; &, Reflections on music / ML417.S36.A3 1972

My Lord, what a morning: an autobiography / ML420.A6 A3 2002

My many years / ML417.R79.A28

My music is my flag: Puerto Rican musicians and their New York communities, 1917-1940 / ML3481.G53 1995

My music, my life / ML338.S475.M9

My song is my weapon: People's Songs, American communism, and the politics of culture, 1930-1950 / ML3795.L44 1989

My young years / ML417.R79.A3

Myself when I am real: the life and music of Charles Mingus / ML418.M45.S26 2000

Mystery of samba: popular music & national identity in Brazil, The / ML3465.V5313 1999

Mystery of the Bayeux tapestry, The / NK3049.B3.B44 1987

Myth into art: poet and painter in classical Greece / NK4645.S47 1994

N.C. Wyeth: a biography / ND237.W94.M53 1998

Nagauta: the heart of kabuki music / ML340.M33

Nam June Paik: video time, video space / N7369.P35.A4 1993

Narrative singing in Ireland: lays, ballads, come-all-yes, and other songs / ML3654.S54 1993

Nashville sound: authenticity, commercialization, and country music, The / ML3524.J46 1998

Nat King Cole / ML420.C63.E67 1999

National Gallery of Art, Washington / N856.W33 1984

National Museum of American Art / N857.A617 1995

National romanticism and modern architecture in Germany and the Scandinavian countries / NA1067.5.N38

National schools of singing: English, French, German, and Italian techniques of singing revisited / MT823.M55 1997

Nationalists, cosmopolitans, and popular music in Zimbabwe / ML3503.Z55

Nationalizing blackness: afrocubanismo and artistic revolution in Havana, 1920-1940 / ML3486.C8.M66 1997

Native genius in anonymous architecture in North America / NA203.M6 1976

Natural house, The / NA7208.W68

Natural man observed: a study of Catlin's Indian gallery, The / ND237.C35.T78 1979

Nature and culture: American landscape and painting, 1825-1875 / ND1351.5.N68

Nature and the idea of a man-made world: an investigation into the evolutionary roots of form and order in the built environment / NA2542.35.C77 1995

Nature near: late essays of Richard Neutra / NA737.N4.A2 1989

Nature's workshop: Renoir's writings on the decorative arts / NK27.H47 2000

Negro in American culture, The / NX512.3.N5.B8 1972

Neo-Baroque: a sign of the times / NX456.C3213 1992

Neoclassical architecture in Canada / NA744.5.N45.M35 1984

Neoclassicism and romanticism, 1750-1850; sources and documents / N6425.N4.E35

New architecture and the Bauhaus, The / NA680.G7 1965

New architecture in Africa / NA1590.K813

New art from the Soviet Union: the known and the unknown / N6988.N47 1977

New art of Cuba / N6603.C26 1994

New Bach reader: a life of Johann Sebastian Bach in letters and documents, The / ML410.B1.D24 1998

New directions in music / ML197.C757 2001

New feminist art criticism: critical strategies / N72.F45.N45 1995

New Finnish architecture, The / NA1455.F5.P66 1992

New French architecture, The / NA1048.L47 1990

New German architecture, The / NA1068.F36 1993

New Grove dictionary of American music, The / ML101.U6.N48 1986

New Grove dictionary of jazz, The / ML102.J3.N48 2000

New Grove dictionary of music and musicians, The / ML100.N48 2001

New Grove dictionary of musical instruments, The / ML102.I5.N48 1984

New Grove dictionary of opera, The / ML102.O6 N5 1992

New Harvard dictionary of music, The / ML100.N485 1986

New history of jazz, A / ML3506.S47 2001

New history of the organ from the Greeks to the present day, A / ML550.W38

New images of man / N7570.S38 1969

New kingdom art in ancient Egypt: during the eighteenth dynasty; 1570 to 1320 B. C. / N5350.A586 1961

New Kobbé's opera book, The / MT95.K52 1997

New landscape in art and science, The / N72.S3.K5

New moderns: from late to neo-modernism, The / NA682.P67.J4 1990

New Monteverdi companion, The / ML410.M77 N5 1985

New Mozart documents: a supplement to O.E. Deutsch's documentary biography / ML410.M9.D4782 Suppl.

New music and the claims of modernity / ML3845.W59 1997

New music, 1900-1960, The / ML197.C76 1968

New musical figurations: Anthony Braxton's cultural critique / ML419.B735.R3 1993

New Oxford companion to music, The / ML100.N5 1983

New Oxford history of music / ML160.N44 1990

New perspectives on Charles Willson Peale: a 250th anniversary celebration / ND237.P27.N48 1990

New sculpture, The / NB467.5.N48.B42 1983

New sounds for woodwind / MT339.5.B37 1982

New Spanish architecture, The / NA1308.Z33 1992

New subjectivism: art in the 1980s, The / N6490.K87 1988

New theory of urban design, A / NA9031.A38 1987

New urbanism: toward an architecture of community, The / NA2542.4.K38 1994

New worlds of Dvoˆrák: searching in America for the composer's inner life / ML410.D99 B42 2003

New York 1880: architecture and urbanism in the gilded age / NA735.N5.S727 1999

Penguin guide to compact discs, The / ML156.9.G73 1999

Penguin guide to jazz on CD, The / ML156.4.J3 C67 2002

Pennies from heaven: the American popular music business in the twentieth century / ML3477.S2 1996

Pennsylvania barn: its origin, evolution, and distribution in North America, The / NA8230.E5 1992

Perceptions and evocations: the art of Elihu Vedder / N6537.V43.A4 1979

Percussion / ML1030.H64 1981

Percussion instruments and their history / ML1030.B6 1992

Percussionists: a biographical dictionary / ML399.B38 2000

Percy Grainger / ML410.G75.M4 1992

Perfect Wagnerite; a commentary on the Niblung's ring, The / MT100.W25.S5 1967

Performance practice, medieval to contemporary: a bibliographic guide / ML128.P235.J3 1988

Performance practices in classic piano music: their principles and applications / ML705.R67 1988

Performance practices of the seventeenth and eighteenth centuries / ML457.N46 1993

Performing baroque music / ML457.C9 1992

Performing Beethoven / ML410.B42.P47 1994

Performing twentieth-century music: a handbook for conductors and instrumentalists / MT75.W38 1993

Persia and the West: an archaeological investigation of the genesis of Achaemenid art / NA225.B63 2000

Persian architecture; the triumph of form and color / NA1480.P6

Persian painting / ND980.G72 1977

Personal recollections of Arnold Dolmetsch / ML424.D65.D57 1980

Perspective as symbolic form / NC750.P2313 1991

Perspectives on American music since 1950 / ML200.5.P48 1999

Perspectives on John Philip Sousa / ML410.S688 P47 1983

Perspectives on Schoenberg and Stravinsky / ML55.B663 P5

Peter Behrens and a new architecture for the twentieth century / NA1088.B4.A827 2000

Peter Paul Rubens: man & artist / N6973.R9.W48 1987

Peter Warlock: the life of Philip Heseltine / ML410.W2953.S6 1994

Peterson's professional degree programs in the visual and performing arts / NX303.P52

Petrus Christus: his place in Fifteenth-Century Flemish painting / ND673.C312.U68 1990

Philip Evergood: never separate from the heart / ND237.E8.T39 1987

Philip Johnson: life and work / NA737.J6.S38 1994

Philip Johnson / NA737.J6.J3

Philosophical perspectives on music / ML3800.B79 1998

Philosophy of mass art, A / NX180.M3.C37 1998

Philosophy of music education, A / MT1.R435 1989

Phrase rhythm in tonal music / MT42.R84 1989

Physics and psychophysics of music: an introduction, The / ML3805.R74 1995

Pianist's bookshelf; a practical guide to books, videos, and other resources, The / ML128.P3 H534 1998

Pianist's guide to pedaling, The / MT227.B2 1985

Pianist's guide to transcriptions, arrangements, and paraphrases, The / ML128.P3.H536 1990

Pianist's problems: a modern approach to efficient practice and musicianly performance, The / MT220.N5 1984

Pianist's reference guide: a bibliographical survey, The / ML128.P3.H54 1987

Piano: a history, The / ML652.E4 1990

Piano in America, 1890-1940, The / ML661.R64 1989

Piano in chamber ensemble: an annotated guide, The / ML128.C4.H5

Piano quartet and quintet: style, structure, and scoring, The / ML1165.S59 1994

Piano roles: three hundred years of life with the piano / ML650.P37 1999

Piano trio: its history, technique, and repertoire, The / ML1165.S6 1989

Pianoforte in the classical era, The / ML655.C63 1998

Piazzetta: a tercentenary exhibition of drawings, prints, and books / N6923.P457.A4 1983

Picasso: creator and destroyer / N6853.P5.S74 1988

Picasso: life and art / N6853.P5.D2613 1994

Picasso and the age of iron / NB1220.P5 1993

Picasso and the Spanish tradition / N6853.P5.P519 1996

Picasso and the war years, 1937-1945 / ND553.P5.A4 1998

Picasso and the weeping women: the years of Marie-Therese Walter & Dora Maar / ND553.P5.A4 1994

Picasso in perspective / ND553.P5.P477

Picasso's Guernica: history, transformations, meanings / ND553.P5.A66 1988b

Picasso--the early years, 1892-1906 / N6853.P5.A4 1997

Pictographs of Adolph Gottlieb, The / ND237.G614.A4 1994

Pictorial arts of the West, 800-1200, The / N5970.D64 1993

Pictorial dictionary of ancient Rome. / NA310.N28 1968

Pictorial history of Chinese architecture: a study of the development of its structural system and the evolution of its types, A / NA1540.L536 1984

Pictorial history of music, A / ML89.L15

Picture theory: essays on verbal and visual representation / NX170.M58 1994

Pictures of innocence: the history and crisis of ideal childhood / N7640.H54 1998

Pictures of people: Alice Neel's American portrait gallery / ND1329.N36.A9 1998

Picturing a nation: art and social change in nineteenth-century America / ND210.L83 1994

Picturing America, 1497-1899: prints, maps, and drawings bearing on the New World discoveries and on the development of the territory that is now the United States / N8214.5.U6.D43 1988

Picturing science, producing art / N72.S3.P53 1998

Piero della Francesca / ND623.P548.L54 1992

Pierre Bonnard, the graphic art / NE2349.5.B66.A4 1989

Pierre Boulez / ML410.B773.J313 1990

Pierre Chareau: designer and architect / NA1053.C43.A4 1998